ESSENTIAL
SCOTLAND

Welcome to Scotland

Scotland packs spectacular landscapes, as well as rich history and tradition, into a small country. From the Lowlands to the Highlands, its lush woodlands, windswept moors, and deep lochs may take your breath away. Impressive castles, whisky distilleries, and golf courses entice, and cities such as Edinburgh and Glasgow tweak tradition with cutting-edge festivals and vibrant cultural scenes. Scotland's classic products and customs—from tartans to bagpipes—may travel the globe, but there's nothing like experiencing them firsthand.

TOP REASONS TO GO

★ **Castles:** Stirling, Glamis, Floors, and others tell tales of a complex, turbulent past.

★ **Cool cities:** Edinburgh's International Festival and Fringe; Glasgow's nightlife.

★ **Islands:** Skye's misty mountains, Islay's seabirds, Orkney's prehistoric remains.

★ **Whisky:** Distillery tours and tastings refine an appreciation for the national drink.

★ **Landscapes:** Crystal-clear lochs and rivers, wooded hills, wide-open moors.

★ **Golf:** The great names here include St. Andrews, Gleneagles, and Western Gailes.

Contents

MAPS

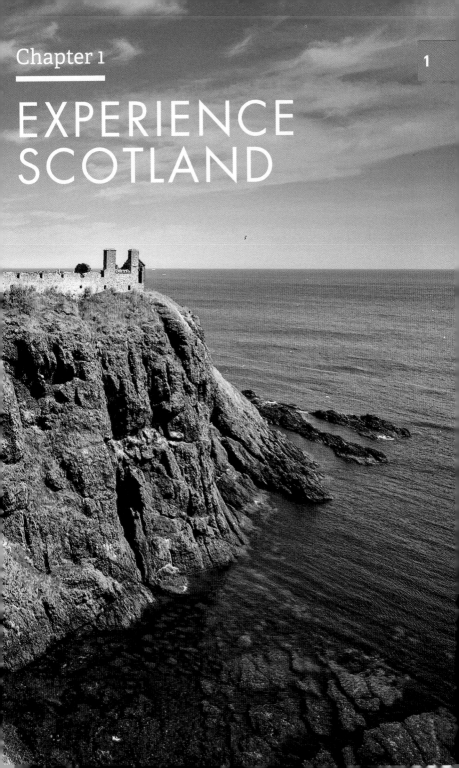

Chapter 1

EXPERIENCE SCOTLAND

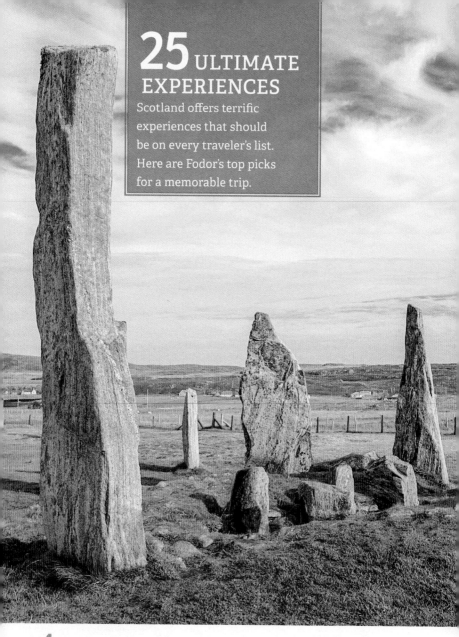

25 ULTIMATE EXPERIENCES

Scotland offers terrific experiences that should be on every traveler's list. Here are Fodor's top picks for a memorable trip.

1 Prehistoric Monuments

Around Scotland, haunting structures like the Calanais Standing Stones on the Isle of Lewis provide an intriguing glimpse into the past. Sights are scattered across the landscape, but Orkney claims a large concentration. (*Ch. 9, 11, 12*)

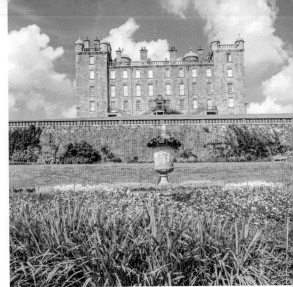

2 Castles

Whether in ruins or full of treasure, castles dating from the medieval period to Victorian times are among Scotland's glories. *(Ch. 3–12)*

3 Isle of Skye

With the misty Cuillin Mountains and rocky shores, Skye has few rivals among the country's islands for sheer loveliness. *(Ch. 11)*

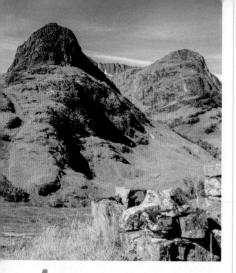

4 Glencoe

The wild beauty of Glencoe's craggy peaks and deep valley provided the background for a tragic massacre in 1692, but today the area is popular for outdoor activities. *(Ch. 10)*

5 Whisky Tours

From Speyside to Islay, whisky distilleries offer tours and tastings of Scotland's signature drink. Their often-spectacular settings are an added bonus. *(Ch. 5, 7–12)*

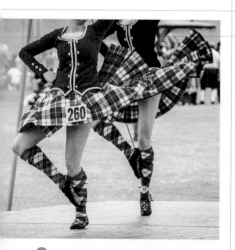

6 Scottish Folk Culture

For a true Scottish experience, attend a *céilidh*, a night of traditional folk dancing, singing, and music. *(Ch. 3–12)*

7 Glasgow

An urban renaissance has brought great shopping and nightlife to complement the city's rich architectural heritage and museums like the Kelvingrove. *(Ch. 4)*

8 Iona Abbey

One of Scotland's most spiritual spots, the abbey located on the island of Iona, in the Inner Hebrides, is considered the birthplace of Christianity in Scotland. *(Ch. 9)*

9 Hiking

Fully immerse yourself into the Scottish landscape by embarking on a hike through the countryside, like on the 93-mile West Highland Way. *(Ch. 7)*

10 Dundee

Once an industrial powerhouse, this Fife city has become a booming art hub in recent years, with impressive museums like the V&A Dundee and the McManus Galleries. *(Ch. 6)*

11 Loch Ness

Scotland's most famous loch continues to charm thanks to its alleged longtime resident, Nessie (aka the Loch Ness Monster). *(Ch. 10)*

12 Loch Lomond and the Trossachs

Its clear water make Loch Lomond a coveted retreat, while the lakes and hills of the Trossachs are the essence of the Highlands. *(Ch. 7)*

13 Robert Burns

Visit the birthplace of Scotland's most famous poet (known for writing "Auld Lang Syne") or celebrate his birthday with a Burns Supper via poetry, haggis, and whisky. *(Ch. 4)*

14 Edinburgh Festival

The Edinburgh Festival is actually a collection of several festivals—including the Fringe, book, and art festivals—all taking place around the same time in August. *(Ch. 3)*

15 Hogmanay

New Year's Eve, or "Hogmanay," is Edinburgh's biggest night of the year. In fact, Edinburgh's Hogmanay party is one of the world's biggest New Year celebrations. *(Ch. 3)*

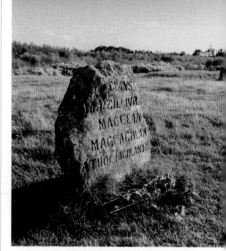

16 Culloden Moor Battlefield

The final Jacobite uprising, in which "Bonnie Prince" Charles Edward Stuart attempted to reclaim the British throne, was decisively and brutally crushed in 1746 at Culloden in the Highlands. *(Ch. 10)*

17 Cairngorms National Park

Many of Scotland's highest peaks are found in the Great Glen in stunning Cairngorms National Park, where you can also hike, ski, and spot wildlife. *(Ch. 10)*

18 The Northern Isles

The beautifully remote Orkney and Shetland islands have a colorful Scandanavian heritage, notable prehistoric artifacts, and rollicking festivals. *(Ch. 12)*

19 Cycling

Another popular way to explore the Central Highlands is via bicycle. The Low/Highland Trail stretches over 60 miles through the Trossachs and Loch Katrine. *(Ch. 7)*

20 Edinburgh

Scotland's capital charms with its Royal Mile and Old Town while the National Museum of Scotland and Edinburgh Castle give history lessons. *(Ch. 3)*

21 Seafood

From salmon to oysters, the superb fish and seafood from the rivers, lakes, and the sea are treats to savor. Delicately smoked fish is a specialty, served hot or cold. *(Ch. 3–12)*

22 Golf

The home of golf, Scotland claims some of the world's most challenging holes but has courses for all levels, many in beautiful settings by lakes, hills, or the ocean. *(Ch. 3–11)*

23 Jacobite Steam Train

The famous trip from Fort William to the coast at Mallaig offers spectacular views of mountains and lochs as well as a ride over the 21 arches of the Glenfinnan Viaduct. *(Ch. 10)*

24 Stirling

One of the best places to explore the country's history is Stirling, with its grand castle and Old Town telling the tales of early Scotland. *(Ch. 7)*

25 Seaside Towns

The country's jagged coastline and many islands create scenic settings for towns such as Tobermory on the Isle of Mull, with its colorfully painted houses. *(Ch. 9)*

WHAT'S WHERE

1 Edinburgh and the Lothians. Scotland's captivating capital is the country's most popular city, famous for its high-perched castle, Old Town and 18th-century New Town, ultramodern Parliament building, Georgian and Victorian architecture, superb museums, and the most celebrated arts festival in the world. For fewer crowds, escape to the Lothians and its coastal towns, beaches, and castles.

2 Glasgow. The country's largest city has evolved from prosperous Victorian hub to depressed urban center to thriving modern city with a strong artistic, architectural, and culinary reputation. Museums and galleries such as the Kelvingrove and Gallery of Modern Art (GoMA) are here, along with the Arts and Crafts architecture of Charles Rennie Mackintosh and iconic institutions such as Glasgow University.

3 The Borders and the Southwest. Scotland's southern gateway from England, the Borders, with its moors and gentle hills and river valleys, is rustic but historically rich. It's known for being the home of Sir Walter Scott and has impressive stately homes such as Floors Castle and ruined abbeys including Melrose. The southwest, or Dumfries and Galloway region, is perfect for scenic drives, castles, and hiking.

4 Fife and Angus. The "kingdom" of Fife is considered the sunniest and driest part of Scotland, with sandy beaches, fishing villages, and stone cottages. St. Andrews has its world-famous golf courses, but this university town is worth a stop even for nongolfers. To the north in Angus are Glamis Castle, the legendary setting of Shakespeare's *Macbeth*, as well as the city of Dundee with its increasing cultural attractions.

5 The Central Highlands. Convenient to both Edinburgh and Glasgow, this area encompasses some of Scotland's most beautiful terrain, with rugged, dark landscapes broken up by lochs and fields. Not to be missed are Loch Lomond and the Trossachs, Scotland's first national park. Perth and Stirling are the main metropolitan hubs and worth a stop; Stirling Castle has epic views that stretch from coast to coast.

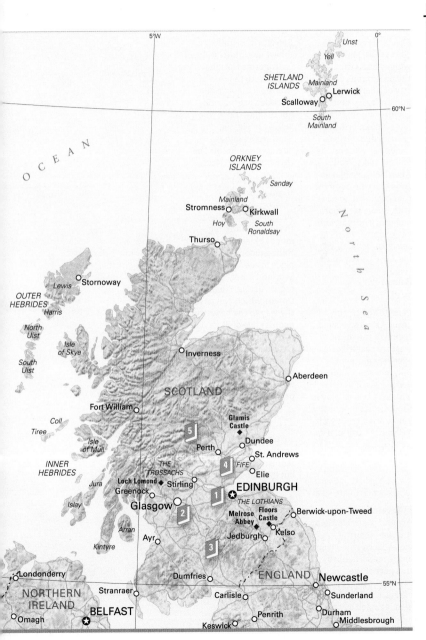

WHAT'S WHERE

6 Aberdeen and the Northeast. Malt-whisky buffs can use the prosperous port city of Aberdeen, known for its silvery granite buildings, as a base for exploring the region's distilleries, including those on the Malt Whisky Trail. Aberdeen also makes a good starting point for touring Royal Deeside, with its purple moors and piney hills as well as the notably rich selection of castles built over many centuries, including Balmoral.

7 Argyll and the Isles. Remote and picturesque, this less visited region of the southwestern coastline has excellent gardens, religious sites, and distilleries. If you like whisky, a trip to Islay is a must; if it's mountains you're after, try Jura; if a Christian site strikes a chord, head to Iona. The Isle of Arran is the place to see Scotland's diversity shrunk down to a more intimate size.

8 Inverness and Around the Great Glen. An awe-inspiring valley laced with rivers and streams defines this part of the country. A top spot for hikers, this Highland glen is ringed by tall mountains, including Ben Nevis, Britain's tallest mountain. Rugged Cairngorms National Park lies to the east of this area. Glencoe and Culloden are historic sites not to miss; those who believe in Nessie, Scotland's famous monster, can follow the throngs to Loch Ness.

9 The Northern Highlands and the Western Isles. This rugged land is home to the lore of clans, big moody skies, and wild rolling moors. It's also the place to see one of Scotland's most picturesque castles, Eilean Donan, which you pass on the way to the beautiful, popular Isle of Skye. The stark, remote Outer Hebrides, or Western Isles, offer ruined forts and chapels. This is where you go for real peace and quiet.

10 Orkney and Shetland Islands. Remote and austere, these isles at the northern tip of Scotland require tenacity to reach but have an abundance of prehistoric sites, including standing circles, *brochs* (circular towers), and tombs, as well as wild, open landscapes. The Shetland Isles, with their barren moors and vertical cliffs, are well known for bird-watching and diving opportunities.

SCOTLAND

ATLANTIC

10°W

IRELAND

Donegal

0   50 mi

0   50 km

What to Eat and Drink in Scotland

SHORTBREAD

The traditional Scottish biscuits may seem simple enough (they're typically made from one part white sugar, two parts butter, and three parts oat flour), but there are countless varieties, from big name brands like Walkers to artisan biscuit makers.

FULL SCOTTISH BREAKFAST

The full Scottish is a hearty, filling, and artery-clogging morning staple, which includes some or all of the following: back bacon, sausages, black pudding, haggis, eggs (fried, poached, or scrambled), baked beans, grilled tomatoes, mushrooms, tattie (potato) scones, and toast.

WHISKY

No trip to Scotland is complete without trying a dram or two of Scotland's most famous tipple. There are several distinct Scotch whisky regions, each producing a single malt with its own complex character, from sweeter Speyside whiskies to smokier Islays.

HAGGIS, NEEPS, AND TATTIES

From the offal-heavy list of ingredients (minced heart, liver, and lungs mixed with onions, oatmeal, and spices) and the unconventional cooking method (the mixture is boiled in a sheep's stomach), haggis may not sound like the most appetizing of meals. But there's a very good reason for its status as Scotland's national dish: it's delicious. Travel the country and you'll see haggis all over menus. It's traditionally served with neeps (turnips) and tatties (potatoes), but is also found at breakfast, in sandwiches, and even on nachos.

SMOKED FISH

From Arbroath smokies to Finnan haddie, smoked fish is a staple of Scottish dining tables nationwide. Smokies are haddock, salted and dried overnight, then smoked in a barrel over a hardwood fire, while Finnan haddies are cold-smoked haddock, cooked over green wood and peat. And that's only the start of the many regional variations of smoked fish all over Scotland. Visitors will also find menus featuring smoked herring (kippers), smoked trout, and, of course, smoked salmon.

REAL ALES

Also known as draught cask ale, real ale is unfiltered, unpasteurized beer that is served directly from a cask. The term was coined in the early 1970s to differentiate traditional English-style beers, containing live yeast and therefore naturally bubbly, from the highly

Smoked fish

processed, artificially carbonated beers made by big breweries of the time. Today real ales (from IPAs and stouts to golden ales and porters) are served in all good Scottish pubs; look for a traditional hand-pulled pump or for beer being served directly from the cask.

FISH-AND-CHIPS

Usually known as a "fish supper" in Scotland, this British staple comprises battered and deep-fried fish (most commonly cod, haddock, or another white fish) served with a portion of thick-cut potato "chips" (a thicker, greasier version of fries). For a true Scottish experience, ask for it with salt and "chippy sauce,"

a pungent mix of malt vinegar and brown sauce, which is similar to American steak sauce.

SCOTCH PIE

Once frowned upon by the Church of Scotland for being too decadent, these savory snacks are now embraced by all. The small, double-crust meat pastries are filled with mutton or similar meat and spiced with pepper. You can pick them up from most Scottish bakeries and fish-and-chips shops to eat on the go.

CULLEN SKINK

Cullen skink is a decadently creamy fish soup that's made with hearty smoked haddock, potatoes, onions, and cream. Think American chowder, but thicker, smokier, and served piping hot with bread. You'll find it on the menu in many Scottish pubs and restaurants, especially on the coasts.

What to Buy in Scotland

KILTS

These knee-length pleated skirts, usually made from woolen cloth in a tartan pattern, are the traditional dress of men in the Highlands. While no longer everyday wear for most modern Scots, you'll still see kilts worn on special occasions like weddings.

TUNNOCK'S TEA CAKES

A small shortbread biscuit covered in a marshmallow dome and then dipped in milk chocolate, these small sweet treats are quintessentially Scottish, with the Tunnock's bakery based just outside Glasgow. You will find the cookies in B&B bedrooms, coffee shops, and hipster bars all across the country, and if you want to take a selection home as a taste of Scotland, you can pick up a pack of six in any Scottish supermarket.

ANYTHING TARTAN PRINT

Like the look of tartan but can't see yourself in a kilt? No problem. You'll find plenty of other tartan print products on sale in Scotland, from sweaters and scarves to coats and cushions to backpacks and bow ties. If you want to go the whole hog, order yourself a statement tartan-clad armchair from ANTA in Edinburgh.

SINGLE-MALT WHISKY

It's no surprise that whisky is one of the most popular Scottish souvenirs. After all, nowhere makes single malt whisky quite like Scotland. If you have a chance to try some drams on a distillery tour, you can then pick up a bottle (or several) to take home. Otherwise, most supermarkets have a good selection of Scottish whiskies. Don't worry if you are low on luggage space; you can pick up a bottle at the airport duty-free.

A SCOTTISH CREST

If you have Scottish heritage or know someone else who does, why not order something decorated with the family crest of a Scottish clan? Whether you are an Armstrong, a McDonald, or a Walker, there are all manner of crest-related gifts available in Scotland, from certificates and cufflinks to embossed hip flasks.

GREYFRIARS BOBBY STUFFED ANIMAL

Every visitor to Edinburgh can recount the tale of Greyfriars Bobby, a Skye Terrier dog who guarded his master's grave for 14 years and who is now immortalized in a popular statue next to Greyfriars Kirk. You will find "cuddly" (stuffed) toys of the city's renowned canine resident for sale all over Edinburgh; it's the perfect gift for a little one.

OOR WULLIE COMIC BOOK

A popular Scottish comic character "born" in 1936, Oor Wullie (real name: William Russell) is considered a

Quaich

Scottish institution. In fact, in a 2004 poll, he was voted "Scotland's Favorite Son" ahead of William Wallace, Sean Connery, and Robert Burns. To see the latest strip, simply pick up a copy of the Sunday Post from any newsstand, or for a longer read, pick up the latest Oor Wullie Annual from any good bookshop.

QUAICH

An old Highland symbol of kinship and friendship, this shallow drinking vessel was the original whisky tumbler. Its distinctive two-handle design means it can be shared amicably between friends and loved ones (and it's still used to toast the bride at weddings). Though traditionally made of wood and modestly decorated, modern quaichs are commonly made from pewter and silver to allow for personalized engraving.

HEATHERGEMS JEWELRY

For a truly unique Scottish souvenir or gift, it's hard to beat Heathergems. This unique range of jewelry is made from the stems of natural heather, a plant that grows throughout Scotland and is recognizable for its purple flowers. Choose from elegant silver drop earrings, stylish animal-shaped brooches, and more.

HARRIS TWEED

A traditional cloth handwoven from pure virgin wool by crofters in the Western Isles (not just Lewis and Harris, but also North Uist, Benbecula, South Uist, and Barra), Harris Tweed is world famous for its warmth, softness, resilience, and breathability. From jackets to scarves to blankets, Harris Tweed items are for sale across the Western Isles but also on the mainland; simply look for the official orb trademark.

IRN-BRU

After whisky, Irn-Bru is the drink most associated with Scotland. The luminous orange carbonated soda even outsells Coca-Cola in these parts. Nobody can quite agree exactly what the flavor is, and it famously isn't to everyone's taste, but you can't say you have truly experienced Scotland without a sip of Irn-Bru. They also make for an inexpensive but distinctly Scottish souvenir.

Best Museums in Scotland

KELVINGROVE ART GALLERY AND MUSEUM, GLASGOW

One of Scotland's most popular museums, Kelvingrove's collection includes works by Rembrandt, van Gogh, and Dali, an impressive collection of arms and armor, a gigantic concert pipe organ, and much more.

NATIONAL MUSEUM OF SCOTLAND, EDINBURGH

From Dolly the Sheep (the world's first cloned mammal) to the Lewis Chessmen (ivory-carved medieval chess pieces), the National Museum of Scotland has a host of fascinating, family-friendly exhibits. It also has one of Edinburgh's best city views; take the elevator to the rooftop terrace for a stunning panorama of the city.

RIVERSIDE MUSEUM, GLASGOW

Set within an eye-catching, Zaha Hadid–designed building on the banks of the Clyde, the award-winning Riverside Museum has an exhaustive collection of transport exhibits, from skateboards to steam trains and everything in between. Also the Tall Ship at Riverside, a Victorian cargo ship, is moored outside.

AUCHINDRAIN MUSEUM, ARGYLL

The open-air Auchindrain Museum is a rarity: a real opportunity to step back in time. As one of the last surviving examples of an 18th-century farming community, this fine museum allows you to wander freely around its furnished thatched buildings and learn about the lives of Highland farmers living in the 1700s.

SCOTTISH FISHERIES MUSEUM, FIFE

This fascinating Fife museum brings to life the history and heritage of Scottish fisherfolk through a series of exhibits, including fishing apparatus, paintings, and model ships, while a look out the window reveals a working boatyard. If the fishing-themed exhibits make you hungry, famous Anstruther Fish Bar is next door.

V&A DUNDEE

The V&A Dundee design museum is not only the first V&A outpost outside London but also the country's first design museum; it features permanent exhibits from designers across Scotland, including Charles Rennie Mackintosh.

MCMANUS GALLERIES, DUNDEE

Another Dundee favorite, the McManus houses one of Scotland's most impressive fine art collections, while the building—a grand Gothic Revival style construction—is a work of art in itself.

ROBERT BURNS BIRTHPLACE MUSEUM, ALLOWAY

Although a little off the beaten track, this interesting little Alloway museum is well worth the journey. As the name suggests, the Robert Burns Birthplace Museum is dedicated to Scotland's national poet, Rabbie Burns, who is perhaps best known for his poem—and now a New Year's Eve staple song—"Auld Lang Syne." Set within the humble cottage where he was born, it houses thousands of his manuscripts and artifacts.

WEST HIGHLAND MUSEUM, FORT WILLIAM

You're unlikely to spend more than a few days in Scotland without hearing the story of Bonnie Prince Charles and the 1745 Jacobite Rebellion (fans of the TV show *Outlander* will be especially familiar with it). This small museum explores this important slice of Scottish history through a host of fascinating and folksy exhibits.

Best Castles in Scotland

CRATHES CASTLE

With a beautiful backdrop of rolling green hills, the impeccably preserved 16th-century Crathes Castle is one of Scotland's lesser-known gems. Situated just outside Aberdeen, it is home to Jacobean rooms with painted ceilings, an impressive collection of portraits, and a vast estate of gardens, fields, and woodland.

EDINBURGH CASTLE

Scotland's most famous medieval fortress, Edinburgh Castle is the capital's crowning glory, having played host to kings, queens, soldiers, and prisoners for close to a millennium.

DUNNOTTAR CASTLE

The site of these captivating castle ruins, perched on a cliff overlooking the turbulent North Sea, is one of the most dramatic in Scotland. Famed for saving the Scottish crown jewels from the grasp of Oliver Cromwell, Dunnottar Castle now provides a fine sea-air stop on a drive from Dundee to Aberdeen.

DRUMLANRIG CASTLE

Owned by one of the wealthiest families in Britain, pink-sandstone Drumlanrig Castle sits at the heart of an enormous estate and has period features dating back to the 16th century, world-class art collection, and a host of activities on offer.

STIRLING CASTLE

Magnificent Stirling Castle was at the heart of the Wars of Independence, and the biggest prize for Robert the Bruce's famous victory at Bannockburn. The castle's royal connections lasted for centuries; it was later the childhood home of Mary, Queen of Scots. Today exhibits tell the story of the castle's roles as a battle site, royal palace, and tourism hot spot.

FLOORS CASTLE
Built in the 1720s as the seat of the Duke of Roxburghe, the enormous Floors Castle remains the property of the duke to this day. That makes it the largest inhabited castle in Scotland; it has grand rooms decorated with plush furnishings, old portraits, and precious porcelain.

BALMORAL CASTLE
This imposing estate house has been an official residence of the royal family since 1852 and remains the Queen's summer home of choice. Its 19th-century design is faux–Scottish baronial, but its grandiose ballroom, formal grounds, and fascinating exhibits make it a worthwhile stop.

EILEAN DONAN
The most postcard-perfect castle, Eilean Donan sits pretty on a loch islet en route to the Isle of Skye. Often obscured by rolling fog, the 14th-century fortification—a merry mess of imposing towers, timber-framed roofs, and crooked staircases—connects to the mainland via a stone-arched bridge.

CAERLAVEROCK CASTLE
A true Scottish landmark, 13th-century Caerlaverock Castle is instantly recognizable for its rare triangular design. Although built to control trade, its strategic location on the border of Scotland and England inevitably led to a key role in the Wars of Independence; it subsequently endured cycles of ruin, repair, and rebuilding.

GLAMIS CASTLE
Beautiful Glamis Castle has a long history of royal connections, from Macbeth, King of the Scots (who was the Thane of Glamis, as well as Cawdor) to Princess Margaret (who was born within its four walls). Consequently, for any lovers of Shakespeare or the British royal family, Glamis Castle is a must-see sight.

Best *Outlander* Filming Locations

CULLODEN BATTLEFIELD

A popular tourist attraction not far outside Inverness, Culloden Battlefield was the site of the last battle of the Jacobite Uprising. Unusual for this list, this is a real-life attraction that plays itself in the series; it appears in the scene where Jamie and Claire say goodbye before he leaves to fight in the historic battle.

BLACKNESS CASTLE

Located about eight miles west of South Queensferry on the shores of the Firth of Forth, the mighty fortification of Blackness Castle ably plays the Fort William base of dastardly Black Jack Randal in the show.

PALACE OF HOLYROODHOUSE

The official Scottish residence of the Queen, this is where Bonnie Prince Charlie established his court for six weeks before the Jacobite Uprising; in the show, Claire and Jamie visit the prince here to beg him to abandon his hopeless cause.

GLENCOE

Even if you've never made it beyond the opening credits of *Outlander*, you will still have seen glimpses of Glencoe, as its lush green valleys, snowcapped peaks, and glistening lakes feature in the title sequence. And no wonder, when it is one of Scotland's most attractive locations.

DOUNE CASTLE

A stand-in for the fictional Castle Leoch in the show (the home of dashing warrior Jamie Fraser's uncle, Colum Mackenzie, and his clan), Doune Castle is a medieval stronghold that dates back to the 14th century. In addition to *Outlander*, the castle has featured in *Game of Thrones*, *Ivanhoe*, and *Monty Python and the Holy Grail*.

CALANAIS STANDING STONES AND CLAVA CAIRNS

The mysterious, prehistoric Calanais Standing Stones were the main inspiration for Craigh na Du, the fictional stones that send Claire back in time in *Outlander*. There's also a touch of the Clava Cairns (a Bronze Age burial site) about Craigh na Du.

CRAIGMILLAR CASTLE

Known to *Outlander* fans as the remote Ardsmuir Prison, the place of Jamie's incarceration in season three, the handsome ruined Craigmillar Castle is in fact situated just a few miles from the center of Edinburgh.

HOPETOUN HOUSE

As perhaps Scotland's finest stately home, the turn-of-the-18th-century building houses stunning interiors and a sprawling English garden–style landscape park. It's been used as several locations in the show, standing in for the home of the Duke of Sandringham and the Hawkins Estate.

LINLITHGOW PALACE

As the birthplace of Mary, Queen of Scots and the seat of Stewart kings, Linlithgow Palace is steeped in real medieval history. But in the fictional world of *Outlander*, the palace stood in as Wentworth Prison, where Jamie is tried and sentenced to hang—though not before being tortured by Black Jack Randall.

CULROSS

As a living museum of 17th-century Scottish life, the seaside town of Culross has played the Black Kirk, the village of Cranesmuir, the location of Balriggan Cottage, and has been a backdrop to the Jacobite encampment and makeshift hospital scenes.

The Best Whisky Distilleries in Scotland

THE GLENLIVET

Founded in 1824, The Glenlivet was the first licensed distillery anywhere in the Highlands, and it's been in operation almost continually since. The signature 12-year-old's smooth, lightly fruity style makes it the biggest selling single malt in the United States, while the full collection features experimental sherry-cask whiskies, light peaty drams, and white oak reserves.

THE MACALLAN

One of the world's most popular single malts, The Macallan has produced whisky here for nigh on two centuries. Its collection is matured in a mix of bourbon oak and oak sherry casks, making for a heady blend of perfumed, spicy, and sweet drams.

HIGHLAND PARK

It may no longer be Scotland's northernmost distillery, but it remains one of Scotland's finest. The Highland Park distillery was founded in Orkney more than 220 years ago and has since won countless global awards for its peat-heavy, Viking-themed spirits.

GLEN GRANT DISTILLERY

A perennial Speyside favorite, Glen Grant Distillery is renowned for three things: it was the first Scottish distillery to be electrically powered; it's surrounded by beautiful gardens that feature rivers and lily ponds; and it consistently produces excellent whisky.

ISLE OF ARRAN DISTILLERS

Located on the southwestern Isle of Arran, this distillery only began producing whisky in 1995, but it has quickly gained an enviable reputation for its fresh, sweet, and spicy single malts. Choose from a series of distillery tours and whisky tastings.

LAPHROAIG

For lovers of peaty whiskies, the Laphroaig distillery is a place of pilgrimage, as Islay's most distinctive single malt is renowned for its smoky flavor and smooth finish. Take a tour of the distillery, which includes great views of the coast and its iconic pagoda-style chimney.

GLENMORANGIE DISTILLERY

One of the Highlands' best-known distilleries, Glenmorangie makes arguably the archetypal Speyside whisky: light, floral, and sweet. The distillery offers a range of experiences, including in-depth tours and tasting master classes.

GLENFIDDICH

The world's most popular single malt whisky and one of the most famous stops on the Malt Whisky Trail, Glenfiddich is a bona fide Scotch superstar. As you would expect, it has a visitor center to suit its status. Knowledgeable guides offer a range of tours and tastings.

TOBERMORY DISTILLERY

For an off-the-beaten-path whisky-tasting experience, look no further than Tobermory Distillery. Situated on the Isle of Mull, it has been producing whisky on and off since 1798. Today you can try its signature Ledaig single malt, as well as its unpeated Tobermory whisky, on a visit to its white-walled visitor center.

BUNNAHABHAIN

A special distillery with an equally special view, Bunnahabhain (pronounced *Boon*-a-*ha*-bin) sits on the northeastern shore of Islay looking across the sea to Jura. Along with its setting, the whisky is also one of a kind—less peaty and more citrusy than its neighbors—and you can try it yourself on a distillery tour.

Scotland Today

It may have just 5.4 million people, but today Scotland has some big ideas about where it's headed socially, culturally, and economically. International sporting events, the lively (but ultimately defeated) 2014 referendum on whether to become an independent nation, and even First Minister Nicola Sturgeon's state visits to the United States and elsewhere continue to focus worldwide attention on Scotland.

TRAVEL IN THE 21ST CENTURY
The experience of traveling in Scotland has changed markedly for the better in recent years, with wholesale improvements in standards of hospitality and food especially.

Today hotels and restaurants charge prices similar to those in the rest of the United Kingdom. On the other hand, most of Scotland's biggest and best museums and galleries are free. Walk through well-tended gardens, along bustling waterfronts, and in beautifully renovated neighborhoods—a good day out can show you everything but cost nothing at all.

In 2020 Scotland presents its Year of Coasts and Waters, celebrating its varied and spectacular coastal scenery. In 2022 the focus will be on the country's rich storytelling traditions in the Year of Scotland's Stories.

INDEPENDENCE AND BREXIT
Dominating Scotland's public life in recent years has been the relationship of Scotland with the United Kingdom. Parliament and the increasingly troubled state of this 300-year-old union. Through devolution, Scotland elected its first parliament in 300 years in 1999. In 2014 the independence referendum saw 55% vote against Scotland becoming an independent country. But that vote by no means resolved the matter, especially given the unpopularity in Scotland of the 2016 U.K. vote to leave the European Union, or Brexit, when only 38% of Scots voted to leave and 62% to remain. With the prospect that leaving the single-market European Union might lead to further economic turmoil across the United Kingdom, First Minister of Scotland Nicola Sturgeon has called for a second independence referendum, due to a significant material change. Sturgeon's Scottish Nationalist Party (SNP) reset the timetable for triggering "IndyRef 2" for when the outcome of Brexit negotiations plays out in late 2019 (or so says the current plan—the official exit date of the United Kingdom has been pushed back several times over the last year).

Besides the prospect of being dragged out of the European Union against the wishes of its people, why are many Scots dissatisfied with the U.K. government? In a time of budget woes, the Westminster government has been slashing public services. Many of these cuts deeply offend the Scots, who are committed to free education and free health care from the publicly owned National Health Service. Many commentators predict that Brexit-induced economic turmoil and further erosions of public services by newly elected (and largely reviled) Prime Minister Boris Johnson will hasten another independence vote.

CULTURE
The arts continue to thrive, a sign of Scotland's creative energy. Edinburgh's arts festivals grow bigger every year, attracting visitors from around the globe. The National Theatre of Scotland has been such a resounding success that productions have made their way to Broadway. Glasgow is renowned for contemporary arts: Glasgow artists often win the Turner Prize, Britain's most prestigious art honor.

In a sign of vitality, culture is not confined only to the large cities. Far to the north, Shetland (already drawing audiences with its folk festivals) has built Mareel, a remarkable live-music venue and cinema. Dundee is the United Kingdom's sole UNESCO City of Design (Detroit represents the United States) and is the location of the first outpost of London's Victoria and Albert Museum, opened in 2018. Perth's renewal will center on the transformation of Perth City Hall into a museum and gallery.

LAND

It's a disturbing fact that just 500 people own half the land in Scotland, many of them wealthy foreigners who have become absentee landlords. Experts say that giving residents a say on what happens to the land they live on is crucial if communities are going to thrive. New models of community ownership and management are being hard won, particularly in the Western Isles. There have been some community buyouts in which farming communities get the government's help to purchase the land where they live and work.

Still the depopulation of rural Scotland continues. The popularity of holiday homes has meant that some villages are fully inhabited for only a few weeks each summer. Those who want to live here permanently find that low wages, a high cost of living, and a lack of affordable housing mean that they are priced out of a home surrounded by such beauty.

WIND POWER

Urged by the government to help the country meet its ambitious targets for renewable energy, Scottish landowners began leasing land to the corporations behind wind farms. Scotland now has many large-scale commercial wind farms—including Europe's largest—and hundreds of smaller ones, many in community ownership. This has sparked vociferous debate. The pro-wind lobby argues in favor of emission-free energy that's better for the environment than coal or nuclear plants, while the anti-wind camp decries the environmental damage to ancient peat bogs and bird populations.

Turbines are now being built offshore, which is another cause for dispute. Donald Trump, who ignored environmental activists while building his sprawling golf estate, had a very public fallout with government officials over the "ugly" planned offshore turbine plant that will be visible from his golf course. Now the American president, Trump continues to withhold the multimillion-dollar investment he promised at the outset.

SCOTLAND, FINALLY WINNING

When it comes to sports, the Scots have reveled in their traditional role as the underdog. But Olympic gold medal–winning cyclist Chris Hoy and tennis Grand Slam winner Andy Murray have shown that this narrative needs rewriting.

As well as regularly hosting major golf tournaments, Scotland has proved itself of late as a worthy and welcoming venue for prestigious international events. After the success of the Glasgow Commonwealth Games in 2014 and with St. Andrews hosting the landmark 150th Open Golf Championship in 2021, pride and participation in Scottish sports is growing.

Playing Golf in Scotland

There are some 550 golf courses in Scotland and only 5.3 million residents, so the country has probably the highest ratio of courses to people anywhere in the world. If you're visiting Scotland, you'll probably want to play the "famous names" sometime in your career.

So by all means play the championship courses such as the Old Course at St. Andrews, but remember they *are* championship courses. You may enjoy the game itself much more at a less challenging course. Remember, too, that everyone else wants to play the big names, so booking can be a problem at peak times in summer. Reserving three to four months ahead is not too far for the famous courses, although it's possible to get a time up to a month (or even a week) in advance if you are relaxed about your timing. If you're staying in a hotel attached to a course, get the concierge to book a tee time for you.

Happily, golf has always had a peculiar classlessness in Scotland. It's a game for everyone, and for centuries Scottish towns and cities have maintained courses for the enjoyment of their citizens. Admittedly, a few clubs have always been noted for their exclusive air, and some newer golf courses are losing touch with the game's inclusive origins, but these are exceptions to the tradition of recreation for all. Golf here is usually a democratic game, played by ordinary folk as well as the wealthy.

TIPS ABOUT PLAYING

Golf courses are everywhere in Scotland. Most courses welcome visitors with a minimum of formalities, and some at a surprisingly low cost. Other courses are very expensive, but a lot of great golf can be played for between about £30 to £100 a round. Online booking at many courses has made arranging a golf tour easier, too.

Be aware of the topography of a course. Scotland is where the distinction between "links" and "parkland" courses was first made. Links courses are by the sea and are subject to the attendant sea breezes—some quite bracing—and mists, which can make them trickier to play. The natural topography of sand dunes and long, coarse grasses can add to the challenge. A parkland course is in a wooded area and its terrain is more obviously landscaped. A "moorland" course is found in an upland area.

Here are three pieces of advice, particularly for North Americans: (1) in Scotland the game is usually played fairly quickly, so don't dawdle if others are waiting; (2) caddy carts are hand-pulled carts for your clubs and driven golf carts are rarely available; and (3) when they say "rough," they really mean "rough."

Unless specified otherwise, hours are generally sunrise to sundown, which in June can be as late as 10 pm. Note that some courses advertise the SSS, "standard scratch score," instead of par (which may be different). This is the score a scratch golfer could achieve under perfect conditions. Rental clubs, balls, and other gear are generally available from clubhouses, except at the most basic municipal courses. Don't get caught by the dress codes enforced at many establishments: in general, untailored shorts, round-neck shirts, jeans, and sneakers are frowned upon.

The prestigious courses may ask for evidence of your golf skills by way of a handicap certificate; check in advance and carry this with you.

COSTS AND COURSES

Many courses lower their rates before and after peak season—at the end of September, for example. It's worth asking about this. ■TIP➜ Some areas offer regional golf passes that save you money. Check with the local tourist board.

For a complete list of courses, contact local tourist offices or VisitScotland's official and comprehensive golf website, ⊕ golf.visitscotland.com. It has information about the country's golf courses, special golf trails, regional passes, special events, and tour operators, as well as on conveniently located accommodations. U.K. Golf Guide (⊕ www.uk-golfguide.com) has user-generated reviews. For information about regional courses, also see individual chapters.

BEST BETS AROUND SCOTLAND

If your idea of heaven is teeing off on a windswept links, then Scotland is for you. Dramatic courses, many of them set on sandy dunes alongside the ocean, are just one of the types you'll encounter. Highland courses that take you through the heather and moorland courses surrounded by craggy mountains have their own challenges.

Boat of Garten Golf Club, Inverness-shire. With the Cairngorm Mountain as a backdrop, this beautiful course has rugged terrain that requires even seasoned players to bring their A game. As an added bonus, a steam railway runs alongside the course.

Carnoustie Golf Links, Angus. Challenging golfers for nearly 500 years, Carnoustie is on many golfers' must-do list. The iconic Championship Course has tested many of the world's top players, while the Burnside and Buddon courses attract budding Players and Watsons.

Castle Stuart Golf Links, Inverness-shire. A more recent addition to Scotland's world-class courses offers cliff-top hazards, sprawling bunkers, and rolling fairways overlooking the Moray Firth.

Cruden Bay Golf Club, Aberdeenshire. This challenging and enjoyable links course was built by the Great North of Scotland Railway Company in 1894. Its remote location beside a set of towering dunes makes it irresistible.

Dunbar Golf Club, East Lothian. This classic and challenging links course has dramatic weather and scenery, with a backdrop of the Firth of Forth, Bass Rock, and a lighthouse.

Gleneagles, Perthshire. Host of the 2014 Ryder Cup championship, Gleneagles has three 18-hole courses that challenge the pros and a 9-hole course that provides a more laid-back game. It's also home to the PGA National Golf Academy.

Machrihanish Golf Club, Argyll. A dramatic location on the Mull of Kintyre and some exciting match play make these links well worth a journey.

Royal Dornoch Golf Club, Sutherland. Extending across a coastal shelf, Royal Dornoch has fast greens, pristine beaches, and mountain views. In spring yellow gorse sets the green hills ablaze.

St. Andrews Links, Fife. To approach the iconic 18th hole in the place where the game was invented remains the holy grail of golfers worldwide.

Western Gailes Golf Club, near Glasgow. This splendid links course is a final qualifying course for the British Open. Sculpted by Mother Nature, it's the country's finest natural links course.

Film Locations Throughout Scotland

Scotland's dramatic scenery and the character of its people have left impressions on viewers since the birth of the moving image. Today visitors not only seek out the locations seen in blockbuster series such as *Outlander*, *Game of Thrones*, and James Bond films, but also classic and cult movie scenes: from *Local Hero* and *Wicker Man* to *Shallow Grave* and *Trainspotting*. Here is a selection of some standout film locations:

EDINBURGH AND THE LOTHIANS

Edinburgh and the Lothians' handsome architecture is the backdrop for many productions. In the 1969 adaptation of Muriel Spark's novel *The Prime of Miss Jean Brodie*, Oscar winner Maggie Smith leads her 1930s schoolgirls around Edinburgh Academy on Henderson Row, Greyfriars Churchyard, and the Vennel (Grassmarket), retreating to Cramond. In *Trainspotting's* (1994) opening sequence Renton and pals flee the police down Princes Street and steps toward Calton Street Bridge. *T2*, the 2017 sequel, revisits this iconic chase scene and also includes Commercial Street, Leith, Arthur's Seat, Scottish Parliament, Royal Circus, and Stockbridge. The feel-good musical *Sunshine on Leith* (2013), based on the Proclaimers' rousing tunes, plays out in the Old Town and on the Port of Leith's cobblestone streets. Auld Reekie's magical skyline and atmosphere is captured in the charming animation *The Illusionist* (2010).

Outlander (2014) season one and two feature Hopetoun House, Blackness Castle, and Linlithgow Palace. For a map of *Outlander* locations, see ⊕ *www.visitscotland.com/see-do/attractions/tv-film/outlander*.

GLASGOW

Glasgow's street grid makes it a good stand-in for U.S. cities including Philadelphia in zombie flick *World War Z* (2013) starring Brad Pitt; while Blythswood Hill resembles San Francisco in *Cloud Atlas* (2012). The grand City Chambers stand in for: belle époque New York mansions in *House of Mirth* (2000); the Vatican in *Heavenly Pursuits* (1986); and the Kremlin in *An Englishman Abroad* (1983). Hutcheson's Hall on Ingram Street appears in *The Wife* (2017), starring Glenn Close. *Mission Impossible's* (2000) railway chase finale is a blur of East Ayrshire countryside and Ballochmyle Viaduct. Brooding landscapes make the Borders and the Southwest ripe for intrigue, murder, and mystery. Hermitage Castle's role in 16th-century regal plotting appears in *Mary Queen of Scots* (1971), starring Vanessa Redgrave and Glenda Jackson; a lavish retelling was filmed in 2017. Chilling cult B-feature *The Wicker Man* centers on a pagan Scottish isle, with many creepy scenes filmed around Newton Stewart, including St. Ninian's Cave, Castle Kennedy, and Logan Botanic Gardens.

FIFE AND ANGUS

Many visitors to Fife and Angus hum Vangelis's *Chariots of Fire* (1984) synthesizer soundtrack, reenacting the slow-motion sprint along St. Andrews West Beach. The Royal and Ancient club and Fife's coastal links also appear in *Tommy's Honour* (2017), telling the story of Old and Young Tom Morris's relationship and golfing history.

CENTRAL HIGHLANDS

Doune Castle in the Central Highlands is synonymous with *Monty Python and the Holy Grail* (1975), the first Winterfell in *Game of Thrones* (2011), and then Castle Leoch for *Outlander*. The Falls of Dochart appear in the *39 Steps* (1959) and *Casino Royale* (1967).

ABERDEEN AND THE NORTHEAST

Fans of the much-loved *Local Hero* (1983) with Burt Lancaster and Peter Reigert make a pilgrimage to Aberdeen and the northeast harbor village Pennan's red telephone box and nearby Banff's Ship Inn. For the fictional west-coast village of Furness's beach and Ben's shack, go west to Camusdarach, Morar. Royal Deeside and Balmoral Estate are at the heart of *The Queen* (2009), *The Crown* (2016), and *Mrs. Brown* (1997).

ARGYLL AND THE ISLES

Duart Castle in Argyll and the Isles has staged real-life kidnap attempts and celluloid dramas including *I Know Where I'm Going* (1945) and *Entrapment* (1999). Mull's Treshnish Peninsula and Oban feature in the spy thriller the *Eye of the Needle* (1981), starring Donald Sutherland.

INVERNESS AND AROUND THE GREAT GLEN

Glen Nevis is clan central in *Braveheart* (1995), while *Rob Roy* (1995) rampages around Glen Coe, Rannoch Moor, Lochs Morar, and Leven, and Eilean Donan Castle. The lochside castle also stars in *Master of Ballatrae* (1953) with Errol Flynn, *Highlander* (1986) with Sean Connery, and *The World Is Not Enough* (1999) as MI6 headquarters Scotland. Another Bond movie, *Skyfall* (2012), has a spectacular A82 driving scene. Billie Wilder's *The Private Life of Sherlock Holmes* (1971) introduces Urquhart Castle for some Loch Ness monster encounters. Glenfinnan Viaduct has become synonymous with the *Harry Potter* films; Claichaig Gully, Glencoe, Steall Falls in Glen Nevis, and Loch Eilt also appear.

NORTHERN HIGHLANDS AND WESTERN ISLES

Skye's Cuillin mountain outcrops are now so popular with jet-setting fans of *Outlander, Macbeth* (2015), *Prometheus* (2012), *Skyfall* (2012), and *Stardust* (2007) that they are best visited in low season. Animation adventure *Brave* (2012) enchants children with its hyper-realistic depictions of Calanais Standing Stones, Glen Affric, and Dunnotar Castle. Dunrobin Castle impersonates a French chateau in Stanley Kubrick's adaptation of William Makepeace Thackeray's novel *Barry Lyndon* (1975). *Whisky Galore* (1949) was filmed on Barra, while the 2016 remake barrels around the mainland (see ⊕ *www.visitscotland.com/blog/films/whisky-galore*).

ORKNEY AND SHETLAND ISLANDS

The essence of Scotland's far-flung isles and the evacuation of St. Kilda inspired *The Edge of the World* (1937), filmed on Foula in the Orkney and Shetland Islands. Pioneering filmmakers Jenny Gilbertson and Margaret Tait were stirred by the landscapes and communities on these archipelagos, directing *The Rugged Island* (1934) and *Blue Black Permanent* (1992), respectively. Four seasons of crime drama *Shetland* (2013–) showcase the windswept Nordic scenery, including extinct volcano Eshaness.

FILM TOURS

Open Roads Scotland Open Roads offers James Bond, *Harry Potter*, and *Outlander*–themed tours. ☎ *0141/634–8444* ⊕ *openroadsscotland.com*.

Mary's Meanders Mary's has themed tours including *Outlander* film locations. ⊕ *www.marysmeanders.co.uk/outlander-tours/* 🎫 *From £80*.

What to Watch and Read Before Your Trip

OUTLANDER

If you're traveling to Scotland in the 21st century, chances are you're going to hear about the cultural phenomenon that is *Outlander*. The book series by Diana Gabaldon first captured the attention of the world in 1991, with many readers becoming dedicated fans of the time-traveling series through eight (and counting) novels. But then the television series debuted in 2014 on Starz and it seems the entire world fell in love with the love story between Claire Randall and Jamie Fraser amid a stunning Scottish Highlands backdrop. Both the book and the television show tell the same story: a nurse in 1946 finds herself sent back in time to 1743 Scotland, where she becomes entangled in the Jacobite uprising and falls in love with a Highland warrior. Many scenes are filmed on location, and you will find many a tour eager to take you to filming spots throughout the country.

BRAVEHEART

This 1995 classic starring Mel Gibson was many a filmgoer's introduction to Scottish history and remains one of the most quoted movies ever. It tells a very embellished story of the real 13-century Scottish warrior, William Wallace, who did lead the Scots in the First War of Scottish Independence against England. While historians will be happy to point out the many historical inaccuracies, the film was nonetheless a commercial and critical success, earning several Academy Awards, including Best Picture.

BRAVE

The first Pixar film directed by a woman (Brenda Chapman) and the first with a female main character, this 2012 animated film tells the story of Merida, the headstrong daughter of a Scottish king and queen who wishes to defy tradition in the name of her independence. Along with a heartwarming tale of mother and daughter love and acceptance, it portrays gorgeous animation of the Scottish Highlands and Highland traditions.

MACBETH BY WILLIAM SHAKESPEARE

Shakespeare may be England's most famous writer, but one of his most famous plays tells a distinctly Scottish tale. The play is based on the lives of actual men who fought for power in 11th-century Scotland although the real life versions of Macbeth, Macduff, and Duncan were quite different. Nevertheless the fiction that the Bard weaves is one of the most powerful stories of ambition, power, and politics (and witchcraft) ever written.

THE HEART OF MIDLOTHIAN BY SIR WALTER SCOTT

Scotland's other famous literary son is Sir Walter Scott, a late 18th-/early 19th-century poet, historian, and writer who wrote several classics with Scotland as the backdrop, including *Ivanhoe* and *The Lady of the Lake*. But perhaps his most truly Scottish work is this 1818 novel that tells the tale of a woman who wishes to receive a royal pardon for her sister amid the 1736 Porteous riots in Edinburgh.

THE PRIME OF MISS JEAN BRODIE BY MURIEL SPARK

One of Scotland's most popular writers of the 20th century, Muriel Spark was born in Edinburgh and went on to write several novels and essays well known for their satire and wit. In her most famous book, written in 1961, she tells the story of Jean Brodie, a free-spirited teacher at a 1930s school for girls, whose emphasis on art and romance inspires a group of young women.

Chapter 2

TRAVEL SMART

Updated by
Nick Bruno

★ **CAPITAL:**
Edinburgh

‌∮ **POPULATION:**
5,438,100

💬 **LANGUAGE:**
English

$ **CURRENCY:**
British pound

☎ **COUNTRY CODE:**
44

⚠ **EMERGENCIES:**
999

🚗 **DRIVING:**
On the left

⚡ **ELECTRICITY:**
230V/50 cycles; plugs have
three rectangular blades

🕗 **TIME:**
Five hours ahead of New
York

🌐 **WEB RESOURCES:**
www.visitbritain.com;
www.visit.scotland.com;
www.nts.org.uk

Know Before You Go

Scotland is indeed one of the most accessible places for a traveler to visit, but there are still some key things to keep in mind before your trip. From tipping to understanding the ever-elusive Scottish accent, here's everything you need to know before a trip to Scotland.

DON'T MIX UP YOUR SCOTS WITH YOUR WELSH.

Remember that although Scotland is part of the United Kingdom politically and does share many cultural links with England, Wales, and Northern Island, Scots do not take kindly to their country being called England or being called English (or increasingly even British). In recent years the Scottish have developed a burgeoning pride in their distinctive identity, which has led to a waning sense of being British. So when in conversation, it's best not to associate Scottish people with the much maligned London-based Parliament and its English elite.

KNOW THE BEST TIMES OF THE YEAR TO VISIT.

Peak tourist season runs from mid-May through mid-September. Crowds at main attractions can be heavy, and prices are at their highest. Summer days are very long, and temperatures can linger in the 60s, 70s, or 80s, with dry spells lasting a week or two. November to March marks the low season for

travel. Winter sees lots of rain, some snow, and icy winds, not to mention the short days. City museums stay open year-round, but some tourist sites such as castles and historic houses close from November to Easter. You can get some excellent deals in spring (April to mid-May) and fall (mid-September to October); weather is cool and often rainy, but crowds are not as intense.

DON'T HUG A SCOT.

Although many Scots are fantastic talkers, they're less enthusiastic with greetings on the physical front. If you're in less familiar company, a handshake is more appreciated than a kiss or hug.

BE PREPARED FOR CHANGING WEATHER.

The weather in Scotland is very temperamental so be prepared for all possibilities, even in summer (including snow); it can be smart to pack layers and have a decent waterproof jacket on you at all times. If you plan on hiking while here, make sure you have decent outdoor equipment, sturdy footwear, food, and

refreshments. If you don't know how to read a map and use a compass, hire an expert hiking guide.

THERE AREN'T REALLY ANY DRESS CODES OR EATING CODES.

When you are visiting houses of worship, modest attire is appreciated, though you will see shorts and even bared midriffs. Photographs are welcome in churches, outside of services. Shorts and other close-fitting attire are allowed just about anywhere else at any time, weather permitting; these days locals tend not to cover up as much as they used to. It's the same with food; Scots eat and drink just about anywhere, and much of the time they do it standing up or even walking.

BUT IT'S STILL GOOD TO KNOW SOME SCOTTISH ETIQUETTE.

In Scotland it's rude to walk away from a conversation, even if it's with someone you don't know. If you're at a pub, keep in mind that it's very important to buy a round of drinks if you're socializing with a group of people. You don't simply buy your own drink; you buy a drink for all the people you're there with, and those people do the same. It can make for a very foggy evening and public drunkenness, especially on Friday and Saturday nights. Conversational topics that are considered taboo are money matters; the Scots are private about their finances.

Driving etiquette is carefully observed, too; be

courteous and allow people to pass. Jaywalking isn't rude or illegal, but it's much safer to cross with the lights, especially if traffic is coming from a direction you might not be used to. As for waiting in lines and moving through crowds, put your best foot forward. The Scots are very polite and you'll be noticed (and not in a good way) if you're not.

BE PREPARED TO NOT UNDERSTAND THE SCOTTISH ACCENT.

The Scots language, which borrows from Scandinavian, Dutch, French, and Gaelic, survives in various forms, with each region having its own dialect. In the northeast they speak Doric, while the Shetland and Orkney "tongue" is influenced by the now-extinct Norn. The Gaelic language, the indigenous language of those from the Western Isles and Highlands, has been given a new lease on life. Many primary schools in the region are teaching a new generation of Gaelic speakers. The language has its own TV channel, BBC Alba, and is being promoted in a huge signage campaign. Otherwise, Scots speak English often with a strong accent (which may be hard for nonnative Brits and Americans to understand), but your ear will soon come to terms with it.

BE AWARE IF YOU'RE HERE ON A BANK HOLIDAY.

The following days are public holidays in Scotland; note that the dates for England and Wales are slightly different. Ne'er Day and a day to recover (January 1–2), Good Friday, May Day (first Monday in May), Spring Bank Holiday (last Monday in May), Summer Bank Holiday (first Monday in August), St. Andrew's Day (November 30; for Scots government but optional for businesses), and Christmas (December 25–26). The majority of businesses might be closed on these days, but some museums and other major sights might be more crowded if they are open.

CHECK OUT THE OPTIONS FOR SIGHTSEEING PASSES.

Discounted sightseeing passes are a great way to save money on visits to castles, gardens, and historic houses. Just check what the pass offers against your itinerary to be sure it's worthwhile. The Explorer Pass, available from any staffed Historic Scotland (HS) property as well as from many tourist information centers, allows visits to HS properties for 5 (£35) or 14 (£45) consecutive days. The Scottish Heritage pass gives free access from April through October to over 120 Heritage Scotland–and National Trust for Scotland–run properties.

YES, YOU SHOULD TIP HERE.

Tipping is done in Scotland as in the United States, but at a lower level. Some restaurants include a service charge on the bill; if not, add about 10% to 15%. Taxi drivers, hairdressers, and barbers should also get 10% to 15%.

DON'T UNDERTAKE HIKES LIGHTLY.

Scotland has a stunning array of landscapes that make for some great walks and hikes, including the Great Glen, the Highlands, and more. But the wilderness of Scotland can still be quite a rugged place, so if you're not experienced as a hiker or camper, check to make sure you're undertaking the easiest trails possible. For longer or overnight hikes, consider going with a guide and always take the necessary precautions: bring plenty of food and water and always notify someone of the path you're taking and when you plan to return.

WATCH OUT FOR MIDGES IN THE HIGHLANDS.

If you're traveling in the Highlands and islands in summer, pack some midge repellent and antihistamine cream to reduce swelling: the Highland midge is a force to be reckoned with. Check ⊕ www.smidgeup.com/midge-forecast for updates on these biting pests.

Getting Here and Around

Air

Scotland's main hubs are Glasgow, Prestwick (near Glasgow), Edinburgh, Inverness, and Aberdeen. Glasgow and Prestwick are the gateways to the west and southwest, Edinburgh the east and southeast, Aberdeen and Inverness the north. All these cities have excellent bus and train transportation services and well-maintained roads that link them with each other and other cities within Scotland. Taxis are also an efficient and reliable option, but they are three to four times the cost of going by public transport.

Traveling by air is straightforward in Scotland. Security is heavy but efficient. You can often breeze through check-in lines by using your airline's online check-in option or bag drop, but confirm this ahead of time.

Flying time to Glasgow and Aberdeen is 6½ hours from New York, 7½ hours from Chicago, 9½ hours from Dallas, 10 hours from Los Angeles, and 21½ hours from Sydney. Flying time to Edinburgh is 7 hours from New York, 8 hours from Chicago, 10 hours from Dallas, 10½ hours from Los Angeles, and 22 hours from Sydney. Not all airlines offer direct flights to Scotland; many go via London. For those flights allow an extra four to five hours of travel (two to three for the layover in London plus an additional hour or two for the duration of the flight).

AIRPORTS

The major international gateways to Scotland are Glasgow Airport (GLA), about 7 miles outside Glasgow, and Edinburgh Airport (EDI), 7 miles from the city. Both offer connections for dozens of European cities and regular flights to London's Gatwick (LGW) and Heathrow (LHR) airports. Aberdeen Airport (ABZ) has direct flights to most major European cities. Prestwick

(PIK) has direct flights to some European cities at discounted rates. Inverness (INV) offers direct flights in and around the United Kingdom.

Airport tax is included in the price of your ticket. Generally the tax for economy tickets within the United Kingdom from European Union countries is £13. For all other flights it is £78. The standard rate for flights from the United Kingdom and European Union is £26; for all other destinations it's £172.

All Scottish airports offer typical modern amenities: restaurants, cafés, shopping, sandwich and salad bars, pubs, pharmacies, bookshops, and newsstands; some even have spas and hair salons. Glasgow and Edinburgh are the most interesting airports when it comes to a delayed flight. Good food and shopping options abound—try Discover Scotland, Scottish Fine Gifts, and Tartan Plus for Scottish-inspired goods.

There are plenty of hotels near all airports, and all airports also have Internet access.

GROUND TRANSPORTATION

The best way to get to and from the airport based on speed and convenience is by taxi. All airport taxi stands are just outside the airport's front doors and are well marked with clear signs. Most taxis have a set price when going to and from the airport to the city center but will turn on the meter at your request. Ask the driver to turn on the meter to confirm the flat-rate price.

If you're traveling with a large party, you can request a people carrier to transport everyone, luggage included. Luggage is included in the taxi fare; you should not be charged extra for it.

If you're traveling alone, a more economical transfer option is public transportation. Buses travel between city centers and Glasgow, Edinburgh, Aberdeen, and Inverness airports. Trams travel between Edinburgh Airport and the city center; Edinburgh Gateway station links the airport to the tram and rail network; trains go direct to Glasgow Prestwick Airport. All are fast, inexpensive, and reliable.

TRANSFERS BETWEEN AIRPORTS

Scottish airports are relatively close to one another and all are connected by a series of buses and trains. Flights between airports add hours to your journey and are very expensive (between £200 and £400). The best way to travel from one airport to another is by bus, train, car, or taxi. Normally you must take a combination of bus and train, which is easy and—if you travel light—quite enjoyable.

From Edinburgh Airport you can take the Citylink Air (£11.60) bus direct to Glasgow Airport in one hour. For those wanting to see Edinburgh and have time on their hands, take a tram (£5.50) or bus (£4.50) to the city center and then a train to Glasgow city center (£13.90) and a shuttle bus to Glasgow Airport (£7.50). This journey should take you less than two hours. Taxis are fast but costly. The price of a taxi from Edinburgh Airport to Glasgow Airport is around £90, a good choice if you're traveling with a few people. Renting a car would be a good choice if you want to get from Edinburgh to, say, Aberdeen Airport and you're traveling with a group of people. Otherwise, take a train from Edinburgh Gateway.

FLIGHTS

Scotland has a significant air network for a small country. British Airways (or British Airways Express) has flights from London's Heathrow Airport or from Glasgow, Edinburgh, Aberdeen, and Inverness to the farthest corners of the Scottish mainland and to the islands.

Among the low-cost carriers, Virgin has service from Heathrow; and easyJet flies from London Luton/Gatwick/Stansted to and between Glasgow, Edinburgh, Aberdeen, and Inverness, plus to and from Belfast. Flybe has services to Sumburgh (Shetland) and Kirkwall (Orkney) from Aberdeen, Inverness, Glasgow, and Edinburgh, where you can continue on to Bristol, Cardiff, Exeter, Manchester, Newquay, and Southampton. Flybe also runs the Dundee–London Stansted route.

Bike

Bicycling in Scotland is variable. The best months for cycling are May, June, and September, when the roads are often quieter and the weather is usually better. Because Scotland's main roads are continually being upgraded, bicyclists can easily reach the network of quieter rural roads in southern and much of eastern Scotland, especially Grampian. In a few areas of the Highlands, notably in northwestern Scotland, the rugged terrain and limited population have resulted in the lack of side roads, making it difficult—sometimes impossible—to plan a minor-road route in these areas.

Several agencies now promote routes for recreational cyclists. These routes are signposted, and agencies have produced maps or leaflets showing where they run. Perhaps best known is the Glasgow–Loch Lomond–Killin Cycleway. VisitScotland has advice on a site dedicated to cycling.

You can take bicycles on car and passenger ferries in Scotland, and it's usually not necessary to book in advance. Arrive early so that your bike can be loaded through the car entrance.

Getting Here and Around

ScotRail strongly advises that you make a train reservation for you and your bike at least one month in advance. On several trains reservations are compulsory.

ScotRail now runs a low-cost cycle-hire program via 12 major city and town stations. It costs £10 to register and the bike hire rate is just £3.80 per day.

BIKING ORGANIZATIONS

The Cyclists' Touring Club publishes a members' magazine, route maps, and guides. Sustrans is a nonprofit organization dedicated to providing environmentally friendly routes for cyclists. Active Scotland, part of the national tourism agency, has a great list of bike routes ranked by area and difficulty.

🧭 Boat and Ferry

Because Scotland has so many islands, plus the great Firth of Clyde waterway, ferry services are of paramount importance. Most ferries transport vehicles as well as foot passengers, although a few smaller ones are for passengers only.

It's a good idea to make a reservation ahead of time, although reservations are not absolutely necessary. Most travelers show up on the day of departure and buy their tickets from the stations at the ports. Keep in mind that these are working ferries, not tourist boats. Although journeys are scenic, most people use these ferries as their daily means of public transportation to and from their hometowns.

The main operator is Caledonian MacBrayne, known generally as CalMac. Services extend from the Firth of Clyde in the south, where there's an extensive network, right up to the northwest of Scotland and all the Hebrides. CalMac offers 25 island-hopping itineraries, called

Hopscotch, valid for 31 days, which can be combined for tailored exploration. Fares can range from £2 to £6 for a short trip to over £50 for a longer trip with several legs.

The Dunoon–Gourock route on the Clyde is served by Western Ferries (for cars) and Argyll Ferries (for passengers and cycles only).

Northlink Ferries operates a car ferry for Orkney between Scrabster, near Thurso, and Stromness, on the main island of Orkney; and between Aberdeen and Kirkwall, which is also on the mainland of Orkney. Northlink also runs an efficient ferry to Lerwick, Shetland, and Kirkwall, Orkney. The journey to Lerwick is overnight, but comfortable cabins are available. These ferries can be busy in summer, so book well in advance.

🚢 Cruise

Many of the crossings from North America to Europe are repositioning sailings for ships that cruise the Caribbean in winter and European waters in summer. Sometimes rates are reduced, and fly-cruise packages are usually available. To get the best deal on a cruise, consult a cruise-only travel agency.

The National Trust for Scotland runs a Cultural Cruising program with natural history, literary, and culinary themes. The destinations change each year but may include the west coast or Northern Isles. Hebridean Island Cruises offers 4- to 10-night luxury cruises aboard the MV *Hebridean Princess* around the Scottish islands, including all the Western Isles. Majestic Line runs small-group cruises on converted wooden fishing boats around Argyll and the Hebrides.

Bus

Long-distance buses usually provide the cheapest way to travel between England and Scotland; fares may be as little as a third of the rail fares for comparable trips and are cheaper if you buy in advance. Nevertheless, the trip is not as comfortable as by train (no dining cart, smaller bathrooms, less spacious seats), and travel takes longer. Glasgow to London by nonstop bus takes 8 hours, 45 minutes; by train it takes about 5 hours, 30 minutes. Scotland's bus (short-haul) and coach (long-distance) network is extensive. Bus service is comprehensive in cities, less so in country districts. Express service links main cities and towns, connecting, for example, Glasgow and Edinburgh to Inverness, Aberdeen, Perth, Skye, Ayr, Dumfries, and Carlisle; or Inverness with Aberdeen, Wick, Thurso, and Fort William. Express service is very fast, and fares are reasonable. Scottish Citylink, National Express, and Megabus are among the main operators; there are about 20 in all. The Royal Mail Post Bus provides a valuable service—generally twice daily—in the Highlands, Argyll, and Bute and the Western Isles. All buses are nonsmoking.

DISCOUNTS AND DEALS

On Scottish Citylink, the Explorer Passes offer complete freedom of travel on all services throughout Scotland. Three permutations give 3 days of travel out of a 5-day period, 5 days of travel out of 10, and 8 days of travel out of 16. They're available from Scottish Citylink offices, and cost £49, £74, and £99 respectively.

National Express offers discounted seats on buses from London to more than 50 cities in the United Kingdom, including Glasgow and Aberdeen. Tickets range from £15 to £70, but only when purchased online. Megabus (order tickets online), a discount service, has similarly competitive prices between major cities throughout Scotland, including Aberdeen, Dundee, Glasgow, Inverness, and Perth.

FARES AND SCHEDULES

Contact Traveline Scotland for information on all public transportation and timetables.

For town, suburban, or short-distance journeys, you buy your ticket on the bus, from a pay box, or from the driver. You need exact change. For longer journeys—for example, Glasgow to Inverness—it's usual (and a good idea; busy routes and times can book up) to reserve a seat online.

Car

If you plan to stick mostly to the cities, you will not need a car. All cities in Scotland are either so compact that most attractions are within easy walking distance of each other (Aberdeen, Dundee, Edinburgh, Inverness, and Stirling) or are accessible by an excellent local public transport system (Glasgow). And there is often good train or bus service from major cities to nearby day-trip destinations. Bus tours are a good option for day trips.

Once you leave Edinburgh, Glasgow, and the other major cities, a car will make journeys faster and much more enjoyable than trying to work out public-transportation connections to the farther-flung reaches of Scotland (though it is possible, if time-consuming, to see much of the country by public transportation). A car allows you to set your own pace and visit off-the-beaten-path towns and sights most easily.

In Scotland your own driver's license is acceptable. International driving permits

Getting Here and Around

(IDPs) are available from the American Automobile Association and, in the United Kingdom, from the Automobile Association and Royal Automobile Club. These international permits, valid only in conjunction with your regular driver's license, are universally recognized; having one may save you a problem with local authorities.

PARKING

On-street parking is a bit of a lottery in Scotland. Depending on the location and time of day, the streets can be packed or empty of cars. In the cities you must pay for your on-street parking by getting a sticker from a parking machine; these machines are clearly marked with a large *P*. Make sure you have the exact change; the cost is around £3 for two hours, but can vary considerably from central to suburban zones, especially in Edinburgh and Glasgow. Put the parking sticker on the inside of your windshield. Parking lots are scattered throughout urban areas and tend to be more or less the same price as on-street parking.

ROAD CONDITIONS

A good network of superhighways, known as motorways, and divided highways, known as dual carriageways, extends throughout Britain. In remote areas of Scotland where the motorway hasn't penetrated, travel is noticeably slower. Motorways shown with the prefix *M* are mainly two or three lanes in each direction, without any right-hand turns. These are the roads to use to cover long distances, though inevitably you'll see less of the countryside. Service areas are at most about an hour apart.

Dual carriageways, usually shown on a map as a thick red line (often with a black line in the center) and the prefix "a" followed by a number perhaps with a bracketed "t" (for example, "a304[t]"), are similar to motorways, except that

From	To	Driving Time
Edinburgh	Glasgow	1 hour
Glasgow	Stirling	¼ hour
Stirling	Dundee	1¼ hours
Dundee	Aberdeen	1½ hours
Aberdeen	Inverness	2¾ hours
Inverness	Glasgow	3½ hours
Edinburgh	Inverness	3¼ hours
Glasgow	Dundee	1¾ hours

right turns are sometimes permitted, and you'll find both traffic lights and traffic circles along the way. The vast network of other main roads, which typical maps show as either single red *A* roads, or narrower brown *B* roads, also numbered, are for the most part the old roads originally intended for horses and carriages. Travel along these roads is slower than on motorways, and passing is more difficult. On the other hand, you'll see much more of Scotland. The A9, Perth to Inverness, is a particularly dangerous road with the worst road accident record in Scotland because of the stopping and starting on the dual carriageway.

Minor roads (shown as yellow or white on most maps, unlettered and unnumbered) are the ancient lanes and byways of Britain, roads that are not only living history but a superb way of discovering hidden parts of Scotland. You have to drive slowly and carefully. On single-track (one-lane) roads, found in the north and west of Scotland, there's no room for two vehicles to pass, and you must use a passing place if you meet an oncoming car or tractor, or if a car behind wishes to overtake you. Never hold up traffic on single-track roads.

RULES OF THE ROAD

The most noticeable difference for most visitors is that when in Britain, you drive on the left and steer the car on the right. Give yourself time to adjust to driving on the left—especially if you pick up your car at the airport. One of the most complicated questions facing visitors to Britain is that of speed limits. In urban areas it's generally 20 mph or 30 mph, but it's 40 mph on some main roads, as indicated by circular red-rimmed signs. In rural areas the official limit is 60 mph on ordinary roads and 70 mph on divided highways and motorways. Traffic police can be hard on speeders, especially in urban areas. Driving while using a cell phone is illegal, and the use of seat belts is mandatory for passengers in front and back seats. Service stations and news-stands sell copies of the Highway Code (£2.50), which lists driving rules and has pictures of signs, or you can download the information or get the mobile app at ⊕ *www.highwaycodeuk.co.uk*

Drunk-driving laws are strictly enforced and penalties are heavy. Be aware that the legal alcohol limit is lower than in the rest of the United Kingdom: just 50 mg in every 100 ml of blood. That equates to just under a pint of beer or glass of wine for an average male, and half a pint or a small glass of wine for a woman. To be safe, avoid any alcohol if you're driving.

CAR RENTALS

You can rent any type of car you desire; however, in Scotland cars tend to be on the smaller side. Many roads are narrow, and a smaller car saves money on gas. Common models are the VW Golf, Ford Focus, and Vauxhall Corsa. Four-wheel-drive vehicles aren't a necessity. Most cars are manual, not automatic, and come with air-conditioning, although you rarely need it in Scotland. If you want an automatic, reserve ahead. Green Motion rents electric, hybrid, and low–carbon dioxide cars with service pick-up points at Edinburgh and Glasgow airports.

When you're returning the car, allow an extra hour to drop it off and sort out any paperwork. If you're traveling to more than one country, make sure your rental contract permits you to take the car across borders and that your insurance policy covers you in every country you visit.

Rates from Edinburgh Airport begin at £200 a week for an economy car with a manual transmission and unlimited mileage. This does not include tax on car rentals, which is 20%. The busiest months are June through August, when rates may go up 30%. During this time, book at least two to four weeks in advance. Online booking is fine.

Companies frequently restrict rentals to people over age 23 and under age 75. If you are over 70, some companies require you to have your own insurance. If you are under 25, a surcharge of around £25 per day plus V.A.T. will apply.

 Taxi

In Edinburgh, Glasgow, and the larger cities, black hackney taxis—similar to those in London—with their "taxi" sign illuminated can be hailed on the street, or booked by phone (expect to pay an extra 80-pence charge for this service in Edinburgh). If you call a private-hire taxi, expect a regular-looking car to pick you up. The only distinctions are that they have a taxi license and a meter stuck on the dashboard, along with an ID card for the driver. Private-hire taxis are cheaper than black hackney taxis and will pick you up only from a specific location, not off the street.

Getting Here and Around

Scottish taxis are reliable, safe, and metered. In Edinburgh, meters begin at £2.10 weekdays and increase in 25-pence increments. Beyond the larger cities, most communities of any size have a taxi service; your hotel will be able to supply telephone numbers.

🚆 Train

Train service within Scotland is generally run by ScotRail, one of the most efficient of Britain's service providers. Trains are generally modern, clean, and comfortable. Long-distance services carry buffet and refreshment cars. Scotland's rail network extends all the way to Thurso and Wick, the most northerly stations in the British Isles. Lowland services, most of which originate in Glasgow or Edinburgh, are generally fast and reliable. A shuttle makes the 50-minute trip between Glasgow and Edinburgh every 15 minutes. It's a scenic trip with plenty of rolling fields, livestock, and traditional houses along the way. Rail service throughout the country, especially the Highlands, is limited on Sunday.

CLASSES

Most trains have first-class and standard-class coaches. First-class coaches are always less crowded; they have wider seats and are often cleaner and newer than standard-class cars, and they're a lot more expensive. Nevertheless, on weekends you can often upgrade from standard to first class for a fee (often £10 to £25)—ask when you book.

FARES AND SCHEDULES

The best way to find out which train to take, which station to catch it at, and what times trains travel to your destination is to call National Rail Enquiries. It's a helpful, comprehensive service that covers all Britain's rail lines. National Rail will help you choose the best train to take, and then connects you with the ticket office for that train company so that you can buy tickets. You can also check schedules and purchase tickets on its website.

Train fares vary according to class of ticket purchased, time (off-peak travel will be much cheaper), and distance traveled. Before you buy your ticket, stop at the Information Office/Travel Centre and request the lowest fare to your destination and information about any special offers. There's sometimes little difference between the cost of a one-way and round-trip ticket, and returns are valid for one month. So if you're planning on departing from and returning to the same destination, buy a round-trip fare upon your departure, rather than purchasing two separate one-way tickets.

It's often much cheaper to buy a ticket in advance than on the day of your trip (except for commuter services); the closer to the date of travel, the more expensive the ticket will be. Try to purchase tickets at least eight weeks in advance during peak-season summer travel to save money and reserve good seats. You must stick to the train you have booked (penalties can be the full price), and you need to keep the seat reservation ticket, which is part of the valid ticket. All the operators now provide the option for a paperless ticket download that can be managed via a smartphone app.

Check train websites, especially ScotRail, for deals. You can also check The Trainline, which sells discounted advance-purchase tickets from all train companies to all destinations in Britain.

TRAIN PASSES

Rail passes may save you money, especially if you're going to log a lot of miles. If you plan to travel by train in Scotland, consider purchasing a BritRail Pass, which also allows travel in England and Wales. There are Scotland-specific passes, too, for the Highlands, central region, and countrywide travel. All BritRail passes must be purchased in your home country; they're sold by travel agents as well as ACP, The Trainline, or Rail Europe. Rail passes do not guarantee seats on the trains, so be sure to reserve ahead. Remember that Eurail Passes aren't honored in Britain.

The cost of an unlimited BritRail adult pass for 4 days is $216/$328 (standard/first class); for 8 days, $314/$467; for 15 days, $467/$690; for 22 days, $584/$876; and for a month, $690/$1,038.

FROM ENGLAND

There are two main rail routes to Scotland from the south of England. The first, the west-coast main line, runs from London Euston to Glasgow Central; it takes 5½ hours to make the 400-mile trip to central Scotland, and service is frequent and reliable. Useful for daytime travel to the Scottish Highlands is the direct train to Stirling and Aviemore, terminating at Inverness. For a restful route, take the overnight sleeper service, with sleeping carriages that arrives the following morning. It runs from London Euston, departing in late evening, splitting into sections heading to different parts of Scotland: one portion stops at Perth, Stirling, Aviemore, and Inverness; another covers the east coast stations Leuchars (for St. Andrews), Dundee, and Aberdeen, while the West Highland route terminates at Fort William. The *Caledonian Sleeper*, now run by Serco, has a revamped service with new cozy sleeping berths, a stylish club car serving food and drink, and luxurious options with en-suite bathrooms and breakfast included.

The east-coast main line from London King's Cross to Edinburgh provides the quickest trip to the Scottish capital. Between 8 am and 6 pm there are usually trains every half hour to Edinburgh; three of them travel directly to Aberdeen. LNER East Coast's limited-stop expresses like the *Flying Scotsman* make the 393-mile London-to-Edinburgh journey in about 4½ hours. Connecting services to most parts of Scotland—particularly the Western Highlands—are often better from Edinburgh than from Glasgow.

Trains from elsewhere in England are good: regular service connects Birmingham, Manchester, Liverpool, and Bristol with Glasgow and Edinburgh.

SCENIC ROUTES

Although many routes in Scotland run through extremely attractive countryside, several stand out: from Glasgow to Oban via Loch Lomond; to Fort William and Mallaig via Rannoch (ferry connection to Skye); from Edinburgh to Inverness via the Forth Bridge and Perth; from Inverness to Kyle of Lochalsh and to Wick; and from Inverness to Aberdeen.

A private train, the *Royal Scotsman,* does all-inclusive scenic tours, with banquets en route. This is a luxury experience: you choose itineraries from two nights (£3,600) to seven nights (£15,760) per person.

Essentials

Lodging

Your choices in Scotland range from small, local B&Bs to large, elegant hotels—some of the chain variety. Bed-and-breakfasts tend to be less expensive than large hotels, and are often different from those in the United States: many consist of spare rooms in someone's home, where breakfasts are cooked in the host's kitchen and served at the dining or kitchen table. Proprietors keep costs down, and guests get a more personal, if less private, Scottish touch. Recent economic stagnation, political uncertainty, and the fall in the value of the pound sterling means there are special deals if you look. Furthermore, some lodgings offer discounted rates for stays of two nights or longer.

If you haven't booked ahead, you're not likely to be stranded. Even in the height of the season—July and August—hotel occupancy runs at about 80%. Nevertheless, your choice of accommodations will be extremely limited if you show up somewhere during a festival or golf tournament. Your best bet will be to try for a room in a nearby village.

VisitScotland classifies and grades accommodations using a simple star system. The greater the number of stars, the greater the number of facilities and the more luxurious they are.

The lodgings we list are the best in each price category. When pricing accommodations, always ask what's included. Many hotels and most guesthouses and B&Bs include a breakfast with the basic room rate. Meal-plan information appears at the end of a review. *Prices in the reviews are the lowest cost of a standard double room in high season, including 20% V.A.T. Hotel reviews have been shortened. For full reviews, visit Fodors.com*

APARTMENT AND HOUSE RENTALS

Rental houses and flats (apartments) are becoming more popular lodging choices for travelers visiting Scotland, particularly for those staying in one place for more than a few days. Some places may rent only by the week. Prices can be cheaper than a hotel (though perhaps not less than a bed-and-breakfast), and the space and comfort are much better than what you'd find in a typical hotel.

In the country your chances of finding a small house to rent are good; in the city you're more likely to find a flat (apartment) to let (rent). Either way, your best bet for finding these rentals is online. Individuals and large consortiums can own these properties, so it just depends on what you're looking for. Citybase Apartments is a handy resource for finding an apartment, from single studios to large apartments suitable for families and groups. Dreamhouse Apartments has swanky, serviced flats in Edinburgh, Glasgow, and Aberdeen. The National Trust for Scotland has many unique properties, from island cottages to castles, for rent. Knight Residence has 19 well-appointed, modern apartments in the heart of the Old Town, Edinburgh; it has 16 similarly smart apartments in Inverness, many with spectacular terrace views.

BED-AND-BREAKFASTS

Common throughout Scotland, B&Bs are a special British tradition and the backbone of budget travel. Prices average about £50 to £140 per night, depending on the region and the time of year. They're usually in a family home, occasionally don't have private bathrooms, and usually offer only breakfast. More upscale B&Bs, along the line of American B&Bs or small inns, can be found in Edinburgh and Glasgow especially, but in other parts of Scotland as well. Guesthouses are a slightly larger, somewhat more luxurious version. All provide a glimpse of everyday life. Note that local tourist offices can book a B&B for you; there may be a small charge for this service.

FARMHOUSE AND CROFTING HOLIDAYS

A popular option for families with children is a farmhouse holiday, combining the freedom of B&B accommodations with the hospitality of Scottish family life. You'll need a car if you're staying deep in the country, though. Information is available from VisitBritain or VisitScotland, and from the Farm Stay UK.

HOTELS

Large hotels vary in style and price. Many lean toward Scottish themes when it comes to decoration, but you can expect the same quality and service from a chain hotel wherever you are in the world. Keep in mind that hotel rooms in Scotland are smaller than what you'd find in the United States. Today hotels of all sizes are trying to be greener, and many newer chains are striving for government environmental awards. Discounted rooms are another trend, as are discounts for room upgrades.

In the countryside some older hotels are former castles or converted country homes. These types of hotels are full of character and charm but can be very expensive, and they may not have elevators. Normally they have all the amenities, if not more, of their urban counterparts. Their locations may be so remote that you must eat on the premises, which may be costly.

Some small regional chains operate in Scotland that are not internationally known. Apex (in Edinburgh, Glasgow, Dundee, and London) is modish and has Scandinavian-inspired bedrooms;

Malmaison (in Aberdeen, Dundee, Edinburgh, and Glasgow) is luxury on a budget; Hotel du Vin (Glasgow, St. Andrews, and Edinburgh), with its chic bistros, sumptuous bedding, and original art, may blow the budget.

🍴 Dining

Today the traditional Scottish restaurant offers more than fish-and-chips, fried sausage, and black pudding. Instead you'll find the freshest of scallops, organic salmon, wild duck, and Aberdeen Angus beef, as well as locally grown vegetables and fruits. There's also a wide array of international restaurants: Chinese, French, Greek, Indian, Italian, Japanese, and Mexican (to name but a few) can be truly exceptional.

Places like Glasgow, Edinburgh, Dundee, and Aberdeen have sophisticated restaurants at various price levels; of these, the more notable tend to open only in the evening. But fabulous restaurants are popping up in the smaller villages as well. Dining in Scotland can be an experience for all the senses. These meals are rarely cheap, so don't forget your credit card.

Note that most pubs do not have a table service, so go to the bar and order your meal. You're not expected to tip the bartender, but you are expected to tip restaurant waitstaff by leaving 10% to 15% of the tab on the table.

There are a couple of vegetarian options on every menu, and most restaurants, particularly pubs that serve food, welcome families with young children. Smoking is banned from pubs, clubs, and restaurants throughout Britain.

The restaurants we review in this book are the best in each price category. Properties are assigned price categories

Essentials

based on dinner prices. *Prices in the reviews are the average cost of a main course at dinner or, if dinner is not served, at lunch.*

DISCOUNTS AND DEALS

Many city restaurants have good pret-heater meals from 5 to 7 pm. Lunch deals can also save you money; some main courses can be nearly half the price of dinner entrées. All supermarkets sell a large variety of high-quality sandwiches, wraps, and salads at reasonable prices. If the weather's dry, opt for a midday picnic.

MEALS AND MEALTIMES

To start the day with a full stomach, try a traditional Scottish breakfast of bacon and eggs served with sausage, fried mushrooms, and tomatoes, and usually fried bread or potato scones. Some places also serve kippers (smoked herring). All this is in addition to juice, porridge, cereal, toast, and other bread products.

"All-day" meal places are becoming prevalent. Lunch is usually served 12:30 to 2:30. A few places serve high tea—masses of cakes, bread and butter, and jam—around 2:30 to 4:30. Dinner is fairly early, around 5 to 8.

Restaurant chains are often more expensive than home-cooked meals in local establishments, where large servings of British comfort food—fish-and-chips, stuffed baked potatoes, and sandwiches—are served. In upscale restaurants cutting costs can be as simple as requesting *tap* water; "water" means a bottle of mineral water that could cost up to £5.

Unless otherwise noted, the restaurants listed in this guide are open daily for lunch and dinner.

PAYING

Credit cards are widely accepted at most types of restaurants. Some restaurants exclude service charges from the printed menu (which the law obliges them to display outside), then add 10% to 15% to the check, or else stamp "service not included" along the bottom, in which case you should add the 10% to 15% yourself. Just don't pay twice for service—unscrupulous restaurateurs add a service charge but leave the total on the credit-card slip blank.

PUBS

A common misconception among visitors to Scotland is that pubs are cozy bars. But they are also gathering places, conversation zones, even restaurants. Pubs are, generally speaking, where people go to have a drink, meet their friends, and catch up on one another's lives. Traditionally, pubs are open until midnight, with last orders called about 20 minutes before closing time. In the bigger cities pubs can stay open until 1 am or later.

Some pubs are child-friendly, but others have restricted hours for children. If a pub serves food, it will generally allow children in during the day. Some are stricter than others, though, and will not admit anyone younger than 18. If in doubt, ask the bartender. Family-friendly pubs tend to be packed with kids, parents, and all of their accoutrements.

RESERVATIONS AND DRESS

It's a good idea to make a reservation if you can. For popular restaurants, book as far ahead as you can (often 30 days), and reconfirm as soon as you arrive. Large parties should always call ahead to check the reservations policy.

Online reservation services make it easy to book a table before you even leave home. Open Table has listings in many Scottish cities.

NIGHTLIFE

Bars and pubs typically sell two kinds of beer: lager is light in color, very carbonated, and served cold, while ale is dark, less fizzy, and served just below room temperature. You may also come across a pub serving "real ales" or "craft beers," which are very flavorful beers from smaller breweries. Both traditional real ale and innovatively crafted brews have a fervent following; check out the Campaign for Real Ale's website, ⊕ www.camra.org.uk.

You can order Scotland's most famous beverage—whisky (most definitely spelled without an e)—at any local pub. All pubs serve single-malt and blended whiskies. It's also possible to tour numerous distilleries, where you can sample a dram and purchase a bottle. Most distilleries are concentrated in Speyside and Islay, but there are notable ones on Orkney and Skye. In recent years a new breed of craft gin producers have opened stills, many producing small batches of botanically infused tipples and offering tours, tastings, and lessons.

The legal drinking age in Scotland is 18.

◉ Shopping

Tartans, tweeds, and woolens may be a Scottish cliché, but nevertheless the selection and quality of these goods make them a must-have for many visitors, whether a made-to-measure traditional kilt outfit or a designer sweater from Skye. Particular bargains can be found in Scottish cashmere sweaters; look for Johnstons of Elgin. Glasgow is great for designer wear, although prices may seem high.

Food items are another popular purchase: whether shortbread, smoked salmon, boiled sweets, *tablet* (a type of hard fudge), marmalade and raspberry jams, Dundee cake, or black bun, it's far too easy to eat your way around Scotland.

Unique jewelry is available all over Scotland, but especially in some of the remote regions where get-away-from-it-all craftspeople have set up shop amid the idyllic scenery.

Scottish antique pottery and table silver make unusual, if sometimes pricey, souvenirs: a WemyssWare pig for the mantelpiece, perhaps, or Edinburgh silver candelabra for the dining table. Antique pebble jewelry is a unique style of jewelry popular in Scotland; several specialized antique jewelry shops can be found in Edinburgh and Glasgow. Antiques shops and one- or two-day antiques fairs held in hotels abound all over Scotland. In general, goods are reasonably priced. Most dealers will drop the price a little if asked "What's your best price?"

⊕ Safety

Overall, Scotland is a very safe country to travel in, but be a cautious traveler and keep your cash, passport, credit cards, and tickets close to you or in a hotel safe. Don't agree to carry anything for strangers. It's a good idea to distribute your cash, credit cards, IDs, and other valuables between a deep front pocket, an inside jacket or vest pocket, and a hidden money pouch. Don't reach for the money pouch once you're in public. Use common sense as your guide.

Scotland is largely welcoming to LGBTQ travelers, with big cities like Edinburgh and Glasgow having especially lively LGBTQ scenes; gay marriage has been legal in Scotland since 2014.

On the Calendar

Winter

DEC. 29–JAN. 2

Hogmanay. Scotland's ancient, still-thriving New Year's celebration, Hogmanay takes place over several days. In rural areas neighbors "first foot" each other's houses—thereby ensuring the good luck of the household—and toast the new year with a dram. ⊠ *Edinburgh* ⊕ *www.edinburghshogmanay.com.*

JAN. 25

Burns Night. Burns Night dinners and other events are held in memory of poet Robert Burns on his birthday, January 25. Haggis and mashed turnips, whisky, and poetry readings are familiar elements of the supper. ⊕ *www.scotland.org/whats-on/burns-night.*

LAST TUES. IN JAN.

Up-Helly-Aa. Every year Shetlanders celebrate their Viking heritage and torch a replica Viking longship. The biggest Up-Helly-Aa is in Lerwick on the last Tuesday in January. ⊕ *www.uphellyaa.org.*

JAN.

Celtic Connections. Glasgow's immensely popular celebration of Celtic music, Celtic Connections hosts national and international musicians from mid-January to early February. ⊠ *Glasgow* ⊕ *www.celticconnections.com.*

Spectra: Aberdeen's Festival of Light. Brightening up four February nights is a light-filled extravaganza staged in prominent city locations featuring international artists and Scots collaborators.

Spring

LATE APR.–EARLY MAY

Shetland Folk Festival. This festival is one of the biggest folk gatherings in Scotland, and musicians from all over the world stay up for four days of fiddle frenzy. It normally falls as April turns to May. ☎ *01595/694757* ⊕ *www.shetlandfolkfestival.com.*

APR. 30

Beltane Fire Festival. This festival celebrates the rites of spring according to the traditional Celtic calendar on April 30. You can witness displays of pyrotechnics and elaborately costumed mythological creatures at Calton Hill in Edinburgh. ⊠ *Edinburgh* ⊕ *www.beltane.org.*

LATE MAY

Orkney Folk Festival. This annual festival brings the folkies back up to the remote far north by the hundreds. Festivities take place over a few days in late May or early June. ⊕ *www.orkneyfolkfestival.com.*

Summer

MAY–SEPT.

Highland Games. Held annually in many Highland towns, the Highland games include athletic and cultural events like hammer throwing, caber tossing, and Highland dancing. The fun takes place from May through September. ⊕ *www.visitscotland.com/highland-games.*

Dundee Design Festival. Dundee is the United Kingdom's sole UNESCO City of Design and home to the V&A Dundee design museum. In late May the city hosts a week of innovative and collaborative events and workshops exploring the world of design. ⊕ *www.dundeecityofdesign.com.*

JUNE

Edinburgh International Film Festival. Concentrating on new films from all over the world, Edinburgh International Film Festival screenings are held over two weeks in June. ⊠ *Edinburgh* ☎ *0131/228–6382* ⊕ *www.edfilmfest.org.uk.*

St. Magnus International Festival. Orkney's weeklong St. Magnus International Festival is a feast of classical and modern music each June, often showcasing new vocal or orchestral compositions. ☎ *01856/871445* ⊕ *www.stmagnusfestival.com.*

JULY

Merchant City Festival. Glasgow's transformed mercantile district–turned–cultural quarter stages a few days of pop-up performances and various artsy gatherings in late July, including comedy, dance, music, markets, fashion and design, family events, tours, heritage walks, and food and drink. ⊠ *Glasgow* ☎ *0141 /287–4350* ⊕ *www.merchantcityfestival.com.*

AUG.

Pitenweem Arts Festival. In early August the picturesque Fife fishing village–turned–artists' retreat favorite opens dozens of small home studios and other intimate venues to the public. ⊕ *www.pittenweemartsfestival.co.uk.*

Edinburgh Festival Fringe. The rowdy, unofficial counterpart to the Edinburgh International Festival, the Edinburgh Festival Fringe takes over the city during three weeks in August. ☎ *0131/226–0000* ⊕ *www.edfringe.com.*

Edinburgh International Festival. The world's largest festival of the arts, the Edinburgh International Festival takes place over three weeks in August. ☎ *0131/473–2000* ⊕ *www.eif.co.uk.*

Edinburgh Military Tattoo. A stirring, colorful show of marching bands and military regiments, the Edinburgh Military Tattoo takes place during three weeks in August. ⊠ *Edinburgh* ☎ *0131/225–1188* ⊕ *www.edintattoo.co.uk.*

EARLY SEPT.

Braemar Royal Highland Gathering. Kilted clansmen from all over Scotland get together for the Braemar Royal Highland Gathering on the first Saturday in September. Bagpipe bands, dancers, and athletes join in the fun and games. ☎ *013397/41098* ⊕ *www.braemargathering.org.*

Fall

MID-OCT.

Royal National Mòd. This weeklong Gaelic festival includes speech competitions and theatrical performances, in addition to piping, choir, and Highland dancing exhibitions. The location changes each year, but it's generally held in mid-October. ⊠ *Inverness* ☎ *01463/709705* ⊕ *www.acgmod.org.*

Festival of the Future. In October the University of Dundee hosts a festival of collaborations, performances, and discussions bringing together scientists, artists, and thinkers. ⊕ *www.dundee.ac.uk/festival-future/.*

LATE NOV.–DEC.

Glasgow Loves Christmas. From late November through December, George Square in Glasgow is transformed into a winter wonderland: sparkling ornaments and an impressive palace facade tower over a gigantic ice rink. Festive markets and other seasonal events are part of the program, too. ⊠ *Glasgow* ⊕ *www.glasgowloveschristmas.com.*

Great Itineraries

Highlights of Scotland in 10 Days

Scotland isn't large, but its most famous cities and most iconic landscapes take time to explore. This itinerary packs in many national icons: Edinburgh's enormous charm and Glasgow's excellent museums; a castle or two; lochs, mountains, and an island. It's a busy pace, but you'll still be able to fit in a whisky distillery visit and even a round of golf. You can do parts of this trip by public transportation, but beyond the cities, a car allows more flexibility.

DAYS 1 AND 2: EDINBURGH

The capital of Scotland is loaded with iconic sights in its Old Town and New Town. Visit **Edinburgh Castle** and the **National Gallery of Scotland,** and take tours of the **National Museum of Scotland** and the modern **Scottish Parliament** building. Walk along Old Town's **Royal Mile** and New Town's **George Street** for some fresh air and retail therapy. Later on, seek out a traditional pub with live music.

Logistics: Fly into Edinburgh Airport if you're flying via London. If you're flying directly into Glasgow from overseas, make your way from Glasgow Airport to Queen Street station via taxi or bus. It takes an hour to travel from Glasgow to Edinburgh by car or bus, about 45 minutes to an hour by train. Explore on foot or by public transportation.

DAY 3: STIRLING TO ST. ANDREWS

Rent a car in Edinburgh and drive to the historic city of **Stirling.** Spend the day visiting **Stirling Castle** and the **National Wallace Monument.** If you're eager to tour a distillery, make time for a stop at the **Glenturret Distillery** in **Crieff.** For your overnight stay, drive to the seaside town of St. Andrews, famous for golf.

Logistics: It's 35 miles or a one-hour drive to Stirling from Edinburgh, and 50 miles and 90 minutes from Stirling to St. Andrews. You can easily take a train or bus to these destinations.

DAY 4: ST. ANDREWS TO AVIEMORE

Spend the morning exploring **St. Andrews,** known for its castle and the country's oldest university as well as its golf courses. If you've booked well in advance, play a round of golf. After lunch, drive to **Aviemore.** Along the way, either make a detour to **Dundee** and its spectacular new V&A Dundee design museum or **Blair Castle** (just off the A9 and 10 miles north of **Pitlochry).** Head to Aviemore, gateway to the Cairngorm Mountains and Britain's largest national park, for two nights. The town is a center for outdoor activities and has many choices for accommodations, dining, and shopping, but you can also consider the more attractive surrounding villages and towns such as **Kingussie** for your stay.

Logistics: It's 120 miles from St. Andrews to Aviemore via the A9, a drive that will take 2½ hours. You can also take a train or bus.

DAY 5: THE CAIRNGORMS

For anyone who enjoys outdoor pursuits or dramatic scenery, the arctic plateau of the Cairngorms is a must. Hiking, biking, and climbing are options (Glenmore Lodge is a renowned outdoor-sports center), but so is visiting attractions such as the **Cairngorm Reindeer Centre** and **Highland Folk Museum.**

DAY 6: THE ISLE OF SKYE

Leave Aviemore early and head to Inverness, which has a busy center suited for a wander. **Inverness Castle** and the **Inverness Museum and Art Gallery** are worth seeing. The drive southwest to Skye is peaceful, full of raw landscapes and big, open horizons. Stop at **Eilean Donan Castle** on the way. Set on an island among three lochs, the castle is the stuff postcards are made of from the outside, although the interiors are comically underwhelming. Explore Skye: **Glen Brittle** is the perfect place to enjoy mountain scenery including the crystal clear **Fairy Pools** at the foot of the Black Cuillins; and **Armadale** is a good place to go crafts shopping. End up in Portree for dinner and the night.

Logistics: It's 30 miles (a 40-minute drive) via the A9 from Aviemore to Inverness, and then it's 80 miles (a two-hour drive) from Inverness to Skye. Public transportation is possible but a car is best.

DAY 7: OBAN VIA BEN NEVIS
Leave Skye no later than 9 am and head for **Fort William.** The town isn't worth stopping for, but the view of Britain's highest mountain, the 4,406-foot Ben Nevis, is. If time permits, take a hike in **Glen Nevis.** Continue on to **Oban,** a traditional Scottish resort town on the water, to overnight. Outside Oban, stop by the **Ocean Explorer Centre.** At night, feast on fish-and-chips in a local pub.

Logistics: It's nearly 100 miles from Skye to Oban; the drive is 3½ hours without stopping. Public transportation is challenging.

DAYS 8 AND 9: LOCH LOMOND AND GLASGOW
Enjoy a waterfront stroll in Oban. Midmorning set off for **Glasgow** via **Loch Lomond.** Arrive in Glasgow in time for dinner; take in a play or concert, or just relax in a pub on the first of your two nights in this rejuvenated city. Spend the next day visiting the sights: **Kelvingrove Art Gallery and Museum,** Charles Rennie Mackintosh's iconic buildings, and the **Riverside Museum** are a few highlights.

Logistics: It's 127 miles (a three-hour drive) from Oban to Glasgow via Balloch. Traveling by train is a possibility, but you won't be able to go via Balloch. Return your rental car in Glasgow.

DAY 10: GLASGOW AND HOME
On your final day, stow your suitcases at your hotel and hit Buchanan and Sauchiehall streets for some of Britain's best shopping. Clothes, whisky, and tartan items are good things to look for.

Logistics: It's less than 10 miles (15 minutes) by taxi to Glasgow's international airport in Paisley but more than 30 miles (40 minutes) to the international airport in Prestwick.

Best Tours in Scotland

📍 General-Interest Tours

Many companies offer fully guided tours in Scotland, from basic to luxury. Most of these are full packages including hotels, all food, and transportation costs in one flat fee. Because each tour company has different specialties, do a bit of research—either on your own or through a travel agent—before booking. You'll want to know about the hotels you'll be staying in, how big your group is likely to be, precisely how your days will be structured, and who the other people are likely to be.

CIE Tours

BUS TOURS | It offers all-inclusive tours of Scotland with various themes, from distillery tours to cruises to Home of Golf and St. Andrews packages. ☎ *0800/680–0611* ⊕ *www.cietours.com* ✉ *From £765 for a 5-day Taste of Scotland tour.*

Globus

BUS TOURS | Covering Scotland and Great Britain, Globus offers many packages including a 7-day Bonnie Scotland tour from Glasgow to Edinburgh, and a 14-day one that also delves into the Highlands and islands. ☎ *866/755–8581* ⊕ *www.globusjourneys.com* ✉ *From $1,819, excluding airfare, for 7-day Bonnie Scotland.*

Heart of Scotland Tours

BUS TOURS | Offered here are small-group (16 maximum) minibus tours that aim to take you off the beaten track. ☎ *0131/228–2888* ⊕ *www.heartofscotlandtours.co.uk* ✉ *From £45 for a Best of Scotland in a Day excursion.*

Rabbie's Trail Burners

BUS TOURS | These minibus guided tours include handy day trips for small groups (16 maximum) and depart from Edinburgh and Glasgow. The company has won numerous awards including the Scottish Thistle award for sustainable tourism. ☎ *0131/226–3133* ⊕ *www.rabbies.com* ✉ *From £29 for day trips (Rosslyn Chapel & Scots Borders); 2-day Loch Ness & Inverness trip starts at £79.*

📍 Special-Interest Tours

You can find tours for many special interests from whisky and vegetarian-friendly to cultural, historic, and wildlife-themed packages.

Celtic Dream Tours

SPECIAL-INTEREST | This outfit specializes in extended Celtic-inspired luxury excursions and custom tours, as well as vegetarian-/vegan-friendly and Burns literary adventures. ☎ *813/317–6039* ⊕ *www.celticdreamtours.com* ✉ *From $4,495 double occupancy for 12-night Dream Tour of Scotland.*

The Wayfarers

SPECIAL-INTEREST | Enjoy walking tours through the countryside and scenic towns, exploring natural and historic sights. ☎ *800/249–4620* ⊕ *www.thewayfarers.com* ✉ *From $4,695 per person (double occupancy) for the Highlands 6-night tour.*

📍 Golf Tours

Scotland has fabulous golf courses; a tour can help enthusiasts make the most of their time. VisitScotland has a dedicated golf website with a list of tour companies.

Golf Scotland

SPECIAL-INTEREST | This company has provided luxury golf tours, including tournament specials and the Gleneagles Experience tour, since 1988.

☎ 866/875–4653 ⊕ www.golfscotland. com ✉ From $1,145 per person for the Gleneagles Experience.

Scotland for Golf
SPECIAL-INTEREST | Established by St. Andrews pros in 1999, this is the company to consider for those seeking to tour Fife's finest fairways, including the Old Course. ☎ 01334/611466 ⊕ www. scotlandforgolf.co.uk ✉ From $1350 per person for 5 nights in St Andrews playing its best courses.

⚲ Private Guides
Scottish Tourist Guides Association
PERSONAL GUIDES | The association has members throughout Scotland who are fully qualified professional guides able to conduct walking tours in the major cities, half- or full-day tours or extended tours throughout Scotland, driving tours, and special study tours. Fees are negotiable. ☎ 01786/447784 ⊕ www.stga.co.uk.

Contacts

✈ Air

AIRPORTS Aberdeen Airport. ☎ 0344/481–6666 ⊕ www.aberdeenairport.com. **Edinburgh Airport.** ⊕ www.edinburghairport.com. **Glasgow Airport.** ☎ 0344/481–5555 ⊕ www.glasgowairport.com. **Glasgow Prestwick Airport.** ☎ 0871/223–0700 ⊕ www.glasgowprestwick.com. **Inverness Airport.** ☎ 01667/464000 ⊕ www.hial.co.uk/inverness-airport.

🚲 Bicycle

BIKE MAPS AND INFORMATION ActiveScotland. ☎ 0131/473–3868 ⊕ active.visitscotland.com. **Cycling UK.** ☎ 01483/238300 ⊕ www.cyclinguk.org. **Sustrans.** ☎ 0131/346–1384 ⊕ www.sustrans.org.uk.

⛴ Boat and Ferry

INFORMATION Argyll Ferries. ☎ 0800/066–5000 ⊕ www.argyllferries.co.uk. **Caledonian MacBrayne.** ☎ 0800/066–5000 ⊕ www.calmac.co.uk. **Northlink Ferries.** ☎ 0845/600–0449 ⊕ www.northlinkferries.co.uk. **Western Ferries.** ☎ 01369/704452 ⊕ www.western-ferries.co.uk.

🚌 Bus

BUS INFORMATION Traveline Scotland. ☎ 0871/200–2233 ⊕ www.traveline-scotland.com.

BUS LINES Megabus. ☎ 0900/160–0900 ⊕ uk.megabus.com. **National Express.** ☎ 0871/781–8181 ⊕ www.nationalexpress.com. **Scottish Citylink.** ☎ 0871/266–3333 ⊕ www.citylink.co.uk.

🚗 Car Rental

LOCAL CAR RENTAL AGENCIES Arnold Clark. ☎ 0141/237–4374 ⊕ www.arnoldclarkrental.com. **Green Motion.** ☎ 03338/884000 in U.K., 0207/186–4000 rest of the world ⊕ www.greenmotion.com.

MAJOR RENTAL AGENCIES Avis. ☎ 0808/284–0014 ⊕ www.avis.co.uk. **Budget.** ☎ 0808/284–4444 ⊕ www.budget.co.uk. **Hertz.** ☎ 020/7026–0077 ⊕ www.hertz.co.uk. **National Car Rental.** ☎ 0800/121–8303 ⊕ www.nationalcar.co.uk.

🚆 Train

INFORMATION National Rail Enquiries. ☎ 03457/484950 ⊕ www.nationalrail.co.uk. **ScotRail.** ☎ 0344/811–0141 ⊕ www.scotrail.co.uk. **The Trainline.** ☎ 0333/202–2222 ⊕ www.thetrainline.com.

TRAIN PASS INFORMATION ACP Rail International. ☎ 866/938–7245 ⊕ www.acprail.com. **BritRail Travel.** ⊕ www.britrail.com. **Rail Europe.** ⊕ www.raileurope.com.

SPECIAL TRAINS Caledonian Sleeper. ☎ 0330/060–0500, 141/555–0888 ⊕ www.sleeper.scot. **LNER.** ☎ 03457/ 225–333 ⊕ www.lner.co.uk. **The Royal Scotsman.** ☎ 0845/077–2222 in U.K., 800/524–2420 in U.S. ⊕ www.royalscotsman.com.

🎟 Sightseeing Passes

DISCOUNT PASSES Historic Scotland. ☎ 0131/668–8600 ⊕ www.historicenvironment.scot. **National Trust for Scotland.** ☎ 0131/458–0303 ⊕ www.nts.org.uk.

📍 Visitor Information

CONTACTS IN BRITAIN VisitScotland. ✉ Princes Mall, 3 Princes St., Edinburgh ☎ 0131/473–3868 ⊕ www.visitscotland.com.

Chapter 3

EDINBURGH AND THE LOTHIANS

Updated by
Joseph Reaney

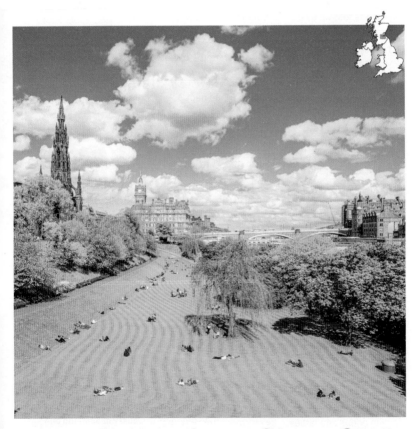

👁 Sights	🍴 Restaurants	🛏 Hotels	🛍 Shopping	🍸 Nightlife
★★★★★	★★★★★	★★★★★	★★★★★	★★★★★

WELCOME TO EDINBURGH AND THE LOTHIANS

TOP REASONS TO GO

★ **Culture:** From floor-stomping *ceilidhs* to avant-garde modern dance, the city's calendar of cultural festivals, including the remarkable Edinburgh Festival Fringe—the world's largest arts festival by a mile—is truly outstanding.

★ **The Royal Mile:** History plays out before your eyes in this centuries-old capital along the Royal Mile. Edinburgh Castle and the Palace of Holyroodhouse were the locations for some of the most important struggles between Scotland and England.

★ **Architecture:** From the Old Town's labyrinthine medieval streets to the neoclassical orderliness of the New Town to imaginative modern developments like the Scottish Parliament, the architecture of Auld Reekie spans the ages.

★ **Food:** The city's ever-expanding restaurant scene attracts celebrity chefs that serve up international dishes and genuine Scottish cuisine, like Cullen skink and haggis with neeps and tatties.

For all its steep roads and hidden alleyways, Edinburgh is not a difficult place to navigate. Most newcomers gravitate to two areas, the Old Town and the New Town. The former funnels down from the castle on either side of High Street, better known as the Royal Mile. Princes Street Gardens and Edinburgh Waverley station separate the oldest part of the city from the stately New Town, known for its neoclassical architecture and verdant gardens. To the north the city sweeps down to the Firth of Forth. It is here you will find the port of Leith, replete with trendy pubs and fine-dining restaurants. The southern and western neighborhoods are mainly residential, but are home to a few attractions, such as Edinburgh Zoo.

1 **Old Town.** The focal point of Edinburgh for centuries, the Old Town is a picturesque jumble of medieval tenements. Here are prime attractions such as Edinburgh Castle and the newer symbol of power, the Scottish Parliament. Here you will find everything from buzzing bars and nightclubs to

ghostly alleyways and vaults.

2 **New Town.** Built in the 18th and 19th centuries to prevent the wealthier residents of overcrowded Old Town from decamping to London, the neoclassical sweep of the New Town is a masterpiece of city planning. Significant sights include the National Gallery of Scotland and Calton Hill, which offers some of the best views of the city from its summit.

3 Haymarket. West of the Old Town and south of the West End is Haymarket, a district with its own down-to-earth character and well-worn charm. It's close to Edinburgh's second train station.

4 West End. Edinburgh's commercial center has boutiques aplenty as well as the Edinburgh Zoo.

5 South Side. Mostly residential, the South Side makes a good base for budget-conscious travelers. It's where most of the city's students live.

6 Leith. On the southern shore of the Firth of Forth, Edinburgh's port of Leith is where you'll find the now-retired Royal Yacht *Britannia*, along with some of the city's smartest restaurants and bars.

7 West Lothian, the Forth Valley, Midlothian, and East Lothian. Known collectively as the Lothians, the areas of green countryside and seafront villages around Edinburgh are replete with historic houses, castles, museums, and world-renowned golf courses.

Edinburgh is "a city so beautiful it breaks the heart again and again," as Alexander McCall Smith once wrote. One of the world's stateliest cities and proudest capitals, it is—like Rome—built on seven hills, making it a striking backdrop for the ancient pageant of history.

In a skyline of sheer drama, Edinburgh Castle looks out over the city, frowning down on Princes Street's glamour and glitz. But despite its rich past, the city's famous festivals, excellent museums and galleries, and the modernist Scottish Parliament are all reminders that Edinburgh has its feet firmly in the 21st century.

Nearly everywhere in Edinburgh (the *burgh* is always pronounced *burra* in Scotland) are spectacular buildings, whose Doric, Ionic, and Corinthian pillars add touches of neoclassical grandeur to the largely Presbyterian backdrop. Large gardens are a strong feature of central Edinburgh, while Arthur's Seat, a craggy peak of bright green-and-yellow furze, rears up behind the spires of the Old Town. Even as Edinburgh moves through the 21st century, its tall guardian castle remains the focal point of the city and its venerable history.

Modern Edinburgh has become a cultural capital, staging the Edinburgh International Festival and the Festival Fringe in every possible venue each August. The stunning National Museum of Scotland complements the city's wealth of galleries and artsy hangouts. Add Edinburgh's growing reputation for food and nightlife and you have one of the world's most beguiling cities.

Today, Edinburgh is the second-most-important financial center in the United Kingdom, and is widely renowned for its exceptional (and ever-expanding) dining and nightlife scenes—some of the reasons it regularly ranks near the top of quality-of-life surveys.

Edinburgh's Old Town, which bears a great symbolic weight as the "heart of Scotland's capital," is a boon for lovers of atmosphere and history. In contrast, if you appreciate the unique architectural heritage of the city's Enlightenment, then the New Town's for you. If you belong to both categories, don't worry—the Old and New Towns are only yards apart. Explore the city's main thoroughfares—peopled by the spirits of Mary, Queen of Scots, Sir Walter Scott, and Robert Louis Stevenson—then get lost among the tiny *wynds* and *closes* (old medieval alleys that connect the winding streets). And remember: you haven't earned your porridge until you've climbed Arthur's Seat.

Head out of the city center and you'll find smaller communities with an abundance of charm. Dean Village, with its cobbled streets and 19th-century water mills, has a character all its own. Duddingston, just southeast of Arthur's Seat, has all the bucolic charm of a country village. Then there's Edinburgh's port, Leith, home to some of Scotland's smartest bars and restaurants. Visible beyond them all, across the Firth of Forth, is the patchwork of fields that is the county of Fife—a reminder, like the mountains to the northwest that can be glimpsed from Edinburgh's highest points, that the rest of Scotland lies within easy reach.

Planning

When to Go

Scotland's reliably unreliable weather means that you could visit at the height of summer and be forced to wear a winter coat. Conversely, conditions can be balmy in early spring and late autumn. You may choose to avoid the crowds (and hotel price hikes) of July and August, but you'd also miss some of the greatest festivals on Earth. May, June, and September are probably the most hassle-free months in which to visit, while still offering hope of good weather. Short days and grim conditions make winter less appealing, though there are few better New Year's Eve celebrations than Edinburgh's Hogmanay.

FESTIVALS

Walking around Edinburgh in late July, you'll likely feel the first vibrations of the earthquake that is festival time, which shakes the city throughout August. You may hear reference to an "Edinburgh Festival," but this is really an umbrella term for five separate festivals all taking place around the same time. For an overview, check out ⊕ *www.edinburgh-festivalcity.com.*

Beltane Fire Festival

FESTIVALS | Held every year on April 30, this flame-filled Calton Hill extravaganza is inspired by an Iron Age Celtic festival, which was held to celebrate the return of summer. Expect drumbeat processions, bonfires, and fireworks, as costumed fire dancers reveal the fates of the May Queen and the Green Man. ⊠ *Calton Hill, Calton* ⊕ *www.beltane.org.*

★ Edinburgh Festival Fringe

ARTS FESTIVALS | FAMILY | During the world's largest arts festival in August, most of the city center becomes one huge performance area, with fire eaters, sword swallowers, unicyclists, jugglers, string quartets, jazz groups, stand-up comedians, and magicians all thronging into High Street and Princes Street. Every available performance space—church halls, community centers, parks, sports fields, nightclubs, and more—is utilized for every kind of event, with something for all tastes. There are even family-friendly shows. Many events are free; others start at a few pounds and rise to £15 or £20. There's so much happening in the three weeks of the festival that it's possible to arrange your own entertainment program from early morning to after midnight. ■ TIP➜ **Be aware that hotels get booked up months in advance during the Fringe and bargains are virtually impossible to come by, so plan your trip as far in advance as possible.** ⊠ *Edinburgh Festival Fringe Office, 180 High St., Old Town* ☏ *0131/226–0026* ⊕ *www.edfringe. com.*

Edinburgh International Book Festival

FESTIVALS | FAMILY | This two-week-long event held every August pulls together a heady mix of authors from around the world, from Nobel laureates to best-selling fiction writers, and gets them talking about their work in a magnificent tent village. There are more than 750 events in total, with the workshops for would-be writers and children proving hugely popular. ⊠ *Edinburgh International Book Festival Admin Office, 5 Charlotte Sq., New Town* ☏ *0131/718–5666* ⊕ *www. edbookfest.co.uk.*

Edinburgh International Festival

ARTS FESTIVALS | FAMILY | Running throughout August, this flagship traditional arts festival attracts international performers and audiences to a celebration of music,

The Festival Fringe started in 1947 at the same time as the International Festival, when eight companies that were not invited to perform in the latter decided to attend anyway.

dance, theater, opera, and art. Programs, tickets, and reservations are available from the Hub, set within the impressive Victorian-Gothic Tolbooth Kirk. Tickets for the festival go on sale in April, and the big events sell out within the month. Nevertheless, you'll still be able to purchase tickets for some events during the festival; prices range from around £4 to £60. ⊠ *The Hub, 348–350 Castlehill, Old Town* ☎ *0131/473–2015* ⊕ *www.eif.co.uk.*

Edinburgh International Film Festival

FESTIVALS | One of Europe's foremost film festivals, promoting the best of global independent cinema since 1947, this event takes place from mid-June to early July each year. It's a great place for a first screening of a new film—movies from *Billy Elliot* to *Little Miss Sunshine* to *The Hurt Locker* have premiered here. ⊠ *Edinburgh Film Festival Office, 88 Lothian Rd., West End* ☎ *0131/228–4051* ⊕ *www. edfilmfest.org.uk.*

Edinburgh International Science Festival

FESTIVALS | FAMILY | Held around Easter each year, the Edinburgh International Science Festival is one of Europe's largest, and aims to make science accessible, interesting, and fun for kids (and adults) through an extensive program of innovative exhibitions, workshops, performances, and screenings. ⊠ *The Hub, 348–350 Castlehill, Old Town* ☎ *0131/553–0320* ⊕ *www.sciencefestival.co.uk.*

Edinburgh Jazz & Blues Festival

FESTIVALS | Held over a week in late July, the Edinburgh Jazz & Blues Festival attracts world-renowned musicians playing everything from blues-rock to soul music, and brings local enthusiasts out of their living rooms and into the pubs, clubs, and Spiegeltents (pop-up performance spaces) around the city. ⊠ *Edinburgh Jazz & Blues Festival, 89 Giles St., Leith* ☎ *0131/467–5200* ⊕ *www. edinburghjazzfestival.com.*

★ Edinburgh's Hogmanay

FESTIVALS | Nowadays most capital cities put on decent New Year's celebrations, but Edinburgh's three-day-long Hogmanay festivities are on a whole other level. There's a reason this city is famous around the world as the best place to ring in the New Year. Yes, it's winter and yes, it's chilly, but joining a crowd of 80,000 people in a monster street party, complete with big-name rock concerts, torchlight processions, ceilidh dancing, and incredible fireworks, is something you won't forget in a hurry. The headline city center events are ticketed (and can be pricey), but there are free parties happening all over the city. ⊠ *Princes St., Old Town* ⊕ *www.edinburghshogmanay. com* ⊠ *From £20.*

The Royal Edinburgh Military Tattoo

FESTIVALS | It may not be art, but The Tattoo (as it's commonly known) is at the very heart of Scottish cultural life. Taking place, like many of the city's festivals, during August, this celebration of martial music features international military bands, gymnastics, and stunt motorcycle teams on the castle esplanade. Each year 22,000 seats are made available, yet it's always a sellout, so book your place early. If you are lucky enough to get tickets, dress warmly for evening shows and always bring a raincoat; the show goes on in all weathers. ⊠ *The Tattoo Box Office , 1–3 Cockburn St., Old Town* ☎ *0131/225–1188* ⊕ *www.edintattoo. co.uk.*

Planning Your Time

One of Edinburgh's greatest virtues is its compact size, which means that it is possible to pack a fair bit into even the briefest of visits. The two main areas of interest are the Old Town and the New Town, where you'll find Edinburgh Castle, the Scottish Parliament, Princes Street Gardens, and the National Gallery of Scotland. You can cover the major attractions in one day, but to give the major sights their due, you should allow at least two. You can also choose between the Palace of Holyroodhouse and the important museums of Edinburgh, or explore

the Royal Botanic Garden and Holyrood Park. Head down to leafy, villagelike Stockbridge, then immerse yourself in the greenery along the Water of Leith, visiting the Scottish National Gallery of Modern Art along the way.

Getting out of town is also an option for longer stays. Hop on a bus out to Midlothian to see the magnificent Rosslyn Chapel (even if you're not a fan of *The Da Vinci Code*, it's still interesting), and Crichton Castle, parts of which date back to the 14th century. Head west along the Firth of Forth to explore South Queensferry, with its three Forth bridges (including the iconic red railway bridge) and palatial Hopetoun House, or head east for the beautiful beaches, bird-watching, and golf courses in and around North Berwick.

■**TIP→ Some attractions have special hours during August, due to the large influx of festivalgoers. If you want to see something special, be sure to check the hours ahead of time.**

Getting Here and Around

AIR

Edinburgh Airport is 7 miles west of the city center. Flights bound for Edinburgh depart virtually every hour from London's Gatwick, Heathrow, and City airports.

Airlines serving Edinburgh, Scotland's busiest airport, include Air France, Aer Lingus, American Airlines, British Airways, Delta Virgin, easyJet, Flybe, Iberia, Jet2, KLM, Lufthansa, and Ryanair.

Delta flies direct to Edinburgh from New York's JFK airport, while United flies direct from Newark. There are also direct flights from Boston and Washington, D.C., (Delta), Chicago (United), and Philadelphia (American). Otherwise, your airline is likely to require a change somewhere in Europe. You could also fly into Glasgow Airport, 50 miles away, or the smaller Glasgow Prestwick, another

30 miles south, but these will add about an hour and a half to your journey.

There are no rail links to the city center, so the most efficient way to do the journey on public transport is by tram; the service runs every 8 to 12 minutes and takes about half an hour. Tickets cost £6 one-way and £8.50 for a round-trip. By bus or car you can usually make it to Edinburgh in a half hour, unless you hit the morning (7:30 to 9) or evening (4 to 6) rush hours. Lothian Buses runs an Airlink express service to Waverley railway station via Haymarket that usually takes around half an hour, depending on traffic. Buses run every 10 minutes (every 30 minutes throughout the night); tickets cost £4.50 one way or £7.50 round-trip and can be purchased from the booth beside the bus. Local buses also run between Edinburgh Airport and the city center every 15 minutes or so from 9 to 5, and roughly every hour during off-peak hours; they are far cheaper—just £1.70 one-way—but can take twice as long.

You can arrange for a chauffeur-driven limousine to meet your flight at Edinburgh Airport through Transvercia Chaffeur Drive, Little's, or W L Sleigh Ltd, for upwards of £50.

Taxis are readily available outside the terminal. The trip takes 20 to 30 minutes to the city center, 15 minutes longer during rush hour. The fare is roughly £25. Note that airport taxis picking up fares from the terminal are any color, not the typical black cabs.

AIRPORT INFORMATION Edinburgh Airport. ⊠ Glasgow Rd., Ingliston ☎ 0844/448–8833 ⊕ www.edinburghairport.com.

AIRPORT TRANSFER CONTACTS
Little's. ⊠ 1282 Paisley Rd. W, Glasgow ☎ 0131/334–2177 ⊕ www.littles.co.uk. **Transvercia Chaffeur Drive.** ⊠ The Harland Bldg., Unit 6, Suite 19, Pilrig Heights, Leith ☎ 0131/555–0459 ⊕ www.transvercia.co.uk. **W L Sleigh.** ⊠ Unit 11A

West Craigs, Turnhouse Rd., Edinburgh ☎ 0131/339–9607 ⊕ sleigh.co.uk.

BUS
National Express provides a coach service to and from London and other major towns and cities. The main terminal, Edinburgh Bus Station, is a short walk north of Edinburgh Waverley station, immediately east of St. Andrew Square. Long-distance coaches must be booked in advance online, by phone, or at the terminal. Edinburgh is approximately eight hours by bus from London.

Lothian Buses provides most of the services between Edinburgh and the Lothians and conducts day tours around and beyond the city. First Bus runs additional buses out of Edinburgh into the surrounding area. Megabus offers dirt-cheap fares to selected cities across Scotland.

Lothian Buses is the main operator within Edinburgh. You can buy tickets from the driver on the bus, though you will need the exact fare. Alternatively, you can buy tickets in advance at a Lothian Buses store or on your phone through the Lothian Buses M-Tickets app. On a limited (but ever-increasing) number of routes, contactless card payment is also available. In all cases, it's £1.70 for a single ticket or £4 for a day ticket, which allows unlimited one-day travel on the city's buses. A single night ticket costs £3, or you can get unlimited travel from 6 pm to 4:30 am with a DAY&NIGHT ticket (£3.50). ■TIP➔ Buses can be packed on Friday and Saturday nights, so you may want to consider a taxi instead.

BUS CONTACTS First Bus. ☎ 0871/200–2233 ⊕ www.firstgroup.com. Lothian Buses. ☎ 0131/554–4494 ⊕ www.lothianbuses.com. Megabus. ☎ 0900/160–0900 ⊕ uk.megabus.com. National Express. ☎ 0871/781–8181 ⊕ www.nationalexpress.co.uk.

CAR

It's not necessary to have a car in Edinburgh, as the city is quite walkable and has an extensive and efficient public transport system. Driving in Edinburgh has its quirks and pitfalls—particularly at the height of festival season. Metered parking in the city center is scarce and expensive, and the local traffic wardens are an unforgiving lot. Note that illegally parked cars are routinely towed away, and getting your car back will be expensive. After 6 pm, the parking situation improves considerably, and you may manage to find a space quite near your hotel, even downtown. If you park on a yellow line or in a resident's parking bay, be prepared to move your car by 8 the following morning. Parking lots are clearly signposted; overnight parking is expensive and not always permitted.

TAXI

Taxi stands can be found throughout the city, mostly in the New Town. The following are the most convenient: the west end of Princes Street, South Street, David Street, and North Street, Andrew Street (both just off St. Andrew Square), Waverley Mall, Waterloo Place, and Lauriston Place. Alternatively, hail any taxi displaying an illuminated "for hire" sign.

TRAIN

Edinburgh's main train hub, Edinburgh Waverley station, is downtown, below Waverley Bridge and around the corner from the unmistakable spire of the Scott Monument. Travel time from Edinburgh to London by train is as little as 4½ hours for the fastest service.

Edinburgh's other main station is Haymarket, about four minutes (by rail) west of Edinburgh Waverley. Most Glasgow and other western and northern services stop here.

TRAIN CONTACTS National Rail Enquiries.
☎ 08457/484950 ⊕ www.nationalrail. co.uk. **ScotRail.** ☎ 0344/811–0141 ⊕ www.scotrail.co.uk.

TRAM

Absent since 1956, trams returned to the streets of Edinburgh in 2014. The 8½-mile stretch of track currently runs between Edinburgh Airport in the west to York Place in the east, although work is under way to extend it up Leith Walk and to The Shore. Useful stops for travelers include Haymarket, Princes Street, and St. Andrew Square (for Edinburgh Waverley station). Tickets are £1.70 for a single journey in the "City Zone" (which is every stop excluding the airport), or £6 for a single to/from the airport (£8.50 return). Day tickets, allowing unlimited travel, cost £4 in the City Zone and £9 including the airport.

TRAM CONTACTS Edinburgh Trams.
☎ 0131/338–5780 ⊕ www.edin-burghtrams.co.uk.

Restaurants

Edinburgh's eclectic restaurant scene has attracted a brigade of well-known chefs, including the award-winning trio of Martin Wishart, Tom Kitchin, and Paul Kitching, who have abandoned the tried-and-true recipes for more adventurous cuisine. Of course, you can always find traditional fare, which usually means the Scottish-French style that harks back to the historical "Auld Alliance" of the 13th century. The Scottish element is the preference for fresh and local foodstuffs; the French supplies the sauces. In Edinburgh you can sample anything from Malaysian *rendang* (a thick, coconut-milk stew) to Kurdish kebabs, while the long-established French, Italian, Chinese, Pakistani, and Indian communities ensure that the majority of the globe's most treasured cuisines are well represented. It's possible to eat well in Edinburgh without spending a fortune. Multicourse prix-fixe options are common, and almost always less expensive than ordering à la carte. Even at restaurants in the highest price category, you can easily spend less than £35 per person. People tend to eat later in Scotland than in England—around 8 pm on average—and then drink on in leisurely Scottish fashion.

Hotels

From stylish boutique hotels to homey bed-and-breakfasts, Edinburgh has a world-class array of accommodation options to suit every taste. Its status as one of Britain's most attractive and fascinating cities ensures a steady influx of visitors, but the wealth of overnight options means there's no need to compromise on where you stay. Grand old hotels are rightly renowned for their regal bearing and old-world charm, but if your tastes are a little more contemporary, the city's burgeoning contingent of chic design hotels offers an equally alluring alternative. For those on a tighter budget, the town's B&Bs are the most obvious choice. If you've previously found B&Bs to be restrictive, keep in mind that Scots are trusting people—many proprietors provide front-door keys and very few impose curfews.

Space is at a premium in August and September, when the Edinburgh International Festival and the Festival Fringe take place, so reserve your room at least three months in advance. B&Bs may prove trickier to find in the winter months (with the exception of Christmas and New Year), as this is when many proprietors choose to close up shop and go on vacation themselves.

To save money and see how local residents live, stay in a B&B in one of the areas away from the city center, such as Pilrig to the north, Murrayfield to the west, or Sciennes to the south. Public buses can whisk you to the city center in 10 to 15 minutes.

Restaurant and hotel reviews have been shortened. For full information, visit Fodors.com. Restaurant prices are the average cost of a main course at dinner or, if dinner is not served, at lunch. Hotel prices are the lowest cost of a standard double room in high season, including 20% V.A.T.

WHAT IT COSTS in Pounds			
$	$$	$$$	$$$$
RESTAURANTS			
under £15	£15–£19	£20–£25	over £25
HOTELS			
under £125	£125–£200	£201–£300	over £300

Nightlife

The nightlife scene in Edinburgh is vibrant—whatever you're looking for, you'll find it here. There are traditional pubs, chic modern bars, and cutting-edge clubs. Live music pours out of many watering holes on weekends, particularly folk, blues, and jazz, while well-known artists perform at some of the larger venues.

Edinburgh's 400-odd pubs are a study in themselves. In the eastern and northern districts of the city, you can find some grim, inhospitable-looking places that proclaim that drinking is no laughing matter. But throughout Edinburgh, many pubs have deliberately traded in their old spit-and-sawdust vibe for atmospheric revivals of the warm, oak-paneled, leather-chaired *howffs* (meeting places). Most pubs and bars are open weekdays, while on weekends they're open from about 11 am to midnight (some until 2 am on Saturday).

The List and *The Skinny* carry the most up-to-date details about cultural events. *The List* is available at newsstands throughout the city, while *The Skinny* is free and can be picked up at a number of pubs, clubs, and shops around town. The *Herald* and *The Scotsman* newspapers are good for reviews and notices of upcoming events throughout the city and beyond.

Performing Arts

Think Edinburgh's arts scene consists of just the elegiac wail of a bagpipe and the twang of a fiddle? Think again. Edinburgh is one of the world's great performing-arts cities. The jewels in the crown are the famed Edinburgh Festival Fringe and Edinburgh International Festival, which attract the best in music, dance, theater, circus, stand-up comedy, poetry, painting, and sculpture from all over the globe in August. The *Scotsman* and *Herald,* Scotland's leading daily newspapers, carry listings and reviews in their arts pages every day, with special editions during the festival. Tickets are generally sold in advance; in some cases they're also available from certain designated travel agents or at the door, although concerts by national orchestras often sell out long before the day of the performance.

Shopping

Despite its renown as a shopping street, **Princes Street** in the New Town may disappoint some visitors with its dull modern architecture, average chain stores, and fast-food outlets. One block north of Princes Street, **Rose Street** has many smaller specialty shops; part of the street is a pedestrian zone, so it's a pleasant place to browse. The shops on **George Street** in New Town tend to be fairly upscale, with London names like Laura Ashley and Penhaligons prominent, though some of the older independent stores continue to do good business.

The streets crossing George Street—Hanover, Frederick, and Castle—are also worth exploring. **Dundas Street,** the northern extension of Hanover Street, beyond Queen Street Gardens, has several antiques shops. **Thistle Street,**

originally George Street's "back lane," or service area, has several boutiques and more antiques shops.

As may be expected, many shops along the **Royal Mile** in Old Town sell what may be politely or euphemistically described as "touristware"—whiskies, tartans, and tweeds. Careful exploration, however, will reveal some worthwhile establishments, including shops that cater to highly specialized interests and hobbies. A street below the Royal Mile, East Market Street, close to the castle end of the Royal Mile, just off George IV Bridge, is **Victoria Street,** with specialty shops grouped in a small area. Follow the tiny West Bow to **Grassmarket** for more specialty stores.

Stafford and William Streets form a small, upscale shopping area in a Georgian setting. Walk to the west end of Princes Street and then along its continuation, Shandwick Place, then turn right onto Stafford Street. William Street crosses Stafford halfway down.

North of Princes Street, on the way to the Royal Botanic Garden Edinburgh, is **Stockbridge,** an oddball shopping area of some charm, particularly on St. Stephen Street. To get here, walk north down Frederick Street and Howe Street, away from Princes Street, then turn left onto North West Circus Place.

Edinburgh's newest (and hippest) shopping area is **The Arches,** which has a number of glass-fronted independent stores set within Victorian-era archways. You'll find it on East Market Street, to the east of Edinburgh Waverley train station and below the Royal Mile. And 2020 saw the opening of the refurbished **Edinburgh St. James,** a vast, state-of-the-art shopping complex between Princes Street and Leith Walk.

Tours

ORIENTATION TOURS

One good way to get oriented in Edinburgh is to take a bus tour. If you want to get to know the area around Edinburgh, Rabbie's Trail Burners leads small groups on several different excursions.

Edinburgh Bus Tours

BUS TOURS | Explore every corner of Edinburgh with this company's range of bus tours. The most popular are the Edinburgh Tour, which mainly covers Old Town sights including Edinburgh Castle, the Royal Mile, and the Palace of Holyroodhouse; and the Majestic Tour, which explores the New Town and farther corners of the city, including the Royal Yacht *Britannia* at Leith and the Royal Botanic Garden. Buses depart from Waverley Bridge, with each tour lasting an hour. ■TIP➔ **If you plan more than one bus tour during a weekend, buy a money-saving Grand 48 ticket.** ⊠ *Waverley Bridge, New Town* ☎ *0131/220–0770* ⊕ *www.edinburghtour.com* ✉ *From £16.*

Rabbie's Trail Burners

EXCURSIONS | Venture farther afield from Edinburgh on day trips run by this cheerful company. Its minibuses will take you a surprisingly long way and back in a day, with sights including Loch Ness, St. Andrews, Rosslyn Chapel, and Loch Lomond National Park. Groups are kept to a guaranteed maximum of 16, giving these a less impersonal feel than some of the big enterprises. ■TIP➔ **Book online for a discount.** ⊠ *207 High St., Old Town* ☎ *0131/226–3133* ⊕ *www.rabbies.com* ✉ *From £29.*

PERSONAL GUIDES

Scottish Tourist Guides Association

PERSONAL GUIDES | This organization can supply guides (in 19 languages) who are fully qualified and will meet clients at any point of entry into the United Kingdom or Scotland. Guides can also tailor tours to your interests. ☎ *01786/451953* ⊕ *www.stga.co.uk* ✉ *From £150.*

WALKING AND CYCLING TOURS

The Cadies and Witchery Tours

WALKING TOURS | Spooky tours tracing Edinburgh's ghouls, murders, and other grisly happenings start outside the Witchery Restaurant. The Cadies and Witchery Tours has built an award-winning reputation for combining entertainment and historical accuracy in its lively and enthusiastic Murder and Mystery and (in summer only) Ghosts and Gore tours. Both take you through the narrow Old Town lanes and closes, with costumed guides and other theatrical characters popping up along the route. ⊠ *The Witchery, 352 Castlehill, Old Town* ☎ *0131/225–6745* ⊕ *www.witcherytours.com* ✉ *£10.*

The Edinburgh Literary Pub Tour

WALKING TOURS | Professional actors invoke local literary characters while taking you around some of the city's most hallowed watering holes on these lively and informative tours. The experience is led by "Clart and McBrain"—one a bohemian, the other an intellectual—who regale you with witty tales of the literary past of Edinburgh's Old and New Towns. Tours run daily from May to September and meet outside the Beehive Inn. ⊠ *The Beehive Inn, 18–20 Grassmarket, Edinburgh* ☎ *0800/169–7410* ⊕ *www.edinburghliterarypubtour.co.uk* ✉ *£14.*

★ The Tartan Bicycle Company

BICYCLE TOURS | Cycling enthusiast and Edinburgh native Johann offers a range of guided and self-guided bike tours in and around the capital. Each half-day or full-day tour includes hotel pickup and your choice of standard or e-bikes. For a relaxed half-day introduction to Edinburgh, including some lesser-visited neighborhoods, opt for the Sky to Sea tour; it starts at leafy Union Canal, passes by The Meadows and Arthur's Seat, visits Portobello Beach, The Shore, and the Water of Leith, and ends in the New

Town. ✉ *Edinburgh* ☎ *0797/394–0924* ⊕ *www.tartanbiketours.co.uk* ✈ *From £45.*

Visitor Information

The VisitScotland Edinburgh iCentre, located close to St. Giles' Cathedral on the Royal Mile, offers an accommodation-booking service, along with regular tourist information services.

VISITOR INFORMATION VisitScotland Edinburgh iCentre. ✉ *249 High St., Old Town* ☎ *0131/473–3868* ⊕ *www.visitscotland.com.*

 ## Activities

FOOTBALL

Like Glasgow, Edinburgh is mad for football (soccer in the United States), and there's an intense rivalry between the city's two professional teams.

Heart of Midlothian Football Club

SOCCER | Better known simply as "Hearts," the Heart of Midlothian Football Club plays in maroon and white and is based at Tynecastle. The club's crest is based on the Heart of Midlothian mosaic on the Royal Mile. ✉ *Tynecastle Stadium, McLeod St., Edinburgh* ☎ *0333/043–1874* ⊕ *www.heartsfc.co.uk.*

Hibernian Football Club

SOCCER | Known to most as simply "Hibs," the green-and-white-bedecked Hibernian Club was founded in 1875—one year after Hearts—and plays its home matches at Easter Road Stadium in Leith. ✉ *Easter Road Stadium, 12 Albion Pl., Leith* ☎ *0131/661–2159* ⊕ *www.hibernianfc.co.uk.*

GOLF

Edinburgh is widely considered to be the birthplace of modern golf, as its first official rules were developed at Leith Links. Naturally, there are a number of great courses in the city. For more information, the VisitScotland website has an extensive, searchable guide to Scottish courses.

Braid Hills

GOLF | This golf course is beautifully laid out over a rugged range of small hills in the southern suburbs of Edinburgh. The views in each direction—the Pentland Hills to the south, the city skyline and Firth of Forth to the north—are worth a visit in themselves. The city built this course at the turn of the 20th century after urban development forced golfers out of the city center. There's also a nine-hole "Wee Braids" course for beginners and younger players. Reservations are recommended for weekend play. ✉ *27 Braids Hill Approach, Edinburgh* ☎ *0131/447–6666* ⊕ *www.edinburghleisure.co.uk* ✈ *Braids: £26.50 weekday, £27.50 weekends; Wee Braids: £15 weekdays, £16 weekends* 🏌 *Braids: 18 holes, 5865 yards, par 71; Wee Braids: 9 holes, 2232 yards, par 31.*

Bruntsfield Links

GOLF | The British Seniors and several other championship tournaments are held at this prestigious Willie Park–designed course. It's located 3 miles west of Edinburgh, and should not be confused with Bruntsfield Links park in the city center. The course meanders among 155 acres of mature parkland and has fine views over the Firth of Forth. A strict dress code applies. Bruntsfield takes its name from one of the oldest golf links in Scotland, in the center of Edinburgh, where the club used to play—all that remains there is a nine-hole pitch-and-putt course. ■ TIP→ **Full-day tickets are available for just £20 more than the cost of a single round on weekends.** ✉ *32 Barnton Ave., Edinburgh* ☎ *0131/336–1479* ⊕ *www.bruntsfieldlinks.co.uk* ✈ *£90 weekdays, £110 weekends Apr.–Sept.; £60 weekdays, £80 weekends Oct.; £30 Nov.–Mar.* 🏌 *18 holes, 6437 yards, par 70* ⚐ *Reservations essential.*

Duddingston Golf Club

GOLF | Founded in 1895, this excellent public parkland course is 2 miles east of the city. The first hole is located in an idyllic deer park (watch out for four-legged spectators). Braid Burn—a stream that flows across the southern part of Edinburgh—also runs through the course, creating a perilous hazard on many holes. Prices drop sharply in the winter months for those willing to risk strong winds and rain. ✉ *Duddingston Rd. W, Duddingston* ☎ *0131/661–7688* ⊕ *www.duddingston-golfclub.co.uk* ✆ *£55 May–Sept.; £29 Mar.–Apr. and Oct.–Nov.; £20 Nov.–Feb.* 🏌 *18 holes, 6466 yards, par 72.*

Royal Burgess Golfing Society

GOLF | Edinburgh's other Victorian courses are newcomers when compared to Royal Burgess, which opened in 1735. Its members originally played on Bruntsfield Links; now they and their guests play on elegantly manicured parkland in the city's northwestern suburbs. It's a challenging course with fine, beautifully maintained greens. There's a fairly conservative dress code—no denim or T-shirts allowed—and you must wear a jacket and tie in the clubhouse. ✉ *181 Whitehouse Rd., Barnton* ☎ *0131/339–2075* ⊕ *www.royal-burgess.co.uk* ✆ *£100 for 1 round; £150 day ticket* 🏌 *18 holes, 6511 yards, par 71* ⚲ *Reservations essential.*

RUGBY

Edinburgh is the home of Scottish rugby, with national stadium Murrayfield hosting regular international matches. It's also home to several amateur clubs and the professional club Edinburgh Rugby, who compete in the international Pro14 League.

★ Murrayfield Stadium

RUGBY | Home of the Scottish Rugby Union, Murrayfield Stadium hosts rugby matches in early spring and fall, as well as prestigious Six Nations tournament games in February and March. Crowds of good-humored rugby fans from all over the world add greatly to the sense of excitement in the streets of Edinburgh. Stick around after the game as there's often live music, food, and drinks to enjoy in the stadium grounds. Outside of the rugby season, you can still see Murrayfield with a stadium tour; tickets are £12 for adults. ✉ *Roseburn St., Murrayfield* ☎ *0131/346–5000* ⊕ *www. scottishrugby.org.*

Old Town

East of Edinburgh Castle, the historic castle esplanade becomes the street known as the Royal Mile, leading down through Old Town to the Palace of Holyroodhouse. The Mile, as it's known locally, is actually made up of one thoroughfare that bears, in consecutive sequence, different names—Castlehill, Lawnmarket, Parliament Square, High Street, and Canongate. This thoroughfare, and the streets and passages that wind off it on both sides, really *were* Edinburgh until the 18th century saw expansions to the south and north. Everybody lived here: the richer folk on the lower floors of houses; the less well-to-do families on the middle floors; and the poor highest up.

Time and progress (of a sort) have swept away some of the narrow closes and tall tenements of the Old Town, but enough survive for you to be able to imagine the original profile of Scotland's capital. There are many guided tours of the area, or you can simply stroll around at your leisure. The latter is often a better choice in summer, when tourists pack the area and large guided groups have trouble making their way through the crowds.

Sights

Arthur's Seat

VIEWPOINT | The high point of 640-acre Holyrood Park is this famously spectacular viewpoint. You'll have seen it before—countless photos have been snapped from this very spot. The "seat" in question is actually the 822-foot-high plateau of a small mountain. A ruined church—the 15th-century Chapel of St. Anthony—adds to its impossible picturesqueness. There are various starting points for the walk, but one of the most pleasant begins at the Scottish Parliament building. Cross the road from Parliament, skirt around the parking lot, cross a second road, and join the gently rising path to the left (rather than the steeper fork to the right). At a moderate pace, this climb takes around 45 minutes up and 30 minutes down, and is easy so long as you're reasonably fit. Even if you aren't, there are plenty of places to stop for a rest and to admire the views along the way. A faster—though less beautiful—way to reach the summit is to drive to the small parking area at Dunsapie Loch, on Queen's Road, then follow the footpath up the hill; this walk takes about 20 minutes. ⊠ *Queen's Dr., Old Town.*

Camera Obscura and World of Illusions

OBSERVATORY | FAMILY | View Edinburgh like a Victorian at the city's 19th-century camera obscura. Head up Outlook Tower for the headline attraction—an optical instrument that affords live bird's-eye views of the city, illuminated onto a concave table. It's been wowing visitors since 1853, and yet it retains a magical quality that can captivate even the most cynical smartphone-toting teen. After you've seen the camera obscura and enjoyed the rooftop views, head down to explore five more floors of interactive optical illusions. They are guaranteed to keep the kids entertained and educated for an hour or two. ⊠ *549 Castlehill, Old Town* ☎ *0131/226–3709* ⊕ *www.camera-obscura.co.uk* ⌸ *£16.*

Canongate

NEIGHBORHOOD | This section of the Royal Mile takes its name from the canons who once ran the abbey at Holyrood. Canongate—in Scots, *gate* means "street"—was originally an independent town, or *burgh,* another Scottish term used to refer to a community with trading rights granted by the monarch. In this area you'll find **Canongate Kirk** and its graveyard, **Canongate Tolbooth,** as well as the **Museum of Edinburgh.** ⊠ *Royal Mile, between High St. and Abbey Strand, Old Town.*

Canongate Kirk

RELIGIOUS SITE | This unadorned Church of Scotland building, built in 1688, is best known for its graveyard. It is the final resting place of some notable Scots, including economist Adam Smith (1723–90), author of *The Wealth of Nations* (1776); Dugald Stewart (1753–1828), the leading European philosopher of his time; and the undervalued Scottish poet Robert Fergusson (1750–74). The fact that Fergusson's grave is even distinguishable is due to the far more famous Robert Burns (1759–96), who commissioned a marker to be made. Incidentally, Robert Burns's literary lover Agnes McLehose (the "Clarinda" to his "Sylvander" as noted in a series of passionate letters) also has a memorial stone here. ⊠ *153 Canongate, Old Town* ☎ *0131/556–3515* ⊕ *canongatekirk.org.uk* ⊗ *Closed Oct.–Apr.*

Canongate Tolbooth and People's Story Museum

MUSEUM | Nearly every city and town in Scotland once had a tolbooth. Originally a customhouse, where tolls were gathered, it soon came to mean town hall and later prison, as there were detention cells in the cellar. The building where Canongate's town council once met now has a museum, the **People's Story Museum,** which focuses on the lives of everyday folk from the 18th century to today. Exhibits describe how Canongate once bustled with the activities of the tradespeople needed to supply life's essentials. There are also displays on the politics, health care, and leisure time (such as it was) in days of yore. Other exhibits leap forward in time to show, for example, a typical 1940s kitchen. ⊠ *163*

Old Town

NEW TOWN

OLD TOWN

TOLLCROSS

Queen St.
Hanover St.
St. David St.
St. Andrew St.
Leith St.

St. James Centre

St Andrews Square

George St.
St. Tram
Frederick St.
Castle St.

Scott Monument

Edinburgh Waverley Station

Princes St.
Waverley Bridge
North Bridge

Princes Street Gardens

Ross Fountain

Market St.
Cockburn St.

New College-University of Edinburgh

High St.
Mercat Cross

Edinburgh Castle

Parliament Sq.

Cowgate
Guthrie St.

Johnston Terrace

King's Stables Rd.
Grassmarket
Candlemaker Row
Chambers St.

Old College

West Port
Spittal St.
E. Fountainbridge

Greyfriars Kirk
Forrest Rd.
Teviot Pl.
Potterrow

Flodden Wall

George Heriot's School

University of Edinburgh-Lauriston Campus

Heriot Pl.
Lauriston Place

University of Edinburgh

Lauriston Gdns.
Chalmers St.
Nightingale Way
Simpson Loan

George Square Gardens

Buccleuch Pl.

The Meadows

KEY

Canongate, Old Town ☎ *0131/529–4057* ⊕ *www.edinburghmuseums.org.uk.*

Castlehill

NEIGHBORHOOD | This street, the upper portion of the Royal Mile, was where alleged witches were brought in the 16th century to be burned at the stake. The cannonball embedded in the west gable of Castlehill's **Cannonball House** was, according to legend, fired from the castle during the Jacobite Rebellion of 1745, led by Bonnie Prince Charlie (1720–88)—though the truth is probably that it was installed there deliberately in 1681 as a height marker for Edinburgh's first piped water-supply system. Atop the Gothic **Tolbooth Kirk,** built in 1844 for the General Assembly of the Church of Scotland, stands the tallest spire in the city, at 240 feet. The church now houses the cheery Edinburgh Festival offices and a pleasant café known as **The Hub.** ✉ *East of Esplanade and west of Lawnmarket, Old Town.*

Craigmillar Castle

CASTLE/PALACE | This handsome medieval ruin, only 3 miles south of the city center, is the archetypal Scottish fortress: forbidding, powerful, and laden with atmosphere. It is best known for its association with Mary, Queen of Scots: during a stay here in 1563, her courtiers hatched the successful plot to murder her troublesome husband, Henry Stuart (possibly with Mary's approval). Today Craigmillar is one of the most impressive ruined castles in Scotland. Stroll its beautiful courtyard, enter the well-preserved great hall, or climb the 15th-century tower for a superb view across the city. Look out for the unusually ornate defensive arrow slits, shaped like inverted keyholes. ✉ *Craigmillar Castle Rd., South Side* ☎ *0131/661–4445* ⊕ *www.historicenvironment.scot* 🎟 *£6* ☯ *Closed Thurs. and Fri. Oct.–Apr.*

Dynamic Earth

MUSEUM | **FAMILY** | Using state-of-the-art technology, the 11 theme galleries at this interactive science museum educate and entertain as they explore the wonders of the planet, from polar regions to tropical rain forests. Geological history, from the big bang to the unknown future, is also examined, all topped off with a 360-degree Showdome movie-theater experience. Book tickets online for a 10% discount. ✉ *112–116 Holyrood Rd., Old Town* ☎ *0131/550–7800* ⊕ *www.dynamicearth.co.uk* 🎟 *£15.95 at door; £14.50 online* ☯ *Closed Mon. and Tues. Nov.–Feb.*

Duddingston Village

TOWN | Tucked behind Arthur's Seat, and about a 45-minute walk through Holyrood Park, lies this small community, which still has the feel of a country village. The **Duddingston Kirk** has a Norman doorway and a watchtower that was built to keep body snatchers out of the graveyard; it overlooks **Duddingston Loch,** popular with bird-watchers. Pathways meander down to lochside **Thomson's Tower,** an octagonal tower built in 1825 and now home to a small museum. Nearby, Edinburgh's oldest hostelry, the **Sheep Heid Inn,** serves a wide selection of beers and hearty food. It also has the oldest *skittle* (bowling) alley in Scotland—once frequented, it's said, by Mary, Queen of Scots. ✉ *Duddingston Low Rd., Duddingston.*

★ Edinburgh Castle

CASTLE/PALACE | **FAMILY** | The crowning glory of the Scottish capital, Edinburgh Castle is popular not only for its pivotal role in Scottish history, but also because of the spectacular views from its battlements: on a clear day the vistas stretch all the way to Fife. You'll need at least three hours to see everything it has to offer (even longer if you're a military history buff), though if you're in a rush, its main highlights can just about be squeezed into an hour and a half.

You enter across the **Esplanade,** the huge forecourt built in the 18th century as a parade ground. The area comes alive with color and music each August when it's used for the Military Tattoo, a festival of

An emblem of the city's history, the rock where Edinburgh Castle stands has been inhabited as far back as 1,000 BC.

magnificently outfitted marching bands and regiments. Head over the drawbridge and through the gatehouse, past the guards, and you'll find the rough stone walls of the **Half-Moon Battery,** where the one-o'clock gun is fired every day in an impressively anachronistic ceremony; these curving ramparts give Edinburgh Castle its distinctive silhouette. Climb up through a second gateway and you come to the oldest surviving building in the complex, the tiny 11th-century **St. Margaret's Chapel,** named in honor of Saxon queen Margaret (1046–93), who persuaded her husband, King Malcolm III (circa 1031–93), to move his court from Dunfermline to Edinburgh. The story goes that Edinburgh's environs—the Lothians—were occupied by Anglian settlers with whom the queen felt more at home, as opposed to the Celts who surrounded Dunfermline. The **Crown Room,** a must-see, contains the "Honours of Scotland"—the crown, scepter, and sword that once graced the Scottish monarch—as well as the **Stone of Scone,** upon which Scottish monarchs once

sat to be crowned (it's still a feature of British coronation ceremonies today). In the section now called **Queen Mary's Apartments,** Mary, Queen of Scots, gave birth to James VI of Scotland. The **Great Hall,** which held Scottish Parliament meetings until 1840, displays arms and armor under an impressive vaulted, beamed ceiling.

Military features of interest include the **Scottish National War Memorial,** the **Scottish United Services Museum,** and the famous 15th-century Belgian-made cannon Mons Meg. This enormous piece of artillery has been silent since 1682, when it exploded while firing a salute for the Duke of York; it now stands in an ancient hall behind the Half-Moon Battery. Contrary to what you may hear from locals, it's not Mons Meg but the battery's gun that goes off with a bang every weekday at 1 pm, frightening visitors and reminding Edinburghers to check their watches.

■ **TIP→** Avoid the queues and save some money by buying tickets in advance online. When you arrive, you can pick up your

The History of Edinburgh Castle

Archaeological investigations have established that the rock on which Edinburgh Castle stands was inhabited as far back as 1,000 BC, in the latter part of the Bronze Age. There have been fortifications here since the mysterious tribal Picts first used it as a stronghold in the 3rd and 4th centuries AD. Anglian invaders from northern England dislodged the Picts in AD 452, and for the next 1,300 years the site saw countless battles and skirmishes.

In the castle you'll hear the story of how Randolph, Earl of Moray and nephew of freedom fighter Robert the Bruce, scaled the heights one dark night in 1313, surprised the English guard, and recaptured the castle for the Scots. During this battle he destroyed every one of the castle's buildings except for St. Margaret's Chapel, dating from around 1076, so that successive Stewart kings had to rebuild the castle bit by bit.

The castle has been held over time by Scots and Englishmen, Catholics and Protestants, soldiers and royalty. In the 16th century Mary, Queen of Scots, gave birth here to the future James VI of Scotland (1566–1625), who was also to rule England as James I. In 1573 it was the last fortress to support Mary's claim as the rightful Catholic queen of Britain, causing the castle to be virtually destroyed by English artillery fire.

ticket from one of the automated collection points at the entrance. ⊠ *Castle Esplanade and Castlehill, Old Town* ☎ *0131/225–9846* ⊕ *www.edinburghcastle.scot* ⊠ *£17.50.*

George IV Bridge

BRIDGE/TUNNEL | Here's a curiosity—a bridge that most of its users don't ever realize is a bridge. With buildings closely packed on both sides, George IV Bridge can feel to many like a regular Edinburgh street, but for those forewarned, the truth is plain to see. At the corner of the bridge stands one of the most photographed sculptures in Scotland, *Greyfriars Bobby*. This statue pays tribute to the legendarily loyal Skye terrier who kept vigil beside his master's grave for 14 years after he died in 1858. The 1961 Walt Disney film *Greyfriars Bobby* tells a version of the heartrending tale. ⊠ *Bank St. and Lawnmarket, Old Town.*

Gladstone's Land

HOUSE | This narrow, six-story tenement, situated next to the Assembly Hall, is one of the oldest buildings on the Royal Mile.

It's a survivor from the early 17th century, and now stands as a re-creation of the living conditions of the time. Rooms are decorated in authentic period furnishings, and the sense of how cramped life must have been, even for the moderately successful, is deftly portrayed. Typical Scottish architectural features are evident on two floors, including an arcaded ground floor (even in the city center, livestock sometimes inhabited the ground floor) and some magnificent painted ceilings. Look out for the lovely spinet in the drawing room; the ingeniously designed instrument, resembling a space-saving piano, plucks strings rather than strikes them, producing a resonantly baroque sound. ⊠ *477B Lawnmarket, Old Town* ☎ *0131/226–5856* ⊕ *www.nts.org.uk* ⊠ *£7.*

Grassmarket

PLAZA | For centuries an agricultural marketplace, Grassmarket is now the site of numerous shops, bars, and restaurants, making it a hive of activity at night. Sections of the Old Town wall can be traced

Grassmarket Gallows

Grassmarket's history is long and gory. The **cobbled cross** at the east end marks the site of the town gallows. Among those hanged here were many 17th-century Covenanters, members of the Church of Scotland who rose up against Charles I's efforts to enforce Anglican or "English" ideologies on the Scottish people. Judges were known to issue the death sentence for these religious reformers with the words,

"Let them glorify God in the Grassmarket." Two Grassmarket pubs have names that reference the hangings; The Last Drop and Maggie Dickson's. The latter references a woman who was hanged and proclaimed dead, but when traveling for her burial, sprang back to life. She lived for another 40 years with the nickname Half-Hangit Maggie.

on the north side by a series of steps that ascend from Grassmarket to Johnston Terrace. The best-preserved section of the wall can be found by crossing to the south side and climbing the steps of the lane called the Vennel. Here the 16th-century **Flodden Wall** comes in from the east and turns south at Telfer's Wall, a 17th-century extension.

From the northeast corner of the Grassmarket, **Victoria Street,** a 19th-century addition to the Old Town, leads to the George IV Bridge. Shops here sell antiques, designer clothing, and souvenirs. ⊠ *Grassmarket, Edinburgh.*

★ Greyfriars Kirkyard

CEMETERY | This sprawling, hillside graveyard, surely one of the most evocative in Europe (particularly at twilight), is a giddy mess of old, tottering tombstones that mark the graves of some of Scotland's most respected heroes and despised villains. Many of these inspired character names in the Harry Potter book series; fans can seek out Potters, McGonagalls, and Moodies, to name a few. Among the larger tombs arranged in avenues and the seemingly random assortment of grave markers, lie two rare surviving *mortsafes*: iron cages erected around graves in the early 1800s to prevent the theft of corpses for sale to medical schools.

At the southern end of the graveyard stands Greyfriars Kirk, the church where the National Covenant—a document declaring the Presbyterian Church in Scotland independent of the monarchy, and which plunged Scotland into decades of civil war—was signed in 1638. Nearby, at the corner of George IV Bridge and Candlemaker Row, stands one of Scotland's most photographed sites: the statue of Greyfriars Bobby, a Skye terrier who supposedly spent 14 years guarding the grave of his departed owner. ⊠ *Greyfriars Pl., Old Town* ☎ *0131/225–1900* ⊕ *www.greyfriarskirk.com/visit-us/kirkyard* ⊠ *Free.*

High Kirk of St. Giles (*St Giles' Cathedral*)
RELIGIOUS SITE | St. Giles, which lies about one-third of the way along the Royal Mile from Edinburgh Castle, is one of the city's principal churches. It may not quite rival Paris's Notre Dame or London's Westminster Abbey—it's more like a large parish church than a great European cathedral—but it has a long and storied history. There has been a church here since AD 854, although most of the present structure dates from either 1120 or 1829, when the church was restored.

The tower, with its stone crown 161 feet above the ground, was completed between 1495 and 1500. Inside the

The Greyfriars Kirkyard, part of the church Greyfriars Kirk, is allegedly one of the most haunted cemeteries in Europe.

church stands a life-size statue of the Scot whose spirit still dominates the place—the great religious reformer and preacher John Knox. But the most elaborate feature is the **Chapel of the Order of the Thistle,** built onto the southeast corner of the church in 1911 for the exclusive use of Scotland's only chivalric order, the Most Ancient and Noble Order of the Thistle. It bears the belligerent national motto "*nemo me impune lacessit*" ("No one provokes me with impunity"). Look out for the carved wooden angel playing bagpipes. ⊠ *High St., Old Town* ☏ *0131/225–9442* ⊕ *www.stgilescathedral.org.uk* ⊠ *Free, but donations welcome.*

High Street

NEIGHBORHOOD | The High Street (one of the five streets that make up the Royal Mile) is home to an array of impressive buildings and sights, including some hidden historic relics. Near Parliament Square, look on the west side for a **heart** mosaic set in cobbles. This marks the site of the vanished Old Tolbooth, the

center of city life from the 15th century until the building's demolition in 1817. The ancient municipal building was used as a prison and a site of public execution, so you may witness a local spitting on the heart as one walks by—for good luck.

Just outside Parliament House lies the **Mercat Cross** (*mercat* means "market"), a great landmark of Old Town life. It was an old mercantile center, where royal proclamations were—and are still—read. Most of the present cross is comparatively modern, dating from the time of William Gladstone (1809–98), the great Victorian prime minister and rival of Benjamin Disraeli (1804–81). Across High Street from the High Kirk of St. Giles stands the **City Chambers,** now the seat of local government. Built by John Fergus, who adapted a design of John Adam in 1753, the chambers were originally known as the Royal Exchange and intended to be where merchants and lawyers could conduct business. Note how the building drops 11 stories to Cockburn Street on its north side.

A *tron* is a weigh beam used in public weigh houses, and the **Tron Kirk** was named after a salt tron that used to stand nearby. The *kirk* (church) itself was built after 1633, when St. Giles's became an Episcopal cathedral for a brief time. In 1693 a minister here delivered an often-quoted prayer: "Lord, hae mercy on a' [all] fools and idiots, and particularly on the Magistrates of Edinburgh." ⊠ *Between Lawnmarket and Canongate, Old Town.*

Lawnmarket

NEIGHBORHOOD | The second of the streets that make up the Royal Mile, this was formerly the site of the city's produce market, with a once-a-week special sale of wool and linen. Now it's home to **Gladstone's Land** and the **Writers' Museum.** At various times, the Lawnmarket Courts housed James Boswell, David Hume, and Robert Burns, while in the 1770s this area was home to the infamous Deacon Brodie, pillar of society by day and a murdering gang leader by night. Robert Louis Stevenson (1850–94) may well have used Brodie as the inspiration for his novella *Strange Case of Dr. Jekyll and Mr. Hyde.* ⊠ *Between Castlehill and High St., Old Town.*

Museum of Childhood

MUSEUM | FAMILY | Even adults tend to enjoy this cheerfully noisy museum—a cacophony of childhood memorabilia, vintage toys, antique dolls, and fairground games. The museum claims to have been the first in the world devoted solely to the history of childhood. ⊠ *42 High St., Old Town* ☎ *0131/529–4142* ⊕ *www. edinburghmuseums.org.uk.*

Museum of Edinburgh

MUSEUM | A must-see if you're interested in the details of Old Town life, this bright yellow, 16th-century building is home to a fascinating museum of local history. It houses some of the most important artifacts in Scottish history—including the National Covenant, a document signed by Scotland's Presbyterian leadership in defiance of a reformed liturgy imposed by King Charles I of England that ignited decades of civil war—alongside Scottish pottery, silver, and glassware, as well as curios like Greyfriars Bobby's dog collar. ⊠ *142–146 Canongate, Old Town* ☎ *0131/529–4143* ⊕ *www.edinburghmuseums.org.uk.*

★ National Museum of Scotland

MUSEUM | FAMILY | This museum traces the country's fascinating story from the oldest fossils to the most recent popular culture, making it a must-see for first-time visitors to Scotland. Two of the most famous treasures are the Lewis Chessmen, 11 intricately carved 12th-century ivory chess pieces found on one of Scotland's Western Isles, and Dolly the sheep, the world's first cloned mammal and biggest ovine celebrity. A dramatic, cryptlike entrance gives way to the light-filled, birdcage wonders of the Victorian grand hall and the upper galleries. Other exhibition highlights include the hanging hippo and sea creatures of the Wildlife Panorama, beautiful Viking brooches, Pictish stones, and Queen Mary's *clarsach* (harp). Take the elevator to the lovely rooftop terrace for spectacular views of Edinburgh Castle and the city below. ⊠ *Chambers St., Old Town* ☎ *0300/123–6789* ⊕ *www.nms.ac.uk* ⊠ *Free.*

★ Palace of Holyroodhouse

CASTLE/PALACE | The one-time haunt of Mary, Queen of Scots with a long history of gruesome murder, destructive fire, and power-hungry personalities, the Palace of Holyroodhouse is now Queen Elizabeth's official residence in Scotland. A doughty, impressive palace standing at the foot of the Royal Mile, it's built around a graceful, lawned central court at the end of Canongate. And when royals are not in residence, you can take a tour. There's plenty to see here, so make sure you have at least two hours to tour the palace, gardens, and the ruins of the 12th-century abbey; pick up the free audio guide for the full experience.

The Building of Edinburgh

Towering over the city, Edinburgh Castle was actually built over the plug of an ancient volcano. Many millennia ago, an eastward-grinding glacier encountered the tough basalt core of the volcano and swept around it, scouring steep cliffs and leaving a trail of matter. This material formed a ramp gently leading down from the rocky summit. On this *crag* and *tail* would grow the city of Edinburgh and its castle.

Castle, Walled Town, and Holyroodhouse

By the 12th century Edinburgh had become a walled town, still perched on the hill. Its shape was becoming clearer: like a fish with its head at the castle, its backbone running down the ridge, and its ribs leading briefly off on either side. The backbone gradually became the continuous thoroughfare now known as the Royal Mile, and the ribs became the closes (alleyways), some still surviving, that were the scene of many historic incidents.

By the early 15th century, Edinburgh had become the undisputed capital of Scotland. The bitter defeat of Scotland at Flodden in 1513, when Scotland aligned itself with France against England, caused a new defensive city wall to be built. Though the castle escaped destruction, the city was burned by the English Earl of Hertford under orders from King Henry VIII (1491–1547). This was during a time known as the "Rough Wooing," when Henry was trying to coerce the Scots into allowing the young Mary, Queen of Scots (1542–87), to marry his son Edward. The plan failed and Mary married Francis, the Dauphin of France.

By 1561, when Mary returned from France already widowed, the guest-house of the Abbey of Holyrood had grown to become the Palace of Holyroodhouse, replacing Edinburgh Castle as the main royal residence. Her legacy to the city included the destruction of most of the earliest buildings of Edinburgh Castle.

Enlightenment and the City

In the trying decades after the union with England in 1707, many influential Scots, both in Edinburgh and elsewhere, went through an identity crisis. Out of the 18th-century difficulties, however, grew the Scottish Enlightenment, during which educated Scots made great strides in medicine, economics, and science.

Changes came to the cityscape, too. By the mid-18th century, it had become the custom for wealthy Scottish landowners to spend the winter in the Old Town of Edinburgh, in town houses huddled between the high Castle Rock and the Royal Palace below. Cross-fertilized in coffeehouses and taverns, intellectual notions flourished among a people determined to remain Scottish despite their Parliament being dissolved. One result was a campaign to expand and beautify the city, to give it a look worthy of its future nickname, the Athens of the North. Thus, the New Town of Edinburgh was built, with broad streets and gracious buildings creating a harmony that even today's throbbing traffic cannot obscure.

The Grand Gallery of the National Museum of Scotland is reminiscent of a classic Victorian arcade mall.

Many monarchs, including Charles II, Queen Victoria, and George V, have left their mark on the rooms here, but it's Mary, Queen of Scots whose spirit looms largest. Perhaps the most memorable room is the chamber in which David Rizzio (1533–66), secretary to Mary, met a nasty end in 1566, stabbed more than 50 times by the henchmen of her second husband, Lord Darnley. Darnley himself was murdered the next year, clearing the way for the queen's marriage to her lover, the Earl of Bothwell.

The **King James Tower** is the oldest surviving section of the palace, containing Mary's rooms on the second floor, and Lord Darnley's rooms below. Though much has been altered, there are fine fireplaces, paneling, tapestries, and 18th- and 19th-century furnishings throughout. At the south end of the palace front, you'll find the **Royal Dining Room,** and along the south side is the **Throne Room,** now used for social and ceremonial occasions.

At the back of the palace is the **King's Bedchamber.** The 150-foot-long **Great Picture Gallery,** on the north side, displays the portraits of 110 Scottish monarchs. These were commissioned by Charles II, who was eager to demonstrate his Scottish ancestry—but most of the people depicted are entirely fictional, and the likenesses of several others were invented and simply given the names of real people. The **Queen's Gallery,** in a former church and school at the entrance to the palace, holds rotating exhibits from the Royal Collection. There is a separate admission charge.

Holyroodhouse has its origins in an Augustinian monastery founded by David I (1084–1153) in 1128. In the 15th and 16th centuries, Scottish royalty, preferring the comforts of the abbey to drafty Edinburgh Castle, settled into Holyroodhouse, expanding the buildings until the palace eclipsed the monastery. Nevertheless, you can still walk around some evocative abbey ruins.

After the Union of the Crowns in 1603, when the Scottish royal court packed its bags and decamped to England, the building began to fall into disrepair. It was Charles II (1630–85) who rebuilt Holyrood in the architectural style of Louis XIV (1638–1715), and this is the style you see today. Queen Victoria (1819–1901) and her grandson King George V (1865–1936) renewed interest in the palace, and the buildings were refurbished and again made suitable for royal residence. ⊠ *Canongate, Old Town* ☎ *0131/123–7306* ⊕ *www.rct.uk* ☎ *£15; £24.50 includes Queen's Gallery and a garden history tour.*

Princes Street Gardens

CITY PARK | These beautifully manicured gardens, directly overlooked by Edinburgh Castle, are just a few steps and yet a whole world away from bustling Princes Street. The 38-acre park, divided into the East and West Gardens, was first laid out in the 1760s, on marshland created by the draining of a (long-since-vanished) loch. It has a host of attractions, including a functioning floral clock on the corner of Princes Street and The Mound, the Ross Fountain, a series of memorials, a children's play park, and a café. The gardens often host free concerts, and have a central role in the city's famed Hogmanay festivities. ⊠ *Princes St., Old Town.*

The Real Mary King's Close

NEIGHBORHOOD | FAMILY | Buried beneath the City Chambers, this narrow, cobbled close (alleyway) provides a glimpse into a very different Edinburgh. It was once a busy open-air thoroughfare with hundreds of residents and a lively market, but in 1753 it was sealed off when the Royal Exchange (now the City Chambers) was built on top. Today costumed guides take you around the claustrophobic remains of the shops and houses, describing life here for the residents from plague and quarantine to rivers of sewage, as well as the odd murder mystery and ghost story. But for all the (somewhat over-the-top) theatricality, the real highlights here are historical; the sealed-in street is a truly fascinating insight into 17th-century Edinburgh. ⊠ *2 Warriston's Cl., Old Town* ☎ *0131/225–0672* ⊕ *www.realmarykingsclose.com* ☎ *£16.50.*

The Scottish Parliament

GOVERNMENT BUILDING | Scotland's now-iconic Parliament building is starkly modernist, with irregular curves and angles that mirror the twisting shapes of the surrounding landscape. Stylistically, it is about as far removed from Westminster as can be. Originally conceived by the late Catalan architect Enric Miralles, and completed by his widow Benedetta Tagliabue, the structure's artistry is most apparent when you step inside. The gentle slopes, the forest's worth of oak, the polished concrete and granite, and the walls of glass create an understated magnificence. Take a free guided tour to see the main hall and debating chamber, a committee room, and other areas of the building, or choose a specialist subject for your tour, from history to literature to art. All tour reservations must be made online. Call well in advance to get a free ticket to view Parliament in action. ⊠ *Horse Wynd, Old Town* ☎ *0131/348–5000* ⊕ *www.parliament.scot* ⊗ *Closed Sun.*

Scotch Whisky Experience

MUSEUM | Transforming malted barley and spring water into one of Scotland's most important exports—that's the subject of this popular Royal Mile attraction. An imaginative approach to the subject has guests riding in low-speed barrel cars and exploring Scotland's diverse whisky regions and their distinct flavors. Sniff the various aromas and decide whether you like fruity, sweet, or smoky, and afterward experts will help you select your perfect dram. Your guide will then take you into a vault containing the world's largest collection of Scotch whiskies. Opt for one of the premium tours (from £28

The Palace of Holyroodhouse is the Queen's official residence in Scotland and the setting of a few key scenes in the television show *Outlander.*

to £75) for extras ranging from additional tastings to a Scottish dining experience. ⊠ *354 Castlehill, Old Town* ☎ *0131/220–0441* ⊕ *www.scotchwhiskyexperience. co.uk* ⊠ *From £16.*

★ Scottish Storytelling Centre and John Knox House

ARTS VENUE | The stripped-down, low-fi, traditional art of storytelling has had something of a resurgence in Britain over the last decade or so, and there are few places better than this to experience a master storyteller in full flow. Housed in a modern building that manages to blend seamlessly with the historic structures on either side, the center hosts a year-round program of storytelling, theater, music, and literary events. A great little café serves lunch, tea, and home-baked cakes.

The center's storytellers also hold tours of John Knox House next door. It isn't certain that the religious reformer ever lived here, but there's evidence he died here in 1572. Mementos of his life are on view inside, and the distinctive dwelling

gives you a glimpse of what Old Town life was like in the 16th century—projecting upper floors were once commonplace along the Royal Mile. ⊠ *43–45 High St., Old Town* ☎ *0131/556–9579* ⊕ *www. scottishstorytellingcentre.com* ⊠ *Story-telling Centre free; John Knox House £6* ⊗ *Closed Sun. Sept.–June.*

Writers' Museum

MUSEUM | Situated down a narrow close off Lawnmarket is the 1662 Lady Stair's House, a fine example of 17th-century urban architecture. Inside, the Writers' Museum evokes Scotland's literary past with such exhibits as the letters, possessions, and original manuscripts of Sir Walter Scott, Robert Burns, and Robert Louis Stevenson. ⊠ *Lady Stair's Close, Old Town* ☎ *0131/529–4901* ⊕ *www. edinburghmuseums.org.uk.*

🍴 Restaurants

The most historic part of the city houses some of its grander restaurants (though, curiously, none of its current Michelin stars). It is also home to some of Edinburgh's oldest and most atmospheric pubs, which serve good, informal meals.

Checkpoint

$ | INTERNATIONAL | Originally run as a pop-up during the Festival Fringe, this supercool café-bar is now a permanent part of the Edinburgh dining scene. The coffee is sensational, but the comfort food is just as much of a draw. **Known for:** excellent coffee and hearty breakfasts; delicious light lunches; hip hangout in the evening. $ Average main: £8 ⊠ 3 Bristo Pl., Old Town ☎ 0131/225–9352 ⊕ www.checkpointedinburgh.com.

★ Cannonball Restaurant

$$ | ITALIAN | The name refers to one of the most delightful quirks of Edinburgh's Old Town—the cannonball embedded in the wall outside, said to have been fired at the castle while Bonnie Prince Charlie was in residence (not true, but a good story). The atmosphere in this three-story restaurant and whisky bar is casual and relaxed, despite the gorgeous art deco dining room with views of the castle esplanade. **Known for:** scrumptious Italian-Scottish cuisine; great views of the castle; bread-crumbed haggis cannonballs. $ Average main: £18 ⊠ 356 Castlehill, Old Town ☎ 0131/225–1550 ⊕ www.contini.com/cannonball.

David Bann

$ | VEGETARIAN | This hip eatery, situated just off the Royal Mile, serves exclusively vegetarian and vegan favorites, and its inventive dishes and modern interior make it a popular place with young locals. The menu changes constantly, but the invariably creative, flavorful dishes often leave carnivores forgetting they're eating vegetarian. **Known for:** superb vegetarian and vegan cuisine; very affordable; lovely setting. $ Average main: £13 ⊠ 56–58 St. Mary's St., Old Town ☎ 0131/556–5888 ⊕ www.davidbann.com.

Hanam's

$ | MIDDLE EASTERN | Kurdish food may not be as well known as other Middle Eastern cuisines, but dishes like *bayengaan surocrau* (marinated slow-roasted eggplant) and lamb *tashreeb* (a flavorful casserole) are worth checking out. Hanam's proudly promotes Kurdish cuisine, but also serves more familiar and equally delicious Middle Eastern fare, from shish kebabs to falafel. **Known for:** traditional Kurdish cooking; BYOB policy; hookah on heated terrace. $ Average main: £14 ⊠ 3 Johnston Terr., Old Town ☎ 0131/225–1329 ⊕ www.hanams.com.

Howies

$ | BRITISH | The Victoria Street branch of this bistro chain is a good choice for contemporary Scottish fare, with lots of fresh local produce. Alongside the daily specials and quality Scottish steaks and salmon, there are some nicely inventive vegetarian options. **Known for:** quality Scottish menu; good value set-price lunch; can get very busy. $ Average main: £14 ⊠ 10–14 Victoria St., Old Town ☎ 0131/225–1721 ⊕ www.howies.uk.com.

La Garrigue

$$$ | FRENCH | Edinburgh is blessed with several excellent French bistros, and this is one of the best. Although the modern decor evokes Paris, the food has the rustic flavor of the southern Languedoc region. **Known for:** rustic French cuisine; attentive service; colorful crockery. $ Average main: £22 ⊠ 31 Jeffrey St., Old Town ☎ 0131/557–3032 ⊕ www.lagarrigue.co.uk.

★ Lovecrumbs

$ | CAFÉ | A bakery-café with an inordinately sweet tooth, Lovecrumbs joyously, deliciously, and unashamedly focuses on what *really* matters in life: cake. It serves delectable confections of all kinds, from sumptuous Victoria sponges to heavenly peanut-butter brownies to mouthwatering lemon tarts. **Known for:** extraordinary cakes galore; junk-shop-esque decor;

large crowds despite unpredictable opening times. ⑤ *Average main: £4* ✉ *155 W. Port, Old Town* ☎ *0131/629–0626* ⊕ *www.lovecrumbs.co.uk.*

Michael Neave Kitchen and Whisky Bar

$$ | MODERN BRITISH | Young chef Michael Neave delivers exceptional cuisine at affordable prices in his restaurant just off the Royal Mile. With a mission to "explore the best of Scotland's larder," quality Scottish produce is the star here, with meaty mains like Aberdeen Angus steaks, Perthshire venison, and Borders lamb appearing alongside Scottish seafood specialties like lobster and sea bream. **Known for:** superb Scottish cuisine; inventive sauces; great-value fixed-price menus. ⑤ *Average main: £19* ✉ *21 Old Fishmarket Cl., Old Town* ☎ *0131/226–4747* ⊕ *www.michaelneave. co.uk* ⊗ *Closed Sun. and Mon.*

★ Oink

$ | BRITISH | For a quick, cheap bite while wandering the Royal Mile, you can't beat Oink—possibly the best hog roast (pulled pork) in Edinburgh. Located at the bottom of the Royal Mile (there are two other outlets, but this one is the best), it was founded by two farmers in 2008, and their high-quality, hand-reared pork has proved a huge hit ever since. **Known for:** unbelievable pulled pork; extra crackling on request; great-value lunch. ⑤ *Average main: £6* ✉ *82 Canongate, Old Town* ☎ *07584/637416* ⊕ *www.oink-hogroast.co.uk.*

Ondine

$$$ | SEAFOOD | This fabulous seafood restaurant just off the Royal Mile makes waves with its expertly prepared dishes from sustainable fishing sources. The menu is populated with Scottish seafood staples, from salmon and sea bream to lobster and langoustines, but these are often served in interesting and surprising ways. **Known for:** spectacular seafood; lavish decor; reservations usually needed for nights and weekends. ⑤ *Average main: £25* ✉ *2 George IV Bridge, Old*

Town ☎ *0131/226–1888* ⊕ *www.ondinerestaurant.co.uk* ⊗ *Closed Sun.*

★ Timberyard

$$ | BRITISH | There are few restaurants that feel so wonderfully, well, *Edinburgh* as this one. The freshest seasonal ingredients, mostly sourced from small local producers, go into creating delicious, inventive fare. **Known for:** exciting dishes; hip interior; pricey multicourse menus. ⑤ *Average main: £15* ✉ *10 Lady Lawson St., Old Town* ☎ *0131/221–1222* ⊕ *www. timberyard.co* ⊗ *Closed Sun. and Mon.*

★ Wedgwood the Restaurant

$$$ | MODERN BRITISH | Rejecting the idea that fine dining should be a stuffy affair, owners Paul Wedgwood and Lisa Channon are in charge at this Royal Mile gem. Local produce and some unusual foraged fronds enliven the taste buds as Scottish and international influences are creatively fused together, from the starters (like the satisfyingly salty Scottish "miso" soup) to the desserts (such as the malt and whisky panna cotta). **Known for:** unfussy fine dining; delicious wild foraged salad; good three-course lunch deal. ⑤ *Average main: £22* ✉ *267 Canongate, Old Town* ☎ *0131/558–8737* ⊕ *www.wedgwoodtherestaurant.co.uk.*

 Hotels

The narrow *pends* (alleys), cobbled streets, and steep hills of the Old Town remind you that this is a city with many layers of history. From medieval to modernist, these hotels all are within a stone's throw of the action.

Radisson Collection Royal Mile Edinburgh

$$$ | HOTEL | The bright primary colors, striking stenciled wallpapers, and bold, eclectic furnishings inside this über-trendy design hotel contrast with the Gothic surroundings of the Royal Mile—and yet, somehow, it works. **Pros:** perfect location in the heart of the city; bold and eclectic decor; complimentary gin-and-tonic on arrival. **Cons:** decor a little Austin Powers in places; expensive during high season; street noise can leak into rooms. $ *Rooms from: £240* ⊠ *1 George IV Bridge, Old Town* ☎ *0131/220–6666* ⊕ *www.radissonhotels.com/en-us/hotels/radisson-collection-edinburgh-royal-mile* ➾ *136 rooms* �‖ *Free Breakfast.*

★ Hotel du Vin

$$ | HOTEL | Leave it to one of the United Kingdom's most forward-thinking hotel chains to convert a Victorian-era asylum into this understated luxury property, which combines a real sense of history with contemporary decor and trappings. **Pros:** unique and historic building; trendy design; lively on-site dining and drinking. **Cons:** quarter-mile walk to nearest parking; neighborhood can be noisy; service can be hit-and-miss. $ *Rooms from: £200* ⊠ *11 Bristo Pl., Old Town* ☎ *0131/285–1479* ⊕ *www.hotelduvin.com* ➾ *47 rooms* �‖ *Free Breakfast.*

The Inn on the Mile

$$$ | B&B/INN | This chic and welcoming boutique inn could hardly be more central—some rooms even overlook the Royal Mile. **Pros:** views of the Royal Mile; excellent on-site bar; great design. **Cons:** lots of steps and no elevator; sometimes noisy; nearest parking at a public lot (three-minute walk). $ *Rooms from: £210* ⊠ *82 High St., Old Town* ☎ *0131/556–9940* ⊕ *www.theinnonthemile.co.uk* ➾ *9 rooms* �‖ *Free Breakfast.*

The Scotsman

$$$ | HOTEL | This magnificent turn-of-the-20th-century building, with its grand marble staircase and its fascinating history—it was once the headquarters of the *Scotsman* newspaper—now houses this modern luxury hotel. **Pros:** gorgeous surroundings; personalized service; ideal Old Town location. **Cons:** no air-conditioning; spa can be noisy; could do with some renovation. $ *Rooms from: £270* ⊠ *20 N. Bridge, Old Town* ☎ *0131/556–5565* ⊕ *scotsmanhotel.co.uk* ➾ *69 rooms* ❼ *Free Breakfast.*

The Witchery by the Castle

$$$$ | HOTEL | Each suite within this lavishly theatrical lodging has a theme—choices include the Library, the Guardroom, and the Turret—and is appointed with grand antiques, champagne chilling in an immense bucket, and the finest-quality bedding. **Pros:** Gothic drama and intriguing antiques; a truly romantic retreat; sumptuous dining. **Cons:** can be noisy at night; decor not for everybody; pricey. $ *Rooms from: £395* ⊠ *352 Castlehill, Old Town* ☎ *0131/225–5613* ⊕ *www.thewitchery.com* ➾ *9 suites* ❼ *Free Breakfast.*

 # Nightlife

BARS AND PUBS
The Canons' Gait

BARS/PUBS | In addition to a fine selection of local real ales and malts, The Canons' Gait has live jazz and blues performances, as well as edgy comedy shows in the cellar bar. ⊠ *232 Canongate, Old Town* ☎ *0131/556–4481* ⊕ *www.gait.bar.*

★ The Holyrood 9A

BARS/PUBS | This warm, wood-paneled hipster hangout has a fine array of craft beers on tap, as well as an impressive whisky collection. It also serves some of Edinburgh's best gourmet burgers. ⊠ *9A Holyrood Rd., Old Town* ☎ *0131/556–5044* ⊕ *www.theholyrood.co.uk.*

The Last Drop

BARS/PUBS | There's plenty of atmosphere (and plenty of tourists) amid the nooks and crannies at The Last Drop. The name has a grim double meaning, as it was once the site of public hangings. ⊠ *74–78 Grassmarket, Old Town* ☎ *0131/225–4851* ⊕ *www.nicholsonspubs.co.uk/restaurants/scotlandandnorthernireland/thelastdropgrassmarketedinburgh.*

The Three Sisters

BARS/PUBS | This pub is a hive of activity during festival season, when the courtyard transforms into a beer garden with food stalls, and is packed wall-to-wall with revelers until the wee hours. Outside of the summer months, it remains a lively local favorite and the best place to watch live sports in Edinburgh. ✉ *139 Cowgate, Old Town* ☎ *0131/622–6802* ⊕ *www.thethreesistersbar.co.uk.*

Under the Stairs

BARS/PUBS | As the name suggests, this shabby-chic cocktail bar-cum-bistro is tucked away below street level. A cozy, low-ceilinged place, full of quirky furniture and hip art exhibits, Under the Stairs serves specialty, seasonal cocktails, as well as superb bar food, to a mostly young crowd. ✉ *3A Merchant St., Old Town* ☎ *0131/466–8550* ⊕ *www. underthestairs.org.*

★ Whiski Rooms

BARS/PUBS | This venerable establishment offers one of Old Town's most enjoyable whisky tastings: an informative and interactive experience with an expert guide. The 90-minute Premium Whisky Tasting features five unusual drams you'll almost certainly not have tasted before. When you're finished, either browse the shop stacked high with tempting bottles or head into the bar for another dram. ✉ *4–7 N. Bank St., Old Town* ☎ *0131/225–7224* ⊕ *www.whiskirooms.co.uk.*

LIVE MUSIC

You can still find folk and jazz musicians performing in pubs and clubs throughout the Old Town.

★ The Jazz Bar

MUSIC CLUBS | This basement music venue delivers exactly what the name promises: jazz, in all its many weird and wonderful forms. Blues, funk, acoustic, electric—there's something new to discover every night of the week. There's usually a small cover charge (cash only), but this all goes to musicians, not the venue. ✉ *1A Chambers St., Old Town* ☎ *0131/220–4298* ⊕ *www.thejazzbar. co.uk.*

The Royal Oak

MUSIC CLUBS | With a piano in the corner, this cozy, friendly pub presents excellent live blues and folk music most nights—usually with no cover charge. ✉ *1 Infirmary St., Old Town* ☎ *0131/557–2976* ⊕ *www.royal-oak-folk.com.*

Whistle Binkies Live Music Bar

MUSIC CLUBS | This atmospheric North Bridge bar, accessible from Niddry Street (as it's *in* the bridge), presents rock, blues, and folk music every night of the week, with as many as six or seven acts on Saturday nights. ✉ *4–6 South Bridge, Old Town* ☎ *0131/557–5114* ⊕ *whistlebinkies.com.*

NIGHTCLUBS
Cabaret Voltaire

DANCE CLUBS | The vaulted ceilings of this subterranean club reverberate with dance music most nights, with an ever-changing lineup of cutting-edge DJs on the decks. The club also hosts regular live gigs and, during the Fringe, stand-up comedy shows. ✉ *36–38 Blair St., Old Town* ☎ *0131/247–4704* ⊕ *www.thecabaretvoltaire.com.*

Performing Arts

Festival Theatre

MUSIC | This theater hosts regular concerts, as well as musical theater and Scottish Opera productions. ✉ *13–29 Nicolson St., Old Town* ☎ *0131/529–6000* ⊕ *www.capitaltheatres.com.*

The Queen's Hall

MUSIC | This intimate venue hosts a range of music events, from indie and rock concerts to jazz and classical music recitals. ✉ *85–89 Clerk St., Old Town* ☎ *0131/668–2019* ⊕ *www.thequeenshall.net.*

🛍 Shopping

BOOKS AND STATIONERY
Armchair Books

BOOKS/STATIONERY | Just a two-minute walk from Grassmarket, Armchair Books

Hogmanay: Hello, New Year

In Scotland New Year's Eve is called Hogmanay. Around Scotland celebrations continue the next day with customs such as "first-footing"—visiting your neighbors with gifts that include whisky, all with the purpose of bringing good fortune. It's so important that January 2 as well as January 1 is a holiday in Scotland, while the rest of the United Kingdom trudges back to work.

What to Expect

Edinburgh's Hogmanay celebrations extend over several days, with music, dance, and theater performances taking place throughout the city. The lineup changes every year, but always includes a number of free events. Festivities featuring fire add a dramatic motif; buildings may open for rare night tours; a ceilidh has everyone dancing outdoors to traditional music; and family concerts and serious discussions during the day round out the agenda. At the heart of Hogmanay, though, is the evening street party on New Year's Eve, with different music stages, food and drink (and people *do* drink), and the cockle-warming sight of glowing fireworks over Edinburgh Castle. And it all ends with communal renditions of "Auld Lang Syne," written by Scotland's own Robert Burns.

Planning Basics

Besides the £30 you'll pay to get into the street party celebrations, expect to shell out extra for some related events. For example, the torchlight procession on December 30 costs around £15, while the big-name concert in the Princes Street Gardens on 30 will run you a wallet-punching £70. Book rooms as far ahead as possible. Obvious but essential is warmth: superfluffy hats and the bundled-up look are de rigueur. Check out ⊕ www.edinburghshogmanay.com for full details.

is a chaotic but characterful bookshop heaving with secondhand and antiquarian books. ⊠ 72–74 W. Port, Old Town ☎ 0131/229–5927 ⊕ www.armchair-books.co.uk.

Carson Clark Gallery

BOOKS/STATIONERY | This gallery specializes in antique maps, sea charts, and prints. ⊠ 34 Northumberland St., Old Town ☎ 0131/556–4710.

Main Point Books

BOOKS/STATIONERY | This bibliophile's haven is stacked high with obscure first editions and bargain tomes. It also hosts regular literary events. ⊠ 77 Bread St., Old Town ☎ 0131/228–4837 ⊕ www.mainpoint-books.co.uk.

CLOTHING

Bill Baber

CLOTHING | One of the more imaginative Scottish knitwear designers, Bill Baber's creative and colorful pieces are a long way from the conservative pastel woolies sold at some of the large mill shops. ⊠ 66 Grassmarket, Old Town ☎ 0131/225–3249 ⊕ www.billbaber.com.

Ragamuffin

CLOTHING | First established on the Isle of Skye, Ragamuffin's Edinburgh outlet sells some of the funkiest, brightest, and most elegant knitwear produced anywhere in Scotland. ⊠ 278 Canongate, Old Town ☎ 0131/557–6007.

GIFTS AND ACCESSORIES
Hannah Zakari

GIFTS/SOUVENIRS | Quirky handmade pieces, including embroidered cushions, are a specialty at Hannah Zakari. Keep an eye out for unusual jewelry, artwork, and accessories, too. ⊠ 43 Candlemaker Row, Old Town ☎ 0131/226–5433 ⊕ www.hannahzakari.co.uk.

JEWELRY
Clarksons of Edinburgh

JEWELRY/ACCESSORIES | A family firm, Clarksons handcrafts a unique collection of jewelry, from Celtic to contemporary styles. The pieces here are made with silver, gold, platinum, and precious gems, with a particular emphasis on diamonds. ⊠ 87 W. Bow, Old Town ☎ 0131/225–8141 ⊕ www.clarksonsedinburgh.co.uk.

SCOTTISH SPECIALTIES
★ Cadenhead's Whisky Shop

WINE/SPIRITS | Edinburgh's most iconic Scotch shop, Cadenhead's has an incredible selection of whisky to purchase (including rare bottles from closed distilleries), and also offers tasting sessions. The friendly and knowledgeable staff can help you pick out the perfect whisky to suit your palate. ⊠ 172 Canongate, Old Town ☎ 0131/556–5864 ⊕ www.cadenhead.scot.

★ Cranachan & Crowdie

FOOD/CANDY | This lovely gourmet shop on the Royal Mile is brimming with the finest Scottish food and drink, from crunchy oatcakes to melt-in-the-mouth shortbread. There's even a chocolate counter for those with a particularly sweet tooth. Staff are happy to put together hampers of food for any occasion—including an impromptu picnic back in your room. They also sell tweeds, handmade candles, and other gift-worthy knickknacks. ⊠ 263 Canongate, Old Town ☎ 0131/556–7194 ⊕ www.cranachanandcrowdie.com.

Geoffrey Tailor Kiltmakers

LOCAL SPECIALTIES | This shop can clothe you in full Highland dress, with high-quality kilts made in its own workshops. ⊠ 57–59 High St., Old Town ☎ 0131/557–0256 ⊕ www.geoffreykilts.co.uk.

New Town

It was not until the Scottish Enlightenment, a civilizing time of expansion in the 1700s, that the city's elite decided to break away from the Royal Mile's craggy slope and narrow closes to create a new neighborhood below the castle. This was to become the New Town, with elegant squares, classical facades, wide streets, and harmonious proportions. Clearly, change had to come. At the dawn of the 18th century, Edinburgh's unsanitary conditions—primarily a result of overcrowded living quarters—were becoming notorious. The well-known Scottish fiddle tune "The Flooers (flowers) of Edinburgh" was only one of many ironic references to the capital's unpleasant environment.

To help remedy this sorry state of affairs, in 1767 James Drummond, the city's lord provost (the Scottish term for mayor), urged the town council to hold a competition to design a new district for Edinburgh. The winner was an unknown young architect named James Craig (1744–95). His plan called for a grid of three main east–west streets, balanced at either end by two grand squares. These streets survive today, though some of the buildings that line them have been altered by later development. Princes Street is the southernmost, with Queen Street to the north and George Street as the axis, punctuated by St. Andrew and Charlotte squares. A look at the map will reveal a geometric symmetry unusual in Britain. Even the Princes Street Gardens are balanced by the Queen Street Gardens, to the north. Princes Street was conceived as an exclusive residential address, with an open vista facing the castle. It has since been altered by the demands of business and shopping, but the vista remains.

The New Town was expanded several times after Craig's death and now covers an area about three times larger than Craig envisioned. Indeed, some of the most elegant facades came later and can be found by strolling north of the Queen Street Gardens.

Sights

Calton Hill

VIEWPOINT | Robert Louis Stevenson's favorite view of his beloved city was from the top of this hill, and it's easy to see why. Located in the heart of the city, Calton Hill offers stunning vistas of the Old and New Towns and out to the Firth of Forth, making it a popular setting for picnicking and watching festival fireworks. Great views aside, the hill is also home to a number of impressive monuments. The most notable is the so-called **National Monument,** also known as "Scotland's Disgrace," which was commissioned in 1822 and intended to mimic Athens's Parthenon. But after just 12 columns had been built, the money ran out, leaving the facade as a monument to high aspirations and poor fundraising. Nearby, the 100-foot-high **Nelson Monument,** completed in 1815 in honor of Britain's greatest naval hero, is topped with a "time ball" that is dropped at 1 pm every day. Other hillside monuments honor notable Scots ranging from mathematician John Playfair to philosopher Dugald Stewart.

The hill is also home to the **City Observatory,** which hosts regular contemporary art exhibitions, as well as upmarket restaurant **The Lookout by Gardener's Cottage**. It also plays host to the **Beltane Fire Festival** every April 30. ⊠ *Bounded by Leith St. to the west and Regent Rd. to the south, New Town* ☎ *0131/529–5151* ⊕ *www.edinburgh.gov.uk* ✉ *Nelson Monument £6.*

George Street

NEIGHBORHOOD | With its high-end shops, upmarket bistros, and five-star hotels, all with handsome Georgian frontages, George Street is a more pleasant, less crowded thoroughfare for strolling than Princes Street. It also has a couple of points of interest. First, there's the **statue of King George IV,** at the intersection of George and Hanover streets, which recalls the visit of George IV to Scotland in 1822; he was the first British monarch to do so since King Charles II in the 17th century. Next, the **Assembly Rooms,** between Hanover and Frederick streets, are where Sir Walter Scott officially acknowledged having written the Waverley novels (the author had hitherto been a mystery, albeit a badly kept one). It's now a popular venue during the Fringe Festival. ⊠ *Between Charlotte Sq. and St. Andrew Sq., New Town.*

Moray Place

PLAZA | With its "pendants" of Ainslie Place and Randolph Crescent, Moray Place was laid out in 1822 by the Earl of Moray. From the start the homes were planned to be of particularly high quality, with lovely curving facades, imposing porticos, and a central secluded garden reserved for residents. ⊠ *Between Charlotte Sq. and Water of Leith, New Town.*

Princes Street

NEIGHBORHOOD | The south side of this dominant New Town street is occupied by the well-kept Princes Street Gardens, which act as a wide green moat to the castle on its rock. The north side is now one long sequence of chain stores with mostly unappealing modern fronts, with one or two exceptions: most notably the handsome Victorian facade that is home to Jenners department store. ⊠ *Waterloo Pl. to Lothian Rd., New Town.*

★ Royal Botanic Garden Edinburgh

GARDEN | FAMILY | Explore Britain's largest rhododendron and azalea gardens at this beautiful 70-acre botanical garden. Founded in 1670 as a physic garden, it now has a range of natural highlights such as soaring palms in the glass-domed Temperate House and the steamy Tropical Palm House, an extensive Chinese garden, and a pretty rock garden and stream. There's a visitor center with exhibits on biodiversity, a fabulous gift shop selling plants, books, and gifts, and two cafeterias. The handsome 18th-century Inverleith House hosts art exhibitions.

It's free to roam the gardens, though it costs extra for greenhouse admission, and you can splash out even more for guided garden walks and private tours. It takes 20 minutes to walk to the garden from Princes Street, or you can take a bus. ⊠ *Arboretum Pl., Inverleith* ☎ *0131/248–2909* ⊕ *www.rbge.org.uk* 🖭 *Free; Glasshouses £7.*

Scott Monument

MEMORIAL | What appears to be a Gothic cathedral spire that's been chopped off and planted on Princes Street is in fact Scotland's tribute to one of its most famous sons, Sir Walter Scott. Built in 1844 and soaring to 200 feet, it remains the largest monument to a writer anywhere in the world. Climb the 287 steps to the top for a stunning view of the city and the hills and coast beyond. ⊠ *E. Princes St. Gardens, New Town* ☎ *0131/529–4068* ⊕ *www.edinburghmu-seums.org.uk* 🖭 *£8; cash only.*

★ Scottish National Gallery

MUSEUM | Opened to the public in 1859, the Scottish National Gallery presents a wide selection of paintings from the Renaissance to the postimpression-ist period within a grand neoclassical building. Most famous are the old-master paintings bequeathed by the Duke of Sutherland, including Titian's *Three Ages of Man*. Many masters are here: works by Velázquez, El Greco, Rembrandt, Goya, Poussin, Turner, Degas, Monet, and van Gogh, among others, complement a fine collection of Scottish art, including Sir Henry Raeburn's *Reverend Robert*

Walker Skating on Duddingston Loch and other works by Ramsay, Raeburn, and Wilkie. The gallery also has an informa-tion center, a quirky gift shop, and the excellent Scottish Cafe and Restaurant.

You can also hop on a shuttle bus (£1 donation requested) from here to the Scottish National Gallery of Modern Art, which has paintings and sculptures by Pablo Picasso, Georges Braque, Henri Matisse, and André Derain, among others. ⊠ *The Mound, New Town* ☎ *0131/624–6200* ⊕ *www.nationalgaller-ies.org.*

Scottish National Portrait Gallery

MUSEUM | Set within a magnificent red-sandstone Gothic building from 1889, this gallery is an Edinburgh must-see. Conceived as a gift to the people of Scotland, it divides into five broad themes, from Reformation to Modernity, with special galleries for photography and contemporary art—all centered around the stunning Great Hall. It also plays host to regular temporary exhibitions, includ-ing the annual BP Portrait Award. ⊠ *1 Queen St., New Town* ☎ *0131/624–6200* ⊕ *www.nationalgalleries.org.*

🍴 Restaurants

The New Town, with its striking street plan, ambitious architecture, and profes-sional crowd, has restaurants where you can get everything from a quick snack to a more formal dinner.

Contini George Street

$$ | ITALIAN | Set within a grand former banking hall on George Street, this superb restaurant serves light but satisfying Italian favorites divided into *primi, secondi,* and *formaggi,* all within a light, airy setting of grand Corinthi-an columns, an open marble-topped bar, intricate wall hangings, and soft gray banquettes. The food choices are strictly seasonal, but regularly appear-ing favorites include the Scotch beef carpaccio and the homemade ravioli with

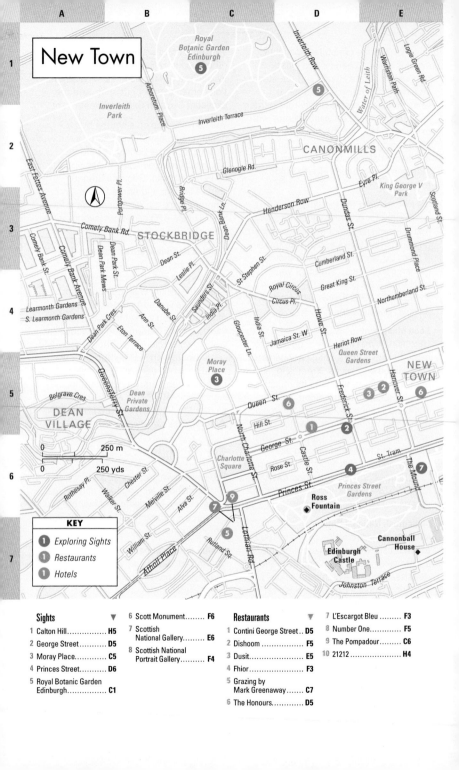

New Town

Sights

1 Calton Hill **H5**
2 George Street **D5**
3 Moray Place **C5**
4 Princes Street **D6**
5 Royal Botanic Garden
   Edinburgh **C1**
6 Scott Monument **F6**
7 Scottish
   National Gallery **E6**
8 Scottish National
   Portrait Gallery **F4**

Restaurants

1 Contini George Street .. **D5**
2 Dishoom **F5**
3 Dusit **E5**
4 Fhior **F3**
5 Grazing by
   Mark Greenaway **C7**
6 The Honours **D5**
7 L'Escargot Bleu **F3**
8 Number One **F5**
9 The Pompadour **C6**
10 21212 .... **H4**

KEY

1 *Exploring Sights*
1 *Restaurants*
1 *Hotels*

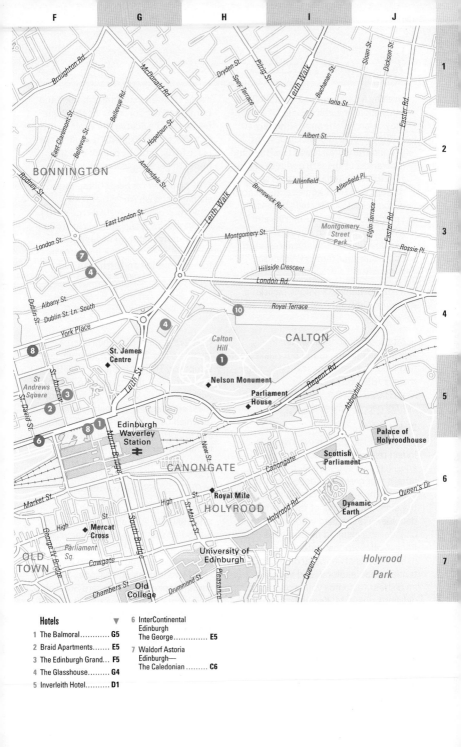

F   G   H   I   J

1
2
3
4
5
6
7

Broughton Rd.
East Claremont St.
Bellevue St.
Bellevue Rd.
McDonald Rd.
Dryden St.
Sper Terrace
Pilrig St.
Leith Walk
Sloan St.
Dickson St.
Easter Rd.

BONNINGTON

Rodney St.
Hopetoun St.
Annandale St.
Buchanan St.
Iona St.
Albert St.

London St.
East London St.
Leith Walk
Brunswick Rd.
Allenfield
Allenfield Pl.
Montgomery St.
Montgomery Street Park
Elgin Terrace
Easter Rd.
Rossie Pl.

Dublin St.
Albany St.
Dublin St. Ln. South
York Place
Hillside Crescent
London Rd.
Royal Terrace

St. Andrew St.
St. Andrews Square
St. David St.
St. James Centre

Calton Hill
CALTON

Nelson Monument
Parliament House

Regent Rd.
Abbeyhill

Market St.
North Bridge
Leith St.
Edinburgh Waverley Station
New St.
CANONGATE
Canongate
Scottish Parliament
Palace of Holyroodhouse

High St.
South Bridge
George IV Bridge
St. Mary's St.
Royal Mile
HOLYROOD
Holyrood Rd.
Dynamic Earth
Queen's Dr.

Mercat Cross
Parliament Sq.
Cowgate
High St.

OLD TOWN
Chambers St.
Old College
Drummond St.
Pleasance
University of Edinburgh
Queen's Dr.

Holyrood Park

Ancestor Hunting

Are you a Cameron or a Campbell, a Mackenzie or a Macdonald? If so, you may be one of the approximately 40 million people of Scottish descent around the world. It was the Highland clearances of the 18th and 19th centuries, in which tenant farmers were driven from their homes and replaced with sheep, that started the mass emigration to North America and Australia. Before or during a trip, you can do a little genealogical research or pursue your family tree more seriously.

VisitScotland (⊕ *www.visitscotland. com/about/ancestry*) has information about clans and surnames, books, and family-history societies. At the Register House, the ScotlandsPeople Centre (⊕ *www.scotlandspeople.gov.uk*) is the place to dip into the past or conduct in-depth genealogical research.

Willing to pay for help? Companies such as Scottish Ancestral Trail (⊕ *www.scottish-ancestral-trail.co.uk*) do the research and plan a trip around your family history. Throughout Scotland, you can check bookstores for information and visit clan museums and societies.

ricotta and spinach. **Known for:** lovely, light Italian cuisine; grand but relaxed setting; Scotch beef carpaccio. ⑤ *Average main: £18* ⊠ *103 George St., New Town* ☎ *0131/225–1550* ⊕ *www.contini.com/ contini-george-street.*

Dishoom
$ | **INDIAN** | The city's most inventive Indian restaurant, Dishoom serves up an all-sensory experience, from the smells that greet you (delicious whiffs of incense mixed with aromatic spices) to the sight and sounds of the interior (the decor is all distressed-wood panels and chandeliers, inspired by Bombay's 1920 Iranian cafés) to the taste of the food itself. A tapas-style menu of deliciously tender meat, seafood, and vegetarian dishes welcomes you, along with delicious desserts. **Known for:** incredible lamb salli boti; great cocktail and mocktail menu; unique Indian breakfast rolls. ⑤ *Average main: £9* ⊠ *3a St. Andrew Sq., Edinburgh* ☎ *0131/2026–406* ⊕ *www. dishoom.com.*

Dusit
$$ | **THAI** | Tucked down narrow Thistle Street, Dusit doesn't register on most travelers' radars, but it has been a local favorite since 2002. An authentic, contemporary Thai restaurant run by Bangkok-born Pom, the menu here delights with deliciously creamy curries, spicy stir-fries, and fragrant seafood specialties, all of which use a mix of fresh local produce and imported Thai vegetables. **Known for:** award-winning Thai food; local haunt; good value lunch menu. ⑤ *Average main: £17* ⊠ *49a Thistle St., New Town* ☎ *0131/220–6846* ⊕ *www.dusit.co.uk.*

Fhior
$$$$ | **BRITISH** | A relative newcomer to Edinburgh's dining scene, Fhior seems here to stay. Owner and chef Scott Smith, who previously ran the award-winning Norn, serves up seasonal, Scandinavian-inspired fare with rare Scottish ingredients, from beremeal (an ancient form of barley) bread to sea buckthorn. **Known for:** modernist decor; old-school Scottish dishes with a Scandinavian flair; multicourse menu options chosen by the chef. ⑤ *Average main: £40* ⊠ *36 Broughton St., Edinburgh* ☎ *0131/477–5000* ⊕ *www.fhior.com* ⊗ *Closed Sun.–Tues.*

Grazing by Mark Greenaway

$$$ | BRITISH | Despite the name and the smattering of shared plates on offer, Grazing is mostly about traditional, hearty bistro fare done brilliantly. Set within a lavish yet unstuffy dining room, the restaurant's menu of seasonal dishes with inventive twists adds a real sense of fun to this consistently excellent, if suprisingly high-priced, dining experience. **Known for:** fun and inventive dishes; attentive service; menu prices that tend to add up. $ *Average main: £25 ⊠ Waldorf Astoria Edinburgh—The Caledonian, Princes St., New Town ☎ 0131/222–8857 ⊕ www.markgreenaway.com.*

★ The Honours

$$$ | BISTRO | Run by Edinburgh restaurant grandee Martin Wishart, the Honours is a more relaxed (though almost as pricey) alternative to his eponymous flagship in Leith. Inside its gorgeous black-and-white, art deco interior, diners can enjoy a range of excellent Scottish seafood dishes; but those in the know order the meat, with extraordinary rare-breed sirloin and fillet beef steaks as well as delicious game like roe deer, guinea fowl, and rabbit. **Known for:** mouthwatering meat dishes; beautiful art deco decor; impeccable service. $ *Average main: £25 ⊠ 58a North Castle St., New Town ☎ 0131/220–2513 ⊕ www.thehonours. co.uk ⊘ Closed Sun. and Mon.*

★ L'Escargot Bleu

$ | FRENCH | When it comes to quality at a good value, this pretty little French bistro, situated on one of Edinburgh's trendiest streets, is almost impossible to beat. You're warmly welcomed into an upmarket but casual space of stripped wooden floors and period French posters, then shown a menu that seems to have a typo: £12.90 for a two-course lunch, or £14.90 for dinner of fine French cuisine as authentic as a withering stare on the Champs-Élysées. **Known for:** authentic French fare; hard-to-believe low prices; friendly service. $ *Average main: £13 ⊠ 56 Broughton St., New Town ☎ 0131/557–1600 ⊕ www.lescargotbleu. co.uk ⊘ Closed Sun.*

Number One

$$$$ | BRITISH | Clublike but unstuffy, this outstanding basement restaurant, set within the Edwardian splendor of The Balmoral hotel, is made for intimate dining. The food is extraordinary, with a menu that highlights the best of Scottish seafood and meat in inventive fashion, but the prices make this a place for serious special occasions; the regular three-course prix-fixe is £90 per person (drinks not included) while the tasting menus will set you back even more. **Known for:** wonderfully intimate setting; inventive dishes; very expensive. $ *Average main: £90 ⊠ The Balmoral, 1 Princes St., New Town ☎ 0131/557–6727 ⊕ www.roccofortehotels.com ⊘ No lunch.*

★ The Pompadour

$$$$ | FRENCH FUSION | Sophisticated surroundings, spectacular views, and sumptuous cuisine make this restaurant, originally opened in 1925, one of Edinburgh's best spots for fine dining. Head chef Dan Ashmore uses his expertise in great Scottish produce, from venison to sea trout, to serve up a stunning, "mystery" seven-course tasting menu (it comes in a sealed envelope; it's up to you when, or if, you want to take a peek). **Known for:** beautiful pastel-floral dining room; subtly sumptuous flavors; gorgeous presentation. $ *Average main: £35 ⊠ Waldorf Astoria Edinburgh–The Caledonian, Princes St., New Town ☎ 0131/222–8857 ⊕ www.thepompadour.com ⊘ Closed Mon. and Tues.*

21212

$$$$ | MODERN FRENCH | Paul Kitching is one of Britain's most innovative chefs, and the theatrical dining experience at 21212 delivers surprises galore. Set within a Georgian town house, the Michelin-starred restaurant is sumptuously appointed while, behind a large glass screen, a small army of chefs

is busy assembling the delicious and intricate dishes. **Known for:** contemporary Franco-Anglo-Scottish cuisine; atmospheric and romantic; enigmatic menu of two starts, two mains, and two desserts with soup and cheese courses in between. ⑤ *Average main: £85* ⊠ *3 Royal Terr., New Town* ☎ *0131/523–1030* ⊕ *www.21212restaurant.co.uk* ⊙ *Closed Sun.–Tues.*

 # Hotels

Calton Hill, which offers some of the best views of the city from its summit, is just one of the reasons to base yourself in the New Town, filled with gorgeous 18th- and 19th-century architecture.

★ The Balmoral

$$$$ | HOTEL | The attention to detail in the elegantly appointed rooms and suites, where colors and patterns echo the country's heathers and moors, and the sheer Edwardian splendor of this grand, former railroad hotel make staying at The Balmoral a special introduction to Edinburgh. **Pros:** big and beautiful Edwardian building; top-hatted doorman; top-notch spa, restaurant, and whisky bar. **Cons:** small lap pool; spa books up fast; some rooms a little tiny. ⑤ *Rooms from: £340* ⊠ *1 Princes St., New Town* ☎ *0131/556–2414* ⊕ *www.roccofortehotels.com* ↪ *188 rooms* ⑪ *Free Breakfast.*

Braid Apartments

$$ | RENTAL | This collection of chic, comfortable, and spacious self-service apartments is tucked away on quiet Thistle Street, meaning that guests can enjoy being in the heart of the New Town and yet out of sight (and sound) of the crowds. **Pros:** good modern facilities; quiet central location; friendly reception staff. **Cons:** no on-site parking; noisy water pumps; no access for people with disabilities. ⑤ *Rooms from: £175* ⊠ *27 Thistle St., New Town* ☎ *0800/304–7160* ⊕ *www.bymansley.com* ↪ *20 rooms* ⑪ *No meals.*

The Edinburgh Grand

$$ | RENTAL | Despite all appearances—the classical Edinburgh exterior, the Corinthian-columned art deco lobby, the friendly and attentive concierges, and the in-house high-end restaurants—The Edinburgh Grand is not a swanky hotel, but rather a collection of grand and luxurious serviced apartments. **Pros:** beautiful apartments with supercomfy beds; ideal location for trams and trains; all amenities included. **Cons:** perilously dark corridors; no doors on some bathrooms; Register Club food disappointing and overpriced. ⑤ *Rooms from: £200* ⊠ *42 St. Andrew Sq., New Town* ☎ *0131/230–0570* ⊕ *www.lateralcity.com* ↪ *50 apartments* ⑪ *No meals.*

★ The Glasshouse

$$ | HOTEL | Glass walls extend from the 19th-century facade of a former church, foreshadowing the daring, modern interior of one of the city's original, and best, boutique hotels. **Pros:** truly stunning rooftop garden; very modern and stylish; near all the attractions. **Cons:** loud air-conditioning and toilet flushing; decor a little sterile for some; continental breakfast extra (hot breakfast even more). ⑤ *Rooms from: £200* ⊠ *2 Greenside Pl., New Town* ☎ *0131/525–8200* ⊕ *www.theglasshousehotel.co.uk* ↪ *77 rooms* ⑪ *No meals.*

Inverleith Hotel

$ | B&B/INN | Across from the Royal Botanic Gardens, this renovated Victorian town house has cozy, well-lit rooms with velour bedspreads, dark-wood furniture, and pale-gold curtains—at an incredible value. **Pros:** quiet surroundings; knowledgeable staff; cheap parking nearby (free on weekends). **Cons:** some rooms are small; far from the Old Town; uphill walk to the city center. ⑤ *Rooms from: £80* ⊠ *5 Inverleith Terr., New Town* ☎ *0131/556–2745* ⊕ *www.inverleithhotel.co.uk* ↪ *9 rooms* ⑪ *Free Breakfast.*

InterContinental Edinburgh The George

$$ | HOTEL | Built in 1775 for Edinburgh's elite, this row of five Georgian town houses in the heart of the New Town now hosts a luxury hotel. **Pros:** excellent central location; stylish and comfortable rooms; fast Wi-Fi throughout. **Cons:** regular wedding parties in reception area; service can be hit-and-miss; not all rooms have air-conditioning. ⑤ *Rooms from: £200* ✉ *19–21 George St., New Town* ☎ *0131/225–1251* ⊕ *www.ihg.com/intercontinental/hotels/gb/en/edinburgh/edigs/hoteldetail* ⇌ *240 rooms* ⑩ *Free Breakfast.*

Waldorf Astoria Edinburgh—The Caledonian

$$$ | HOTEL | An imposing and ornate red-sandstone building situated at the west end of Princes Street Gardens, "The Caley" has dramatic Victorian decor, beautifully restored interiors, and more castle-view rooms than anywhere else—not to mention the best hotel dining in Edinburgh. **Pros:** impeccable service; not as pricey as some other grande dame hotels; outstanding restaurants. **Cons:** expensive parking (£25 per night); no wow factor for some; location a little away from the action. ⑤ *Rooms from: £250* ✉ *Princes St., New Town* ☎ *0131/222–8888* ⊕ *waldorfastoria3.hilton.com* ⇌ *241 rooms* ⑩ *Free Breakfast.*

Nightlife

BARS AND PUBS

The Basement

BARS/PUBS | This funky, cheerful bar has something of the 1950s jet-setter vibe—which might explain its happy-go-lucky mash-up of cocktails, Mexican food, and Hawaiian-shirted bar staff. ✉ *10A–12A Broughton St., New Town* ☎ *0131/557–0097* ⊕ *www.basement-bar-edinburgh.co.uk.*

Bramble Bar

BARS/PUBS | This easily walked-by basement bar on Queen Street—take the stairs down to a clothing-alteration shop and you'll see a small sign—is one of Edinburgh's great hidden gems. Expect superb cocktails, eclectic music (DJs spin most nights), young crowds, and lots of nooks and crannies. ✉ *16A Queen St., New Town* ☎ *0131/226–6343* ⊕ *www.bramblebar.co.uk.*

★ Cafe Royal Circle Bar

BARS/PUBS | Famed for its atmospheric Victorian interiors—think ornate stucco, etched mirrors, tiled murals, stained glass, and leather booths—the Cafe Royal Circle Bar has been drawing a cast of Edinburgh characters since it opened in 1863. Regulars and newcomers alike pack in for the drinks (a host of real ales and malt whiskies) and tasty bar food—everything from yummy sandwiches and small plates to elaborate seafood platters. ✉ *19 W. Register St., New Town* ☎ *0131/556–1884* ⊕ *www.caferoyaledinburgh.co.uk.*

Cask and Barrel

BARS/PUBS | A spacious, traditional pub on trendy Broughton Street, the Cask and Barrel serves hand-pulled ales from a horseshoe-shaped bar, ringed by a collection of brewery mirrors. ✉ *115 Broughton St., New Town* ☎ *0131/556–3132* ⊕ *www.caskandbarrelbroughton.co.uk.*

★ Guildford Arms

BARS/PUBS | Like the Café Royal Circle Bar on the other corner of the same Victorian block, the Guildford Arms has a spectacular interior of intricate plasterwork, elaborate cornices, and wood paneling. The ornate ceiling alone is worth the visit. Stay for the range of excellent Scottish ales on tap. ✉ *1 W. Register St., New Town* ☎ *0131/556–4312* ⊕ *www.guildfordarms.com.*

Joseph Pearce's

BARS/PUBS | FAMILY | One of eight Swedish bars and restaurants in Edinburgh owned by the Boda group, Joseph Pearce's has a distinctly northern European feel, despite its solidly Edwardian origins. Scandi-themed cocktails are popular here, as are the meatballs, open sandwiches, and other Swedish dishes. There's a children's corner with toys to keep the little ones occupied, and a sunny outdoor space in summer. ⊠ 23 Elm Row, New Town ☎ 0131/556–4140 ⊕ www.bodabar.com.

★ Juniper

BARS/PUBS | Situated right opposite Edinburgh Waverley Station, Juniper cultivates an air of glamorous fun, helped by its postcard-worthy views of the city and the castle. The wine list is good (if a little pricey), but it's the wildly imaginative cocktails that really make this place. A long-standing favorite is Strawberries and Steam, a strawberry-infused gin cocktail served in a teapot that's bubbling over with dry ice. You can soak up your drinks with nibbles from the modern Scottish "street food" menu. ⊠ 20 Princes St., New Town ☎ 0131/652–7370 ⊕ www. juniperedinburgh.co.uk.

Kay's Bar

BARS/PUBS | Housed in a former Georgian coach house, this diminutive but friendly spot serves 50 single-malt whiskies, a range of guest ales, and decent bottled beers. Check out the cute little wood-paneled library room, with its tiny fireplace and shelves full of books. ⊠ 39 Jamaica St., New Town ☎ 0131/225–1858 ⊕ www.kaysbar.co.uk.

★ Panda and Sons

BARS/PUBS | The very definition of a hidden gem, this Prohibition-style speakeasy is cunningly tucked away behind a barbershop exterior. Venture inside and downstairs to discover a quirky bar serving some seriously refined cocktails. And yes, we're baffled by the fictional bar-owning panda, too. ⊠ 79 Queen St., New Town ☎ 0131/220–0443 ⊕ www. pandaandsons.com.

Starbar

BARS/PUBS | Well worth seeking out, the tucked-away Starbar has a beer garden, table soccer, and—a rarity—a very good jukebox. It is also rumored to be haunted—get the owners to regale you with scary stories, including a specific clause in their lease that prevents them from removing a human skull from the building. ⊠ 1 Northumberland Pl., New Town ☎ 0131/539–8070 ⊕ www.starbar.co.uk.

Tonic

BARS/PUBS | This stylish basement bar has bouncy stools, comfy sofas, and a long list of superb cocktails. There's relaxing music Monday to Thursday, acoustic acts Friday, and resident DJs on the weekend. ⊠ 34A N. Castle St., New Town ☎ 0131/225–6431 ⊕ www.bar-tonic. co.uk.

COMEDY CLUBS

The Stand

COMEDY CLUBS | Laugh until your sides split at The Stand, a legendary basement comedy club that hosts both famous names and up-and-coming acts all throughout the year, though it's particularly popular during the Fringe. There's a free improv show every Sunday lunchtime. ⊠ 5 York Pl., East End ☎ 0131/558–7272 ⊕ www.thestand.co.uk.

LGBTQ BARS

There's an ever-expanding LGBTQ scene in Edinburgh, and the city has many predominantly gay clubs, bars, and cafés. Nevertheless, don't expect the scene to be quite as varied as in London, New York, or even Glasgow. The List and The Skinny have sections that focus on gay and lesbian venues.

CC Blooms

BARS/PUBS | Modern and colorful, CC Blooms is a club spread over two levels, playing a mix of musical styles and with regular cabaret nights. Open nightly, it's been a mainstay on the gay scene since the early '90s, and can now count several other gay-friendly bars and clubs as neighbors. ✉ *23–24 Greenside Pl., New Town* ☎ *0131/556–9331* ⊕ *www. ccblooms.co.uk.*

Regent Bar

BARS/PUBS | Billing itself as "the best real ale gay pub in Edinburgh," this popular drinking hole is warm, homey, and welcoming—and it's dog-friendly, too. As advertised, the real ales selection is great. ✉ *2 Montrose Terr., Abbeyhill* ☎ *0131/661–8198* ⊕ *www.theregentbar. co.uk.*

NIGHTCLUBS
The Liquid Room

DANCE CLUBS | Top indie bands and an eclectic mix of club nights (techno, hip-hop, and alternative, to name a few) have made the Liquid Room a favorite after-dark venue since 1997. ✉ *9C Victoria St., New Town* ☎ *0131/225–2564* ⊕ *www. liquidroom.com.*

Performing Arts

Edinburgh Playhouse

THEATER | Big-ticket concerts and musicals, along with the occasional ballet and opera production, are staged at the popular Playhouse, with its enormous 3,000-seat auditorium. ✉ *18–22 Greenside La., East End* ☎ *0844/871–3014* ⊕ *www. atgtickets.com.*

Shopping

ANTIQUES
★ Unicorn Antiques

ANTIQUES/COLLECTIBLES | This Victorian basement is crammed with fascinating antiques, including artworks, ornaments, silverware, and other such curios. ✉ *65 Dundas St., New Town* ☎ *0131/556–7176* ⊕ *www.unicornantiques.co.uk.*

CLOTHING
Concrete Wardrobe

CLOTHING | For an eclectic mix of quirky knitwear and accessories, dive into Concrete Wardrobe. You can also find vintage furnishings and other crafty items. ✉ *50a Broughton St., New Town* ☎ *0131/558–7130.*

Elaine's Vintage Clothing

CLOTHING | This wee boutique in trendy Stockbridge is crammed full of vintage threads for women and men. The finds span the 20th century, but most are from the '40s to the '70s. The friendly owner is happy to share her knowledge of the many elegant and quirky outfits on her rails. ✉ *55 St. Stephen St., New Town* ☎ *0131/225–5783.*

DEPARTMENT STORES
Harvey Nichols

DEPARTMENT STORES | Affectionately (and almost universally) known as Harvey Nicks, this high-style British fashion chain has its Scottish outpost on St. Andrew Square, carrying the store's chic, upscale style options. ✉ *30–34 St. Andrew Sq., New Town* ☎ *0131/524–8388* ⊕ *www. harveynichols.com.*

★ Jenners

DEPARTMENT STORES | Jenners, a long-standing Edinburgh landmark that is now part of the U.K.-wide House of Fraser chain, specializes in traditional china and glassware, as well as Scottish tweeds and tartans—though you'll find everything else you'd expect from a large department store, too. Its famous food hall, run by Valvona & Crolla, stocks traditional culinary delights including shortbread, marmalade, and honey. ✉ *48 Princes St., New Town* ☎ *0343/909–2031* ⊕ *www.houseoffraser.co.uk.*

John Lewis

DEPARTMENT STORES | John Lewis specializes in furnishings and household goods, but also stocks designer clothes. It's part of the Edinburgh St. James shopping complex, which is currently closed for extensive redevelopment (due to finish in 2020), but John Lewis remains open as usual with access from Leith Street. ✉ *Edinburgh St. James, Leith St., New Town* ☎ *0131/556–9121* ⊕ *www.johnlewis.com.*

Marks & Spencer

DEPARTMENT STORES | Fairly priced, stylish clothes and accessories are on offer at Marks & Spencer. You can also buy quality food and household goods. ✉ *54 Princes St., New Town* ☎ *0131/225–2301* ⊕ *www.marksandspencer.com.*

JEWELRY

Hamilton & Inches

JEWELRY/ACCESSORIES | Established in 1866, this jeweler is worth visiting not only for its gold and silver pieces, but also for its late-Georgian interior. Designed by David Bryce in 1834, it's all columns and elaborate plasterwork. ✉ *87 George St., New Town* ☎ *0131/225–4898* ⊕ *www.hamiltonandinches.com.*

Joseph Bonnar

JEWELRY/ACCESSORIES | Tucked behind George Street, Joseph Bonnar stocks Scotland's largest collection of antique jewelry, including 19th-century agate jewels. ✉ *72 Thistle St., New Town* ☎ *0131/226–2811* ⊕ *www.josephbonnar. com.*

★ Sheila Fleet

JEWELRY/ACCESSORIES | As much art gallery as jewelry shop, designer Sheila Fleet's store in Stockbridge displays a variety of stunning jewelry inspired by her native Orkney, from wind and waves to Celtic spirals to island wildlife. ✉ *18 St. Stephen St., Stockbridge* ☎ *0131/225–5939* ⊕ *www.sheilafleet.com.*

OUTDOOR SPORTS GEAR

Cotswold Outdoor

SPORTING GOODS | This specialist chain store sells outdoor clothing for all weather, as well as accessories, maps, guides, and more. The staff are invariably helpful and informed. ✉ *72 Rose St., New Town* ☎ *0131/341–2063* ⊕ *www.cotswoldoutdoor.com.*

Haymarket

West of the Old Town and south of the West End is Haymarket, a district with its own down-to-earth character and well-worn charm. It offers varied shopping and dining options that become more upmarket as you head toward the West End and Leith.

Restaurants

This area has many restaurants that tend to be more affordable than those in the center of town.

First Coast

$$ | INTERNATIONAL | This laid-back bistro, just a few minutes from Haymarket Station, has a loyal following—and for good reason. Its multicultural menu has everything from Thai mango salads to Brazilian seafood stews to Korean rice cakes, as well as an unusually good selection of vegetarian options. **Known for:** great international fare; big on flavor; relaxing interior. ⑤ *Average main: £15* ✉ *97–101 Dalry Rd., Haymarket* ☎ *0131/313–4404* ⊕ *www.first-coast. co.uk* ⊗ *Closed Sun.*

🛏 Hotels

Close to one of Edinburgh's two main train stations, Haymarket—beyond the west end of Princes Street—can make a good base for exploring the city.

★ The Dunstane Houses

$$ | HOTEL | Set within two Victorian town houses that sit across the road from one another, with each offering a selection of beautifully appointed rooms and suites, this hotel is one of Edinburgh's most luxurious boutique options. **Pros:** beautifully decorated; excellent food and service; quiet, residential area. **Cons:** no elevator (and stairs to climb); a 20-minute walk to Princes Street; some traffic noise from outside. ⑤ *Rooms from: £200* ✉ *4 W. Coates, Haymarket* ☎ *0131/337–6169*

⊕ *www.thedunstane.com* ⤴ *35 rooms* ⦿ *Free Breakfast.*

The Victorian Town House

$ | **B&B/INN** | This handsome B&B, situated in a quiet, leafy crescent but within walking distance of Princes Street, offers bright and spacious rooms with a quirky mix of Edwardian and modern furnishings. **Pros:** serene surroundings; gracious staff; beautiful Water of Leith at your doorstep. **Cons:** no parking nearby; a little way from the Old Town. ⑤ *Rooms from: £120* ✉ *14 Eglinton Terr., Haymarket* ☎ *0131/337–7088* ⊕ *the-victorian-town-house.edinburgh-hotel.org* ⤴ *3 rooms* ⦿ *Free Breakfast.*

West End

Handsome Georgian town houses give this neighborhood a dignified feel. People head here for the small boutiques and cafés, as well as the wide range of cultural venues.

Sights

Edinburgh Zoo

ZOO | **FAMILY** | Home to star attractions Tian Tian and Yang Guang, the United Kingdom's only two giant pandas, Edinburgh's Zoo hosts more than 1,000 animals over 80 acres. Don't miss the famous Penguin Parade, which takes place every afternoon (as long as the penguins are willing), or the ever-popular Koala Territory, where you can get up close to the zoo's four koalas—including joey Kalari, who was born in 2019. Discounted tickets are available online. ✉ *Royal Zoological Society of Scotland, 134 Corstorphine Rd., Corstorphine* ☎ *0131/334–9171* ⊕ *www.edinburghzoo.org.uk* 🎫 *£19.95.*

★ Dean Village

NEIGHBORHOOD | Founded as a milling community in the 12th century, this pretty residential area offers a pleasant respite from the noise and crowds of the city. Head down cobbled Bells Brae Street and you'll be met by a charming assortment of old mill buildings, stone bridges, and lush greenery, all lining the Water of Leith. Walk two minutes east for a dramatic view of an imposing, 19th-century viaduct (Dean Bridge) or a little farther west to visit the Scottish National Gallery of Modern Art. ✉ *Dean Village, Dean Village* ⊕ *history.business. site.*

★ Edinburgh Gin Distillery

WINERY/DISTILLERY | Whisky may be Scotland's most famous spirit, but gin also has a long and storied history here and as any visit to an Edinburgh bar will tell you, it's currently all the rage. Edinburgh Gin is a small distillery and visitor center just off Princes Street, offering tours and tastings that give a fascinating insight into craft gin production. You'll see two copper stills, Flora and Caledonia, which helped kick-start the now award-winning operation, and are still used to make some of their experimental, small-batch gins. (Note that the main range, including the navy-strength Cannonball Gin and the coastal botanical-infused Seaside Gin, are now produced at a larger facility in Leith). Take a discovery tour (£10) or, if you'd like a tasting too, a connoisseur tour (£25), then head into the Heads & Tales bar to sample some Scottish gin cocktails. ✉ *1a Rutland Pl., West End* ☎ *0131/656–2810* ⊕ *www.edinburghgin.com* 🎫 *£10.*

🍴 Restaurants

Even after business hours, the city's commercial center is a good place to find a variety of international restaurants.

★ Bread Meats Bread

$ | **BURGER** | This family-run burger joint, first opened in Glasgow in 2012 and expanded to Edinburgh in 2016, has already gained a nationwide reputation for its over-the-top add-ons like bone-marrow butter, kimchi, 'Nduja (spicy salami

Sights ▼

1 Dean Village.............. **E6**
2 Edinburgh
  Gin Distillery.............. **E7**
3 Edinburgh Zoo........... **A8**
4 The Meadows........... **F8**
5 The Royal Yacht
  Britannia................. **G3**
6 Water of Leith
  Walkway................. **H4**

Restaurants ▼

1 Aurora.................... **H4**
2 Bonsai.................... **G7**
3 Bread Meats Bread **E7**
4 First Coast **D8**
5 Kalpna.................... **G8**
6 The King's Wark........ **H3**
7 The Kitchin **H3**
8 Mimi's Bakehouse–
  Leith **H4**
9 Restaurant
  Martin Wishart.......... **H4**

Hotels ▼

1 AmarAgua............... **H9**
2 B+B Edinburgh.......... **D6**
3 The Bonham.............. **E6**
4 The Chester
  Residence **E7**
5 The Conifers............. **G5**
6 The Dunstane
  Houses.................. **D7**
7 Fingal..................... **H3**
8 Glenalmond House **H9**
9 Malmaison................**I3**
10 94DR......................**H8**
11 Prestonfield House **I8**
12 Rutland Hotel............ **E7**
13 The Victorian
  Town House **D7**

spread), and pomegranate molasses. Take a seat inside the chic, reclaimed-wood interior and choose from a menu packed with amped-up burgers, as well as chicken, veggie, and halal options. **Known for:** signature Wolf of St. Vincent Street burger; no reservations so usually long waits; smart, modern interior. ⓢ *Average main: £14* ✉ *92 Lothian Rd., West End* ☎ *0131/225–3000* ⊕ *www.breadmeatsbread.com.*

Hotels

With easy access to some of the city's trendiest shops and cafés, the West End has lodgings that take advantage of the neighborhood's handsome Georgian-style town houses.

B+B Edinburgh

$$ | **B&B/INN** | **FAMILY** | Standing out along an elegant and tranquil West End terrace, this excellent B&B is the first Scottish outpost of supertrendy B+B Belgravia of London; an imposing Victorian mansion that combines grand public spaces with affordable modern accommodation. **Pros:** fascinating building in tranquil area; superb views; nice library and lounge bar. **Cons:** no night porter; hint of previous institutional use; basement rooms are dark. ⓢ *Rooms from: £135* ✉ *3 Rothesay Terr., West End* ☎ *0131/225–5084* ⊕ *www.bb-edinburgh.com* ↝ *27 rooms* ⷩ *Free Breakfast.*

The Bonham

$$ | **HOTEL** | There's a clubby atmosphere throughout this hotel, where the typical high-ceilinged town-house rooms have gorgeous late-19th-century architectural features mixed with pastel-shade furnishings and distinctly Scottish patterned fabrics. **Pros:** smart and stylish; excellent restaurant; quiet location. **Cons:** few common areas; needs upgrading in places; no air-conditioning. ⓢ *Rooms from: £165* ✉ *35 Drumsheugh Gardens, West End* ☎ *0131/226–6050* ⊕ *www.thebonham.com* ↝ *49 rooms* ⷩ *Some meals.*

★ The Chester Residence

$$$ | **RENTAL** | A decadent hideaway located just off from the main drag, these elegant self-service apartments offer a lot of space and a plethora of peace in a city where both can be hard to find. **Pros:** quiet but convenient location; well-stocked kitchens; beautiful gardens. **Cons:** lots of stairs and no elevators; no washing machines; no free on-site parking. ⓢ *Rooms from: £225* ✉ *9 Rothesay Pl., West End* ☎ *0131/226–2075* ⊕ *www.chester-residence.com* ↝ *23 apartments* ⷩ *No meals.*

Rutland Hotel

$$ | **HOTEL** | Nominated for several style awards, this chic boutique hotel at the west end of Princes Street offers 12 guest rooms with flamboyant fabrics and classic furnishings, as well as eight stylish serviced apartments, a flexible option for a family or two couples traveling together. **Pros:** friendly staff; casual and unpretentious; great bar and restaurant. **Cons:** decor too loud and busy for some; no elevators to apartments; no free on-site parking. ⓢ *Rooms from: £155* ✉ *1–3 Rutland St., West End* ☎ *0131/229–3402* ⊕ *www.therutlandhotel.com* ↝ *20 rooms* ⷩ *Free Breakfast* Ⓜ *West End-Princes St.*

Nightlife

BARS AND PUBS

Blue Blazer

BARS/PUBS | This cozy and characterful bar has an extensive selection of real ales, malt whiskies, and rums, all of which are enjoyed by a friendly, diverse crowd. ✉ *2 Spittal St., West End* ☎ *0131/229–5030.*

The Hanging Bat

BARS/PUBS | A favorite with beer-loving locals, this stylish modern bar of reclaimed wood and exposed brickwork has an extensive, regularly changing selection of craft beers from across the country on tap, from IPAs to saisons to porters. The food, cooked in the in-house smoker, is great, too (try the smoked pulled pork). ⊠ *133 Lothian Rd., West End* ☏ *0131/229–0759* ⊕ *www.thehangingbat.com.*

★ The Jolly Botanist
BARS/PUBS | Gin lovers are spoiled for choice at this self-proclaimed "liquor emporium." Take a seat amid the quirky period furnishings and flick through a menu of 72 gins from around the world, which can be enjoyed with your choice of tonic or as part of an inventive gin cocktail. There's also good bar food available. ⊠ *256–260 Morrison St., West End* ☏ *0131/228–5596* ⊕ *www.thejollybotanist.co.uk.*

Performing Arts

Cameo Picturehouse
FILM | Cameo has one large and two small auditoriums, both of which are extremely comfortable, showing a good mix of mainstream and art-house films. There's also a bar serving snacks late into the evening. ⊠ *38 Home St., Tollcross* ☏ *0871/902–5747* ⊕ *www.picturehouses.com.*

★ Filmhouse
FILM | Widely considered to be among the best independent cinemas in Britain, the excellent three-screen Filmhouse is the go-to venue for modern, foreign-language, offbeat, and any other less-commercial films. It also holds frequent live events and mini-festivals for the discerning cinephile, and is the main hub for the International Film Festival each summer. The café and bar here are open late on weekends. ⊠ *88 Lothian Rd., West End* ☏ *0131/228–2688* ⊕ *www.filmhousecinema.com.*

King's Theatre
THEATER | Built in 1906 and adorned with vibrant murals by artist John Byrne, the art nouveau King's Theatre has a great program of contemporary dramatic works. ⊠ *2 Leven St., Tollcross* ☏ *0131/529–6000* ⊕ *www.capitaltheatres.com.*

The Lyceum
THEATER | Traditional plays and contemporary works, including previews or tours of London West End productions, are presented here. ⊠ *30b Grindlay St., West End* ☏ *0131/248–4848* ⊕ *www.lyceum.org.uk.*

Traverse Theatre
THEATER | With its specially designed space, the Traverse Theatre has developed a solid reputation for new, stimulating plays by Scottish dramatists, as well as innovative dance performances. ⊠ *10 Cambridge St., West End* ☏ *0131/228–1404* ⊕ *www.traverse.co.uk.*

Usher Hall
MUSIC | Edinburgh's grandest concert venue, Usher Hall hosts a wide range of national and international performers, from Kaiser Chiefs and Vampire Weekend to the Royal Scottish National Orchestra. ⊠ *Lothian Rd., West End* ☏ *0131/228–1155* ⊕ *www.usherhall.co.uk.*

Shopping

CLOTHING
Herman Brown
CLOTHING | This secondhand clothing store is where cashmere twinsets and classic luxe labels are sought and found. ⊠ *151 W. Port, West End* ☏ *0131/228–2589* ⊕ *www.hermanbrown.co.uk.*

South Side

This residential district, which includes the suburbs of Morningside, Marchmont, and Newington (among others), offers a peek at the comings and goings of regular Edinburghers. Cost-conscious visitors can find lots of affordable restaurants and budget B&Bs here.

Sights

★ The Meadows

CITY PARK | FAMILY | Edinburgh's most popular green space, The Meadows is the first port of call for nearby workers, students, and families when the sun is out (or even when it isn't). You'll find people making the most of the grass here: picnicking, barbecuing, playing soccer, throwing frisbees, and flying kites. More formal sports facilities include tennis courts, a small golf putting course, and the biggest kids' play area in Edinburgh. Come during one of the city's many cultural festivals and there's likely to be a show on, too. ⊠ *Melville Dr., South Side* ☎ *0131/529–5151* ⊕ *www.themeadowsofedinburgh.co.uk.*

 Restaurants

The presence of university professors and students means eateries that are both affordable and interesting.

Bonsai

$ | JAPANESE | The owners of Bonsai regularly visit Tokyo to research the casual dining scene, and their expertise is setting a high standard for Japanese cuisine in Edinburgh. The succulent *gyoza* (steamed dumplings) are pliant and tasty, while the wide variety of noodle, teriyaki, and sushi dishes balance sweet and sour deliciously. **Known for:** authentic sushi; great dragon gaijin-zushi (inside-out roll); friendly and informal vibe. ⑤ *Average main: £6* ⊠ *46 W. Richmond St., South Side* ☎ *0131/668–3847* ⊕ *www.bonsaibarbistro.co.uk.*

★ Kalpna

$ | INDIAN | Amid an ordinary row of shops, the facade of this vegetarian Indian restaurant may be unremarkable, but the food is exceptional and a great value, too. You'll find south- and west-Indian specialties, including *dam aloo kashmiri* (a medium-spicy potato dish with a sauce made from honey, pistachios, and almonds) and *bangan achari* (super-spicy marinated eggplants). **Known for:** authentic veggie Indian fare; lively interior with exotic mosaics; great lunchtime buffet. ⑤ *Average main: £10* ⊠ *2–3 St. Patrick Sq., South Side* ☎ *0131/667–9890* ⊕ *www.kalpnarestaurant.com.*

 Hotels

The B&Bs and guesthouses in this residential area offer good value.

AmarAgua

$ | B&B/INN | Four-poster beds, a tranquil location, and bountiful breakfasts set this Victorian town-house B&B apart. **Pros:** quiet setting; snug rooms; wonderful and varied breakfasts. **Cons:** far from the city center; minimum two-night stay; early checkout (10 am) and late check-in (5 pm). ⑤ *Rooms from: £105* ⊠ *10 Kilmaurs Terr., Newington* ☎ *0131/667–6775* ⊕ *www.amaragua.co.uk* ⊗ *Closed Jan* ⤢ *5 rooms* ⦿| *Free Breakfast.*

Glenalmond House

$ | B&B/INN | Elegantly furnished rooms, a friendly atmosphere, and a hearty breakfast are three big factors that make this town-house B&B a popular budget stay. **Pros:** knowledgeable owners; elegant furnishings; amazing sausages at breakfast. **Cons:** a 30-minute walk to the Royal Mile; some rooms small; street noise can be audible. ⑤ *Rooms from: £100* ⊠ *25 Mayfield Gardens, South Side* ☎ *0131/668–2392* ⊕ *www.glenalmondhouse.com* ⤢ *9 rooms* ⦿| *Free Breakfast.*

94DR

$$ | B&B/INN | Like the infectiously optimistic owners, Paul and John, 94DR reaches for the stars with its stylish decor and contemporary trappings, while maintaining a comfortable, homey feel. **Pros:** warm welcome; gay-friendly vibe; smashing breakfast. **Cons:** 25-minute walk to the city center; some bathrooms small; a little pricey. ⑤ *Rooms from: £175* ⊠ *94 Dalkeith Rd., South Side*

☎ 0131/662–9265 ⊕ www.94dr.com ⚑ 7 rooms ⦿ Free Breakfast.

★ Prestonfield House

$$$ | HOTEL | The Highland "coos" (cows), peacocks, and grouse wandering around this hotel's 20-acre grounds transport you to a whole new world; one that's only five minutes by car from the Royal Mile. **Pros:** baroque grandeur; comfortable beds; extensive grounds. **Cons:** underwhelming showers; brooding decor can look gloomy; bit pretentious for some. Ⓢ *Rooms from: £260* ✉ *Priestfield Rd., Prestonfield* ☎ *0131/225–7800* ⊕ *www. prestonfield.com* ⚑ *23 rooms* ⦿ *Some meals.*

Nightlife

BARS AND PUBS

Cloisters

BARS/PUBS | Set within an old church parsonage, Cloisters now offers a very modern form of sanctuary: real ales, fine whisky, and good food at reasonable prices, with a total absence of music and game machines. ✉ *26 Brougham St., Tollcross* ☎ *0131/221–9997* ⊕ *www. cloistersbar.com.*

Leslie's Bar

BARS/PUBS | Retaining its original mahogany island bar, the late-Victorian-era Leslie's Bar is renowned for its gorgeous interior and for serving a range of traditional Scottish ales and malt whiskies. ✉ *45–47 Ratcliffe Terr., South Side* ☎ *0131/667–7205.*

CEILIDHS AND SCOTTISH EVENINGS

★ Edinburgh Ceilidh Club

THEMED ENTERTAINMENT | One of Edinburgh's most popular ceilidhs, this traditional Scottish music and dance night is held each Tuesday at Summerhall. It's ideal for beginners, as a caller teaches the dance steps before the live band begins each song. The club also holds irregular nights at Assembly Roxy near South Bridge. ✉ *Summerhall, 1 Summerhall Pl.,*

South Side ☎ *0131/560–1580* ⊕ *www. edinburghceilidhclub.com* ⚑ *£7.*

Performing Arts

Church Hill Theatre

THEATER | The intimate, 335-seat Church Hill Theatre, managed by the city council, hosts high-quality productions by local amateur dramatic societies. ✉ *33 Morningside Rd., Morningside* ☎ *0131/220–4348* ⊕ *www.assemblyroomsedinburgh. co.uk.*

⬤ Shopping

ANTIQUES

Courtyard Antiques

ANTIQUES/COLLECTIBLES | This lovely shop, tucked down a tiny alleyway, stocks a mixture of high-quality antiques, toys, and militaria. ✉ *108a Causewayside, Sciennes* ☎ *0131/662–9008* ⊕ *www. edinburghcourtyardantiques.co.uk.*

Leith

Just north of the city is Edinburgh's port, a place brimming with seafaring history and undergoing a supercharged revival after years of postwar neglect. It may not be as pristine as much of modern-day Edinburgh, but there are plenty of cobbled streets, dockside buildings, and bobbing boats to capture your imagination. Here along the lowest reaches of the Water of Leith (the river that flows through town), you'll find an ever-growing array of modish shops, pubs, and restaurants. Leith's major attraction is the Royal Yacht *Britannia,* moored outside the huge Ocean Terminal shopping mall. You can reach Leith from the center by walking down Leith Walk from the east end of Princes Street (20 to 30 minutes)—or, better yet, walk along the beautiful Water of Leith Walkway (a great way to forget you're in a capital city). Alternatively, you can hop on a bus.

Sights

The Royal Yacht *Britannia*

LIGHTHOUSE | FAMILY | Moored on the waterfront at Leith is the Royal Yacht *Britannia*—launched in Scotland in 1953, retired in 1997, and now returned to her home country. A favorite of Queen Elizabeth II (she is reported to have shed a tear at its decommissioning ceremony), it is now open for the public to explore, from the royal apartments on the upper floors to the more functional engine room, bridge, galleys, and captain's cabin. The visitor center, based within the hulking, onshore Ocean Terminal shopping mall, has a variety of fascinating exhibits and photographs relating to the yacht's history. ⊠ *Ocean Dr., Leith* ☎ *0131/555–5566* ⊕ *www.royalyachtbritannia.co.uk* ⊠ *£16.50.*

★ Water of Leith Walkway

TRAIL | The Water of Leith, Edinburgh's main river, rises in the Pentland Hills, skirts the edges of the city center, then heads out to the port at Leith, where it flows into the Firth of Forth. For a scenic stroll from the West End out to Leith, you can join this waterside walkway at the Scottish National Gallery of Modern Art, follow it through pretty Dean Village and Stockbridge, and continue past the Royal Botanic Garden, before emerging at The Shore. It takes about 90 minutes at a leisurely pace—and with all the tree-lined paths, pretty stone bridges, colorful wildflowers, and stunning birdlife (including herons, kingfishers, and buzzards) to see, we do suggest taking your time. Keep an eye out, too, for Anthony Gormley's "6 Times" artwork, a series of life-sized human sculptures dotted along the river. ⊠ *Leith* ☎ *0131/455–7367* ⊕ *www.waterofleith.org.uk.*

🍽 Restaurants

Seafood lovers are drawn to the old port of Leith to sample the freshest seafood amid the authentic seafaring setting.

Some of Scotland's most renowned chefs have made Leith—and more specifically, The Shore, its upmarket waterfront—their home.

★ Aurora

$ | BRITISH | Probably the best quality-to-value dining option in Leith, Aurora offers deliciously inventive three-course lunch menus (with plenty of tasty sourdough bread) for the price of a pub main. This modern, Nordic-style bistro also serves heavenly brunches, as well as a varied dinner menu—choose anything from informal, tapas-style sharing plates to elaborate, six-course tasting menus with a wine pairing. **Known for:** high quality at a low cost; sumptuous braised pork cheeks; interior of reclaimed materials. ⑤ *Average main: £9* ⊠ *187 Great Junction St., Leith* ☎ *0131/554–5537* ⊕ *www.auroraedinburgh.co.uk* ⊙ *Closed Mon. and Tues.*

The King's Wark

$$ | BRITISH | This gastro-pub at The Shore in Leith combines a beautiful historic setting with great quality food and a wide selection of Scottish gins. At lunchtime, the dark-wood bar does a roaring trade in simple fare such as gourmet burgers, fish cakes, and haggis (traditional or vegetarian), but in the evening, the kitchen ups the ante with a chalkboard menu of locally caught seafood specialties, from hake to monkfish. **Known for:** affordable quality cuisine; atmospheric setting; Leith's best roast dinner. ⑤ *Average main: £16* ⊠ *36 The Shore, Leith* ☎ *0131/554–9260* ⊕ *www.kingswark.co.uk.*

The Kitchin

$$$$ | FRENCH | A perennially popular high-end dining option, Tom Kitchin's Michelin-starred venture packs in the crowds. Kitchin, who trained in France, runs a tight ship, and his passion for using seasonal and locally sourced produce to his own creative ends shows no sign of waning. **Known for:** nose-to-tail philosophy; lovely setting; very expensive dinners. ⑤ *Average main: £35* ⊠ *78 Commercial*

Leith's most famous sight is the moored Royal Yacht *Britannia*, which once carried Queen Elizabeth and is now open to the public to explore.

Quay, Leith ☎ 0131/555–1755 ⊕ thekitch-in.com ⊗ Closed Sun. and Mon.

★ Mimi's Bakehouse—Leith

$ | **BAKERY** | **FAMILY** | Despite its large interior with acres of seating, this bakery-café still regularly has lines out the door. The reason is simple: it does the best cakes in Edinburgh, using everything from Oreos to Reese's Pieces to strawberries and cream. **Known for:** delicious and creative cakes; to-die-for breakfasts; fun and cheeky decor. $ *Average main:* £10 ⊠ 63 The Shore, Leith ☎ 0131/555–5908 ⊕ www.mimisbakehouse.com ⊗ No dinner.

★ Restaurant Martin Wishart

$$$$ | **FRENCH** | Leith's premier dining experience, this high-end restaurant combines imaginative cuisine, luxuriously understated decor, and a lovely waterfront location. Renowned Michelin-starred chef Martin Wishart woos diners with his inspired menu of artistically presented, French-influenced dishes. **Known for:** impeccable cuisine; beautiful location; multicourse tasting menus (with vegetarian versions of each). $ *Average main:* £35 ⊠ 54 The Shore, Leith ☎ 0131/553–3557 ⊕ www.restaurantmartinwishart.co.uk ⊗ Closed Sun. and Mon.

Hotels

Staying in Leith means you'll be away from the main Old and New Town sights, but near to the Royal Yacht *Britannia* and some of the city's best dining options.

The Conifers

$ | **B&B/INN** | This small family-run guesthouse in a red-sandstone town house offers simple, traditionally decorated rooms and warm hospitality. **Pros:** nice mix of old and new; many original fittings; hearty breakfasts. **Cons:** a bit of a walk to the city center; just as far to The Shore; one bathroom not en suite. $ *Rooms from:* £100 ⊠ 56 Pilrig St., Leith ☎ 0131/554–5162 ⊕ www.conifersguesthouse.com ⇆ 4 rooms ⦿ Free Breakfast.

Leith, Edinburgh's Seaport

Situated on the south shore of the Firth of Forth, Leith was a separate town until it merged with the city in 1920. After World War II and up until the 1980s, the declining seaport became known as an impoverished corner of Edinburgh, but in recent years it has been completely revitalized with the restoration of commercial buildings and the construction of new luxury housing, boutique hotels, hipster cafés, and upmarket restaurants. All the docks have been redeveloped, looked over variously by a shopping mall, a government building, and office and apartment blocks.

In earlier times Leith was the stage for many historic happenings. In 1560 Mary of Guise—mother of Mary, Queen of Scots—ruled Scotland from Leith; her daughter landed in Leith the following year to embark on her infamous reign. A century later Cromwell led his troops to Leith to root out Scottish royalists. And in 1744 Leith became the so-called "home of golf," as official rules to the game were devised on Leith Links, a lovely park that remains to this day.

Fingal

$$$ | HOTEL | For something completely different, step aboard this floating boutique hotel, permanently moored near the Royal Yacht *Britannia* in Leith, and discover 23 luxurious cabins and a chic restaurant and bar, all set above a lovingly preserved engine room. **Pros:** out-of-the-ordinary luxury; close to Leith's best bars and restaurants; quiet and peaceful. **Cons:** no room service; dinner is overpriced; a little way out of the center. ⑤ *Rooms from: £220* ⊠ *Alexandra Dock, Leith* ☎ *0131/357–5000* ⊕ *www.fingal. co.uk* ⌸ *23 rooms.*

Malmaison

$$ | HOTEL | Once a seamen's hostel, this French-inspired boutique hotel, which is part of a pioneering U.K.-wide chain, draws a refined clientele to its superchic shorefront rooms. A dramatic black-and-taupe color scheme prevails in the public areas, while the hip rooms are dominated by tartan designs and shades of heather, with bolder fabrics and brighter features in the suites. **Pros:** impressive building; elegant interiors; great waterfront location. **Cons:** price fluctuates wildly; bar sometimes rowdy at night; a long way from the center of town. ⑤ *Rooms from: £135* ⊠ *1 Tower Pl., Leith* ☎ *0131/285– 1478* ⊕ *malmaison.com-edinburgh.com* ⌸ *100 rooms* ⦿ *Free Breakfast.*

Nightlife

BARS AND PUBS

The Lioness of Leith

BARS/PUBS | This historic pub has always been a popular Leith Walk haunt for locals, but recent acclaim for their gourmet, gargantuan Lioness Burgers has brought them wider attention. ⊠ *21–26 Duke St., Leith* ☎ *0131/629–0580* ⊕ *www.thelionessofleith.co.uk.*

Malt & Hops

BARS/PUBS | First opening its doors in 1749, Malt & Hops has a fine waterfront location and serves microbrewery cask ales—with a selection good enough to be endorsed by CAMRA (the Campaign for Real Ale). It also has a resident ghost. ⊠ *45 The Shore, Leith* ☎ *0131/555–0083.*

★ Teuchters Landing

BARS/PUBS | Tucked away down a side street near The Shore, Teuchters Landing is a perennially popular pub for its wide range of whiskies and beers, its excellent pub food (try the nachos with cheddar and haggis), and its pontoon for sunny days. It's also a great place for watching live sports. If you're feeling lucky, try the Hoop of Destiny game, for your chance to land a vintage dram for a fraction of its usual price. ⊠ *1c Dock Pl., Leith* ☎ *0131/554–7427* ⊕ *www.aroomin.co.uk.*

🛍 Shopping

SHOPPING CENTERS
Ocean Terminal

SHOPPING CENTERS/MALLS | As well as being home to the Royal Yacht *Britannia,* this on-the-water mall also has an impressive range of big-name brand stores and independent craft shops, as well as bars, restaurants, and a cinema. ⊠ *Ocean Dr., Leith* ☎ *0131/555–8888* ⊕ *www.oceanterminal.com.*

OUTDOOR SPORTS GEAR
Tiso Edinburgh Outdoor Experience

SPORTING GOODS | This sizable store stocks outdoor clothing, boots, and jackets ideal for hiking in the Highlands. It also sells tents and camping accessories for the truly hardy. There's a good little café inside, too. ⊠ *41 Commercial St., Leith* ☎ *0131/554–0804* ⊕ *www.tiso.com.*

West Lothian and the Forth Valley

If you stand on an Edinburgh eminence—the castle ramparts, Arthur's Seat, Calton Hill—you can plan a few Lothian excursions without even the aid of a map. The Lothians is the collective name given to the swath of countryside south of the Firth of Forth and surrounding Edinburgh. Many courtly and aristocratic families lived here, and the region still has the castles and mansions to prove it. And with the rich came deer parks, gardens in the French style, and Lothian's fame as a seed plot for Lowland gentility.

West Lothian comprises a good bit of Scotland's central belt. The River Forth snakes across a widening floodplain on its descent from the Highlands, and by the time it reaches the western extremities of Edinburgh, it has already passed below the mighty Forth bridges and become a broad estuary. Castles and historic houses sprout thickly on both sides of the Forth. You can explore a number of them, and the territory north of the River Forth, in a day or two, or you can just pick one excursion for a day trip from Edinburgh.

GETTING HERE AND AROUND
BUS TRAVEL
First Bus and Lothian Buses link most of this area. If you're planning to see more than one sight in the region by bus, it's worth planning an itinerary in advance.

CAR TRAVEL
The Queensferry Road, also known as the A90, is the main thoroughfare running through this region. After crossing the Forth Bridge, it joins the M90 heading north, with branches off to Culross (on the A985), Dunfermline (on the A823), and the Ochil Hills (on the A91).

TRAIN TRAVEL
Dalmeny (for South Queensferry), Linlithgow, and Dunfermline all have rail stations and can be reached from Edinburgh stations.

South Queensferry

7 miles west of Edinburgh.

This pleasant little waterside community, a former ferry port, is completely dominated by the Forth Bridges, three dramatic structures of contrasting architecture (dating from the 19th, 20th, and 21st centuries) that span the Firth of Forth at this historic crossing point. It's near a number of historic and cultural sights.

West Lothian
and the Forth Valley

| 0 | | 10 mi |
| 0 | | 10 km |

GETTING HERE AND AROUND

The Queensferry Road, also known as the A90, is the main artery west from Edinburgh toward the Forth Bridge, Hopetoun House, the House of the Binns, and Blackness Castle.

◉ Sights

Dalmeny House

HOUSE | The first of the stately houses clustered on the western edge of Edinburgh, Dalmeny House is the home of the Earl and Countess of Rosebery. This 1815 Tudor Gothic mansion displays among its sumptuous interiors the best of the family's famous collection of 18th-century French furniture. Highlights include the library, the Napoléon Room, the Vincennes and Sevres porcelain collections, and the drawing room, with its tapestries and intricately wrought

French furniture. Admission is by guided tour in June and July only. ⊠ *South Queensferry* ☎ *0131/331–1888* ⊕ *www. roseberyestates.co.uk* ⊠ *£10* ⊗ *Closed Aug.–May and Thurs.–Sat. in June and July.*

Forth Bridge

BRIDGE/TUNNEL | Opened in 1890, when it was hailed as the eighth wonder of the world, this iconic red cantilevered rail bridge is a UNESCO World Heritage site. The extraordinary, 1½-mile-long crossing expands by another yard or so on a hot summer's day. The famous 19th-century bridge has since been joined by two neighbors; the 20th-century Forth Road Bridge (opened 1964) and the 21st-century Queensferry Crossing (opened 2017). ⊠ *South Queensferry* ⊕ *www.theforth-bridges.org.*

A quick day trip from Edinburgh, one of Inchcolm Island's most interesting sights is its 12th-century abbey.

Hopetoun House

HOUSE | The palatial premises of Hopetoun House are among Scotland's grandest courtly seats, and are now home to the Marquesses of Linlithgow. The enormous property was started in 1699 to the original plans of Sir William Bruce, then enlarged between 1721 and 1754 by William Adam and his sons Robert and John. The house has decorative work of the highest order and a notable painting collection, plus all the trappings to keep you entertained: a nature trail, a restaurant in the former stables, a farm shop, and a museum. The estate also specializes in clay pigeon shooting; groups of six or more can book an expert-led introductory session, with prices starting at £45 per person. ⊠ *South Queensferry* ☎ *0131/331–2451* ⊕ *www. hopetoun.co.uk* ✉ *£10.50; grounds only £4.75* ⊙ *Closed Oct.–Mar.*

★ Inchcolm Island

BOAT TOURS | Accessible by boat tour from South Queensferry, Inchcolm Island is home to a beautifully preserved 12th-century abbey, a First World War fortress, green cliffs, sandy beaches, and an abundance of wildlife, from playful gray seals to brightly colored puffins. Prepare to be dive-bombed by seagulls if you visit during nesting season. The island is run by Historic Scotland, which levies an entry fee of £6, but boat tours (run by Maid of the Forth and Forth Boat Tours) include this in the price of their tickets. ⊠ *Inchcolm Island* ☎ *01383/823332* ⊕ *www.historicenvironment.scot* ✉ *£20 (boat tour and island entry)* ☞ *Closed Nov.–Mar.*

🍴 Restaurants

The Boat House

$$ | **MODERN BRITISH** | Scotland's natural larder is on display at this romantic restaurant on the banks of the Forth. Seafood is the star of the show, and chef Paul Steward is the man behind the imaginative yet unfussy recipes. **Known for:** delicious seafood; freshly caught daily specials; spectacular views from the patio. ⑤ *Average main: £18* ⊠ *22 High*

St. ☎ 0131/331–5429 ⊕ www.theboat-house-sq.co.uk.

Jupiter Artland

10 miles west of Edinburgh.

For anyone drawn to interesting art and beautiful open spaces, a visit to this open-air collection of sculptures by world-renowned artists is a must.

GETTING HERE AND AROUND

To reach Jupiter Artland from Edinburgh, take the A71 southwest toward Kilmarnock. Just after Wilkieston, turn right onto the B7015. It's also easy to reach by bus: the X27 departs from Princes Street, while Bus 27 leaves from Dalry Road near Haymarket.

Sights

★ Jupiter Artland

MUSEUM | The beautiful grounds of a Jacobean manor house have been transformed by an art-loving couple, Robert and Nicky Wilson, into an impressive sculpture park. With the aid of a map you can explore the magical landscapes and encounter works by renowned artists including Andy Goldsworthy, Anya Gallaccio, Jim Lambie, Nathan Coley, Ian Hamilton Finlay, and Anish Kapoor, among many others. A highlight is walking around Charles Jencks's *Cells of Life*, a series of shapely, grass-covered mounds. ⊠ *Bonnington House Steadings, Wilkieston, Edinburgh* ☎ 01506/889900 ⊕ *www.jupiterartland.org* 🎫 *£9* ⏱ *Closed Oct.–mid May.*

Linlithgow

12 miles west of Edinburgh.

Linlithgow is best known for its lochside palace, the impressive remnants of what was once the seat of the Stewart kings,

but there are other fortified sights to see, too.

GETTING HERE AND AROUND

From Edinburgh, take the A90 westward, continuing onto the A904 and M9, to reach Linlithgow. You can also board a train to Linlithgow station, which is just a short walk from the palace.

Sights

Blackness Castle

CASTLE/PALACE | Standing like a grounded ship on the very edge of the Forth, this curious 15th-century structure has had a varied career as a strategic fortress, state prison, powder magazine, and youth hostel. The countryside is gently green and cultivated, and open views extend across the blue Forth to the distant ramparts of the Ochil Hills. ⊠ *Blackness, Linlithgow* ☎ 01506/834807 ⊕ *www.historicenvironment.scot* 🎫 *£6.*

House of the Binns

HOUSE | The 17th-century general "Bloody" Tam Dalyell (c. 1599–1685) transformed a fortified stronghold into a gracious mansion, the House of the Binns. The name derives from *bynn,* the old Scottish word for hill. The present exterior dates from around 1810 and shows a remodeling into a kind of mock fort with crenellated battlements and turrets. Inside, see magnificent Elizabethan-style plaster ceilings. ⊠ *Off A904, Linlithgow* ☎ 01786/812664 ⊕ *www.nts.org.uk* 🎫 *£10.50* ⏱ *House closed Jan.–Mar.*

Linlithgow Palace

CASTLE/PALACE | On the edge of Linlithgow Loch stands the splendid ruin of Linlithgow Palace, the birthplace of Mary, Queen of Scots. Burned, perhaps accidentally, by Hanoverian troops during the last Jacobite rebellion in 1746, this impressive shell stands on a site of great antiquity, though an earlier fire in 1424 destroyed any hard evidence of medieval life here. The palace gatehouse was built

Due to its role as a living museum, the entire town of Culross is considered a National Trust sight.

in the early 16th century, and the central courtyard's elaborate fountain dates from around 1535. The halls and great rooms are cold, echoing stone husks now in the care of Historic Scotland. ✉ *Kirkgate, Linlithgow* ☎ *01506/842896* ⊕ *www. historicenvironment.scot* 🗒 *£7.20.*

Culross

17 miles northwest of Edinburgh.

With its mercat cross, cobbled streets, tolbooth, and narrow *wynds* (alleys), sea-side Culross is a picturesque little town. It's also a living museum of 17th-century Scottish life, with preserved historic properties open to the public. Culross once had a thriving industry and export trade in coal and salt (the coal was used in the salt-panning process), but as local coal became exhausted, the impetus of the Industrial Revolution passed Culross by, while other parts of the Forth Valley prospered. Culross became a backwater town, and the merchants' houses of the 17th and 18th centuries were never

replaced by Victorian developments or modern architecture. In the 1930s the National Trust for Scotland started to buy up the decaying properties with a view to preservation. Today ordinary citizens live in many of these properties, but others are available to explore. Walking tours of the town are available for a small fee.

GETTING HERE AND AROUND
To get here by car, head north of the Forth Bridge on the A90, then westward on the A985. You can get here by bus (No. 8) from Dunfermline, which in turn is easily reached by train from Edinburgh.

Sights

★ Culross Palace
MUSEUM VILLAGE | Don't let the name fool you: this 16th-century merchant's house was never a royal residence, and lacks the ostentatious grandeur of a palace. It is, however, a fascinating slice of social history—the owner was a pioneer in local coal mining and salt production—and its interiors of Baltic pine, Durch floor

tiles, and Staffordshire pottery was pretty flashy for its time. It was also visited by King James VI in 1617. Today it retains its period charms, including a garden that grows herbs and vegetables typical of the period. ✉ *Culross Palace* ☎ *01383/880359* ⊕ *www.nts.org.uk* 🎫 *£10.50* ⊗ *Closed weekends Oct.–Mar.*

Dunfermline

16 miles northwest of Edinburgh.

Oft-overlooked Dunfermline was once the world center for the production of damask linen, but the town is better known today as the birthplace of millionaire industrialist and philanthropist Andrew Carnegie (1835–1919). Undoubtedly Dunfermline's most famous son, Carnegie endowed the town with a park, library, fitness center, and, naturally, a Carnegie Hall, still the focus of the town's culture and entertainment.

GETTING HERE AND AROUND
When you're driving, head north on the A90, turning off onto the A823 a few miles north of the Forth Bridge. You can also reach the town by train from Edinburgh in about 35 minutes.

 ## Sights

Andrew Carnegie Birthplace Museum
MUSEUM | Scottish-American industrialist and noted philanthropist Andrew Carnegie was born here in 1835. Don't be misled by the simple exterior of this 18th-century weaver's cottage—inside it opens into a larger hall, where documents, photographs, and artifacts relate his fascinating life story. The collection includes art from a wide range of periods, from medieval to 19th century to art deco, as well as displays on the genus of Jurassic dinosaur named after the great man—*Diplodocus carnegii.* ✉ *Moodie St.* ☎ *01383/724302* ⊕ *www.carnegiebirthplace.com* 🎫 *Free.*

Dunfermline Abbey and Palace
RELIGIOUS SITE | This impressive complex, the literal and metaphorical centerpiece of Dunfermline, was founded in the 11th century as a Benedictine abbey by Queen Margaret, the English wife of Scottish king Malcolm III. The present church is a mishmash of medieval and Norman work, and a decorative brass tomb here is the final resting place of Robert the Bruce (1274–1329). A palace was also part of the complex here, and was the birthplace of Charles I (1600–49); its ruins lie beside the abbey. Dunfermline was the seat of the royal court of Scotland until the end of the 11th century, and its central role in Scottish affairs is explored by means of display panels dotted around the drafty but hallowed buildings. ✉ *St. Margaret St.* ☎ *01383/739026* ⊕ *www.historicenvironment.scot* 🎫 *£6* ⊗ *Closed Thurs. and Fri. Oct.–Mar.*

Midlothian and East Lothian

Stretching east to the sea and south to the Lowlands from Edinburgh, the regions of Midlothian and East Lothian, and their many attractions, are all within an hour's reach of Edinburgh.

Despite its countless tourist draws, including Scotland's finest stone carvings at Rosslyn Chapel, associations with Sir Walter Scott, outstanding castles, and miles of rolling countryside, Midlothian (the area immediately south of Edinburgh) remained off the beaten path for years. Fortunately, things are starting to change, as visitors look beyond the capital and the well-manicured charm of East Lothian to explore the pretty working towns and suburbs of Midlothian.

East Lothian, on the other hand, has been a draw for decades. An upmarket stockbroker belt, East Lothian's biggest draws are its golf courses of world rank,

Midlothian and East Lothian

most notably Muirfield, plus a scattering of stately homes and interesting hotels. Its photogenic villages, active fishing harbors, dramatic cliff-side castles, and vistas of pastoral Lowland Scotland seem a world away from bustling Edinburgh—yet excellent transport links mean they're easy and quick to reach.

GETTING HERE AND AROUND
BUS TRAVEL
Buses from Edinburgh serve towns and villages throughout Midlothian and East Lothian. For details of all services, inquire at the Edinburgh Bus Station, immediately east of St. Andrew Square in Edinburgh.

CAR TRAVEL
A quick route to Rosslyn Chapel follows the A701, while the A7 heads toward Gorebridge and the National Mining Museum Scotland. The A1

passes Newhailes, Haddington, and Dunbar. Take the A198 to Gullane, North Berwick, and Tantallon Castle.

TRAIN TRAVEL
There is very limited train service in Midlothian. In East Lothian there are tracks running east along the coast with regular services to North Berwick and Dunbar.

Newhailes

5 miles east of Edinburgh.

With sumptuous interiors and relaxing grounds, this neo-Palladian villa a few miles east of Edinburgh hosted many luminaries of the Scottish Enlightenment.

GETTING HERE AND AROUND
To get here from Edinburgh, take the A1 east, then transfer to the A6095. You can also get here by Lothian Bus 30 or by

train to Newcraighall station, a 20-minute walk from the villa.

 Sights

Newhailes

CASTLE/PALACE | This fine late-17th-century house was designed by Scottish architect James Smith in 1686 as his own home. He later sold it to Lord Bellendon, and in 1707 it was bought by Sir David Dalrymple, first Baronet of Hailes, who improved and extended the house, adding one of the finest rococo interiors in Scotland. The library here played host to many famous figures from the Scottish Enlightenment, as well as inveterate Scot-basher Dr. Samuel Johnson, who dubbed the library "the most learned room in Europe." Most of the original interiors and furnishings remain intact, and there are beautiful walks around the landscaped grounds and through the surrounding woodland. ✉ *Newhailes Rd., Musselburgh* ☎ *0131/653–5599* ⊕ *www. nts.org.uk* ✉ *£12.50* ⊗ *Entire property closed Nov.–mid-Apr. House closed Tues. and Wed. mid-Apr.–Oct.*

Roslin

7 miles south of Edinburgh.

It may be best known for its extraordinary chapel, but Roslin itself is a pleasant place to while away some time. There are some lovely walks from the village along the North River Esk.

GETTING HERE AND AROUND

By car take the A701 south from Edinburgh, turning off onto the B7006 just north of the town. Lothian Buses also shuttle passengers from Edinburgh: Bus 37 from North Bridge is the most direct way.

 Sights

★ Rosslyn Chapel

RELIGIOUS SITE | This chapel has always beckoned curious visitors intrigued by the various legends surrounding its magnificent carvings, but today it pulses with tourists as never before. Much of this can be attributed to Dan Brown's best-selling 2003 mystery novel *The Da Vinci Code*, which featured the chapel heavily, claiming it has a secret sign that can lead you to the Holy Grail. Whether you're a fan of the book or not, this Episcopal chapel (services continue to be held here) remains an imperative stop on any traveler's itinerary. Originally conceived by Sir William Sinclair (circa 1404–80) and dedicated to St. Matthew in 1446, the chapel is outstanding for the quality and variety of the carving inside. Covering almost every square inch of stonework are human figures, animals, and plants. The meaning of these remains subject to many theories; some depict symbols from the medieval order of the Knights Templar and from Freemasonry. The chapel's design called for a cruciform structure, but only the choir and parts of the east transept walls were fully completed. Free talks about the building's history are held daily. ✉ *Chapel Loan* ☎ *0131/440–2159* ⊕ *www.rosslynchapel.com* ✉ *£9.*

 Restaurants

The Original Rosslyn Inn

$ | **BRITISH** | This atmospheric inn, on the crossroads in the center of Roslin village, serves tasty, hearty pub grub, including fish-and-chips, burgers, and pies, plus good veggie options. The inn is very close to Rosslyn Chapel; walk past the car park for a few minutes and you'll see it on the other side of the main road. **Known for:** traditional Scottish pub; great steak-and-ale pie; convenient location.

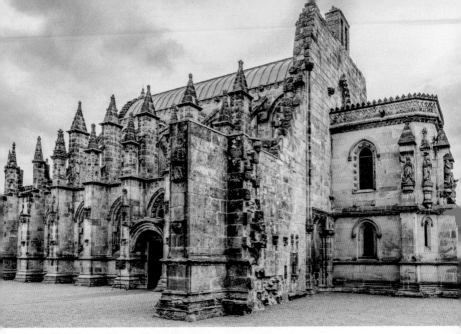

Rosslyn Chapel is one of Scotland's most intact 15th-century churches.

$ Average main: £9 ⊠ 2–4 Main St., Roslin ☎ 0131/440–2384 ⊕ www.theoriginal-rosslyninn.co.uk.

The Pentlands

20 miles south of Edinburgh.

These unmistakable hills begin almost in the suburbs of Edinburgh, and they make for a very welcome escape from the city crowds. There are access points to the hills along the A702, but the best two are Snowsports Centre and Flotterstone. At each of these you can find a parking lot, a lovely pub, and quiet walking paths leading up into the hills.

GETTING HERE AND AROUND

The easiest way to reach the Pentlands is by car—simply follow the A702 south. Bus 101 from Edinburgh town center also follows this route. Alternatively, you can cycle into the hills in under an hour.

🍴 Restaurants

The Steading

$ | BRITISH | This pleasant pub, set within a converted farm building on the roadside of the A702, serves traditional, freshly prepared pub food, along with hearty snacks like sandwiches, baked potatoes, and nachos. It is right by the parking lot for the Snowsports Centre, from which several Pentlands walking trails begin. **Known for:** hearty pub grub; beautiful building; great location. $ *Average main: £10 ⊠ 118–120 Biggar Rd., Edinburgh ☎ 0131/445–1128 ⊕ www.thesteadinged-inburgh.co.uk.*

National Mining Museum Scotland

9 miles southeast of Edinburgh.

The museum provides visitors with a sobering look into the lives of coal miners and the difficult conditions they endured down Scotland's mines.

GETTING HERE AND AROUND

To get here by car, head south on the A1 (turning into the A6106 and A7) to Newtongrange. You can also take a train from Edinburgh Waverley to Newtongrange (the museum is a six-minute walk away), or come by bus: 29 and X95 stop right outside the museum.

 Sights

National Mining Museum Scotland

MUSEUM | In the former mining community of Newtongrange, the National Mining Museum Scotland provides a good introduction to the history of the country's mining industry. With the help of a guided tour and video exhibits, you can experience life deep below the ground. Interactive displays and "magic helmets" also bring the tour to life and relate the power that the mining company held over the lives of workers in Scotland's largest planned mining village. This frighteningly autocratic system, in which the company owned the houses, shops, and even the pub, survived well into the 1930s. Tours are conducted by ex-miners. ⊠ *Lady Victoria Colliery, A7, Newtongrange* ☎ *0131/663–7519* ⊕ *www.nationalminingmuseum.com* 🎟 *£9.50.*

Crichton Castle

14 miles southeast of Edinburgh.

Sitting on a terrace overlooking a beautiful river valley, this 14th-century structure with diamond-faceted facade was home to the Crichtons, and later the earls of Bothwell.

GETTING HERE AND AROUND

Head south on the A1 and A68, then take the turnoff to the B6372 just before Pathhead.

 Sights

Crichton Castle

CASTLE/PALACE | Standing amid rolling hills that are interrupted here and there by patches of woodland, Crichton was a Bothwell family castle. Mary, Queen of Scots, attended the wedding here of Bothwell's sister, Lady Janet Hepburn, to Mary's brother, Lord John Stewart. The curious arcaded range reveals diamond rustication on the courtyard stonework; this particular geometric pattern is unique in Scotland and is thought to have been inspired by the Renaissance styles in Europe, particularly Italy. The oldest part of the structure is the 14th-century keep (square tower). Note that there are no toilets at the castle. ⊠ *Off B6367, Pathhead* ☎ *01875/320017* ⊕ *www. historicenvironment.scot* 🎟 *£6* 🕑 *Closed Oct.–Mar.*

Dunbar

29 miles east of Edinburgh.

In the days before tour companies started offering package deals to the Mediterranean, Dunbar was a popular holiday beach resort. Now a bit faded, the town is still lovely for its spacious Georgian-style properties, characterized by the astragals, or fan-shaped windows, above the doors; the symmetry of the house fronts; and the parapeted rooflines. Though not the popular seaside playground it once was, Dunbar has an attractive beach and a picturesque harbor. It's also one end of the John Muir Way, a cross-Scotland hiking trail.

GETTING HERE AND AROUND

From Edinburgh head east on the A1 to get to Dunbar. You can also take a direct train from Edinburgh Waverley.

Sights

John Muir Country Park

NATIONAL/STATE PARK | Set on the estuary of the River Tyne, winding down from the Moorfoot Hills, the John Muir Country Park encompasses varied coastal scenery: rocky shoreline, golden sands, and the mixed woodlands of Tyninghame, teeming with wildlife. Dunbar-born conservationist John Muir (1838–1914), whose family moved to the United States when he was a child, helped found Yosemite and Sequoia national parks in California. ⊠ *Off A1087.*

St. Mary's Parish Church

RELIGIOUS SITE | In the village of Whitekirk, on the road from Dunbar to North Berwick, lies the unmistakable St. Mary's Parish Church, with its beautiful red-sandstone Norman tower. Occupied since the 6th century, the church was a place of pilgrimage in medieval times because of its healing well. Behind the kirk, in a field, is a tithe barn—the tithe is the portion of a farmer's produce that was given to the local church. Beside this stands a 16th-century tower house, once used to accommodate visiting pilgrims. In the 15th century, the church was visited by a young Italian nobleman, Aeneas Sylvius Piccolomini, after he was shipwrecked off the East Lothian coast; two decades later, Piccolomini became Pope Pius II. ⊠ *A198, Whitekirk* ☞ *Free.*

Activities

GOLF

Dunbar Golf Club

GOLF | There's a lighthouse at the 9th hole of this seaside course, first laid out in 1856. It's a good choice for experiencing a typical east coast links, including the unique challenges presented by coastal winds. Within easy reach of Edinburgh, Dunbar Golf Club has stunning views of the Firth of Forth and Bass Rock. The club is currently undergoing an expansion that may see some changes to the course, as well as a new clubhouse and a hotel. Greens fees drop by nearly half in winter, when it's open midweek only. ⊠ *East Links, Golf House Rd.* ☎ *01368/862317* ⊕ *www.dunbargolfclub. com* ☞ *£85 weekdays, £115 weekends* ⚐ *18 holes, 6597 yards, par 71* ⚑ *Reservations essential.*

HIKING

John Muir Way

HIKING/WALKING | Completed in 2014, this much-praised scenic hiking path stretches from Helensburgh, northwest of Glasgow, to Dunbar. The trail's terminus is outside John Muir's birthplace, on the town's High Street. The 130-mile coast-to-coast route passes through some spectacular scenery (especially at the Helensburgh end). It takes about a week to traverse completely, but the official website has maps covering all the various sections. ⊠ *The John Muir Way (East End), 125 High St.* ⊕ *www. johnmuirway.org.*

North Berwick

24 miles northeast of Edinburgh.

The pleasant little seaside resort of North Berwick manages to retain a small-town personality even when it's thronged with city visitors on warm summer days. Eating ice cream, the city folk stroll on the beach and in the narrow streets or gaze at the sailing craft in the small harbor. The town is near a number of castles and other sights.

GETTING HERE AND AROUND
Travel east on the A1 and A198, or take one of the regular trains from Edinburgh Waverley.

Sights

★ Isle of May

ISLAND | This small island in the middle of the Firth of Forth is home to many interesting sights, from the ruins of a medieval priory to a Gothic lighthouse to a wartime signal station. But it's the sea-birds that really bring in the visitors. The Isle of May is the largest puffin colony on the east coast of Britain and is home to a quarter of a million birds nesting on the cliffs during late spring and early summer, as well as seals basking on the shore. To visit the island, you'll need to take a 12-seat RIB (rigid inflatable boat) across choppy waters, including a sail by Bass Rock—the world's largest colony of gannets. Tours start from the Scottish Seabird Centre and last four hours, including two hours on the island. ■ **TIP→ Book in advance online to avoid disappointment.** ✉ North Berwick ⊕ www.seabird.org 🎟 Tour £48 ⊗ Closed Oct.–Mar.

Scottish Seabird Centre

NATURE PRESERVE | FAMILY | An observation deck, exhibits, and films at this excellent family-friendly attraction provide a captivating introduction to the world of the gannets and puffins that nest on the Firth of Forth islands. Live interactive cameras let you take an even closer look at the bird colonies and marine mammals. Kids will enjoy the "Flyway Tunnel," a 3-D multimedia exhibit that simulates walking through an underwater passage, learning all about local nesting birds and sea life along the way. There are plenty of family-focused activities, nature walks, and photography shows, as well as a great on-site café and gift shop. ✉ The Harbour 🕾 01620/890202 ⊕ www.seabird.org 🎟 £9.95.

★ Tantallon Castle

CASTLE/PALACE | Travel east along the flat fields from North Berwick, and the imposing silhouette of Tantallon Castle, a substantial, semiruined medieval fortress, comes dramatically into view. Standing on a headland with the sea on three sides, the red-sandstone walls are being chipped away by time and sea spray, with the earliest surviving stonework dating from the late 14th century.

The fortress was besieged in 1529 by the cannons of King James V and again (more damagingly) during the civil war of 1651. Despite significant damage, much of the curtain wall of this former Douglas stronghold survives and is now cared for by Historic Scotland. From the grounds you can see Bass Rock out to sea, which looks gray during winter but bright white in summer. Look through the telescope here and you'll see why. ✉ Off A198 🕾 01620/892727 ⊕ www.historicenvironment.scot 🎟 £6.

🍴 Restaurants

★ The Lobster Shack

$ | **SEAFOOD** | North Berwick's most talked-about dining option isn't a traditional restaurant, or even a restaurant at all—it's a shack. That's testament to the sheer quality of the seafood served at this take-out stand, where freshly caught lobster (£19.95), sea bass, and haddock are cooked before your eyes and served in a box with double-dipped chips, ready to eat on a fold-up chair, a harbor wall, or while strolling along the beach. **Known for:** amazing lobster and chips; beautiful harborside location; good value. ⑤ Average main: £10 ✉ North Berwick Harbour 🕾 07910/620480 ⊕ www.lobstershack.co.uk ⊗ Closed Oct.–Mar.

🛏 Hotels

The Glebe House

$$ | **B&B/INN** | This dignified 18th-century building was once a manse (minister's house), but is now a delightful and luxurious B&B. **Pros:** peaceful atmosphere; interesting antiques; sociable breakfast around a mahogany table. **Cons:** books up well in advance; too precious for some; expensive per-person rate for B&B. ⑤ Rooms from: £150 ✉ Law Rd. 🕾 01620/892608 ⊕ www.glebehouse-nb.co.uk ⇨ 4 rooms ⦿ Breakfast.

Gullane

20 miles northeast of Edinburgh.

Follow the coastline on either side of Gullane and you're faced with golf course after golf course. Fairways are laid out wherever there is available links space along this stretch of East Lothian, with Muirfield just one of the courses here replete with players clad in expensive golfing sweaters. Apart from golf, visitors can enjoy restful summer-evening strolls along Gullane's sandy beach.

GETTING HERE AND AROUND

From Edinburgh, drive east on the A1, then head north along the coast on the A198. There are also two regular direct buses from the capital, run by East Coast Buses: 124 and X5.

Sights

Dirleton Castle

CASTLE/PALACE | In the center of tiny Dirleton, 2 miles east of Gullane, sits the impressive-looking 12th-century Dirleton Castle. It's now a ruin, but its high outer wall is relatively complete, and the grounds behind the walls feature a 17th-century bowling green, set in the shade of yew trees and surrounded by a herbaceous flower border that blazes with color in high summer. King Edward I of England occupied the castle in 1298 as part of his campaign for the continued subjugation of the unruly Scots. ⊠ *Dirleton Ave., Off A198* ☎ *01620/850330* ⊕ *www.historicenvironment.scot* ☜ *£6.*

Restaurants

★ The Bonnie Badger

$$ | **BRITISH** | A charming concoction of sandstone walls, raftered roofs, and roaring fireplaces, as well as a lovely garden area, this upmarket inn is the ideal spot for a pub lunch. Owned by star Edinburgh chef Tom Kitchin, the menu at first appears to be fairly by-the-numbers British pub fare—think fish-and-chips, steak pie, and sausage and mash—but with superior local produce and a dash of culinary imagination, classic dishes are transformed into something special. **Known for:** pigs' ears as a pre-meal snack; delicious desserts; beautiful garden. ⑤ *Average main: £17* ⊠ *Main St.* ☎ *01620/621111* ⊕ *www.bonniebadger. com.*

Activities

Gullane Golf Club

GOLF | Often overshadowed by Muirfield, Gullane provides an equally authentic links experience, as well as a far-more-effusive welcome than its slightly snooty neighbor along the road. The three championship courses here crisscross Gullane Hill, and all command outstanding views of the Firth of Forth and particularly the beaches of Aberlady Bay. No. 1 is the toughest, but No. 2 and No. 3 offer up equally compelling sport and for significantly lower greens fees. Day tickets can also be purchased, and for No. 3 it's little more than the price of a single round. ⊠ *W. Links Rd.* ☎ *01620/842255* ⊕ *www.gullanegolfclub.com* ☜ *No. 1: £155 weekdays, £180 weekends; No. 2: £62 weekdays, £69 weekends; No. 3: £42 weekdays, £49 weekends* ⅃ *No. 1 Course: 18 holes, 6583 yards, par 71; No. 2 Course: 18 holes, 6385 yards, par 71; No. 3 Course: 18 holes, 5259 yards, par 68* ⌂ *Reservations essential.*

Muirfield

GOLF | Home of the Honourable Company of Edinburgh Golfers and the world's oldest golfing club, Muirfield has a pedigree that few other courses can match. Although this course overlooking the Firth of Forth is considered one of golf's most challenging, players also talk about it being "fair," which means it has no hidden bunkers or sand traps. The club has a well-deserved reputation for being stuffy and traditional; you will be refused entry to the restaurant if you aren't wearing a jacket and tie. In addition, its first female members were only admitted in 2019, 275 years after it first opened (and this was only after threats of losing hosting rights to The Open). Visitors are permitted only on Tuesday and Thursday, and you must apply for a tee time well in advance. ✉ *Duncur Rd.* ☎ *01620/842123* ⊕ *www.muirfield.org.uk* 🎟 *£270 Apr.–Oct., £110 Nov.–Mar.* 🏌 *18 holes, 7245 yards, par 71.*

Haddington

18 miles east of Edinburgh.

One of the best-preserved medieval street plans in the country can be explored in Haddington. Among the many buildings of architectural and historical interest is the Town House, designed by William Adam in 1748 and enlarged in 1830. A wall plaque at the Sidegate recalls the great heights of floods from the River Tyne. Beyond is the medieval Nungate footbridge, with the Church of St. Mary a little way upstream.

GETTING HERE AND AROUND
From Edinburgh, simply drive east on the A1. Alternatively, take the bus: East Coast Buses 104 and X7, plus Borders Buses 253, will get you there.

 ## Sights

Lennoxlove House
HOUSE | Majestic Lennoxlove House has been the grand ancestral home of the very grand dukes of Hamilton since 1947 and the Baird family before them. This turreted country house, with parts dating from the 15th century, is a cheerful mix of family life and Scottish history. The beautifully decorated rooms house portraits, furniture, porcelain, and items associated with Mary, Queen of Scots, including her supposed death mask. Sporting activities from falconry to fishing take place on the stunning grounds. ✉ *Estate Office* ☎ *01620/823720* 🎟 *£10* 🕐 *Closed Nov.–Apr., Mon., Tues., Fri., and Sat.*

Chapter 4

GLASGOW

Updated by
Mike Gonzalez

◉ Sights   🍴 Restaurants   🛏 Hotels   ● Shopping   🍸 Nightlife

★★★★☆   ★★★★★   ★★★★☆   ★★★★★   ★★★★☆

WELCOME TO GLASGOW

TOP REASONS TO GO

★ **Architecture:** The Victorians left a legacy of striking architecture, and Glasgow's buildings manifest the city's love of grand artistic statements—just remember to look up. The Arts and Crafts buildings by Charles Rennie Mackintosh are reason alone to visit.

★ **Art museums:** Some of Britain's best art galleries are in Glasgow. The Hunterian Art Gallery, the Kelvingrove Art Gallery and Museum, and the Gallery of Modern Art are worth a visit.

★ **Parks and gardens:** From Kelvingrove Park to the Glasgow Botanic Gardens, the city has more parks per square mile than any other in Europe. Stop by the Botanic Gardens for outdoor theatrical productions in summer or Glasgow Green for the annual piping festival.

★ **Food and drink:** Whether you fancy a Guinness in a traditional pub like the Scotia or a Pinot Noir in a fashionable wine bar, there's a place to quench all thirsts. Locals love their cafés and tearooms too.

1 City Centre. From Buchanan Street west to Hope Street and beyond, look up to see grand Victorian and neo-Gothic buildings expressing the confidence of an industrial capital. George Square's City Chambers are worth a visit before you trawl the shops, duck into one of the trendy eateries, or explore the bars and music venues.

2 Merchant City. In the Middle Ages, the city grew up around Glasgow Cathedral. As the city expanded along with the growing transatlantic trade, wealthy tobacco and cotton traders built palatial houses here. They were laid to rest in the glorious tombs of the Necropolis, which overlooks the city. Today the area is busy with restaurants, clubs, and high-end shops.

3 West End. In the quieter, slightly hillier western part of the city is Glasgow University and the more bohemian side of Glasgow. The West End's treasures include the Botanic Gardens, Kelvingrove Park, and the Kelvingrove Art Gallery and Museum. Along Byres Road, there are well-priced restaurants and lively bars that attract weekend revelers from across the city.

4 Finnieston. Once lined with shipyards, the River Clyde has been reborn as a relaxing destination that entrances visitors and locals. The Glasgow Science Centre and the Museum of Transport face each other across the water, while the Scottish Exhibition Centre and the SSE Hydro are major event venues. Argyle Street has been transformed into a fashionable strip of restaurants and bars.

5 East End. What was once the poorest area of Glasgow is being treated to a major face-lift. Glasgow Green's wonderful People's Palace draws visitors throughout the year, and on weekends the nearby Barras market is a reminder of the area's past. Its famous dance hall has also been reborn as a major arts center.

6 South Side. Often overlooked, this less-visited side of the city includes beautiful Pollok Park as well as Pollok House, with its art collection and its elegant gardens. Art-filled Mackintosh's House sits in Bellahouston Park.

7 Side Trips from Glasgow. Just outside Glasgow, you can find Robert Owen's famous community at New Lanark, and in Ayrshire, you'll find many monuments to the life and times of Scottish poet Robert Burns. Alternatively you can follow generations of Glaswegians who took their summer holidays in the coastal resorts of the Clyde Coast.

Trendy stores, a booming cultural life, fascinating architecture, and stylish restaurants reinforce Glasgow's claim to being Scotland's most exciting city. After decades of decline, it finally experienced an urban renaissance uniquely its own. The city's grand architecture reflects a prosperous past built on trade and shipbuilding. Today buildings by Charles Rennie Mackintosh hold pride of place along with the Zaha Hadid–designed Riverside Museum.

Glasgow (the "dear green place," as it was known) was founded some 1,500 years ago. Legend has it that the king of Strathclyde, irate about his wife's infidelity, threw a ring he had given her into the River Clyde. (Apparently she had passed it on to an admirer.) When the king demanded to know where the ring had gone, the distraught queen asked the advice of her confessor, St. Mungo. He suggested fishing for it—and the first salmon to emerge had the ring in its mouth. The moment is commemorated on the city's coat of arms.

The vast profits from American cotton and tobacco built the grand mansions of the Merchant City in the 18th century. The tobacco lords financed the building of wooden ships, and by the 19th century the River Clyde had become the center of a vibrant shipbuilding industry, fed by the city's ironworks and steelworks. The city grew again, but its internal divisions grew at the same time. The West End

harbored the elegant homes of the newly rich shipyard owners. Down by the river, areas like the infamous Gorbals, with its crowded slums, or Govan, sheltered the laborers who built the ships. They came from the Highlands, expelled to make way for sheep, or from Ireland, where the potato famines drove thousands from their homes.

During the 19th century the city's population grew from 80,000 to more than a million. The new prosperity gave Glasgow its grand neoclassical buildings, such as those built by Alexander "Greek" Thomson, as well as the adventurous visionary buildings designed by Charles Rennie Mackintosh and others who produced Glasgow's Arts and Crafts movement.

The decline of shipbuilding and the closure of the factories in the later 20th century led to much speculation as to what direction the city would take. The curious thing is that, at least in part, the past gave the city its new lease on life. It was as if people looked at their city and saw Glasgow's beauty for the first time: its extraordinarily rich architectural heritage, its leafy parks, its artistic heritage, and its complex social history. Today Glasgow is a dynamic cultural center and a commercial hub, as well as a launching pad from which to explore the rest of Scotland, which, as it turns out, is not so far away. In fact, it takes only 40 minutes to reach Loch Lomond, where the other Scotland begins.

Planning

When to Go

The best times to visit Glasgow are spring and summer and into early fall. Although you may encounter crowds, the weather is more likely to be warm and dry. In summer the days can be long and pleasant—if the rain holds off—and festivals and outdoor events are abundant. Fall can be nice, although cold weather begins to set in after mid-September and the days grow shorter. From November to February it is cold, wet, and dark. Although thousands of people flock to Glasgow for New Year's celebrations, the winter months are relatively quiet in terms of crowds.

Getting Oriented

Glasgow's layout is hard to read at a single glance. The River Clyde, around which Glasgow grew up as a trading city, runs through the center of the city—literally cutting it in two. To the north, the oldest part of Glasgow, the Merchant City, stretches from High Street (the heart of the medieval city) as far as Queen Street, bounded by George Square and Argyle Street to the north and south. Victorian Glasgow, which grew with the shipbuilding boom, extends as far as what is now

the M8 motorway and the River Clyde to the south. Beyond the M8 is the West End, originally the wealthy area around Glasgow University. Its main street is Byres Road. Across Kelvingrove Park, what was once a fading and neglected area has sprung back to life; Finnieston is now the city's trendiest neighborhood, with shipbuilding giving way to riverside concerts and exhibition venues. The opposite bank of the river was the city's poorer quarter, where the workers lived, though beyond it are Pollok Park and Pollok House, with its fine collection of art and furniture.

Planning Your Time

You could quite easily spend five comfortable days here, although in a pinch, two would do. The best strategy for seeing the city is to start at High Street on the east side of Merchant City and work your way west. On the first day explore the city's medieval heritage, taking in Glasgow Cathedral, the Museum of Religious Life, and Provand's Lordship, as well as the Necropolis with its fascinating crumbling monuments. The gentle walk west from here to the Merchant City is also a walk through time, to 17th- and 18th-century Glasgow, and George Square, around which spread the active and crowded shopping areas. For those interested in architect Charles Rennie Mackintosh, the Mackintosh Trail connects the many buildings designed by this outstanding Glasgow designer and architect. Full information on all his buildings can be found online at ⊕ *www. crmsociety.com*, where you can also purchase tickets, as well as at the individual sites. Another day could be well spent between the Kelvingrove Art Gallery (you can lunch here and listen to the daily concert on its magnificent organ) and the nearby Hunterian Museum and Gallery in the university. From here it's only minutes to lively Byres Road and its shops, pubs, and cafés or to the Finnieston strip along Argyle Street. The redevelopment of the riverside offers another route—to the Transport Museum and the Science Centre.

If you have a few extra days, head out to Robert Burns country and the extraordinary Burns Birthplace Museum in Ayrshire. It's a scenic 45-minute drive from Glasgow. Most destinations on the Clyde Coast are easily accessible from Glasgow. Direct trains from Glasgow Central station take you to Paisley, Irvine, and Lanark in less than an hour. These small towns need no more than a day to explore. To get a flavor of island life, take the hour-long train ride to Wemyss Bay and then the ferry to the Isle of Bute.

FESTIVALS

Aye Write

CULTURAL FESTIVALS | This highly successful literary festival brings together writers from Scotland and the world to discuss their work and exchange ideas. It is held in the Mitchell Library and other venues over one week in July. ⊠ *Mitchell Library, North St., West End* ☎ *0141/287–2999* ⊕ *www.ayewrite.com* Ⓜ *St. George's Cross.*

★ Celtic Connections

FESTIVALS | Continually expanding, this music festival is held throughout the second half of January in venues across the city. Musicians from Scotland, Ireland, and other countries celebrate Celtic music, both traditional and contemporary. There are a series of hands-on workshops and a popular late-night club at the Royal Concert Hall. ⊠ *Glasgow* ☎ *0141/353–8000* ⊕ *www.celticconnections.com.*

Glasgow Jazz Festival

CONCERTS | For five days in late June, Glasgow hosts jazz musicians from around the world in venues throughout the city, though mainly in the City Centre. ⊠ *City Centre* ☎ *0141/552–3552* ⊕ *www. jazzfest.co.uk* ☞ *Tickets from Scottish Music Centre* Ⓜ *Buchanan St.*

Getting Here and Around

AIR

Airlines flying from Glasgow Airport to the rest of the United Kingdom and to Europe include Aer Lingus, Air Canada, BMI Regional, British Airways, easyJet, Flybe, Icelandair, Jet 2, and KLM. Several carriers fly from North America, including Air Canada, American Airlines, United, Westjet, and Icelandair (service via Reykjavík).

Ryanair and Vueling offer budget airfares between Prestwick and London and European destinations. Budget-minded easyJet has similar services from Glasgow Airport. Loganair flies to the islands.

Glasgow Airport (GLA) is about 7 miles west of the City Centre on the M8 to Greenock. The airport serves international and domestic flights, and most major European carriers have frequent and convenient connections to many cities on the continent; it closes overnight. There's a frequent shuttle service from London, as well as regular flights from Birmingham, Bristol, East Midlands, Leeds/Bradford, Manchester, Southampton, Isle of Man, and Jersey. There are also flights from Wales (Cardiff) and Ireland (Belfast, Dublin, and Londonderry). Local Scottish connections can be made to Aberdeen, Barra, Benbecula, Campbeltown, Inverness, Islay, Kirkwall, Shetland (Sumburgh), Stornoway, and Tiree.

Prestwick Airport (PIK), on the Ayrshire coast about 30 miles southwest of Glasgow, is known mainly as an airport for budget airlines like Ryanair and Vueling.

Although there's a railway station about 2 miles from Glasgow Airport (Paisley Gilmour Street), it is not very accessible. Transport to the City Centre is by bus or taxi and takes about 20 minutes. Metered taxis cost around £22. Express buses depart every 15 minutes from Glasgow Airport to Central and Queen Street stations and to the Buchanan

Street bus station. The fare is £7.50 one way, £13.50 open round-trip per person.

The drive from Glasgow Airport into the City Centre via the M8 motorway (Junction 29) is normally quite easy. Most companies that provide chauffeur-driven cars and tours will also do limousine airport transfers. TBR Global Chauffeuring is a worldwide organization offering chauffeur-driven transport in Glasgow and across the United Kingdom.

There's a rapid half-hourly train service (hourly on Sunday) direct from Prestwick Airport's terminal to Glasgow Central. Strathclyde Passenger Transport and ScotRail offer a discount ticket that allows you to travel for half the standard fare; just show a valid airline ticket for a flight to or from Prestwick Airport. An hourly coach service makes the same trip but takes much longer than the train. Travelers arriving after 11 pm can take a late bus (X99); book this online with Dodds of Troon. The fare is £14.

The City Centre is reached by car from Prestwick via the fast M77 in about 40 minutes. Metered taxis are available at the airport. The fare to Glasgow is about £40.

AIRPORT CONTACTS Glasgow Airport.
✉ *Caledonia Way, Paisley* ☎ *0844/481–5555* ⊕ *www.glasgowairport.com.* **Prestwick Airport.** ✉ *A79, Prestwick* ☎ *0871/223–0700* ⊕ *www.glasgowprestwick.com.*

AIRPORT TRANSFER CONTACTS Dodds
of Troon. ☎ *01292/288100* ⊕ *www.doddsoftroon.com.* **Little's Chauffeur Drive.** ☎ *0141/883–2111* ⊕ *www.littles.co.uk.* **Strathclyde Passenger Transport Travel Centre.** ✉ *Buchanan Street Bus Station, Killermont St., City Centre* ☎ *0141/332–6811* ⊕ *www.spt.co.uk* Ⓜ *Buchanan St..* **TBR Global Chauffeuring.** ☎ *0141/280–4800* ⊕ *www.tbrglobal.com.*

BIKE
Increasingly bike-friendly, Glasgow has networks of off-road cycle paths. The city has a public bike-rental scheme run by nextbike; ranks of blue cycles at over 30 stations around the city are available for rent. You provide a credit card number and a £10 deposit on the smartphone app, over the phone, or on the on-bike computer, and give the cycle number. You'll be given the number for the combination lock and off you go. It's a great way to see the city, and you can return the bike at any station. Bikes cost £1 per 30 minutes up to 5 hours or £10 for 5–24 hours. The Glasgow Cycle Map available at information centers provides comprehensive route information, or see ⊕ *www.glasgow.gov.uk/cycling.* Companies like Glasgow Bike Tours also offer tours of the city on bike.

BIKE CONTACTS Glasgow Bike Tours.
☎ *7786/683445* ⊕ *www.glasgowbiketours.co.uk.* **nextbike.** ☎ *0208/166–9851* ⊕ *www.nextbike.co.uk.*

BUS
The main intercity operators are National Express, Scottish Citylink, and Megabus, which serve numerous towns and cities in Scotland, Wales, and England, including London and Edinburgh. Glasgow's bus station is on Buchanan Street, not far from Queen Street station.

When traveling from the City Centre to either the West End or the South Side, it's easy to use the city's integrated network of buses, subways, and trains. Service is reliable and connections are convenient from buses to trains and the subway. Many buses require exact fare, which is usually around £1.75.

Traveline Scotland provides information on schedules, fares, and route planning, as does the Strathclyde Passenger Transport Travel Centre, which has an information center.

BUS CONTACTS Buchanan Street Bus Station. ⊠ *Killermont St., City Centre* ☏ *0141/333–3708* ⊕ *www.spt.co.uk* Ⓜ *Buchanan St..* **Megabus.** ☏ *0141/352–4444* ⊕ *uk.megabus.com.* **National Express.** ☏ *0871/781–8181* ⊕ *www. nationalexpress.com.* **Scottish Citylink.** ☏ *0871/266–3333* ⊕ *www.citylink.co.uk.* **Traveline Scotland.** ☏ *0871/200–2233* ⊕ *www.travelinescotland.com.*

CAR

If you're driving to Glasgow from England and the south of Scotland, you'll approach the city via the M6, M74, and A74. From Edinburgh, the M8 leads to the City Centre. From the north, the A82 from Fort William and the A82/M80 from Stirling join the M8 in the City Centre.

You don't need a car in Glasgow, and you're probably better off without one. In the City Centre meters are expensive, running about £2.40 per hour during the day. In the West End they cost 80 pence per hour. Don't park illegally, as fines are upward of £30. Multistory garages are open 24 hours a day at Anderston Centre, George Street, Waterloo Place, Mitchell Street, Cambridge Street, and Concert Square. Rates run between £1 and £2 per hour. More convenient are the park-and-ride operations at some subway stations (Kelvinbridge, Bridge Street, and Shields Road).

SUBWAY

Glasgow's small subway system—it has 15 stations—is useful for reaching all the City Centre and West End attractions. Stations are signposted by a prominent letter "S." You can choose between a flat fare (£1.75) and a one-day pass (£4.20) that can be used after 9 am on weekdays and all day on weekends. A Smart Card, which you can get free online or at stations for £3, will give you reduced fares. A Roundabout ticket costs £7.20 a day and covers subway and trains. A Day Tripper ticket is well worth it for families, covering bus, subway, trains, and some ferries. It costs £12.70 for one adult and

up to two children or £22.50 for two adults and up to four kids. The distance between many central stops is no more than a 10-minute walk. More information is available from Strathclyde Passenger Transport Travel Centre or its website, including transportation maps.

TAXI

Taxis are a fast and cost-effective way to get around. You'll find metered taxis (usually black and of the London sedan type) at stands all over the City Centre. Most have radio dispatch. Some have also been adapted to take wheelchairs. You can hail a cab on the street if its "for hire" sign is illuminated. A typical ride from the City Centre to the West End or the South Side costs around £7. Uber is also available in Glasgow.

TAXI CONTACTS Glasgow Taxis. ☏ *0141/429–7070* ⊕ *www.glasgowtaxis. co.uk.*

TRAIN

Glasgow has two main rail stations: Central and Queen Street. Central serves Virgin trains from London's Euston station (five hours). Trains for Ayr and to the south of Glasgow also depart from Central. East Coast trains run from London's Kings Cross (via Edinburgh) to Glasgow's Queen Street station. For details, contact National Rail. All routes heading north from Glasgow depart from Queen Street.

A regular bus service links the Queen Street and Central stations (although you can easily walk if you aren't too encumbered with bags). Queen Street is near the Buchanan Street subway station, and Central is close to St. Enoch. Taxis are available at both stations.

The Glasgow area has an extensive network of suburban railway services. Locals still call them the Blue Trains, even though most are now painted maroon and cream. For more information and a free map, contact the Strathclyde Passenger Transport Travel Centre or National Rail.

📠 *08457/484950* ⊕ *www.nationalrail.co.uk*. **Trainline.** ⊕ *www.thetrainline.com*.

Restaurants

Glasgow's vibrant restaurant culture is constantly renewing itself. More recently, the city has responded enthusiastically to the small-plate and sharing-platter trends, but there are still plenty of fine-dining options on the one hand, and steak houses and burger places on the other. The city continues to present the best that Scotland has to offer: grass-fed beef, free-range chicken, wild seafood, venison, duck, and goose, not to mention superb fruits and vegetables. The growing emphasis on organic food is reflected on menus that increasingly provide detailed information about the source of their ingredients. Around the city, an explosion of coffee shops offer artisanal macchiatos and mochas. And brunch is becoming an increasingly popular option.

You can eat your way around the world in Glasgow. A new generation of Italian restaurants serves updated versions of classic Italian dishes. Chinese, Indian, and Pakistani foods, longtime favorites, are now more varied and sophisticated, and Thai and Japanese restaurants have become popular. Spanish-style tapas are now quite common, and the small-plate trend has extended to every kind of restaurant. Seafood restaurants have moved well beyond the fish-and-chips wrapped in newspaper that were always a Glasgow staple, as langoustines, scallops, and monkfish appear on menus with ever more unusual accompaniments. And Glasgow has an especially good reputation for its vegan and vegetarian restaurants.

Eating in Glasgow can be casual or lavish. For inexpensive dining, consider the benefit of lunch or pretheater set menus. Beer and spirits cost much the same as they would in a bar, but wine is relatively expensive in restaurants. Increasing numbers of pubs offer food, but their kitchens usually close early. ■ TIP➔ **Some restaurants allow you to bring your own bottle of wine, charging just a small corkage fee. It's worth the effort.**

Hotels

Glasgow has a whole range of hotel options, from revamped grand hotels to basic budget options to stylish boutique properties. Glasgow's City Centre never sleeps, so downtown hotels may be noisier than those in the leafy and genteel West End or in fashionable Finnieston. Downtown hotels are within walking distance of all the main sights, while West End lodgings are more convenient for museums and art galleries.

Although big hotels are spread out all around the city, B&Bs are definitely a more popular, personal, and cheaper option. For country-house luxury you should look beyond the city—try Mar Hall, near Paisley. Regardless of the neighborhood, hotels are about the same in price. Some B&Bs as well as the smaller properties may also offer discounts for longer stays. Make your reservations in advance, especially when there's a big concert, sporting event, or holiday (New Year's Eve is popular). Glasgow is busiest in summer, but it can fill up when something special is going on. If you arrive in town without a place to stay, contact the Glasgow Tourist Information Centre.

It is always worthwhile to inquire about special deals or rates, especially if you book online and in advance. Another money-saving option is to rent an apartment. B&Bs are the best-priced short-term lodging option, and you're sure to get breakfast.

Most smaller hotels and all guesthouses include breakfast in the room rate. Larger hotels usually charge extra for breakfast. Also note that the most expensive hotels often exclude V.A.T. (Value-Added Tax, the sales tax) in the initial price quote but budget places include it.

Restaurant and hotel reviews have been shortened. For full information, visit Fodors.com. Restaurant prices are the average cost of a main course at dinner or, if dinner is not served, at lunch. Hotel prices are the lowest cost of a standard double room in high season, including 20% V.A.T.

WHAT IT COSTS in Pounds			
$	$$	$$$	$$$$
RESTAURANTS			
under £15	£15–£19	£20–£25	over £25
HOTELS			
under £125	£125–£200	£201–£300	over £300

Nightlife

Glasgow's music scene is vibrant and creative, and many successful pop artists began their careers in its pubs and clubs. When it comes to nightlife, the City Centre and the West End are alive with pubs and clubs offering an eclectic mix of everything from bagpipes to salsa to punk. The biweekly magazine *List,* available at newsstands and many cafés and arts centers, is an indispensable guide to Glasgow's bars and clubs.

Performing Arts

Because the Royal Scottish Conservatoire is in Glasgow, a pool of impressive young talent is always pressing the city's artistic boundaries in theater, music, and film. The city has a well-deserved reputation for its theater, with everything from cutting-edge plays to over-the-top pantomimes. The Citizens Theatre is one of Europe's leading companies, and the

Kings and the Theatre Royal play host to touring productions.

TICKETS
Scottish Music Centre
TICKETS | As well as a library, the Scottish Music Centre serves as the main ticket office for all music events at venues like the Royal Concert Hall and for annual events like the Glasgow Jazz Festival. ✉ *Candleriggs, City Centre* ☎ *0141/353–8000* ⊕ *www.scottishmusiccentre.com* Ⓜ *Buchanan St.*

Ticketmaster
TICKETS | Tickets for theatrical performances can be purchased at theater box offices or online through Ticketmaster. ⊕ *www.ticketmaster.co.uk.*

Shopping

You'll find the mark of the fashion industry on Glasgow's hottest shopping streets. In the Merchant City, Ingram Street is lined on either side by high-fashion and designer outlets like Cruise. Buchanan Street, in the City Centre, is home to many chains geared toward younger people, including Diesel, Monsoon, and USC, and malls like the elegant Princes Square and Buchanan Galleries. The adjacent Argyle Street Arcade is filled with jewelry stores. Antiques tend be found on and around West Regent Street in the City Centre. The West End has a number of small shops selling crafts, vintage clothing, and trendier fashions—punctuated by innumerable cafés and restaurants. The university dominates the area around West End, and many shops cater to students.

Tours

BOAT TOURS
Both Sweeney's and Cruise Loch Lomond offer a range of tours. For cruises along the River Clyde, contact Glasgow Tourist Information Centre for details.

Cruise Loch Lomond

BOAT TOURS | Based in Tarbet on Loch Lomond's western shore, this company offers tours that include the picturesque village of Luss to the west and journeys towards the eastern shore at Inversnaid and Balmaha, sailing around the island of Inchcailloch. ☎ *1301/702356* ⊕ *www.cruiselochlomond.co.uk* ✉ *From £13.*

Sweeney's Cruise Co. Loch Lomond

BOAT TOURS | This company offers a range of cruises on Loch Lomond, departing from Balloch Pier at the southern end of the loch. Tours sail toward the two main islands, Inchmurrin and Inchcailloch, with views of Ben Lomond. ☎ *1389/ 752376* ⊕ *www.sweeneyscruiseco.com* ✉ *From £12.*

BUS TOURS

The Glasgow Tourist Information Centre can give information about city tours and about longer tours northward to the Highlands and islands.

City Sightseeing

TOUR—SIGHT | Daily hop-on, hop-off bus tours of Glasgow in open-topped double-decker buses are offered by City Sightseeing. The full tour lasts just under two hours, with an English-speaking guide aboard and a multilingual commentary. Tours begin at George Square. ✉ *City Centre* ☎ *0141/204–0444* ⊕ *www.citysightseeingglasgow.co.uk* ✉ *From £16.*

Rabbie's Trail Burners

TOUR—SIGHT | Choose from a range of well-regarded one-, two-, and three-day minibus tours with guides to Loch Lomond, Loch Ness, Stirling, and the Highlands. There is also a one-day Outlander tour from Glasgow. Glasgow-based tours depart from George Street beside the City Chambers, near George Square. ☎ *0131/226–3133* ⊕ *www.rabbies.com.*

PRIVATE GUIDES

Glasgow Taxis

TOUR—SIGHT | Few people know the city better than taxi drivers. Glasgow Taxis will organize a guided Mackintosh tour around Glasgow, a Burns tour to Ayrshire, or a trip to Loch Lomond, including pickup and drop-off at your place of choice. These black cabs carry up to five passengers. ✉ *City Centre* ☎ *0141/429–7070* ⊕ *www.glasgowtaxis.co.uk* ✉ *From £45 per taxi.*

Little's Chauffeur Drive

TOUR—SIGHT | You can arrange personally tailored car-and-driver tours, both locally and throughout Scotland. ☎ *0141/883–2111* ⊕ *www.littles.co.uk.*

Scottish Tourist Guides Association

TOUR—SIGHT | The association provides qualified and accredited Blue Badge Guides with specific areas of expertise; guides also speak a range of languages. Tours start at half a day, and driver guides are available. Book online in advance. ✉ *Glasgow* ☎ *01786/451953* ⊕ *www.stga.co.uk* ✉ *From £150 for half-day tours.*

WALKING TOURS

The Glasgow Tourist Information Centre can provide information on a whole range of self-guided walks around the city.

Glasgow Street Art Tour

WALKING TOURS | A two-hour walking tour takes you around Glasgow to view its diverse and often surprising street murals. Tours occur on Friday, Saturday, and Sunday at 2 pm between June and October. ✉ *Entrance to the Lighthouse, Mitchell Ln.* ⊕ *www.walkingtoursin.com/street-art-tour* ✉ *From £10* Ⓜ *Buchanan Street.*

Visitor Information

The Glasgow Tourist Information Centre provides information about different types of tours and has an accommodations-booking service. Books, maps, and souvenirs are also available. There's a branch at Glasgow Airport, too. You can also find helpful information online at ⊕ *www.peoplemakeglasgow.com.*

CONTACT Visit Scotland icentre Glasgow.
✉ *156a/158 Buchanan Street, City Centre* ☏ *0141/566–4083* ⊕ *www.visitscotland. com/glasgow.*

Activities

You can't go far these days in Glasgow without seeing a runner or cyclist; numerous parks provide plenty of opportunities, and the nextbike (⊕ *www.next-bike.co.uk*) public bike-rental program has been a boon to cyclists. It rains a lot in Glasgow, but don't let the weather stop you. It doesn't deter the locals who play soccer, tennis, hike, bike, run, swim, and walk in the rain.

FOOTBALL

The city has been sports mad, especially for football (soccer), for more than 100 years. The historic rivalry between its two main football clubs, Rangers and Celtic, is legendary, so the low-key club Partick Thistle is a less contentious alternative for football fans. Matches are held usually on Saturday or Sunday in winter. Admission prices start at about £20, and don't go looking for a family-day-out atmosphere. Football remains a fiercely contested game attended mainly by rowdy fans, though the stadiums at Ibrox and Celtic Park are becoming more family-friendly.

Celtic

SOCCER | This famous football club wears white-and-green stripes and plays in the east at Celtic Park, or Perkhead as it is know locally. Daily stadium tours must be booked ahead, and the Celtic Museum is also in the stadium. To get here, take a taxi from central Glasgow or a train from Central station to Dalmarnock (10-minute walk from station). Match tickets start at £90. ✉ *Celtic Park, 18 Kerrydale St., East*

End ☏ *0871/226–1888* ⊕ *www.celticfc. net* ⍓ *Stadium tours £15.*

Partick Thistle

SOCCER | Soccer in Glasgow isn't just blue or green, nor is it dominated by international players and big money. Partick Thistle Football Club, known as the Jags, wears red and yellow, and its home field is Firhill Park. ✉ *80 Firhill Rd., West End* ☏ *0141/579–1971* ⊕ *www.ptfc.co.uk* Ⓜ *St. George's Cross.*

Rangers

SOCCER | The Rangers wear blue and play at Ibrox, on the south side of the Clyde. Stadium tours are on Friday, Saturday, and Sunday; booking ahead is essential. ✉ *150 Edmiston Dr., South Side* ☏ *0871/702–1972* ⊕ *www.rangers.co.uk* ⍓ *Stadium tours £8* Ⓜ *Ibrox.*

GOLF

Several municipal courses are operated within Glasgow proper by the local authorities. Bookings are relatively inexpensive and should be made directly to the course 24 hours in advance to ensure prime tee times (courses open at 7 am). A comprehensive list of contacts, facilities, and greens fees of the 30 or so other courses near the city is available from the tourist board.

Carrick at Loch Lomond

GOLF | Located on the banks of legendary Loch Lomond, this imaginatively designed course pays homage to the surrounding landscapes. ✉ *Alexandria* ☏ *0141/276–0810* ⊕ *www.glasgowlife. org.uk* ⍓ *£50–£80* ⚐ *18 holes, 7082 yards, par 71.*

Douglas Park Golf Club

GOLF | A charming parkland course at Milngavie, on the western outskirts of Glasgow, this attractive and varied course is set among lush rhododendron bushes and birch and pine trees. Each hole is highly individual, and though shorter than many courses it tests the careful, accurate golfer rather than the big swing. The Campsie Fells form a pleasant

Glasgow City Chambers is most charming lit up at night over George Square.

backdrop. ✉ *Milngavie Rd., Hillfoot, Bearsden* ☎ *0141/942–0985* ⊕ *www. douglasparkgolfclub.co.uk* ✈ *Apr.–Oct., £44 weekdays, £55 weekends; Nov.– Mar., £15 weekdays, £20 weekends* 🏌 *18 holes, 5981 yards, par 69.*

City Centre

Some of the city's most important historical buildings are found in the City Centre close to George Square, many of them converted to very different purposes now. Along the streets of this neighborhood are some of the best examples of the architectural confidence and vitality that so characterized the burgeoning Glasgow of the turn of the 20th century. There are also plenty of shops, trendy eateries, and pubs.

GETTING HERE

Every form of public transportation can bring you here, from bus to train to subway. Head to George Square and walk from there.

Sights

Central Station

TRANSPORTATION SITE (AIRPORT/BUS/FERRY/ TRAIN) | It was the railways that first brought hordes of Victorian tourists to Scotland, and the great station hotels were places of luxury for those wealthier Victorian travelers; Central Station and its accompanying hotel are excellent examples of this. The Grand Central Hotel (once the Station Hotel) demonstrates how important this building was to the city. It remains a busy active train station from which to travel south to England or west to the Ayrshire coast and Prestwick Airport. The Champagne Bar in the Grand Central Hotel is a good vantage point for watching the station concourse and its comings and goings. The railway bridge across Argyll Street behind the station is known as the Highlandman's Umbrella because immigrants from the north once gathered there to look for work in the early 20th-century. ✉ *Gordon St., bounded by Gordon, Union, Argyle,*

City Centre and Merchant City

KEY

1 *Exploring Sights*

1 *Restaurants*

1 *Hotels*

Jamaica, Clyde, Oswald, and Hope Sts., City Centre.

★ City Chambers

BUILDING | Dominating the east side of George Square, this exuberant expression of Victorian confidence, built by William Young in Italian Renaissance style, was opened by Queen Victoria in 1888. Among the interior's outstanding features are the entrance hall's vaulted ceiling, sustained by granite columns topped with marble, the marble-and-alabaster staircases, and Venetian mosaics. The enormous banqueting hall has murals illustrating Glasgow's history. Free guided tours lasting about an hour depart weekdays at 10:30 and 2:30; tours are very popular, so pick up a ticket beforehand from the reception desk. The building is closed to visitors during civic functions. ⊠ 80 George Sq., City Centre ☎ 0141/287–2000 ⊕ www.glasgow.gov.uk ⊠ Free ⊗ Closed weekends Ⓜ Buchanan St.

Compass Gallery

ART GALLERIES | The gallery is something of an institution, having opened in 1969 to provide space for young and unknown artists—a role it continues. It shares space with Cyril Gerber Fine Arts, which specializes in British paintings from 1880 to the present. ⊠ 178 W. Regent St., City Centre ☎ 0141/221–6370 ⊕ www.compassgallery.co.uk Ⓜ Cowcaddens.

Glasgow School of Art

BUILDING | Scotland's only public art school's main claim to fame used to be the iconic architecture of its main building, designed by architect Charles Rennie Mackintosh; sadly, the building was badly damaged by fires in 2014 and 2018. Glaswegians mourned its passing, but plans are in place to rebuild it although officials have admitted that its restoration will be a long and complicated process. Fortunately, there are other wonderful Mackintosh buildings in and around the city. Stephen Holl's newer interpretation of the **Reid Building,** directly opposite the original, is a spectacular modern homage to it. ⊠ 164 Renfrew St., City Centre ☎ 0141/353–4526 ⊕ www.gsa.ac.uk/tours Ⓜ Cowcaddens.

The Lighthouse

BUILDING | Charles Rennie Mackintosh designed these former offices of the *Glasgow Herald* newspaper, with the emblematic Mackintosh Tower, in 1893. On the third floor, the **Mackintosh Interpretation Centre** is a great place to start exploring this groundbreaking architect's work, which is illustrated in a glass wall with alcoves containing models of his buildings. From here you can climb the more than 130 steps up the tower and, once you have caught your breath, look out over Glasgow. (Alternatively, a viewing platform on the sixth floor can be reached by elevator.) Today the Lighthouse serves as Scotland's **Centre for Architecture, Design and the City,** celebrating all facets of architecture and design. The fifth-floor Doocot Café is a great place to take a break from sightseeing. ⊠ 11 Mitchell La., City Centre ☎ 0141/271–5365 ⊕ www.thelighthouse.co.uk ⊠ Free Ⓜ St. Enoch.

Mackintosh at the Willow

BUILDING | One of Charles Rennie Mackintosh's most admired commissions was the tearooms he designed in 1903 for Miss Cranston, whose tearooms across the city were a magnet for Glasgow's middle class. She commissioned the young Mackintosh for several projects; the Willow Tea Rooms were among the best known. The tearooms have now been restored to their 1903 state, with furniture to match Makintosh's design. You'll find other beautiful examples of his work in the building, too, including the Billiard Room, the Board Room, and the aptly named Salon de Luxe. An interactive exhibition focuses on the great artist in his time and place, together with his contemporaries, including the Glasgow Girls. ⊠ 215-217 Sauchiehall St. ☎ 141/204–1903 ⊕ www.

The streets of Glasgow are filled with terrace houses like these.

mackintoshatthewillow.com Ⓜ *Buchanan Street.*

Regimental Museum of the Royal Highland Fusiliers

MUSEUM | Exhibits of medals, badges, and uniforms relate the history of a famous, much-honored regiment and the men who served in it. ✉ *518 Sauchiehall St., City Centre* ☎ *0141/332–5639* ⊕ *www.rhf.org.uk* 🖃 *Free* ⊙ *Closed weekends* Ⓜ *Cowcaddens.*

St. Vincent's Street Church

RELIGIOUS SITE | This 1859 church, the work of Alexander Thomson, stands high above the street. The building exemplifies his Greek Revival style, replete with Ionic columns, sphinxlike heads, and rich interior color. Owned by Glasgow City Council, it is currently used by the Free Church of Scotland. You can see the interior by attending a service Sunday at 11 am or 6 pm or by appointment. ✉ *265 St. Vincent St., City Centre* ⊕ *www.glasgowcityfreechurch.org* 🖃 *Free* ⊙ *Closed Mon.–Sat. except by appointment* Ⓜ *Buchanan St.*

★ Tenement House

HOUSE | This ordinary first-floor apartment is anything but ordinary inside: it was occupied from 1937 to 1982 by Agnes Toward (and before that by her mother), both of whom seem never to have thrown anything away. Agnes was a dressmaker, and her legacy is this fascinating time capsule, painstakingly preserved with her everyday furniture and belongings. A small museum explores the life and times of its careful occupant. The red-sandstone building dates from 1892 and is in the Garnethill area near the Glasgow School of Art. ✉ *145 Buccleuch St., City Centre* ☎ *0141/333–0183* ⊕ *www.nts.org.uk* 🖃 *£7.50* ⊙ *Closed Nov.–Mar* Ⓜ *Cowcaddens.*

🍴 Restaurants

The City Centre has restaurants catering to the 9-to-5 crowd, meaning there are a lot of fine-dining establishments as well as good restaurants catching people as they leave work, drawing them in with pretheater menus.

Anchor Line

$$$ | STEAKHOUSE | Occupying the former headquarters of the Anchor Line, whose ships sailed from Scotland to America, this bar and restaurant near George Square has been impressively refurbished to create the sense of fine dining aboard a luxury ocean liner. The menu reflects the voyage, too, including Scottish seafood and lamb, and a full range of steaks and their sauces to represent America. **Known for:** high-end cocktails; luxurious fine dining; steak of all kinds. ⑤ *Average main: £20* ☒ *12 St. Vincent Pl., City Centre* ☎ *0141/248–1434* ⊕ *www. theanchorline.co.uk* Ⓜ *Buchanan St.*

The Butterfly and the Pig

$ | BRITISH | Down an innocuous-looking flight of stairs, this intimate restaurant is the type of place young locals love: flickering candles, mix-and-match crockery, and inventive, inexpensive food that offers new twists on the familiar. The menu reads like a comedic narrative, with descriptions like "traditional fish-and-chips, battered to death" or "Supreme Commander chicken." Although vegetarians are not well catered to, they at least can try the portobello-mushroom burgers with extra-thick potato chips. **Known for:** shabby chic atmosphere; quirky takes on familiar dishes; tea shop upstairs. ⑤ *Average main: £14* ☒ *153 Bath St., City Centre* ☎ *0141/221–7711* ⊕ *www.thebutterflyandthepig.com* Ⓜ *Buchanan St.*

★ Chaophraya

$ | THAI | You can experience dining at its most sumptuous and elegant for a good price in the grand surroundings of what was the Glasgow Conservatoire, where today golden Buddhas sit comfortably beside busts of great composers. The delicate flavors of Thai cooking are at their finest here in the chef's wonderful signature Massaman lamb (and beef) curry, flavorsome Fisherman's Soup, and fusion dishes like scallops with black pudding. **Known for:** Massaman lamb curry; luxurious surroundings; extensive menu of Thai classics. ⑤ *Average main: £14* ☒ *The Town House, Nelson Mandela Pl., City Centre* ☎ *0141/332–0041* ⊕ *www.chaophraya.co.uk* Ⓜ *Buchanan St.*

Halloumi

$$ | GREEK | Greek cuisine was not well represented in Glasgow until Halloumi arrived to fill the gap. Its large windows onto the street invite you in to a simply decorated interior with white walls and wooden tables, where you will find a reassuringly familiar menu of small plates, or meze. **Known for:** shared small plates of traditional Greek meze; excellent moussaka; good lunch deal. ⑤ *Average main: £17* ☒ *161 Hope St., City Centre* ⊹ *Near Central station* ☎ *0141/204–1616* ⊕ *www.halloumiglasgow.co.uk* Ⓜ *Buchanan St.*

Ibérica

$$ | SPANISH | The Spanish small-plates revolution has arrived in Glasgow in this grand former bank, going a step beyond tapas with portions that are larger and encourage sharing and combining flavors at the table. The qualities of each dish are patiently explained: the different kinds of Serrano ham, the flavors of cheese, how aioli (homemade garlic mayonnaise) is made. **Known for:** black-rice dishes; Galician-style octopus; range of Serrano ham. ⑤ *Average main: £18* ☒ *140 St. Vincent St., City Centre* ☎ *0141/530 7985* ⊕ *www.ibericarestaurants.com* Ⓜ *Buchanan St.*

Las Iguanas

$$ | SOUTH AMERICAN | The bright interior of this restaurant, part of a popular chain, echoes the Latin American–themed menu in its vibrant colors and decoration. The extensive menu features items like Argentine steak, Brazilian Xinxim (a type of curry stew), and classics like tapas and burritos. **Known for:** Xinxim, a stew of chicken and crayfish in a coconut sauce; colorful cocktails; equally colorful decor. ⑤ *Average main: £15* ☒ *15–20 W. Nile St.,*

City Centre ☎ 0141/248–5705 ⊕ www.
iguanas.co.uk Ⓜ Buchanan St.

Loon Fung

$$ | **CANTONESE** | **FAMILY** | The friendly staff at this huge, popular Cantonese eatery guide you through the dishes here, including barbecued duck, deep-fried wontons with prawns, and more challenging dishes like pork with jellyfish or king prawn with salted egg. On most days you will see local Chinese families seated at the huge round tables enjoying the dim sum for which the restaurant is rightly famous. **Known for:** Glasgow's best dim sum; authentic Cantonese cuisine; lively family atmosphere. Ⓢ Average main: £16 ⊠ 417–419 Sauchiehall St., City Centre ☎ 0141/332–1240 ⊕ www.
loonfungglasgow.com/Ⓜ Cowcaddens.

★ Macintosh at the Willow

$ | **BRITISH** | Miss Cranston's Willow Tea Rooms were the ultimate place to be seen in Glasgow in 1903, not only for the tasty tea but for the beautiful art nouveau decor and furniture designed by a young architect by the name of Charles Rennie Mackintosh. The original tearooms have now been fully restored here, and you can lunch on traditional Scottish cuisine or take an elegant high tea in the exquisite surroundings of the Salon de Luxe. **Known for:** traditional high tea in a stunning location; historic Mackintosh furniture; great steak pie and haggis. Ⓢ Average main: £12 ⊠ 215–217 Sauchie-hall Street, City Centre ☎ 0141/204–1903 ⊕ www.mackintoshatthewillow.com/ ⊘ No dinner Ⓜ Buchanan St.

★ Mussel Inn

$$ | **SEAFOOD** | West-coast shellfish farmers own this sleek restaurant and feed their customers incredibly succulent oysters, scallops, and mussels. The pots of mussels, steamed to order and served with any of a number of sauces, are revelatory, and scallops, prawns, and oysters come together in a wonderful seafood pasta. **Known for:** delicious seafood pasta and chowder; famed Queenie oysters;

mussels Moroccan style. Ⓢ Average main: £18 ⊠ 157 Hope St., City Centre ☎ 0141/572–1405 ⊕ www.mussel-inn.
com Ⓜ Buchanan St.

★ Opium

$$ | **ASIAN** | This eatery has completely rethought Asian cuisine, taking Chinese, Malaysian, and Thai cooking in new directions and using sauces that are fragrant and spicy but never overpowering. Subdued lighting, neutral tones, and dark wood create a calm setting for specialties including superb dim sum and crisp wontons filled with delicious combinations of crab, shrimp, and chicken. **Known for:** creative Asian-fusion food; great cocktails; excellent dim sum. Ⓢ Average main: £17 ⊠ 191 Hope St., City Centre ☎ 0141/332–6668 ⊕ www.
opiumrestaurant.co.uk Ⓜ Buchanan St.

★ Rogano

$$ | **MODERN EUROPEAN** | Two things have made the Rogano a Glasgow institution: its beautiful art deco decor, which echoes the luxury Clyde-built oceanliners of the thirties, and its seafood menu, which has held its own despite the competition of the city's new generation of restaurants. The main restaurant is a formal affair, but the downstairs Café Rogano is more intimate and relaxed, serving oysters and a signature fish soup among many other options. **Known for:** gorgeous art deco bar; excellent old-school seafood options, including famed fish soup; exquisite cocktails. Ⓢ Average main: £19 ⊠ 11 Exchange Pl., City Centre ☎ 0141/248–4055 ⊕ www.roganoglas-gow.com Ⓜ Buchanan St.

Stereo

$ | **VEGETARIAN** | Down a quiet lane near Glasgow Central station, this ultracool eatery dishes up a fantastic range of vegan food, from paella and gnocchi to a colorful platter with hummus, red-pepper pâté, and home-baked flatbread. The decor is homey and relaxed, and someone always seems to be nearby reading or writing. **Known for:** imaginative vegan food; hipster vibe with good art and music; perfect side dish of roasted sweet potato chips. $ *Average main: £10* ⊠ *20–28 Renfield La., City Centre* ☎ *0141/222–2254* ⊕ *www.stereocafebar. com* Ⓜ *Buchanan St.*

Two Fat Ladies

$$$ | SEAFOOD | From its start in 1989 in a tiny West End space, Two Fat Ladies raised the standards of seafood in the city well before the Finnieston revolution, and superb fish still dominates the limited menu. This City Centre branch retains a feeling of intimacy even if the decor and large window give off an airy vibe. **Known for:** some of the city's best seafood; intimate vibe; lamb shank with rosemary mash for non–fish lovers. $ *Average main: £20* ⊠ *118A Blythswood St., City Centre* ⊹ *Just off Blythswood Sq.* ☎ *0141/847–0088* ⊕ *www.twofatladiesrestaurant.com* Ⓜ *Cowcaddens.*

Where the Monkey Sleeps

$ | CAFÉ | This quirky basement café, in a series of small rooms with brightly colored sofas, serves huge sandwiches with amusing names—the "Wytchfinder" has chorizo sausage and cheese, while the "Serious Operation" contains practically everything on the menu. Enjoy your choice with soup or one of the wonderful smoothies. **Known for:** brilliant sandwiches made-to-order (so expect a bit of a wait); atmosphere that invites hanging out; cheerful service. $ *Average main: £6* ⊠ *182 W. Regent St., City Centre* ☎ *0141/226–3406* ⊕ *www. monkeysleeps.com* ⊙ *Closed weekends. No dinner* Ⓜ *Cowcaddens.*

 ## Hotels

Here you'll be close to everything—the main sights, shops, theaters, restaurants, and bars—the pulse of the city. You don't have to worry about transportation in the center of town, but it can get noisy on weekend nights.

Abode Glasgow

$$ | HOTEL | Stylish and modern, this boutique hotel in an Edwardian building was once the grand home of a prime minister, hence the high ceilings and huge windows. **Pros:** stylish rooms; great location; echoes of Edwardian grandeur. **Cons:** limited public areas; some front rooms noisy; pricey parking. $ *Rooms from: £129* ⊠ *129 Bath St., City Centre* ☎ *0141/221–6789* ⊕ *www.abodeglasgow.co.uk* ⊅ *59 rooms* ⑩ *Free Breakfast* Ⓜ *Buchanan St.*

Apex City of Glasgow Hotel

$$ | HOTEL | The extraordinary floor-to-ceiling windows here set this modern chain hotel apart, providing a panoramic view over Glasgow and beyond from the upper floors (sixth and seventh). **Pros:** bright rooms; central location; awesome city views from higher floors. **Cons:** lower-floor rooms overlook other buildings; no parking facility and nearby lot closes at night; corridors quite cramped. $ *Rooms from: £127* ⊠ *110 Bath St., City Centre* ☎ *0141/375–3333* ⊕ *www. apexhotels.co.uk* ⊅ *106 rooms* ⑩ *Free Breakfast* Ⓜ *Buchanan St.*

Carlton George

$ | HOTEL | A narrow revolving doorway, a step back from busy West George Street, creates the illusion of a secret passageway leading into this lavish boutique hotel. **Pros:** near City Centre attractions and beside Queen Street station; nice resturant with stunning views; great value. **Cons:** entrance very small and often crowded; area sometimes noisy at night; parking at nearby paid car park. $ *Rooms from: £117* ⊠ *44 W. George St., City Centre* ☎ *0141/353–6373* ⊕ *www.carlton. nl/george* ⊅ *64 rooms* ⑩ *Free Breakfast* Ⓜ *Buchanan St.*

★ citizenM Glasgow

$$ | HOTEL | There's no lobby at the futuristic citizenM—no reception area at all, because you can only book online—but there are chic "living spaces" with ultra-modern furnishings where guests can

congregate and streamlined rooms that are smartly designed. **Pros:** wonderful and creative design; central location; free Wi-Fi. **Cons:** not for the claustrophobic; breakfast costs more if you don't book ahead; the absence of reception staff can be confusing. ⑤ *Rooms from: £139 ✉ 60 Renfrew St., corner of Hope St., City Centre* ☎ *01782/488–3490* ⊕ *www. citizenm.com* ⟿ *198 rooms* ⦿ *No meals* Ⓜ *Buchanan St.*

★ Dakota Deluxe Glasgow
$$ | HOTEL | At this extremely stylish addition to Glasgow's hotel scene, the textured, neutral decor creates a restful, subdued atmosphere. **Pros:** relaxing public rooms; spacious, well-appointed bedrooms; lovely bathrooms. **Cons:** unexciting views from hotel; not right in the middle of the action; slightly corporate feel. ⑤ *Rooms from: £145 ✉ 179 W. Regent St., City Centre* ☎ *0141/404–3680* ⊕ *glasgow.dakotahotels.co.uk* ⟿ *83 rooms* ⦿ *Free Breakfast* Ⓜ *Cowcaddens.*

★ Grand Central Hotel
$$ | HOTEL | One of Europe's great Victorian hotels built when train travel was a luxury, this hotel located within Glasgow's historic train station deserves its name, as everything about it, from the magnificent marble-floor champagne bar to the ballroom fully restored to its original glory, is grand. **Pros:** a real air of luxury; generally spacious rooms; great champagne bar for lingering. **Cons:** occasional noise from street; parking a couple of blocks away; some small rooms. ⑤ *Rooms from: £125 ✉ 99 Gordon St., City Centre* ☎ *0141/240–3700* ⊕ *www. grandcentralhotel.com* ⟿ *233 rooms* ⦿ *Free Breakfast* Ⓜ *Buchanan St.*

Grasshoppers Hotel Glasgow
$ | HOTEL | Not visible from the street, this hotel occupies a sixth floor above Central station; guest rooms are on the small side but have expansive windows overlooking the glass roof of the station on one side and across the rooftops of Glasgow on the other. **Pros:** bright and

clean; complimentary cakes and ice cream; quiet despite its central location. **Cons:** no lobby; rooms are quite small; no parking at hotel. ⑤ *Rooms from: £118 ✉ 87 Union St., City Centre* ⚓ *Door marked "Caledonian Chambers" leads to elevator* ☎ *0141/222–2666* ⊕ *www. grasshoppersglasgow.com* ⟿ *30 rooms* ⦿ *Breakfast* Ⓜ *St. Enoch.*

Hallmark Hotel Glasgow
$$ | HOTEL | FAMILY | Behind a rather austere exterior built on to what was once a mill, the Hallmark clearly sees itself as a family-oriented hotel, with the facilities of a large chain but decor and ambience that are unpretentious and comfortable. **Pros:** pleasant atmosphere; good spa and leisure center available to guests; close to City Centre. **Cons:** no views; some noise from nearby elevated motorway; hotel vehicle entrance not easy to find. ⑤ *Rooms from: £128 ✉ 27 Washington St., City Centre* ☎ *0141/222–2929* ⊕ *www.hallmarkhotels.co.uk* ⟿ *129 rooms* ⦿ *Free Breakfast* Ⓜ *St. Enoch.*

Hotel Indigo Glasgow
$$ | HOTEL | In the center of the city, the fashionable Indigo is awash with bold colors and modern designs that emphasize comfort and calm. **Pros:** well-designed rooms; vivid colors, patterns, and lighting; good on-site dining. **Cons:** narrow corridors; only showers in the bathrooms; restaurant has an anonymous, corporate feel. ⑤ *Rooms from: £145 ✉ 75 Waterloo St., City Centre* ☎ *0141/226–7700* ⊕ *www.hinglasgow.co.uk* ⟿ *94 rooms* ⦿ *No meals* Ⓜ *St. Enoch.*

★ Kimpton Blythswood Square
$$ | HOTEL | History and luxury come together at this smart conversion of the former headquarters of the Royal Automobile Club of Scotland, which occupies a classical building on peaceful Blythswood Square. **Pros:** airy and luxurious; glorious bathrooms; great spa, restaurant, and bar. **Cons:** room lighting may be too dim for some; some street noise; the square itself is in need of

some care and attention. ⑤ *Rooms from: £185* ✉ *11 Blythswood Sq., City Centre* ☎ *0141/248–8888* ⊕ *www.kimpton-blythswoodsquare.com* ⌨ *113 rooms* ❍ *Free Breakfast* Ⓜ *Cowcaddens.*

Malmaison Glasgow

$$ | **HOTEL** | Housed in a converted church, this modern boutique hotel prides itself on personal service and outstanding amenities like plasma televisions and high-end stereo systems. **Pros:** stunning lobby; attention to detail; five-minute walk to Sauchiehall Street. **Cons:** bland views; dark hallways; no on-site parking. ⑤ *Rooms from: £129* ✉ *278 W. George St., City Centre* ☎ *0141/572–1000* ⊕ *www.malmaison.com* ⌨ *72 rooms* ❍ *Free Breakfast* Ⓜ *Cowcaddens.*

Premier Inn Glasgow City Centre Buchanan Galleries

$ | **HOTEL** | It would be easy to miss the big City Centre branch of this popular budget hotel chain, since its entrance on Renfield Street is quite small, but it's worth seeking out for its winning location just around the corner from the pedestrian precinct in Sauchiehall Street. **Pros:** great location; bargain rates; modern rooms. **Cons:** some front rooms a bit noisy; entrance easily missed at street level; no parking facilities. ⑤ *Rooms from: £90* ✉ *Buchanan Galleries, 141 W. Nile St., City Centre* ☎ *0871/527–9360* ⊕ *www.premierinn.com* ⌨ *220 rooms* ❍ *No meals* Ⓜ *Buchanan St.*

Radisson Blu Hotel, Glasgow

$$ | **HOTEL** | You can't miss this eye-catching edifice behind Central station: its glass facade makes the interior, particularly the lounge, seem as though it were part of the street. **Pros:** charming kilted doorman; access to gym and pool; free Wi-Fi and other amenities. **Cons:** neighborhood is very busy; most rooms have poor views; no on-site parking. ⑤ *Rooms from: £135* ✉ *301 Argyle St., City Centre* ☎ *0141/204–3333* ⊕ *www.radissonblu.com* ⌨ *250 rooms* ❍ *Breakfast* Ⓜ *St. Enoch.*

Victorian House

$ | **B&B/INN** | This unpretentious hotel sits on a quiet residential area above Sauchiehall Street but still close to Glasgow's Chinatown. **Pros:** appealing and quiet location; basement rooms very spacious; close to bars and restaurants. **Cons:** not all rooms are en-suite; no elevator; on-street parking sometimes difficult to find. ⑤ *Rooms from: £89* ✉ *212 Renfrew St., City Centre* ☎ *0141/332–0129* ⊕ *www.thevictorian.co.uk* ⌨ *56 rooms* ❍ *Free Breakfast* Ⓜ *Cowcaddens.*

Nightlife

BARS AND PUBS

Bloc+

BARS/PUBS | Step behind a curious version of the Iron Curtain where burgers and Tex-Mex diner food mix with an eclectic musical mash of DJs and live rock and folk bands. ✉ *117 Bath St., City Centre* ☎ *0141/574–6066* ⊕ *www.bloc.ru* Ⓜ *Cowcaddens.*

King Tut's Wah Wah Hut

MUSIC CLUBS | An intimate venue showcasing up-and-coming independent bands since 1990, King Tut's Wah Wah Hut claims to have been the venue that discovered the U.K. pop band Oasis. Indeed, the list of those who have played here reads like a catalog of indie music history. It's a favorite with students and hosts live music most nights, but the cozy and traditional pub setting draws people of all ages, and the refurbished bar is a pleasant and comfortable place for a drink or a meal. ✉ *227A St. Vincent St., City Centre* ☎ *0141/221–5279* ⊕ *www.kingtuts.co.uk* Ⓜ *Cowcaddens.*

La Cheetah

MUSIC CLUBS | A tiny club in the basement of Max's Bar, La Cheetah is popular precisely because it's small and intimate. It plays a variety of dance and electronic music, with some surprising well-known guests who just like the atmosphere. ✉ *73 Queen St., City Centre*

🖷 0141/221–1379 ⊕ www.maxsbar.co.uk
Ⓜ Buchanan St.

★ Sloans
BARS/PUBS | One of Glasgow's oldest and most iconic pubs, the wood-paneled Sloans is always lively and welcoming; it serves traditional pub food like fish-and-chips throughout the day. The upstairs ballroom is a magnificent mirrored affair, and on the floor above there's dancing and a *ceilidh*—traditional music and dancing—every Friday night (booking essential). The pub has a good selection of beers and spirits, and the outdoor area is always lively when the weather cooperates. ✉ *108 Argyle St., City Centre* ⊹ *Entrance during the day is through the Argyll Arcade, otherwise from a nearby alley off Argyle St. when the Argyll Arcade is closed.* 🖷 *0141/221–8886* ⊕ *www.sloansglasgow.com* Ⓜ *St. Enoch.*

CLUBS

Argyle Street Arches
DANCE CLUBS | As the name suggests, this enormous and endlessly flexible space occupies the railway arches beneath Glasgow Central station. Most nights it's a popular music venue, but on weekends it becomes a street food market called Platform. Despite its appearance, this industrial space and its glass roof can be a surprisingly intimate place to see a show. ✉ *253 Argyle St., City Centre* 🖷 *1345/6253* ⊕ *argylestarches.com* Ⓜ *St Enoch.*

Stereo
DANCE CLUBS | The small downstairs music venue gets crowded quickly when bands play Sunday to Thursday night, but that only adds to the electric atmosphere at Stereo. There's also a hopping nightclub where DJs spin on Friday and Saturday nights until the wee hours of the morning. Upstairs, the café-bar serves tasty vegan food and organic drinks. ✉ *20–28 Renfield La., City Centre* 🖷 *0141/222–2254* ⊕ *www.stereocafebar.com* Ⓜ *Buchanan St.*

Sub Club
DANCE CLUBS | This atmospheric underground venue has staged cutting-edge music events since its jazz club days in the '50s. Legendary favorites like Saturday's SubCulture (House) and Sunday's Optimo (a truly eclectic mix for musical hedonists) pack in friendly and sweaty crowds on its large dance floor. ✉ *22 Jamaica St., City Centre* 🖷 *0141/248–4600* ⊕ *www.subclub.co.uk* Ⓜ *St. Enoch.*

Swing
MUSIC CLUBS | Hidden behind a narrow doorway on Hope Street, Swing comes as a surprise. It is an art deco bar that has survived the city's changes, and jazz bands play here three times a week. Blues and soul are heard other nights. Cocktails enhance the atmosphere, so go ahead and ask for a Manhattan. ✉ *183A Hope St., City Centre* 🖷 *0141/332–2147* ⊕ *www.swingltd.co.uk* Ⓜ *Buchanan St.*

🎭 Performing Arts

Centre for Contemporary Arts
ART GALLERIES—ARTS | The center hosts regular major art exhibitions and other arts events and regularly screens classic, independent, and children's films. It also has a restaurant, the Saramago, which serves vegan dishes; an upstairs bar; and a very good small independent bookshop. ✉ *350 Sauchiehall St., City Centre* 🖷 *0141/352–4900* ⊕ *www.cca-glasgow.com* Ⓜ *Cowcaddens.*

Cineworld Glasgow
FILM | An 18-screen facility, this is Glasgow's busiest movie multiplex. A glass-walled elevator whisks you to the top of the 170-foot-tall building, which is also the world's tallest cinema. ■ **TIP→ Book your tickets online and collect them from machines at the venue to avoid the often very long queues.** ✉ *7 Renfrew St., City Centre* 🖷 *0871/200–2000* ⊕ *www.cineworld.co.uk* Ⓜ *Cowcaddens.*

★ Glasgow Film Theatre

FILM | An independent operation, the three-screen Glasgow Film Theatre shows the best new releases, documentaries, and classic films. It has several programs for young people and hosts the annual Glasgow Film Festival. ⊠ *12 Rose St., City Centre* ☎ *0141/332–6535* ⊕ *www.glasgowfilm.org* Ⓜ *Cowcaddens.*

Glasgow Royal Concert Hall

CONCERTS | The 2,500-seat Glasgow Royal Concert Hall is the venue for a wide range of concerts, from classical to pop. It also hosts the very popular late-night club during the annual Celtic Connections music festival. ⊠ *2 Sauchiehall St., City Centre* ☎ *0141/353–8000* ⊕ *www.glasgowconcerthalls.com* Ⓜ *Buchanan St.*

King's Theatre

THEATER | Dramas, variety shows, and musicals are staged at the King's Theatre, open since 1904. Check ticket websites to see what's on. ⊠ *297 Bath St., City Centre* ☎ *0141/240–1111* ⊕ *www.atgtickets.com* Ⓜ *Cowcaddens.*

Pavilion Theatre

THEATER | FAMILY | This traditional variety theater hosts family-friendly entertainment, some plays, the occasional hypnotist, and concerts, most with a very strong Glasgow flavor. ⊠ *121 Renfield St., City Centre* ☎ *0141/332–1846* ⊕ *www.paviliontheatre.co.uk* Ⓜ *Cowcaddens.*

Royal Scottish Conservatoire

CONCERTS | An important venue for music and drama, the Royal Scottish Conservatoire hosts regular concerts by well-known performers, as well as by its own students. The lunchtime concert series is popular. ⊠ *100 Renfrew St., City Centre* ☎ *0141/332–4101* ⊕ *www.rcs.ac.uk* Ⓜ *Cowcaddens.*

Theatre Royal

DANCE | Glasgow is home to the Scottish Opera and Scottish Ballet and plays hosts to a range of events throughout the year by visiting dance and theater companies. ⊠ *282 Hope St., City Centre* ☎ *844/871–7647* ⊕ *www.atgtickets.com* Ⓜ *Cowcaddens.*

 # Shopping

ARCADES AND SHOPPING CENTERS

Argyll Arcade

JEWELRY/ACCESSORIES | An interesting diversion off Argyle Street is the covered Argyll Arcade, the region's largest collection of jewelers under one roof. The L-shaped edifice, built in 1827, houses several locally based jewelers and a few shops specializing in antique jewelry, as well as the famed Sloans pub. ⊠ *Buchanan St., City Centre* ⊕ *www.argyll-arcade.com* Ⓜ *St. Enoch.*

Buchanan Galleries

SHOPPING CENTERS/MALLS | Next to the Glasgow Royal Concert Hall, Buchanan Galleries houses the John Lewis department store and more than 80 high-quality shops. ⊠ *220 Buchanan St., City Centre* ☎ *0141/333–9898* ⊕ *www.buchanangalleries.co.uk* Ⓜ *Buchanan St.*

★ Princes Square

SHOPPING CENTERS/MALLS | The city's best shopping center is the art nouveau Princes Square, a lovely space filled with impressive shops and pleasant cafés and restaurants. A stunning glass dome was fitted over the original building, which dates back to 1841. ⊠ *48 Buchanan St., City Centre* ☎ *0141/221–0324* ⊕ *www.princessquare.co.uk* Ⓜ *St. Enoch.*

St. Enoch's Shopping Centre

SHOPPING CENTERS/MALLS | Eye-catching if not especially pleasing, this modern glass building resembles an overgrown greenhouse. It has dozens of stores, including the huge Hamley's toy store. ⊠ *55 St. Enoch Sq., City Centre* ☎ *0141/204–3900* ⊕ *www.st-enoch.com* Ⓜ *St. Enoch.*

BOOKS, PAPER, AND MUSIC
Cass Art Glasgow

CRAFTS | One of the country's largest suppliers of art and craft materials operates this store near the Glasgow Gallery of Modern Art. There's plenty to inspire your creativity, and good choices for kids as well. ⊠ 63–67 Queen St., City Centre ☎ 0141/248–5899 ⊕ www.cassart.co.uk Ⓜ Buchanan St.

Monorail Music

MUSIC STORES | For the latest on the city's ever-thriving music scene, try this independent record store located within a café-bar called Mono, that is also an occasional music venue. The shop specializes in indie music and has a large collection of vinyl with everything from rock to jazz. ⊠ 12 Kings Ct., City Centre ✛ Close to the Tron Theatre ☎ 0141/552–9458 ⊕ www.monorailmusic.com Ⓜ St. Enoch.

Paperchase

BOOKS/STATIONERY | For everything that stationery has to offer—cards, notebooks, books—Paperchase is the place. And there's a café where you can ponder which notebook you want to buy. ⊠ 185–221 Buchanan St., City Centre ☎ 0141/353–3491 ⊕ www.paperchase.co.uk Ⓜ Buchanan St.

Waterstones

BOOKS/STATIONERY | In an age of online sales, bookstores seem to be becoming scarcer. Waterstones remains the city's main bookshop, and it has an excellent selection throughout its four floors. There's also a good basement café. ⊠ 153–57 Sauchiehall St., City Centre ☎ 0141/248–4814 ⊕ www.waterstones.com Ⓜ Buchanan St.

CLOTHING
Mr. Ben

CLOTHING | Here you'll find a large, funky selection of vintage and retro clothing for men and women. ⊠ 6 King's Ct., City Centre ☎ 0141/553–1936 ⊕ mrbenretroclothing.com Ⓜ St. Enoch.

Primark

CLOTHING | Invariably crowded, Primark is a huge store where clothing is sold at marked-down prices. It caters to every generation. ⊠ 56 Argyle St., City Centre ☎ 0141/229–1343 ⊕ www.primark.co.uk Ⓜ St. Enoch.

Zara

CLOTHING | This hugely successful Spanish-owned chain offers high contemporary fashion for men, women, and children at affordable prices. ⊠ 10–16 Buchanan St., City Centre ☎ 0141/227–4770 ⊕ www.zara.com Ⓜ St. Enoch.

DEPARTMENT STORES
Debenham's

DEPARTMENT STORES | One of Glasgow's principal department stores, Debenham's has fine china and crystal as well as women's and men's clothing. ⊠ 97 Argyle St., City Centre ☎ 0844/561–6161 ⊕ www.debenhams.com Ⓜ St. Enoch.

★ House of Fraser

DEPARTMENT STORES | A Glasgow institution, the House of Fraser stocks wares that reflect the city's material aspirations, including European designer clothing. There are also more locally produced articles, such as tweeds, tartans, glass, and ceramics. The magnificent interior is set off by a grand staircase rising to various floors and balconies. ⊠ 21–45 Buchanan St., City Centre ☎ 0343/909–2025 ⊕ www.houseoffraser.co.uk Ⓜ St. Enoch.

John Lewis

DEPARTMENT STORES | This store is a favorite for its stylish mix of clothing, household items, electronics, and practically everything else. John Lewis claims to have "never been knowingly undersold" and prides itself on its customer service. It also has an elegant second-floor balcony café. ⊠ Buchanan Galleries, 220 Buchanan St., City Centre ☎ 0141/353–6677 ⊕ www.johnlewis.com/glasgow Ⓜ Buchanan St.

Marks & Spencer

DEPARTMENT STORES | Selling sturdy, practical clothing and accessories at moderate prices, Marks & Spencer also offers gourmet foods and household goods. There's a second location at 172 Sauchiehall Street. ⊠ *2–12 Argyle St., City Centre* ☎ *0141/552–4546* ⊕ *www.marksandspencer.com* Ⓜ *St. Enoch.*

SCOTTISH SPECIALTIES

Hector Russell Kiltmakers

CLOTHING | Primarily for men, this shop specializes in Highlands outfits, wool, and cashmere clothing. ⊠ *110 Buchanan St., City Centre* ☎ *0141/221–0217* ⊕ *www.hector-russell.com* Ⓜ *Buchanan St.*

Slanj Kilts

CLOTHING | For kilts, trews, and all things tartan, this shop offers a nice variety of traditional Scottish clothing to rent and for sale. ⊠ *49 Bath St., City Centre* ☎ *0333/320–1977* ⊕ *www.slanjkilts.com* Ⓜ *Buchanan St.*

SHOPPING DISTRICTS

Argyle Street

SHOPPING NEIGHBORHOODS | On the often-crowded pedestrian area of Argyle Street you'll find chain stores like Debenham's and some of the more popular and less expensive chains like Gap, Next, and Schuh as well as Primark and H&M. There are current plans for the area to be extended and modernized starting in 2020 and lasting through 2021. ⊠ *City Centre* Ⓜ *St. Enoch.*

Buchanan Street

SHOPPING NEIGHBORHOODS | This pedestrian-only street has become increasingly upmarket, with Monsoon, Topshop, Burberry, Jaeger, Pretty Green, and All Saints as well as House of Fraser and other chain stores along its length. Always crowded with shoppers, it has also become a mecca for the growing community of buskers in Glasgow's streets, playing every kind of music. ⊠ *City Centre* Ⓜ *Buchanan St.*

OUTDOOR GEAR

Tiso Glasgow Outdoor Experience

CLOTHING | You'll find good-quality gear and outerwear at Tiso Glasgow Outdoor Experience, handy if you're planning some Highlands walks or just need protection from the weather. ⊠ *129 Buchanan St., City Centre* ☎ *0141/248–4877* ⊕ *www.tiso.com* Ⓜ *Buchanan St.*

Merchant City

Near the remnants of medieval Glasgow, around Glasgow Cathedral, is the Merchant City, with some of the city's most important 18th-century buildings. Many of them, like the great mansions along Ingram Street, were built by tobacco merchants with profits from the tobacco trade. Today those palatial homes hold restaurants and designer stores; one especially grand example houses the Gallery of Modern Art. Many of Glasgow's young and upwardly mobile have made their home here, in converted buildings ranging from warehouses to the old Sheriff's Court.

GETTING HERE

Buchanan Street is the handiest subway station when you want to explore the Merchant City, as it puts you directly on George Square. You can also easily walk from Central station or the St. Enoch subway station.

 Sights

Gallery of Modern Art (*GoMA*)

MUSEUM | One of Glasgow's boldest, most innovative galleries occupies the neoclassical former Royal Exchange building. The modern art, craft, and design collections include works by Scottish conceptual artists such as David Mach, and also paintings and sculptures from around the world, including Papua New Guinea, Ethiopia, and Mexico. Each floor of the gallery reflects one of the elements—air, fire, earth, and water—which

One of the highlights of Glasgow Cathedral is its 20th-century stained glass windows.

creates some unexpected juxtapositions and also allows for various interactive exhibits. In the basement is a café, a tourist information center, and an extensive library. The building, designed by David Hamilton (1768–1843) and finished in 1829, was first a meeting place for merchants and traders; later it became Stirling's Library. It also incorporates the mansion built in 1780 by William Cunninghame, one of the city's wealthiest tobacco lords. ⊠ *Queen St., Merchant City* ☎ *0141/287–3050* ⊕ *www.glasgow-life.org.uk* ⊠ *Free* Ⓜ *Buchanan St.*

George Square

PLAZA | The focal point of Glasgow is lined with an impressive collection of statues: Queen Victoria; Scotland's national poet, Robert Burns (1759–96); the inventor and developer of the steam engine, James Watt (1736–1819); Prime Minister William Gladstone (1809–98); and, towering above them all atop a column, Scotland's great historical novelist, Sir Walter Scott (1771–1832). That column was originally intended for George III (1738–1820), after whom the square is named, but when he was found to be insane toward the end of his reign, a statue of him was never erected. On the square's east side stands the magnificent Italian Renaissance–style **City Chambers**; the handsome **Merchants' House** fills the corner of West George Street, crowned by a globe and a sailing ship. The fine old Post Office building, now converted into flats, occupies the northern side. There are plenty of benches in the center of the square where you can pause and contemplate. Glasgow's Queen Street Station is on the western corner. ⊠ *Merchant City* ⊠ *Free* Ⓜ *Buchanan St.*

★ Glasgow Cathedral

RELIGIOUS SITE | The most complete of Scotland's cathedrals (it would have been more complete had 19th-century vandals not pulled down its two rugged towers), this is an unusual double church, one above the other, dedicated to Glasgow's patron saint, St. Mungo. Consecrated in 1136 and completed about 300 years later, it was spared the ravages of the

Reformation—which destroyed so many of Scotland's medieval churches—mainly because Glasgow's trade guilds defended it. A late-medieval open-timber roof in the nave and lovely 20th-century stained glass are notable features.

In the lower church is the splendid crypt of St. Mungo, who was originally known as St. Kentigern (*kentigern* means "chief word"), but who was nicknamed St. Mungo (meaning "dear one") by his early followers. The site of the tomb has been revered since the 6th century, when St. Mungo founded a church here. Mungo features prominently in local legends; one such legend is about a pet bird that he nursed back to life, and another tells of a bush or tree, the branches of which he used to miraculously relight a fire. The bird, the tree, and the salmon with a ring in its mouth (from another story) are all found on the city's coat of arms, together with a bell that Mungo brought from Rome. ✉ *Cathedral St., Merchant City* ☎ *0141/552–6891* ⊕ *www.glasgow-cathedral.com* ⌷ *Free* Ⓜ *Buchanan St.*

★ Necropolis

CEMETERY | A burial ground since the beginning of recorded history, the large Necropolis, modeled on the famous Père-Lachaise Cemetery in Paris, contains some extraordinarily elaborate Victorian tombs. A great place to take it all in is from the monument of John Knox (1514–72), the leader of Scotland's Reformation, which stands at the top of the hill at the heart of the Necropolis. Around it are grand tombs that resemble classical palaces, Egyptian tombs, or even the Chapel of the Templars in Jerusalem. You'll also find a smattering of urns and broken columns, the Roman symbol of a great life cut short. The Necropolis was designed as a place for meditation, which is why it is much more than just a graveyard. The main gates are behind the St. Mungo Museum of Religious Life and Art. The Friends of the Necropolis run regular and informative tours, but booking ahead is essential; the tours are free but donations are welcome. ✉ *2 Castle St., Merchant City* ☎ *0141/287–3961* ⊕ *glasgownecropolis. org* ⌷ *Free* Ⓜ *Buchanan St.*

Provand's Lordship

HOUSE | Glasgow's oldest house, one of only four medieval buildings surviving in the city, was built in 1471 by Bishop Andrew Muirhead. Before it was rescued by the Glasgow City Council, this building had been a pub, a sweetshop, and a soft drinks factory. It is now a museum that shows the house as it might have looked when it was occupied by officers of the church. The furniture is 17th century, and the top floor is a gallery with prints and paintings depicting the characters who might have lived in the surrounding streets. Behind the house is a medicinal herb garden, and the cloisters house and its rather disturbing carved stone heads. ✉ *3 Castle St., Merchant City* ☎ *0141/276–1625* ⊕ *www.glasgowlife. org.uk* ⌷ *Free* ⊙ *Closed Mon.* Ⓜ *Buchanan St.*

St. Mungo Museum of Religious Life and Art

MUSEUM | An outstanding collection of artifacts, including Celtic crosses and statuettes of Hindu gods, reflects the many religious groups that have settled throughout the centuries in Glasgow and the west of Scotland. A Zen garden creates a peaceful setting for rest and contemplation, and elsewhere stained-glass windows include a depiction of St. Mungo himself. Pause to look at the beautiful Chilkat Blanketwofven, made from cedar bark and wool by the Tlingit people of North America. ✉ *2 Castle St., Merchant City* ☎ *0141/276–1625* ⊕ *www. glasgowlife.org.uk* ⌷ *Free* ⊙ *Closed Mon.* Ⓜ *Buchanan St.*

🍽 Restaurants

Despite covering a relatively small area, the Merchant City has a wide variety of restaurants. The selection of cafés and eateries includes many budget-friendly options that cater to the working population.

Café Gandolfi

$$ | MODERN BRITISH | Occupying what was once the tea market, this trendy café draws a style-conscious crowd and can justly claim to have launched the dining renaissance of the Merchant City. The café opens early, serving its wonderful signature breakfasts, and the main menu is varied but resolutely Scottish; don't miss the scorched mackerel, the roast rack of Dornoch lamb, or the smoked haddie and Stornaway black pudding. **Known for:** Stornaway black pudding with mushrooms; unique, locally made furniture; intimate second-floor bar offering the same menu. $ *Average main: £15* ⊠ *64 Albion St., Merchant City* ☎ *0141/552–6813* ⊕ *www.cafegandolfi. com* Ⓜ *Buchanan St.*

Corinthian Club

$$ | MODERN BRITISH | Inside what was once the mansion of tobacco merchant George Buchanan, the Corinthian Club includes two bars, a nightclub, and a casino in its maze of rooms. At the heart of the building, the main restaurant, the steak-and-seafood-focused Brasserie makes a dramatic first impression with its glass dome and statues. **Known for:** extravagant central restaurant; range of menus and spaces; spectacular columns under the roof. $ *Average main: £17* ⊠ *191 Ingram St., Merchant City* ☎ *0141/552–1101* ⊕ *www.thecorinthian-club.co.uk* Ⓜ *Buchanan St.*

Hutchesons City Grill

$$$ | BRITISH | Located in another of the Merchant City's iconic buildings, what was originally the 17th-century Hutchesons Hospital, is now an elegant restaurant specializing in steak and seafood. The steaks are sold by weight, while the main menu includes roast monkfish tail alongside an impressive array of beef. **Known for:** subdued elegance in an iconic building; one of Glasgow's best luxurious

dining options; great Sunday roast with champagne. $ *Average main: £20* ⊠ *158 Ingram St., Merchant City* ☎ *0141/552–4050* ⊕ *www.hutchesonsglasgow.com* Ⓜ *Buchanan St.*

★ Kool Ba

$$ | ASIAN FUSION | Thick wooden tables, tapestries, and soft candlelight make you feel at home in the comfortable dining room of this atmospheric haven serving an intriguing mix of Indian and Persian fare. A family-owned restaurant, it's all about healthy, flavorful cooking; chicken tikka masala in a yogurt sauce or lamb korma with coconut cream and fruit or the Persian shashlik are good picks. **Known for:** Indian-Persian fusion cuisine; wide-ranging menu; weekend reservations a must. $ *Average main: £16* ⊠ *109–113 Candleriggs, Merchant City* ☎ *0141/552–2777* ⊕ *www.koolba.com* ☾ *Closed Mon.* Ⓜ *Buchanan St.*

★ Schottische Restaurant at Babbity Bowster's

$$ | MODERN EUROPEAN | This warm and welcoming old merchant's house in the heart of the Merchant City offers excellent Scottish food, a barbecue menu, and a lively charming bar area. On Wednesday or Saturday traditional musicians gather for an impromptu session in the bar; the rest of the time there is just conversation. **Known for:** classy Scottish pub with rooms upstairs to stay the night; traditional Scottish food with a French twist including saddle of Highland deer; convivial bar atmosphere. $ *Average main: £18* ⊠ *16–18 Blackfriars St.* ☎ *0141/552–5055* ⊕ *www.babbity-bowster.com* Ⓜ *Buchanan Street.*

 Hotels

The hotels in the Merchant City are best for those who plan to spend most of their time out and about. In general, this busy area is not the place to come if you want peace and quiet.

Millennium Hotel Glasgow

$ | HOTEL | This huge hotel behind an original Georgian facade occupies almost a whole side of George Square and stretches above the rail station next door. **Pros:** central location; ample comfortable public areas; competitive prices. **Cons:** very long corridors; views of the square only from some (more expensive) rooms; can feel very anonymous. $ *Rooms from: £90* ✉ *40 George Sq., City Centre* ☎ *0141/332–6711* ⊕ *www.millenniumhotels.co.uk* ⇗ *116 rooms* ❍❘ *Free Breakfast* Ⓜ *Buchanan St.*

Moxy Merchant City Hotel

$ | HOTEL | With a youthful, defiantly anti-institutional vibe, the Moxy is perfect for those looking to capture Glasgow's lively energy. **Pros:** simple but comfortable rooms; relaxed informal environment; fun bar great for meeting new people. **Cons:** can get a little rowdy on weekends; surrounding area is a little shabby; grab-and-go food options a little sparse. $ *Rooms from: £90* ✉ *210 High St.* ☎ *0141/846–0256* ⊕ *moxy-hotels. marriott.com/en/hotels/glasgow-merchant-city* ⇗ *81 rooms* ❍❘ *Free Breakfast* Ⓜ *Buchanan Street.*

The Z Hotel Glasgow

$ | HOTEL | Just a few yards from George Square, this good-value modern hotel is one of the newer additions to Merchant City's accommodation options. **Pros:** central location close to Queen Street Station; good beds and bedding; great value. **Cons:** internal rooms have small (or no) windows; no restaurant; no parking facilities. $ *Rooms from: £80* ✉ *36 N. Frederick St., Merchant City* ☎ *0141/212⊞4550* ⊕ *www.thezhotels. com* ⇗ *104 rooms* ❍❘ *No meals.*

Nightlife

BARS AND PUBS

Arta

WINE BARS—NIGHTLIFE | Built on the site of Glasgow's traditional cheese market, Arta has transformed the place into what feels and looks like a Spanish hacienda. It is a labyrinth of different spaces and unexpected rooms on the ground and basement levels, where a live DJ, a salsa night, or a live band might be in action. You can also stay with the cocktails and tapas on the ground floor. ✉ *62 Albion St., Merchant City* ☎ *0141/552–2101* ⊕ *www.arta.co.uk* Ⓜ *Buchanan St.*

Boteco do Brasil

BARS/PUBS | Glasgow's only Brazilian bar-restaurant-club has salsa nights Wednesdays and Latin music to dance to on weekends until 3 am. ✉ *62 Trongate, Merchant City* ☎ *0141/548–1330* ⊕ *www. botecodobrasil.com* Ⓜ *St. Enoch.*

★ Scotia Bar

BARS/PUBS | This place is a survivor of a different, older city, but it offers a taste of an authentic Glasgow pub, with traditional folk music performances happening regularly. Dark wood, a wood-beamed ceiling, and a classic L-shaped bar set the mood. ✉ *112 Stockwell St., Merchant City* ☎ *0141/552–8681* ⊕ *www.scotia-bar-glasgow.co.uk* Ⓜ *St. Enoch.*

CLUBS

Polo Lounge

DANCE CLUBS | Oozing with Edwardian style, the Polo Lounge is Glasgow's largest gay club. Upstairs is a bar that resembles an old-fashioned gentlemen's club. On the two dance floors downstairs, the DJs spin something for everyone. ✉ *84 Wilson St., Merchant City* ☎ *0141/553–1221* ⊕ *www.pologlasgow. co.uk* Ⓜ *Buchanan St.*

Performing Arts

City Halls

CONCERTS | One of the top music venues in the Merchant City, the stone-fronted City Halls hosts orchestral, jazz, and folk concerts. ✉ *Candleriggs, Merchant City* ☎ *0141/353–8000* ⊕ *www.glasgowconcerthalls.com* Ⓜ *Buchanan St.*

Old Fruitmarket

MUSIC CLUBS | A wonderful venue for almost every type of music, this was once the city's fruit and vegetable market. The first-floor balcony, with its intricate iron railings, still carries some of the original merchants' names. It's adjacent to City Halls in the heart of the Merchant City. ✉ *Candleriggs, Merchant City* ☎ *0141/353–8000* ⊕ *www.glasgow-concerthalls.com* Ⓜ *Buchanan St.*

★ Sharmanka Kinetic Theatre

ART GALLERIES—ARTS | **FAMILY** | A unique spectacle, Sharmanka Kinetic Theatre is the brainchild of Eduard Bersudsky, who came to Glasgow from Russia in 1989 to continue making the mechanical sculptures that are his stock in trade. They are witty and sometimes disturbing, perhaps because they are constructed from scrap materials. They move in a kind of ballet to haunting, specially composed music punctuated by a light show. The shows are 45 or 70 minutes. ✉ *103 Trongate, Merchant City* ☎ *0141/552–7080* ⊕ *www.sharmanka.com* 🎫 *£8* Ⓜ *St. Enoch.*

Trongate 103

ART GALLERIES—ARTS | This vibrant contemporary arts center, housed in a converted Edwardian warehouse, is home base for diverse groups producing film, photography, paintings, and prints. It contains the Russian Cultural Centre and the Sharmanka Kinetic Theatre, as well as the Glasgow Print Studio, a well-established outlet for Glasgow artists; Street Level Photoworks, which aims at making photography more accessible; and the Transmission Gallery, a key exhibition space supporting nonconceptual art in the city. ✉ *103 Trongate, Merchant City* ☎ *0141/276–8380* Ⓜ *St. Enoch.*

Tron Theatre

THEATER | Come here for contemporary theater from Scotland and around the world; there are three performance spaces. ✉ *63 Trongate, Merchant City* ☎ *0141/552–4267* ⊕ *www.tron.co.uk* Ⓜ *St. Enoch.*

🛍 Shopping

Many of Glasgow's young and upwardly mobile types make their home in Merchant City. Shopping here is expensive, but the area is worth visiting if you're seeking the youthful Glasgow style.

ANTIQUES AND FINE ART

★ Glasgow Print Studio

ART GALLERIES | Essentially an artists' cooperative, the Glasgow Print Studio's facilities launched a generation of outstanding painters, printers, and designers. The work of members past and present can be seen (and bought) at the Print Studio Gallery on King Street. ✉ *103 Trongate, Merchant City* ☎ *0141/552–0704* ⊕ *www.gpsart.co.uk* Ⓜ *St. Enoch.*

CLOTHING

Cruise

CLOTHING | As one of the first haute couture stores in central Glasgow, Cruise can claim to have launched a new commercial era in the city. It now has two stores in the Merchant City, where its high-fashion clothes and accessories for men and women are beautifully and characteristically displayed to those who can stretch their budgets to its levels. ✉ *180 Ingram St., Merchant City* ☎ *0141/332–5797* ⊕ *www.cruisefashion.com* Ⓜ *Buchanan St.*

Jigsaw

CLOTHING | You'll find a wide and ever-changing range of fashion items for women and men at Jigsaw, well tailored and glamorous but at accessible prices. A U.K.-based chain, its Glasgow store is especially dramatic, occupying one of the tobacco lords' mansions on Ingram Street. ✉ *177 Ingram St., Merchant City* ☎ *0141/552–7639* ⊕ *www.jigsaw-uk.co.uk* Ⓜ *Buchanan St.*

JEWELRY

Orro

JEWELRY/ACCESSORIES | The beautiful and contemporary jewelry here uses modern designs and new materials in unexpected

Locals head to the Botanic Gardens and its Victorian greenhouse on sunny days.

ways. The shop has a gallery feel, and you can browse uninterrupted. ⊠ *12 Wilson St., Merchant City* ☎ *0141/552–7888* ⊕ *www.orro.co.uk* Ⓜ *Buchanan St.*

West End

Glasgow University dominates the West End, creating a vibrant neighborhood. Founded in 1451, the university is the third oldest in Scotland, after St. Andrews and Aberdeen. The industrialists and merchants who built their grand homes on Great Western Road and adjacent streets endowed museums and art galleries and commissioned artists to decorate and design their homes, as a stroll will quickly reveal. In summer the Glasgow Botanic Gardens, with the iconic glasshouse that is the Kibble Palace, becomes a stage for new and unusual versions of Shakespeare's plays. A fun way to save money is to picnic in the park; you can buy sandwiches, salads, and other portable items at shops on Byres Road. Alternatively, stroll past the university

and down Gibson Street and Woodlands Road with their cafés and pubs.

GETTING HERE

The best way to get to the West End from the City Centre is by subway; get off at the Hillhead station. A taxi is another option.

Sights

★ Botanic Gardens

GARDEN | FAMILY | It is a minor Glasgow miracle how as soon as the sun appears, the Botanics (as they're known to locals) fill with people. Beautiful flower displays and extensive lawns create the feeling that this is a large back garden for the inhabitants of the West End's mainly apartment homes. At the heart of the gardens is the spectacular circular greenhouse, the **Kibble Palace,** a favorite haunt of Glaswegian families. Originally built in 1873, it was the conservatory of a Victorian eccentric. Kibble Palace and the other greenhouses contain tree ferns, palm trees, and the Tropicarium, where you can experience the lushness of a rain forest or see its world-famous collection of orchids. There is a tearoom, and in June and July the gardens host presentations of Shakespeare's plays (⊕ *www.bardinthebotanics.co.uk*). ⊠ *730 Great Western Rd., West End* ☎ *0141/276–1614* ⊕ *www.glasgowbotanicgardens.com* ☎ *Free* ⊘ *Closed dusk–7 am* Ⓜ *Hillhead.*

Glasgow University

COLLEGE | Gorgeous grounds and great views of the city are among the many reasons to visit this university. The Gilbert Scott Building, the university's main edifice, is a lovely example of the Gothic Revival style. **Glasgow University Visitor Centre,** near the main gate on University Avenue, has exhibits on the university and a small coffee bar; one-hour guided walking tours of the campus (Thursday–Sunday at 2) start here. A self-guided tour starts at the visitor center and takes in the east and west quadrangles, the cloisters, Professor's Square, Pearce Lodge, and the not-to-be-missed University Chapel. The university's Hunterian Museum and Art Gallery are also well worth a visit. ⊠ *University Ave., West End* ☎ *0141/330–2000* ⊕ *www.glasgow.ac.uk* ☎ *Free* Ⓜ *Hillhead.*

★ Hunterian Art Gallery

MUSEUM | Opposite Glasgow University's main gate, this gallery houses William Hunter's (1718–83) collection of paintings. You'll also find prints, drawings, and sculptures by Tintoretto, Rembrandt, and Auguste Rodin, as well as a major collection of paintings by James McNeill Whistler, who had a great affection for the city that bought one of his earliest paintings. Also in the gallery is a replica of Charles Rennie Mackintosh's town house. Between 1906 and 1914, famed architect Mackintosh and his wife Margaret Macdonald lived at 78 Southpark Avenue, just one street away from where their house has been faithfully rebuilt as part of the gallery. Its stunning rooms contain Mackintosh's art nouveau chairs, tables, beds, and cupboards. The upstairs sitting room, with its famous desk, echoes the Japanese motifs so popular with his generation. Free guided tours are available. ⊠ *Hillhead St., West End* ☎ *0141/330–5431* ⊕ *www.gla.ac.uk/hunterian* ☎ *Free; Macintosh House £6* ⊘ *Closed Mon.* Ⓜ *Hillhead.*

Hunterian Museum

MUSEUM | Set within Glasgow University, this museum, dating from 1807, showcases part of the collections of William Hunter, an 18th-century Glasgow doctor who assembled a staggering quantity of valuable material. Check out Hunter's hoards of coins, manuscripts, scientific instruments, and archaeological artifacts in this striking Gothic building. A permanent exhibit chronicles the building of the Antonine Wall, the Romans' northernmost defense. ⊠ *University Ave., West End* ☎ *0141/330–4221* ⊕ *www.gla.ac.uk/hunterian* ☎ *Free* ⊘ *Closed Mon.* Ⓜ *Hillhead.*

★ Kelvingrove Art Gallery and Museum

MUSEUM | FAMILY | Worthy of its world-class reputation, the Kelvingrove Art Gallery and Museum attracts local families as well as international visitors. This combination of cathedral and castle was designed in the Renaissance style and built between 1891 and 1901. The stunning red-sandstone edifice is an appropriate home for works by Botticelli, Rembrandt, Monet, and others, not to mention the collection of arms and armor. The Glasgow Room houses extraordinary works by local artists. Whether the subject is Scottish culture, design, or storytelling, every room entices you to look deeper; labels are thought-provoking and sometimes witty. You could spend a weekend here, but in a pinch three hours would do one level justice—there are three. Leave time to visit the gift shop and the attractive basement restaurant. Daily free recitals on the magnificent organ (usually at 1) are well worth the trip. ⊠ *Argyle St., West End*

4

Glasgow WEST END

Charles Rennie Mackintosh

Not so long ago, the furniture of innovative Glasgow-born architect Charles Rennie Mackintosh (1868–1928) was broken up for firewood. Today art books are devoted to his distinctive, astonishingly elegant Arts and Crafts—and art nouveau—influenced interiors, and artisans around the world look to his theory that "decoration should not be constructed, rather construction should be decorated" as holy law. Mackintosh's stripped-down designs ushered in the modern age.

An Architect's Career

Mackintosh trained in architecture at the Glasgow School of Art and was apprenticed to the Glasgow firm of John Hutchison at the age of 16. Early influences on his work included the Pre-Raphaelites, James McNeill Whistler (1834–1903), Aubrey Beardsley (1872–98), and Japanese art. But by the 1890s a distinct Glasgow style developed.

The building for the *Glasgow Herald* newspaper, which he designed in 1893, is now the Lighthouse Centre for Architecture, Design, and the City. Other major buildings followed: the Martyrs Public School in Glasgow; Hill House, in Helensburgh, now owned by the National Trust for Scotland; and Queen's Cross Church, completed in 1899 and now the headquarters of the Charles Rennie Mackintosh Society (⊕ *www.crmsociety.com*). In 1897 Mackintosh began work on a new home for the Glasgow School of Art, recognized as one of his major achievements.

Mackintosh married Margaret Macdonald in 1900, and in later years her decorative work enhanced the buildings' interiors. It was she who inspired the Glasgow Girls group of women artists. In 1904 Mackintosh became a partner in Honeyman and Keppie, and in the same year he designed what is now the Scotland Street School Museum. Until 1913, when he moved to England, Mackintosh's projects included buildings over much of Scotland, and their interiors were always part of his overall design.

Commissions in England after 1913 included design challenges not confined to buildings, such as fabrics, furniture, and even bookbindings. After 1904 architectural taste turned against Mackintosh's style, however, his work was seen as strange. Mackintosh could not conform to the times; he lost commissions, drank heavily, and ended up poor and sick. He died in London in 1928. Mackintosh's reputation revived only in the 1950s and has continued to grow over time. It seems fitting that his unique style has become so emblematic of his home city.

How to See His Work

Glasgow is the best place to admire Mackintosh's work. In addition to the buildings mentioned above, most of which can be visited, the Hunterian Art Gallery contains magnificent reconstructions of the Mackintoshes' home at 78 Southpark Avenue, along with original drawings, documents, and records. The Kelvingrove Art Gallery and Museum also has displays of his work in several galleries. His iconic Glasgow School of Art building is being reconstructed after a fire and plans to reopen to visitors in 2020.

☎ 0141/276–9599 ⊕ www.glasgowlife.
org.uk 🖅 Free (some special exhibitions
require admission) Ⓜ Kelvinhall.

Kelvingrove Park

NATIONAL/STATE PARK | FAMILY | Both
a peaceful retreat and a well-used
playground, the park was purchased
by the city in 1852. The River Kelvin
flows through its green spaces. The
park's numerous statues of prominent
Glaswegians include one of Lord Kelvin
(1824–1907), the Scottish mathemati-
cian and physicist remembered for his
pioneering work in electricity. The shady
park has a massive fountain commemorating a lord provost of Glasgow from the
1870s, a duck pond, two children's play-
grounds, and a skateboard park. The An
Clachan café beside the children's play
area is an excellent daytime eatery and a
boon to parents looking for a refuge. Public bowling and croquet greens are free,
as are the tennis courts. The Bandstand,
a 2,300-seat open-air theater, hosts
major concerts in summer. ⊠ Bounded
by Sauchiehall St., Woodlands Rd., and
Kelvin Way, West End ⊕ www.glasgow-
life.org.uk 🖅 Free Ⓜ Kelvinhall.

Mitchell Library

LIBRARY | The largest public reference
library in Europe houses more than a
million items, including what is claimed
to be the world's largest collection about
Robert Burns. The Mitchell also houses
the remarkable private collection of
outstanding puppeteer John Blundell.
Minerva, goddess of wisdom, looks
down from the library's dome, encour-
aging the library's users and frowning at
the drivers thundering along the nearby
motorway. This is a genuinely public
library with open access to all its materi-
als, nearly 100 computers for public use,
and a comfortable on-site café. A bust
in the entrance hall commemorates the
library's founder, Stephen Mitchell, who
died in 1874. The Aye Write Literature
Festival takes place here every March,
as do many other events celebrating

Glasgow's history. ⊠ North St., West End
☎ 0141/287–2999 ⊕ www.glasgowlife.
org.uk 🖅 Free ۞ Closed Sun. Ⓜ St.
George's Cross.

Queen's Cross Church

RELIGIOUS SITE | The only church Mack-
intosh designed houses the Charles
Rennie Mackintosh (CRM) Society Headquarters and is the ideal place to learn
more about the famous Glasgow-born
architect and designer. The church has
beautiful stained-glass windows and a
light-enhancing, carved-wood interior. The
center's library and shop provide further
insight into Glasgow's other Mackin-
tosh-designed buildings. A taxi is probably the best way to get here, but you can
also take a bus toward Queen's Cross
from stops along Hope Street or walk
up Maryhill Road from the St. George's
Cross subway station. ⊠ 870 Garscube
Rd., West End ☎ 0141/946–6600 ⊕ www.
crmsociety.com 🖅 £4; free Wed. after
1 pm ۞ Closed weekends year-round
and Tues. and Thurs. Nov.–Mar. Ⓜ St.
George's Cross.

🍴 Restaurants

Because of Glasgow University, the
eateries in this area were once just the
domain of students and professors. In
recent years this elegant residential area
has also attracted fine restaurants that
appeal to a wide range of visitors.

Balbir's

$$ | INDIAN | Don't let the tinted windows
discourage you: this place is a temple
for pure, healthy Indian food that's
impressive in taste and presentation.
Try the chicken tikka chasni (with mango
chutney, lemon juice, and mint), lamb
korma, or the traditional celebration dish
of Goanese fish curry. **Known for:** healthy
but delicious Indian food; multiple spice
(and heat) combinations; everything on
a grand scale. ⑤ Average main: £17 ⊠ 7
Church St., West End ☎ 0141/339–7711

⊕ *www.balbirs.co.uk* ⊙ *No lunch*
Ⓜ *Kelvinhall.*

Bay Tree

$ | **MIDDLE EASTERN** | This popular small café in the university area is unpretentious and quite cheap. It serves wonderful Middle Eastern food—mostly vegetarian dishes, but there are a few lamb and chicken creations as well. **Known for:** wide variety of meze; Turkish and Lebanese dishes; BYOB-policy (and a great wine store nearby). $ *Average main: £11* ✉ *403 Great Western Rd., West End* ☎ *0141/334–5898* ⊕ *www.thebaytreewestend.co.uk* Ⓜ *Kelvinbridge.*

Bistro du Vin

$$$ | **FRENCH** | Here you can enjoy fine dining in the luxurious surroundings of a grand terrace set back from Great Western Road. Located within the Hotel du Vin, this bistro specializes in French cuisine, with a strong commitment to locally sourced fare. **Known for:** elegant and romantic surroundings; adventurous starters; iconic curries. $ *Average main: £20* ✉ *Hotel du Vin, 1 Devonshire Gardens, West End* ☎ *0141/339–2001* ⊕ *www.hotelduvin.com* Ⓜ *Hillhead.*

Bread Meats Bread

$ | **BURGER** | One of a new breed of burger joints that has emerged in the city, this casual spot with long wooden tables, stools, and benches is also a meeting place for coffee or a drink. The many creatively stuffed burgers and sauces are accompanied by different poutines and cheese toasties, a variation on the British classic known as rarebit. **Known for:** creative and delicious burgers; best poutines outside of Canada; cheerful sociable vibe. $ *Average main: £10* ✉ *701 Great Western Rd., West End* ☎ *0141/648⍰0399* ⊕ *www.breadmeatsbread.com* Ⓜ *Hillhead.*

Cafe Andaluz

$$ | **TAPAS** | With Iberian flair, this lively basement eatery is beautifully decorated using Spanish tiles throughout. The first tapas place to make an impact in Glasgow, it has been followed by others (and has opened a second location in the City Centre) but remains one of the most successful. **Known for:** nice Spanish wine selection; lively but intimate atmosphere; delicious paella. $ *Average main: £15* ✉ *2 Cresswell La., West End* ☎ *0141/339–1111* ⊕ *www.cafeandaluz.com* Ⓜ *Hillhead.*

Cafe Zique

$$ | **BRITISH** | This small but inviting café has a vibrant, bustling atmosphere while remaining unhurried. Its changing breakfast, lunch, and dinner menus of British fare are always fresh and exciting. **Known for:** wonderful breakfasts; tasty sobrasada (a chorizo spread); vibrant atmosphere. $ *Average main: £15* ✉ *66 Hyndland St., West End* ☎ *0141/339–7180* ⊕ *www.cafezique.com* Ⓜ *Hillhead.*

Celino's Deli and Trattoria

$$ | **ITALIAN** | After over 20 years on Glasgow's east side, Celino's has expanded into the city's West End, with a setup that's really two establishments in one. First you enter an overstuffed marketplace, packed from floor-to-ceiling with every conceivable Italian product and an impressive display of take-out antipasti; then, there's the sit-down restaurant, where the range of pastas, risottos, and pizzas is just as varied. **Known for:** classic Italian wines and food; perfect saltimbocca à la romana; open-kitchen setup in the restaurant. $ *Average main: £18* ✉ *235 Dumbarton Rd., West End* ☎ *0141/341–0311* ⊕ *www.celinos.com* Ⓜ *Kelvinhall.*

Hanoi Bike Shop

$$ | **VIETNAMESE** | Glasgow's first Vietnamese canteen offers a different style of dining, which is apparent from the moment you walk through the door and see the rustic setting, low tables, and stools. This is classic street food (all cooked on the premises and arriving when it is ready) and choices include blood sausage with razor clam salad, hot-and-sour fish soup, and plenty of pho, the fragrant Vietnamese soup with noodles and sliced meat.

Known for: excellent pho; street food in small plates; organic tofu options. $ *Average main: £15* ✉ *8 Ruthven La., West End* ✛ *Down the alley opposite Hillhead subway station* ☎ *0141/334–7165* ⊕ *hanoibikeshop.co.uk* Ⓜ *Hillhead.*

The Left Bank

$$ | ECLECTIC | Close to Glasgow University, this popular bar and restaurant attracts a more mature student crowd. It's an airy spot with high ceilings, leather sofas, and wood floors, and the specialty is good, eclectic international food at reasonable prices. **Known for:** delicious small plates of varied cuisine; casual atmosphere; tasty brunch. $ *Average main: £15* ✉ *33–35 Gibson St., West End* ☎ *0141/339–5969* ⊕ *www.theleftbank. co.uk* Ⓜ *Kelvinbridge.*

Little Italy

$ | ITALIAN | FAMILY | Offering all things Italian, this constantly busy, noisy, and extremely friendly café sits in the heart of the West End. Its pizzas, made on the premises while you wait with a coffee or a glass of Italian wine, are probably the best around, and the house-made pastas are just as consistently good. **Known for:** perhaps Glasgow's best pizza; wide variety of Italian wines; perfect tiramisu for dessert. $ *Average main: £14* ✉ *205 Byres Rd., West End* ☎ *0141/339–6287* ⊕ *littleitalyglasgow.com* Ⓜ *Hillhead.*

Number Sixteen

$$ | BRITISH | This tiny, intimate restaurant serves only the freshest ingredients, superbly prepared, on a constantly changing menu. Halibut is served with choucroute and a passion-fruit dressing—a typically unpredictable meeting of flavors. **Known for:** excellent set menus; surprising flavor combinations; cozy interior, so reservations are a good idea. $ *Average main: £18* ✉ *16 Byres Rd., West End* ☎ *0141/339–2544* ⊕ *www. number16.co.uk* Ⓜ *Kelvin Hall.*

★ Stravaigin

$$$ | ECLECTIC | For many years Stravaigin has maintained the highest quality of cooking, creating adventurous dishes that often combine Asian and local flavors and unusual marriages of ingredients. You can try the *piri piri* quail (the seasoning is used in Africa) or the restaurant's famous haggis and neeps (turnips), symbolizing its commitment to local produce. **Known for:** buzzy bar with a quieter restaurant downstairs; classic haggis and neeps; daily-changing curry option. $ *Average main: £20* ✉ *28 Gibson St., West End* ☎ *0141/334–2665* ⊕ *www.stravaigin. co.uk* Ⓜ *Kelvinbridge.*

Ubiquitous Chip

$$$ | MODERN BRITISH | Occupying a converted stable behind the Hillhead subway station on busy Ashton Lane, this restaurant is a Glasgow institution, with an untarnished reputation for creative Scottish cooking. Its street-level restaurant is a beautiful courtyard protected by a glass roof, and the more informal brasserie upstairs also serves less expensive dishes like haggis with neeps and tatties or a plate of mussels. **Known for:** creative Scottish cuisine like venison haggis; popular upstairs bar great for socializing; lovely courtyard. $ *Average main: £24* ✉ *12 Ashton La., West End* ☎ *0141/334–5007* ⊕ *www.ubiquitouschip.co.uk* Ⓜ *Hillhead.*

Wudon

$ | JAPANESE | Pleasant and relaxed, this Japanese restaurant with white walls, simple furniture, subdued lighting, and a large window onto the street offers beautifully prepared food presented with great charm by the staff. Whether your taste is for hearty broths, just-made sushi, or savory rice and noodle dishes, the chef will combine the elements to your taste. **Known for:** noodle broth bowls; huge sushi menu; reasonable prices, including a great weekday lunch special. $ *Average main: £11* ✉ *535 Great Western Rd.,*

West End ☎ 0141/357–3033 ⊕ www.
wudon-noodlebar.co.uk Ⓜ Kelvinbridge.

 # Hotels

Many lodgings are on quieter Great
Western Road, set apart from busy Byres
Road.

Amadeus Guest House

$ | B&B/INN | This attractive Victorian town
house has comfortably furnished rooms
that are flooded with plenty of natural
light. **Pros:** near West End attractions;
two-minute walk from subway; kids
under six free. **Cons:** some rooms small;
finding parking sometimes difficult; a bit
pricey for the location. ⑤ Rooms from:
£108 ✉ 411 N. Woodside Rd., West End
☎ 0141/339–8257 ⊕ www.amadeus-
guesthouse.co.uk ↩ 9 rooms ⑩ Free
Breakfast Ⓜ Kelvinbridge.

Ambassador Hotel

$ | HOTEL | FAMILY | Opposite the West
End's peaceful Glasgow Botanic Gardens, this hotel is within minutes of
busy Byres Road yet well away from its
noisy weekend activity. **Pros:** views of
Botanic Gardens; great for families with
kids; five-minute walk to public transportation and West End amenities. **Cons:** no
elevator; on-street parking difficult after
6 pm; on the corner of a fairly busy road.
⑤ Rooms from: £82 ✉ 7 Kelvin Dr., West
End ☎ 0141/946–1018 ⊕ www.ambas-
sador-hotel.net ↩ 26 rooms ⑩ Free
Breakfast Ⓜ Hillhead.

Clifton Hotel

$ | HOTEL | Occupying two of the grand
houses along a collection of town houses
above Great Western Road, this popular
hotel offers wallet-friendly rates and simply furnished rooms done up in cheerful
shades. **Pros:** conveniently located; free
Wi-Fi; good budget option. **Cons:** basic
amenities; no elevator; some rooms
have a shared bathroom. ⑤ Rooms
from: £59 ✉ 26–27 Buckingham Terr.,
West End ☎ 0141/334–8080 ⊕ www.

cliftonhotelglasgow.co.uk ↩ 26 rooms
⑩ Free Breakfast Ⓜ Hillhead.

Heritage Hotel

$ | HOTEL | This small, unpretentious, but
well-established hotel in a very central
West End location has cozy, simply decorated rooms. **Pros:** very good location;
lovely breakfast; on a quiet street. **Cons:**
rooms quite small; no parking spaces and
on-street parking is expensive; main road
can get noisy. ⑤ Rooms from: £80 ✉ 4/5
Albert Terr., West End ✛ Entrance by
Hillhead St. ☎ 0141/339–6955 ⊕ www.
theheritagehotel.net ↩ 27 rooms ⑩ Free
Breakfast Ⓜ Hillhead.

Hilton Glasgow Grosvenor

$ | HOTEL | Behind a row of grand terrace
houses, this modern hotel overlooks the
Glasgow Botanic Gardens. **Pros:** close
to Byres Road; some rooms have good
views; tasty restaurant. **Cons:** rooms at
the back overlook a parking lot; a rather
institutional feel; Wi-Fi in guest rooms
costs extra. ⑤ Rooms from: £111 ✉ 1–9
Grosvenor Terr., West End ☎ 0141/339–
8811 ⊕ hiltongrosvenor.com-glasgow.
com ↩ 96 rooms ⑩ Free Breakfast
Ⓜ Hillhead.

★ Hotel du Vin Glasgow

$$ | HOTEL | Consisting of a group of
Victorian houses on a tree-lined street,
well away from the bustle of Byres
Road, this hotel is all about elegance,
from the sophisticated drawing room to
the individually decorated guest rooms
with flowing draperies, Egyptian linens,
and mahogany furnishings like four-post-
er beds. **Pros:** stunning Scottish-style
rooms; understated luxury; complimen-
tary whisky on arrival. **Cons:** no elevator;
on-street parking can be difficult after 6
pm; a little too much tartan in the decor.
⑤ Rooms from: £146 ✉ 1 Devonshire
Gardens, West End ☎ 0330/016–0390
⊕ www.hotelduvin.com ↩ 49 rooms
⑩ Free Breakfast Ⓜ Hillhead.

171

Nightlife

BARS AND PUBS

Dram!

BARS/PUBS | With mismatched furnishings and the odd stag's head on the wall, the four large rooms here are decorated in a style that can only be described as "ultra eclectic." It's no place for a quiet, intimate evening, but Dram feels like a traditional bar while being brashly youthful and up-to-the-minute. There's a wide range of beers, and the place takes special pride in the 75 whiskies. On Thursday and Sunday, musicians gather in an informal jam session. Food is served every night until 9. ✉ *232–246 Woodlands Rd., West End* ☎ *0141/332–1622* ⊕ *www.dramglasgow.co.uk* Ⓜ *Kelvinbridge.*

Òran Mór

BARS/PUBS | At the top of Byres Road, Òran Mór has estabished itself as the heart of West End nightlife. Located in what was once a church, it still has beautiful stained-glass windows and a lovely nave gloriously decorated by outstanding Glasgow artist Alasdair Gray. The bar fills with different types of people at different times of day, but its late license means crowds surge Friday and Saturday nights. In the basement, the hugely successful lunchtime theater series "A Play, a Pie, and a Pint" plays to capacity crowds. It also houses a busy bistro, a brasserie, and an evening music venue, as well as a late-night club. The small beer garden fills up quickly in good weather. ✉ *731 Great Western Rd., West End* ☎ *0141/357–6200* ⊕ *www.oran-mor.co.uk* Ⓜ *Hillhead.*

Tennents

BARS/PUBS | A spacious corner bar, Tennents prides itself on its comprehensive selection of beers. You can expect lively conversation, as there's a refreshing lack of loud music. ✉ *191 Byres Rd., West End* ☎ *0141/341–1021* ⊕ *www.thetennentsbarglasgow.co.uk* Ⓜ *Hillhead.*

COMEDY CLUBS

Stand Comedy Club

COMEDY CLUBS | In the basement of a former school, the Stand Comedy Club has live shows every night of the week and is most popular on Thursday and Friday. Prices vary according to who is appearing, and the doors open at 7:30. ✉ *333 Woodlands Rd., at Park Rd., West End* ☎ *0141/212–3389* ⊕ *www.thestand. co.uk* Ⓜ *Kelvingrove.*

Performing Arts

Grosvenor

FILM | This popular, compact cinema has two screens and extremely comfortable leather seats (some of them big enough for two). It's part of a small complex in the always busy Ashton Lane, immediately behind the subway station, that also includes bars, cafés, and restaurants. ✉ *Ashton La., West End* ☎ *0845/339–8444* ⊕ *www.grosvenorcafe.co.uk* Ⓜ *Hillhead.*

★ A Play, a Pie, and a Pint

THEATER | In a former church, Glasgow's hugely successful lunchtime theater series called "A Play, a Pie, and a Pint" (and you do get all three) showcases new writing from Scotland and elsewhere. ■TIP➔ **Performances sell out quickly, particularly late in the week, so book well in advance on the website.** Doors open at 12:15 pm and shows begin at 1 pm Monday through Saturday. ✉ *Òran Mór, 731 Great Western Rd., Byres Rd. and Great Western Rd., West End* ☎ *0141/357–6200* ⊕ *www.playpiepint.com* Ⓜ *Hillhead.*

Shopping

BOOKS, PAPER, AND MUSIC

Caledonia Books

BOOKS/STATIONERY | This well-organized and well-stocked secondhand bookstore fills the gap left by the departure of other bookstores. The owners are knowledgeable and willing to search for even the most obscure volumes. ✉ *483 Great*

4

Glasgow WEST END

Western Rd., West End ☎ 0141/334–
9663 ⊕ www.caledoniabooks.co.uk
Ⓜ Kelvinbridge.

Fopp
MUSIC STORES | This funky shop is an
extravaganza of music, books, and DVDs.
It's a small space, but the selection is
huge. The prices are a lot more reasonable than those at most other chain
stores. ⊠ 358 Byres Rd., West End
☎ 0141/222–2128 ⊕ www.fopp.com
Ⓜ Hillhead.

CLOTHING
Charles Clinkard
SHOES/LUGGAGE/LEATHER GOODS | This
traditional shoe store—a rare thing
these days—has an impressive range of
choices, often unusual lines, principally
for women but for men, too. There are
also regular bargains here, and the staff
knows their shoes. ⊠ 149 Byres Rd.,
West End ☎ 0345/241–7742 ⊕ www.
charlesclinkard.co.uk Ⓜ Hillhead.

Glasgow Vintage Co.
CLOTHING | You can find plenty of genuine
bargains here for upmarket vintage
clothes at down-market prices. There
are choices for men, women, and
children from the 1950s to the 1980s.
⊠ 453 Great Western Rd., West End
☎ 0141/338–6633 ⊕ www.glasgowvin-
tage.co.uk.

Strawberry Fields
CLOTHING | Designer clothing for children
is the specialty of Strawberry Fields.
⊠ 517 Great Western Rd., West End
☎ 0141/339–1121 Ⓜ Kelvinbridge.

FOOD
Demijohn
FOOD/CANDY | Specializing in infused
wines, spirits, oils, and vinegars, Demi-
john calls itself a "liquid deli."⊠ 382 Byres
Rd., West End ☎ 0141/337–3600 ⊕ www.
demijohn.co.uk Ⓜ Hillhead.

Iain Mellis Cheesemonger
FOOD/CANDY | This shop has a superb,
seemingly endless selection of fine

Scottish cheeses, in addition to others
from England and across Europe, as well
as bread and olives. ⊠ 492 Great Western
Rd., West End ☎ 0141/339–8998 ⊕ www.
mellischeese.net Ⓜ Kelvinbridge.

HOME FURNISHINGS AND TEXTILES
Nancy Smillie
HOUSEHOLD ITEMS/FURNITURE | Local to
the floorboards, Nancy Smillie is a
one-of-a-kind boutique that sells unique
glassware, jewelry, and furnishings. It
also runs a jewelry boutique at 425 Great
Western Road. ⊠ 53 Cresswell St., West
End ☎ 0141/334–0055 ⊕ www.nancys-
millieshop.com Ⓜ Hillhead.

Time and Tide
HOUSEHOLD ITEMS/FURNITURE | Loosely
described as a household goods store,
Time and Tide sells an eclectic mix of
lamps and candleholders and cushions
and things you never realized you needed
until you see them. ⊠ 398 Byres Rd.,
West End ☎ 0141/357–4548 ⊕ www.
timeandtidestores.co.uk Ⓜ Hillhead.

Finnieston

The River Clyde has long been the city's
main artery, bearing Clyde-built ships,
from warships to ocean liners, to the
sea. Few of the yards remain open, and
the Finnieston Crane, which once moved
locomotives onto ships, is no longer
active. But the area around it, bounded
by the river on one side and Sauchiehall
Street on the other, has undergone a
great transformation since the 1990s.
The riverside has been reborn, with
Zaha Hadid's Transport Museum and the
Tall Ship, as well as the Scottish Event
Campus (SEC) occupying pride of place
on the Finnieston bank and the Science
Museum on the opposite side. The SSE
Hydro, an ultramodern concert arena, has
generated a new fashionable strip of bars
and restaurants along Argyle Street as
well as several new hotels.

GETTING HERE

From the Partick subway station it's a 10-minute walk to the Riverside Museum. From that museum it's a short stroll along the river (and across a bridge) to the Glasgow Science Centre. Argyle Street is a short walk from Kelvin Hall subway station or across Kelvingrove Park from Glasgow University.

◉ Sights

Glasgow Science Centre

MUSEUM | FAMILY | Fun and engaging, this museum for children has three floors packed with games, experiments, and hands-on machines from pendulums to small-scale whirlpools, soundscapes to optical illusions. Its space-age home on the south side of the Clyde has a whole wall of glass looking out onto the river. The *BodyWorks* exhibition explores every aspect of our physical selves—you can even try and reconstruct a brain. There are daily events and science shows, a lovely play area for under-sevens, a planetarium, an IMAX theater, and the spectacular Glasgow Tower, 400 feet high, where you can survey the whole city from the river to the surrounding hills. All carry an additional charge. Always inquire whether the tower is open—even moderate winds will close it down. ■ TIP→ **Admission is expensive, but the tower and planetarium cost less if you buy all the tickets at the same time.** ✉ *50 Pacific Quay, Finnieston* ☎ *0141/420–5000* ⊕ *www.glasgowsciencecentre. org* ✆ *£11.50; planetarium £2.70 with museum admission; Glasgow Tower £3.15 with museum admission; Tower only £6.50* ⊗ *Closed Mon., Tues., and Thurs. Nov.–Mar.* Ⓜ *Cessnock.*

★ Riverside Museum: Scotland's Museum of Transport and Travel

MUSEUM | FAMILY | Designed by Zaha Hadid to celebrate the area's industrial heritage, this huge metal structure with curving walls echoes the covered yards where ships were built on the Clyde. Glasgow's shipbuilding history is remembered with a world-famous collection of ship models. Locomotives built at the nearby St. Rollox yards are also on display, as are cars from every age and many countries. You can wander down Main Street, circa 1930, without leaving the building: the pawnbroker, funeral parlor, and Italian restaurant are all frozen in time. Relax with a coffee in the café, wander out onto the expansive riverside walk, or board the Tall Ship that is moored permanently behind the museum. Take Bus 100 from the City Centre, or walk from Partick subway station. ✉ *100 Poundhouse Pl., Finnieston* ☎ *0141/287–2720* ⊕ *www.glasgowlife. org.uk* ✆ *Free* Ⓜ *Partick.*

Tall Ship at Riverside

LIGHTHOUSE | FAMILY | Built in 1896, this fine tall sailing ship now sits on the River Clyde immediately behind the Riverside Museum. The *Glenlee* once belonged to the Spanish Navy (under a different name), but carried cargo all over the world in her day. She returned to Glasgow and the River Clyde in 1993, and now forms part of the museum. You can wander throughout this surprisingly large cargo ship with or without an audio guide, peer into cabins and holds, and stand on the forecastle as you gaze down the river (but bring your own binoculars). Bus 100 from George Square brings you here, or you can walk from the Partick subway station in 10 minutes. ✉ *150 Pointhouse Pl., Finnieston* ☎ *0141/357–3699* ⊕ *www.thetallship.com* ✆ *Free* Ⓜ *Partick.*

🍴 Restaurants

A small strip of Argyle has been transformed into an exciting new restaurant area, dominated by seafood restaurants, hip steak houses, old pubs transformed into trendy cocktail bars, and small-plate innovators. It caters to the visitors brought in by the music arena and the riverside development.

West End and Finnieston

KEY
- ① Exploring Sights
- ① Restaurants
- ① Hotels

Sights ▼

1 Botanic Gardens........ **E2**
2 Glasgow
   Science Centre **D7**
3 Glasgow University..... **F5**
4 Hunterian Art Gallery... **F4**
5 Hunterian Museum..... **F5**
6 Kelvingrove Art Gallery
   and Museum **F6**
7 Kelvingrove Park....... **G6**
8 Mitchell Library **I7**
9 Queen's Cross Church ... **I2**
10 Riverside Museum:
   Scotland's Museum of
   Transport and Travel ... **B7**
11 Tall Ship at Riverside ... **B7**

Restaurants ▼

1 Baffo **E6**
2 Balbir's **D5**
3 Bay Tree **H4**
4 Bistro du Vin............ **C1**
5 Bread Meats Bread **F3**
6 The Brunch Club........ **E6**
7 Butchershop
   Bar and Grill............. **F6**
8 Cafe Andaluz **E3**
9 Cafe Zique **C4**
10 Celino's Deli
   and Trattoria............. **C5**
11 Crabshakk **G7**
12 The Finnieston **G7**

| F | G | H | I | J |

Baffo

$ | **ITALIAN** | There has been something of an explosion of new pizzerias in Glasgow, many of them newer chains, but Baffo has made its mark and won approval from a demanding audience. Not only are the pizzas beautifully crispy and varied, they are also very large: if you need a half-meter of pizza (about 1½ feet), it's available as an economical choice. **Known for:** famous half-meter pizza; busy but friendly atmosphere; good pasta at decent prices. $ *Average main: £10* ⊠ *1377 Argyle St., Finnieston* ☎ *0141/583–0000* ⊕ *www.baffo.co.uk* Ⓜ *Kelvin Hall.*

The Brunch Club

$ | **CAFÉ** | The name says it all: this pleasant, airy café pays homage to all things brunch. There are eggs in every combination, decadent waffles and French toast, and a delicious array of classic brunch cocktails from Bloody Marys to mimosas. **Known for:** best brunch in Glasgow; great cocktails; relaxing vibe. $ *Average main: £9* ⊠ *67 Old Dumbarton Rd., Finnieston* ☎ *0141/237–7374* ⊕ *www.thebrunchclub. co* ⊘ *No dinner* Ⓜ *Kelvin Hall.*

Butchershop Bar and Grill

$$ | **STEAKHOUSE** | An early arrival in the redeveloping Finnieston area, Butchershop occupies what was once a pub and overlooks the bowling greens in Kelvingrove Park. Modern, open, and airy, it preserves the sociable atmosphere of its predecessor, though it is now a quality steak house offering a range of cuts from rump to T-bone. **Known for:** steaks of every variety; good value fixed-price menus; publike atmosphere. $ *Average main: £19* ⊠ *1055 Sauchiehall St., Finnieston* ☎ *0141/339–2999* ⊕ *www.butchershop-glasgow.com* Ⓜ *Kelvin Hall.*

★ Crabshakk

$$ | **SEAFOOD** | Anything but a shack, this intimate dining room has heavy wooden tables and chairs, an elegantly ornate ceiling, and a bar so shiny and inviting that it seems to almost insist you have a drink. The food comes from the sea—oysters, lobster, and squid—and you can have your choice served iced, grilled, roasted, or battered. **Known for:** local and sustainably sourced Scottish seafood; art deco decor; reservations essential. $ *Average main: £15* ⊠ *1114 Argyle St., Finnieston* ☎ *0141/334–6127* ⊕ *www. crabshakk.com* Ⓜ *Kelvin Hall.*

★ The Finnieston

$$ | **SEAFOOD** | A 19th-century inn turned into an elegant restaurant, the Finnieston retains the dark wood and narrow cubicles of earlier times, but today it is one of the new high-quality seafood restaurants that have transformed the faded Finnieston area into a fashionable district. The menu allows you to choose the fish and how it is prepared, the sauce, and salad or vegetable sides. **Known for:** impressive seafood cuisine; stunning array of cocktails; comfy wooden booths. $ *Average main: £18* ⊠ *1125 Argyle St., Finnieston* ☎ *0141/222–2884* ⊕ *www.thefinnieston-bar.com* Ⓜ *Kelvin Hall.*

The Gannet

$$$ | **MODERN EUROPEAN** | One of the early occupants of the new Finnieston, the Gannet has maintained its stellar reputation. Its comfortable wood-and-brick interior denotes the emphasis on the natural provenance and unencumbered presentation of their food. **Known for:** varied seafood menu; tasting menus for both carnivores and vegetarians; local produce. $ *Average main: £20* ⊠ *1155 Argyle St., Finnieston* ☎ *0141/204–2081* ⊕ *www.thegannetgla.com* ⊘ *Closed Mon. No lunch Tues. and Wed.* Ⓜ *Kelvin Hall.*

Mother India

$$ | **INDIAN** | The brand known as Mother India really covers four adjacent restaurants rather than just one location, all highlighting small plates of impressive Indian cuisine. What makes this place across from Kelvingrove Art Gallery so popular is the combination of high-quality cooking and an extensive range of tastes,

from the vegetarian dal to spicy ginger chicken. **Known for:** casual small-plate Indian food; no reservations, which means there are crowds and usually some wait; BYOB policy. $ *Average main: £15* ⊠ *1355 Argyle St., Clyde* ☎ *0141/339–9145* ⊕ *www.motherindiaglasgow.co.uk* Ⓜ *Kelvin Hall.*

★ Ox and Finch

$$$ | ECLECTIC | This immensely popular restaurant shines at every level—service, presentation, and taste. The stripped-back, rustic decor encourages chatter and the sharing of the eclectic small plates that are its specialty. **Known for:** small-plates dining with a wide variety of options; relaxed and buzzy atmosphere; huge wine list. $ *Average main: £20* ⊠ *920 Sauchiehall St., Finnieston* ☎ *0141/339–8627* ⊕ *www.oxandfinch.com* Ⓜ *Kelvin Hall.*

Rioja

$$ | SPANISH | Rioja belongs to the second generation of tapas restaurants, combining classic small plates with new and innovative interpretations. At this dark, rustic spot with exposed brick, wood floors, and dark walls, *patatas riojanas* go a stage beyond *patatas bravas,* adding pork and chorizo, while the spring lamb with almond crust adds new flavors. **Known for:** contemporary take on tapas; good Spanish wines; late-night dining. $ *Average main: £15* ⊠ *1116 Argyle St., Clyde* ☎ *0141/334–0761* ⊕ *www.riojafinnieston.co.uk* Ⓜ *Kelvin Hall.*

The Sisters Kelvingrove

$$$ | BRITISH | Walk up the smooth sandstone steps to this restaurant, which aims to inspire your palate with a menu that is locally sourced and always changing; a typical dish might be Carluke ham with buttered savoy cabbage and colcannon mash. Douglas Gray tartan pads the pristine room, and polished floorboards reflect the natural light shining in from the long windows around the unusual oval-shaped room. **Known for:** fine Scottish cooking carefully sourced;

intimate and stylish decor; homegrown Arran-gooseberry fool for dessert. $ *Average main: £20* ⊠ *36 Kelvingrove St., Finnieston* ☎ *0141/564–1157* ⊕ *www.thesisters.co.uk* Ⓜ *Kelvin Hall.*

Six by Nico

$$$ | BRITISH | In a street of adventurous eateries, Six by Nico adds a new dimension of fun and wit. The concept at this intimate, modern restaurant with black tile, wood floors and tables, and black chairs is a six-course tasting menu linked to a theme that changes every six weeks, whether it's fish-and-chips or Route 66, with dishes that deconstruct and reconstruct the familiar. **Known for:** highly original approach to a tasting menu; imaginative dishes (with wine-pairing option); reservations essential. $ *Average main: £25* ⊠ *1132 Argyle St., Finnieston* ☎ *0141/334⦿5661* ⊕ *www.sixbynico.co.uk* ⊘ *Closed Mon.* Ⓜ *Kelvin Hall.*

🛏 Hotels

Besides a handful of interesting museums and a popular cluster of busy bars and restaurants, this up-and-coming area near the river also has a few lodgings, mostly on Sauchiehall Street.

Argyll Guest House

$ | B&B/INN | In this budget-minded annex to the Argyll Hotel, across the road on Sauchiehall Street, the rooms are plainly furnished but scrupulously clean. **Pros:** close to Kelvingrove Park and public transportation; tasty breakfast; bargain prices. **Cons:** front rooms noisy on weekends; no elevator; basic amenities. $ *Rooms from: £65* ⊠ *966–970 Sauchiehall St., Finnieston* ☎ *0141/357–5155* ⊕ *www.argyllhotelglasgow.co.uk* ⊷ *20 rooms* ⦿❙ *Free Breakfast* Ⓜ *Kelvin Hall.*

Argyll Hotel

$ | HOTEL | The tartan in the reception area reflects the clan theme throughout the hotel; each room is named after a clan, but each is also very different from the next. **Pros:** centrally located; comfortable rooms; reasonable prices. **Cons:** street can get noisy on weekends; metered parking on the street; downstairs breakfast area and bar need refurbishing. $ Rooms from: £79 ⊠ 973 Sauchiehall St., Finnieston ☎ 0141/337–3313 ⊕ www.argyllhotelglasgow.co.uk ⇥ 38 rooms ⊙| Free Breakfast Ⓜ Kelvin Hall.

Hilton Garden Inn Glasgow City Centre
$ | HOTEL | Overlooking the Clyde, this hotel is within sight of the SSE Hydro entertainment arena and a short walk along the water from the Riverside Museum, and a slightly longer walk from Argyle Street in Finnieston. **Pros:** convenient location; lovely terrace; some great views. **Cons:** isolated from the rest of the city; no nearby metro; prices rise if there is a performance at the Hydro. $ Rooms from: £87 ⊠ Finnieston Quay, Finnieston ☎ 0141/240–1002 ⊕ www3.hilton.com ⇥ 164 rooms ⊙| Breakfast.

Radisson Red
$ | HOTEL | Located within the increasingly busy Finnieston Quay area, the stylish rooms here have large windows that take full advantage of the river view, which can be more fully enjoyed from the ninth-floor rooftop bar. **Pros:** close to all riverside amenities; fun rooftop bar overlooking the river; riverside rooms have lovely views. **Cons:** not all rooms have riverside views; reception area can be confusing; not the easiest area to get to by public transport. $ Rooms from: £108 ⊠ Finnieston Quay, 25 Tunnel St., Finnieston ☎ 0141/471–1700 ⊕ www.radissonhotels.com/en-us/hotels/radisson-red-glasgow ⇥ 174 rooms.

The Sandyford
$ | HOTEL | The Victorian exterior of this hotel anticipates the colorful decor you'll find inside, where the large windows in the reception area let in lots of light. **Pros:** extremely well located; minutes from several good restaurants; very competitive prices. **Cons:** front rooms can get late-night noise; no elevator; parking on

the street is metered. $ Rooms from: £54 ⊠ 904 Sauchiehall St., Finnieston ☎ 0141/334–0000 ⊕ www.sandyford-hotelglasgow.com ⇥ 55 rooms ⊙| Free Breakfast Ⓜ Kelvin Hall.

Nightlife

BARS AND PUBS
Ben Nevis
BARS/PUBS | A traditional pub still holding its own on the trendy Finnieston strip, this eccentric spot is full of Highland artifacts. There are more than 180 whiskies from which to choose and traditional live music on Wednesday, Thursday, and Sunday. ⊠ 1147 Argyle St., Finnieston ☎ 0141/576–5204 ⊕ www.thebennevis.co.uk Ⓜ Kelvinhall.

78
BARS/PUBS | Enjoy cozy sofas, a real coal fire, and tasty vegan food throughout the day. There's live music every night, with jazz on Sunday. ⊠ 10–14 Kelvinhaugh St., Finnieston ☎ 0141/576–5018 ⊕ www.the78cafebar.com Ⓜ Kelvinhall.

Performing Arts

SEC Armadillo
CONCERTS | The 3,000-seat riverside SEC is known as the Armadillo for its distinctive, curved design by Norman Foster. It hosts large-scale pop concerts and other events. ⊠ Exhibition Way, Finnieston ⊹ Train to Exhibition Centre station from Glasgow Central Low Level station ☎ 0141/248–3000 ⊕ www.sec.co.uk.

SSE Hydro
CONCERTS | This dramatic addition to the banks of the Clyde is a 12,000-seat arena under a silver dome. Built for the 2014 Commonwealth Games, it has proved enormously popular as a music and event venue. ⊠ SEC Exhibition Way, Finnieston ☎ 0844/395–4000 ⊕ www.thessehydro.com.

Nelson Column towers over Glasgow Green, the city's oldest park.

East End

Glasgow Green has always been the heart of Glasgow's East End, a formerly down-at-heel neighborhood that has seen many changes over time. One of the top attractions is the People's Palace, which tells the story of daily life in the city. On Sunday head to the nearby Barras market to hunt for bargains.

GETTING HERE

To get to the East End, take the subway to the St. Enoch station and walk along Argyle Street to the Tron Cross. From there, London Road takes you to Glasgow Green.

 ## Sights

Glasgow Cross

HISTORIC SITE | This crossroads was the center of the medieval city. The Mercat Cross (*mercat* means "market"), topped by a unicorn, marks the spot where merchants met, where the market was held, and where criminals were executed. Here, too, was the *tron,* or weigh beam, installed in 1491 and used by merchants to check weights. The Tolbooth Steeple dates from 1626 and served as the civic center and the place where travelers paid tolls. ⊠ *Intersection of Saltmarket, Trongate, Gallowgate, and London Rds., East End* Ⓜ *St. Enoch.*

Glasgow Green

CITY PARK | FAMILY | Glasgow's oldest park has a long history as a favorite spot for public recreation and political demonstrations. Note the Nelson Column, erected long before London's; the McLennan Arch, originally part of the facade of the old Assembly Halls in Ingram Street; and the Templeton Business Centre, a former carpet factory built in the late 19th century in the style of the Doge's Palace in Venice. There is an adventure playground for kids and a small cycle track beside it, with children's bikes for rent. Don't miss the **People's Palace** and the Doulton Fountain that faces it. The Green also hosts the World Piping Championship in summer and a major firework display for Guy Fawkes night (November 5). ✉ *East End ✢ North side of River Clyde between Green St. and Saltmarket St.*

Hampden Park

SPORTS VENUE | FAMILY | A mecca for soccer enthusiasts who come from far and near to tread the famous turf, the home field for the country's national team was the largest stadium in the world when it was built in 1903. There are stadium tours on non-match days at 11, 12:30, 2, and 3. You can then visit the Scottish Football Museum, which traces the history of the game; the museum may close on game days. ✉ *Letherby Dr., East End ✢ Nearest rail stations are Mount Florida and Kings Park. Buses from City Centre* ☎ *0141/616–6139* ⊕ *www.hampdenpark. co.uk* ✉ *Stadium tour £8, museum entrance £8, combined ticket £13.*

People's Palace and Winter Gardens

MUSEUM | FAMILY | The excited conversations among local visitors are the evidence that this museum tells the story of everyday lives in Glasgow. There is always something that sparks a memory: a photo, an object, a sound. Inside you'll find the writing desk of John McLean (1879–1923), the famous "Red Clydeside" political activist, and the banana boots worn onstage by Glasgow-born comedian Billy Connolly. On the top floor a sequence of fine murals by Glasgow artist Ken Currie tells the story of the city's working-class citizens. In contrast, the Doulton Fountain opposite the entrance celebrates the British empire. The museum is housed in a Victorian red-sandstone building at the heart of Glasgow Green, and behind it are the restored Winter Gardens (a Victorian conservatory) and a popular café. To get here from the St. Enoch subway station, walk along Argyle Street past Glasgow Cross. ✉ *Glasgow Green, Monteith Row, East End* ☎ *0141/276–0788* ⊕ *www.glasgow- life.org.uk* ✉ *Free* ⊙ *Closed Mon.* Ⓜ *St. Enoch.*

🍴 Restaurants

The East End doesn't have a huge selection of great places to dine, but there are a few gems.

A'Challtainn Fish Restaurant

$$ | SEAFOOD | A welcome addition for East End diners, A'Challtainn (which means "Hazel Wood," the area's original name) occupies the central courtyard space of the Barras Architecture and Design Centre within the heart of Glasgow's original flea market, the Barras. The menu showcases Scottish seafood, with both small plates and a fine dining menu. **Known for:** excellent seafood; nice selection of shared plates; great Sunday brunch. Ⓢ *Average main: £16* ✉ *Barras Architecture and Design Centre, 54 Calton Entry, East End* ☎ *0141/237–9220* ⊕ *www.achalltainn.com* ⊙ *Closed Mon.*

West on the Green

$ | GERMAN | This microbrewery serves beer brewed "according to German purity laws of 1516"—in other words, no additives to muddy the flavor. The German theme is continued with the slightly cavernous dining space dotted with large wooden tables, and the food, which includes wursts, Wiener schnitzel, and goulash. **Known for:** classic German cuisine like wurst and potato salad; variety of its own beer served in a popular beer garden; weekend brewery tours with tasting. Ⓢ *Average main: £13* ✉ *Templeton Bldg., Templeton St., East End* ☎ *0141/550–0135* ⊕ *www.westbeer. com* Ⓜ *St. Enoch.*

🛍 Shopping

★ Barras

OUTDOOR/FLEA/GREEN MARKETS | Scotland's largest indoor market—named for the barrows, or pushcarts, formerly used by the stallholders—prides itself on selling everything "from a needle to an anchor" and is a must-see for anyone addicted to searching through piles of junk for bargains. Open on weekends only, the atmosphere is always good-natured, and you can find just about anything here, in any condition, from dusty model railroads to antique jewelry. Haggling is mandatory. You can reach the Barras by walking along Argyle Street from the St. Enoch subway station. The Barrowland Ballroom, which forms part of the market, was once where Glaswegians went to dance; today it is a venue for concerts of every kind. ■**TIP➔ Across the road is one of Glasgow's oldest pubs, the Saracen's Head; enter with caution—ghosts are said to abound.** ⊠ *Gallowgate, East End* ⊕ *www.theglasgowbarras.com.*

South Side

Just southwest of the City Centre in the South Side are two of Glasgow's dear green spaces—Bellahouston Park and Pollok Country Park—which have important art collections: Charles Rennie Mackintosh's House for an Art Lover in Bellahouston, and Pollok House in Pollok Country Park. A respite from the buzz of the city can also be found in the parks, where you can have a picnic or ramble through greenery and gardens. The famous Burrell Collection is also in the area, but the museum will be closed through 2020 for a substantial renovation.

GETTING HERE
Both parks are off Pollokshaws Road, about 3 miles southwest of City Centre. You can take a taxi or car, city bus, or a train from Glasgow Central station to Pollokshaws West station or Dumbreck.

 Sights

House for an Art Lover
HOUSE | Within Bellahouston Park is a "new" Mackintosh house, based on a competition entry Charles Rennie Mackintosh submitted to a German magazine in 1901. The house was never built in his lifetime, but took shape between 1989 and 1996. It is home to Glasgow School of Art's postgraduate study center, and displays show designs for the various rooms and decorative pieces by Mackintosh and his wife, Margaret. The main lounge is spectacular. There's also a café and shop filled with art. Buses 9, 53, and 54 from Union Street will get you here. Call ahead, as opening times can vary. ⊠ *Bellahouston Park, 10 Dumbreck Rd., South Side* ☎ *0141/353–4770* ⊕ *www. houseforanartlover.co.uk* ⊠ *£6* ⊙ *Closed weekdays Oct.–Mar.* Ⓜ *Ibrox.*

Pollok House
HOUSE | This classic Georgian house, dating from the mid-1700s, sits amid landscaped gardens and avenues of trees that are now part of Pollok Country Park. It still has the tranquil air of a wealthy but unpretentious country house. The Stirling Maxwell Collection includes paintings by Blake and a strong grouping of Spanish works by El Greco, Murillo, and Goya. Lovely examples of 18th- and early-19th-century furniture, silver, glass, and porcelain are also on display. The house has beautiful gardens that overlook the White Cart River. The downstairs servants' quarters include the kitchen, which is now a café-restaurant. The closest train station is Pollokshaws West, from Glasgow Central station; or you can take Buses 45, 47, or 57 to the gate of Pollok County Park. ⊠ *Pollok County Park, 2060 Pollokshaws Rd., South Side* ☎ *0141/616–6410* ⊕ *www.nts.org.uk* ⊠ *£7.50.*

Scotland Street School Museum
MUSEUM | FAMILY | A former school designed by Charles Rennie Mackintosh, this building houses a fascinating museum of education. Classrooms re-create school life in Scotland during Victorian times and World War II, and a cookery room recounts a time when education for Scottish girls consisted of little more than learning how to become a housewife. There's also an exhibition space and

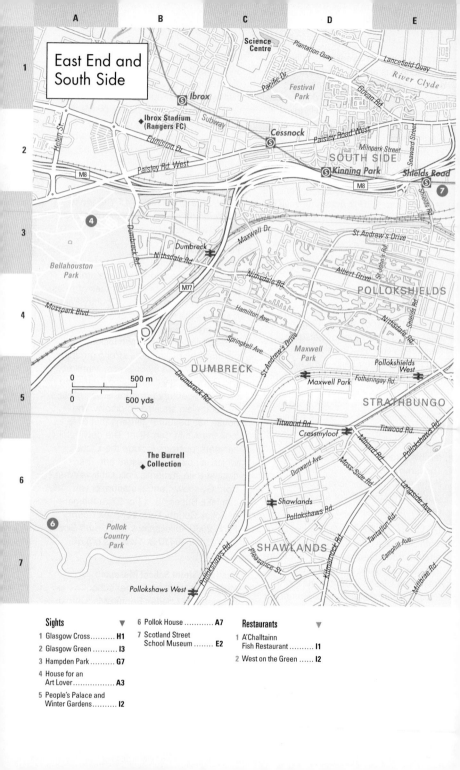

East End and South Side

	A	B	C	D	E
1			Science Centre	Plantation Quay	Lancefield Quay
					River Clyde
2	Helen St.	Ibrox · Ibrox Stadium (Rangers FC) · Edmiston Dr.	Subway · Cessnock · Paisley Road West	SOUTH SIDE · Milnpark Street · Kinning Park	Seaward Street · Shields Road
	M8 · Paisley Rd. West			M8	Shields Rd.
3	④ · Bellahouston Park	Dumbreck Rd. · Dumbreck · Nithsdale Rd.	Maxwell Dr. · Nithsdale Rd.	St Andrew's Drive · Albert Drive · POLLOKSHIELDS	St John's Rd. · Shields Rd.
4	Mosspark Blvd.	M77	Hamilton Ave. · Springkell Ave. · St Andrew's Drive	Maxwell Park · Pollokshields West · Nithsdale Rd.	
5	0 — 500 m · 0 — 500 yds	Drumbreck Rd.	DUMBRECK	Maxwell Park · Fotheringay Rd. · STRATHBUNGO · Titwood Rd. · Crossmyloof	Pollokshaws Rd.
6	⑥ · Pollok Country Park	The Burrell Collection		Durward Ave. · Moss-Side Rd. · Shawlands · Pollokshaws Rd.	Longside Ave. · Tantallon Rd. · Campbill Ave.
7		Pollokshaws West · Pollokshaws Rd.	Pleasance St.	SHAWLANDS · Kilmarnock Rd.	Millbrae Rd.

a café. The building sits opposite Shields Road subway station. ⊠ *225 Scotland St., South Side* ☎ *0141/287–0513* ⊕ *www. glasgowlife.org.uk* ✉ *Free* ⊘ *Closed Mon.* Ⓜ *Shields Rd.*

🎭 Performing Arts

Tramway

ART GALLERIES—ARTS | **FAMILY** | South of the City Centre, this innovative arts center is well worth seeking out. It hosts regular exhibitions in its two galleries, and plays—often of a very experimental nature—in its flexible theater space. The city's famed Citizens Theatre Company is also currently performing here while its permanent space undergoes a major renovation. Tramway has a café and a more formal restaurant on the first floor. Don't miss the Hidden Garden, which has transformed an empty lot behind the building into a sculpture park. To get here, take the train from Glasgow Central station to Pollokshields East (one stop). ⊠ *25 Albert Dr., South Side* ☎ *0845/330–3501* ⊕ *www.tramway.org.*

Ayrshire, Clyde Coast, and Robert Burns Country

The jigsaw puzzle of firths and straits and interlocking islands that you see as you fly into Glasgow Airport harbors numerous tempting one-day excursion destinations. You can travel south to visit the fertile farmlands of Ayrshire or west to the Firth of Clyde. Besides the spots related to celebrated Scottish poet Robert Burns, key treasures in this area include Culzean Castle, as famous for its Robert Adam (1728–92) design as it is for its spectacular seaside setting and grounds.

For many people a highlight of this region is Robert Burns country, a 40-minute

drive from Glasgow. The poet was born in Alloway, beside Ayr, and the towns and villages where he lived and loved make for an interesting day out. English children learn that Burns (1759–96) is a good minor poet, but Scottish children know that he's Shakespeare, Dante, Rabelais, Mozart, and Karl Marx rolled into one. As time goes by, it seems that the Scots have it more nearly right, as Burns increases in stature both as a poet and humanist. When you plunge into Burns country, don't forget that he's held in extreme reverence by Scots of all backgrounds. They may argue about Sir Walter Scott and Bonnie Prince Charlie, but there's no disputing the merits of the author of "Auld Lang Syne" and "A Man's a Man for A' That."

GETTING HERE AND AROUND
From Glasgow you can take the bus or train (from Glasgow Central station) to Ayr for the Burns Heritage Trail; and Troon, Prestwick, and Ayr to play golf. Bus companies also operate one-day guided excursions; for details, contact the tourist information center in Glasgow or the Strathclyde Passenger Transport Travel Centre. Traveline Scotland has helpful information.

If you're driving from Glasgow, there are two main routes to Ayr. The quickest is to take the M77 to the A77, which takes you to Ayr, where Alloway is well signposted. The alternative and much slower route is the coast road; take the M8 to Greenock and continue down the coast on the A78 until you meet the A77 and continue on into Burns Country.

Paisley

7 miles west of Glasgow.

The industrial prosperity of Paisley came from textiles and, in particular, from the woolen paisley shawl. The internationally recognized paisley pattern is based on the shape of a palm shoot, an ancient

Ayrshire and
the Clyde Coast

Babylonian fertility symbol brought from Kashmir. Today you can explore this history at several attractions in town.

GETTING HERE AND AROUND
Paisley-bound buses depart from the Buchanan Street bus station in Glasgow. Trains to Paisley's Gilour Street depart daily every 5 to 10 minutes from Glasgow Central station. If you're driving, take the M8 westbound and turn off at Junction 27, which is clearly signposted to Paisley.

◎ Sights

Paisley Abbey
RELIGIOUS SITE | Paisley's 12th-century abbey dominates the town center. Founded as a Cluniac monastery and almost completely destroyed by the English in 1307, the abbey was not totally restored until the early 20th century. It's

associated with Walter Fitzallan, the high steward of Scotland, who gave his name to the Stewart monarchs of Scotland (Stewart is a corruption of "steward"). Outstanding features include the vaulted stone roof and stained glass of the choir. ✉ 13 High St. ☎ 0141/889–7654 ⊕ www.paisleyabbey.org.uk ☞ Free.

Sma' Shot Cottages
HOUSE | To get an idea of the life led by textile industry workers, visit the Sma' Shot Cottages. These re-creations of mill workers' houses contain displays of linen, lace, and paisley shawls. Two typical cottages, built 150 years apart, are open to visitors. ✉ 11–17 George Pl. ☎ 0141/889–1708 ⊕ www.smashotcottages.co.uk ☞ Free ⊗ Closed Oct.–Mar. and Sun.–Tues. and Thurs. in Apr.–Sept.

Hotels

Mar Hall

$$$ | **HOTEL** | This imposing baronial house, now a luxurious golf and spa resort, sits amid formal gardens and overlooks the River Clyde and verdant woodlands. **Pros:** spacious rooms; fantastic pool; wonderful country setting but also near airport. **Cons:** quite remote; very expensive; not ideal for families. $ *Rooms from: £220* ✉ *Earl of Mar Estate, Mar Hall Dr., Bishopton* ☎ *0141/812–9999* ⊕ *www.marhall.com* ⇨ *53 rooms* ⦿ *Breakfast.*

Irvine

24 miles south of Glasgow.

Beyond Irvine's cobbled streets and grand Victorian buildings, look for a peaceful crescent-shaped harbor and fishermen's cottages huddled in solidarity against the Atlantic winds. The Scottish Maritime Museum pays homage to the town's seafaring past. Scotland's national poet, Robert Burns, lived here in 1781. Golf clubs Western Gailes and nearby Royal Troon make the area popular with golfers.

GETTING HERE AND AROUND

By car take the M8 from Glasgow, then the A726 and the A736 to Irvine. By rail it's a 40-minute journey from Glasgow Central station.

Sights

★ Scottish Maritime Museum

MUSEUM | **FAMILY** | On the waterfront in the coastal town of Irvine, this museum brings together ships and boats—both models and the real thing—to tell the tale of Scotland's maritime history, as well as chronicle the lives of its boatbuilders, fishermen, and sailors. The atmospheric Linthouse Engine Building, part of a former shipyard, hosts most of the displays. The museum also includes a shipyard

worker's tenement home that you can explore. In Dumbarton, 35 miles to the north, you can visit the Denny Tank (part of the museum), where ship designs were tested. ■**TIP**➔ **Children are admitted free.** ✉ *6 Gottries Rd.* ☎ *01294/278283* ⊕ *www.scottishmaritimemuseum.org* ▣ *£8.50.*

Hotels

Piersland House Hotel

$$ | **HOTEL** | Formerly the home of a whisky magnate, this late-Victorian mansion on the southern edge of town is now a country-house hotel. **Pros:** gorgeous gardens and grounds; close to golf courses; near Prestwick Airport. **Cons:** helps to have a car to get around; can get crowded with private functions; not much nearby besides golf courses. $ *Rooms from: £135* ✉ *15 Craigend Rd., Troon* ✛ *7 miles south of Irvine via the A78* ☎ *01292/314747* ⊕ *www.piersland.co.uk* ⇨ *37 rooms* ⦿ *Breakfast.*

Activities

★ Royal Troon Golf Club

GOLF | Of the two courses at Royal Troon, it's the Old or Championship Course—a traditional links course with superb sea views frequently used for the British Open—that is renowned among golfers. The second, Portland, shares the challenges of strong sea breezes and the gorse beside the fairways. Advance payment and a deposit are required, as is a handicap certificate. It is a good idea to check the tournament calendar before you go. ✉ *Craigend Rd., Troon* ✛ *9 miles south of Irvine via the A78* ☎ *01292/311555* ⊕ *www.royaltroon.com* ▣ *Old Course, £250; Portland Course, £85; both courses £290 total in Sept.* ⚲ *Old Course: 18 holes, 7208 yards, par 71; Portland Course: 18 holes, 6349 yards, par 72* ☞ *Closed for visitors Nov.–mid-Apr.*

★ Western Gailes Golf Club

GOLF | Known as the finest natural links course in Scotland, Western Gailes is entirely nature-made, and the greens are kept in truly magnificent condition. This is the final qualifying course when the British Open is held at Royal Troon or Trump Turnberry. Tom Watson lists the par-5 6th hole as one of his favorites. Visitors can play during restricted hours through the week; reserve online. ⊠ *Gailes Rd.* ☎ *01294/311649* ⊕ *www.westerngailes. com* ⊠ *Nov.–Feb £70 per round; Mar. £100 per round; Apr. and Oct. £140 per round; May–Sept. £175 per round* 🏌 *18 holes, 6640 yards, par 71.*

Ayr and Alloway

10 miles south of Irvine, 34 miles south of Glasgow.

The commercial port of Ayr is Ayrshire's chief town, a peaceful and elegant place with an air of prosperity. Poet Robert Burns was baptized in the Auld Kirk (Old Church) here and wrote a humorous poem about the Twa Brigs (Two Bridges) that cross the river nearby. Burns described Ayr as a town unsurpassed "for honest men and bonny lasses."

If you're on the Robert Burns trail, head for Alloway, on B7024 in Ayr's southern suburbs. A number of sights here are part of the **Burns National Heritage Park**, including the magnificent Robert Burns Birthplace Museum.

GETTING HERE AND AROUND

From Glasgow you can take the bus or train to Ayr; travel time is about an hour (a bit less by train). Drivers can use the A78 and A77 near the coast; a car would provide more flexibility to see the Burns sites around Alloway.

Remembering Mr. Burns

Born in Ayrshire, Robert Burns (1759–96) is one of Scotland's treasures. The poet and balladeer had a style that was his and his alone. His most famous song, "Auld Lang Syne," is heard everywhere on New Year's Day. Burns's talent, charisma, and good looks made him an icon to both the upper and lower classes (and made him quite popular with the ladies). Today his birthday (January 25) is considered a national holiday; on "Burns Night" young and old alike get together for Burns Suppers and recite his work over neeps, tatties, and drams of the country's finest whisky.

👁 Sights

Auld Kirk Alloway

RELIGIOUS SITE | This small ruined church is famous for its role in Burns's epic poem, "Tam o' Shanter," which many Scots know by heart and is often recited at Burns Suppers. In the poem, the kirk is where a rather drunk Tam o' Shanter unluckily passed a witches' revel—with Old Nick himself playing the bagpipes—on his unsteady way home. In flight from the witches, Tam managed to cross the medieval Brig o' Doon (*brig* is Scots for *bridge*; you can still see the bridge) just in time. His gray mare, Meg, however, lost her tail to the closest witch. (Any resident of Ayr will tell you that witches cannot cross running water.) ⊠ *Murdoch's Lone, Alloway* ⊠ *Free.*

Burns Cottage

HOUSE | In the delightful Burns Heritage Park, this thatched cottage is where Scotland's national poet lived for his first seven years. It has a living room, a kitchen, and a stable, one behind the other. The life and times of Burns, born in 1759,

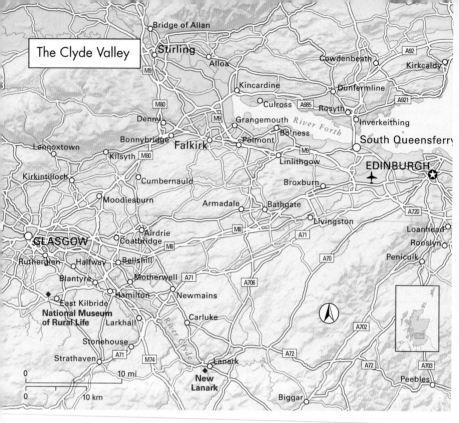

are beautifully and creatively illustrated in the fly-on-the-wall videos of daily life in the 18th century. The garden is lush with the types of vegetables the poet's father might have grown. From the cottage, take the Poet's Path through the village to the Robert Burns Birthplace Museum, the spooky churchyard where Tam o' Shanter faced fearsome ghosts, and the Brig o' Doon, all included in the museum entry ticket. ⊠ *Greenfield Ave., Alloway* ☎ *0844/493–2601* ⊕ *www.burnsmuseum.org.uk* ⊠ *£10.50, includes Burns Monument and Robert Burns Birthplace Museum.*

Burns Monument

MEMORIAL | This neoclassical structure, built in 1823, overlooks the Brig o' Doon. You can climb to the top (with some care!). Entrance is included in the Burns Museum ticket. ⊠ *Murdoch's Lone,*

Alloway ⊕ *www.burnsmuseum.org.uk* ⊠ *Free; also included in £10.50 ticket to Burns Cottage and Robert Burns Birthplace Museum.*

Dumfries House

HOUSE | Built in the 1750s by the Adam brothers, Dumfries House has preserved the living conditions of the landed aristocracy of the time. The restored house contains a large collection of furniture by Chippendale that is original to the property, as well as pieces by other great designers of the period. Run by a charity headed by Prince Charles, the surrounding 2,000-acre estate is currently in development as a site for an eco-village and centers practicing historic crafts. Entry is by guided tour only; booking ahead is essential. There are 22 guest rooms, some cottages, and a restaurant on the property as well. ⊠ *Cumnock*

⊕ From Ayr, take the A70 to Cumnock; it's about 10 miles ☎ 01290/421742 ⊕ www.dumfries-house.org.uk ⌖ Guided tour £10; extended tour £14; grounds free ⊗ Closed weekdays Nov.–Mar.

★ Robert Burns Birthplace Museum

MUSEUM VILLAGE | Besides being a poet of delicacy and depth, Robert Burns was also a rebel, a thinker, a lover, a good companion, and a man of the country-side. This wonderful museum explains why the Scots so admire this complex "man o' pairts." The imaginative displays present each of his poems in context, with commentaries sensitively written in a modern version of the Scots language in which he spoke and wrote. Headsets let you hear the poems sung or spoken. The exhibits are vibrant and interactive, with touch screens that allow you to debate his views on politics, love, taxation, revolution, and Scottishness. An elegant café offers a place to pause, while the kids can play in the adjoining garden. Included in the ticket are the Burns Cottage, a few minutes' walk down a Burns-themed walkway, and the Burns Monument. ⌗ Murdoch's Lone, Alloway ☎ 01292/443700 ⊕ www.burnsmuseum.org.uk ⌖ £10.50, includes Burns Cottage and Burns Monument.

Restaurants

Brig o' Doon House

$$ | BRITISH | Originally built in 1827, this attractive hotel restaurant often has a piper by the door to greet hungry travelers ready for a Scottish setting and some Scottish fare. Tartan carpets, dark-wood paneling, and buck heads mounted on the walls set the mood, and the bar is a shrine to Robert Burns. **Known for:** riverside location; Scottish food and decor; great venison casserole. ⑤ Average main: £15 ⌗ High Maybole Rd., Alloway ☎ 01292/442466 ⊕ www.brigodoonhouse.com.

Cafe Le Monde

$ | ITALIAN | This Italian-style café with alfresco seating for good weather serves lunch and smaller bites to a mainly day-visitor crowd. The ciabattas and soups are well made and substantial, if not enormously adventurous, and the staff is attentive. **Known for:** tasty soups and toasted cheese sandwiches; good coffee; outdoor seating. ⑤ Average main: £12 ⌗ 36 Newmarket St., Ayr ☎ 01292/611219 ⊗ No dinner.

Activities

GOLF

Prestwick Golf Club

GOLF | Tom Morris helped design this challenging Ayrshire coastal links course, which saw the birth of the British Open Championship in 1860. The first hole is reputed to be among the most challenging in Scotland, since the railway line runs along the length of the hole. But it doesn't get any easier after that. Some of its bunkers are especially threatening, and the bumps at the 5th are high enough to be called the Himalayas. Prestwick has excellent, fast rail links with Glasgow. There are a limited number of tee times on Saturday afternoon. ⌗ 2 Links Rd., Prestwick ⊕ 4 miles south of Ayr via the A79 ☎ 01292/477404 ⊕ www.prestwickgc.co.uk ⌖ Apr. and Oct., £160 weekdays, £210 weekends; May–Sept., weekdays £190, weekends £225; Nov.–Mar. Mon.–Sat. £110, Sun. £145 ⚐ 18 holes, 6544 yards, par 71.

Trump Turnberry

GOLF | One of the most famous links courses in Scotland, the main course here is the iconic Ailsa Course, which is open to the waterside elements, and the 9th hole requires you to hit the ball over the open sea. The British Open was famously hosted here in 1977, and again in 1986, 1994, and 2009. A second course, the King Robert the Bruce, has an 11th hole that overlooks a lighthouse and Ailsa Craig; it redesigned the old

Kintyre and Arran courses. ✉ *Trump Turnberry Resort, Maidens Rd., Turnberry* ✛ *Off A719, 15 miles south of Ayr* ☎ *01655/331000* ⊕ *www.turnberryresort. co.uk* ✉ *Ailsa: Dec.–Mar. weekdays £175, weekends £200; Apr. and May weekdays £200, weekends £250; June–Oct. weekdays £325, weekends £375; Nov. Tues.–Thurs. £200; Fri.–Mon. £250. King Robert the Bruce: Dec.–Mar £70; Apr. and May £90; June–Oct. £120; Nov. £90* ⛳ *Ailsa: 18 holes, 7448 yards, par 71; King Robert the Bruce: 18 holes, 7203 yards, par 71.*

Culzean Castle and Country Park

12 miles south of Ayr, 50 miles south of Glasgow.

There's plenty to do at this popular spot between visiting the Robert Adam–designed house and touring the extensive grounds.

GETTING HERE AND AROUND

Stagecoach buses run from Ayr to the park entrance; the nearest train station from Glasgow is at Maybole, 4 miles to the east, but there is Stagecoach bus service to the park entrance. Note that the park entrance is a mile walk from the castle visitor center.

Sights

★ Culzean Castle and Country Park

CASTLE/PALACE | FAMILY | The dramatic cliff-top castle of Culzean (pronounced ku-*lain*) is quite a long drive from Glasgow, but it's the National Trust for Scotland's most popular property. Robert Adam designed the neoclassical mansion, complete with a walled garden, in 1777. The grounds are enormous and beautifully kept, combining parkland, forests, and a beach looking out over the Atlantic Ocean; the surprisingly lush shrubberies reflect the warm currents that explain the

mild climate. There are caves in the cliffs; tours are occasionally available. In the castle itself you can visit the armory, luxuriously appointed salons and bedchambers, and a nursery with its lovely cradle in a boat. Adam's grand double spiral staircase is the high point of its design. There's a free audio tour, and guided tours are available daily at 11 and 2:30. A short walk through the woods brings you to the visitor center with shops and a restaurant. ✉ *Culzean Castle, A719, Maybole* ☎ *01655/884455* ⊕ *www.nts. org.uk* ✉ *Park and castle £17, park only £11.50* ⊗ *Castle closed Nov.–Mar.*

Hotels

Eisenhower Hotel

$$$ | HOTEL | It would be hard to imagine a more spectacular location for an overnight stay than the upper floors of Culzean Castle, which looks out toward Arran and the Atlantic Ocean. **Pros:** beautiful setting; luxurious lodging; a strong sense of history. **Cons:** a little remote; rather formal; not for minimalists. ⑤ *Rooms from: £250* ✉ *Culzean Castle, A719, Maybole* ☎ *0844/493–2149* ⊕ *www.culzean-eisenhower.com* ⤴ *6 rooms* ⦿ *Free Breakfast.*

The Clyde Valley

The River Clyde is (or certainly was) famous for its shipbuilding, yet its upper reaches flow through some of Scotland's most fertile farmlands, rich with crops of tomatoes and fruit. It's an interesting area with some museums, most notably at New Lanark, that tell the story of the growth of manufacturing.

GETTING HERE AND AROUND

If you're driving from Glasgow, head south on the M74 and turn on to the A72. This is the main road through the Clyde Valley, ending at Lanark. Train service runs from Glasgow Central station to Lanark; for details check National Rail.

To experience life in an 18th-century industrial community, visit New Lanark.

National Museum of Rural Life

9 miles south of Glasgow.

The effect of farming on the land and on people's lives is the focus of this museum near Glasgow.

GETTING HERE AND AROUND

From Glasgow, take the M77 and then the A726 at Junction 4 to East Kilbride, or the A725 from Blantyre to East Kilbride; it's a 20-minute drive. You can take the train from Glasgow Central station to East Kilbride, then taxi or bus. By bus take First Bus 31 from St. Enoch Centre in Glasgow.

Sights

★ **National Museum of Rural Life**
FARM/RANCH | FAMILY | Set in a rural area, this lovely museum exploring every aspect of the country's agricultural heritage is slightly off the beaten track but well worth the trip. It is a whole day out. In a modern building resembling a huge barn you learn about how farming transformed the land, experience the life and hardships of those who worked it, and see displays of tools and machines from across the ages. Take a tractor ride to a fully functioning 1950s farmhouse. There are also some great exhibits geared toward children and a range of summer events. ⊠ *Wester Kittochside, Philipshill Rd., East Kilbride* ☎ *0300/123–6789* ⊕ *www.nms.ac.uk/rural* ⊠ *£8.*

New Lanark

25 miles southeast east of Glasgow.

Set in pleasing, rolling countryside, New Lanark was a model workers' community that is now a museum and World Heritage site. It's about a mile to the south of the old Scottish town of Lanark.

GETTING HERE AND AROUND

If you're driving, take the M74 to the A72. The train from Glasgow Central station to Lanark takes 50 minutes or so; then take a taxi or bus. New Lanark is signposted from Lanark; you drive to the parking lot and walk down into New Lanark.

Sights

★ New Lanark

HISTORIC SITE | FAMILY | Now a UNESCO World Heritage site, New Lanark was home to a social experiment at the beginning of the Industrial Revolution. Robert Owen (1771–1858), together with his father-in-law, David Dale (1739–1806), set out to create a model industrial community with well-designed worker homes, a school, and public buildings. Owen went on to establish other communities on similar principles, both in Britain and in the United States. Robert Owen's son, Robert Dale Owen (1801–77), went on to help found the Smithsonian Institution.

After many changes of fortune, the mills eventually closed. One of the buildings has been converted into a visitor center that tells the story of this brave social experiment. You can also explore Robert Owen's house, the school, and a mill worker's house, and enjoy the Annie McLeod Experience, a fairground ride that takes you through the story of one mill worker's life. Other restored structures hold various shops and eateries; one has a rooftop garden with impressive views of the entire site. Another now houses the New Lanark Mill Hotel.
■ TIP➜ **It's a good idea to book your ticket ahead in summer to avoid lines.**

The River Clyde powers its way through a beautiful wooded gorge here, and its waters were once harnessed to drive textile-mill machinery. Upstream it flows through some of the finest river scenery anywhere in Lowland Scotland, with woods and waterfalls. ⊠ *New Lanark Rd., New Lanark* ☎ *01555/661345* ⊕ *www. newlanark.org* ⊠ *£12.50.*

Hotels

New Lanark Mill Hotel

\$\$ | HOTEL | Housed in a converted cotton mill by the river in the 18th-century village of New Lanark, this hotel is decorated in a spare, understated style that allows the impressive architecture of barrel-vaulted ceilings and elegant Georgian windows to speak for itself. **Pros:** beautiful river views; large rooms; impressive spa. **Cons:** bland bar; some rooms can get cold; restaurant is the only one in the vicinity. ⑤ *Rooms from: £135* ⊠ *New Lanark Rd., New Lanark* ☎ *01555/667200* ⊕ *www.newlanarkmillhotel.co.uk* ⇱ *38 rooms* ¶◯¶ *Breakfast.*

THE BORDERS AND THE SOUTHWEST

Updated by
Mike Gonzalez

WELCOME TO
THE BORDERS AND THE SOUTHWEST

TOP REASONS TO GO

★ **Ancient abbeys:** The great abbeys of the Border regions and the wonderful Sweetheart Abbey in the Southwest are mainly in ruins, but they retain an air of their former grandeur.

★ **Outdoor activities:** You can walk, bicycle, or even ride horses across Galloway or through the Borders. Abandoned railway tracks make good paths, and there are forests and moorlands if you prefer wilder country.

★ **Stately homes and castles:** Some of the landed aristocracy still lives in these grand mansions, and most of the homes are open to visitors, like Floors Castle, Threave, Drumlanrig, and the magical Caerlaverock Castle near Dumfries.

★ **Literary Scotland:** The Borders region has enough monuments dedicated to Sir Walter Scott to make him the focus of a visit. The poet Robert Burns spent much of his working life in Dumfries, and the Moat Brae Centre in Dumfries was where J. M. Barrie first came up with *Peter Pan*.

1 Jedburgh. A pretty town dominated by a glorious abbey.

2 Kelso. A charming market town close to imposing Floors Castle.

3 Melrose. Home to a ruined abbey and the house once belonging to Sir Walter Scott.

4 Selkirk. Another small town with beautiful landscapes and Sir Walter Scott history.

5 Hawick. A larger Borders town central to the region's wool industry.

6 Innerleithen. A former industrial boomtown of wool mills now popular for its outdoor activities.

7 Peebles. A busy market town with great shopping.

8 Gretna Green. A town right on the Scottish-English border with a quirky reputation as a haven for married couples.

9 Dumfries. A tranquil market town that was once home to Robert Burns and J. M. Barrie.

10 North of Dumfries. Where you'll find Drumlanrig Castle, *Crawick Multiverse*, and the Museum of Lead Mining.

11 Solway Firth. One the area's best-kept secrets with an extraordinary population of wildlife and plants centered around Caerlaverock Castle.

0   10 mi

0   10 km

12 Castle Douglas. A pleasant town specializing in local food products and home to Threave Castle.

13 Kirkcudbright. A lovely harbor town once a haven for artists, including one of the "Glasgow Boys."

14 Newton Stewart. The gateway to Galloway Forest Park.

15 Gatehouse of Fleet. A peaceful small town with a traditional Scottish castle.

16 Whithorn. Home to the historic early Christian settlement Whithorn Abbey.

17 Stranraer. Once the main ferry port for Ireland and now in the midst of redevelopment.

18 Portpatrick. A lovely village with dramatic cliff walks.

In the Borders region, south of Edinburgh, are more stately homes, fortified castles, and medieval abbeys than in any other part of Scotland. This is also Sir Walter Scott territory, including his pseudo-baronial home at Abbotsford.

The area embraces the whole 90-mile course of one of Scotland's great rivers, the Tweed. Passing woodlands luxuriant with game birds, the river flows in rushing torrents through this fertile land. To the west of the Borders is Dumfries and Galloway, an area of gentle coasts, forests, and lush hills, ideal country for walkers and cyclists.

For centuries the Borders was a battlefield, where English and Scottish troops remained locked in a struggle for its possession. At different times, parts of the region have been in English hands, just as slices of northern England (Berwick-upon-Tweed, for example) have been under Scottish control. The castles and fortified houses as well as the abbeys across the Borders are the surviving witnesses to those times. After the Union of 1707, fortified houses gradually gave way to the luxurious country mansions that pepper the area. And by the 19th century they had become grand country houses like Mellerstain House, built by fashionable architects.

All the main routes between London and Edinburgh traverse the Borders, whose hinterland of undulating pastures, woods, and valleys is enclosed within three lonely groups of hills: the Cheviots, the Moorfoots, and the Lammermuirs. Hamlets and prosperous country towns dot the

land, giving valley slopes a lived-in look, yet the total population is still sparse. The sheep that are the basis of the region's prosperous textile industry outnumber human beings by 14 to 1.

To the west is the region of Dumfries and Galloway, on the shores of the Solway Firth. It might appear to be an extension of the Borders, but the southwest has a history all its own. From its ports ships sailed to the Americas, carrying country dwellers driven from their land to make room for sheep. Inland, the earth rises toward high hills, forest, and bleak but captivating moorland, whereas nearer the coast you can find pretty farmlands, small villages, and unassuming towns. The shoreline is washed by the North Atlantic Drift (Scotland's answer to the Gulf Stream), and first-time visitors are always surprised to see palm trees and exotic plants thriving in gardens and parks along the coast.

At the heart of the region is Dumfries, the "Queen o' the South." Once a major port and commercial center, its glamour is now slightly faded. But the memory of poet Robert Burns, who spent several years living and working here and who is buried in the town, remains very much alive. In addition, Moat Brae can claim to be the location of Neverland, the imaginary world of *Peter Pan*, which was written there.

MAJOR REGIONS

The Borders. Borders towns cluster around and between two rivers—the Tweed and its tributary, the Teviot. Borders folk take great pride in the region's fame as Scotland's main woolen-goods manufacturing area. Its main towns—Jedburgh, Hawick, Selkirk, Peebles, Kelso, and Melrose—retain an air of prosperity and confidence with their solid stone houses and elegant town squares. Although many mills have closed since the 1980s, the pride in local identity is still evident in the fiercely contested Melrose Sevens rugby competition in April and the annual Common Ridings—local events commemorating the time when towns needed to patrol their borders—throughout June and July. A visit to at least one of the region's four great ruined abbeys makes the quintessential Borders experience. The monks in these powerful, long-abandoned religious communities were the first to work the fleeces of their sheep flocks, thus laying the groundwork for what is still the area's main manufacturing industry.

Although the Borders has many attractions, it's most famous for being the home base for Sir Walter Scott (1771–1832), the early-19th-century poet, novelist, and creator of *Ivanhoe*. Scott single-handedly transformed Scotland's image from that of a land of brutal savages to one of romantic and stirring deeds and magnificent landscapes. The novels of Scott are not read much nowadays—frankly, some of them are difficult to wade through—but the mystique that he created, the aura of historical romance, has outlasted his books. The ruined abbeys, historical houses, and grand vistas of the Borders provide a perfect backdrop.

Dumfries and Galloway. Galloway covers the southwestern portion of Scotland, west of the main town of Dumfries; it's a quiet and less-visited region of Scotland, in general. Here a gentle coastline gives way to farmland and then breezy uplands that gradually merge with coniferous forests. The region now claims two extraordinary public art projects—Charles Jencks's *Crawick Multiverse* and Andy Goldsworthy's *Striding Arches*. The Solway Firth is a vast nature preserve, and the climate of the west sustains the surprising tropical plants at the Logan Botanic Gardens and the gardens at Threave Castle. Even farther west, Galloway draws active visitors to its forests to hike or cycle.

Planning

When to Go

Because many lodgings and some sights are privately owned and shut down from early autumn until early April, the area is less suited to off-season touring than some other parts of Scotland. The best time to visit is between Easter and late September. The region does look magnificent in autumn, especially along the wooded river valleys of the Borders. Late spring is the time to see the rhododendrons in the gardens of Dumfries and Galloway.

FESTIVALS
Common Ridings
FESTIVALS | More than 10 Borders communities have reestablished their identities through the annual summer gatherings known as the Common Ridings. In medieval times it was essential that each town be able to defend its area by "riding the marches," or patrolling the boundaries. The Common Ridings that celebrate this history are more authentic than the Highland Games concocted by the Victorians. Although this is above all a celebration for native Borderers, you will be welcome to share the excitement of clattering hooves and banners proudly

displayed. ⊕ *www.returntotheridings.
co.uk.*

Dumfries & Galloway Arts Festival
FESTIVALS | Celebrated every year since
1979, this festival with music, theater,
dance, and other events is usually held
at the end of May at several venues
throughout the region. ☎ *01387/260447*
⊕ *www.dgartsfestival.org.uk.*

Getting Oriented

What was once for centuries a battle-
ground region separating Scotland and
England, today the Borders area is a
bridge between the two countries. This
is a place of upland moors and hills,
farmland, and forested river valleys. Yet
it also embraces the rugged coastline
between Edinburgh and Berwick. It's
rustic and peaceful, with textile mills,
abbeys, castles, and gardens. The area is
a big draw for hikers and walking enthusiasts, especially thanks to the lovely
Tweed Valley Forest Park in the east and
the Galloway Forest Park in the west.
The Borders region is steeped in history,
with Mary, Queen of Scots, a powerful
presence despite the relatively short
time she spent here. The moorlands of
the Southwest feature dramatic art projects like the Striding Arches and *Crawick
Multiverse* as well as peaceful seascapes
like the Solway Firth and wilder ones on
the Galloway coast.

Planning Your Time

The Borders Railway has opened the
route between Edinburgh and the Borders, running from Edinburgh's Waverley
Station to Tweedbank, in the heart of
the Borders. Its 30-mile journey passes
through Galashiels (for connections to
Traquair House) and ends at Tweedbank,
which is near Melrose and Walter Scott's
home at Abbotsford. Beyond the Borders
Railway, it is still more convenient to
explore by car. If you're driving north

along the A1 toward Edinburgh, it's easy
to take a tour around the prosperous
Borders towns. Turn onto the A698 at
Berwick-upon-Tweed, which will take you
along the Scottish–English border toward
Kelso, Jedburgh, Dryburgh, and Melrose.
It's 36 miles from Jedburgh to Peebles, a
good place to stay overnight. Another day
might begin with a visit to Walter Scott's
lovely Abbotsford House, and then some
shopping in any of these prosperous
towns.

To the west, Dumfries and Galloway
beckon. If you're traveling north toward
Glasgow on the M6/A74, take the A70
west toward Dumfries. From the A1, on
the east coast, travel west on the A708
to Moffat and pick up the A70 there.
From Glasgow take the A74 south to
Beattock and pick up the A701 there.
Two days would give you time to explore
Burns sites and more in Dumfries. From
Dumfries you can visit Sweetheart Abbey
(8 miles away), Caerlaverock Castle (9
miles away), and Threave Castle and Gardens (20 miles away). Castle Douglas is
a good place to stop for lunch. The A710
and A711 take you along the dramatic
coastline of the Solway Firth. Farther
west along the A75 are the towns of
Newton Stewart and Portpatrick, and on
the A714, Glen Trool. The region does not
have good rail links but there is good bus
service, and by car it is a charming and
compact region.

Getting Here and Around

AIR
The nearest Scottish airports are at Edin-
burgh, Glasgow, and Prestwick (outside
Glasgow).

BOAT AND FERRY
P&O European Ferries and Stena Line
operate from Larne, in Northern Ireland,
to Cairnryan, near Stranraer, several
times daily. The crossing takes one hour
on the Superstar Express, two hours on
other ferries.

BOAT AND FERRY CONTACTS P&O
European Ferries. ☎ *0800/130–0030*
⊕ *www.poferries.com.* **Stena Line.**
☎ *08447/707070* ⊕ *www.stenaline.co.uk.*

BUS

If you're approaching from the south, check with Scottish Citylink, National Express, or First about buses from Edinburgh and Glasgow. In the Borders, Firstborders and Borders Buses offer service within the region. Stagecoach Western is the main bus company serving Dumfries and Galloway.

BUS CONTACTS Borders Buses.
☎ *01896/754350* ⊕ *www.bordersbuses.co.uk.* **First Bus.** ☎ *01224/650000*
⊕ *www.firstgroup.com.* **Firstborders.**
☎ *01896/754350* ⊕ *www.firstborders.co.uk.* **National Express.** ☎ *0871/781–8181* ⊕ *www.nationalexpress.com.*
Scottish Citylink. ☎ *0871/266–3333*
⊕ *www.citylink.co.uk.* **Stagecoach Western.** ☎ *0141/552–4961 in Glasgow, 01387/253496 in Dumfries* ⊕ *www.stagecoachbus.com.*

CAR

Traveling by car is the best and easiest way to explore the area, especially if you get off the main, and often crowded, arterial roads and use the little back roads. The main route into both the Borders and Galloway from the south is the M6, which becomes the M74 at the border. You can then take the scenic and leisurely A7 northwestward through Hawick toward Edinburgh, or the A75 and other parallel routes westward into Dumfries, Galloway, and the former ferry ports of Stranraer (nearby Cairnryan is an active ferry port) and Portpatrick.

There are several other possible routes: starting from the east, the A1 brings you from the English city of Newcastle to the border in about an hour. Moving west, the A697, which leaves the A1 north of Morpeth (in England) and crosses the border at Coldstream, is a leisurely back-road option. The A68 is probably the most scenic route to Scotland: after climbing to Carter Bar, it reveals a view of the Borders hills and windy skies before dropping into the ancient town of Jedburgh.

TRAIN

Apart from the main London–Edinburgh line, the Borders had no train service until 2015, when the rail link from Edinburgh to Tweedbank began service. The Borders Railway website has information about using it to explore the area. In the Southwest, trains headed from London's Euston to Glasgow stop at Carlisle, just south of the border, and some also stop at Lockerbie. Trains between Glasgow and Carlisle stop at Gretna Green, Annan, and Dumfries. From Glasgow there is service on the coastal route to Stranraer.

First Bus provides connections between Hawick, Selkirk, and Galashiels and train service at Carlisle, Edinburgh, and Berwick.

TRAIN CONTACTS Borders Railway.
☎ *0344/811–0141* ⊕ *www.scotrail.co.uk.*
National Rail. ☎ *03457/484950* ⊕ *www.nationalrail.co.uk.* **ScotRail.** ☎ *0344/811–0141* ⊕ *www.scotrail.co.uk.* **Trainline.**
☎ *0871/244–1545* ⊕ *www.thetrainline.com.*

Restaurants

Most good restaurants in the region used to be located in hotels, but today things are changing. Good independent eateries are popping up in small (and sometimes unlikely) towns and villages, and many new establishments specialize in fresh local ingredients. Seasonal menus are now popular. It is important to remember that restaurants here usually serve lunch between noon and 2 and dinner until 8:30 only.

Hotels

From top-quality, full-service hotels to quaint 18th-century drovers' inns to cozy bed-and-breakfasts, the Borders has all manner of lodging options. Choices in Dumfries and Galloway may be a little less expensive than in the Borders (with the same full range of services). These days many establishments are willing to lower their rates depending on availability.

Restaurant and hotel reviews have been shortened. For full reviews, see Fodors. com. Restaurant prices are the average cost of a main course at dinner or, if dinner is not served, at lunch. Hotel prices are the lowest cost of a standard double room in high season, including 20% V.A.T.

WHAT IT COSTS in Pounds

	$	$$	$$$	$$$$
RESTAURANTS				
	under £15	£15–£19	£20–£25	over £25
HOTELS				
	under £125	£125–£200	£201–£300	over £300

Visitor Information

Visit Scottish Borders has offices in Jedburgh, Hawick, and Peebles. The Dumfries & Galloway Tourist Board can be found in Dumfries and Stranraer. Seasonal information centers are at Castle Douglas, Eyemouth, Galashiels, Gretna Green, Kelso, Kirkcudbright, Langholm, Moffat, Sanquhar, and Selkirk. Liveborders provides online information on cultural and sporting activities in the Borders.

CONTACTS Dumfries & Galloway Tourist Board. ⊠ *64 Whitesands, Dumfries* ☏ *01387/253862* ⊕ *www.visitscotland. com.* **Liveborders.** ⊠ *Melrose Rd., Galashiels* ☏ *01896/661166* ⊕ *www.liveborders. org.uk.* **Visit Scottish Borders.** ⊠ *Murray's Green, Jedburgh* ☏ *01835/863170* ⊕ *www.visitscotland.com.*

Activities

Rugby Sevens

RUGBY | The Borders invented the fast-and-furious, cut-down version of rugby in 1883, though it has now spread worldwide. Teams are made up of 7 players rather than 15, and the matches are shorter. Although the population of the Borders is about 100,000, the region boasts a total of 17 clubs and some of Scotland's best players. Each spring, 10 teams compete for the Kings of the Sevens title. ⊕ *www.kingsofthesevens.net.*

7stanes Mountain Biking

BICYCLING | The Dumfries and Galloway region is something of a mecca for mountain bikers, offering trails and routes of every level of difficulty in beautiful and varying landscapes. This outfitter offers full equipment rental, skills training, advice, and local route maps organized by degree of difficulty. You can bring your own bike or rent one and ride gentle forest routes or tough hill climbs. There are eight centers across Dumfries and Galloway and the Borders; the most popular is Glentress located near Peebles. Each center has showers and changing facilities, as well as good cafés. Specific information on each is available on the comprehensive website. ⊠ *Campbell House, Crichton Business Park, Bankend Rd., Dumfries* ☏ *01721/721180* ⊕ *www.7stanesmountainbiking.com.*

Jedburgh

50 miles south of Edinburgh, 95 miles southeast of Glasgow, 14 miles northeast of Hawick.

The town of Jedburgh (*burgh* is always pronounced *burra* in Scots) was for centuries the first major Scottish target of invading English armies. In more peaceful times it developed textile mills, most of which have since languished. The large landscaped area around the town's tourist information center was once a mill but now provides an encampment for the armies of modern tourists. The past still clings to this little town, however. The ruined abbey dominates the skyline, a reminder of the formerly strong governing role of the Borders abbeys.

GETTING HERE AND AROUND

By car from Edinburgh, you can take the A68 (about 45 minutes) or the A7 (about an hour). From Glasgow take the M8, then the A68 direct to Jedburgh (about two hours).

There are fairly good bus connections from all major Scottish cities to Jedburgh. From Edinburgh direct routes to Melrose take about two hours. From Glasgow it takes 3½ hours to reach Melrose. From Melrose it's just 20 minutes to Jedburgh.

The Borders Railway runs between Edinburgh and Tweedbank, about 15 miles northwest of Jedburgh.

ESSENTIALS

VISITOR INFORMATION Jedburgh Visitor Centre. ⊠ *Murray's Green* ☎ *01835/863170* ⊕ *www.visitscotland. com.*

Sights

Harestanes Countryside Visitor Centre

MUSEUM | FAMILY | Housed in a former farmhouse 4 miles north of Jedburgh, this visitor center portrays life in the Scottish Borders through art exhibitions and natural history displays. Crafts such as woodworking and tile making are taught here, and finished projects are often on display. Outside are meandering paths, quiet roads for bike rides, and the biggest children's play area in the Borders. There's plenty for children, including a fascinating puzzle gallery full of sturdy wooden games. It is also on one of the best-known walking routes in the Borders, the St. Cuthbert's Path. ⊠ *Junction of A68 and B6400, 4 miles north of Jedburgh* ☎ *01835/830306* ⊕ *www.liveborders.org.uk* ⊠ *Free* ☉ *Closed Nov.–Mar.*

Hermitage Castle

CASTLE/PALACE | To appreciate the famous 20-mile ride of Mary, Queen of Scots, in 1566—she rushed to the side of her wounded lover, the Earl of Bothwell—travel southwest from Jedburgh to this, the most complete remaining example of the bare and grim medieval border castles. Restored in the early 19th century, it was built in the 13th century to guard what was at the time one of the important routes from England into Scotland. Local folklore maintains that the 14th-century Lord Soulis, a descendant of the original owner and notorious for diabolical excess, was captured by the local populace, who wrapped him in lead and boiled him in a cauldron—a much better story than the reality, which is that he died in Dumbarton Jail. ⊠ *Hawick* ✛ *2 miles west of B6399, about 21 miles south of Jedburgh* ☎ *01387/376222* ⊕ *www.historicenvironment.scot* ⊠ *£6* ☉ *Closed Oct.–Mar.*

★ Jedburgh Abbey

RELIGIOUS SITE | The most impressive of the Borders abbeys towers above Jedburgh. Built by David I, king of Scots in the 12th century, the abbey was nearly destroyed by the English Earl of Hertford's forces in 1544–45, during the destructive time known as the Rough Wooing. This was English king Henry VIII's (1491–1547) armed attempt to persuade the Scots that it was a good idea to unite the kingdoms by the marriage of his young son to the infant Mary, Queen of Scots (1542–87); the Scots disagreed and sent Mary to France instead. The story is explained in vivid detail at the visitor center, which also has information about the ruins and an audio tour. The arched abbey walls, the nave, and the cloisters still give a sense of the power these buildings represented. ⊠ *High St.* ☎ *01835/863925* ⊕ *www. historicenvironment.scot* ⊠ *£6.*

Jedburgh Castle Jail and Museum

JAIL | FAMILY | This building might look like a castle, but it's actually a prison that sits where a castle originally once stood. Named for the prison reformer John Howard, who campaigned for improved prison conditions, today you can inspect prison cells, rooms with period furnishings, and costumed figures. The audio guide, which recounts the history of the prison and the town, is useful. In what was once the prison governor's house, you'll now find an exhibition about the town of Jedburgh. ⊠ *Castlegate* ☎ *01835/864750* ⊕ *www.scotborders. gov.uk/museums* ⊠ *Free* ⊗ *Closed Nov.–Mar.*

Mary, Queen of Scots Visitor Centre

HOUSE | This *bastel* (from the French *bastille*) was the fortified town house in which, as the story goes, Mary stayed before embarking on her famous 20-mile ride to Hermitage Castle to visit her wounded lover, the Earl of Bothwell (circa 1535–78) in 1566. Displays relate the tale and other episodes in her life, including her questionable choices of lovers and husbands and her own reflections on her life. Still, Mary's death mask suggests that she was serene at the end. There are tapestries and furniture of the period, and the house's ornamental garden has pear trees leading down to the river. ⊠ *Queen St.* ☎ *01835/863331* ⊕ *www.scotborders. gov.uk* ⊠ *Free* ⊗ *Closed Dec.–Feb.*

🍴 Restaurants

Born in the Borders

$ | BRITISH | FAMILY | This family-friendly complex is built around a café and brewery producing Born in the Borders beer. The café serves breakfast and lunch while a shop sells the on-site brewed beer along with a "ginnery," where visitors can learn about how gin is made and sample a gin-and-tonic after a tour (£5). **Known for:** craft beer and gin; classic café cuisine; surrounding farmland in a remote location. ⑤ *Average main: £10* ⊠ *Lanton Mill* ✛ *Off the A78 near Jedburg* ☎ *01835/830495* ⊕ *www.bornintheborders.com* ⊗ *No dinner.*

The Caddy Mann Restaurant

$$ | BRITISH | This unpretentious restaurant comes with antique tables, decor of assorted bric-a-brac, and an adventurous menu cooked to order. Each day, the chef builds the menu around what local suppliers can offer. **Known for:** dishes focusing on wild game, including the surprisingly popular squirrel; expansive vegetarian menu; famous Sunday roasts. ⑤ *Average main: £18* ⊠ *Mounthooly* ✛ *On the A698, 2 miles outside Jedburgh* ☎ *01835/850787* ⊕ *www.caddymann.com* ⊗ *Closed Mon. and Tues. No dinner Wed., Thurs., and Sun.*

The Capon Tree Town House

$$ | BRITISH | The interiors of this traditional red-sandstone house in central Jedburgh are quite conservative, but the fine-dining menu is creative. Food presentation is artistic, and the taste of what is always local produce confirms the artistry. **Known for:** venison three ways; Thursday steak nights; great cheese board. ⑤ *Average main: £19* ⊠ *61 High St.* ☎ *01835/869596* ⊕ *www.thecapontree.com* ⊗ *Closed Sun. and Mon.*

Hotels

Hundalee House

$ | **B&B/INN** | **FAMILY** | The richly decorated Victorian-style rooms of this 18th-century stone manor house have nice touches such as four-poster beds and cozy fireplaces; 15 acres of gardens and woods surround the B&B. **Pros:** fantastic views of apple orchards; hearty breakfasts; lovely views. **Cons:** farm aromas; far from shops and restaurants; small rooms. *⑤ Rooms from: £80 ⊠ Off A68 ✛ 1 mile south of Jedburgh ☎ 01835/863011 ⊕ www.accommodation-scotland.org ⊗ Closed Jan.–Mar ⌁ 5 rooms ⦿ Free breakfast.*

Meadhon House

$ | **B&B/INN** | On a row of medieval buildings in the heart of town, Meadhon House is a charming 17th-century house with a history to match; rooms are bright and clean, with views onto the street or over the large and fragrant garden behind the house. **Pros:** central location; pleasant rooms; welcoming atmosphere. **Cons:** rooms on the small side; some street noise; garden not open to guests. *⑤ Rooms from: £75 ⊠ 48 Castlegate ☎ 01835/862504 ⊕ www.meadhon.co.uk ▭ No credit cards ⌁ 5 rooms ⦿ Free breakfast.*

Shopping

Edinburgh Woollen Mill

CLOTHING | The shelves at this shop burst with sweaters, kilts, tartan knitwear, and scarves. It's a good place to stock up on gifts. ⊠ *Bendek North, Edinburgh Rd.* ☎ *01835/863773 ⊕ www.ewm.co.uk.*

Kelso

12 miles northeast of Jedburgh.

One of the most charming Borders burghs, Kelso is often described as having a Continental flavor—some people think its broad, paved square makes it resemble a Belgian market town. The community also has some fine examples of Georgian and Victorian Scots town architecture.

GETTING HERE AND AROUND

There are direct bus routes from Jedburgh to Kelso. Edinburgh has direct buses to Jedburgh; buses from Glasgow aren't direct. Your best option is to travel by car. From Jedburgh to Kelso take the A698, which is 12 miles, or about 20 minutes. Alternatively, the A699 is a scenic half-hour drive.

ESSENTIALS

VISITOR INFORMATION Kelso Tourist Information Centre. ⊠ *Town House, The Square* ☎ *01573/221119 ⊕ www.kelso. bordernet.co.uk.*

Sights

★ Floors Castle

CASTLE/PALACE | The palatial Floors Castle, the largest inhabited castle in Scotland, is an architectural extravagance bristling with pepper-mill turrets. Not so much a castle as the ancestral seat of a wealthy and powerful landowning family, the Roxburghes, it stands on the "floors," or flat terrain, on the banks of the River Tweed. The enormous home was built in 1721 by William Adam (1689–1748) and modified by William Playfair (1789–1857), who added the turrets and towers in the 1840s. Rooms are crowded with valuable furniture, paintings, porcelain, and an eerie circular room full of stuffed birds; each room has a knowledgeable guide at the ready. The surrounding 56,000-acre estate is home to more than 40 farms. Although the castle itself is closed to visitors in winter, the grounds and café are open year-round. ⊠ *A6089* ☎ *01573/223333 ⊕ www.floorscastle. com ⌑ Castle and grounds £11.50 ⊗ Castle closed Nov.–Mar. and weekdays in Oct.*

Kelso Abbey

RELIGIOUS SITE | The least intact ruin of the four great abbeys, Kelso Abbey is just a bleak fragment of what was once the largest of the group. It was here in 1460 that the nine-year-old James III was crowned king of Scotland. On a main invasion route, the abbey was burned three times in the 1540s alone, on the last occasion by the English Earl of Hertford's forces in 1545, when the 100 men and 12 monks of the garrison were butchered and the structure all but destroyed. ⊠ *Bridge St.* ☎ *0131/668–8600* ⊕ *www.historicenvironment. scot* ⊠ *Free* ⊙ *Closed Thurs. and Fri. Oct.–Mar.*

Mellerstain House and Gardens

HOUSE | One fine example of the Borders area's ornate country homes is Mellerstain House, begun in the 1720s and finished in the 1770s by Robert Adam (1728–92); it is considered one of his finest creations. Sumptuous plasterwork covers almost all interior surfaces, and there are outstanding examples of 18th-century furnishings, porcelain and china, and paintings and embroidery. The beautiful terraced gardens (open an hour before the house itself) are as renowned as the house. ⊠ *Off A6089, Gordon* ✛ *7 miles northwest of Kelso* ☎ *01573/410636* ⊕ *www.mellerstain.com* ⊠ *Gardens £6, house and gardens £10* ⊙ *Closed Tues.–Thurs. and Oct.–Mar.*

★ Smailholm Tower

BUILDING | Standing uncompromisingly on top of a barren, rocky ridge in the hills south of Mellerstain, this 16th-century peel tower, characteristic of the Borders, was built solely for defense, and its unadorned stones contrast with the luxury of Mellerstain House. If you let your imagination wander at this windy spot, you can almost see the rising dust of an advancing raiding party. Sir Walter Scott found this spot inspiring, and he visited the tower often during his childhood. Anne Carrick's tableaux in the tower illustrate some of Scott's Borders ballads, and the ticket includes an audio tour of the building. ⊠ *Kelso* ✛ *Off B6404, 4½ miles south of Mellerstain House* ☎ *01573/460365* ⊕ *www.historicenvironment.scot* ⊠ *£6* ⊙ *Closed Oct.–Mar.*

Restaurants

The Cobbles

$$ | **BRITISH** | Just off the town's cobbled square, this well-established pub and restaurant with wooden tables and a bustling, cheerful atmosphere seems to be permanently busy. The extensive menu combines generously sized burgers, steaks, and meat pies with the ever-popular fish-and-chips. **Known for:** homemade desserts; craft beer menu; generous portions of classic Scottish cuisine. ⑤ *Average main: £16* ⊠ *7 Bowmont St.* ☎ *01573/223548* ⊕ *www.thecobbleskelso.co.uk.*

🛏 Hotels

Edenwater House

$$ | **B&B/INN** | Overlooking Edenwater, a trout stream that runs into the River Tweed, this handsome stone house has three guest rooms that are luxuriously furnished in a traditional style with flower-pattern fabrics; they offer fine views of the river and the Cheviot hills. **Pros:** excellent food; romantic atmosphere; peaceful surroundings. **Cons:** restaurant open only on weekend evenings; far from urban amenities; popular, so book well ahead. ⑤ *Rooms from: £130* ⊠ *Off B6461, Ednam* ☎ *01573/224070* ⊕ *www. edenwaterhouse.co.uk* ⊅ *3 rooms* ⑩ *Breakfast* ⊄ *No children under 10 allowed.*

★ Ednam House Hotel

$$ | **HOTEL** | This rather grand building on the banks of the River Tweed is close to Kelso's great abbey and sprawling market square. **Pros:** great outdoor activities; atmospheric lobby; impressive restaurant. **Cons:** some rooms need a

The grand Abbotsford House was once home to Sir Walter Scott.

makeover; popular for weddings and other events, so can be crowded; rooms with a river view cost more. ⑤ *Rooms from: £189* ✉ *Bridge St.* ☎ *01573/224168* ⊕ *www.ednamhouse.com* ⊗ *Closed late Dec.–early Jan.* ⇴ *32 rooms* ⑩ *Free breakfast.*

Melrose

15 miles west of Kelso, 4 miles southeast of Galashiels.

Though it's small, there is nevertheless a bustle about Melrose, the perfect example of a prosperous Scottish market town and one of the loveliest in the Borders. It's set around a square lined with 18th- and 19th-century buildings housing myriad small shops and cafés. Despite its proximity to the much larger Galashiels, Melrose has rejected industrialization. You'll likely hear local residents greet each other by first name in the square.

GETTING HERE AND AROUND

Buses do go to Melrose, and the Borders Railway ends at Tweedbank, just 2 miles to the northwest. Driving remains the easiest way to get here from the south or east. From Galashiels, take the A6091 (10 minutes).

Sights

★ Abbotsford House

HOUSE | In this great house overlooking the Tweed, Sir Walter Scott lived, worked, and received the great and the good in luxurious salons. In 1811 the writer bought a farm on this site named Cartleyhole, which was a euphemism for the real name, Clartyhole (*clarty* is Scots for "muddy" or "dirty"). The romantic Scott renamed the property after a ford in the nearby Tweed used by the abbot of Melrose. Scott eventually had the house entirely rebuilt in the Scottish baronial style. It was an expensive project, and Scott wrote feverishly to keep his creditors at bay. John Ruskin, the art critic, disapproved, calling it an "incongruous pile," but most contemporary visitors find it fascinating, particularly because of its expansive views and delightful gardens.

A free audio tour guides you around the salon, the circular study, and the library with its 9,000 leather-bound volumes. Perhaps more than anyone else, Scott redefined Scotland as a place of mystery and romance, and awoke the English, who read him avidly, to its natural beauty and its past—or at least a heavily drama-tized version of it. The visitor center hous-es displays about Scott's life, a gift shop, and a restaurant serving lunch. To get here, take the A6091 from Melrose and follow the signs for Abbotsford. ⊠ B6360 ⊹ Between Melrose and Tweedbank ☎ 01896/752043 ⊕ www.scottsabbots-ford.co.uk ⊠ House and gardens £11.20; gardens only £5.60 ☉ House closed Dec.–Feb.

Dryburgh Abbey
RELIGIOUS SITE | The final resting place of Sir Walter Scott and his wife, and the most peaceful and secluded of the Borders abbeys, the "gentle ruins" of Dryburgh Abbey sit on parkland in a loop of the Tweed. The abbey, founded in 1150, suffered from English raids until, like Melrose, it was abandoned in 1544. The style is transitional, a mingling of rounded Romanesque and pointed early English. The north transept, where the Haig and Scott families lie buried, is lofty and pillared, and once formed part of the abbey church. ⊠ St. Boswell's, B6404 ☎ 01835/822381 ⊕ www.historicenviron-ment.scot ⊠ £6.

★ Melrose Abbey
RELIGIOUS SITE | Just off Melrose's town square sit the ruins of Melrose Abbey, one of the four Borders abbeys: "If thou would'st view fair Melrose aright, go visit it in the pale moonlight," wrote Scott in The Lay of the Last Minstrel. So many of his fans took the advice literally that a custodian begged him to rewrite the lines. Today the abbey is still impres-sive: a red-sandstone shell with slender windows, delicate tracery, and carved capitals, all carefully maintained. Among the carvings high on the roof is one of a bagpipe-playing pig. An audio tour is included in the admission price. The heart of 14th-century national hero Robert the Bruce is rumored to be buried here. You can tour the on-site museum and its historical artifacts for free in July and August, but be sure to book in advance. ⊠ Abbey St. ☎ 01896/822562 ⊕ www.historicenvironment.scot ⊠ £6.

Priorwood Garden and Harmony Garden
GARDEN | The National Trust for Scotland's Priorwood Garden, next to Melrose Abbey, specializes in flowers for drying, and dried flowers are on sale in the shop. Next to the gardens is an orchard with some old apple varieties. The walled Harmony Garden, belonging to the lovely Georgian house at its heart, sits nearby opposite the abbey. ⊠ Abbey St. ☎ 01896/822493 ⊕ www.nts.org.uk ⊠ Free ☉ Closed Nov.–Mar.

Scott's View
VIEWPOINT | This is possibly the most photographed rural view in the south of Scotland. (It's almost as iconic as Eilean Donan Castle, far to the north.) The sinuous curve of the River Tweed and the gentle landscape unfolding to the triple peaks of the Eildons and then rolling out into the shadows beyond are certainly worth seeking out. ⊠ B6356, Dryburgh ⊹ 3 miles east of Melrose.

Thirlestane Castle
CASTLE/PALACE | This large, turreted, and castellated house, part of which was built in the 13th century and part in the 16th century, looks for all the world like a French château, and it brims with history. The former home of the Duke of Lauder-dale (1616–82), one of Charles II's advis-ers, Thirlestane is said to be haunted by the duke's ghost. Exquisite 17th-century plaster ceilings and rich collections of paintings, porcelain, and furniture fill the rooms. In the nursery, children are invited to play with Victorian-style toys and to

dress up in masks and costumes. Guided tours are available 11 to 2. ⊠ *Off A68 at Lauder, Lauder ✛ 11 miles north of Melrose* ☎ *01578/722430* ⊕ *www.thirlestanecastle.co.uk* ✉ *Castle and grounds £9.50; grounds only £4* ⊙ *Closed Fri., Sat., and Nov.⬚Apr.*

Trimontium Museum and Three Hills Roman Heritage Centre

MUSEUM | Run by extremely knowledgeable enthusiasts, this museum has such artifacts as tools, weapons, and armor retrieved from the largest Roman settlement in Scotland, Trimontium, which was located at nearby Newstead. The center offers walking tours to the site every Thursday at 1:30 pm (and Tuesdays in July and August). It is well worth taking the tour, which lasts four hours. Within the small museum, a blacksmith's shop, several examples of pottery, and scale models of the fort are also on display. ⊠ *The Ormiston, Market Sq.* ☎ *01896/822651* ⊕ *www.trimontium. org.uk* ✉ *Museum £2, tour £4* ⊙ *Closed Nov.–Mar.*

Restaurants

Hergés on the Loch

$$ | **ECLECTIC** | At this light and airy place, a wall of windows allows you to contemplate swans and ducks as they float serenely across Gunknowe Loch, and, if the weather allows, you can dine on the terrace. The elegant but understated food, well presented and served in generous portions, includes familiar dishes like steak-and-ale pie, fish-and-chips, and steak. **Known for:** restful setting with loch views; reasonable prices; familiar food prepared imaginatively. ⑤ *Average main: £15* ⊠ *Tweedbank Dr., Tweedbank* ☎ *01896/759909* ⊕ *www.hergesontheloch.com.*

Seasons

$$$ | **BRITISH** | A family-run restaurant in an appealing village setting, Seasons has a reputation for using local produce

consistently well in imaginative ways. White walls and wooden tables create an uncluttered setting for the elegant and creative dishes offered. **Known for:** fresh local ingredients; delicious bread; on-site garden provides herbs and vegetables. ⑤ *Average main: £21* ⊠ *Main St., Gattonside* ☎ *01896/823217* ⊕ *www.seasonsborders.co.uk* ⊙ *Closed Mon. and Tues. No lunch Wed. and Thurs.*

Hotels

Burts Hotel

$$ | **HOTEL** | Dating from the 18th century, this charming whitewashed building in the center of Melrose has individually decorated and different rooms filled with floral pastels. **Pros:** walking distance to restaurants and pubs; good restaurant on-site; central location. **Cons:** rooms can be tiny; slightly overpriced for some rooms; bar can get noisy. ⑤ *Rooms from: £148* ⊠ *Market Sq.* ☎ *01896/822285* ⊕ *www.burtshotel.co.uk* ⟿ *20 rooms* ⑩ *Free breakfast.*

Dryburgh Abbey Hotel

$ | **HOTEL** | Mature woodlands and verdant lawns surround this imposing, 19th-century mansion-turned-hotel, which is adjacent to the ruins of Dryburgh Abbey on a sweeping bend of the River Tweed. **Pros:** beautiful grounds; romantic setting; swimming pool, a rarity in this part of the country. **Cons:** some rooms need to be freshened up; service can be on the slow side; some (but not all) rooms look out onto the grounds. ⑤ *Rooms from: £114* ⊠ *Off B6404, St. Boswells* ☎ *01835/822261* ⊕ *www.dryburgh.co.uk* ⟿ *38 rooms* ⑩ *Free breakfast.*

Shopping

Abbey Mill

CLOTHING | Take a break from sightseeing at Abbey Mill, where you'll find hand-woven knitwear as well as homemade jams and fudge. The wee tearoom is also popular. ⊠ *Annay Rd.* ☎ *01896/822138.*

Selkirk

6 miles south of Galashiels, 11 miles north of Hawick.

Selkirk is a hilly outpost with a smattering of antiques shops and an assortment of bakers selling Selkirk bannock (fruited sweet bread) and other cakes. It is the site of one of Scotland's iconic battles, Flodden Field, commemorated here with a statue in the town. Sir Walter Scott was sheriff (judge) of Selkirkshire from 1800 until his death in 1832, and his statue stands in Market Place. Selkirk is also near Bowhill, a stately home.

The town claims its Common Riding (⊕ *returntotheridings.co.uk*) is the largest mounted gathering anywhere in Europe. More than 400 riders take part in the event in June. It's also the oldest Borders festival, with roots back to the Battle of Flodden in 1513.

GETTING HERE AND AROUND

If you're driving, take the A7 south to Galashiels. The scenic journey is less than 7 miles and takes around 10 minutes. First Edinburgh Bus offers a regular service between Galashiels and Selkirk.

ESSENTIALS

VISITOR INFORMATION Selkirk Visitor Information Centre. ⊠ *Halliwell's House, Market Pl.* ☎ *01750/20054* ⊕ *www. visitscotland.com.*

 ## Sights

Bowhill

HOUSE | Home of the Duke of Buccleuch, Bowhill dates from the 19th century and houses an outstanding collection of works by Gainsborough, Van Dyck, Canaletto, Reynolds, and Raeburn, as well as porcelain and period furniture. Although the grounds are mostly accessible from April through September, access to the house is only by guided tours on specific days in the summer; check the website for exact dates. There is an excellent adventure playground for the kids and a 57-mile country ride for those who prefer horseback riding. A local stable hires out horses. ⊠ *Off A708* ✢ *3 miles west of Selkirk* ☎ *01750/22204* ⊕ *www.bowhill-house.co.uk* ⊡ *Grounds £5.50, house and grounds £11* ☉ *Closed Oct.–Mar. and Mon.–Thurs. in June and Sept.*

Halliwell's House Museum

MUSEUM | Tucked off the main square, Halliwell's House Museum was once an ironmonger's shop, which is now re-created downstairs. Upstairs, an exhibit tells the town's story, illustrates the working lives of its inhabitants, and provides useful background information on the Common Ridings. ⊠ *Halliwell's Close, Market Pl.* ☎ *01750/20096* ⊕ *www.scotborders. gov.uk* ⊡ *Free* ☉ *Closed Nov.–Mar.*

Lochcarron Visitor Centre

FACTORY | You can take an informative guided tour of this world-renowned working textile mill and also purchase some of the best woolen goods on offer, from knitwear to tartans and tweeds. The shop also sells Scottish jewelry. ⊠ *Dinsdale Rd.* ☎ *01750/726100* ⊕ *www.lochcarron. com* ⊡ *Tour £9.95* ☉ *Closed Sun.*

Philiphaugh Salmon Viewing Centre

LOCAL INTEREST | On the site of a famous battle in 1645 in which the Scottish Covenanters drove off the pro-English armies under the Earl of Montrose, the Philiphaugh Salmon Viewing Centre is devoted to more peaceful pursuits: watching salmon. Its viewing platforms and underwater cameras allow you to follow the life cycle of the salmon. There are also country walks and cycling routes to follow, and a tearoom. The website has a self-guided audio tour of the battlefield. ⊠ *A708* ✢ *1 mile outside Selkirk* ☎ *01750/21766* ⊕ *www.salmonviewing-centre.com* ⊡ *Free.*

Sir Walter Scott's Courtroom

MUSEUM | The historic courtroom where Sir Walter Scott presided as sheriff from 1804 to 1832 contains a display examining his life, writings, and time on the bench. It uses models to re-create the atmosphere of a 19th-century Scottish court and includes an audio-visual presentation. A statue of the famous writer overlooks the comings and goings outside the court. ⊠ *Market Sq.* ☎ *01750/720761* ⊕ *www.scotborders. gov.uk* ⊠ *Free* ⊙ *Closed Nov.–Feb.*

The Three Brethren

VIEWPOINT | These three identical cairns, 9 feet high and 6 feet around at the base, are the end point of a fairly strenuous 11-mile walk that begins 4 miles north of Selkirk on the A707. The view from the Three Brethren is spectacular and embraces the whole of the Borders. Park at the car park at Philipburn on the A707, 4 miles from Selkirk. The path is signposted from there. ⊠ *A707* ⊠ *Free.*

Hotels

Best Western Philipburn House Hotel

$$ | HOTEL | West of Selkirk, this Alpine-style hotel enjoys a lovely setting among the woods and hills. **Pros:** pleasant rural setting; bright rooms; on-site parking. **Cons:** no elevator; restaurant closes rather early; breakfast is extra. ⑤ *Rooms from: £130* ⊠ *Linglie Rd.* ⊹ *Opposite Salmon Viewing Centre* ☎ *01750/720747* ⊕ *www.bw-philipburnhousehotel.co.uk* ⇨ *24 rooms* �◎ *No meals.*

Hawick

10 miles south of Selkirk, 14 miles southwest of Jedburgh.

Hawick (pronounced *hoyk*) is a busy town at the center of the region's textile industry, commemorated in the interesting Borders Textile Towerhouse. The Victorian buildings along its High Street recall the town's heyday. The largest community in the Borders, it's a good place to buy the delicate cashmere and woolen goods that made the region famous. Hawick's

Common Riding festival, held each June, draws onlookers from all over Scotland.

GETTING HERE AND AROUND

Driving here from Selkirk or Jedburgh is no trouble—it's a straight shot on major roads. There is also bus service from many of the other Borders towns.

ESSENTIALS

VISITOR INFORMATION Hawick Visitor Centre. ⊠ *Towermill, Kirkstile* ☎ *01450/373993* ⊕ *www.visitscotland. com.*

Sights

Borders Textile Towerhouse

MUSEUM | **FAMILY** | In the former Drumlanrig Tower, this museum includes a good exhibition about the textile industry, once the lifeblood of the Borders. Plenty of interactive elements make it interesting for children as well. One room commemorates the demonstrations by textile workers who were demanding the right to vote in the 1880s. On the upper floor are up-to-the-minute fabrics that define the 21st century. Check out the shop, too. ⊠ *1 Tower Knowe* ☎ *01450/377615* ⊠ *Free* ⊙ *Closed Tues. and Sun. Nov.–Mar.*

Restaurants

★ Damascus Drum

$ | CAFÉ | Decorated in muted colors, this lovely little café and bookshop named for a traditional folktale (you can find it on the tables) provides a tranquil refuge in the town center. It's a perfect spot for a light lunch; choose from a limited menu that includes soup, delicious meze, and burgers with or without meat. **Known for:** vegetarian burgers; quiet atmosphere; lovely bookstore that is regularly host to readings and book launches. ⑤ *Average main: £10* ⊠ *2 Silver St.* ☎ *07707/856123* ⊕ *www.damascusdrum.co.uk* ⊙ *Closed Sun. No dinner.*

🛍 Shopping

Hawick Factory Visitor Centre

CLOTHING | This is a good place to see knitwear in the making—literally. In the shop you can buy knitwear and cashmere goods for discounted prices. ✉ *Trinity Mills, Duke St.* ☎ *01450/371221* ⊕ *www.hawico.com.*

Innerleithen

17 miles northwest of Hawick.

Innerleithen is one of the larger Borders towns; you'll feel that you've entered a hub of activity when you arrive. It's also dramatically beautiful. Surrounded by hills and glens, the town is where the Tweed and Leithen rivers join, then separate. Historically, Innerleithen dates back to pre-Roman times, and there are artifacts all around for you to see. Once a booming industrial town of wool mills, today it's a great destination for outdoor activities including hiking, biking, and fly-fishing.

GETTING HERE AND AROUND

To drive to Innerleithen, take the A7 north from Hawick and then the A707 northwest from Selkirk. There are no trains between the two towns.

👁 Sights

Robert Smail's Printing Works

FACTORY | **FAMILY** | Try your hand at printing the way it used to be done: painstakingly setting each letter by hand. Robert Smail's print shop, founded in 1866 to produce materials for nearby factories, boat tickets, theater posters, and the local newspaper, is still a working print shop as well as a museum. Two great waterwheels once powered the presses, and they are still running. The guided tour, which includes making your own bookmark, takes 90 minutes. ✉ *7–9 High St.* ☎ *01896/830206* ⊕ *www.nts.*

org.uk ✉ *£7* ⊙ *Closed Oct.–Mar. and Tues.–Thurs.*

★ Traquair House

HOUSE | Said to be the oldest continually occupied home in Scotland (since 1107), Traquair House has secret stairways and passages, a library with more than 3,000 books, and a bed said to be used by Mary, Queen of Scots in 1566. You can walk freely through the rooms, and each has an explanatory leaflet as well as helpful guides. The top floor of the house is an interesting small museum. Outside is a reasonably scary maze, an adventure playground, and some lovely woodland walks as well as pigs, goats, and chickens. The 18th-century brew house still makes highly recommended ale, and there's a café on the grounds near the beautiful walled garden. The Traquair Fair in August is the nearest you are likely to get to a medieval fair, and well worth the visit. You may even spend the night, if you wish. ✉ *B709* ⊹ *From the A70 some 6 miles south of Peebles, take the B709 for 7 miles; the car entrance into the house is in the village* ☎ *01896/830323* ⊕ *www.traquair.co.uk* ✉ *Grounds £4, house and grounds £8.80, guided tours £10* ⊙ *Closed Dec.–Mar. and weekdays in Nov.*

Hotels

Traquair House

$$ | **B&B/INN** | Staying in one of the guest rooms in the 12th-century wing of Traquair House is to experience a slice of Scottish history. **Pros:** stunning grounds; spacious rooms; great breakfast. **Cons:** nearly 2 miles to restaurants and shops; rooms fill up quickly in summer; parking can be difficult in summer months. 💲 *Rooms from: £200* ✉ *B709* ☎ *01896/830323* ⊕ *www.traquair.co.uk* ⇴ *3 rooms* ⧀ *Free breakfast.*

Windlestraw Lodge

$$ | **HOTEL** | This elegant bed-and-breakfast and restaurant occupies a grand

Edwardian country home surrounded by extensive gardens. **Pros:** beautifully designed rooms; excellent restaurant; lovely location. **Cons:** a bit expensive for what you get; not all rooms have Tweed views; restaurant is pricey. *$ Rooms from: £190 ⊠ 9 Galashiels Rd., Walkerburn ⊕ On the A72 between Galashiels and Innerleithen ☎ 01896/870636 ⊕ www.windlestraw.co.uk ↪ 6 rooms ⦿ Free breakfast.*

Peebles

6 miles west of Innerleithen.

Thanks to its excellent though pricey shopping, Peebles gives the impression of catering primarily to leisured country gentlefolk. Architecturally, the town is nothing out of the ordinary, just a very pleasant burgh. Don't miss the splendid dolphins ornamenting the bridge crossing the River Tweed.

GETTING HERE AND AROUND
Because of its size and location, direct buses run from both Edinburgh and Glasgow to Peebles. There are also buses here from Innerleithen, though driving from here is more direct. (Take the A72; it's about a 10-minute drive.)

ESSENTIALS
VISITOR INFORMATION Peebles
Visitor Information Centre. ⊠ *23 High St.* ☎ *01721/728095 ⊕ www.visitscotland. com.*

 Sights

Peebles War Memorial
MEMORIAL | The exotic, almost Moorish mosaics of the Peebles War Memorial are unique in Scotland, although most towns have a memorial to honor those killed in service. It's a remarkable tribute to the 225 Peebleans killed in World War II. ⊠ *Chambers Quadrangle, High St.* ☞ *Free.*

 Restaurants

★ Adam Room
$$ | BRITISH | FAMILY | With a minstrels' gallery, crystal chandeliers, and tall windows with views over the Tweed, the dining room at the Tontine Hotel has a grand feel. It's a bit surprising, therefore, that it also serves good home cooking for the family at reasonable prices. **Known for:** traditional home cooking; luxurious dining room; solid wine list. *$ Average main: £18 ⊠ Tontine Hotel, High St.* ☎ *01721/720892 ⊕ www.tontinehotel. com.*

Coltman's Delicatessen and Kitchen
$$$ | DELI | The pleasant white-walled, modern dining room of this bright, airy eatery sits behind the tempting deli counter, and its windows overlook the Tweed. All-day options include salads, platters, and sandwiches, while the compact but finely balanced dinner menu offers choices such as cod with a mussel-and-saffron broth and a hanger steak with braised shallots. **Known for:** tasty deli lunches; tempting desserts; well-balanced dinner menu. *$ Average main: £24 ⊠ 71–73 High St.* ☎ *01721/720405 ⊕ www.coltmans.co.uk ⊙ No dinner Sun.–Wed.*

Horseshoe Inn
$$ | BRITISH | The opulent dining room at the Horseshoe has large gold-framed mirrors and heavy drapes to emphasize its grand style. The dinner menu combines well-established favorites with fine dining, from fish-and-chips to roast lamb and baked cod. **Known for:** Scottish fine dining; Sunday roast menu; luxurious surroundings. *$ Average main: £18 ⊠ Horseshoe Inn, Eddleston* ☎ *01721/730225 ⊕ www.horseshoeinn. co.uk.*

Hotels

Cringletie House

$$ | **HOTEL** | With medieval-style turrets and crow-step gables, this small-scale, peaceful retreat manages to be fancy *and* homey, Victorian (it was built in the 1860s) and modern (flat-screen TVs). **Pros:** elegant bedrooms; cozy fireplaces; decadent dining. **Cons:** some bedrooms have low ceilings; atmosphere can be almost too quiet; some public rooms a little faded. $ *Rooms from: £197* ✉ *Edinburgh Rd.* ✛ *Off the A703, 2 miles north of Peebles* ☎ *01721/725750* ⊕ *www.cringletie.com* ☉ *Closed Nov.–Feb.* ⛺ *13 rooms* ⦿ *Breakfast.*

Peebles Hydro

$$ | **HOTEL** | **FAMILY** | One of the great "hydro hotels" built in the 19th century for those anxious to "take the waters," the family-friendly Peebles Hydro has comfortable if rather old-fashioned rooms that are slowly but surely being renovated. **Pros:** plenty of activities available, including a gin school and archery; interesting history; delicious breakfast. **Cons:** can feel impersonal; some rooms have bland decor; still an air of faded glory despite renovations. $ *Rooms from: £170* ✉ *Innerleithen Rd.* ☎ *01721/720602* ⊕ *www.peebleshydro.co.uk* ⛺ *132 rooms* ⦿ *Breakfast.*

Tontine Hotel

$ | **HOTEL** | A small and charming facade hides a spacious, lovingly refurbished (an ongoing process) hotel that stretches back from Peebles High Street and has lovely views of the Tweed River. **Pros:** centrally located; pleasant rooms; good restaurant on-site. **Cons:** some small rear rooms; old-fashioned decor in some areas; no elevator. $ *Rooms from: £104* ✉ *High St.* ☎ *01721/729732* ⊕ *www.tontinehotel.com* ⛺ *36 rooms* ⦿ *Breakfast.*

Performing Arts

Eastgate Theatre

CONCERTS | A year-round program of films, concerts, and theater as well as community activities for adults and children are on offer here. The theater also has a very pleasant café. ✉ *1 School Brae* ☎ *01721/725777* ⊕ *www.eastgatearts.com.*

Shopping

Be prepared for temptations at every turn as you browse the shops on High Street and in the courts and side streets leading off it.

Caledonia

CLOTHING | For anything and everything Scottish, from kilts to dirks and jams to tablecloths, look no further than Caledonia. You can also rent kilts here. ✉ *57 High St.* ☎ *01721/722343* ⊕ *caledonialifestyle.com.*

Head to Toe

GIFTS/SOUVENIRS | The shop stocks natural beauty products, handmade pine furniture, and handsome linens—from patchwork quilts to silk flowers. ✉ *43 High St.* ☎ *01721/722752* ⊕ *www.headtotoepeebles.co.uk.*

Keith Walter

JEWELRY/ACCESSORIES | Among the many jewelers on High Street, Keith Walter is a master of gold and silver who makes his creations on the premises. He also stocks jewelry made by other local designers. ✉ *28 High St.* ☎ *01721/720650* ⊕ *www.keithwalterjeweller.co.uk.*

Activities

Glentress Bike Shop

BICYCLING | Located just outside of Peebles, the 7Stanes mountain biking center at Glentress is widely regarded as one of the best in Europe. Its trails take cyclists and hikers through forestry commission lands; the trail lengths vary between 2 and 18 miles long and from fairly basic to extremely difficult. On-site, there's also an information center, a bike shop with rentals (from £25), and an excellent café as well as changing rooms and showers. Entry is free, but all-day parking costs £3.50. ⊠ *On A68* ✛ *2 miles outside Peebles* ☎ *01721/724522* ⊕ *www.tiso.com/shops/glentress.*

Go Ape Glentress

ZIP LINING | In the forests of Glentress, Go Ape is made for those who prefer treetop adventures to cycling or walking. With a combination of climbing and ziplines, you'll explore the treetops of Glentress; your adventure lasts between two and three hours (and the Glentress Cycling Centre café is nearby for post-treetop relaxation). ⊠ *Glentres Forest, Falla Brae* ☎ *01721/722361* ⊕ *www.goape.co.uk* ☞ *From £26.40.*

Gretna Green

10 miles north of Carlisle, England, 87 miles south of Glasgow, 92 miles southwest of Edinburgh.

The first town across the English–Scottish border, Gretna Green (not to be confused with nearby Gretna) was historically where runaway couples went to be married by the local blacksmith under Scotland's more lenient laws. No one could accuse the town of failing to exploit its reputation as the place to tie the knot. Although it is highly commercialized, it is still a favorite venue for weddings, even though the original reasons for going have long since changed.

GETTING HERE AND AROUND

From Glasgow you can reach Gretna Green via the M74 and A74; it's an hour-and-a-half drive. From Edinburgh take the A74 (about two hours). Buses and trains travel daily to Gretna Green from Glasgow and Edinburgh.

ESSENTIALS

VISITOR INFORMATION Gretna Green Tourist Information Centre. ⊠ *Gretna Gateway Outlet Village, Glasgow Rd., Gretna* ☎ *01461/337834* ⊕ *www.gretnagreen.com.*

 Sights

Blacksmith's Shop

HISTORIC SITE | Today the 18th-century house of the village blacksmith, known as the "anvil priest," contains a collection of blacksmithing tools, as well as the anvil over which many weddings may have been conducted to symbolize the forging of the link between two people. The village was on the new coaching road from London to Edinburgh when the marriage laws in England became more restrictive than Scotland's, where, for a time at least, boys and girls in their early teens could marry without parental permission. Gretna Green was the first place in Scotland runaway couples reached after crossing the border, hence its fame and the fact that over 1,000 couples a year still go there to marry. Today it also contains a shop, restaurant, and museum, as well as the Courtship Maze, which couples enter separately in the hope of finding each other. ⊠ *Headless Cross* ☎ *01461/338441* ⊕ *www.gretnagreen.com* ▣ *Museum £4.20.*

 Activities

Powfoot Golf Club

GOLF | A pleasant mix of links and parkland holes, this course looks out across the Solway Firth. Its roughs and the tough thorny whins (local bushes with yellow flowers) make the course quite challenging, especially when the wind blows off the firth in summer, but it is the views from here that make it memorable and a pleasure to play. Powfoot is included in the Gateway to Golf Pass. The club is 14 miles west of Gretna Green via the A75. ⊠ *Off B724, Cummertrees, Annan*

☎ 01461/204100 ⊕ www.powfootgolf-club.com ⊠ Mid-Mar.–Sept., £40 week-days, £46 weekends; Oct.–early Mar., £23 ⅃. 18 holes, 6250 yards, par 71.

Dumfries

24 miles west of Gretna Green, 76 miles south of Glasgow, 81 miles southwest of Edinburgh.

The River Nith meanders through Dum-fries, and the pedestrian-only center of this town of 31,000 makes wandering and shopping a pleasure. Author J. M. Barrie (1860–1937) spent his childhood in Dumfries, and the garden of Moat Brae House is said to have inspired his boyish dreams in *Peter Pan*. But the town also has a justified claim to Robert Burns, who lived and worked here for several years. His house and his favorite *howff* (pub), The Globe Inn, are here, too, as is his final resting place in St. Michael's Churchyard.

The Dumfries & Galloway Tourist Board has a lodging service and also sells golf passes for the region at £70 for three rounds.

GETTING HERE AND AROUND
Public transportation is a good option for reaching Dumfries—there's a good train station here, and most major Scottish cities have regular daily bus routes to the town. If you're driving from Gretna Green, take the A75; it's a 35-minute drive. From Glasgow take the M74 to the A701. From Edinburgh take the A701.

ESSENTIALS
VISITOR INFORMATION Dumfries & Galloway Tourist Board. ⊠ 64 Whitesands ☎ 01387/253862 ⊕ www.visitscotland. com.

⊙ Sights

Dumfries Museum and Camera Obscura
MUSEUM | A camera obscura is essentially a huge reflecting mirror that projects an extraordinarily clear panoramic view of the surrounding countryside onto an internal wall. The one at the Dumfries Museum, which claims to be the oldest in the world, is housed in the old Wind-mill Tower, built in 1836. The museum itself covers the culture and daily life of the people living in the Dumfries and Galloway region from the earliest times. ⊠ Rotchell Rd. ☎ 01387/253374 ⊕ www.dumgal.gov.uk/artsandmuseums ⊠ Museum free; Camera Obscura £3.60 ⊙ Closed Nov.–Mar.

Globe Inn
HISTORIC SITE | Poet Robert Burns spent quite a lot of time at the Globe Inn, where he frequently fell asleep in the tack room beside the stables; today it's still an active pub where you can eat and drink. Burns later graduated to the upstairs bedroom where he slept with his wife, Jean Armour, and scratched some lines of poetry on the window. The room is preserved (or at least partly re-created), and the bar staff will happily show you around if you ask. But beware, if you choose to sit in Burns's chair in the bar, tradition has it that you have to buy a round for the whole pub. ⊠ 56 High St. ☎ 01387/252335 ⊕ www.globeinndum-fries.co.uk ⊠ Free.

Gracefield Arts Centre
ARTS CENTERS | With galleries hosting changing exhibits of Scottish art mostly from the 1840s to today, Gracefield Arts Centre also has a well-stocked crafts shop. A café serves lunch and snacks. ⊠ 28 Edinburgh Rd. ☎ 01387/262084 ⊕ www.exploreart.co.uk ⊠ Free.

John Paul Jones Museum
MUSEUM | The little community of Kirk-bean is the backdrop for the bright-green landscape of the Arbigland Estate; in a cottage here, now the John Paul Jones

Museum, John Paul (1747–92), the son of an estate gardener, was born. He eventually left Scotland, added "Jones" to his name, and became the founder of the U.S. Navy. The cottage where he was born is furnished as it would have been when he was a boy. There is an informative video, which you watch in a reconstruction of his captain's cabin. Jones returned to raid the coastline of his native country in 1778, an exploit recounted in an adjoining visitor center. ⊠ *Off A710, Kirkbean ⊕ 12 miles south of Dumfries on the A710* ☎ *01387/880613* ⊕ *www. jpj.demon.co.uk* ⊠ *£4.50* ⊘ *Closed Oct.–Mar.*

Moat Brae and the Neverland Garden

HOUSE | FAMILY | Writer J.M. Barrie was a regular visitor to the Gordon family's grand Edwardian home at Moat Brae. The stories he told their children would eventually go on to become the tale of *Peter Pan*, and the house's on-site garden was the inspiration for Neverland. Today the garden has a replica of Captain Hook's ship, where kids can play. After coming perilously close to demolition, the house was saved and restored to its original state over several years, and the on-site center has been conceived as a National Storytelling Centre rather than simply a historical museum. It's meant to be a place where today's children can exercise their own imaginations. In the children's bedroom, Tinkerbell flies around the walls, and you can try to catch her. ⊠ *101 George St.* ☎ *01387/255549* ⊕ *www.peterpanmoatbrae.org* ⊘ *Closed Mon. Sept.–Apr.*

Sweetheart Abbey

RELIGIOUS SITE | At the center of the village of New Abbey are the impressive red-tinted, roofless remains of Sweetheart Abbey, founded in 1273 by the Lady of Galloway Devorgilla (1210-90), who, it is said, kept her dead husband's heart in a tiny casket she carried everywhere. After she died, she was laid to rest in the Abbey with the casket resting

on her breast. The couple's son John Balliol (1249–1315) was the puppet king installed in Scotland by Edward of England when the latter claimed sovereignty over Scotland. After John's appointment the Scots gave him a scathing nickname that would stay with him for the rest of his life: Toom Tabard (Empty Shirt). Currently the higher section of the abbey is closed for restoration, leaving only the lower parts accessible for visitors. Entry is free. ⊠ *A710, New Abbey ⊕ 7 miles south of Dumfries* ☎ *01387/253849* ⊕ *www.historic-scotland.gov.uk* ⊠ *Free.*

Robert Burns Centre

MUSEUM | Not surprisingly, Dumfries has its own Robert Burns Centre, housed in a sturdy 18th-century former mill overlooking the River Nith. The center has an audiovisual program and an extensive exhibit about the life of the poet. It also now houses Dumfries's only cinema. ⊠ *Mill Rd.* ☎ *01387/264808* ⊕ *www.dum-gal.gov.uk/artsandmuseums* ⊠ *Free.*

Robert Burns House

HOUSE | Poet Robert Burns (1759–96) lived here, on what was then called Mill Street, for the last three years of his life, when his salary from the customs service allowed him to improve his living standards. Many distinguished writers of the day visited him here, including William Wordsworth. The house contains some of his writings and letters, a few pieces of furniture, and some family memorabilia. ⊠ *Burns St.* ☎ *01387/255297* ⊕ *www.dumgal.gov.uk/ artsandmuseums* ⊠ *Free.*

St. Michael's Churchyard

CEMETERY | When he died in 1796, Robert Burns was buried in a modest grave in St. Michael's Churchyard. English poet William Wordsworth, visiting a few years later, was horrified by the small gravestone and raised money to build the much grander monument that stands there today. ⊠ *39 Cardiness St.* ☎ *01387/253849* ⊕ *www.dumgal.gov.uk/ artsandmuseums* ⊠ *Free.*

Restaurants

Cavens Arms

$ | **BRITISH** | This lively, welcoming traditional pub in the center of town has a separate bar and dining area, comfortable seating, and a large selection of beers. It's a magnet for locals at dinnertime and always seems to be busy, a testimony to the quality of its food as well as the large portions. **Known for:** local beers; good food in generous pub portions; vibrant atmosphere. ⑤ *Average main: £13* ✉ *20 Buccleuch St.* ☎ *01387/252896.*

Home Restaurant

$$ | **MEDITERRANEAN** | This tiny family-run restaurant has quickly gained a considerable reputation for fine cooking. The menu is small and changes regularly but is consistently of high quality. **Known for:** fine cooking with local ingredients; excellent slow beef with polenta; reservations a must. ⑤ *Average main: £16* ✉ *Above the Coach and Horses, Whitesands* ☎ *01387/262296* ⊕ *www.facebook.com/ homedumfries/* ☾ *Closed Sun.–Wed. No lunch.*

The Stove Cafe

$ | **BAKERY** | In the very center of Dumfries, this café offers wholesome breakfasts, sandwiches, and cakes. It's also a blossoming arts center with music and other events throughout the year. **Known for:** good coffee; relaxed atmosphere good for hanging out; popular breakfasts and brunches. ⑤ *Average main: £10* ✉ *100 High St.* ☎ *01387/252435* ⊕ *www. thestove.org* ☾ *Closed Sun.*

🛏 Hotels

Cairndale Hotel

$ | **HOTEL** | Centrally located, the Cairndale has a Victorian Gothic appearance and spacious and comfortable rooms. **Pros:** central location; comfortable rooms; pool, sauna, and gym. **Cons:** generally old-fashioned feel; can get very crowded; small lobby. ⑤ *Rooms from: £93* ✉ *132–6*

English St. ☎ *01387/354111* ⊕ *www. cairndalehotel.co.uk* ⇱ *91 rooms* ⑂�’ *Free breakfast.*

Holiday Inn

$ | **HOTEL** | With the secluded feel of a country hotel, this modern Holiday Inn less than 2 miles from the center of Dumfries is set in the Crichton Estate (owned by the University of the West of Scotland), with its lush plantings, rock gardens, and elegant Victorian buildings. **Pros:** beautiful setting; very different from your standard Holiday Inn; easy access to Dumfries. **Cons:** slightly institutional feel; a little remote from the town; frequently used for weddings and large events. ⑤ *Rooms from: £79* ✉ *Bankend Rd., Crichton* ☎ *01387/272410* ⊕ *www.hidumfries.co.uk* ⇱ *71 rooms* ⑂�’ *Breakfast.*

Shopping

Dumfries is the main shopping center for the region, with all the big-name chain stores as well as specialty shops.

★ Loch Arthur Creamery and Farm Shop

FOOD/CANDY | Known for its high-quality dairy products, this lively and active farm run by the Camphill community in the charmingly named village of Beeswing has an expansive café and retail store selling a range of organic products. Much of what you eat or buy is produced on the farm, where they make their own bread, butcher their meat, and cook the delicious food served here. The building itself has large windows opening directly on to the fields beyond; on a nice day, you can eat outside. There's always freshly baked bread, cakes, cheeses, cold meats, and soups to choose from, all made on the farm. ✉ *On A711, Beeswing* ✛ *6 miles south of Dumfries* ☎ *01387/259669* ⊕ *www.locharthur.org.uk.*

🏃 Activities

G&G Cycle Centre

BICYCLING | You can rent bicycles here, and the staff gives good advice on route options. ✉ *10–12 Academy St.* ☎ *01387/259483* ⊕ *www.cycle-centre. co.uk.*

North of Dumfries

18 miles northwest of Dumfries.

Travel north along the A70 from Dumfries for a short trip through time at some very different attractions. Drumlanrig Castle is one of Scotland's grandest houses, set amid hills, moorland, and forest. In contrast, the world of lead miners, explored at the Museum of Lead Mining, was a great deal harsher. A spectacular modern addition to the area, the land artwork *Crawick Multiverse,* transforms the landscape into a mirror of the heavens. Sculptor Andy Goldsworthy's *Striding Arches* frame a natural space and invite the walker to explore them.

GETTING HERE AND AROUND

Trains run from Dumfries to Sanquhar, near *Crawick Multiverse.* You can get a bus from Dumfries to Drumlanrig and Sanquhar along the A701. For Ledhills and the mining museum, it's best to drive. The same is true for *Striding Arches*: Take the A76 from Dumfried to Thornhill, and then the A702 toward Monaive.

👁 Sights

★ Crawick Multiverse

PUBLIC ART | The extraordinary 2015 land artwork by Charles Jencks, 45 minutes north of Dumfries near the village of Sanquhar, must surely become a focus for visitors to the region for years to come. Jencks has transformed a 55-acre site, once an open-pit mine, into a beautiful and inspiring created landscape, at the heart of which are two grass spiral mounds that represent the Milky Way and the Andromeda Constellation. But they are simply the heart of a site where woodland, moor, mountain, and desert meet. Local rocks have been lifted to form avenues and labyrinths across the site. As you look across from its highest point, it is as if you were looking in a mirror in which the skies were reflected on the earth. Set aside two or three hours at least for the experience. ✉ *Crawick, Off B740, by Sanquhar* ✛ *Take the A75 toward Kirkconnel from Sanquhar, then turn on to the B740 (signposted Crawfordjohn)* ☎ *01659/50242* ⊕ *www. crawickmultiverse.co.uk* 🎟 *£5.*

★ Drumlanrig Castle

CASTLE/PALACE | FAMILY | A spectacular estate, Drumlanrig Castle is as close as Scotland gets to the treasure houses of England—which is not surprising, since it's owned by the dukes of Buccleuch, one of the wealthiest British peerages. Resplendent with romantic turrets, this pink-sandstone palace was constructed between 1679 and 1691 by the first Duke of Queensbury, who, after nearly bankrupting himself building the place, stayed one night and never returned. The Buccleuchs inherited the palace and filled the richly decorated rooms with paintings by Holbein, Rembrandt, and Murillo, among others. Because of the theft of a Leonardo da Vinci painting in 2003, all visits are conducted by guided tour. There is also a playground, a gift shop, and a tearoom. The grounds are varied and good for mountain biking; bikes can be rented at the castle. ✉ *Off A76, Thornhill* ✛ *18 miles northwest of Dumfries* ☎ *01848/600283* ⊕ *www.drumlanrig.com* 🎟 *Park £6, castle and park £12* 🕑 *Closed Oct.–Mar.*

Museum of Lead Mining

MUSEUM | The Lochnell Mine was abandoned in 1861, after 150 years of operation, and the mine and miners' homes now form part of this museum re-creating their lives. The isolated village of Warnlockhead, where the mine was located, has not changed a great deal since then—there was little alternative employment for the miners and their families. The visitor center, housed in the old smithy, exhibits some of the minerals the mine yielded. The nearby Leadhills and Warnlockhead Narrow Gauge Railway runs on weekends throughout the summer and costs £4, with a 10% reduction for a joint ticket with the museum. ✉ *Off B797, Wanlockhead* ✛ *32 miles north of Dumfries* ☏ *01659/74387* ⊕ *www.leadminingmuseum.co.uk* ✉ *£12.95 for mine, cottages, and library; £5 mine only* ⊙ *Closed Oct.–Mar.*

Striding Arches

PUBLIC ART | British sculptor Andy Goldsworthy's extraordinary piece of public landscape art enriches the great natural amphitheater at Cairnhead in the southern uplands of Dumfries and Galloway. His three red-sandstone arches stand 13 feet high and mark out the area, "striding" across the landscape and symbolizing all those who have left the area and migrated in search of work or better lives. ✉ *Cairnhead Forest, near Moniaive* ✛ *Take the A702 (off the A76 at Thornhill) to Moniaive, then the road to Benbuie until you reach The Byre. From there it is a walk to the viewpoint* ☏ *07801/232229* ⊕ *www.stridingarches.com* ✉ *Free.*

Solway Firth

10 miles south of Dumfries.

Mostly undiscovered by travelers, the Solway Firth is a must for walkers, cyclists, and bird-watchers. This lovely and protected inlet, guarded by beautiful Caerlaverock Castle, is a haven for a great variety of seabirds. You can see them at the nature reserve behind the castle. Cycling or on foot, you can stroll gentle coastal paths beside the firth that link the villages of Sandyhills, Rockcliffe, and Kippford.

GETTING HERE AND AROUND

There is a bus from Dumfries to Kippford (one hour), but a car is best for visiting this area. Take the A710 from Dumfries and then the A711.

 Sights

★ Caerlaverock Castle

CASTLE/PALACE | The stunningly beautiful moated Caerlaverock Castle stands in splendid isolation amid the surrounding wetlands. Built in a unique triangular design, this 13th-century fortress has solid-sandstone masonry and an imposing double-tower gatehouse. King Edward I of England (1239–1307) besieged the castle in 1300, when his forces occupied much of Scotland at the start of the Wars of Independence. A splendid residence was built inside in the 1600s. Now largely in ruins, the interior is still atmospheric, and the siege engines on the grounds give some sense of what medieval warfare was like. The castle has a pleasant café for coffee, cakes, or lunch. ✉ *Off B725, Ruthwell* ✛ *10 miles south of Dumfries* ☏ *01387/770244* ⊕ *www.historicenvironment.scot* ✉ *£6.*

★ Caerlaverock Wildfowl and Wetlands Centre

NATURE PRESERVE | This wild and beautiful wetland provides a stunning backdrop to Caerlaverock Castle. Here you can observe wintering wildfowl, including migrating geese, spy ducks, swans, and raptors. In summer, ospreys patrol the waters of this northernmost outpost of the Wildfowl and Wetlands Trust. The triops, the tadpole shrimp that is one of the oldest known species, lives in the aquarium here. There are bats and badgers, sparrows, and natterjack toads as well. Free guided walks are available in the afternoons throughout the year. ✉ *Eastpark Farm, Off B725, Dumfries* ✛ *9 miles southeast of Dumfries off the A75* ☏ *01387/770200* ⊕ *www.wwt.org.uk* ✉ *£7.28.*

Hotels

Clonyard House Hotel

$ | HOTEL | A modest hotel occupying a stone house, most of the comfortable rooms here look out on a well-tended, pleasant garden. **Pros:** good location; hearty breakfasts; beautiful setting. **Cons:** not all rooms look onto the garden; lounge bar rather small; limited access to public transport. ⑤ *Rooms from: £80* ✉ *Colvend, Dalbeattie, Kippford* ☎ *01556/630732* ⊕ *www.clonyardhotel. co.uk* ⇆ *4 rooms* ❍ *Free Breakfast.*

Castle Douglas

18 miles southwest of Dumfries, 25 miles west of Caerlaverock Castle, 84 miles south of Glasgow, 90 miles southwest of Edinburgh.

A quaint town that sits beside Carlingwark Loch, Castle Douglas is a popular base for exploring the surrounding countryside. The loch sets off the town perfectly, reflecting its dramatic architecture of sharp spires and soft sandstone arches. Its main thoroughfare, King Street, has unique shops and eateries.

GETTING HERE AND AROUND

There's no train station in Castle Douglas, and buses from Dumfries make several stops along the way. The best way to get here is by car. From Dalbeattie take the A711/A745 (10 minutes). From Glasgow take the A713 (just under two hours). From Edinburgh take the A70 (a little over 2 hours).

BICYCLING TOURS

Galloway Cycling Holidays

BICYCLE TOURS | For a slower-paced look at the sights in the region, take a bike tour that begins in Castle Douglas. This small outfit is run by local residents and offers tours, self-guided or otherwise, varying from weekend packages to weeklong explorations of the region for castle seekers, nature watchers, or passionate cyclists. ✉ *Castle Douglas* ☎ *1556/502979* ⊕ *www.gallowaycycling. com.*

Sights

★ Threave Castle

CASTLE/PALACE | Once home to the Black Douglases, who were the earls of Nithsdale and lords of Galloway, Threave's imposing towers reflect well the Lord of Galloway who built it, Archibald the Grim, in the 14th century. Not to be confused with the mansion in Threave Gardens, the castle was dismantled in the religious wars of the mid-17th century, though enough of it remained to have housed prisoners from the Napoleonic Wars two centuries later. It's a few minutes from Castle Douglas by car and is signposted from the main road. To get here, leave your car in a farmyard and make your way down to the edge of the river. Ring the bell (loudly) and, rather romantically, a boatman will come to ferry you across to the great stone tower looming from a marshy island in the river. ✉ *A75* ✛ *3 miles west of Castle Douglas* ☎ *07711/223101* ⊕ *www.historicenvironment.scot* ☞ *£6 including ferry; buy tickets online or from the NTS Osprey Centre on the site (cash only)* ⊗ *Closed Nov.–Mar.*

Threave Garden and Estate

GARDEN | The National Trust for Scotland cares for the gently sloping parkland and gardens around an 1867 mansion built by William Gordon, a Liverpool businessman. The house, fully restored in the 1930s, gives a glimpse into the daily life of a prosperous 19th-century family. The grounds demand an army of gardeners, and today many of them are students at the National Trust's School of Heritage Gardening, which has developed the variety of gardens here. Bats, ospreys, and other birds and animals share the space. Entry to the house is by timed guided tour, and it's wise to book ahead. There's an on-site restaurant. ✉ *South*

To get to moody Threave Castle, you must be ferried across the River Dee by boat.

of A75 ✛ 1 mile west of Castle Douglas ☎ 01556/502575 ⊕ www.nts.org.uk/Visits 🖼 Gardens £9, house and gardens £15, nature reserve free ⊙ Gardens closed Dec.–Feb. House closed Nov.–Apr.

Restaurants

The Café at Designs Gallery

$ | CAFÉ | For a good balance of art and food, look no further than this café at a contemporary art and crafts gallery in the town center. You'll find the freshest ingredients here, from soup to salads, sandwiches to quiches; everything is made on-site, including the bread, and it's all organic. **Known for:** good lunch menu; homemade soups; lovely garden. $ Average main: £9 ⊠ 179 King St. ☎ 01556/504552 ⊕ www.designsgallery. co.uk ⊙ Closed Sun. No dinner.

🛍 Shopping

A. D. Livingston and Sons

HOUSEHOLD ITEMS/FURNITURE | Fine-furniture restorers and makers in wood and raffia, the Livingstons have a shop in the main street, and some of their work is displayed two doors down under an arch into a charming lane. ⊠ 183 King St. ☎ 01556/504234 ⊕ www.livingstons-antiques.co.uk.

By the Book

BOOKS/STATIONERY | This well-stocked and (more important) well-organized second-hand bookshop on Castle Douglas's main shopping street has large windows that invite you in to browse, which you can do without interruption—there's bound to be something you want, though it may be in a box or under the table. ⊠ 201 King St. ☎ 01556/503338.

Galloway Gems and Craft Centre and Outback Yarns

CRAFTS | In this glittery shop you can purchase mineral specimens, polished stone slices, and a range of Celtic- and Nordic-inspired jewelry, as well as craft materials of every kind. For fiber artists and sewers, it's a real find. ⊠ 130–132 King St. ☎ 01556/503254 ⊕ www.outbackyarns.co.uk.

Activities

BICYCLING

Castle Douglas Cycle Centre

BICYCLING | You can rent bicycles for everyone in the family from Castle Douglas Cycle Centre. It also handles repairs and service. ✉ *Church St.* ☎ *01556/504542* ⊕ *www.cdbikes.co.uk.*

BOATING

Galloway Activity Centre

BICYCLING | With dinghies, kayaks, and canoes for rent, the Galloway Activity Centre on the banks of Loch Ken specializes in water sports. "Dry" sports include mountain biking, archery, and rock climbing. ✉ *Shirmers Bridge, Loch Ken ✛ 10 miles northwest of Castle Douglas off A713* ☎ *01556/502011* ⊕ *www.lochken. co.uk.*

GOLF

Southerness Golf Club

GOLF | Mackenzie Ross designed this course, the first built in Scotland after World War II. Southerness is a long course, played over extensive links with fine views southward over the Solway Firth. The greens are hard and fast, and the frequent winds make for some testing golf. Thursday is reserved for women. ✉ *Southerness St., Southerness ✛ 19 miles west of Castle Couglas via the A745 and B793* ☎ *01387/880677* ⊕ *www. southernessgolfclub.com* ✉ *Apr.–Sept. £60 weekdays, £70 weekends; Oct.–Mar. £35 weekdays, £40 weekends ✠ 18 holes, 6110 yards, par 69 ⚑ Reservations essential.*

Kirkcudbright

9 miles southwest of Castle Douglas, 89 miles south of Glasgow, 99 miles southwest of Edinburgh.

Kirkcudbright (pronounced kir -*coo*-bray) is an 18th-century town of Georgian and Victorian houses, some of them washed in pastel shades and roofed with the blue slate of the district. It sits on an inlet from the Solway Firth. In the early 20th century the town became a haven for artists, and its L-shaped main street is full of crafts and antiques shops.

GETTING HERE AND AROUND

Driving is your best and only real option. From Castle Douglas take the A711 (15 minutes). From Glasgow take the A713 (about two hours). From Edinburgh take the A701 (about 2½ hours).

ESSENTIALS

VISITOR INFORMATION Kirkcudbright Tourist Information Centre. ✉ *Harbour Sq.* ☎ *01557/330494* ⊕ *www.visitscotland. com.*

Sights

★ Broughton House

HOUSE | The 18th-century Broughton House was the home of the artist E. A. Hornel from 1901 until his death in 1933 and remains largely as it was in his time. Hornel was a member of the school of painters called the "Glasgow Boys," who were influenced by the Vienna Secession and art nouveau. You can see many of his paintings in the gallery Hornel built onto the house to impress the guests and buyers who came to see his work. His use and love of color is obvious in the beautiful garden, which combines lawns, ponds, and formal and wildflower beds. The knowledgeable guides will gladly provide information about the life and work of the painter. ✉ *12 High St.* ☎ *01557/330437* ⊕ *www.nts.org.uk* ✉ *£8* ⊙ *House closed Nov.–Mar. Garden closed Nov.–Jan.*

MacLellan's Castle

CASTLE/PALACE | Conspicuous in the center of town are the stone walls of MacLellan's Castle, a once-elaborate castellated mansion dating from the 16th century. You can walk around the interior, still atmospheric even though the rooms are bare. The "Lairds Lug," behind the fireplace, allowed the *laird* (lord) to listen in to what his guests were saying about him. You can also get a glimpse of life below stairs in the kitchen vaults beneath the main staircase. The mansion has lovely views over the town. ⊠ *Off High St.* ☎ *01557/331856* ⊕ *www.histori-cenvironment.scot* ☒ *£4.80* ⊘ *Closed Oct.–Mar.*

Stewartry Museum

MUSEUM | Stuffed with all manner of local paraphernalia, the delightfully old-fashioned Stewartry Museum allows you to putter and absorb as much or as little as takes your interest in the display cases. Stewartry is the former name of Kirkcudbright. ⊠ *St. Mary St.* ☎ *01557/331643* ⊕ *www.dumgal.gov.uk* ☒ *Free.*

Tolbooth Arts Centre

ARTS VENUE | In the 17th-century tolbooth (a combination town hall–courthouse–prison), the Tolbooth Arts Centre describes how the town attracted famous artists, among them E. A. Hornel, Jessie King, and Charles Oppenheimer. Some of their paintings are on display, as are works by contemporary artists. ⊠ *High St.* ☎ *01557/331556* ⊕ *www.dumgal.gov.uk* ☒ *Free* ⊘ *Closed Sun. Oct.–May.*

Restaurants

Artistas at the Selkirk Arms

$$ | MODERN BRITISH | Paintings of Scotland, starched white tablecloths, and giant windows overlooking the well-kept garden beckon you into this highly praised eatery. Locals love that the food on the bar and regular menus is locally sourced and full of imagination. **Known for:** local produce; both familiar and more exotic dishes; charming location in town. ⑤ *Average main: £16* ⊠ *Selkirk Arms, High St.* ☎ *01557/330402* ⊕ *www.selkirkarmshotel.co.uk.*

Hotels

★ Selkirk Arms

$ | HOTEL | Bursting with charm, this elegant 18th-century hotel has a lot going for it, including spacious guest rooms that are individually decorated with cozy beds, contemporary wood furniture, and soft lighting. **Pros:** free Wi-Fi; massive breakfast; lively traditional pub. **Cons:** rooms closest to restaurant can be noisy; bar gets crowded during sporting events; some rooms are small. ⑤ *Rooms from: £99* ⊠ *High St.* ☎ *01557/330402* ⊕ *www.selkirkarmshotel.co.uk* ⌫ *16 rooms* ⚭ *Free breakfast.*

Gatehouse of Fleet

9 miles west of Kirkcudbright, 90 miles southwest of Glasgow, 103 miles southwest of Edinburgh.

A peaceful, pleasant, backwoods sort of place, Gatehouse of Fleet has a castle guarding its southern approach.

GETTING HERE AND AROUND

There's no train station in Gatehouse of Fleet. Local buses are available, but you may need to make several transfers. Driving is your best option. From Kirkcudbright take the A755/B727 (15 minutes). From Glasgow take the A713 (about two hours). From Edinburgh take the A701 (about 2½ hours).

Sights

Cardoness Castle

CASTLE/PALACE | The castle was a typical Scottish tower house, severe and uncompromising. The 15th-century structure once was the home of the McCullochs of Galloway, then the Gordons—two of the area's important and occasionally infamous families. Though ruined, it is well preserved with fireplaces and some carvings intact. ⊠ *A75* ⊹ *1 mile southwest of Gatehouse of*

Fleet ☎ *01557/814427* ⊕ *www.histor-ic-scotland.gov.uk/places* 🎫 *£6* 🕙 *Closed Oct.⬚Mar.*

Mill on the Fleet

FACTORY | For more than a hundred years, Gatehouse of Fleet was the center of the region's cotton industry, and you can learn more at this converted mill, where arts and crafts are on display. The tearoom serves light lunches and delicious home-baked goods. The building also houses the town's tourist information center. ✉ *High St.* ☎ *01557/814099* ⊕ *www.millonthefleet.co.uk* 🎫 *Free* 🕙 *Closed Nov.⬚Mar.*

 ## Hotels

Cally Palace

$$ | **HOTEL** | Many of the public rooms in this Georgian hotel, built in 1763 as a private mansion, retain their original grandeur, with elaborate plaster ceilings and marble fireplaces. **Pros:** beautiful views from balconies; impressive setting; piano music at dinner. **Cons:** decor is bland and rather old-fashioned; some beds are past their prime; slightly isolated from other sites. ⑤ *Rooms from: £168* ✉ *Off A75* ⊹ *About 1 mile south of Gatehouse of Fleet* ☎ *01557/814341* ⊕ *www.mcmillanhotels.co.uk* 🕙 *Closed Jan. and Feb.* 🛏 *56 rooms* ⑩ *Breakfast.*

 ## Shopping

Galloway Lodge Preserves

FOOD/CANDY | This family-run shop sells marmalades, mustards, chutneys, jams, and jellies, all made in the village. You can also pick up some Scottish pottery and eat at the café. ✉ *24–28 High St.* ☎ *01557/814001* ⊕ *www.gallowaylodge.co.uk.*

Newton Stewart

18 miles northwest of Kirkcudbright, 77 miles southwest of Glasgow, 105 miles southwest of Edinburgh.

The bustling town of Newton Stewart is the place to stop when touring the western region of Galloway. It is the gateway to the Galloway Forest and Glen Trool.

GETTING HERE AND AROUND
Newton Stewart does not have a train station, but the town is served by regular buses from Glasgow and Edinburgh as well as local buses from neighboring towns. By car from Glasgow, take the A77 (about two hours). From Edinburgh take the A702 (about 2¾ hours).

 ## Sights

Creetown Gem Rock Museum

MUSEUM | In the village of Creetown outside Newton Stewart, this museum has an eclectic mineral collection, a dinosaur egg, an erupting volcano, and a crystal cave. There's also an Internet café, a tearoom, and a shop selling stones and crystals—both loose and in settings. Entry is good for two weeks. ✉ *Chain Rd., Creetown* ⊹ *Off A75* ☎ *01671/820357* ⊕ *www.gemrock.net* 🎫 *£5* 🕙 *Closed Dec. and Jan.*

★ Galloway Forest Park

NATIONAL/STATE PARK | The expansive facilities in Galloway Forest Park are evidence of the growing enthusiasm for active vacations in Scotland; it offers chances for cycling, walking, kayaking on the rivers, bird-watching, and mountain-biking. You can walk or bicycle along the paths through moorland and forests, by lochs and over hills—all contained within the 300 square miles of the forest. The Forestry Commission, which manages the forest, has three visitor centers at Glen Trool, Kirroughtree, and Clatteringshaws and also offers exhibits about the region's wildlife, a reconstructed Iron Age dwelling, and 7Stanes mountain-biking centers. The forest is designated as a Dark Sky Park; the low light pollution here ensures exceptional stargazing. ✉ *A712* ✛ *7 miles northeast of Newton Stewart* ☎ *01671/402420* ⊕ *www.gallowayforestpark.com* ✉ *Free.*

Glen Trool

FOREST | With high purple-and-green hilltops shorn rock-bare by glaciers, and with a dark, winding loch and thickets of birch trees sounding with birdcalls, Glen Trool's setting almost looks more highland than the real Highlands. Note **Bruce's Stone,** just above the parking lot, marking the site where in 1307 Scotland's champion Robert the Bruce (King Robert I, 1274–1329) won his first victory in the Scottish Wars of Independence. A little road off A714 leads through increasingly wild woodland scenery to a parking lot. The visitor center is open daily. Only after you have climbed for a few minutes onto a heathery knoll does the full, rugged panorama become apparent. Driving is really the only way to get to Glen Trool, which is part of Galloway Forest Park. From Glasgow take the A77 (about 2¼ hours). From Edinburgh take the A702 (about three hours). ✉ *Off A714, Bargrennan* ✛ *A714 north from Newton Stewart for about 15 mins; turn right at the signpost for Glen Trool* ☎ *01671/840302* ⊕ *www.forestry.gov.uk* ✉ *Free.*

Wood of Cree Nature Reserve

NATURE PRESERVE | Birders love the Wood of Cree Nature Reserve, managed by the Royal Society for the Protection of Birds. In the reserve you can see such species as the redstart, pied flycatcher, and wood warbler. You might also spot otters and roe deer. To get there, take the minor road that travels north from Newton Stewart alongside the River Cree east of the A714. The entrance is next to a small parking area at the side of the road. ✉ *Off A714* ✛ *4 miles north of Newton Stewart* ☎ *01988/402130* ⊕ *www.rspb.org.uk* ✉ *Donations accepted.*

 Hotels

Creebridge House Hotel

$ | HOTEL | Close to the River Cree and set among gardens and woodland, the Creebridge places the emphasis on comfort and quiet rural surroundings. **Pros:** practical center for exploring the area; comfort in a rural setting; within easy reach of Newton Stewart. **Cons:** slightly conservative feel; not easy to reach without a car; gets busy and noisy with weddings. ⑤ *Rooms from: £89* ✉ *Minigaff, Off B7079* ☎ *01671/402121* ⊕ *www.creebridge.co.uk* ⇄ *18 rooms* ❙⊙❙ *Breakfast.*

Whithorn

17 miles south of Newton Stewart, 94 miles southwest of Glasgow, 121 miles southwest of Edinburgh.

Known for its early Christian settlement, Whithorn is full of history. The main street is notably wide, with pretty pastel buildings nestled up against each other, their low doorways and small windows creating images of years long past. It's still mainly a farming community but is fast becoming a popular tourist destination. Several scenes from the original *Wicker Man* (1973) were shot in and around the area. During the summer months, it's a popular place for festivals. The Isle of Whithorn, just beyond the town, is not an island at all but a fishing village of great charm.

GETTING HERE AND AROUND

There's no train station in Whithorn, and most of the buses are local (getting to main Scottish cities from Whithorn takes careful planning and several transfers). To drive from Newton Stewart, take the A714 and then A746. From Glasgow take the A77 (about 2½ hours). From Edinburgh take the A702 (about three hours).

Sights

St. Ninian's Chapel

ARCHAEOLOGICAL SITE | The Isle of Whithorn (a fishing village on the mainland) holds the ruins of the 14th-century St. Ninian's Chapel, where pilgrims who came by sea prayed before traveling inland to Whithorn Priory. Some people claim that this, and not Whithorn Priory, is the site of the Candida Casa, a 4th-century church. The structure seems to have been erected on top of a much older chapel built around 1100. It's 4 miles south of Whithorn. ✉ *Isle of Whithorn* ⊹ *Take A746 and B7004 from Whithorn* ⊕ *www.historic-scotland.gov.uk* ✉ *Free.*

Whithorn Priory and Museum

ARCHAEOLOGICAL SITE | The road that is now the A746 was a pilgrims' path that led to the royal burgh of Whithorn, where sat Whithorn Priory, one of Scotland's great medieval cathedrals, now an empty shell. It was built in the 12th century and is said to occupy the site of a former stone church, the Candida Casa, built by St. Ninian in the 4th century. As the story goes, the church housed a shrine to Ninian, the earliest of Scotland's saints, and kings and barons tried to visit the shrine at least once in their lives. As you approach the priory, observe the royal arms of pre-1707 Scotland—that is, Scotland before the Union Act with England—carved and painted above the *pend* (covered walkway). The museum houses restored stonework from the period, including crosses. ✉ *6 Bruce St.* ⊕ *www.historicenvironment.scot* ✉ *£6 (includes the Whithorn Story and Visitor Centre)* ⊗ *Closed Nov.–Mar.*

Restaurants

Steam Packet Inn

$$ | BRITISH | Lovely and old-fashioned, this inn is always full, mainly because of its good beer and hearty, well-cooked food including fish-and-chips and lamb shanks. Located directly on the harbor, it has few local rivals, but customers come from far and wide to eat here and walk the headland behind the pub to the rocky shore of the Solway Firth. **Known for:** superior pub food; outstanding desserts; garden dining in nice weather. *$ Average main: £15* ✉ *Harbour Row, Isle of Whithorn* ☎ *01988/500334* ⊕ *www.thesteampacketinn.biz.*

Stranraer

31 miles northwest of Whithorn, 86 miles southwest of Glasgow via A77, 131 miles southwest of Edinburgh.

Stranraer was for more than a century the main ferry port between Scotland and Northern Ireland. Its closure, and the transfer of ferry traffic to nearby Cairnryan, continues to bring changes to the town. The city center has had a major face-lift, and there are plans to redevelop the harbor as a leisure center and transportation hub. Stranraer has a lovely garden.

GETTING HERE AND AROUND

Stranraer's train station is directly accessible from Glasgow; bus services are also good (with many connections to smaller towns). If you're driving, take the A747 from Whithorn (about 45 minutes). From Glasgow take the M77/A77 (two hours), and from Edinburgh take the A77 (three hours).

Sights

★ Castle Kennedy Gardens

GARDEN | The lovely Castle Kennedy Gardens surround the shell of the original Castle Kennedy, which burned down in 1716. Parks scattered around the property were built by the second Earl of Stair in 1733. The earl was a field marshal and used his soldiers to help with the heavy work of constructing banks, ponds, and other major landscape features. When the rhododendrons are in bloom (April through July, depending on the variety), the effect is kaleidoscopic. There's also a pleasant tearoom. ⊠ *, Sheuchan ⊕ 3 miles east of Stranraer on the A875* ☎ *01776/702024* ⊕ *www.castlekenne-dygardens.co.uk* ✉ *£4.95* ☉ *Closed Nov.– Jan. and weekdays in Feb. and Mar.*

Portpatrick

8 miles southwest of Stranraer, 94 miles southwest of Glasgow, 139 miles south-west of Edinburgh.

The holiday town of Portpatrick lies across the Rhinns of Galloway from Stranraer. Once an Irish ferry port, Portpatrick's harbor eventually proved too small for larger vessels.

GETTING HERE AND AROUND

Direct buses travel between Portpatrick to Stranraer and some of the neighboring towns, but travel to and from the larger Scottish cities can prove more difficult. There is no train station in Portpatrick (though there is one in nearby Stran-raer). Driving is probably your best bet. From Stranraer take the A77; it's about a 15-minute journey. Take the M77/A77 from Glasgow (just over two hours) and the M8/A77 from Edinburgh (about three hours).

 Sights

Logan Botanic Garden

GARDEN | One of the four major sites belonging to the Edinburgh-based National Botanic Gardens of Scotland, the spectacular Logan Botanic Garden is a must-see for garden lovers. Displayed here are plants that enjoy the prevail-ing mild climate, especially tree ferns, cabbage palms, and other Southern Hemisphere exotica. There are free guided walks every second Tuesday of the month at 10:30 am; at other times there is a free audio guide. ⊠ *Port Logan, Port Logan* ⊕ *On B7065, 16 miles south*

of Portpatrick ☎ *01776/860231* ⊕ *www. rbge.org.uk* ✉ *£7* ☉ *Closed Jan. and weekdays in Feb.*

Mull of Galloway

NATURE PRESERVE | If you wish to visit the southern tip of the Rhinns of Galloway, called the Mull of Galloway, follow the B7065/B7041 until you run out of land. The cliffs and seascapes here are rugged, and there's a lighthouse and the Mull of Galloway bird reserve. ⊕ *www.rspb.org. uk* ☉ *Reserve closed Nov.–mid-Mar.*

Southern Upland Way

TRAIL | The village of Portpatrick is the starting point for Scotland's longest offi-cial long-distance footpath, the Southern Upland Way, which runs a switchback course for 212 miles to Cockburnspath, on the east side of the Borders. The path begins on the cliffs just north of the town and follows the coastline for 1½ miles before turning inland. ⊕ *www.souther-nuplandway.gov.uk* ✉ *Free.*

 Hotels

Crown Hotel Portpatrick

$ | HOTEL | From the terrace of this simple small hotel in a working fishing village, you can look out across the sea to Ireland while eating some delicious seafood. **Pros:** beautiful location; very good restau-rant; base for lots of outdoor activities. **Cons:** fairly remote town; rooms are fairly basic; extra cost for sea-view rooms. ⑤ *Rooms from: £100* ⊠ *9 N. Crescent* ☎ *01776/810261* ⊕ *www.crownportpat-rick.com* ⤴ *12 rooms* � *Breakfast.*

Chapter 6

FIFE AND ANGUS

Updated by
Nick Bruno

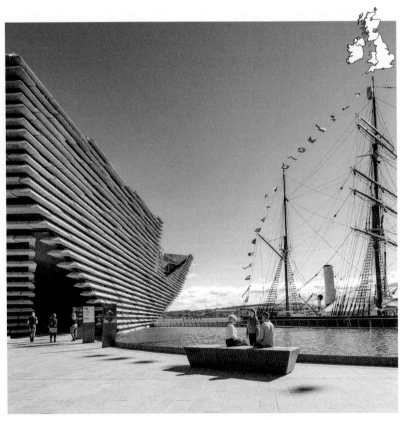

◉ Sights	🍴 Restaurants	🛏 Hotels	🛍 Shopping	🍸 Nightlife
★★★★☆	★★★☆☆	★★★☆☆	★★☆☆☆	★★★☆☆

WELCOME TO FIFE AND ANGUS

TOP REASONS TO GO

★ **St. Andrews:** With its medieval streets, ruined cathedral and castle, and peculiarly posh atmosphere, St. Andrews is one of the most incongruous yet beguiling places in Scotland—even without its famous golf course.

★ **East Neuk:** As you take in crowstep-gabled fishermen's cottages, winding cobbled lanes, seaside harbor scenes, and lovely beaches, you can almost imagine the harsh lives of the hardworking Fifers who lived in tiny hamlets such as Crail, Anstruther, Pittenweem, and Elie. Today artists and visitors make it all pleasantly picturesque.

★ **Dundee:** This former industrial city is becoming better known for its vibrant arts, music, theater, restaurant, and nightlife scenes.

★ **The glens:** The long Angus glens (such as Glen Clova) that run into the wild Grampian Mountains are magical places beloved by outdoors enthusiasts and those just wanting to rediscover nature.

1 St. Andrews. A university town famed for golfing.

2 Crail. A East Neuk fishing village.

3 Anstruther. A working port.

4 Pittenweem and St. Monans. Harbor villages with impressive art.

5 Elie. A Victorian resort.

6 Falkland. A royal burgh.

7 Cupar. A busy market town.

8 Dundee. One of Scotland's most vibrant cities.

9 Arbroath. Famed for its smoked fish.

10 Montrose. A charming town by an estuary.

11 Brechin. A market village.

12 The Angus Glens. Rolling glens that cut into the Cairngorms.

13 Kirriemuir. Peter Pan's hometown.

14 Forfar. Farming and ancient stone carvings.

15 Glamis. Home to a grand castle.

16 Meigle. Notable Pictish stones.

17 Alyth. A rural market town.

Breezy cliff-top walkways, fishing villages, and open beaches characterize Fife and Angus. They sandwich Scotland's fourth-largest city, the rejuvenated city of Dundee. Scotland's east coast has only light rainfall throughout the year; northeastern Fife, in particular, may claim the record for the most sunshine and the least rainfall in Scotland, which all adds to the enjoyment when you're touring the coast or the famous golf center of St. Andrews.

Fife proudly styles itself as a "king-dom," and its long history—which really began when the Romans went home in the 4th century and the Picts moved in—lends some substance to the boast. From medieval times its earls were first among Scotland's nobility and crowned her kings. For many, however, the most historic event in the region was the birth of golf, in the 15th century, which, legend has it, occurred in St. Andrews, an ancient university town with stone houses and seaside ruins. The Royal & Ancient Golf Club, the ruling body of the game worldwide, still has its headquarters here.

Not surprisingly, fishing and seafaring have also played a role in the history of the East Neuk coastal region. From the 16th through the 19th century a large population lived and worked in the small ports and harbors that form a chain around Fife's coast, which James V once called "a beggar's mantle fringed with gold." When the sun shines, this golden fringe—particularly at Tentsmuir, St. Andrews, and Elie—gleams like the beaches of Normandy. Indeed, the houses of the East Neuk villages have a similar character, with color-washed fronts, fishy weather vanes, outdoor stone stairways to upper floors, and crude carvings of anchors and lobsters on their lintels. All the houses are crowded on steep wynds (narrow streets), hugging pint-size harbors that in the golden era supported village fleets of 100 ships apiece.

North, across the Firth of Tay, lies the region of Angus, whose charm is its variety: in addition to its seacoast and pleasant Lowland market centers, there's also a hinterland of lonely rounded hills with long glens running into the typical Grampian Highland scenery beyond. One of Angus's interesting features, which it shares with the eastern Lowland edge of Perthshire, is its fruit-growing industry, which includes raspberries.

Known as the "City of Discovery" (after the RRS *Discovery*, a polar exploration vessel that set sail from this port in 1901), and as the United Kingdom's UNESCO City of Design, Dundee has a sophisticated arts and cultural scene and some beguiling sights. The ongoing regeneration of the city's waterfront has created a buzz, with the cliff-shaped V&A Dundee design museum making a bold statement beside the Tay. Today's Dundee makes a superb base for a cultural stay and from which to launch a number of day trips.

MAJOR REGIONS

St. Andrews and East Neuk. In its western parts Fife still bears the scars of heavy industry, especially coal mining, but these signs are less evident as you move east. Northeastern Fife, around the town of St. Andrews, seems to have played no part in the Industrial Revolution; instead, its residents earned a living from the grain fields or from the sea. Fishing has been a major industry, and in the past a string of Fife ports traded across the North Sea. Today the legacy of Dutch-influenced architecture, such as crowstepped gables (the stepped effect on the ends of the roofs)—gives these East Neuk villages a distinctive character. St. Andrews is unlike any other Scottish town. Once Scotland's most powerful ecclesiastical center as well as the seat of the country's oldest university and then, much later, the very symbol and spiritual home of golf, the town has a comfortable, well-groomed air, sitting almost smugly apart from the rest of Scotland. Its latest cachet is being the place where the riveting 21st-century royal romance between Prince William and Kate Middleton began, which boosted university applications from around the world.

Dundee and Angus. The small, friendly city of Dundee sits near the mouth of the River Tay surrounded by the farms and glens of rural Angus and the coastal grassy banks and golf courses of northeastern Fife. A vibrant, industrious, and cultural city, it's undergoing a postindustrial renaissance of sorts, with the V&A museum as the centerpiece of the emerging waterfront regeneration. The first outpost of London's world-famous Victoria and Albert Museum, a repository of the decorative arts and design, is housed in a sculptural building jutting into Britain's most powerful river. Dundee is the United Kingdom's sole UNESCO City of Design, with a large student population, a lively arts and nightlife scene, and several historical and nautical sights. The tree-lined country roads of the Angus heartlands roll through strawberry and raspberry fields to busy market towns, wee villages, and Glamis Castle. Angus combines coastal agriculture on rich, red soils with dramatic inland glens that pierce their way into the foothills of the Grampian mountain range to the northwest. ■TIP➔ **The main road from Dundee to Aberdeen—the A90—requires special care with its mix of fast cars and unexpectedly slow farm traffic.**

Planning

When to Go

Spring in the Angus glens can be quite captivating, with the hills along Angus's northernmost boundary still covered in snow. Similarly, the moorland colors of autumn are appealing. But Fife and Angus are really summer destinations, when most of the sights are open to visitors. Note that during the summer, St. Andrews hosts several international golf tournaments that effectively take over the town. Nongolfers may become incredibly frustrated when searching for accommodations or places to eat during these times, so check ahead.

Getting Oriented

Fife lies north of the Lothians, across the iconic bridges of the Firth of Forth. A headland, Fife's northeastern coast (or East Neuk) is fringed with golden sands, rocky shores, fishermen's cottages, and, of course, the splendor of St. Andrews, home of golf. Northwest of Fife and across the glorious Firth of Tay, the city of Dundee is undergoing a postindustrial reinvention. Its rural hinterland, Angus, hugs the city, which, stretching north toward the foothills of the Grampian Mountains, houses agricultural and fishing communities, and Glamis, one of Scotland's best-loved castles.

Planning Your Time

St. Andrews, 52 miles from Edinburgh, is not to be missed, for its history and atmosphere as much as for the golf; allot an overnight stop and at least a whole day if you can. The nearby East Neuk of Fife has some of Scotland's finest coastline, now becoming gentrified by the Edinburgh second-home set but still evoking Fife's past. A day's drive along A917 (allow for exploring and stops for ice cream and fish) will take you through the fishing villages of Elie, Pittenweem, Anstruther, and Crail. Dundee, with its rich maritime history, stunning riverside setting, and grand museums, is an ideal base for a drive round the Angus towns of Arbroath, Kirriemuir, and Alyth; if you make a three-hour stop at Glamis Castle, this trip will take about a day.

Getting Here and Around

AIR

There are handy flight options via Edinburgh and the small Dundee airport. For international flights, Edinburgh Airport is the easiest gateway into the region. The Dundee airport has twice daily connections with London Stansted.

CONTACTS Dundee Airport.
☎ *01382/662200* ⊕ *www.hial.co.uk/dundee-airport.* **Edinburgh Airport.**
☎ *0844/448–8833* ⊕ *www.edinburghairport.com.*

BUS

Among the various bus operators that serve much of the region, Stagecoach ⊕ *www.stagecoachbus.com* has the most coverage through Angus and Fife. Xplore Dundee ⊕ *www.nxbus.co.uk/dundee* serves the city and runs the airport transfer bus to and from Edinburgh Airport. Visit ⊕ *www.travelinescotland.com* to plan any bus or train journey through the region.

CAR

For seeing the most of Fife and Angus, car travel is basically essential, although there are some public transport alternatives. The major roads that span the region are not big motorways, but second-tier A roads; many of these roads are single-lane only, so be especially cautious when driving in this region.

TRAIN

The East Coast Main Line makes stops at Cupar, Leuchars (for St. Andrews), Dundee, Arbroath, and Montrose.

CONTACTS East Coast Main Line. ⊕ *www.scotrail.co.uk.*

Restaurants

With an affluent population, St. Andrews supports several stylish hotel restaurants. Because it's a university town and popular tourist destination, there are also many good cafés and bistro-style restaurants. Bar lunches are the rule in large and small hotels throughout the region, and in seaside places the carry-*oot* (to-go) meal of fish-and-chips is an enduring tradition.

Hotels

If you're staying in Fife, the obvious choice for a base is St. Andrews, with ample accommodations of all kinds. Dundee and its hinterlands have a number of diverse accommodations, including an influx of smart city center hotels, many of which offer good value.

Restaurant and hotel reviews have been shortened. For full information, visit Fodors.com. Restaurant prices are the average cost of a main course at dinner or, if dinner is not served, at lunch. Hotel prices are the lowest cost of a standard double room in high season, including 20% V.A.T.

WHAT IT COSTS in Pounds			
$	$$	$$$	$$$$
RESTAURANTS			
under £15	£15–£19	£20–£25	over £25
HOTELS			
under £125	£125–£200	£201–£300	over £300

Visitor Information

The Dundee and St. Andrews tourist offices are open year-round. Smaller tourist information centers operate seasonally in Arbroath, Crail, Forfar, Kirriemuir, and Montrose.

St. Andrews

52 miles northeast of Edinburgh, 83 miles northeast of Glasgow.

It may have a ruined cathedral and a grand university—the oldest in Scotland—but the modern claim to fame for St. Andrews is mainly its status as the home of golf. Forget that Scottish kings were crowned here, or that John Knox preached here and that Reformation reformers were burned at the stake here. Thousands flock to St. Andrews to play at the Old Course, home of the Royal & Ancient Club, and to follow in the footsteps of Hagen, Sarazen, Jones, and Hogan.

The layout is pure Middle Ages: its three main streets—North, Market, and South—converge on the city's earliest religious site, near the cathedral. Like most of the ancient monuments, the cathedral ruins are impressive in their desolation—but this town is no dusty museum. The streets are busy, the shops are stylish, the gray houses sparkle in the sun, and the scene is particularly brightened during the academic year by bicycling students in scarlet gowns.

GETTING HERE AND AROUND

If you arrive by car, be prepared for an endless drive round the town as you look for a parking space. The parking lots around Rose Park (behind the bus station and a short walk from the town center) are your best bet. If you arrive by local or national bus, the bus station is a five-minute walk from town. The nearest train station, Leuchars, is 10 minutes away by taxi (£15) or bus (£3.30), both of which can be found outside the station. St. Andrews can be fully enjoyed on foot without too much exertion.

ESSENTIALS

VISITOR INFORMATION St. Andrews. ✉ *70 Market St.* ☎ *01334/472021* ⊕ *www. visitscotland.com/destinations-maps/ st-andrews.*

Sights

★ Bell Pettigrew Museum of Natural History

MUSEUM | Founded by Elsie Bell Pettigrew in memory of her husband, James, a former professor of medicine, this fascinating collection of zoological specimens takes you from sea to jungle, mountain to sky. The antiquated manner

St Andrews

Sights ▼

1 Bell Pettigrew Museum of Natural History.......... **D4**
2 British Golf Museum **C2**
3 Museum of the University of St. Andrews **D3**
4 Royal & Ancient Golf Club of St. Andrews **B2**
5 St. Andrews Botanic Garden **B5**
6 St. Andrews Castle.... **D3**
7 St. Andrews Cathedral **E4**
8 St. Andrews Preservation Trust Museum and Garden.. **D4**
9 St. Rule's Tower **E4**
10 Tentsmuir Forest and Beach............... **A3**
11 University of St. Andrews **D3**

Restaurants ▼

1 The Grange Inn **E5**
2 The Saint.................. **C4**
3 The Seafood Risorante.. **C2**
4 Surf & Turf **B3**
5 Tailend Restaurant...... **C4**

Hotels ▼

1 Fairmont St. Andrews ... **E5**
2 Macdonald Rusacks ... **B3**
3 Old Course Hotel........ **A2**
4 Rufflets Country House Hotel **A5**

KEY

- 1 Exploring Sights
- 1 Restaurants
- 1 Hotels

of their presentation reminds you of their significance in an age when most of these creatures were still unknown to most people. In the handsome 16th-century St. Mary's Quadrangle, home to the St. Andrews University's divinity and psychology departments, it is dominated by a holm oak and also contains a thorn tree supposedly planted by Mary, Queen of Scots. ⊠ *Bute Medical Bldg., Queens Gardens, off South St.* ☏ *01334/461660* ⊕ *www.st-andrews.ac.uk/museums/visit-us/bell-pettigrew* ☒ *Free.*

British Golf Museum

MUSEUM | Just opposite the Royal & Ancient Golf Club, this museum explores the centuries-old relationship between St. Andrews and golf and displays golf memorabilia from the 18th century to the 21st century. ⊠ *Bruce Embankment* ☏ *01334/460046* ⊕ *www.britishgolfmuseum.co.uk* ☒ *£8.50.*

Museum of the University of St. Andrews

MUSEUM | With a cluster of intimate and engaging galleries, the Museum of the University of St. Andrews exhibits more than a few austere paintings from the 1600s all the way up to the present day. You'll also find ecumenical regalia, decorative arts, and early scientific instruments including Humphrey Cole's astrolabe of 1575. It also has sweeping views over St. Andrews Bay. ⊠ *7A the Scores* ☏ *01334/461660* ⊕ *www.st-andrews. ac.uk/musa* ☒ *Free* ☽ *Closed Mon.–Wed. Nov.–Mar.*

Royal & Ancient Golf Club of St. Andrews

SPORTS—SIGHT | The ruling house of golf worldwide is the spiritual home of all who play or follow the game. Founded in 1754, its clubhouse on the dunes—open to members only, including women since September 2014—is a mix of classical, Victorian, and neoclassical styles; it's adjacent to the famous Old Course. ⊠ *The Scores* ⊕ *www.randa.org.*

★ St. Andrews Botanic Garden

GARDEN | FAMILY | Immerse yourself in these verdant botanics, replete with 2,000 square feet of heated greenhouses, woodland, rock gardens, allotments, and an enchanting butterfly house. It's just 15 minutes out of town via the Lade Braes footpath. ■ TIP➜ **Bring a picnic or enjoy the on-site tearoom. There are picnic tables around the gardens plus a plant nursery and gift shop.** ⊠ *Canongate* ☏ *01334/ 476452* ⊕ *www.standrewsbotanic.org.*

St. Andrews Castle

ARCHAEOLOGICAL SITE | On the shore north of the cathedral stands ruined St. Andrews Castle, begun at the end of the 13th century. The remains include a rare example of a cold and gruesome bottle-shaped dungeon, in which many prisoners spent their last hours. Even more atmospheric is the castle's mine and countermine. The former was a tunnel dug by besieging forces in the 16th century; the latter, a tunnel dug by castle defenders in order to meet and wage battle belowground. You can stoop and crawl into this narrow passageway—an eerie experience, despite the addition of electric light. The visitor center has a good audiovisual presentation on the castle's history. In summer the beach below is popular with sunbathers and tide-pool investigators, weather permitting. ⊠ *N. Castle St.* ☏ *01334/477196* ⊕ *www.historicenvironment.scot* ☒ *£6, £12 with St. Andrews Cathedral and St. Rule's Tower.*

★ St. Andrews Cathedral

RELIGIOUS SITE | These are the poignant remains of what was once the largest and most magnificent church in Scotland. Work on it began in 1160, and after several delays it was finally consecrated in 1318. The church was subsequently damaged by fire and repaired but fell into decay during the Reformation. Only ruined gables, parts of the nave's south wall, and other fragments survive. The on-site museum helps you interpret the remains and gives a sense of what

Although it is considered to be in ruins, St. Andrews Castle is still one of the city's prettiest sites.

the cathedral must once have been like. ✉ *Off Pends Rd.* ☎ *01334/472563* ⊕ *www.historicenvironment.scot* 🎫 *£6, includes St. Rule's Tower; £12 includes St. Andrews Castle.*

★ St. Andrews Preservation Trust Museum and Garden

MUSEUM | Housed in a stone 17th-century house and former fisherfolk dwelling, this charming museum run by friendly volunteers contains furniture, shop fittings, curious objects, and displays relating to St. Andrews's history. The real draw though—especially in bonnie weather—is the flower-filled garden and curious outbuildings including a laundry and twin-bowled privy. ✉ *12 North St.* ☎ *01334/477629* ⊕ *www.standrewspreservationtrust.co.uk* 🎫 *Free (donations welcome)* 🕐 *Closed Oct.–late Apr.*

St. Rule's Tower

VIEWPOINT | Local legend has it that St. Andrews was founded by St. Regulus, or Rule, who, acting under divine guidance, carried relics of St. Andrew by sea from Patras in Greece. He was shipwrecked on this Fife headland and founded a church. The holy man's name survives in the cylindrical tower, consecrated in 1126 and the oldest surviving building in St. Andrews. Enjoy dizzying views of town from the top of the 108-foot high tower, reached via a steep staircase. ✉ *Off Pends Rd.* ☎ *01334/472563* ⊕ *www.historicenvironment.scot* 🎫 *£6, includes St. Andrews Cathedral; £12 includes St. Andrews Castle.*

★ Tentsmuir Forest and Beach

FOREST | FAMILY | Ten miles north of St. Andrews, this wonderful 50-square-mile nature reserve contains a Scots and Corsican pine forest and the birdlife-rich Morton Lochs, fringing dynamic sand dunes and the long, sandy Kinshaldy Beach. Popular with families, beachcombers, and naturalists, the beach is 5 miles long and has enough space for everyone. If you don't bring a picnic, the Crepe Shack at the car park is a decent food-and-drink option. ✉ *B945, Leuchars* ⊕ *www.tentsmuir.org* 🎫 *Parking £2.*

University of St. Andrews

COLLEGE | Scotland's oldest university is the alma mater of John Knox (Protestant reformer), King James II of Scotland, the Duke and Duchess of Cambridge (William and Kate), and Chris Hoy, Scotland's Olympic cyclist. Founded in 1411, the university's buildings pepper the town. For the quintessential University of St. Andrews experience, **St. Salvator's Quadrangle** reveals the magnificence of this historic institution. Looking out onto this impressive college green is the striking St. Salvator's Chapel, founded in 1450. It bears the marks of a turbulent past: the initials PH, carved into the paving stones under the bell tower, are those of Patrick Hamilton, who was burned alive outside the chapel for his Protestant beliefs. ⊠ *St. Mary's Pl.*

 Restaurants

★ The Grange Inn

$$$$ | CONTEMPORARY | Fife foodies flock to this beautifully converted 17th-century farmhouse surrounded by verdant fields just 10 minutes outside town. The prix-fixe menus offer exquisitely crafted dishes using the best seasonal Scots produce such as beef, pork, mackerel, and wild sea trout. **Known for:** stunning location; great lunch deals; lovely views of St. Andrews. ⑤ *Average main: £30* ⊠ *Grange Rd.* ☎ *01334/472670* ⊕ *www.thegrange-inn.com* ☉ *Closed Sun. and Mon.*

The Saint

$ | MODERN BRITISH | FAMILY | Once local favorite the Westport, this reliable lunch and brunch stop has been revamped with swanky contemporary interiors complimented by a relaxed vibe, tasty cocktails, and excellent pub food. The reasonably priced menu offers everything from chunky gourmet sandwiches to seared scallops to heaped salads—all are best enjoyed in the flowery garden on sunny afternoons. **Known for:** gorgeous sun-draped beer garden; first-rate food from breakfast until late night; friendly youthful staff. ⑤ *Average main: £14* ⊠ *170 South St.* ☎ *01334/473186* ⊕ *www.the-saint-bar.co.uk.*

★ The Seafood Ristorante

$$$$ | SEAFOOD | The striking glass-walled venue perched above the West Sands consistently delivers the freshest and most refined seafood dishes in St. Andrews. Scottish-Italian owner Stefano keeps the emphasis on prime Scots seafood while adding *il bel paese* flourishes and menu staples like risotto, agnolotti (stuffed pasta pockets), and *cicchetti* (Venetian-style tapas). **Known for:** sea or car-park views (ask for the bay-watching tables); seasonal Scots delights like hand-dived Orkney scallops; halibut straight off a Pittenweem boat. ⑤ *Average main: £32* ⊠ *Bruce Embankment* ☎ *01334/479475* ⊕ *www.theseafoodrestaurant.com.*

Surf & Turf

$$$$ | MODERN BRITISH | With grandstand views of the Old Course's 18th green and a menu combining subtle and robust flavors, this is a superb venue for a celebratory meal. The head chef often circulates to introduce the mix of delicate seafood bites with bold meat flavors, which regularly hit the sweet spot between sophistication and lip-smacking gluttony. **Known for:** aged, marinated, and spiced meats; exquisite seafood; mesmerizing views. ⑤ *Average main: £26* ⊠ *Macdonald Rusacks Hotel, Pilmour Links* ☎ *0344/879–9136* ⊕ *www.macdonaldhotels.co.uk/our-hotels/scotland/st-andrews/macdonald-rusacks-hotel.*

Tailend Restaurant

$ | SEAFOOD | The line of customers outside might be a bit off-putting, but just focus on the sweet smell of fish-and-chips from St. Andrews's best chipper. There's a busy light-filled dining room and modish seating area, or you can carry out and eat on the university grounds (though be wary of the dive-bombing gulls). The menu also offers tiger prawns, seared scallops, burgers, and a fish of the day, but you can't go wrong with the

The Evolution of Golf

The matter of who invented golf has been long debated, but there's no doubt that its development into one of the most popular games in the world stems from Scotland. The first written reference to golf, variously spelled as *gowf* or *goff*, was in 1457, when James II (1430–60) of Scotland declared that both golf and football (soccer) should be "*utterly cryit doune and nocht usit*" (publicly criticized and prohibited) because they distracted his subjects from archery practice. Mary, Queen of Scots (1542–87) was fond of golf. When in Edinburgh in 1567, she played on Leith Links and on Bruntsfield Links. When in Fife she played at Falkland and at St. Andrews itself.

Golf Expands

Golf clubs (i.e., organizations) arose in the middle of the 18th century. The Honourable Company of Edinburgh Golfers, now residing at Muirfield, was founded in 1744. From then on, clubs sprang up all over Scotland: Royal Aberdeen (1780), Crail Golfing Society (1786), Dunbar (1794), and the Royal Perth Golfing Society (1824).

As for the town of St. Andrews, which now prospers on golf, golf schools, and golf equipment (the manufacture of golf balls is a local industry), locals say that the game was first played here with a piece of driftwood, a shore pebble, and a rabbit hole on the sandy, coastal turf. Residents were playing

golf on the town links as far back as the 15th century. Rich golfers eventually formed exclusive clubs. The Royal & Ancient Golf Club of St. Andrews was founded in 1754.

By the early 19th century, clubs had been set up in England, and the game was being carried all over the world by enthusiastic Scots. These golf missionaries spread their knowledge not only of the sport but also of the courses. Large parts of the Scottish coast are natural golf courses; indeed, the origins of bunkers and the word *links* (courses) are found in the sand dunes of Scotland's shores. Willie Park of Musselburgh, James Braid, and C. K. Hutchison are some of the best known of Scotland's golf-course architects.

Changes in the Game

The original balls, called *featheries*, were leather bags stuffed with boiled feathers and often lasted only one round. In 1848 the gutta-percha ball, called a *guttie*, was introduced. It was in general use until the invention of the rubber-core ball in 1901. Clubs were made of wood with shafts of ash (later hickory), and heads of thorn, apple, or pear. Heads were spliced, then bound to the shaft with twine. Later in the 19th century, manufacturers began to experiment with metal in clubfaces and shafts. The technology of golf continues to change, but its addictive qualities are timeless.

battered haddock supper with chips. **Known for:** the best fish-and-chips in St. Andrews; Arbroath smokies; fabulous starters and desserts. ⑤ *Average main: £14* ✉ *130 Market St.* ☎ *01334/474070* ⊕ *www.thetailend.co.uk.*

 Hotels

Fairmont St. Andrews

$$ | **HOTEL** | Two miles from St. Andrews, this modern hotel has spectacular views of the bay and two superb golf courses. **Pros:** spacious feel; spacious spa; golf at your doorstep. **Cons:** the huge atrium

feels like a shopping center; paintings made to match the decor; food menu needs updating. $ *Rooms from: £199* ✉ *A917* ☎ *01334/837000* ⊕ *www. fairmont.com/standrews* ⬐ *209 rooms* ⍥ *Free breakfast.*

Macdonald Rusacks

$$$ | **HOTEL** | The grand Victorian hotel building with grandstand views of the Old Course's 18th hole and West Sands offers affordable luxury and an unstuffy atmosphere. **Pros:** fabulous views; affordable food options; golf enthusiasts' heaven. **Cons:** service can fall short; bathrooms and bedroom decor lack the wow factor; golf-dominated vibe not for everyone. $ *Rooms from: £220* ✉ *Pilmour, The Links* ☎ *0344/879–9136* ⊕ *www.macdonaldhotels.co.uk* ⬐ *70 rooms* ⍥ *Free breakfast.*

Old Course Hotel

$$$$ | **HOTEL** | Regularly hosting international golf stars and jet-setters, the Old Course Hotel has much-coveted guest room fairway views, grand public spaces, and fabulous facilities including a swanky spa. **Pros:** fabulous location and lovely views; unpretentious service; golfer's heaven. **Cons:** all the golf talk might bore nongolfers; standard rooms small and need an update; expensive. $ *Rooms from: £416* ✉ *Old Station Rd.* ☎ *01334/474371* ⊕ *www.oldcoursehotel. co.uk* ⬐ *179 rooms* ⍥ *Free breakfast.*

★ Rufflets Country House Hotel

$$$ | **HOTEL** | Ten acres of formal and informal gardens surround this vine-covered country house with individually designed rooms, a wonderful restaurant, and a cozy lounge-bar with a handsome fireplace and terrace. **Pros:** attractive gardens; cozy drawing room; family-friendly lodges. **Cons:** too far to walk to St. Andrews; primarily venue for those celebrating, so can get noisy; no elevator in the main house. $ *Rooms from: £220* ✉ *Strathkinness Low Rd.* ☎ *01334/472594* ⊕ *www.rufflets.co.uk* ⬐ *26 rooms* ⍥ *Free breakfast.*

 Nightlife

Central Bar

BARS/PUBS | There are still some old-fashioned pubs to be found among the cocktail bars of St. Andrews, and this wood-and-leather-furnished haunt is a good bet for a friendly mingle with a pint in hand. You'll find a good range of beers (bottled and on tap) and decent pub food. ✉ *77 Market St.* ☎ *01334/478296.*

 Performing Arts

Byre Theatre

THEATER | Experimental plays, small-scale operatic performances, contemporary dance, musical performances, and film screenings are on the bill at the Byre. Its handsome café-bar and bistro serves excellent food. ✉ *Abbey St.* ☎ *01334/475000* ⊕ *byretheatre.com.*

New Picture House Cinema

FILM | A lovely old cinema shows a well-chosen mix of Hollywood and independent films. ✉ *117 North St.* ☎ *01334/474902* ⊕ *nph.nphcinema.co.uk.*

 Shopping

Artery

CRAFTS | This well-curated shop sells work by local, Scottish, and British artists, including jewelry, ceramics, paintings, and intriguing handmade clocks. ✉ *183 South St.* ☎ *01334/473153* ⊕ *arterygifts. com.*

Balgove Larder

FOOD/CANDY | Here you'll discover a huge selection of Scottish items, from spurtles (for stirring your porridge) to tablet (sugary toffee) to big, thick sausages made in its butchery. Foodies should check out the Farm Shop and monthly Night Market, while carnivores can follow their noses to the Steak Barn, where platters piled with huge hunks of beef and sausages are combined with twice-fried chips and onion rings. ⊠ *A91* ☎ *01334/898145* ⊕ *www.balgove.com.*

Mellis

FOOD/CANDY | This heady-smelling store is truly a cheese lover's mecca. Look for a soft, crumbly, and citrusy cheese (called Anster) made thanks to a local herd of Holstein-Friesians. ⊠ *149 South St.* ☎ *01334/471410* ⊕ *www.mellischeese.net.*

★ Topping and Company Booksellers

BOOKS/STATIONERY | This is a bibliophile's dream haunt, with high ceilings and alcoves lined with over 45,000 titles, knowledgeable staff, and frequent readings and literary events. ⊠ *7 Greyfriars Garden* ☎ *01334/585111* ⊕ *www.topping-books.co.uk.*

 Activities

GOLF

What serious golfer doesn't dream of playing at world-famous St. Andrews? Seven St. Andrews courses, all part of the St. Andrews Trust, are open to visitors, and more than 40 other courses in the region offer golf by the round or by the day.

Balgove Course

GOLF | At the beginner-friendly Balgove Course you can turn up and tee off without prior reservation. ⊠ *West Sands Rd., A91* ⊕ *www.standrews.com* 🏌 *£8–£15* 🏌. *9 holes, 1520 yards, par 30.*

Castle Course

GOLF | Designed by David McLay Kidd in 2008, the Castle Course hugs the rugged coastline and has jaw-dropping views. It's 2 miles from the town center. ⊠ *A917* ⊕ *www.standrews.com* 🏌 *£60–£120* 🏌. *18 holes, 6759 yards, par 71.*

Eden Course

GOLF | The aptly named Eden Course, designed in 1914 by Harry S. Colt, winds through inland fields bordered with lovely foliage. It's a bit more forgiving

compared to other St. Andrews courses. ⊠ *West Sands Rd.* ⊕ *www.standrews.com* 🏌 *£25–£50* 🏌. *18 holes, 6250 yards, par 70.*

★ Jubilee Course

GOLF | This windswept course offers quite a challenge even for experienced golfers. When it opened in 1897 it was intended for beginners, but the popularity of its seaside location encouraged the powers that be to convert it into a championship course. Many golfers say the 15th hole is one of the best in the sport. ⊠ *West Sands Rd.* ⊕ *www.standrews.com* 🏌 *£40–£80* 🏌. *18 holes, 6742 yards, par 72.*

New Course

GOLF | Not exactly new—it opened in 1895—the New Course is rather overshadowed by the Old Course, but it has a firm following of golfers who appreciate the loop design. ⊠ *West Sands Rd.* ⊕ *www.standrews.com* 🏌 *£40–£80* 🏌. *18 holes, 6625 yards, par 71.*

★ Old Course

GOLF | Believed to be the oldest golf course in the world, the Old Course was first played in the 15th century. Each year, more than 44,000 rounds are teed off, and no doubt most get stuck in one of its 112 bunkers. A handicap certificate and some very early morning waits for a possible tee-off are required. ⊠ *West Sands Rd.* ⊕ *www.standrews.com* 🏌 *£90–£190* 🏌. *18 holes, 6721 yards, par 72.*

Strathtyrum Course

GOLF | Those with a high handicap will enjoy this course, opened in 1993, without the worry or embarrassment of holding up more experienced golfers. ⊠ *West Sands Rd., A91* ⊕ *www.standrews.com* 🏌 *£15–£30* 🏌. *18 holes, 5620 yards, par 69.*

Crail

10 miles south of St. Andrews.

The oldest and most aristocratic of East Neuk burghs, pretty Crail is where many fish merchants retired and built cottages. The town landmark is a picturesque Dutch-influenced town house, or *tolbooth,* which contains the oldest bell in Fife, cast in Holland in 1520. Crail may now be full of artists, but it remains a working harbor; take time to walk the streets and beaches and to sample fish by the harbor. ■TIP→ **As you head into East Neuk from this tiny port, look about for market crosses, merchant houses, and little doocots (dovecotes, where pigeons were kept)—typical picturesque touches of this region.**

GETTING HERE AND AROUND

Stagecoach bus No. 95 operates between Crail and St. Andrews. This service also takes you on to Anstruther, Pittenweem, St. Monans, and Lower Largo. Crail is about 15 minutes from St. Andrews by car via A917.

Sights

Crail Museum and Heritage Centre

MUSEUM | The story of this trading and fishing town can be found in the delightfully crammed Crail Museum and Heritage Centre, entirely run by local volunteers. There is a small tourist information desk within the center and fascinating guided walks start here Wednesday and Sunday from June through October. ✉ *62–64 Marketgate* ☎ *01333/450869* ⊕ *www. crailmuseum.org.uk* ✇ *Free* ⊗ *Closed Oct.–Mar. Limited hrs Apr. and May.*

Restaurants

★ Reilly Shellfish Lobster Hut

$$ | SEAFOOD | This hut on the pier, a hidden gem, sells beautifully cooked lobsters for £12–£20 each (depending on size) and other items at times, including lobster rolls and dressed crab. They'll crack the lobster for you to allow for easy eating on a nearby bench; there is no seating, but the lobster is wonderful. **Known for:** freshest seafood; casual alfresco eating in a beach and harbor setting; varying, sometimes random hours. ⑤ *Average main: £15* ✉ *34 Shoregate* ☎ *01333/450476* � *Closed winter and Mon. No dinner* ▬ *No credit cards.*

🛏 Hotels

Hazelton

$ | B&B/INN | Beautifully polished wood, exquisitely restored period features, and gentle hues put the Hazelton head and shoulders above the typical seaside B&B. **Pros:** handsome building; central location near pub and harbor; decent breakfast. **Cons:** a couple of rooms on the small side; unreliable communication via email; intermittent traffic noise. ⑤ *Rooms from: £85* ✉ *29 Marketgate N* ☎ *01333/450250* ⊕ *www.thehazelton.co.uk* �

 Closed Jan 💤 *5 rooms* 🍴 *Free breakfast.*

Anstruther

4 miles southwest of Crail.

Anstruther, locally called Ainster, has a lovely waterfront with a few shops brightly festooned with children's pails and shovels, a gesture to summer vacationers.

GETTING HERE AND AROUND
Stagecoach bus No. 95 operates between St. Andrews, Crail, Anstruther, Pittenweem, St. Monans, and Lower Largo. By car Anstruther is 5 to 10 minutes from Crail via A917.

Sights

Isle of May Boat Trip

BOAT TOURS | Take to the waves (April through September) on the compact *May Princess* for a round-trip to the Isle of May, a rocky bird reserve near the mouth of the Forth. Measuring just under a mile long and a third of a mile wide, it harbors 14 species of breeding birds including arctic terns, guillemots, and puffins. The round-trip takes five hours, with three hours on shore to explore the island's history, monastery remains, and the breathtaking sights, sounds, and smells of the avian multitudes. ✉ *Middle Pier, Anstruther Harbour* ☎ *07957/585200* ⊕ *www.isleofmayferry.com* 🎫 *£28.*

★ Scottish Fisheries Museum

MUSEUM | FAMILY | Facing Anstruther Harbor, the Scottish Fisheries Museum is inside a colorful cluster of buildings, the earliest of which dates from the 16th century. A charming trail around the various buildings and odd spaces illustrates the life of Scottish fisherfolk; you can spend a couple of hours examining the many documents, artifacts, model ships, paintings, and displays (complete with the reek of tarred rope and net). There are floating exhibits at the quayside and a window onto a working boatyard. ✉ *Harbourhead* ☎ *01333/310628* ⊕ *www.scotfishmuseum.org* 🎫 *£9.*

Restaurants

★ Anstruther Fish Bar and Restaurant

$ | SEAFOOD | Next door to the Scottish Fisheries Museum, this popular fish-and-chips shop has a functional space to eat, but most people order takeout. Try local specialties including Pittenweem prawns in batter or the catch of the day, which could be mackerel (line caught by the owners), hake, or local crab. **Known for:** consistently excellent fish-and-chips; friendly staff; ice-cream counter with novel flavors. ⑤ *Average main: £11* ✉ *42–44*

Shore St. ☎ *01333/310518* ⊕ *www.anstrutherfishbar.co.uk.*

The Cellar

$$$$ | **EUROPEAN** | Entered through a cobbled courtyard, this unpretentious, atmospheric restaurant is run by talented head chef Billy Boyter and family. The three-course prix-fixe meals feature locally sourced seafood and meat such as crab, hake, mussels, beef, lamb, and quail. **Known for:** elegant yet informal dining; exquisite produce; wine-pairing option. ⑤ *Average main: £70* ⊠ *24 E. Green* ☎ *01333/310378* ⊕ *www.thecellaranstruther.co.uk* ⊘ *Closed Mon. and Tues. No lunch Wed.*

Nightlife

★ Dreel Tavern

BARS/PUBS | A 16th-century coaching inn, the Dreel Tavern was resurrected and refurbished in 2017 by two young sisters who have built on the characterful stone building and added some tasteful improvements including an impressive food menu. Alongside decent draft beers, the excellent food showcases local produce such as lobster and smoked fish. The low-ceilinged wood-beamed bar makes for a lively atmosphere, especially during the ocassional low-key musical gigs and gourmet events that happen here. A pretty beer garden overlooks the Dreel Burn and the family garden where much of the produce on the menu grows. ⊠ *16 High St.* ☎ *01333/279238* ⊕ *www.dreeltavern.co.uk.*

Activities

East Neuk Outdoors

BICYCLING | **FAMILY** | The back roads of Fife make pleasant places for biking. You can rent bicycles from East Neuk Outdoors, which also has equipment for archery, climbing, kayaking, and canoeing. ⊠ *Cellardyke Park* ☎ *01333/310370* ⊕ *www.eastneukoutdoors.co.uk.*

Fife Coastal Path

Fife's green and undulating landscape includes the Lomond Hills, which are easy to climb and offer fabulous views of both the Tay and Forth estuaries. The Fife Coastal Path (⊕ *www.fifecoastalpath.co.uk*) can be a bracing epic or a wandering amble. The 7-mile stretch between East Wemyss and Lower Largo is the easiest going, with some of it along the beaches of Elie. The 8-mile route between Pittenweem and Fifeness (four to six hours) can be rougher in patches, but takes you through Anstruther and Crail.

Pittenweem and St. Monans

1½ and 3 miles southwest of Anstruther.

These neighboring harbors are places to wander among lobster creels, fishing nets, and rocks, discovering quirky local artworks and architectural features. Many examples of East Neuk architecture serve as the backdrop for the working harbor at Pittenweem. Look for the crow-stepped gables, white *harling* (the rough mortar finish on walls), and red *pantiles* (roof tiles with an S-shaped profile). The *weem* part of the town's name comes from the Gaelic *uaime*, meaning cave. Nearby St. Monans has an attractive working fishing harbor, small pebbly beach, and a trio of free sights: pop in first to the wonderful, volunteer-run heritage center by the harbor and curious Wellington boot garden; nearby to the west is the parish church dating from 1265; nearly a mile east along the coastal path is St. Monans Windmill (collect keys from the post office), where Fife salt production is explained.

GETTING HERE AND AROUND

Stagecoach bus No. 95 operates between St. Andrews, Crail, Anstruther, Pittenweem, St. Monans, and Lower Largo. Pittenweem is about five minutes from Anstruther by car via A917.

Sights

Kellie Castle and Garden

CASTLE/PALACE | Dating from the 16th to 17th century and restored in Victorian times, Kellie Castle stands among the grain fields and woodlands of northeastern Fife. Four acres of pretty gardens surround the castle, which is in the care of the National Trust for Scotland. In summer you can buy berries grown in the walled garden, and baked goods are sold in the tearoom. The garden and estate are open year-round, even when the castle itself is closed. ⊠ B9171 ✛ 3 miles northwest of Pittenweem ☎ 01337/720271 ⊕ www.nts.org.uk ⛉ £10.50 ⊘ Castle closed Nov.–Mar. and Fri. Apr.–Oct.

★ Pittenweem Arts Festival

FESTIVAL | There is nothing quite like August's Pittenweem Arts Festival. Exhibitions, which involve hundreds of local and international artists, take place in the town's public buildings and in private homes and gardens. It's a week of events, workshops, and live music. ☎ 01333/313109 ⊕ www.pittenweemarts-festival.co.uk.

St. Fillan's Cave

CAVE | This town's cavern, St. Fillan's Cave, contains the shrine of St. Fillan, a 6th-century hermit who lived here. It's up a pend (alleyway) behind the waterfront. If the cave isn't open, ask at the Cocoa Tree on High Street. Those who can are asked to make a donation of £1 to cover the upkeep of the spooky, spiritual site. ⊠ Cove Wynd ⛉ Free ⊘ Closed Sun.

Restaurants

Craig Millar @ 16 West End

$$$$ | SEAFOOD | This eatery overlooking the harbor run by Dundonian chef Craig Millar put St. Monans on Scotland's culinary map. The fixed-price menu has vegetarian and meat options, but with salty fruits of the North Sea on the Fife quayside—such as crab, cod, hake, and mackerel—it's all about Craig's expertise with seafood. Known for: elegant seafood dining; gorgeous terrace with sea views; attentive service. ⑤ Average main: £45 ⊠ 16 West End, St. Monans ✛ 2 miles west of Pittenweem ☎ 01333/730327 ⊕ www.16westend.com ⊘ Closed Mon. and Tues. No dinner Sun.

East Pier Smokehouse

$ | SEAFOOD | Painted powder-blue, this long harborside building-turned-eatery and foodie shop is the place to pick up freshly netted and smoked local seafood. After ordering at the shop counter, head up the stairs round the back to feast on lobster, langoustine, and crab accompanied by salads and chips. Known for: fresh seafood; imaginative salads; great views from the rooftop terrace. ⑤ Average main: £13 ⊠ East Shore, St. Monans ☎ 01333/405030 ⊕ www.eastpier.co.uk ⊘ Closed Nov.–Mar., weekdays in Apr. and Oct., and Mon. and Tues. in May–Sept. No dinner.

Shopping

★ Pitenweem Chocolate Company

FOOD/CANDY | Open daily, this place stocks the most imaginative and comprehensive range of fine chocolates you'll find in this part of the world. Its lovely Cocoa Tree Café serves cakes, drinks, light meals, and, of course, handmade chocolates from the Pittenweem Chocolate Company. ⊠ 9 High St. ☎ 01333/311495 ⊕ www.pittenweemchocolate.co.uk.

Elie

5 miles south of Pittenweem.

To give it its full name, the Royal Burgh of Elie and Earlsferry is an old trading port with a handsome harbor that loops around one of the most glorious stretches of sand in the British Isles. Since Victorian times, when a railway (sadly defunct since the 1960s) linked it with the capital, Elie has been a weekend and summer retreat for the great and the good of Edinburgh. The beach to the south of the harbor is a mile long and has clean sands, clear waters, and tide pools to interest young and old.

Restaurants

★ Ship Inn

$$ | BRITISH | FAMILY | Overlooking Elie's sandy beach, the Ship Inn combines a nautically themed pub-restaurant serving superb Scottish cuisine with six pristine, tastefully white-shuttered rooms, four with stunning views of the sea. The relaxed atmosphere and views—with the comedy of a cricketing contest on shifting sands a bonus—make for an afternoon you'll never forget, especially if the weather is nice. **Known for:** buzzy, stylish community hub; dining with sea views; excellent seafood. $ *Average main: £17* ⊠ *The Toft* 🕾 *01333/330246* ⊕ *www.shipinn.scot.*

Activities

GOLF
Leven Links

GOLF | A fine Fife course that has been used as a British Open qualifier, Leven Links has a whiff of the more famous St. Andrews, with a hummocky terrain and a tang of salt in the air. The 1st and 18th holes share the same fairway, and the 18th green has a creek running beside it. Saturday play must be booked at least a week in advance. ⊠ *The Promenade,*

Leven 🕾 *01333/421390* ⊕ *www.leven-links.com* ⊠ *£30–£100* 🏌 *18 holes, 6551 yards, par 71* ⚐ *Reservations essential.*

Lundin Golf Club

GOLF | One of a string of fantastic links courses, Lundin Golf Club is a worthy addition to any Scottish golfing itinerary. Designed by the great James Braid, the course is always in prime condition and the greens are a joy. The pick of the holes is the par-3 14th, played from an elevated tee back toward the sea. ⊠ *Golf Rd., Lundin Links* 🕾 *01333/320202* ⊕ *www. lundingolfclub.co.uk* ⊠ *£85 weekdays, £100 weekends* 🏌 *18 holes, 6371 yards, par 71.*

Falkland

24 miles northwest of Pittenweem, 15 miles northwest of Elie.

One of the loveliest communities in Scotland, Falkland is a royal burgh of twisting streets and crooked stone houses.

GETTING HERE AND AROUND
Stagecoach bus No. 64 is the only direct service connecting Falkland to St. Andrews as well as Cupar and Ladybank (both of which are train stations on the Edinburgh to Dundee line). Falkland is about 15 minutes from Cupar and a half hour from St. Andrews by car via A91 and A912, or A91 to A914 to A912.

Sights

Falkland Palace

CASTLE/PALACE | A former hunting lodge of the Stuart monarchs, Falkland Palace dominates the town and is one of the country's earliest and finest examples of the French Renaissance style. Overlooking the main street is the palace's most impressive feature, the walls and chambers on its south side, all rich with buttresses and stone medallions, built by French masons in the 1530s for

King James V (1512–42). He died here, and the palace was a favorite resort of his daughter, Mary, Queen of Scots (1542–87). The beautiful gardens behind Falkland Palace contain a rare survivor: a royal tennis court, built in 1539. In the gardens, overlooked by the palace turret windows, you may easily imagine yourself back at the solemn hour when James on his deathbed pronounced the doom of the house of Stuart: "It cam' wi' a lass and it'll gang wi a lass." ✉ *Main St.* ☎ *01337/857397* ⊕ *www.nts.org.uk* 🎫 *£13* ⏱ *Closed Nov.–Feb.*

 Restaurants

★ Pillars of Hercules

$ | **VEGETARIAN** | **FAMILY** | Head down a country lane to this organic farm and café-bistro for a tasty vegetarian meal made of produce grown in the wonderful gardens. On a sunny day take your crepe or heaped salad to a bench outside by the nursery, or grab some take-out deli foods from the shop. **Known for:** organic produce grown on-site; inventive dishes; beautiful grounds. $ *Average main: £8* ✉ *A912* ⊹ *1 mile northwest of Falkland* ☎ *01337/857749* ⊕ *www.pillars.co.uk* ⏱ *No dinner.*

Cupar

21 miles northwest of Loch Leven, 10 miles west of St. Andrews.

Cupar is a busy market town with several interesting sites, including a museum about Fife.

GETTING HERE AND AROUND

Cupar has a train station on the Edinburgh–Aberdeen line (which passes through Dundee), and there are trains almost every hour. Stagecoach buses serve the town as well. By car you can reach Cupar from Loch Leven via M90 and A91; take A91 if you're traveling from St. Andrews.

 Sights

★ Fife Folk Museum

MUSEUM | To learn more about the history and culture of rural Fife, visit the wonderful Fife Folk Museum in the attractive nearby village of Ceres. The life of local rural communities is reflected in fascinating artifacts and documents housed in a former weigh house and adjoining weavers' cottages. Refreshments and food are served in the Weigh House Tearoom with views of Ceres Burn. The museum is 3 miles southeast of Cupar via A916 and B939. ✉ *High St., Ceres* ☎ *01334/828180* ⊕ *www.fifefolkmuseum.org* 🎫 *Free (donations welcome)* ⏱ *Closed Mon., Tues., and Nov.–Mar.*

Hill of Tarvit Mansion and Kingarrock Hickory Golf

HOUSE | On rising ground near Cupar stands the National Trust for Scotland's Hill of Tarvit House, a 17th-century mansion that was altered in the high-Edwardian style in the late 1890s and early 1900s by the Scottish architect Sir Robert Lorimer (1864–1929). The extensive wood and parklands offer an enjoyable place for a picnic or stroll, and the house itself is well worth a visit. Golfers will also want to play a round on the old Lorimer family course, the Hickory, which was brought back to life in 2008 after being ploughed up for agricultural use during World War II. ✉ *Off A916* ⊹ *2 miles south of Cupar* ☎ *01334/653127* ⊕ *www.nts.org.uk* 🎫 *£10.50; golf £45–£60* ⏱ *Closed Nov.–Mar.*

Scottish Deer Centre

ZOO | **FAMILY** | At the Scottish Deer Centre, many types of deer can be seen at close quarters or on ranger-guided tours. There are falconry displays every two hours, woodland walks, and a café. The zoolike center, west of Cupar, is one of the few places you can spot the red squirrel, as well as wolves, lynx, wildcat, and European brown bear. ✉ *A91*

☎ 01337/810391 ⊕ www.tsdc.co.uk ✉ £9.50.

Restaurants

Ostlers Close Restaurant

$$$ | BRITISH | Tucked away in an alley off the main street, this cottage-style restaurant has earned a well-deserved reputation for top-quality cuisine that is imaginative without trying to be showy. Elegantly presented in the warm-hued, smart dining room, dishes show off the locally sourced meat and fish, as well as homegrown and foraged produce to best advantage. **Known for:** fine produce; daily menus including vegetarian options; intimate atmosphere that can get crowded. $ Average main: £25 ✉ 25 Bonnygate ☎ 01334/655574 ⊕ www.ostlersclose. co.uk ⊘ Closed Sun. and Mon. No lunch.

Hotels

★ The Peat Inn

$$$ | B&B/INN | With eight bright and contemporary two-room suites, this popular "restaurant with rooms" is perhaps best known for its outstanding, modern, Scottish-style restaurant. **Pros:** exceptional restaurant; supercomfy and large beds; verdant gardens and views. **Cons:** books up quickly; you need a car to get here; hard to get a restaurant reservation. $ Rooms from: £235 ✉ B941, at intersection of B940 ☎ 01334/840206 ⊕ www.thepeatinn.co.uk ⊘ Closed Sun. and Mon ➷ 8 suites ❀ Breakfast.

Activities

Ladybank Golf Club

GOLF | Fife is known for its coastal courses, but this one provides an interesting inland layout. Although Ladybank, designed by Tom Morris in 1876, is on fairly level ground, the fir and birch trees and heathery rough give it a Highland flavor among the gentle Lowland fields. Qualifying rounds of the British Open are played here when the main championship is played at St. Andrews. ✉ A92, Annsmuir, Ladybank ☎ 01337/830814 ⊕ www.ladybankgolf.co.uk ✉ £65–£85 ⚐ 18 holes, 6580 yards, par 71 ⚑ Reservations essential.

Dundee

14 miles northwest of St. Andrews, 58 miles north of Edinburgh, 79 miles northeast of Glasgow.

Dundee makes an excellent base for a cultural stay and Fife and Angus exploration at any time of year. The Dundee Contemporary Arts center gave the city a much-needed boost in 1999; today artsy and foodie hangouts and a vibrant mix of student and creative life make it a beguiling stop. As you explore the streets and new waterfront, including the green expanse of Slessor Gardens, you may glimpse contrasting bold lines of the 2018 V&A Dundee museum of design, 1966 Tay Road Bridge, and 1888 Tay Rail Bridge. Those ever-changing views of the Tay led actor and wordsmith Stephen Fry to describe Dundee's setting as "ludicrously ideal." Heading southwest down cobbled Roseangle you reach Magdalen Green, where landscape artist James McIntosh Patrick (1907–98) found inspiration from the river and skyscapes. Dundonians' deadpan humor was distilled in the popular comic strips *The Beano* and *The Dandy,* first published here in the 1930s; statues by Scottish sculptors Tony and Susie Morrow depicting characters Desperate Dan, Dawg, and a catapult-wielding Minnie the Minx are in City Square.

GETTING HERE AND AROUND

The East Coast train line runs through the city, linking it to Edinburgh (and beyond, to London), Glasgow (and the West Coast of England), and Aberdeen, with trains to all every hour or half hour at peak times. Cheaper bus service is available to all these locations, as well as St. Andrews and several other towns in Fife and Angus.

If you're traveling by car, the A92 will take you north from Fife to Abroath and the Angus coast towns. The A90, from Perth, heads north to Aberdeen.

Most of the sights in Dundee are clustered together, so you can easily walk around the city. If the weather is bad or your legs are heavy, hail one of the many cabs on the easy-to-find taxi ranks for little more than a few pounds.

ESSENTIALS

VISITOR INFORMATION Angus and Dundee Tourist Board. ⊠ *16 City Sq.* ☎ *01382/527527* ⊕ *www.dundee.com, www.visitangus.com, www.visitscotland.com.*

 # Sights

Broughty Castle

MUSEUM | FAMILY | Originally built to guard the Tay Estuary, Broughty Castle is now a museum focusing on fishing, ferries, and the history of the area's whaling industry. The cannons and ramparts make for fine photo opportunities, and inside (up a very narrow stairway) are four floors of displays, including some of the lovely art collection of the Victorian inventor and engineer Sir James Orchar. To the north of the castle lies beautiful Broughty Ferry Beach, which, even in midwinter, is enjoyed by the locals; there is regular bus service from Dundee's city center. ⊠ *Castle Approach, Broughty Ferry* ⊕ *4 miles east of city center* ☎ *01382/436916* ⊕ *www.leisureandculturedundee.com/ broughty-castle* ⌦ *Free* ⌚ *Closed Mon. Oct.–Mar.*

Dundee Botanic Garden

GARDEN | FAMILY | This renowned botanical garden contains an extensive collection of native and exotic plants outdoors and in tropical and temperate greenhouses. There are some beautiful areas for picnicking, as well as a visitor center, an art gallery, and a coffee shop. ⊠ *Riverside Dr.* ☎ *01382/381190* ⊕ *www.dundee. ac.uk/botanic* ⌦ *£3.90.*

★ Dundee Contemporary Arts

MUSEUM | FAMILY | Between a 17th-century mansion and a cathedral, this strikingly modern building houses one of Britain's most exciting artistic venues. The two galleries house changing shows by internationally acclaimed contemporary artists. There are children's and adult's workshops, special events, and meet-the-artist events throughout the year. Two movie theaters screen mainly independent, revival, and children's films. There's also a craft shop and a buzzing café-bar that's open until midnight. ⊠ *152 Nethergate* ☎ *01382/432444* ⊕ *www.dca. org.uk* ⌦ *Free.*

The Law

VIEWPOINT | For sweeping views of the city, the Angus Glens to the north, and Fife's coastline to the south, head up to Dundee's very own extinct volcano. This 1,640-feet-above-sea-level hill (*law* means hill in Scots) has a World War II memorial, parking lot, and seating area. ⊠ *Law Rd.*

★ McManus Galleries

MUSEUM | Dundee's principal museum and art gallery, housed in a striking Gothic Revival–style building, has an engaging collection of artifacts that document the city's history and the working, social, and cultural lives of Dundonians throughout the Victorian period and the 20th century. Its varied fine art collection includes paintings by Rossetti, Raeburn, and Peploe as well as thought-provoking yet accessible contemporary works and visiting exhibitions. ⊠ *Albert Sq.* ☎ *01382/307200* ⊕ *www.mcmanus.co.uk* ⌦ *Free.*

Mills Observatory

OBSERVATORY | At the top of a thickly forested hill, Mills Observatory is the only full-time public observatory in Britain. There are displays on astronomy, space exploration, scientific instruments, and a 12-inch refracting telescope for night viewing of the stars and planets. ■ TIP➔ Dundonians flock here when there's a solar or lunar event. If one happens during your visit, don't miss this universally happy experience. ⊠ *Balgay Hill* ✛ *2 miles west of city center* ☎ *01382/435967* ⊕ *www. leisureandculturedundee.com/mills* 🖾 *Free* ⊘ *Closed Sun.–Tues., Thurs., and Fri. in Apr.–Aug.*

Newport-on-Tay

PROMENADE | Across the Tay River, this charming shoreline suburb has spectacular river views, handsome Victorian architecture, and an interesting collection of independent shops and restaurants, plus some beguiling walks. Once just a small village with cottages, Newport was transformed and renamed "New Dundee" when the city's Victorian jute barons and middle classes made it a fashionable enclave. Dundee's mill workers folllowed suit, traveling on the *Fifie* steam ferries to escape the cachaphonous and polluted city; you can follow in their brogues and barefoot soles by walking along the Braes Riverside Park. Although the Victorian bathing establishments once there have gone, the ornate 1878 ferry port has been partly restored. You'd be brave to take a dip even on a warm Tayside day, so opt for a sunset sit-down here instead. ■ TIP➔ Head here by bus from Dundee midafternoon to walk the Braes, landscaped gardens, and woodland of nearby Tayfield Estate (aka Berry's Den). Then head to the Boat Brae for refreshments while watching the sunset over the Tay. ⊠ *Boat Brae* ✛ *Take bus 77 or X54 from Dundee.*

North Carr Lightship

HISTORIC SITE | Moored next to the *Unicorn*, you'll see a strange rusting red ship, the *North Carr Lightship.* After playing a significant role in World War II, Scotland's only remaining lightship was wrecked on the Fife shore during a storm in 1959; seven crew members were lost. ■ TIP➔ The ship is sadly closed awaiting funds for refurbishment but is worth a look from the dock. Donations for restoration welcomed by the Taymara charity, which also runs boat trips (see below). ⊠ *Broughty Ferry Harbour, Beach Crescent* ☎ *01382/542516* ⊕ *www. taymara.org.*

★ RRS *Discovery*

HISTORIC SITE | FAMILY | Dundee's urban-renewal program—the city is determined to celebrate its industrial past—was motivated in part by the arrival of the RRS (Royal Research Ship) *Discovery*, the vessel used by Captain Robert F. Scott (1868–1912) on his polar explorations. The steamer was originally built and launched in Dundee; now it's a permanent resident, sitting by the suitably clifflike V&A museum. At Discovery Point, under the handsome cupola, the story of the ship and its famous expedition unfold; you can even feel the Antarctic chill as if you were there. The ship, berthed outside, is the star: wander the deck, then explore the quarters to see the daily existence endured by the ship's crew and captain. ⊠ *Discovery Quay, Riverside Dr.* ☎ *01382/309060* ⊕ *www.rrsdiscovery.com* 🖾 *£11.50, £18.65 includes Verdant Works.*

Tay River Trips

TOUR—SIGHT | FAMILY | Taymara, the nonprofit group that looks after the *North Carr Lightship,* runs exhilarating dolphin-watching trips on its other vessel, the *Missel Thrush.* Hour-long excursions leave from Broughty Ferry Harbour (weekdays) and Tayport Harbour (weekends), and take you around the mouth of the delta, where dolphins jump and play. Booking in advance is essential. ⊠ *Broughty Ferry Harbour, Beach Crescent* ☎ *01382/542516* ⊕ *www.taymara. org* 🖾 *£16.*

Unicorn

HISTORIC SITE | FAMILY | It's easy to spot this 46-gun wood warship, as it's fronted by a figurehead of a white unicorn. This frigate has the distinction of being the

6

Fife and Angus DUNDEE

Dundee

KEY

- ① *Exploring Sights*
- ① *Restaurants*
- ① *Hotels*

✈ **Dundee Airport**

Hotels ▼

The McManus Galleries are home to many artifacts on local history and culture from the 19th and 20th centuries.

oldest British-built warship afloat, having been launched in 1824 at Chatham, England. You can clamber right down into the hold, or see the models and displays about the Royal Navy's history. Live events like jazz concerts and theater performances are staged on board. ✉ Victoria Dock ✛ East of Tay Rd. bridge ⊕ www.frigateunicorn.org ✍ £7.25 ⊘ Closed Mon. and Tues. Nov.–Mar.

★ V&A Dundee

MUSEUM | Opened to worldwide acclaim in 2018, the first outpost of the Victoria and Albert Museum of London is housed in an arresting riverside building by Japanese architect Kengo Kuma. Scotland's first-ever design museum contains seminal works and inspiring displays by Scots and international designers. The Scottish Design Galleries present the past, present, and future through the V&A collections and loans from around the world. Among the many highlights is Charles Rennie Mackintosh's Oak Room, unveiled for the first time in 50 years. Stellar shows, exclusively created for the new V&A galleries, spark inspiration among young and old. This "living room for the city," as Kuma described his design, is worth a visit for the building and setting alone: the vistas in and around its sea-cliff-like edges and perches provide places to linger, mingle, and reflect. If the weather is bad, the Living Room Café here is a great place to linger, refuel, and admire the views of the architecture and river, plus the gift shop has a wealth of quirky design gift ideas. ✉ Discovery Quay ⊕ www.vam. ac.uk ✍ Free for permammet collection; £12 for temporary exhibits.

Verdant Works

MUSEUM | FAMILY | In a former jute mill, Verdant Works houses a multifaceted exhibit on the story of jute and the town's involvement in the jute trade. Restored machinery, audiovisual displays, and tableaux all bring to life the hard, noisy life of the jute worker. A light and airy café serves lovely little cakes. ✉ W. Hendersons Wynd ☎ 01382/309060 ⊕ www. verdantworks.com ✍ £11.50, £18.65

includes RRS Discovery ⊗ Closed Mon. and Tues. Nov.–Mar.

🍴 Restaurants

Boat Brae

$$ | **BRITISH** | Located within Newport's handsome former Victorian ferry terminal, this is a stunning spot to dine casually while spellbound by views of the Tay River and the Dundee skyline across the water. A versatile menu includes seafood shared platters and maritime mains, Scots steaks and lamb, and plenty of vegetarian options. **Known for:** historic building associated with the Thomas Telford-desgned pier; excellent breakfasts, sandwiches, and a cozy wood-filled bar; huge west-facing windows for sunset dining. ⑤ Average main: £16 ⊠ 2–14 Boat Brae ✛ In Newport across the Tay; take bus 77 or X54 ☎ 01382/540540 ⊕ www. boatbrae.com.

Castlehill

$$$ | **BRITISH** | This spot delivers elegant and inventive dishes in a stylish yet relaxed contemporary setting on trendy Exchange Street. The young, talented team here showcase quality Scottish ingredients in their well-crafted seasonal menus, complemented by an expert mixologist serving alluring aperitifs, a decent wine list, and cheeky cocktails. **Known for:** good-value lunch and à la carte menus; epic tasting menus with wine flights; tempting cocktail bar. ⑤ Average main: £22 ⊠ 22-26 Exchange St. ☎ 01382/220008 ⊕ www.castlehillrestaurant.co.uk ⊗ Closed Sun. and Mon.

★ Jute

$$ | **BRITISH** | Downstairs at Dundee Contemporary Arts, this lively eatery serves breakfast at the bar, cocktails and snacks on the terrace in fine weather, or dinner in the open-plan dining area with huge windows that offer views of artists at work in the printmakers studio. There are plenty of handsomely presented dishes featuring quality Scottish meat, fish, and vegetables. **Known for:** open-plan dining in artsy atmosphere; good for lunch and bar snacks; busy on weekends. ⑤ Average main: £16 ⊠ 152 Nethergate ☎ 01382/909246 ⊕ www.jutecafebar. co.uk.

Manchurian Chinese Restaurant

$ | **CHINESE** | This family-run restaurant above a Chinese supermarket will not win any style awards (it feels a little like a hotel conference suite), but thanks to its food it has won a loyal following. Dishes are fresh and light, from plump and fragrant dim sum to more unusual offerings. **Known for:** authentic Chinese with modern twist; Chinese supermarket downstairs; handy takeout service. ⑤ Average main: £14 ⊠ 15a Gellatly St. ☎ 01382/228822 ⊕ www.manchuriandundee.com ⊗ Closed Wed.

Piccolo

$$ | **ITALIAN** | This small basement eatery on Perth Road, with wooden tables and chairs and a quirky staff, attracts a diverse clientele. It serves well-crafted pasta dishes and mains that showcase fresh Scottish ingredients. **Known for:** candlelit intimacy; reservations needed on weekends; Italian pancakes with ice cream. ⑤ Average main: £18 ⊠ 21 Perth Rd. ☎ 01382/201419 ⊕ www.piccolodundee.co.uk ⊗ Closed Sun. and Mon.

★ Sol y Sombra Tapas Bar

$$$ | **TAPAS** | It looks like an old Scottish pub, and it is, but the vibrant ceramics, tapas, and sangria are so authentic they'll make you feel as if you're in España. Choose from the set menus, like a £10 lunch or £25 dinner, and you'll be served a steady stream of cracking little dishes. **Known for:** boisterous atmosphere; revelatory tapas; occasional live music. ⑤ Average main: £25 ⊠ 27 Gray St., Broughty Ferry ☎ 01382/776941 ⊕ www. solysombratapasbar.co.uk.

The acclaimed V&A Dundee features exhibits from designers across Scotland, including local legend Charles Rennie Mackintosh.

 ## Hotels

Apex City Quay

$ | **HOTEL** | Scandinavian-style rooms with easy chairs, plump bedding, and flat-screen TVs with DVD players help you unwind at this contemporary quayside hotel. **Pros:** stylish rooms; lively, especially on weekends; dockside location and riverside walks. **Cons:** outside is popular with seagulls, too; the bar is often mobbed; conference venue feel. *⑤ Rooms from: £117 ⊠ 1 W. Victoria Dock Rd. ☎ 01382/202404 ⊕ www.apexhotels. com ⇶ 151 rooms ⑩ Breakfast.*

Duntrune House

$ | **B&B/INN** | Set among acres of tidy lawns and rustling trees, this mansion is a genteel contrast to the city and even has a resident ghost. **Pros:** owners are keen genealogists and can offer advice to ancestor seekers; the house and gardens are full of interesting decor; self-catering flat available, too. **Cons:** might be too cluttered for some tastes; minimum two-night stay; five miles out of town. *⑤ Rooms from: £110 ⊠ Off A90, Duntrune ⊹ 5 miles northeast of Dundee ☎ 01382/350239 ⊕ duntrunehouse.co.uk ⊙ Closed Nov.–Feb. ⇶ 3 rooms ⑩ Free breakfast.*

Malmaison

$ | **HOTEL** | British brand Malmaison has brought life and a dash of panache to a dilapidated but much-loved Dundee landmark near the new waterfront. **Pros:** beautifully restored old building; stylish rooms; central location. **Cons:** pricey restaurant and bar; some bathrooms need a refresh; busy location, so there's traffic and other noise. *⑤ Rooms from: £110 ⊠ 44 Whitehall Crescent ☎ 0330/016–0380 ⊕ www.malmaison.com/locations/dundee/ ⇶ 91 rooms ⑩ Breakfast.*

★ Shaftesbury Lodge

$ | **HOTEL** | Just off Perth Road, this Victorian-era villa set among well-tended shrubs is a find for those who like smaller, more intimate hotels. **Pros:** first-rate service; handsome Victorian details; close, but not too close, to the city. **Cons:** some bathrooms are small; 15-minute walk into town; decor a tad dated. **⑤** *Rooms from: £90 ⊠ I Hyndford St.* ☏ *01382/669216* ⊕ *www.shaftesburylodge.co.uk* ⇨ *12 rooms* ⚙ *Free breakfast.*

Nightlife

BARS AND PUBS

Dundee's pub scene, centered in the West End–Perth Road area, is one of the liveliest in Scotland.

Draffens

BARS/PUBS | Secreted down a wynd (alley), this small speakeasy has stylish, exposed-brick interiors, with decorative nods to the defunct Draffens department store and plenty of cocktail shaking going on. ⊠ *Couttie's Wynd, Nethergate.*

Fisherman's Tavern

BARS/PUBS | If you find yourself in Broughty Ferry, you can't leave without a tipple in what the locals call The Fisherman's. It's a great place to mingle with locals and catch some folk music. ⊠ *10–16 Fort St., Broughty Ferry* ☏ *01382/775941* ⊕ *www.fishermanstavern-broughtyferry.co.uk.*

Jute

BARS/PUBS | Better known as the bar at Dundee Contemporary Arts, this café-bar attracts film fans (the art-house cinema's entrance is next door), students, and the well-heeled for European beers, wine, cocktails, or coffee. It serves tasty bar snacks every night and hosts events related to the arts and cinema. ⊠ *152 Nethergate* ☏ *01382/909246* ⊕ *www.jutecafebar.co.uk.*

Ship Inn

BARS/PUBS | Right on Broughty Ferry's promenade, this bright and breezy pub has a friendly atmosphere and decent bar food. ⊠ *121 Fisher St., Broughty Ferry* ☏ *01382/779176* ⊕ *www.theship-inn-broughtyferry.co.uk.*

★ Speedwell Bar

BARS/PUBS | Called Mennie's by locals, the Speedwell Bar is in a mahogany-paneled building brimming with Dundonian characters and architectural features. It's renowned for its superb cask beers, choice of malts, and Edwardian interior. ⊠ *165–168 Perth Rd.* ☏ *01382/667783.*

Performing Arts

Caird Hall

MUSIC | One of Scotland's finest concert halls, Caird Hall stages a wide range of music and events. ⊠ *City Sq.* ☏ *01382/434940* ⊕ *www.leisureandculturedundee.com/culture/caird-hall.*

★ Clarks on Lindsay Street

MUSIC | This busy bar hosts live music until the early hours. Get in early to avoid the lines. ⊠ *80 N. Lindsay St.* ☏ *01382/224925* ⊕ *www.clarksonlindsaystreet.com.*

★ Dundee Repertory Theatre

THEATER | This is home to the award-winning Dundee Rep Ensemble and to Scotland's preeminent contemporary-dance group, Scottish Dance Theatre. Popular with locals, the restaurant and bar welcome late-night comedy shows and jazz bands. ⊠ *Tay Sq.* ☏ *01382/223530* ⊕ *www.dundeerep.co.uk.*

Shopping

COFFEE AND TEA

J. Allan Braithwaite

FOOD/CANDY | Established in 1868 and in its current home since 1932, this enticingly aromatic emporium has large old vats of many freshly roasted coffee blends and tea that you can pop into one of the quaint teapots you'll find here. ⊠ *6 Castle St.* ☏ *01382/322693.*

JEWELRY

DCA

JEWELRY/ACCESSORIES | Just as you enter Dundee Contemporary Arts, the shop on the left sells artist-made jewelry, housewares, books, prints, and gifts. ⊠ *DCA, 152 Nethergate* ☏ *01382/909240* ⊕ *dca.org.uk.*

Gallery Q

JEWELRY/ACCESSORIES | A compelling
selection of jewelry, ceramics, textiles,
sculptures, prints, and paintings by Scottish artists awaits at Gallery Q. ⊠ *160
Nethergate* ☎ *01382/220600* ⊕ *www.
galleryq.co.uk.*

MUSIC

★ Groucho's Record Store

MUSIC STORES | Music lovers, film buffs,
and the curious drop by for some crate
digging in this store founded by the
much-missed music and jukebox collec-
tor Alistair "Breeks" Brodie in 1976. The
Victorian interior spins you right around
with a dizzying display of rare vinyl, CDs,
DVDs, books, T-shirts, and vintage audio
supplies. It's also a great place to pick
up info, flyers, and tickets for gigs and
to chat about the local scene. ⊠ *132
Nethergate* ☎ *01382/228496* ⊕ *www.
grouchos.co.uk.*

Activities

GOLF

East of Perthshire, near the city of Dundee, lies a string of demanding courses
along the shores of the North Sea and
inland into the foothills of the Grampian
Mountains. Golfers who excel in windy
conditions particularly enjoy the breezes
blowing westward from the sea.

★ Carnoustie Golf Links

GOLF | The venue for the British Open in
1999, 2007, and 2018, the coastal links
around Carnoustie have challenged
golfers since at least 1527. Winners
here have included many of the sport's
biggest names: Armour, Hogan, Cotton,
Player, and Watson. There are three
courses, the most famous of which is
the breathtaking Championship Course,
ranked among the very best in the
world. The choice Burnside course is
full of historical interest and local color,
as well as being tough and interesting.
The Buddon course, designed by Peter
Allis and Dave Thomas, is recommended

for links novices. ⊠ *20 Links Parade,
Carnoustie* ☎ *01241/802270* ⊕ *www.
carnoustiegolflinks.co.uk* ⊠ *Championship, £210; Buddon, £75; Burnside, £75*
⛳ *Championship Course: 18 holes, 6948
yards, par 72; Buddon Course: 18 holes,
5921 yards, par 68; Burnside Course: 18
holes, 6028 yards, par 68* ⚐ *Reservations
essential.*

Panmure Golf Club

GOLF | Down the road from the famous
Carnoustie Golf Links, this traditional
course offers an excellent challenge with
its seaside setting, undulating greens,
and sometimes excruciating—but always
entertaining—burrows. The signature 6th
is named after British Open Championship winner Ben Hogan, who practiced
here prior to his triumphant tournament
at Carnoustie in 1953. ⊠ *Burnside Rd., off
Station Rd., Carnoustie* ☎ *01241/855120*
⊕ *www.panmuregolfclub.co.uk* ⊠ *£35–
£105* ⛳ *18 holes, 6551 yards, par 70*
⚐ *Reservations essential.*

Arbroath

15 miles north of Dundee.

You can find traditional boatbuilding in the
fishing town of Arbroath. It has several
small curers and processors as well, and
shops sell the town's most famous delicacy, Arbroath smokies—whole haddock
gutted and lightly smoked. The town is
also known for its association with the
Declaration of Arbroath, a key document in Scotland's history. A few miles
north along the coast is the old fishing
village of Auchmithie, with a beautiful
little beach that you can walk to via a
short path. The jagged, reddish cliffs and
caves are home to a flourishing seabird
population.

GETTING HERE AND AROUND

The East Coast train line stops at
Arbroath. The Abbey and Signal Tower
are all within walking distance, but you'll

Around Angus

NORTH SEA

0   5 mi
0   5 km

---

need a car to get to Auchmithie. If you're driving from Dundee, take A92.

ESSENTIALS

VISITOR INFORMATION Arbroath Tourist Information. ✉ *Fish Market Quay, A92* ☎ *01241/872609* ⊕ *www.visitscotland. com, www.visitangus.com.*

Sights

Arbroath Abbey

ARCHAEOLOGICAL SITE | Founded in 1178 and linked to the famous Declaration of Arbroath, Arbroath Abbey is an unmistakable presence in the town center; it seems to straddle whole streets, as if the town were simply ignoring the redstone ruin in its midst. Surviving today are remains of the church, as well as one of the most complete examples in existence of an abbot's residence. From here in 1320 a passionate plea was sent by King Robert the Bruce (1274–1329) and the Scottish Church to Pope John XXII (circa 1249–1334) in far-off Rome. The pope had until then sided with the English kings, who adamantly refused to acknowledge Scottish independence. The Declaration of Arbroath stated firmly, "It is in truth not for glory, nor riches, nor honours that we are fighting, but for freedom—for that alone, which no honest man gives up but with life itself." Some historians describe this plea, originally drafted in Latin, as the single most important document in Scottish history. The pope advised English king Edward II (1284–1327) to make peace, but warfare was to break out along the border from time to time for the next 200 years. The excellent visitor center recounts this history in well-planned displays. ✉ *Abbey*

St. ☎ *01241/878756* ⊕ *www.historicenvironment.scot* 🎫 *£9.*

Signal Tower Museum

MUSEUM | In the early 19th century, Arbroath was the base for the construction of the Bell Rock lighthouse on a treacherous, barely exposed rock in the Forth of Tay. A signal tower was built to facilitate communication with the builders working far from shore. That structure now houses the Signal Tower Museum, which tells the story of the lighthouse, built by Robert Stevenson (1772–1850) in 1811. The museum also houses a collection of items related to the history of the town, its customs, and the local fishing industry: look out for the 1813 Book of Signals and the witch's eye, a blue-glass buoy hung from the window to ward off evil spirits. ✉ *Ladyloan* ✛ *West of harbor* ☎ *01241/464554* 🎫 *Free* ⊗ *Closed Sun. and Mon.*

Restaurants

Bellrock

$ | **FAST FOOD** | You can't go to Arbroath and not sample some fish-and-chips. Just across the road from the Signal Museum and painted in nautical white and blue, this local favorite has outside benches for warmer days. You'll find all the classics—breaded or battered—but if you are in the mood for something a little different, the spicy fish (in a spiced batter) has certainly won over discerning locals. **Known for:** great fish suppers; weekday buffet; extensive menu that also includes pizza and burgers. ⑤ *Average main: £10* ✉ *33 Ladyloan* ☎ *01241/873656* ⊕ *www.thebellrock.com.*

★ But 'n' Ben

$$ | **BRITISH** | This homey restaurant serves lunches and dinners that offer a taste of quality Scottish home cooking, including Arbroath smokie pancakes, mince and tatties, venison with rowan jelly, and rich moist gingerbread, all at reasonable prices. It's next to Auchmithie's lovely shingle beach; a stroll here is the perfect way to work up an appetite or work off overindulgence. **Known for:** low-ceilinged crofthouse surroundings; traditional Scottish fare; Sunday high tea. ⑤ *Average main: £15* ✉ *Ethie St., Auchmithie* ✛ *3 miles off A92* ☎ *01241/877223* ⊕ *www.thebutnben.com* ⊗ *Closed Tues. No dinner Sun.*

Hotels

The Brucefield

$ | **B&B/INN** | This old manor house, set among well-tended grounds, offers luxurious rooms for very reasonable rates. **Pros:** all the touches you'd expect in a five-star hotel; quality bedding; tranquil gardens. **Cons:** two-night minimum in high season; a 20-minute walk to the city center; books up quickly. ⑤ *Rooms from: £120* ✉ *Cliffburn Rd.* ☎ *01241/875393* ⊕ *www.brucefieldbandb.com* ⇱ *4 rooms* ⑪ *Breakfast.*

Harbour Nights

$ | **B&B/INN** | An excellent and somewhat plush budget option, this B&B is right on the harbor, affording you the most authentic Arbroath stay possible. **Pros:** splendid seafront location; delicious breakfasts; thoughtful decor. **Cons:** only one room with a private bathroom; you must book far in advance; some may find it cluttered. ⑤ *Rooms from: £90* ✉ *4 Shore* ☎ *01421/434343* ⊕ *www.harbournights.co.uk* ⇱ *4 rooms* ⑪ *Breakfast.*

Montrose

14 miles north of Arbroath via A92.

An unpretentious and attractive town with some charming museums and a selection of shops, Montrose sits beside a wide estuary known as the Montrose Basin.

GETTING HERE AND AROUND

On the main East Coast train line, the town is easily accessed by public transportation. Nevertheless, you'll need a car to get to attractions outside town.

ESSENTIALS

VISITOR INFORMATION Montrose Tourist Information Point. ⊠ *Montrose Museum, Panmure Pl.* ☎ *01674/673232* ⊕ *www. visitangus.com.*

Sights

★ House of Dun

HOUSE | The National Trust for Scotland's leading attraction in this area is the stunning House of Dun, which overlooks the Montrose Basin. The mansion was built in the 1730s for lawyer David Erskine, otherwise known as Lord Dun (1670–1755). Designed by architect William Adam (1689–1748), the house is particularly noted for its magnificently ornate plasterwork and curious Masonic masonry. Showing everything from Lady Dun's collection of embroidery to the working kitchens, this house tells the story of the Seat of Dun and the eminent family's history. The sprawling grounds have a restored hand-loom weaving workshop, plus an enchanting walled Victorian garden and wooded den. ⊠ *A935* ✛ *4 miles west of Montrose* ☎ *01674/810264* ⊕ *www.nts.org.uk* ⊠ *£12* ⊙ *House closed mid-Oct.–Mar., Thurs., and Fri.*

Montrose Basin Local Nature Reserve

NATURE PRESERVE | Run by the Scottish Wildlife Trust, the Montrose Basin Local Nature Reserve hosts migrating geese, ducks, and swans. Several nature trails can take you up close to the reserve's residents if you're quiet. In October, at least 20,000 pink-footed geese arrive: come in the morning and the evening to see them fill the sky. ⊠ *Rossie Braes* ☎ *01674/676336* ⊕ *www.montrosebasin. org.uk* ⊠ *£4.50* ⊙ *Closed Tues.–Thurs. Nov.–mid-Feb.*

Montrose Museum

MUSEUM | The town's museum—housed in a neoclassical building that also contains the tourist information center—exhibits some fascinating bequests by the local gentry, including an early-19th-century ship carved from bone by French prisoners in the Napoleonic Wars. ⊠ *Panmure Pl.* ☎ *01674/907447* ⊕ *archive. angus.gov.uk* ⊠ *Free* ⊙ *Closed Sun. and Mon.*

★ William Lamb Studio

MUSEUM | A visit to the studio of renowned Montrosian artist and sculptor William Lamb (1893–1951) provides a glimpse into his intriguing life, travels, and obsessions. In the intimate studio you can walk among the heads of 20th-century royalty, society figures, and everyday Montrose folk. The museum is open only in July and August and by appointment; ask the lovely staff at the Montrose Museum. ⊠ *24 Market St.* ☎ *01674/662660* ⊕ *www.friendswilliamlambstudio.uk* ⊠ *Free* ⊙ *Closed Sept.–June.*

Restaurants

★ The Pavilion Cafe

$ | CAFÉ | Bringing new purpose to an old bowling pavilion, this café's owner freshly painted its clapboard, spruced up the delightful color-glazed fanlights, and gently restored many of the unusual features of this late-Victorian beauty. Expect light meals, breakfasts, salads, buttermilk pancakes, and superfresh home bakes: the seasonal fruit-festooned cream sponges are a treat. **Known for:** bowling-green-scene jollity; scrumptious cakes; quirky setting. ⑤ *Average main: £10* ⊠ *Melville Gardens* ☎ *01674/958188* ⊙ *Closed Sun. and Mon.*

Beautiful Beaches

Scotland's east coast enjoys many hours of sunshine, compared with its west coast, and is blessed with lots of sandy beaches under the ever-changing backdrop of the sky. Take time to explore the beaches and walk along the coast for a change of pace whatever the time of year.

In Fife, Tentsmuir's Beach near St. Andrews is popular with kite flyers and horseback riders, and the famous and lovely West Sands in St. Andrews is where the running sequences in the movie *Chariots of Fire* were filmed. The small cove beach at Elie, south of Crail, hosts cricket matches in summer.

In Angus the beach at Broughty Ferry, near the city of Dundee, fills with families and children on weekends and during school holidays—even on the most blustery of days.

North of Arbroath lies Auchmithie Beach, more shingly (pebbly) than the others and offering a bracing breath of North Sea air. And finally, near the Montrose Basin you can discover the enchanting crescent of Lunan Bay, home to many species of seabirds.

Brechin

10 miles northwest of Montrose.

The small market town of Brechin has a cathedral that was founded around 1200 and contains an interesting selection of antiquities, including the Mary Stone, a Pictish relic.

GETTING HERE AND AROUND
Brechin is not on the East Coast train line but can be reached by bus from Montrose or Arbroath (Stagecoach Strathtay No. 30). It's on the A935, just off the main A90 road between Dundee and Aberdeen.

◉ Sights

Brechin Cathedral and Round Tower
RELIGIOUS SITE | The town's 13th-century Brechin Cathedral and Round Tower is on the site of a former Celtic monastery (priory of the Culdee monks) and has some unusual examples of medieval sculpture. The tower is one of only two on mainland Scotland. This type of structure is more frequently found in Ireland. ⊠ *6 Church St.* ☎ *01356/629360* ⊕ *brechincathedral. org.uk* ▧ *Free.*

Brechin Town House Museum
MUSEUM | Located in the old courtroom that had cells in its cellars, the Brechin Town House Museum houses a small but interesting collection of objects from inhabitants of the area: from Bronze Age jewelry to a Jacobite sporran to a letter from a World War I soldier. There is a small tourist information desk within the museum. ⊠ *28 High St.* ☎ *01356/627458* ⊕ *www.brechintownhouse.org.uk* ▧ *Free* ◔ *Closed Sun. and Mon.*

🍽 Restaurants

Brechin Castle Garden Centre
$ | CAFÉ | FAMILY | Just off the A90, this small country park has lots of children's activities, including a giant sand pit, go-karts, a barrel train, and a wooden maze). Most essentially, there's an excellent café, serving door-stop-size sandwiches, full breakfasts, tasty soups, meringues, and warm scones. **Known for:** hearty food; family-friendly dining; vegan options. ⑤ *Average main: £9* ⊠ *Haughmuir* ☎ *01356/626813* ⊕ *www.brechincastlecentre.co.uk* ◔ *No dinner.*

The Angus Glens

25 miles northwest of Brechin.

You can rejoin the hurly-burly of the A90 for the return journey south from Montrose or Brechin; the more pleasant route, however, leads southwesterly on minor roads (there are several options) that travel along the face of the Grampians, following the fault line that separates Highlands and Lowlands. The **Angus Glens** extend north from points on A90. Known individually as the glens of Isla, Prosen, Clova, and Esk, these long valleys run into the high hills of the Grampians and some clearly marked walking routes. Those in Glen Clova are especially appealing.

Be aware that Thursday is a half day in Angus; many shops and attractions close at lunch.

GETTING HERE AND AROUND

You really need a car to reach the Angus Glens and enjoy the gentle (and not so gentle) inclines here. Glamis and Kirriemuir are both on the A928 (just off the A90), and the B955—which loops round at Glen Clova—is one of the loveliest Scottish roads to drive along, especially when the heather is blooming in late summer.

Hotels

Glen Clova Hotel

$$ | HOTEL | Since the 1850s, the hospitality of this hotel has lifted the spirits of many a bone-tired hill walker, and it remains as comfortable a spot as ever today. **Pros:** stunning location; great base for outdoor pursuits; spacious accommodations. **Cons:** lack of decent public transportation; bar and live-music nights may be noisy; poor email communication. $ *Rooms from: £125* ⊠ *B955, Glen Clova* ☎ *01575/550350* ⊕ *www.clova.com* ⇨ *10 rooms* ⦿ *Free breakfast.*

Kirriemuir

15 miles southwest of Brechin.

Kirriemuir stands at the heart of Angus's red-sandstone countryside and was the birthplace of the writer J. M. Barrie (1860–1937), best known abroad as the author of *Peter Pan* (a statue of whom you can see in the town's square). *Kirrie*, as it's known here, salutes favorite son Bon Scott (1946–80)—the rasping AC/DC vocalist—in a bronze-and-Caithness-rock memorial statue at Bellies Brae. Metal pilgrims gather each springtime for Bonfest.

GETTING HERE AND AROUND

A number of roads lead to Kirriemuir, but A928 (off A90), which also passes Glamis Castle, is one of the loveliest. Stagecoach Strathtay runs buses to this area; Nos. 20 and 22 from Dundee are the most regular.

Sights

Camera Obscura

VIEWPOINT | FAMILY | J. M. Barrie donated this Camera Obscura to the town; located within a cricket pavilion, it magically projects an image of the wonderful landscape views onto the opposite wall. It is one of only four in the country and run by lovely volunteers. ⊠ *Kirrie Hill* ☎ *01575/575885* ⊕ *www.kirriemuircameraobscura.com* ⊡ *Free (donations welcome)* ⊙ *Closed Nov.–Mar. and Tues.–Fri.*

J.M. Barrie's Birthplace

HOUSE | At J. M. Barrie's Birthplace, the National Trust pays tribute to the man who sought to preserve the magic of childhood more than any other writer of his age. The house's upper floors are furnished as they might have been in Barrie's time, complete with domestic necessities, while downstairs is his study, replete with manuscripts and personal mementos. The outside washhouse is said to have served as Barrie's first theater. ⊠ *9 Brechin Rd.* ☎ *01575/572646* ⊕ *www.nts.org.uk/Property/J-M-Barries-Birthplace/* 🎟 *£7* 🕙 *Closed Oct.–Mar. and Tues.–Fri.*

Kirriemuir Gateway to the Glens Museum

MUSEUM | As is the style in Angus, the local museum doubles as the visitor center, meaning you can get all the information you need and admire a few stuffed birds and artifacts at the same time. Rock fans will appreciate the exhibit celebrating local lad made good (or rather bad), the late Bon Scott, original lead singer of the rock band AC/DC. ⊠ *32 High St.* ☎ *01575/526006* ⊕ *archive. angus.gov.uk* 🎟 *Free* 🕙 *Closed Sun. and Mon.*

 ## Restaurants

88 Espresso

$ | **CAFÉ** | **FAMILY** | If you're not in a rush (service can be slow), take time to savor excellent coffee, inventive sandwiches, pizzettes, cakes, and handmade chocolates at this appealing café and shop selling quality fare. If you're in a hurry, buy delicious cheese or chocolates to go or pick up a cheese and apple scone. **Known for:** creative home-baking including sourdough bread; handmade chocolates and truffles; cash-only policy. 🟦 *Average main: £8* ⊠ *17 High St.* ☎ *07449/345089* 🕙 *Closed Mon. and Tues. No dinner* ⊟ *No credit cards.*

Forfar

7 miles east of Kirriemuir.

Forfar goes about its business of being the center of a farming hinterland without being preoccupied with (or even that interested in) tourism.

GETTING HERE AND AROUND

Buses are slow here. The quickest route is by car: take the A90 north, then the A926 turnoff. Alternatively, the A932/ A933 route from Arbroath takes you through farmland and Angus villages.

 ## Sights

Aberlemno

ARCHAEOLOGICAL SITE | You can see excellent examples of Pictish stone carvings about 5 miles northeast of Forfar alongside the B9134. Carvings of crosses, angels, serpents, and other animals adorn the stones, which date from the 7th to the early 9th century. Note the stone in the nearby churchyard—one side is carved with a cross and the other side depicts the only known battle scene in Pictish art, complete with horsemen and foot soldiers. During the winter months, the stones are covered to protect them from the elements. ⊠ *Forfar.*

Meffan Museum and Art Gallery

MUSEUM | The high point of a visit to Forfar is the Meffan Museum and Art Gallery, which displays an interesting collection of Pictish carved stones, a recreation of Forfar's cobbled street The Vennel, and artifacts from the dark days of burning witches. Two galleries host frequently changing exhibitions by leading local and Scottish artists. The museum also houses a tourist information desk. ⊠ *20 W. High St.* ☎ *01307/491771* ⊕ *archive. angus.gov.uk/historyaa/museums/* 🎟 *Free* 🕙 *Closed Sun. and Mon.*

Glamis

5 miles southwest of Forfar, 6 miles south of Kirriemuir.

Set in rolling countryside is the little village of Glamis (pronounced *glahms*), the highlight of which is nearby famous Glamis Castle.

GETTING HERE AND AROUND

The drive to Glamis Castle, along beech- and yew-lined roads, is as majestic as the castle itself. Take the A90 north from Dundee, then off onto the A928. The

Majestic Glamis Castle and its Duncan's Hall is also the setting for Shakespeare's *Macbeth*.

village of Glamis can be reached by the Stagecoach Strathtay No. 22, but service is rather infrequent.

Sights

★ Glamis Castle

CASTLE/PALACE | One of Scotland's best known and most beautiful castles, Glamis Castle connects Britain's royalty through 10 centuries, from Macbeth (Thane of Glamis) to the late Queen Mother and her daughter, the late Princess Margaret, born here in 1930 (the first royal princess born in Scotland in 300 years). The property of the earls of Strathmore and Kinghorne since 1372, the castle was largely reconstructed in the late 17th century; the original keep, which is much older, is still intact. One of the most famous rooms in the castle is Duncan's Hall, the legendary setting for Shakespeare's *Macbeth*. Guided tours allow you to see fine collections of china, tapestries, and furniture. Within the castle is the delightful Castle Kitchen restaurant; the grounds contain a huge

gift shop, a shop selling local produce, and a pleasant picnic area. **■ TIP→ If you are looking to hear the pipes and see some Highland dancing and games of strength, the Strathmore Highland Games are held here around the second weekend of June. See www.strathmorehighlandgames.co.uk for more information.** ⊠ *A94* ✛ *1 mile north of Glamis* ☎ *01307/840393* ⊕ *www. glamis-castle.co.uk* ✉ *£15.50* ⊙ *Closed Nov.–Feb.*

Meigle

7 miles southwest of Glamis, 11 miles northwest of Dundee.

The historic village of Meigle, nestled in the rich agricultural land of the Strathmore Valley, is well known to those with an interest in Pictish stones. Said to be built on an 11th-century Pictish monastery, the village has a number of elaborate Victorian buildings.

GETTING HERE AND AROUND

Meigle is an easy and pleasant drive from Glamis on the A94 (or from Dundee on the B954). The hourly Stagecoach Strathtay from Dundee (No. 57) stops here.

 Sights

Meigle Sculptured Stone Museum

MUSEUM | The town of Meigle, in the wide swathe of Strathmore, has one of the most notable collections of sculpted stones in western Europe, housed at the Meigle Sculptured Stone Museum. It consists of some 25 monuments from the Celtic Christian period (8th to 11th century), nearly all of which were found in or around the local churchyard. The large 9th-century prayer cross-slab known as Meigle 2 shows Daniel in the lions' den. Local legend holds the slab marked the grave of Guinevere, wife of King Arthur; in the story, Arthur sentences her to death by being torn apart by wild animals. ⊠ *A94* ☎ *01828/640612* ⊕ *www.historicenvironment.scot* ⊴ *£6* ⊘ *Closed Oct.–Mar.*

 Sights

Alyth Museum

MUSEUM | This small but intriguing local-history museum has a collection of old photos and an engaging audio Story Box mining tales of local legend, history, and today's community, as well as nearly every type of tool used by the resourceful Alyth folk. ⊠ *Commercial St.* ☎ *01828/633474* ⊴ *Free* ⊘ *Closed Mon., Tues., and Oct.–Apr.*

 Hotels

Tigh Na Leigh

$ | B&B/INN | This grand house turned classy B&B, originally built by the Earl of Airlie, is a relaxing place with spacious, elegant rooms. **Pros:** lovingly restored building; charming rooms; evening meals made with local produce. **Cons:** away from the action; books up quickly; a car needed to explore the area. ⑤ *Rooms from: £100* ⊠ *22–24 Airlie St.* ☎ *01828/632372* ⊕ *www.tighnaleigh.com* ⇌ *6 rooms* †⊙ *Breakfast.*

Alyth

4 miles north of Meigle, 15 miles northwest of Dundee.

Dating back to the Dark Ages, this market town just over the county line in Perth and Kinross was completely transformed by the Industrial Revolution, which lined its streets with mills and factories. The 20th century saw the closing of most of these companies, but the town had never forgotten its agricultural heritage, retaining a rural allure today.

GETTING HERE AND AROUND

Just 4 miles farther along the B954 from Meigle, Alyth is also served by Stagecoach Strathtay No. 57.

Chapter 7

STIRLING AND THE CENTRAL HIGHLANDS

Updated by
Mike Gonzalez

7

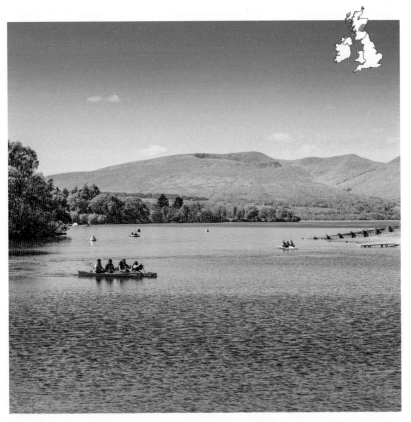

⊙ Sights	🍴 Restaurants	🛏 Hotels	🛍 Shopping	🍸 Nightlife
★★★★☆	★★☆☆☆	★★☆☆☆	★★☆☆☆	★★☆☆☆

WELCOME TO STIRLING AND THE CENTRAL HIGHLANDS

TOP REASONS TO GO

★ **Loch Lomond:** You can see the sparkling waters of Scotland's largest loch by car, by boat, or on foot. A popular option is the network of bicycle tracks that creep around Loch Lomond and the Trossachs National Park, offering every conceivable terrain.

★ **Castles:** Choosing among Scotland's most splendid fortresses and mansions is a challenge. Among the highlights are Stirling Castle, Scone Palace, and Doune Castle.

★ **Great hikes:** The way to experience the Central Highlands is to head out on foot. The less-demanding woodland paths and gentle rambles of the Trossachs will stir even the least adventurous rambler.

★ **Whisky tours and tastes:** The Scots love their whisky, and what better way to participate in Scottish life and culture than to learn about the land's finest? There are some exceptional distilleries in this region, from the Edradour Distillery to Glenturret in Crieff.

1 Stirling. A historic town dominated by its castle.

2 Falkirk. A key medieval city.

3 Dunblane. A small town with an 12th-century cathedral.

4 Callander. The gateway to the Trossachs.

5 The Trossachs. A national park with every kind of landscape.

6 Aberfoyle. Easy access to Queen Elizabeth Forest Park and the eastern banks of Loch Lomond.

7 Loch Lomond. Scotland's largest and perhaps most famous loch.

8 Perth. Once Scotland's capital and now a gateway to the Highlands.

9 Dunkeld. The land of Beatrix Potter.

10 Pitlochry. An old Victorian spa town.

11 Blair Atholl. Home to Blair Castle, one of Scotland's great houses.

12 Aberfeldy. A town with a unique bridge and a popular distillery.

13 Crieff. Home to a glass-making community.

14 Auchterarder. A small Highland town dominated by a famous golf course.

A9

Blair Atholl
Killiecrankie
Loch Tummel
11

Pitlochry
10

ANGUS

A93

Kirriemuir

Glamis Castle

Aberfeldy
12

A9

A924

Alyth

Meigle   Glamis

Blairgowrie

Dunkeld
9

Coupar Angus

MOUNTAINS

Loch Rannoch

Loch Tay

Loch Freuchie

PERTH & KINROSS

A93   A94   A923

A827

Killin

A85

Loch Earn

A85

Crieff
13

Stanley
Scone Palace
Scone

Perth
8

Dundee

Firth of Tay

A90

A92

A9

Abernethy

A84

Callander
4

A9

Auchterarder
14

Earn

Bridge of Earn

M90

Cupar

FIFE

Dunblane
3

Stirling Castle

Kinross

Glenrothes

A92   Methil

A811

Stirling
1

Alloa

Kincardine

M90

Cowdenbeath

Dunfermline

Kirkcaldy

STIRLING

M80

Rosyth

Firth of Forth

Falkirk
2

Cumbernauld

Kirkintilloch

Broxburn

EDINBURGH

Bathgate

GLASGOW   Airdrie   Livingston

The Central Highlands are home to superb castles, moody mountains, and gorgeous glens that are best explored at a leisurely pace. The waters of Loch Lomond reflect the crags and dark woods that surround it, and attract those in search of a more romantic and nostalgic Scotland enshrined in the verses of the famous song that bears its name. When you finish a day of exploring, celebrate with a glass of one of the region's top-notch whiskies.

The Carse of Stirling, the wide plain guarded by Stirling Castle, was the scene of many important moments in Scotland's history—from the Roman invasion commemorated by the Antonine Wall to the castles that mark the site of medieval kingdoms and the battles to preserve them. Look up at Stirling Castle from the valley and you can see why so many battles were fought over its possession. The Battle of Bannockburn Centre, just outside Stirling, commemorates the most emblematic battle of them all.

North from Stirling, past Dunblane, are the birch-, oak-, and pine-covered Highland hills and valleys of the Trossachs, whose high peaks attract walkers and a tougher breed of cyclist. From Callander, a neat tourist town, the hills stretch westward to the "bonnie, bonnie banks" of Loch Lomond. The Victorians were drawn here by the lyrical descriptions of the area by romantic poets like Sir Walter Scott (1771–1832), who set his dramatic

verse narrative of 1810, "The Lady of the Lake," in the landscape of the Trossachs. From the peaks of the Trossachs, on a good day, you can see Edinburgh Castle to the east and the tower blocks of Glasgow's housing projects to the west.

Farther north is Perth, once Scotland's capital; its wealthy mansions reflect the prosperous agricultural land that surrounds the city, and it is still an important market town today. Overlooking the River Tay, the city can reasonably claim to be the gateway to the Highlands, sitting as it does on the Highland Fault that divides Lowlands from Highlands. From Perth the landscape begins to change on the road to Pitlochry and the high, rough country of Rannoch Moor.

The region is full of reminders of heroic struggles, particularly against the English, from the monument to William Wallace to Bannockburn, where Robert the Bruce took on the invader. In Balquhidder near

Callander, Rob Roy MacGregor, the Scottish Robin Hood, lived (and looted and terrorized) his way into the storybooks.

MAJOR REGIONS

Stirling. Famous for its castle and vibrant with history, Stirling has a small Old Town on the hill that is worth covering on foot. Look down from the Stirling Castle crag that dominates the plains below and you can see the stages of the city's growth descending from the hill. The town is a good center from which to explore the changing landscape of central Scotland.

The Trossachs and Loch Lomond. Immortalized by Wordsworth and Sir Walter Scott, the Trossachs (the name means "bristly country") contains some of Scotland's loveliest forest, hills, and glens, well justifying the area's designation as a national park. The area has a special charm, combining the wildness of the Highlands with the prolific vegetation of an old Lowland forest. Its open ground is a dense mat of bracken and heather, and its woodland is of silver birch, dwarf oak, and hazel—trees that fasten their roots into the crevices of rocks and stop short on the very brink of lochs. There are also many small towns to visit along the way, some with their roots in a medieval world; others sprang up and expanded in the wake of the first tourists who came to Scotland in the late 19th century in search of wild country or healing waters. Dunblane has a magnificent cathedral; Doune's castle will make you stare in awe. This area is small but incredibly varied—from dramatic mountain peaks that attract walkers and climbers, to the gentler slopes and forests that stretch from Perth westward to Aberfoyle and the shores of Loch Lomond. The glens and streams that pepper the region create a romantic landscape that is a perfect habitat for the figure of Rob Roy McGregor—Robin Hood or bandit according to taste, but undeniably Scottish. Loch Lomond's western side is more accessible, if busier, than the east, but the views across the loch are spectacular.

The most colorful season is fall, particularly October, a lovely time when most visitors have departed, and the hares, deer, and game birds have taken over. Even in rainy weather the Trossachs of "darksome glens and gleaming lochs" are memorable: the water filtering through the rocks by Loch Lomond comes out so pure and clear that the loch is like a sheet of glass. The best way to explore this area is by car, by bike, or on foot; the latter two depend, of course, on the weather. Keep in mind that roads in this region of the country are narrow and winding, which can make for dangerous conditions in all types of weather.

Perthshire. The prosperous air of Perth, once the capital of Scotland, testifies to its importance as a port exporting wool, salmon, and whisky to the world. Scone Palace serves as a monument to that era. If Perthshire's castles invoke memories of past conflicts, the grand houses and spa towns here are testimony to the continued presence of a wealthy landed gentry. This is also a place for walking, cycling, and water sports. In some ways Perthshire is a crossing point where Lowlands and Highlands, two Scottish landscapes and two histories, meet. Perthshire itself is rural, agricultural Scotland, fertile and prosperous. Its woodlands, rivers, and glens (and agreeable climate and strategic position) drew the Romans and later the Celtic missionaries. In fact, the motto of the capital city, Perth, is "the perfect center." The route northward leads across the Highland Boundary and into the changing landscapes beyond Pitlochry to Rannoch Moor, where the wind sweeps across the hardy heather.

7

Stirling and the Central Highlands

Planning

When to Go

The Trossachs and Loch Lomond are in some ways a miniature Scotland, from the tranquil east shore of Loch Lomond to the hills and glens of the Trossachs and the mountains to the west—and all within a few hours' drive. In spring and summer, despite the erratic weather, the area is always crowded; this is a good time to go. Nevertheless, the landscape is notably dramatic when the trees are turning red and brown in autumn, and evening skies are spectacular. Scotland in winter has a different kind of beauty, especially for skiers and climbers. ■TIP➔ **Pack clothes for wet and dry weather, and carry both types on hikes, as the weather can change quickly. Summer evenings attract midges; bring some repellent.**

Getting Oriented

The starting point for your trip is Stirling, an ancient, historic town from whose castle you can see central Scotland laid out before you. That is why it has been fought for so often over the centuries. Perth, 36 miles away is the gateway to the Highlands. North from Stirling, you cross the fertile open plain (the Carse of Stirling) dotted with historic cathedral towns like Dunblane and fortified castles like Doune. To the east, Falkirk was historically important and later an industrial center, now reborn around its canals. The Trossachs are the Scotland of the romantic imagination, lochs and woodland glens, drovers' inns, and grand country houses. The small towns of the region, like Callander, Aberfoyle, and Pitlochry are bases from which to explore this varied countryside. The great Victorian Hydro hotels are reminders of how popular the region became for Victorian travelers anxious to "take the healing waters" and discover the Scotland described by Sir Walter Scott. To the west lies Loch Lomond, along whose banks the road leads from industrial Glasgow to the hills and glens of the Highlands

Planning Your Time

Scotland's beautiful interior is excellent touring country, though the cities of Stirling and Perth are worth your time, too; Stirling is a good starting point, and exploring its castle can take a half day. Two (slightly rushed) days would be enough to explore the Trossachs loop, to gaze into the waters of Loch Venachar and Loch Achray. The glens, in some places, run parallel to the lochs, including those along Lochs Earn, Tay, and Rannoch, making for satisfying loops and round-trips. Loch Lomond is easily accessible from either Glasgow or Stirling, and is well worth exploring. Don't miss the opportunity to take a boat trip on a loch, especially on Loch Lomond or on Loch Katrine.

Getting Here and Around

AIR
Perth and Stirling can be reached easily from the Edinburgh, Dundee, and Glasgow airports by train, car, or bus.

BUS
A good network of buses connects with this area via Edinburgh and Glasgow. For more information contact Scottish Citylink or National Express. The Perth and Kinross Council supplies a map (available in tourist information centers) showing all public transport routes in Perthshire, marked with nearby attractions.

First, Scottish Citylink, and Stagecoach organize reliable local service on routes throughout the Central Highlands.

BUS CONTACTS First Bus. ☎ *0345/646–0707* ⊕ *www.firstgroup.com.* **National**

Express. ☎ 0871/781–8181 ⊕ www. nationalexpressgroup.com. **Scottish Citylink.** ☎ 0141/352–4444 ⊕ www. citylink.co.uk. **Stagecoach.** ☎ 0843/208–2338 ⊕ www.stagecoachbus.com.

CAR

It's easy to access the area from the central belt of Scotland via the motorway network. The M80 connects Glasgow to Stirling, and then briefly joins the M9 from Edinburgh, which runs within sight of the walls of Stirling Castle. From there the A9 runs from Stirling to Perth, and onward to Pitlochry; it is a good road but a little too fast (so take care). Perth can also be reached via the M90 over the Forth Bridge from Edinburgh. Three signed touring routes are useful: the Perthshire Tourist Route, the Deeside Tourist Route, and the Pitlochry Tourist Route, a beautiful and unexpected trip via Crieff and Loch Tay. Local tourist information centers can supply maps of these routes, or you can check online (⊕ www. visitscotland.com). Once you leave the major motorways, roads become narrower and slower, with many following the contours of the lochs. Be prepared for your journey to take longer than distances might suggest.

TRAIN

The Central Highlands are linked to Edinburgh and Glasgow by rail, with through routes to England (some direct-service routes from London take fewer than five hours). Several discount ticket options are available, although in some cases on the ScotRail system a discount card must be purchased before your arrival in the United Kingdom. Note that families with children and travelers younger than 26 or older than 60 are eligible for significant discounts. Contact Trainline, Traveline Scotland, National Rail, or ScotRail for details.

The West Highland Line runs through the western portion of the area. Services also run to Stirling, Dunblane, Perth, and Gleneagles; stops on the Inverness–Perth line include Dunkeld, Pitlochry, and Blair Atholl.

TRAIN CONTACTS National Rail Enquiries. ☎ 03457/484950 ⊕ www.nationalrail. co.uk. **ScotRail.** ☎ 0344/811–0141 ⊕ www.scotrail.co.uk. **Trainline.** ☎ 0871/244–1545 ⊕ www.thetrainline. com. **Traveline Scotland.** ☎ 0871/200–2233 ⊕ www.travelinescotland.com.

Restaurants

Regional country delicacies—loch trout, river salmon, lamb, and venison—appear regularly on even modest menus in Central Highlands restaurants. In all the towns and villages in the area, you will find simple pubs, often crowded and noisy, many of them serving substantial food at lunchtime and in the evening until about 9 (eaten balanced on your knee, perhaps, or at a shared table). The more luxurious restaurants tend to be in upscale hotels, with prices to match. It can be difficult to find a place to eat later in the evening.

Hotels

A wide selection of accommodations is available throughout the region, especially in Stirling, Bridge of Allan, Callander, and Pitlochry. They range from bed-and-breakfasts to private houses with a small number of rooms to rural accommodations (often on farms). The grand houses of the past—family homes to the landed aristocracy—have for the most part become country-house hotels. Their settings, often on ample grounds, offer an experience of grand living—but the area also has modern hotels, for those who prefer 21st-century amenities.

Restaurant and hotel reviews have been shortened. For full information, visit Fodors.com. Restaurant prices are the average cost of a main course at dinner or, if dinner is not served, at lunch, excluding tax. Hotel prices are the lowest cost of a standard double room in high season, including 20% V.A.T.

WHAT IT COSTS in Pounds			
$	$$	$$$	$$$$
RESTAURANTS			
under £15	£15–£19	£20–£25	over £25
HOTELS			
under £125	£125–£200	£201–£300	over £300

Visitor Information

The tourist offices in Stirling and Perth are open year-round, as are offices in larger towns; others are seasonal (generally from April to October).

Activities

This area of the country is ideal for outdoor enthusiasts. Hiking and bicycling are especially popular, and there are routes that cater to one or the other of these sports, including long paths that traverse the Lowlands and the Highlands, covering multiple towns. The town of Callander in particular has several hiking paths. Information on trails throughout Scotland is supplied on the country's main tourism website (⊕ *www.visitscotland.com/see-do/active/walking/routes-trails* or ⊕ *www.visitscotland.com/see-do/active/cycling/national-routes*).

Lowland-Highland Trail

BICYCLING | The region's big attraction for cyclists is the Lowland-Highland Trail, which stretches more than 60 miles and passes through Drymen, Aberfoyle, the Trossachs, Callander, Lochearnhead, and Killin. This route runs along former railroad-track beds, as well as private and minor roads, to reach well into the Central Highlands. Another almost completely traffic-free option is the roadway around Loch Katrine. Almost every town along the route has cycle-hire shops.

★ The Rob Roy Way

HIKING/WALKING | Want a weeklong walk? The Rob Roy Way is a 79-mile footpath from Drymen to Pitlochry. The route takes you past Loch Venachar and Loch Lubnaig, perfect examples of the beauties of the region. And you may be following in the footsteps of famous Jacobite warrior Rob Roy MacGregor, who for a time was a fugitive from justice . Want to add in some inclines? Along the way are Ben Lawers and Ben Ledi, popular hills for those who prefer climbs. Details of the route are on the website. ⊕ *www.robroyway.com.*

★ West Highland Way

HIKING/WALKING | The long-distance walkers' route, the West Highland Way, begins at Milngavie, outside Glasgow, running 96 miles from the Lowlands of central Scotland to the Highlands at Fort William. Along its course the landscape changes as you walk from the banks of Loch Lomond into the hills beyond, through the dramatic Glencoe, across Ranooch Moor and beyond it to Fort William and the heart of the Central Highlands. Nearly 50,000 people discover the glens each year, climbing the hills and listening to birds singing in the tree canopy. For the most part, this is not an especially difficult walk,though it can be demanding at moments, but keep Scotland's ever-changing weather in mind and go properly prepared. ⊕ *www.west-highland-way.co.uk.*

Stirling

26 miles northeast of Glasgow, 36 miles northwest of Edinburgh.

Stirling is one of Britain's great historic towns. An impressive proportion of the Old Town walls can be seen from Dumbarton Road, a cobbled street leading to Stirling Castle, built on a steep-sided plug of rock. From its esplanade there is a commanding view of the surrounding Carse of Stirling. The guns on the castle battlements are a reminder of the military advantage to be gained from its position.

GETTING HERE AND AROUND

Stirling's central position in the area makes it ideal for travel to and from Glasgow and Edinburgh (or north to Perth and the Highlands) by rail or bus. The town itself is compact and easily walkable, though a shuttle bus travels to and from the town center up the steep road to Stirling Castle every 20 minutes. You can stroll the Back Walk on a circuit around the base of the castle walls—set aside at least 30 minutes for a leisurely walk. The National Wallace Monument (2 miles away) is on the outskirts of the town and can be reached by taxi or on foot.

ESSENTIALS

VISITOR INFORMATION Stirling Visitor Information Centre. ⊠ *Old Town Jail, St. John St.* ☎ *01786/475019* ⊕ *my.stirling. gov.uk/tourism-visitors.*

 Sights

★ Battle of Bannockburn Visitor Centre

MILITARY SITE | FAMILY | You can almost hear the trotting of horses' hooves and the zip of arrows in this 21st-century re-creation of the battle that changed the course of Scotland's history in 1314. Robert the Bruce's defeat of the armies of the English king, despite a 2-to-1 disadvantage, is the stuff of legend. Using 3-D technology, the visitor center allows you to see a battle raging across screens that ring the central hall. Participants on both sides speak directly to you, courtesy of holograms. Later you can play a role in a Bannockburn battle game (reservations essential; age seven and older only). Bruce pursued the Scottish crown, ruthlessly sweeping aside enemies; but his victory here was masterful, as he drew the English horses into marshy land (now the area around the new center), where

they sank in the mud. A circular monument commemorates the battlefield. ■**TIP➔ Book ahead; tickets are for timed entry.** ⊠ *Glasgow Road, Bannockburn* ☎ *01786/812664* ⊕ *www.nts.org.uk/visit/ places/bannockburn* ⊠ *£11.50.*

Church of the Holy Rude

RELIGIOUS SITE | The nave of this handsome church survives from the 15th century, and a portion of the original medieval timber roof can also be seen. This is the only Scottish church still in use to have witnessed the coronation of a Scottish monarch—James VI (1566–1625) in 1567. The origin of the name Holy Rude (similar to Holyrood in Edinburgh) is Holy Cross. *October through April, the building is often open only during service time on Sunday morning (10 am January through June, 11:30 am July through December).* ⊠ *Top of St. John's St.* ⊕ *www.holyrude. org.*

National Wallace Monument

MEMORIAL | This Victorian-era shrine to William Wallace (circa 1270–1305), the Scottish freedom fighter reborn as "Braveheart" in Mel Gibson's 1995 film of the same name, was built between 1856 and 1869. It sits on Abbey Craig, from which Wallace watched the English armies struggle across the old Stirling Bridge before attacking them and winning a major victory in 1297. A steep stone spiral staircase leads to the roof gallery, with views of the bridge and the whole Carse of Stirling. A less flamboyant version of Wallace's life is told in an exhibition and audiovisual presentation on the second floor. To reach the monument, follow the Bridge of Allan signs (A9) northward, crossing the River Forth by the New Bridge of 1832, next to the old one. The monument is signposted at the next traffic circle. From the car park a free shuttle will take you to the monument, or you can walk (15 minutes). ⊠ *Abbey Craig, Hillfoot Rd.* ☎ *01786/472140* ⊕ *www.nationalwallace-monument.com* ⊠ *£10.50.*

Stirling

Stirling (inset)

Stirling Castle

Royal Gardens

Victoria Sq.

Stirling Station

BRIDGE OF ALLAN

University of Stirling

River Forth

Stirling
see inset
to right

FALLIN

WHINS OF MILTON

COWIE

OLD PLEAN

River Forth

KEY

1 Exploring Sights

1 Restaurants

1 Hotels

Sights ▼

1 Battle of Bannockburn
   Visitor Centre............ **B5**

2 Church of the
   Holy Rude................. **D2**

3 National Wallace
   Monument................. **C2**

4 Old Town Jail............ **D2**

5 Smith Art Gallery
   and Museum **D3**

6 Stirling Castle **C2**

Restaurants ▼

1 Allanwater Cafe......... **A1**

2 The Birds and
   the Bees **B2**

3 Brea **E3**

Hotels ▼

1 Colessio Hotel........... **D3**

2 Friars Wynd **E3**

3 Portcullis Hotel.......... **D2**

4 Victoria Square
   Guest House............. **D3**

5 West Plean House....... **C7**

Old Town Jail

JAIL | Though an improvement on the original jail across the road at the Tolbooth, the new county jail was still a pretty grim place. You can visit the cells and explore the corridors in the company of a costumed guide who recounts in gory detail what went on here. There are audio guides and ample information, but it's best to go on the entertaining "performance tours." ■ TIP→ **Summer is busy, so book ahead if you can.** ⊠ St. John St. ☎ 01786/464640 ⊕ www.oldtownjail. co.uk ⌑ £7.50 ⊘ Closed Sept.⊠May (Check website for special openings in September and October.).

Smith Art Gallery and Museum

MUSEUM | **FAMILY** | This small but intriguing museum in a neoclassical building, founded in 1874, houses The Stirling Story, a comprehensive social history of the town. It holds the oldest football in the world, as well as the charming 16th-century portraits of the Five Stirling Sybils. Closer to the present are banners and memorabilia from the great miners' strike of 1984–85. The chiming clocks remind us, on the hour, of the present. The museum also holds regular temporary art and historical exhibitions and has a pleasant café. ⊠ Dumbarton Road ⊕ A few minutes' walk along Albert Place from the town center ☎ 01786/471917 ⊕ www.smithartgalleryandmuseum. co.uk ⌑ Free ⊘ Closed Mon.

★ Stirling Castle

CASTLE/PALACE | **FAMILY** | Its magnificent strategic position on a steep-sided crag made Stirling Castle the grandest prize in the Scots Wars of Independence during the late 13th and early 14th centuries. Robert the Bruce's victory at Bannockburn won both the castle and freedom from English subjugation for almost four centuries. Take time to visit the **Castle Exhibition** beyond the lower gate to get an overview of its evolution as a stronghold and palace. ■ TIP→ **It's a good idea to book tickets online before your visit.**

The daughter of King Robert I (Robert the Bruce), Marjory, married Walter Fitzallan, the high steward of Scotland. Their descendants included the Stewart dynasty of Scottish monarchs (Mary, Queen of Scots, was a Stewart, though she preferred the French spelling, Stuart). The Stewarts were responsible for many of the works that survive within the castle walls. They made Stirling Castle their court and power base, creating fine Renaissance-style buildings that were never completely obliterated, despite reconstruction for military purposes.

You enter the castle through its outer defenses, which consist of a great curtained wall and batteries from 1708. From this lower square the most conspicuous feature is the **Palace,** built by King James V (1512–42) between 1538 and 1542. The decorative figures festooning the ornate outer walls show the influence of French masons. An orientation center in the basement, designed especially for children, lets you try out the clothes and musical instruments of the time. Across a terrace are the **Royal Apartments,** which re-create the furnishings and tapestries found here during the reign of James V and his French queen, Mary of Guise. The queen's bedchamber contains copies of the beautiful tapestries in which the hunt for the white unicorn is clearly an allegory for the persecution of Christ. Overlooking the upper courtyard is the **Great Hall,** built by King James IV (1473–1513) in 1503. Before the Union of Parliaments in 1707, when the Scottish aristocracy sold out to England, this building had been used as one of the seats of the Scottish Parliament.

Among the later works built for regiments stationed here, the **Regimental Museum** stands out; it's a 19th-century baronial revival on the site of an earlier building. Nearby, the **Chapel Royal** is unfurnished. The oldest building on the site is the **Mint,** or **Coonzie Hoose,** perhaps dating as far back as the 14th century.

Below it is an arched passageway leading to the westernmost ramparts, the **Nether Bailey,** with a view of the *carselands* (valley plain) of the Forth Valley.

To the castle's south lies the hump of the Touch and the Gargunnock Hills, which diverted potential direct routes from Glasgow and the south. For centuries all roads into the Highlands across the narrow waist of Scotland led through Stirling. If you look carefully northward, you can still see the Old Stirling Bridge, the site of William Wallace's most famous victory. ⊠ *Castlehill* ☎ *01786/450000* ⊕ *www.stirlingcastle.gov.uk* ⊠ *£16.*

 Restaurants

Allanwater Cafe

$ | **BRITISH** | **FAMILY** | Run by the Bechelli family for four generations, this casual, light, and airy café in Bridge of Allan, just a couple of miles from Stirling, is a popular spot with locals. It is a well-tried Scottish combination of fish-and-chip restaurant and ice-cream parlor. **Known for:** "fish tea"; ice cream; quick service. ⑤ *Average main: £12* ⊠ *15 Henderson St., Bridge of Allan* ☎ *01786/833060* ⊕ *www.allanwatercafe.co.uk.*

The Birds and the Bees

$$ | **BRITISH** | **FAMILY** | This lively pub is a little hard to find but worth the effort for the extensive menu—from burgers and steaks to jambalaya, curry and (this is, after all, Scotland) haggis "draped" in a whisky-and-mustard sauce. The feel is of good home cooking, without pretensions, and the servings are more than generous. **Known for:** hearty home-style cooking; delicious desserts; lovely location. ⑤ *Average main: £15* ⊠ *Easter Cornton Road, Causewayhead* ⊹ *From the Wallace Monument head southeast on Hillfoots Road/B998 (if walking, you can take the Logie Road/B998 shortcut), then take the A9 toward Stirling. Make a right at Easter Cornton Road and follow*

it about one-half mile. ☎ *01786/473663* ⊕ *www.thebirdsandthebees-stirling.com.*

Brea

$$ | **BRITISH** | This unpretentious and very popular place with wooden tables and chairs has a menu that celebrates Scottish food, though well-made burgers and steaks are also permanent features. The food offers some new takes on traditional favorites such as the rolled haddock with salmon, the Cullen skink soup, and haggis in various guises. **Known for:** burgers; good seafood; homemade desserts. ⑤ *Average main: £18* ⊠ *5 Baker St.* ⊹ *Down the hill from Stirling Castle* ☎ *01786/446277* ⊕ *www.brea-stirling. co.uk.*

 Hotels

Colessio Hotel

$$ | **HOTEL** | Occupying a large stone landmark neoclassical building in the center of town and near the castle, this is a modern hotel in the grand style, with 21st-century amenities. **Pros:** great central location; modern facilities; comfortable bedrooms. **Cons:** difficult parking, though there is a parking lot behind the hotel; black-and-white decor may overpower; limited views in some rooms. ⑤ *Rooms from: £140* ⊠ *33 Spittal St.* ☎ *01786/448880* ⊕ *www.hotelcolessio. com* ⇝ *40 rooms* ❍| *Free breakfast.*

Friars Wynd

$ | **HOTEL** | This small boutique hotel in a restored town house is situated in the heart of Stirling. **Pros:** pleasant and relaxing atmosphere; tasteful decor; reasonably priced. **Cons:** Wi-Fi in public areas only; no parking; limited social space. ⑤ *Rooms from: £109* ⊠ *17 Friars St.* ☎ *01786/447501* ⊕ *www.friarswynd. co.uk* ⇝ *8 rooms* ❍| *Free breakfast.*

Portcullis Hotel

$$ | **B&B/INN** | This small hotel with a lively traditional pub scores above all on location: it is just outside the walls of Stirling Castle, and the views are spectacular,

especially from the upper floors where the guest rooms are located. **Pros:** excellent location close to the castle; fine views; a distinctly local atmosphere. **Cons:** can get noisy; snug rooms; not cheap in high season. $ *Rooms from: £145 ⊠ Castle Wynd ☎ 01786/472290 ⊕ www.theportcullishotel.com ⊸ 4 rooms ⦿ Free breakfast.*

Victoria Square Guest House

$$ | **B&B/INN** | Looking out over a pleasant grassy square, this rather grand and completely modernized Victorian house has a conveniently central location. **Pros:** big and bright rooms; sumptuous; quiet spot (first-floor rooms not so much). **Cons:** no children under 12; Orangery restaurant is pricey; rooms are on the expensive side. $ *Rooms from: £142 ⊠ 12 Victoria Sq. ☎ 01786/473920 ⊕ www.victoriasquareguesthouse.com ⊸ 7 rooms ⦿ Free breakfast.*

West Plean House

$ | **B&B/INN** | Dating from 1803, this handsome, rambling B&B with spacious rooms is part of a working farm. **Pros:** beautiful gardens; plenty of peace and quiet; huge and hearty breakfast. **Cons:** a little off the beaten track; a 3-mile walk to Stirling; occasional noise from the farm. $ *Rooms from: £100 ⊠ Denny Road ☎ 01786/812208 ⊕ www.westpleanhouse.com ⊗ Closed Dec. ⊸ 4 rooms ⦿ Free breakfast.*

⊙ Performing Arts

Macrobert Arts Centre

ARTS CENTERS | On the campus of the University of Stirling, this arts center has a theater, gallery, and cinema with programs that range from films to pantomime. It's off the A9 as you're heading toward Bridge of Allan. ⊠ *University of Stirling, West Link Road ☎ 01786/466666 ⊕ www.macrobert.org.*

Tolbooth

ARTS CENTERS | Built in 1705, the Tolbooth has been many things: courthouse, jail, meeting place. At one time the city's money was kept here. Today it serves as an entertainment venue, an art gallery, and a 200-seat theater for concerts and performances of all kinds. The bar is open for performances. *It has retained its traditional Scottish steeple and gilded weathercock, and a newer tower lets you survey the surrounding country.* ⊠ *Broad Street ☎ 01786/274000 ⊕ stirlingevents.org/tolbooth-event.*

Shopping

CLOTHING

House of Henderson

CLOTHING | A Highland outfitter of the old school, House of Henderson sells tartans, woolens, and accessories, and offers a made-to-measure kilt service. ⊠ *6–8 Friars St. ☎ 01786/473681 ⊕ www.houseofhenderson.co.uk.*

Mill Trail

CLOTHING | East of Stirling is Mill Trail country, along the foot of the Ochil Hills. As you travel from Stirling toward Tillicoutry, Alva, and Alloa, mill shops offer woolen clothing and cashmere at good prices.

GIFTS

Fotheringham Gallery

ART GALLERIES | This upscale gallery specializes in contemporary Scottish art as well as striking modern jewelry by Leigh Fortheringham. ⊠ *78 Henderson St., Bridge of Allan ☎ 01786/832861 ⊕ www.fotheringhamgallery.co.uk.*

Stirling Bagpipes

MUSIC STORES | This small shop sells bagpipes of every type and at every price, including antiques by legendary craftspeople that are displayed in glass cases. The owner, who tunes the chanters and drones in a room behind the shop, has been known to take time to walk shoppers through the history of these wonderful instruments, upon request. ✉ *8 Broad St.* ☎ *01786/448886* ⊕ *www.stirlingbagpipes.com* ⊙ *Closed Sun. and Wed.*

Falkirk

14 miles southeast of Stirling, along the M9 motorway.

Falkirk has a fascinating history and some striking attractions. It was here, at the impressive Antonine Wall, that the Roman occupiers drove back the warlike Picts. You can visit parts of the wall and imagine the fierce battles between the Romans and early Scottish natives over this strategic location.

In the late 18th century Falkirk was an important industrial town because of its network of canals linking Glasgow and Edinburgh, but with the arrival of the railways, the town's fortunes flagged. The canals have been brought back to life with the Millennium Link Project, which has revived the waterways with the spectacular Falkirk Wheel, a boat lift that has become a major visitor draw, and the Kelpies Country Park. The restored canal side towpaths are now a network of cycle paths and walking routes; you can hire a bike at the Wheel and cycle to the Kelpies.

GETTING HERE AND AROUND

The M9 from Stirling to Falkirk follows the widening estuary of the River Forth, the view dominated by the huge Grangemouth oil refinery in the distance.

ESSENTIALS

VISITOR INFORMATION Falkirk Council/ Falkirk Community Trust. ✉ *The Falkirk Stadium, 4 Stadium Way, Unit 2A* ⊕ *www. visitfalkirk.com.*

 Sights

Antonine Wall

ARCHAEOLOGICAL SITE | West of Falkirk, Bonnybridge is home to the most extensive remains of the Antonine Wall, a 37-mile-long Roman earthwork fortification that marked the northernmost limit of the Roman Empire. Built around AD 140 as a defense against the warlike Picts of the north, it was abandoned some 20 years later. A UNESCO World Heritage site, the wall was the site of a famous battle in 1298, when William Wallace was defeated by the English. Notable sections of the wall can also be seen in other towns, including Tamfourhill, Callendar Park, Kinneil Estate, and Bridgeness. To get to the Bonnybridge section from Falkirk, take the A803 west. ■ **TIP → You can download a walking map of the wall from** ⊕ **www. visitfalkirk.com.** ✉ *Off A803, Bonnybridge* ⊕ *2 miles west of Falkirk off the A803* ⊕ *www.antoninewall.org* ✉ *Free.*

Callendar House

HOUSE | **FAMILY** | Near the town center, this grand country house gives you a glimpse of a family's daily life in the early 1800s. In the kitchen, local guides explain cooking in the early 19th century and may even offer you a sample. Entry is through an impressive wooden hallway, and the first-floor morning and drawing rooms are the grandest in the region. There are exhibits on the Romans and the Antonine Wall, as well as on the history of Falkirk. The second floor is a gallery space and houses the town's archives. You can relax in the grand tearoom before you move on to the beautiful grounds of Callendar Park, which has activities year-round. The house is something of a secret, but it's well worth a visit. ✉ *Callendar Park , Off Callendar Road* ☎ *01324/503770* ⊕ *www.falkirkcommunitytrust.org* ✉ *Free* ⊙ *Closed Tues.*

The *Kelpies,* located just outside of Falkirk, are the largest works of art in all of Scotland.

★ Falkirk Wheel

TOUR—SIGHT | FAMILY | The only rotating boat lift in the world, the Falkirk Wheel links two major waterways, the Forth and Clyde Canal and the Union Canal, between Edinburgh and Glasgow. Opened in 2001, this extraordinary engineering achievement lifts and lowers boats using four giant wheels shaped like Celtic axes; it can transport eight or more boats at a time from one canal to the other in about 45 minutes. The Falkirk Wheel replaced 11 locks. You can take a 50-minute trip as the wheel turns, and you're transported up or down to the other canal. The site offers children's play areas, as well as children's canoes and bicycle rentals. An on-site office has information on canal boat cruises. There are also several canal path walkways and cycleways. The excellent Heritage Centre provides plenty of information and has a good café and gift shop. ■ **TIP→ Booking your trip ahead is recommended in summer.** ✉ *Lime Road, Tamfourhill* ✛ *Signposted off the A803* ☎ *08700/500208* ⊕ *www.thefalkirkwheel.co.uk* ✍ *£13.50.*

★ The *Kelpies*

PUBLIC ART | FAMILY | The Helix, a country park on the edges of Falkirk with cycle and walking paths, play areas, and a wetland, is home to sculptor Andy Scott's extraordinary *The Kelpies*, two horse heads forged in steel, 85 and 98 feet high respectively. The largest works of art in Scotland, they sit at the center of the park, their beautiful heads framed against the Ochil Hills behind, paying homage to Falkirk's industrial past. The heads are modeled on Clydesdales, the huge draft horses that hauled barges along the canals before the advent of the railways. A special guided tour (book online for convenience) gives you an insight into the area's past and takes you inside the sculptures, and there is a visitor center with a café and gift shop. ✉ *The Helix, A9 and Falkirk Road* ✛ *You can get here from the A9 or the M9, or through Falkirk, where the route is well signposted* ☎ *01324/506850* ⊕ *www.thehelix.co.uk* ✍ *Park free; £7.50 sculpture tour.*

Dunblane

6 miles north of Stirling.

The small, quiet town of Dunblane has long been an important religious center; it is dominated by its cathedral, which dates mainly from the 13th century. The town also boasts one of Scotland's most impressive libraries, the Leighton Library, as well as a castle that may seem familiar to you, especially if you're an *Outlander* fan.

GETTING HERE AND AROUND

Dunblane station is on the main line to Perth and Inverness, and regular bus service links the town to Stirling. For drivers it is easily reached along the main A9 artery.

 Sights

Blair Drummond Safari and Adventure Park

AMUSEMENT PARK/WATER PARK | FAMILY | As unlikely as it might seem in this gentle valley, the Blair Drummond Safari and Adventure Park is the place to see sea lions bobbing their heads above the water or monkeys swinging from the branches. Take a footbridge to Lemur Land or watch hawks and falcons in the *Birds of Prey* exhibit. Beware the llamas, who are more bad-tempered than they may appear. The enclosures are spacious, so the place doesn't feel like a zoo. There are rides, slides, and an adventure playground for the kids, as well as some fairground rides that cost extra. ⊠ *Blair Drummond, Doune* ✛ *Off the A84, between Dunblane and Callander* ☎ *01786/841456* ⊕ *www.blairdrummond. com* ✒ *£17.75 (£16.50 if booked online)* ⊘ *Closed Nov.–Feb.*

Doune Castle

CASTLE/PALACE | This medieval castle may seem eerily familiar because it is a favorite with filmmakers: *Monty Python and the Holy Grail* was filmed here, and more recently it was used in the *Game* of *Thrones* and *Outlander* series (and the admission price has risen since *Outlander* aired). In 1361 the castle became the seat of Robert Stewart, the Duke of Albany and Governor of Scotland, who embarked on various building projects. The semi-ruined Doune is grim and high-walled, with a daunting central keep and echoing, drafty stairways up to the curtain-wall walk. Climb the wall; the views over the countryside will make it worthwhile. Monty Python's Terry Jones narrates a good audio guide. ■ **TIP➡ The best place to photograph this squat, walled fort is from the bridge, a little way upstream.** *In the past, the village of Doune was known for its gunsmiths, and no self-respecting Highland chief's attire was complete without an ornate pair of pistols made here.* ⊠ *Castle Road, Doune* ✛ *5 miles west of Dunblane* ☎ *01786/841742* ⊕ *www.historicenvironment.scot* ✒ *£9.*

Dunblane Cathedral

RELIGIOUS SITE | The oldest part of Dunblane—with its narrow winding streets—huddles around this church's square. Bishop Clement built the cathedral in the early 13th century on the site of St. Blane's tiny 8th-century cell; with the Reformation of the 16th century, it ceased to be a cathedral. In 1996 it was the scene of a moving memorial service for the 15 children and one teacher killed in the local school by Thomas Hamilton. There are free guided tours on Sunday afternoons. Be sure to view the medieval carvings in the choir stalls. ⊠ *The Cross* ☎ *01667/460232* ⊕ *www.dunblanecathedral.org.uk* ✒ *Free.*

Leighton Library

LIBRARY | A 17th-century bishop of Dunblane, and later an archbishop of Glasgow, Robert Leighton donated his collection of roughly 1,400 books for clergy to use, along with funds to build this library to store them. Today the library—which is no longer a lending library but operates like a museum of books—owns more than 4,500 books, and you can

The Trossachs
and Loch Lomond

view an assortment of old and interesting maps and books here. Donations are encouraged. ⊠ *13 Buccleuch Court, Doune* ☎ *01786/822034 Library custodian* ⊕ *www.leightonlibrary.org.uk* ⊗ *Closed Sun. and Oct.–Apr.*

 Hotels

★ Cromlix House
$$$$ | HOTEL | A grand refurbished Victorian country house set amid beautiful grounds, Cromlix House is owned by Scottish tennis champion Andy Murray, and you might notice the sound of ball on racket from the tennis court. **Pros:** luxurious facilities; lovely grounds for walking; comfortable beds. **Cons:** not much for children; a little hard to find; an expensive indulgence. $ *Rooms from: £395* ⊠ *Off B8033, beyond the village of Kinbuck, Kinbuck* ⊹ *Keep looking for the*

entrance, 4½ miles north of Dunblane ☎ *01786/822125* ⊕ *www.cromlix.com* ⊷ *16 rooms* ¶◎¶ *Breakfast.*

DoubleTree by Hilton Dunblane Hydro
$$ | HOTEL | One of the grandes dames where Victorians would come to "take the waters," this hotel on sprawling grounds has retained its original building and the high style of its interior. **Pros:** fine views; lovely grounds; leisure center included in the rates. **Cons:** slightly old-fashioned feel; some rooms are small; charge for Wi-Fi. $ *Rooms from: £129* ⊠ *Perth Rd.* ☎ *01786/822551* ⊕ *www.doubletreedunblane.com* ⊷ *200 rooms* ¶◎¶ *Free Breakfast.*

Old Churches House
$ | HOTEL | In a row of 18th-century houses overlooking the Cathedral Square, this comfortable hotel has a quiet, restful air. **Pros:** quiet location;

all rooms (but one) look out onto the square; traditional and modern Scottish dishes at on-site restaurant. **Cons:** could be too quiet; slightly distant from major sights; parking not on-site, but nearby (and free). $ *Rooms from: £100* ✉ *1–7 Kirk St.* ☎ *01786/823663* ⊕ *www.old-churcheshouse.com* ↗ *11 rooms* ♥ *Free Breakfast.*

Callander

8 miles northwest of Doune.

A traditional Highland-edge resort, the little town of Callander bustles throughout the year, largely with visitors and coach parties from Glasgow and Edinburgh. It is a gateway to the beauty of Loch Lomond and the Trossachs National Park, yet never too far from the cities of the central belt. There's plenty of window-shopping here, plus lively pubs and a selection of mainly bed-and-breakfast accommodations.

GETTING HERE AND AROUND
You can access Callander by bus from Stirling, Glasgow, or Edinburgh. If you're traveling by car from Stirling, take the M8 to Dunblane, then the A820 (which becomes the A84) to Callander. If you are coming from Glasgow, take the A81 through Aberfoyle to Callander; an alternative route (longer but more picturesque) is to take the A821 around Loch Venachar, then the A84 east to Callander.

ESSENTIALS
VISITOR INFORMATION Callander Visitor Information Centre. ✉ *52–54 Main St.* ☎ *01877/330342* ⊕ *incallander.co.uk/visitorcentre.*

Sights

Balquhidder Glen
VIEWPOINT | A 20-minute drive from Callander, through the Pass of Leny and beyond Strathyre, the lovely Balquhidder Glen (pronounced *bal*-kwidd- *er*) is a

typical Highland glen, with a flat-bottom, U-shaped profile, indicating it was formed by prehistoric glaciers. This was MacGregor country, the most famous of whom was Rob Roy MacGregor, the Jacobite hero who is buried in the churchyard here. It is also walkers country, and several walkers routes pass through here. Gentler walks will take you to Kirkton Glen, past Monachyle Mhor, after the road ends. From there the view opens toward the mountain country around Ben More, where the hardier, well-equipped hillwalker may prefer to go. ✉ *Balquhidder* ✛ *From Callander take the A84 and turn left at Kingshouse; the road ends in the glen.*

Hamilton Toy Museum
MUSEUM | FAMILY | This is one of those eccentric museums born of one person's (or one family's) passionate obsession. The small, crowded house and shop on Callander's main street contains one of the most extensive toy collections in Britain. The rooms throughout the house are crammed with everything from Corgi cars and an enormous number of toy soldiers, carefully organized by regiment, to Amanda Jane dolls and Beatles memorabilia. The collection of model railways has extended into tracks in the back garden. The museum is jammed and quirky, but full of reminders of everyone's childhood. ✉ *111 Main St.* ☎ *01877/330004* ⊕ *www.thehamiltontoycollection.co.uk* 🎟 *£3* ⊗ *Closed Nov.–Mar.*

🍴 Restaurants

Deli Ecosse
$ | **CAFÉ** | Don't miss it: in one corner of the square, a narrow door opens into a high-ceilinged old church hall crowded with good things to eat there or take away. You can order tasty soups, homemade cakes, and plump sandwiches from the counter, or try the excellent coffee or a glass of wine. **Known for:** homemade cakes; excellent breakfast; inexpensive lunch. $ *Average main:*

£10 ✉ 10 Ancaster Sq. ☎ 01877/331220 ⊕ deliecosse.co.uk ☾ No dinner.

Mhor Bread and Tearoom

$ | BRITISH | Retaining the feel of an old fashioned bakery, Mhor Bread delights with not only its homemade sourdough and other delicious breads, but also doughnuts, shortbread, and more. The café/tearoom is open for breakfast and lunch, with menu items such as fine sandwiches, soups, and desserts, including an amazing array of pies with different fillings. **Known for:** bread; fine pies of every variety; good breakfasts. *⑤ Average main: £10 ✉ 8 Main St. ☎ 01877/339518 ⊕ www.mhorbread.net ☾ No dinner.*

MHOR Fish

$ | SEAFOOD | Simple white walls and black-and-white floors provide the backdrop for great fish at this very superior, and nicely busy, "chippy" (fish-and-chips shop) and fish restaurant. The fish is fresh and sustainable, so it might be pollock or coley rather than cod or haddock. **Known for:** sustainable fish; great chips (fried in beef fat); homemade bread. *⑤ Average main: £12 ✉ 75☒77 Main St. ☎ 01877/330213 ⊕ monachylemhor.net.*

★ Venachar Lochside

$$ | MODERN BRITISH | All you see from the road is what seems to be a large shed, but inside is a busy restaurant. There's also a view—the restaurant's glass wall affords a lovely panorama of the water and surrounding hills. **Known for:** smoked-fish platter; fine seafood; lochside dining. *⑤ Average main: £15 ✉ Loch Venachar ✛ On the A821 about 6 miles from Callander, at Brig o' Turk ☎ 01877/330011 ⊕ www.venachar-lochside.co.uk ☾ No dinner.*

 Hotels

The Crags Hotel

$ | HOTEL | A traditional establishment on Callander's main street, the Crags Hotel has recently been fully refurbished in a restrained, elegant style. **Pros:** friendly staff and atmosphere; appealing restaurant on-site; reasonably priced. **Cons:** some rooms facing the street may be noisy; small reception area and bar; rooms are quite small. *⑤ Rooms from: £90 ✉ 101 Main St. ☎ 01877/330257 ⊕ www.cragshotel.co.uk ⇌ 8 rooms ⑩ Free Breakfast.*

MHOR 84

$ | B&B/INN | FAMILY | Balquhidder Glen is the perfect place for walkers and cyclists, and this modest but casually chic hotel has been designed with them in mind. **Pros:** beautiful setting; great quality for the price; game room for kids. **Cons:** a rather isolated spot; breakfast extra; used above all by walkers (thus not for intimate retreats). *⑤ Rooms from: £90 ✉ Balquhidder, Lochearnhead ✛ Off the A84 from Callander to Crianlarich, turn at Kingshouse; 11 miles north of Callender ☎ 01877/384646 ⊕ www.mhor84.net ⇌ 7 rooms ⑩ No meals.*

★ Monachyle MHOR

$$$$ | HOTEL | Splendidly isolated, this beautiful converted farmhouse with contemporary interiors is set amid forests and moorland, looking out onto Lochs Voil and Doine. **Pros:** stunning scenery; delicious food; complimentary salmon and trout fishing. **Cons:** remote location; rooms are on the small side; bar can get very crowded. *⑤ Rooms from: £325 ✉ Off A84, Balquhidder ✛ From Callander, drive northwest 17 miles (40 minutes) ☎ 01877/384622 ⊕ www.mhor.net ⇌ 14 rooms ⑩ All-inclusive.*

★ Roman Camp

$$ | B&B/INN | Within a hundred yards of Callander's main street, on the other side of an unpretentious arch, is this 17th-century hunting lodge hidden among ornate gardens. **Pros:** beautiful grounds; luxurious rooms; close to everything in town. **Cons:** restaurant is expensive; no Internet in rooms; much sought after for weddings, so could be busy. *⑤ Rooms from: £160 ✉ Off Main Street ☎ 01877/330003*

⊕ www.romancamphotel.co.uk ⇥ 15 rooms ⊚ Free breakfast.

Shopping

Trossachs Woollen Mill
CLOTHING | The Edinburgh Woollen Mill Group owns this mill shop in Kilmahog, a mile west of Callander. It has a vast selection of woolens on display, including luxurious cashmere and striking tartan throws, and will provide overseas mailing and tax-free shopping. The shop has a small café and a couple of resident animals. ✉ Main St., Kilmahog ☎ 01877/330178 ⊕ www.ewm.co.uk.

Activities

BICYCLING
Wheels
BICYCLING | You can rent bikes of every sort by the hour, the half day, or the day from this friendly firm. Most popular are the mountain bikes, which go for £20 per day. The staff can also help you find the best mountain-bike routes around the Trossachs. ✉ Invertrossachs Road ☎ 01877/331100 ⊕ www.scottish-cycling.com ⇥ Closed Nov.–Feb.

GOLF
Callander Golf Club
GOLF | Designed by Tom Morris in 1890 and extended to 18 holes in 1913 by Willie Fernie, Callander has a scenic upland feel in a town well prepared for visitors. Pine and birch woods and hilly fairways afford fine views, especially toward Ben Ledi, and the tricky moorland layout demands accurate hitting off the tee. The challenging 15th is one of Scotland's most famous holes. ✉ Aveland Road ☎ 01877/330090 ⊕ www.callandergolfclub.co.uk ⇥ £30 weekdays, £40 weekends ⛳ 18 holes, 5208 yards, par 66.

HIKING
Bracklinn Falls
HIKING/WALKING | A walk is signposted from the east end of Callander's main street to the Bracklinn Falls, over whose lip Sir Walter Scott once rode a pony to win a bet.

Callander Crags
HIKING/WALKING | It's a 1½-mile walk through the woods up to the Callander Crags, with views of the Lowlands as far as the Pentland Hills behind Edinburgh. The walk begins at the west end of Callander's main street. ✉ Callander.

Pass of Leny
HIKING/WALKING | Just north of Callander, the mountains squeeze both the road and rocky river into the narrow Pass of Leny. An abandoned railway—now a pleasant walking or biking path—also goes through the pass, past Ben Ledi and Loch Lubnaig. ✉ Brig o'Turk.

The Trossachs

10 miles west of Callander.

The Trossachs has been a popular touring region since the late 18th century, at the dawn of the age of the romantic poets. Influenced by the writings of Sir Walter Scott, early visitors who strayed into the Highlands from the central belt of Scotland admired this as the first "wild" part of Scotland they encountered. Perhaps because the Trossachs represent the very essence of what the Highlands are supposed to be, the whole of this area, including Loch Lomond, is now protected as a national park. Here you can find birch and pine forests, vistas down lochs where the woods creep right to the water's edge, and, in the background, peaks that rise high enough to be called mountains, though they're not as high as those to the north and west.

GETTING HERE AND AROUND
To reach the Trossachs, take the A84 from Callander through the Pass of Leny, then on to Crianlarich on the A85; from here you can continue down the western shore of Loch Lomond or carry on toward

Did You Know?

In 1810, Scottish writer Sir Walter Scott was inspired to write his famous poem *Lady of the Lake* after a visit to Loch Katrine.

Fort William. Alternately, turn onto the A821 outside Callander and travel past Loch Katrine through the Duke's Pass to Aberfoyle.

Sights

Loch Achray

BODY OF WATER | Between Loch Katrine and Loch Venachar, this small and calm man-made lake is popular for fishing. Hikers climb nearby Ben A'an for the views. ⊠ *Off A821, Aberfoyle* ✛ *11 km (6.8 miles) west of Callander.*

★ Loch Katrine

BODY OF WATER | **FAMILY** | This loch was a favorite among Victorian visitors—mysterious and wide and, at times, quite wild. Today it's the source of Glasgow's freshwater. Take a cruise around the loch if time permits, as the shores remain undeveloped and scenic. The steamship *Sir Walter Scott* and the motor launch *Lady of the Lake* sail from the lake's eastern end several times a day in season. You can make the round-trip journey around the loch, or head directly across to Stronachlachar, where you can pause for a coffee and to admire the beauty of the loch from the pier head and then return by bicycle on the lochside road. There are café facilities and cycle-hire shops at the head of the loch; reservations are required if you're taking a bike on the boat. Sailings continue through the year but are reduced in number between October and May. ⊠ *Trossachs Pier, Aberfoyle* ✛ *Off A821* ☎ *01877/376316* ⊕ *www.lochkatrine.com* 🕮 *Sir Walter Scott £17 round-trip, £14 one way; Lady of the Lake £14 round-trip, £10.50 one way. There are also shorter scenic cruises, £14 on the Sir Walter Scott, £10.50 on the Lady of the Lake.*

Loch Venachar

BODY OF WATER | The A821 runs west together with the first and gentlest of the Trossachs lochs, Loch Venachar. A sturdy gray-stone building, with a small dam at the Callander end, controls the water that feeds into the River Teith (and, hence, into the Forth). ⊠ *A821, Brig o'Turk.*

Trossachs National Park

NATIONAL/STATE PARK | Scotland's first national park, designated in 2002, the Trossachs were first discovered and developed as an area for Victorian tourists and visitors. It was Queen Victoria's fascination with the novels of Sir Walter Scott that stimulated an interest in the brooding glens and lochs of the area, as well as the healing qualities of its waters. The park sits on a geological fault that divides the fertile lowlands from the highlands and its hills and mountains, 21 of which are more than 3,000 feet (and known as "Munros"). For hikers there are woodland valleys for pleasant and leisurely walks, long-distance footpaths like the West Highland Rob Roy Ways for more determined walkers, and mountains like the demanding Cobbler and Ben Lomond, as well as shorter hikes on hills surrounding scenic lochs. For cyclists there are exciting routes, and for the nature lover there are many varieties of birds and animals in this protected habitat—capercaillie, golden eagles, red deer, and beavers among them. As the number of visitors has grown, lochside diners and charming country hotels have also multiplied. ⊕ *www.lochlomond-trossachs.org.*

Aberfoyle

11 miles south of Loch Katrine, in the Trossachs.

This small tourist-oriented town has a somewhat faded air, but the surrounding hills (some snowcapped) and the green slopes visible from the town are the reason so many people pause here before continuing up to Duke's Pass or on to Inversnaid on Loch Lomond. Access to nearby Queen Elizabeth Forest Park and the Lodge Forest Centre is another reason to visit.

GETTING HERE AND AROUND

The main route out of Glasgow, the A81, takes you through Aberfoyle and on to Callander and Stirling. There are regular buses from Stirling and Glasgow to Aberfoyle.

ESSENTIALS

VISITOR INFORMATION Trossachs Discovery Centre. ☒ *Main Street* ☎ *01877/381221.*

Sights

★ Inchmahome

ISLAND | The 13th-century ruined priory on the tiny island of Inchmahome, on the Lake of Menteith, is a lovely place for a picnic after you explore the building's chapter house and other remains. It was a place of refuge in 1547 for the young Mary, Queen of Scots. In season, a seven-minute ferry takes passengers to the island, now owned by the National Trust for Scotland. The ferry jetty is just past the Port of Menteith (a village). ☒ *Off A81 ✛ Take the A81 to the B8034; it's 4 miles east of Aberfoyle* ☎ *01786/385294* ⊕ *www.historicenvironment.scot* ☒ *Ferry £9* ⊗ *Closed. Nov.–Mar.*

★ Queen Elizabeth Forest Park

NATURE PRESERVE | For exquisite nature, drive north from Aberfoyle on the A821 and turn right at signposts to Queen Elizabeth Forest Park. Along the way you'll be heading toward higher moorland blanketed with conifers. The conifers hem in the views of Ben Ledi and Ben Venue, which can be seen over the spiky green waves of trees as the road snakes around heathery knolls and hummocks. There's another viewing area, and a small parking lot, at the highest point of the road. Soon the road swoops off the Highland edge and leads downhill.

At the heart of the Queen Elizabeth Forest Park, the **Lodge Forest Visitor Centre** leads to four forest walks, a family-friendly bicycle route, and the 7-mile 3 Lochs Forest Drive, open April to October. Or you can sit on the terrace of the Bluebell Cafe and scan the forests and hills of the Trossachs. The visitor center has a wildlife-watch room, where you can follow the activities of everything from ospreys to water voles. ☒ *Off A821 ✛ 1 mile north of Aberfoyle* ☎ *01877/382383* ⊕ *forestryandland.gov.scot/visit/forest-parks/queen-elizabeth-forest-park* ☒ *Free, but parking costs £3 for the day.*

Scottish Wool Centre

STORE/MALL | **FAMILY** | Besides selling a vast range of woolen garments and knitwear, the Scottish Wool Centre has a small café and some activities. Three times a day from April to September it presents an interactive "gathering" during which dogs herd sheep and ducks in the large amphitheater, with a little help from the public. ☒ *Off Main Street* ☎ *01877/382850* ⊕ *www.ewm.co.uk* ☒ *Free.*

Restaurants

Pier Café

$ | **BRITISH** | At the historic Stronachlachar Pier, this light-filled coffee shop has a satisfying lunch menu (burgers and sandwiches) and a deck with expansive views over Loch Katrine. Cakes, scones, and soups are made on the premises. **Known for:** home baking; good coffee; loch views. ⑤ *Average main: £10* ☒ *B829, Stronachlachar* ☎ *01877/386374* ⊕ *www.thepiercafe.com* ⊗ *No dinner Sun.–Thur.*

Hotels

★ Lake of Menteith Hotel

$$ | **HOTEL** | At this beautifully located hotel overlooking the Lake of Menteith, muted colors and simple but elegant rooms create a restful atmosphere, enhanced, perhaps, by the silent hills that ring the hotel and the tranquil lake. **Pros:** elegant, unpretentious bedrooms; beautiful setting; lakeside seating at restaurant. **Cons:** not well signposted; not all rooms have lake views and those that do are more expensive; no elevator. $ *Rooms from: £160* ✉ *Off A81* ☎ *01877/385258* ⊕ *www.lake-hotel.com* ⤵ *17 rooms* ¦○¦ *Free breakfast.*

Macdonald Forest Hills Hotel

$$$ | HOTEL | This is a traditional Scottish country resort hotel for families and those who simply want to take it easy, though it also offers numerous sporting and fitness activities. **Pros:** stunning views; 20-plus acres of grounds to explore; good children's programs. **Cons:** restaurant is pricey; a great deal of tartan; feels slightly anonymous. $ *Rooms from: £163* ✉ *B829, Kinlochard* ✛ *4 miles west of Aberfoyle* ☎ *08448/799057* ⊕ *www. macdonaldhotels.co.uk/foresthills* ⤵ *55 rooms* ¦○¦ *All-inclusive.*

 Activities

BOATING
Sir Walter Scott

TOUR—SIGHT | The steamer *Sir Walter Scott* embarks on cruises of Loch Katrine every day between April and late October. The boat leaves from Trossachs Pier at 10:30, 1:00, 2:30 and 4. If you're feeling vigorous, hire a bicycle at the pier and pedal back around the loch. It's a not-too-difficult 10-mile ride. A second boat, the *Lady of the Lake,* sails at 12:45 and 3:15, and also has room for bikes. ✉ *Trossachs Pier* ☎ *01877/376316* ⊕ *www.lochkatrine.com* ✉ *£13 one way, £15.50 round-trip.*

GOLF
Aberfoyle Golf Club

GOLF | Queen Elizabeth Forest Park provides the backdrop for this hilly course. One of the area's many James Braid–designed parkland courses, it dates back to 1890. There are views of Ben Lomond and Stirling Castle from different points on the course, which is relatively short but varied and challenging even for quite experienced players, with several uphill shots and undulating ground. ✉ *Braeval* ✛ *Off A821* ☎ *01877/382493* ⊕ *www.*

aberfoylegolf.co.uk ✉ *£20 weekdays, £25 weekends* ⬆. *18 holes, 5158 yards, par 66.*

HIKING
★ Ben A'an

VIEWPOINT | The climb up the steep, heathery Ben A'an requires a couple of hours and good lungs, but it's a worth-while trip, providing you with some of the best Trossachs views, including those of Loch Achray and Loch Katrine. ✉ *Off A821* ✛ *Access the beginning of the path near the Loch Achray parking lot.*

ZIPLINING
Go Ape High Wire Forest Adventure

CITY PARK | FAMILY | Near the Lodge Forest Visitor Centre in the Queen Elizabeth Forest Park, this is an exhilarating experience for thrill seekers age 10 and over. After a short orientation course, you can travel 40 feet above the forest via ziplines and rope ladders on a sort of midair assault course. ✉ *Queen Elizabeth Forest Park, A821* ✛ *1 mile north of Aberfoyle* ☎ *0845/094–9032* ⊕ *www.goape.com* ✉ *The Treetop Challenge (~2.5 hours), £33* ⊙ *Closed weekdays in Nov., Feb., and Mar.*

Loch Lomond

14 miles west of Aberfoyle.

The waters of Scotland's largest loch, which also happens to be one of its most beautiful, create a perfect reflection of the surrounding hills. You can cruise among its small islands or follow the low road that carries you from Glasgow to the beginning of the Highlands.

GETTING HERE AND AROUND

To reach Loch Lomond from Aberfoyle, take the A81 toward Glasgow, then the A811 to Drymen and then the B837 as far as it will take you. From Glasgow take the A82 to the Balloch roundabout, and either go right through Balloch for Drymen and the eastern shore, or continue along the A82 as it hugs the west bank all the way to Crianlarich.

You can drive, cycle, or walk along the 32 miles of Loch Lomond along its western shores, and watch the changing face of the loch as you go, or look up toward the shifting slopes of Ben Lomond.

ESSENTIALS

VISITOR INFORMATION Loch Lomond and the Trossachs National Park Headquarters. ⌧ *Carrochan Road, Balloch* ☎ *01389/722600* ⊕ *www.lochlomond-trossachs.org.*

Sights

★ Loch Lomond

BODY OF WATER | Known for its "bonnie, bonnie banks," Loch Lomond is Scotland's most well-known loch and its largest in terms of surface area. Its waters reflect the crags that surround it.

On the western side of the loch, the A82 follows the shore for 24 miles, continuing a farther 7 miles to Crianlarich, passing picturesque Luss, which has a pier where you can hop aboard boats cruising along the loch, and Tarbert, the starting point for the *Maid of the Loch.* On the eastern side of the loch, take the A81 to Drymen, and from there the B837 signposted toward Balmaha, where you can hire a boat or take the ferry to the island of Inchcailloch. Once you're there, a short walk takes you to the top of the hill and a spectacular view of the loch. Equally spectacular, but not as wet, is the view from Conic Hill behind Balmaha, a short but exhilarating climb. The hill marks the fault that divides the Lowlands and Highlands. If you continue along the B837 beyond Rowardennan to where it ends at a car park, you can join the walkers at the beginning of the path up Ben Lomond. ⚠ **Don't underestimate this innocent-looking hill; go equipped for sudden changes in the weather.** Hikers can also try part of the 96-mile West Highland Way (⊕ *www.west-highland-way.co.uk*) that

runs along the shore of Loch Lomond on its way north.

Loch Lomond Shores

SHOPPING CENTERS/MALLS | This lakeside shopping complex contains restaurants, pubs, and a visitor center. Some cruises set sail from here. ⌧ *Ben Lomond Way, Balloch* ☎ *01389/751031* ⊕ *www.lochlomondshores.com.*

Restaurants

★ Coach House Coffee Shop

$ | **BRITISH** | With its over-the-top Scottishness, this lively restaurant and café serving Scottish classics fits perfectly into its surroundings. Long wooden tables, a large chimney with an open fire in the winter months, and a cabinet full of mouthwatering cakes baked by the owner create a cheerful atmosphere. **Known for:** teapots; stovies; Scottish style. $ *Average main: £12* ⌧ *Church Road, Luss* ✢ *Off A82* ☎ *01436/860341* ◷ *No dinner.*

Drovers Inn

$ | **BRITISH** | Knowing its clientele, this quirky, noisy, friendly inn serves huge, hearty portions that are what you need after a day's walking on the nearby West Highland Way. Scottish staples like sausage and mash, minced beef, and haggis jostle for a place beside occasionally more adventurous dishes. **Known for:** big portions; old stuffed animals; good bar. $ *Average main: £12* ⌧ *On A82 toward Crianlarich, Balloch* ✢ *North of Ardlui, just north of Loch Lomond* ☎ *01301/704234* ⊕ *www.thedroversinn.co.uk.*

Hotels

Balloch House

$ | **HOTEL** | Cute, cozy, and very Scottish, this small hotel offers simple but clean rooms along with tasty breakfasts and good, hearty pub meals like fish-and-chips and local smoked salmon for reasonable prices. **Pros:** beautiful building;

peat fires; near shopping. **Cons:** noisy pinball machine next to bar; not all rooms have views; has a busy pub. $ *Rooms from: £98* ✉ *Balloch Road, Balloch* ☎ *01389/752579* ⊕ *www.innkeeperslodge.com/loch-lomond* ⇨ *12 rooms* ⦿ *Free breakfast.*

The Lodge on Loch Lomond

$$ | **HOTEL** | Known for its views, this hotel overlooking Loch Lomond sits beside the picturesque village of Luss. **Pros:** wonderful setting; big and comfortable rooms; excellent restaurant with full loch views. **Cons:** not all rooms overlook the loch; can be busy with weddings and conferences; beach area is small and gets crowded in summer. $ *Rooms from: £174* ✉ *Luss, Alexandria* ☎ *01436/860201* ⊕ *www.loch-lomond.co.uk* ⇨ *48 rooms* ⦿ *Free Breakfast.*

 Activities

BOATING

Cruise Loch Lomond

BOATING | **FAMILY** | You can take scenic boat tours of Loch Lomond year-round with this company. What you see on your journey depends on where you embark. From April to October boats depart from various ports around the loch, including Tarbet, Luss, Balmaha, and Inversnaid, while from November to March the boats operate on demand. During the warmer months there is also a Two-Loch Tour taking in Loch Lomond and Loch Katrine. ✉ *Tarbet* ⊹ *Off A82* ☎ *01301/702356* ⊕ *www.cruiselochlomond.co.uk* ⊠ *From £11.*

Macfarlane and Son

BOATING | At this longtime favorite, boats with outboard motors rent for £20 per hour or £50 per day. Rowboats rent for £10 per hour or £30 per day. From Balmaha, it is a short trip to the lovely island of Incailloch. Macfarlane's also runs a ferry to the island for £5 per person. ✉ *Balmaha Boatyard, B837, Balmaha* ⊹ *From* *Drymen take the B837* ☎ *01360/870214* ⊕ *www.balmahaboatyard.co.uk.*

Sweeney's Cruises

BOAT TOURS | This operator runs trips and tours on Loch Lomond from Balloch, Luss, and Tarbert. ✉ *Riverside, Balloch Road, Balloch* ☎ *01389/752376* ⊕ *www.sweeneyscruiseco.com* ⊠ *From £10.50.*

Perth

36 miles northeast of Stirling, 43 miles north of Edinburgh, 61 miles northeast of Glasgow.

For many years Perth was Scotland's capital, and central to its history. One king (James I) was killed here, and the Protestant reformer John Knox preached in St. John's Kirk, where his rhetoric moved crowds to burn down several local monasteries. Perth's local whisky trade and the productive agriculture that surrounds the town have sustained it through the centuries. Its grand buildings, especially on the banks of the River Tay, testify to its continued wealth. The open parkland within the city (the Inches) gives the place a restful air, and shops range from small crafts boutiques to department stores. Impressive Scone Palace is nearby.

GETTING HERE AND AROUND

Perth is served by the main railway line to Inverness, and regular and frequent buses run here from Glasgow, Edinburgh, and Stirling. The central artery, the A9, passes through the city en route to Pitlochry and Inverness, while a network of roads opens the way to the glens and hills around Glen Lyon, or the road to Loch Lomond (the A85) via Crianlarich.

ESSENTIALS

VISITOR INFORMATION Perth Visitor Centre. ✉ *45 High St.* ☎ *01738/450600* ⊕ *www.visitscotland.com/info/services/perth-icentre-p234431.*

Sights

Elcho Castle

CASTLE/PALACE | Built around 1560 by the River Tay, the castle marks a transition period when these structures began to be built as grand houses rather than fortresses, and it's easy to see that Elcho was built for both comfort and defense. The well-preserved but uncluttered rooms let you imagine how life might have been here in the 17th century. The staircases still give access to all floors, and a flashlight is provided for the darker corners. From the battlements of the castle you can see the river stretching east and west. ⊠ Off A912 ✛ Close to Rhynd ☎ 01738/639998 ⊕ www.histori-cenvironment.scot/visit-a-place/places/elcho-castle ⊠ £6 ⊗ Closed Oct.–Mar.

Fergusson Gallery

MUSEUM | Originally a waterworks, this gallery with a magnificent dome and rotunda shelters a collection of 6,000 works—paintings, drawings, and prints—by the Scottish artist J. D. Fergusson (1874–1961) and his wife, Margaret Morris, an artist in her own right and a pioneer of modern dance. Fergusson was the longest-lived member of the group called the Scottish Colourists, who took their inspiration from the French impressionist painters in their use of color and light. ⊠ Marshall Place ☎ 01738/783425 ⊕ www.culturepk.org.uk ⊠ Free ⊗ Closed Mon. and Nov.–Mar.

Perth Art Gallery and Museum

MUSEUM | This museum has a wide-ranging collection, including exhibits on natural history, local history, archaeology, and art, as well as an important glass collection. It also includes work by the great painter of animals Sir Edwin Landseer and some botanical studies of fungi by Beatrix Potter, and presents temporary exhibitions from its own collection and elsewhere. ⊠ *78 George St.* ☎ *01738/632488* ⊕ *www.culturepk.org. uk* ✉ *Free* ⊘ *Closed Mon.*

Regimental Museum of the Black Watch

MILITARY SITE | Some will tell you the Black Watch was a Scottish regiment whose name is a reference to the color of its tartan. An equally plausible explanation, however, is that the regiment was established to keep an undercover watch on rebellious Jacobites. The Gaelic word for black is *dubh,* meaning, in this case, "hidden" or "covert." A wide range of uniforms, weaponry, and marching banners are displayed in this museum in Balhousie Castle, and there's a very good café and shop. ⊠ *Balhousie Castle, Hay Street* ☎ *01738/638152* ⊕ *www.theblack-watch.co.uk* ✉ *£8.50, guided tour (book ahead) £15.*

★ Scone Palace

CASTLE/PALACE | **FAMILY** | The current residence of the Earl of Mansfield, Scone Palace (pronounced *skoon*) is much more cheerful than the city's other castles. Although it incorporates various earlier works, the palace today has mainly a 19th-century theme, with mock castellations that were fashionable at the time. There's plenty to see if you're interested in the acquisitions of an aristocratic Scottish family: magnificent porcelain, some sumptuous furniture, a fine collection of ivory, clocks, and 16th-century needlework. Each room has a guide who will happily talk you through its contents and their associations. In one bedroom hangs a portrait of Dido Elizabeth Belle, a young black slave adopted by the family, who became a well-known society beauty in the 1760s. (The 2013 film *Belle* is based on her life). A coffee shop, restaurant, gift shop, and play area are on-site. The palace has its own mausoleum nearby,

on the site of a long-gone abbey on **Moot Hill,** the ancient coronation place of the Scottish kings. To be crowned, they sat on the Stone of Scone, which was seized in 1296 by Edward I of England, Scotland's greatest enemy, and placed in the coronation chair at Westminster Abbey, in London. The stone was returned to Scotland in November 1996 and is now on view in Edinburgh Castle. There is a maze and a children's playground in the grounds, which are free to enter. ⊠ *Braemar Road* ✛ *2 miles north of Perth* ☎ *01738/552300* ⊕ *www.scone-palace. co.uk* ✉ *£12.50. Free for grounds only.* ⊘ *House closed Nov.–Mar. Grounds closed Mon.–Thurs. Nov.–Mar.*

St. John's Kirk

RELIGIOUS SITE | In this impressive cruciform-plan church dating from the 12th century, religious reformer John Knox preached a fiery sermon in May 1559 against idolatry. An enraged crowd stripped the church and poured into the street to attack the wealthy religious institutions; this helped start the Reformation in Scotland. The interior was divided into three parts at the Reformation, but in the 1920s Sir Robert Lorimer restored it to something closer to its medieval state. ⊠ *St. John Street* ☎ *01738/633192* ⊕ *www.st-johns-kirk. co.uk* ✉ *Free* ⊘ *Closed Oct.–Apr. except for services.*

 # Restaurants

Deans Restaurant

$$$ | BRITISH | The varied clientele reflects the broad appeal of noted chef Willie Deans's imaginative and satisfying cuisine, including a dinner menu with starters such as ceviche of sea bream, passion fruit, and lime, and Shetland fish curry and delicious Orkney steak for main courses. Deans is airy and pleasant, merging warm colors and light woods with comfortable sofas perfect for a pred-inner drink. **Known for:** pretheater menu; good lunch menu; Shetland fish curry.

$ *Average main: £23* ✉ *77–79 Kinnoull St.* ☎ *01738/643377* ⊕ *www.letseatperth.co.uk.*

★ 63 Tay Street

$$$ | BRITISH | Dine looking out onto the River Tay in this elegant but relaxed restaurant with tall windows, gray-and-white walls, and wooden tables. Known for imaginative fare with an emphasis on seasonal and local produce, chef Graeme Pallister produces combinations that are adventurous, such as the "witch sole" with curry and sprouting broccoli or red deer with pear, parsnips, and licorice. **Known for:** imaginative use of seasonal ingredients; excellent tasting menu; wine list. $ *Average main: £22* ✉ *63 Tay St.* ☎ *01738/441451* ⊕ *www.63taystreet.com.*

Hotels

Huntingtower Hotel

$$ | HOTEL | Less than 5 miles from Perth, this tranquil, traditional country hotel with an air of understated elegance has a spacious garden and trees that make it feel more rural than it really is. **Pros:** restful setting; amply sized rooms; dining room overlooks gardens. **Cons:** no elevator; perhaps a slight excess of tartan; no air conditioning. $ *Rooms from: £161* ✉ *Crieff Road* ☎ *01738/583771* ⊕ *www.huntingtowerhotel.co.uk* ⇆ *34 rooms* ⫢ *Free breakfast.*

Sunbank House Hotel

$ | B&B/INN | This handsome early-Victorian gray-stone mansion near Perth's Branklyn Gardens overlooks the River Tay and the city of Perth. **Pros:** reasonably priced; friendly staff; delicious local cuisine. **Cons:** some rooms are very small; some traffic noise from the main road; 15 minutes' walk to town center. $ *Rooms from: £105* ✉ *50 Dundee Rd.* ☎ *01738/624882* ⊕ *www.sunbankhouse.com* ⇆ *9 rooms* ⫢ *Free breakfast.*

Performing Arts

Perth Concert Hall

MUSIC | The city's main concert venue hosts musical performances of all types. ✉ *Mill Street* ☎ *01738/621031* ⊕ *www.horsecross.co.uk.*

Perth Theatre

THEATER | Receiving a major face-lift of its Edwardian building in 2017, this respected repertory theater presents a varied theatrical program as well as musical events. ✉ *185 High St.* ☎ *01738/621031* ⊕ *www.horsecross.co.uk.*

Shopping

Cairncross of Perth

JEWELRY/ACCESSORIES | The Romans coveted freshwater pearls from the River Tay. If you do, too, then head to Cairncross of Perth, where you can admire a display of some of the more unusual shapes and colors. Some of the delicate settings take their theme from Scottish flowers. ✉ *18 St. John's St.* ☎ *01738/624367* ⊕ *www.cairncrossofperth.co.uk.*

Whispers of the Past

JEWELRY/ACCESSORIES | This lovely shop has a collection of jewelry, china, and other gift items, some vintage and some new. ✉ *15 George St.* ☎ *01738/635472* ⊕ *whispers-of-the-past.weebly.com.*

Dunkeld

14 miles north of Perth.

The historic town of Dunkeld remains intact and beautifully preserved with its rows of white houses around the town square. The original village was destroyed in 1689 in a ferocious battle during the Jacobite Rebellion and was rebuilt after its defeat by the Atholl family. Today it survives as part of the National Trust for Scotland's Little Houses Project, which helps maintain the houses. The town is overlooked by the grand but semiruined

12th-century cathedral (still used for services). Atholl Street, leading down to the River Tay, has several crafts shops and a hotel.

The bridge across the River Tay takes you to Birnam Wood, where Shakespeare's Macbeth met the three witches who issued the prophecy about his death. Witty wooden notices lead you to the right tree, a gnarled hollow oak.

GETTING HERE AND AROUND

Dunkeld is on the A9 between Perth and Pitlochry. The town is also on the main train line to Inverness.

ESSENTIALS

VISITOR INFORMATION Dunkeld and Birnam Tourist Information Centre. ⊠ *The Cross* ☎ *01350/727674* ⊕ *www.visitscotland.com.*

Sights

Beatrix Potter Exhibition and Garden

GARDEN | FAMILY | The interactive exhibition, specifically designed for children, celebrates the life and work of this much-beloved children's writer who, for many years, spent her family holidays in the area. You're free to walk around the enchanting garden where you can peep into the homes of Peter Rabbit and Mrs. Tiggy-Winkle, her best-known characters. The visitors center has a well-stocked shop and a small café serving breakfast, lunch, and coffee and cake. The garden is a mile south of Dunkeld, in Birnam. ⊠ *Birnam Arts Centre, Station Road, Birnam* ☎ *01350/727674* ⊕ *www.birnamarts.com* ☑ *£3 exhibition, garden free.*

Birnam Wood

HISTORIC SITE | In Shakespeare's *Macbeth*, the future king meets three witches who prophesy his downfall "when Birnam Wood comes to Dunsinane." They were right. The trees of the once dense wood camouflaged the besieging armies approaching Macbeth's castle at Dunsinane. The Birnam Oak (now sustained by crutches) and the Birnam Sycamore are all that remain of the once great wood, though perhaps not as Macbeth knew it in the 11th century. ⊠ *The Birnam Oak, Birnam* ⊹ *Signposted opposite the Birnam Arts Centre.*

Hermitage

FOREST | On the outskirts of Dunkeld, the Hermitage is a 1½-mile woodland walk that follows the River Braan. In the 18th century, the dukes of Atholl constructed two follies (fantasy buildings) here, **Ossian's Cave** and the awesomely decorated **Ossian's Hall,** above a spectacular—and noisy—waterfall. (Ossian was a fictional Celtic poet invented by James MacPherson in the 18th century for an era fascinated by the "primitive" past.) You'll also be in the presence of Britain's tallest tree, a Douglas fir rising to 214 feet. ⊠ *Hermitage Car Park, Off A9* ⊹ *2 miles west of Dunkeld* ⊕ *www.nts.org.uk* ☑ *Free, parking lot £2.*

Loch of the Lowes

NATURE PRESERVE | FAMILY | From the lochside hides at this Scottish Wildlife Trust reserve near Dunkeld, you can observe the area's rich birdlife through a powerful telescope. The main attractions are always the ospreys, one of Scotland's conservation success stories, which can be observed between April and August. But there is much to see throughout the year, like the great crested grebe at feeding stations. The enthusiastic staff will willingly describe what is happening around the center. ⊠ *Off A923* ⊹ *About 2 miles northeast of Dunkeld off the A9* ☎ *01350/727337* ⊕ *scottishwildlifetrust. org.uk* ☑ *£4.50* ⊙ *Closed Mon.–Thurs. Nov.–Feb.*

Restaurants

The Taybank

$$ | BRITISH | This lovely spot overlooking the River Tay is a musical meeting place once owned by Scottish singer and composer Dougie MacLean. It serves unpretentious but plentiful traditional pub food, like haggis, Cullen skink (fish soup), and stovies (a beef-and-potato dish) in the friendly, rough-and-ready bar. **Known for:** traditional Scottish fare; excellent music; beer garden. $ *Average main: £15* ⊠ *Tay Terrace* ☎ *01350/727340* ⊕ *www. thetaybankdunkeld.com.*

Shopping

Jeremy Law of Scotland
SHOES/LUGGAGE/LEATHER GOODS | At this family-owned business you can purchase deerskin shoes and moccasins, as well as leather items including jackets, gloves, shoes, and wallets. ⊠ *City Hall, Atholl Street* ☎ *0800/146780* ⊕ *www.moccasin. co.uk.*

Pitlochry

15 miles north of Dunkeld.

In the late 19th century Pitlochry was an elegant Victorian spa town, famous for its mild microclimate and beautiful setting. Today it is a busy tourist town, with wall-to-wall gift shops, cafés, B&Bs, large hotels, and a huge golf course. The town itself is oddly nondescript, but it's a convenient base from which to explore the surrounding hills and valleys.

GETTING HERE AND AROUND
The main route through central Scotland, the A9, passes through Pitlochry, as does the main railway line from Glasgow/Edinburgh to Inverness. From here the B8019 connects to the B846 west to Rannoch Moor or south to Aberfeldy.

ESSENTIALS
VISITOR INFORMATION Pitlochry Visitor Information Centre. ⊠ *22 Atholl Rd.* ☎ *01796/472215* ⊕ *www. visitscotland.com/info/services/ pitlochry-icentre-p234421.*

Sights

Edradour Distillery
WINERY/DISTILLERY | If you have a whisky-tasting bent, visit Edradour Distillery, which claims to be the smallest single-malt distillery in Scotland (but then, so do others). There's a fun, informative tour of the distillery where you get to see how the whisky is made; you also get to savor a free dram at the end of the tour. ⊠ *Off A924* ⊹ *2½ miles east of Pitlochry* ☎ *01796/472095* ⊕ *www.edradour.com* ⊠ *Tours £12. There is a charge of £2 for using the toilet* ⊗ *Closed Sun. and Nov.–Mar.*

★ Loch Rannoch
BODY OF WATER | With its shoreline of birch trees framed by dark pines, Loch Rannoch is the quintessential Highland loch, stretching more than 9 miles from west to east. Fans of Robert Louis Stevenson (1850–94), especially of *Kidnapped* (1886), will not want to miss the last, lonely section of road. Stevenson describes the setting: "The mist rose and died away, and showed us that country lying as waste as the sea, only the moorfowl and the peewees crying upon it, and far over to the east a herd of deer, moving like dots." ⊠ *B846* ⊹ *20 miles west of Pitlochry.*

Pass of Killiecrankie Visitor Centre
INFO CENTER | Set among the oak woods and above a rocky river just north of Pitlochry, the Pass of Killiecrankie was the site of a famous battle won by the Jacobites in 1689. The battle was noted for the death of the central Jacobite leader, John Graham of Claverhouse (1649–89), also known as Bonnie Dundee, who was hit by a stray bullet. Another soldier escaped by leaping the river nearby at a point still known as "Soldier's Leap." After Dundee's death the rebellion petered out. The National Trust for Scotland's visitor center at Killiecrankie explains the significance of this battle, which was the first attempt to restore

the Stewart monarchy. ✉ *B8079* ⊹ *3 miles north of Pitlochry* ☎ *01796/473233* ⊕ *www.nts.org.uk* 🖅 *Free* ⊙ *Closed Nov.–Apr.*

Pitlochry Dam Visitor Visitor Centre and Fish Ladder

DAM | Seeming to float above the dam at Loch Faskally, the visitor center for the dam has a permanent exhibition that explains how hydroelectricity works. The fish ladder built in 1952 is still here, allowing salmon to make their journey upstream safely, leap by leap, to their spawning grounds. There is a café and gift shop. ✉ *Armoury Road* ⊹ *Off A924, ½ mile from town* ☎ *01796/484111* ⊕ *www.pitlochrydam.com* 🖅 *Free.*

 ## Restaurants

Fern Cottage Restaurant

$$ | **BRITISH** | The stone-built cottage set in pleasant surroundings reflects the cooking within, with its emphasis on local fish, game, and meat. Sharing the menu are Mediterranean, and especially Turkish, elements—tzatziki, kebabs, and lamb cooked in Turkish fashion. **Known for:** Turkish dishes; tea and coffee; pre-theater options. ⑤ *Average main: £18* ✉ *Ferry Road* ☎ *01796 /473840* ⊕ *www.ferncottagepitlochry.co.uk.*

Moulin Pub

$$ | **BRITISH** | At this traditional pub at the Moulin Hotel, you can eat in the pleasant dining room or at the lively bar, which has dark, wooden interiors and some stuffed animals on the walls. Expect standard Scottish fare in generous quantities, including venison, scallops, and mussels; local produce is favored and the menu is spiced with some humorous naming. **Known for:** Scottish cuisine; ales made on-site; choice of lively or quiet dining. ⑤ *Average main: £16* ✉ *11–30 Kirkmichael Rd.* ⊹ *Between Pitlochry and Edradour* ☎ *01796/472196* ⊕ *www. moulinhotel.co.uk.*

Two Sisters Restaurant

$$ | **BRITISH** | **FAMILY** | Just outside Pitlochry, this well-regarded and bright, airy restaurant is within East Haugh House, a country hotel in a turreted 17th-century stone house. Two Sisters serves mainly local produce in these charming surroundings, with an emphasis on Scottish fare. **Known for:** seafood and game; country-house setting; Sunday roast. ⑤ *Average main: £18* ✉ *East Haugh House, Off A924* ⊹ *1 mile south of Pitlochry* ☎ *01796/473121* ⊕ *www. easthaugh.co.uk.*

 ## Hotels

Claymore Guest House

$$ | **B&B/INN** | One of the large Victorian houses set back from the main road, this B&B is a quiet refuge with spacious, updated rooms with large windows. **Pros:** large, well-lit rooms with comfortable seating areas; dog-friendly; welcoming and attentive proprietors. **Cons:** no children allowed; slightly old-fashioned feel; no elevator. ⑤ *Rooms from: £126* ✉ *162 Atholl Rd.* ☎ *01796/472888* ⊕ *www.claymorehotel.com* ⇲ *10 rooms* ⑩ *Breakfast.*

★ Green Park Hotel

$$$ | **HOTEL** | Set among woods and on the shores of Loch Faskally, Green Park is a genuinely luxurious country-house hotel. **Pros:** great location; very attentive staff; country-house comfort. **Cons:** a slightly conservative feel; very popular, thus fills up far in advance; not as suitable for younger visitors. ⑤ *Rooms from: £248* ✉ *Clunie Bridge Road* ⊹ *5 mins north of Pitlochry center on A924* ☎ *01796/473248* ⊕ *www.thegreenpark. co.uk* ⇲ *51 rooms* ⑩ *All-inclusive.*

Killiecrankie Hotel

$$$ | **HOTEL** | A neat oasis, this hotel is set amid the wooded hills and streams of the Pass of Killiecrankie. **Pros:** lovely location; pleasant rooms; fine dining. **Cons:** books up fast; rate generally includes dinner (though it's good); not cheap. ⑤ *Rooms from: £300* ✉ *B8079, Killiecrankie* ✚ *3 miles north of Pitlochry* ☎ *01796/473220* ⊕ *www.killiecrankiehotel.co.uk* ☞ *10 rooms* ❙❁❙ *All-inclusive.*

Pitlochry Hydro Hotel
$ | HOTEL | FAMILY | A grand hotel in the best Victorian style, the Pitlochry Hydro is a 19th-century vision of a medieval castle on 50 acres with views of hills and valleys. **Pros:** lovely grounds; lots for kids to do; high comfort. **Cons:** old-fashioned feel; long, anonymous corridors; breakfast can get busy (get there early). ⑤ *Rooms from: £90* ✉ *A924* ☎ *01796/472400* ⊕ *www.coastandcountryhotels.com* ☞ *73 rooms* ❙❁❙ *Breakfast.*

Performing Arts

Pitlochry Festival Theatre
THEATER | The theater presents six plays each season, hosts Sunday concerts, and holds art exhibitions. It also has a café and restaurant overlooking the River Tummel. ✉ *Port Na Craig* ☎ *01796/484626* ⊕ *pitlochryfestivaltheatre.com.*

Activities

BUNGEE JUMPING
Highland Fling Bungee Jumping
FLYING/SKYDIVING/SOARING | Based at the National Trust's Visitor Centre at Killiecrankie, this newest addition to the local adventure-sports scene has proved very popular for some. The Killiecrankie Gorge, once famous for the historic Soldier's Leap, now offers a more dangerous jump—140 feet from the nearby Garry Bridge attached to an elastic rope, or bungee. Also on offer are organized rafting and canyoning trips. Activities should be booked in advance. *There are age and weight limits.* ✉ *Killiecrankie Visitor Centre, Off A94* ✚ *4 miles north of Pitlochry* ☎ *0345/366–5844* ⊕ *www.bungeejumpscotland.co.uk* ☞ *£79 per jump* ☞ *Closed Mon. and Tues. Nov.–Mar.*

GOLF
Blairgowrie Golf Club
GOLF | Well known to area golfers looking for a challenge, the Blairgowrie Golf Club's Rosemount Course is laid out on rolling land in the pine, birch, and fir woods, which bring a wild air to the scene. There are, however, wide fairways and at least some large greens. If Rosemount is hosting a tournament, you can play on Lansdowne, another 18-hole course, or Wee, a 9-hole course. ✉ *Golf Course Road, Blairgowrie* ☎ *01250/872622* ⊕ *www.theblairgowriegolfclub.co.uk* ☞ *Rosemount/Lansdowne, May–Sept. £95, Apr. and Oct. £70, Nov.–Mar. £25; Wee, May–Sept. £20, Apr. and Oct. £17.50, Nov.–Mar. £7.50* ⚐ *Rosemount: 18 holes, 6630 yards, par 72; Lansdowne: 18 holes, 6886 yards, par 72; Wee: 9 holes, 2327 yards, par 32.*

Pitlochry Golf Course
GOLF | A decent degree of stamina is needed for the first three holes at Pitlochry, where steep climbs are involved. The reward is magnificent Highland scenery. Despite its relatively short length, this beautiful course has more than its fair share of surprises. The course offers golf with food packages. ✉ *Golf Course Road* ☎ *01796/472792* ⊕ *www.pitlochrygolf.co.uk* ☞ *Apr.–Oct.: £42 weekdays, £50 weekends; Nov.–Mar. (restricted course) £10 weekdays, £20 weekends.* ⚐ *18 holes, 5681 yards, par 69.*

Blair Atholl

10 miles north of Pitlochry.

Located where the Tilt and Garry rivers flow together, this small town sits in the middle of the Grampian Mountains and is home to Blair Castle, one of Scotland's grandest of grand houses.

GETTING HERE AND AROUND
Popular Blair Castle is just off the A9 Pitlochry-to-Inverness road, beyond the village of Blair Atholl. The village has a

railway station that is on the main Inverness line.

Sights

★ Blair Castle

CASTLE/PALACE | Its setting among woodlands and gardens, together with its war-torn past, make Blair Castle one of Scotland's most highly rated sights. The turreted white castle was home to successive dukes of Atholl and their families, the Murrays, one of the most powerful in the land. During the Jacobite Rebellion of 1745, the loyalties of the Atholls were divided—a preserved piece of floor shows the marks of red-hot shot fired when the castle was under siege. In the end the supporters of the English king held off the rebels and were well rewarded for it. The dukes were allowed to retain a private army, the Atholl Highlanders. The castle entrance hall presents some of the dukes' collections of weapons, while a rich collection of furniture, china, and paintings occupies the family rooms. The grounds contain a 9-acre walled garden, an 18th-century folly, and a play area for children. ⊠ *Off B8079* ☎ *01796/481207* ⊕ *www.blair-castle.co.uk* ⊠ *Castle and gardens £13, grounds only £7.70* ⊘ *Closed Nov.–Mar.*

House of Bruar

SHOPPING CENTERS/MALLS | An upscale shopping complex, the House of Bruar has a heavy emphasis on traditional tweeds and cashmeres. A large supermarket sells local produce and food, and a restaurant serves breakfast and lunch. When you're done shopping, take a walk up the path that crosses Bruar Falls, behind the complex. The complex is also a popular stop for coach tours. ⊠ *Off A9* ✛ *3 miles west of Blair Castle* ☎ *01796/483236* ⊕ *www.houseofbruar.com*

Aberfeldy

15 miles southwest of Pitlochry, 25 miles southwest of Blair Castle.

The most dramatic thing about Aberfeldy is the high humpbacked bridge into the town, built by William Adam in 1733 and commissioned by General Wade, who marched through Scotland suppressing local resistance after the Jacobite Rebellion. The town itself is rather sleepy, but this is a popular base for exploring the region. There's also a whisky distillery and plenty of local golf courses.

GETTING HERE AND AROUND

To get here from Pitlochry, take the A9 and then the A827. You can also reach Aberfeldy from Dunkeld via the A9 and the A827. A longer but very pretty route is the A85 from Crieff, then through Killin on the A827. Aberfeldy is served by regular buses from Perth and Pitlochry.

ESSENTIALS

VISITOR INFORMATION Aberfeldy Tourist Information Centre. ⊠ *The Square* ☎ *01887/820276* ⊕ *www.visitscotland.com/aberfedy.*

Sights

Castle Menzies

CASTLE/PALACE | A 16th-century fortified tower house, Castle Menzies contains the **Clan Menzies Museum,** which displays many relics of the clan's history. The rooms have been carefully restored, including the bedroom where Bonnie Prince Charlie once took refuge. The castle stands west of Aberfeldy, on the opposite bank of the River Tay. A walled garden is nearby. *The castle has a tearoom that is open on some Saturdays and Sundays.* ⊠ *Aberfeldy Road, Weem* ✛ *Off the B846* ☎ *01887/820982* ⊕ *www.castlemenzies.org* ⊠ *£7* ⊘ *Closed Nov.–Mar.*

Dewar's Aberfeldy Distillery

WINERY/DISTILLERY | This established distillery offers tours that demonstrate how Aberfeldy single-malt whisky is made (with a tasting at the end, of course); audio guides and interactive screens add to the appeal. There's also a worthwhile Heritage Center and a pleasant restaurant. The basic tours are £9.50, but there are more expensive tours for whisky experts, including cask tastings. Dewar's also makes blended whiskies. ✉ *A827* ☎ *01887/822010* ⊕ *www.dewars.com* ⛟ *Basic tour £10.50; cask tasting tour £18* ⏱ *Closed Sun. Nov.–Mar.*

Glen Lyon

SCENIC DRIVE | One of central Scotland's most attractive glens, 34-mile-long Glen Lyon is also one of its longest. It has a rushing river, thick forests, and the typical big house hidden on private grounds. There's a dam at the head of the loch, a reminder that little of Scotland's scenic beauty is unadulterated. The winding road lends itself to an unrushed, leisurely drive, past the visitor center (⊕ *www.nts. org.uk*) at the access to Ben Lawers, a popular climb. ✉ *A827* ✛ *15 miles west of Aberfeldy* ⛟ *Free.*

Scottish Crannog Centre

ARCHAEOLOGICAL SITE | **FAMILY** | Here's your chance to travel back 2,500 years to a time when this region's inhabitants lived in circular homesteads known as crannogs. Standing on stilts in the middle of lochs, these dwellings were approachable only by narrow bridges that could be easily defended from intruders. This center reveals the strength of these communal homes that were built entirely of wood, right down to the nails. Visits are by guided tour, beginning with an interesting exhibit on construction methods, followed by some fun with Neolithic lathes and tips on lighting a fire without matches. You can also reserve ahead to paddle a dugout canoe onto beautiful Loch Tay. It has limited hours of operation in November, February, and March. ✉ *Off A827* ✛ *6 miles west of Aberfeldy* ☎ *01887/830583* ⊕ *www.crannog.co.uk* ⛟ *£10* ⏱ *Closed Dec. and Jan.*

Restaurants

Habitat Cafe

$ | **CAFÉ** | This café with handmade wooden tables and windows overlooking the main town square offers excellent coffee and tea, sandwiches and burgers, platters, and soup in the central square of Aberfeldy. Habitat takes great pride in its coffee making and has awards to prove it; it works closely with sustainable farmers. **Known for:** double burgers; excellent coffee; lunch platters. ⓢ *Average main: £10* ✉ *The Square* ☎ *01877/822944* ⊕ *www.habitatcafe.co.uk* ⏱ *No dinner.*

Shopping

John A. Lacey

SPECIALTY STORES | Carver John Lacey has worked at this house on the road between Killin and Aberfeldy since 1984. Its front room is a treasure trove of horn carving, from a full-masted galleon to knives in their sheaths. He also has deerskins for sale. Lacey says the egg spoons are the most popular items. ✉ *A827* ✛ *15 miles west of Aberfeldy on north side of Loch Tay* ☎ *01567/820561* ⊕ *www. horncarver.co.uk.*

The Watermill

BOOKS/STATIONERY | At this converted mill you can visit an excellent independent bookshop with a large children's section. The mill also has a gallery with frequently changing exhibitions, a home-goods store (called Homer), and a café. ✉ *Mill Street* ☎ *01887/822896* ⊕ *www.aberfeldywatermill.com.*

Activities

Highland Safaris

TOUR—SPORTS | **FAMILY** | This center just outside Aberfeldy offers a full range of outdoor activities, from encounters with the red deer in the neighboring field to off-road driving, fishing, bike rental, and "safaris" into the nearby hills in Land Rovers or on foot. Activities come in a range of prices and lengths, or you can create your own experience. There is a shop and café on the site. ⊠ *Aberfeldy* ✛ *2½ miles west of Aberfeldy on B846* ☎ *01887/820071* ⊕ *www.highlandsafaris. net* 🖾 *Mountain Safari £45.*

Crieff

24 miles south of Aberfeldy

Crieff retains the prosperous air of its Victorian heyday as a place to "take the waters." Its central square, where local farmers may once have gathered to trade, is still a lively focus. For a different view of the town, you could climb Knock Hill, which is signposted from the town center.

GETTING HERE AND AROUND
Crieff once prospered because of the arrival of the railway. No station exits here today, but there are regular buses from Stirling and Glasgow. By car take the A85 from Perth, or the A9 from Stirling, turning onto the A822 after Dunblane. From Aberfeldy take the A826 and A822 for a direct route, or explore the longer, scenic A827/A85 route.

ESSENTIALS
VISITOR INFORMATION Crieff Visitor Information Centre. ⊠ *Muthill Road* ☎ *01764/654065* ⊕ *www.crieff.co.uk.*

Sights

★ Drummond Castle Gardens
GARDEN | These formal Victorian gardens, regarded as some of the finest of their kind in Europe, celebrate family and Scottish heraldry. Combining the formal French and more relaxed Italian styles, the flower beds are planted and trimmed in the shapes of various heraldic symbols, such as a lion rampant and a checkerboard, associated with the coat of arms of the family that owns the castle. The gardens were on display in the filming of *Outlander*. ⊠ *Off A822* ✛ *6 miles southwest of Crieff* ☎ *01764/681433* ⊕ *www.drummond-castlegardens.co.uk* 🖾 *£6* ⊙ *Closed Nov.–Apr.*

Glenturret Distillery
WINERY/DISTILLERY | To discover the delights of whisky distilling, sign up for the Distillery Tour at the Glenturret Distillery, which claims to be Scotland's oldest. Here you learn how whisky is made and why time, water, soil, and air are so important to the taste. A guide takes you through the distillery and to the bar where you can have a glass of Glenturret's famous single malt and try your skill at "nosing." You might cap your tour with lunch in the Wild Thyme café and restaurant. Signs lead to the distillery on the west side of the town. ⊠ *The Hosh, Comrie Road* ☎ *01764/656565* ⊕ *www. thefamousgrouseexperience.com* 🖾 *Tour £10; Fudge Tour £25.*

Hotels

Crieff Hydro
$$$ | HOTEL | FAMILY | One of Scotland's great Victorian hydropathy centers (treating illnesses using water), this grand resort hotel on 900 acres has been owned by the same family for more than 100 years. **Pros:** extensive grounds; variety of activities; spa. **Cons:** some rooms are rather dull; some activities are quite expensive; can feel a little impersonal. ⑤ *Rooms from: £209* ⊠ *Off A85* ☎ *01764/655555* ⊕ *www.crieffhydro.com* 🖙 *220 rooms* ¶⦿¶ *Breakfast.*

Shopping

Caithness Glass at Crieff Visitor Centre
CERAMICS/GLASSWARE | Crieff was once best known for its glass. You can watch

Some of Scotland's most impressive formal gardens, the Drummond Castle Gardens were first laid-out in the 1630s.

the glassblowing process (weekdays only) and then browse the sales gallery here for paperweights and other gift items. There's also a garden center and a restaurant. ⊠ *Muthill Road* ☎ *01764/654014* ⊕ *www.crieff.co.uk*.

Auchterarder

11 miles southeast of Crieff.

Famous for the Gleneagles Hotel (including its restaurant by Andrew Fairlie) and nearby golf courses, Auchterarder also has a flock of tiny antiques shops to amuse Gleneagles's golf widows and widowers.

GETTING HERE AND AROUND
Gleneagles station is on the main Inverness line, while the A9 gives direct access to Gleneagles and Auchterarder via the A823.

ESSENTIALS
VISITOR INFORMATION **Auchterarder Visitor Information Centre.** ⊠ *90 High St.* ☎ *01764/663450* ⊕ *www. visitscotland.com/info/towns-villages/ auchterarder-p244491*.

Restaurants

★ Andrew Fairlie at Gleneagles
$$$$ | BRITISH | Chef Andrew Fairlie established his restaurant in the Gleneagles Hotel in 2001, winning two Michelin stars for his elegant and restrained dishes. It is universally agreed that Fairlie set in motion a food revolution that changed Scottish cooking. **Known for:** two Michelin stars; cuisine marrying France and Scotland; a commitment to local produce. Ⓢ *Average main: £110* ⊠ *Gleneagles Hotel, Off A823, Auchterarder* ☎ *01764/694267* ⊕ *www.andrewfairlie. co.uk* ⊗ *Closed Sun.*

Hotels

★ Gleneagles Hotel

$$$$ | **HOTEL** | One of Britain's most famous hotels, Gleneagles is the very essence of modern grandeur, a vast palace that stands hidden in breathtaking countryside amid its world-famous golf courses. **Pros:** luxurious rooms; famous Andrew Fairlie restaurant; the three courses are a golfer's paradise. **Cons:** quite conservative decor; restaurants get very crowded; nongolfers may feel out of place. ⑤ *Rooms from: £595* ✉ *Off A823* ☎ *01764/662231* ⊕ *www.gleneagles.com* ⤵ *258 rooms* ⥄ *Free breakfast.*

 Activities

GOLF

★ Gleneagles

GOLF | Its superb courses have made Gleneagles a part of golfing history. The 18 holes of the King's Course, designed by James Braid in 1919, have quirky names, such as the Warslin' Lea (Wrestling Ground)—the tough 17th hole that many golfers have grappled with. The Queen's Course mixes varied terrain, including woods and moors. Jack Nicklaus designed the PGA Centenary Course (host of the 2014 Ryder Cup), which sweeps into the Ochil Hills and has views of the Grampians. The 9-hole Wee Course provides challenges for beginners and pros. Gleneagles is also home to the PGA National Academy, a good place to improve your skills. ✉ *A823* ☎ *01764/662231* ⊕ *www.gleneagles. com* ⛳ *King's, Queen's, and PGA Centenary courses: May £150, June £180, July–Sept. 15 £220, Sept. 16–30 £250, Oct.1–15 £150, Oct.16–30 £99, Nov.– Mar. £80, Apr. £90* ⛳ *King's: 18 holes, 6790 yards, par 71; Queen's: 18 holes, 6790 yards, par 68; PGA Centenary: 18 holes, 6815 yards, par 72; Wee Course: 9 holes, 1418 yards, par 27.*

Chapter 8

ABERDEEN AND THE NORTHEAST

8

Updated by
Robin Gauldie

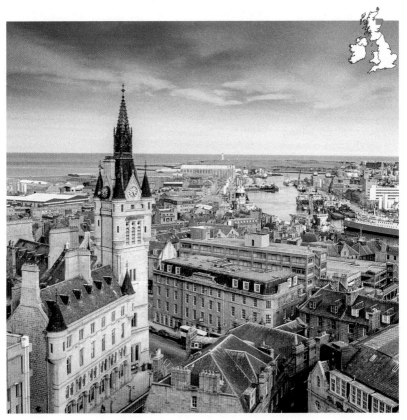

⊙ Sights	🍴 Restaurants	🛏 Hotels	🛍 Shopping	♥ Nightlife
★★★☆☆	★★★☆☆	★★☆☆☆	★☆☆☆☆	★★☆☆☆

WELCOME TO ABERDEEN AND THE NORTHEAST

TOP REASONS TO GO

★ **Castles:** With more than 75 castles, some Victorian and others dating back to the 13th century, this area has everything from ravaged ruins like Dunnottar to opulent Fyvie Castle.

★ **Distilleries:** The valley of the River Spey is famous for its single-malt distilleries, including those connected by the signposted Malt Whisky Trail.

★ **Seaside cities and towns:** The fishing industry may be in decline, but the big-city port of Aberdeen and the colorful smaller fishing towns of Stonehaven and Cullen in the northeast are great (and very different) places to soak up the seagoing atmosphere—and some seafood.

★ **Walking:** There are all types of walking for all kinds of walkers, from the bracing but spectacular inclines of the Grampian Hills to the wooded gardens and grounds of Balmoral and Haddo House.

★ **Golf:** The northeast has more than 50 golf clubs, some of which have championship courses.

Aberdeen, on the North Sea in the eastern part of the region, is Scotland's third-largest city; many people start a trip here. Once you have spent time in the city, you may be inclined to venture west into rural Deeside, with its royal connections and looming mountain backdrop. To the north of Deeside is Castle Country, with many ancient fortresses. Speyside and the Whisky Trail lie at the western edge of the region and are equally accessible from Inverness. From Speyside you might travel back east along the pristine coastline at Scotland's northeastern tip.

1 Aberdeen. The gateway to the northeast.

2 Stonehaven. A seaside town with an iconic castle nearby.

3 Banchory. A popular stop on the way to Deeside.

4 Ballater. A handsome riverside town with royal connections.

5 Braemar. Home of the original Highland Games.

6 Corgarff Castle. A lodge that became a redcoat garrison.

7 Alford. An unassuming village next to mighty Castle Fraser.

8 Dufftown. Speyside's whisky capital.

9 Craigellachie. An angler's delight located beside the River Spey.

10 Aberlour. A charming small town surrounded by distilleries.

11 Elgin. A seaside town with a splendid ruined cathedral.

12 Fochabers. A charming market town.

13 Cullen. Harbor village famed for seafood and white sands.

14 Banff. A fishing haven surrounded by Georgian houses.

15 Fyvie Castle. Grand Edwardian retreat with a superb art collection.

16 Ellon. A pretty suburb with magnificent gardens.

Here in this granite shoulder of Grampian, are some of Scotland's most enduring travel icons: Royal Deeside, the countryside that Queen Victoria made her own; the Castle Country route, where fortresses stand hard against the hills; and the Malt Whisky Trail, where peaty streams embrace the country's greatest concentration of distilleries.

The region's gateway is the city of Aberdeen. Once a prosperous merchant port, it became a boomtown in the 1970s with the discovery of oil beneath the North Sea, but as oil and gas reserves dwindle, the city is looking in new directions for its wealth.

More than 125 miles north of the central belt of Glasgow and Edinburgh, Aberdeen has historically been a fairly autonomous place. Even now it's perceived by many U.K. inhabitants as lying almost out of reach in the northeast. In reality it's a 90-minute flight from London or a little more than two hours by car from Edinburgh. Its 18th- and early-19th-century city center amply rewards exploration. Yet even if this popular base for travelers vanished from the map, an extensive portion of the northeast would still remain at the top of many travelers' wish lists.

Balmoral, the Scottish baronial–style house built for Queen Victoria as a retreat, is merely the most famous castle in the area, and certainly not the oldest. There are so many others that in one part of the region a Castle Trail has been established. In later structures, such as Castle Fraser, you can trace the changing styles and tastes of each of their owners over the centuries. Grand mansions such as 18th-century Haddo House, with its symmetrical facade and elegant interior, surrender any defensive role entirely.

A trail leading to a more ephemeral kind of pleasure can be found south of Elgin and Banff, where the glens embrace Scotland's greatest concentration of malt-whisky distilleries. With so many in Morayshire, where the distilling is centered on the valley of the River Spey and its tributaries, there's now a Malt Whisky Trail. Follow it, and visit other distilleries as well, to experience a surprising wealth of flavors.

The northeast's chief topographical attraction lies in the gradual transition from high mountain plateau—by a series of gentle steps through hill, forest, and farmland—to the Moray Firth and North Sea coast, where the word *unadulterated* is redefined. Here you'll find some of the United Kingdom's most perfect wild shorelines, both sandy and sheer cliff, and breezy fishing villages like Cullen on the Banffshire coast and Stonehaven, south of Aberdeen. The Grampian Mountains, to the west, contain some of the highest ground in the nation, in the area of the Cairngorms.

MAJOR REGIONS

Aberdeen. Family connections or Royal Deeside often take travelers to this part of Scotland, but many are surprised by how grand and rich in history Aberdeen is. The august granite-turreted buildings and rose-lined roads make this a surprisingly pleasant city to explore; don't miss Old Aberdeen in particular.

Royal Deeside and Castle Country. Deeside, the valley running west from Aberdeen down which the River Dee flows, earned its "royal" appellation when Prince Albert designed Balmoral Castle for Queen Victoria, and so began the royal family's love affair with Deeside—and Deeside's love affair with it. To this day, where royalty goes, lesser aristocracy and freshly minted millionaires follow. Many still aspire to own a grand shooting estate in Deeside, and you may appreciate this yearning when you see the piney hills, purple moors, and blue river intermingling. As you travel deeper into the Grampian Mountains, Royal Deeside's gradual scenic change adds a growing sense of excitement. This area has long been the retreat or the fortress of distinguished families, as the clutter of castles throughout the region shows. There are castles along the Dee as well as to the north in Castle Country, a region that illustrates the gradual geological change in the northeast: uplands lapped by a tide of farms. All the Donside and Deeside castles are picturesquely sited, with most fitted out with tall, slender turrets, winding stairs, and crooked chambers that epitomize Scottish baronial style. All have tales of ghosts and bloodshed, siege and torture. Many were tidied up and "domesticated" during the 19th century. Although best toured by car, much of this area is accessible either by public transportation or on tours from Aberdeen. The majesty of the countryside also guarantees a superlative stop for everyone interested in history and romance.

The Northeast and the Malt Whisky Trail. North of Deeside another popular area of this region lies inland, toward Speyside—the valley, or strath, of the River Spey—famed for its whisky distilleries, some of which it promotes in another signposted trail. Distilling Scotch is not an intrinsically spectacular process. It involves pure water, malted barley, and sometimes peat smoke, then a lot of bubbling and fermentation, all of which cause a number of odd smells. The result is a prestigious product with a fascinating range of flavors that you may either enjoy immensely or not at all. Unique in their architecture, their ingredients, and the end product, the distilleries of Speyside are keen to share with you their passion for "the water of life." This region also has rolling hills and, to the north, the beautiful, wild coastline of the North Sea. Instead of closely following the Malt Whisky Trail, dip into it and blend visits to distilleries with some other aspects of the county of Moray, particularly its coastline. Whisky notwithstanding, Moray's scenic qualities, low rainfall, and other reassuring weather statistics are worth remembering. You can also sample the northeastern seaboard, including some of the best but least-known coastal scenery in Scotland.

Planning

When to Go

May and June are probably the loveliest times to visit, but many travelers arrive from late spring to early fall. The National Trust for Scotland tends to close its properties in winter, so many of the northeast's castles are not open for off-season travel, though you can always see them from the outside. Many distilleries are open much of the year, but some close during winter months, so check before visiting.

Planning Your Time

How you allocate your time may depend on your special interests—castles or whisky, for example. But even if you can manage only a morning or an afternoon, do not miss a walk around the granite streets of Old Aberdeen, and take in St. Nicholas Kirk and a pint in the Prince of Wales pub. A trip southward to the fishing town of Stonehaven and the breathtaking cliff-top fortress of Dunnottar makes a rewarding afternoon. Royal Deeside, with a good sprinkling of castles and grandeur, needs a good two days; even this might be tight for those who want to lap up every moment of majesty at Balmoral, Crathes, Fraser, and Fyvie, the best of the bunch. A visit to malt-whisky country should include tours of Glenfiddich, Glenfarclas, Glenlivet, and Glen Grant distilleries, and although it's not technically a maker of malt whisky, Strathisla. Real enthusiasts should allot two days for the distilleries, and they shouldn't pass up a visit to Speyside Cooperage, one of the few remaining cooperages in Scotland. Cullen and Duff House gallery in Banff, on the coast, can be done in a day before returning to Aberdeen.

Getting Here and Around

AIR

The city is easy to reach from other parts of the United Kingdom as well as Europe. British Airways, EasyJet, Loganair, and Ryanair are some of the airlines with service to other parts of Britain. Aberdeen Airport—serving both international and domestic flights—is in Dyce, 7 miles west of the city center on the A96 (Inverness). The drive to the center of Aberdeen is easy via the A96 (which can be busy during rush hour).

CONTACTS Aberdeen Airport. ⊠ *Dyce Dr., Dyce* ☎ *0344/481–6666* ⊕ *www.aberdeenairport.com.*

BOAT AND FERRY

Northlink Ferries has service between Aberdeen, Lerwick (Shetland), and Kirkwall (Orkney).

CONTACTS Northlink Ferries. ⊠ *Jamieson's Quay, Aberdeen* ☎ *0845/600–0449* ⊕ *www.northlinkferries.co.uk.*

BUS

Long-distance buses run to Aberdeen from most parts of Scotland, England, and Wales. Contact Megabus, National Express, and Scottish Citylink for bus connections with English and Scottish towns. There's a network of local buses throughout the northeast run by Stagecoach, but they can take a long time and connections are not always well timed.

CONTACTS Megabus. ☎ *0900/160–0900* ⊕ *uk.megabus.com.* **National Express.** ☎ *08717/818181* ⊕ *www.nationalexpress.com.* **Scottish Citylink.** ☎ *0871/266–3333* ⊕ *www.citylink.co.uk.* **Traveline.** ☎ *0871/200–2233* ⊕ *www.travelinescotland.com.*

CAR

A car is the best way to see the northeast. If you are coming from the south, take the A90, continuing on from the M90 (from Edinburgh) or the M9/A9 (from Glasgow), which both stop at Perth. The coastal route, the A92, is a more leisurely alternative, with its interesting resorts and fishing villages. The most scenic route, however, is the A93 from Perth, north to Blairgowrie and into Glen Shee. The A93 then goes over the Cairnwell Pass, the highest main road in the United Kingdom. This route isn't recommended in winter, when snow can make driving difficult.

Around the northeast roads can be busy, with speeding and erratic driving a problem on the main A roads.

TRAIN

You can reach Aberdeen directly from Edinburgh (2½ hours), Inverness (2½ hours), and Glasgow (3 hours). ScotRail timetables have full details. There are also London–Aberdeen routes that go through Edinburgh and the east-coast main line connecting Aberdeen to all corners of the United Kingdom.

CONTACTS ScotRail. ⊠ *Aberdeen railway station, Guild St., Aberdeen* ☎ *0344/811–0141* ⊕ *www.scotrail.co.uk.*

Restaurants

As in much of the rest of Scotland, Aberdeen and the northeast have rediscovered the quality and versatility of the local produce. Juicy Aberdeen Angus steaks, lean lamb, and humanely reared pork appear on local menus, and there's a great choice of locally sourced seafood, from old-school fish-and-chips to dishes that fuse Mediterranean, Asian, and Latin influence. Traditional favorites like *Cullen skink* (a creamy smoked-fish soup) are on many menus.

Hotels

The northeast has some splendid country hotels with log fires and old Victorian furnishings, where you can also be sure of eating well. Many hotels in Aberdeen are in older buildings that have a baronial feel. The trend for serviced apartments has caught on here, with some extremely modish and good-value options for those who want a bit more privacy. This trend is now extending into Deeside, where it's been notoriously difficult to find good accommodations beyond some country-house hotels, even though it's a popular tourist spot.

Restaurant and hotel reviews have been shortened. For full information, visit Fodors.com. Restaurant prices are the average cost of a main course at dinner or, if dinner is not served, at lunch. Hotel prices are the lowest cost of a standard double room in high season, including 20% V.A.T.

WHAT IT COSTS In Pounds

	$	$$	$$$	$$$$
RESTAURANTS				
	under £15	£15–£19	£20–£25	over £25
HOTELS				
	under £125	£125–£200	£201–£300	over £300

Visitor Information

The tourist information center in Aberdeen supplies information on all of Scotland's northeast. There are also year-round tourist information offices in Braemar and Elgin. In summer, also look for tourist information centers in Alford, Ballater, Banchory, Braemar, Elgin, and Stonehaven.

CONTACT Aberdeen Visitor Information Centre. ⊠ *23 Union St., Aberdeen* ☎ *01224/269180* ⊕ *www.visitscotland.com, www.visitabdn.com.*

Aberdeen

As a gateway to Royal Deeside and the Malt Whisky Trail, Aberdeen attracts visitors, though many are eager to get out into the countryside. Today, though, the city's unique history is finally being recognized as more impressive than many Scots had previously realized, and Aberdeen is being rediscovered. Distinctive architecture, some fine museums, universities, and good restaurants, nightlife, and shopping add to the appeal of Scotland's third-largest city (population 217,000). Union Street is the heart of the city, but take time to explore the university and the pretty streets of Old Aberdeen.

In the 18th century local granite quarrying produced a durable silver stone that would be used boldly in the glittering blocks, spires, columns, and parapets of

Victorian-era Aberdonian structures. The city remains one of the United Kingdom's most distinctive, although some would say it depends on the weather and the brightness of the day. The mica chips embedded in the rock look like a million mirrors in the sunshine. In rain (and there is a fair amount of driving rain from the North Sea) and heavy clouds, however, their sparkle is snuffed out.

The city lies between the Dee and Don rivers, with a working harbor that has access to the sea; it has been a major fishing port and is the main commercial port in northern Scotland. The North Sea has always been important to Aberdeen. In the 1850s the city was famed for its sleek, fast clippers that sailed to India for cargoes of tea. In the 1970s exploitation of newly discovered offshore oil and gas turned Aberdeen into a world energy capital. As reserves dwindle and the oil industry winds down, the city is seeking new ways to diversify its economy.

GETTING HERE AND AROUND

AIR

Stagecoach Bluebird Jet Service 727 operates between the airport terminal in Dyce and Union Square in the center of Aberdeen. Buses (£3.40) run frequently at peak times, less often at midday and in the evening; the journey time is approximately 40 minutes.

Dyce is on ScotRail's Inverness–Aberdeen route. The rail station is a short taxi ride from the terminal building (£12). Trains run approximately every two hours.

BUS

First Aberdeen has easy and reliable service within the city of Aberdeen. Timetables are available from the tourist information center in Union Street.

CONTACTS First Aberdeen.
☎ 0345/6460707 ⊕ www.firstgroup.com.

CAR

Aberdeen is a compact city with good signage. Its center is Union Street, the main east–west thoroughfare, which tends to get crowded with traffic. Anderson Drive is an efficient ring road on the city's west side; be extra careful on its many traffic circles. It's best to leave your car in one of the parking garages (arrive early to get a space) and walk around, or use the convenient park-and-ride stop at the Bridge of Don, north of the city. Street maps are available from the tourist information center, newsstands, and booksellers.

TAXI

You can find taxi stands throughout the center of Aberdeen: at the railway station and at Back Wynd, Chapel Street, Dee Street, and Hadden Street. The taxis have yellow plates, meters, and might be saloon cars (sedans) or black cabs. They are great ways to travel between neighborhoods.

TRAIN TRAVEL

Aberdeen has good ScotRail service.

Sights

Aberdeen centers on Union Street, with its many fine survivors of the Victorian and Edwardian streetscape. Marischal College, dating from the late 16th century, is a city-center landmark, and has many grand buildings that are worth exploring.

Very much a separate area of the city, Old Aberdeen is north of the modern center, clustered around St. Machar's Cathedral and the many fine buildings of the University of Aberdeen. Take a stroll on College Bounds; handsome 18th- and 19th-century houses line this cobbled street in the oldest part of the city.

Aberdeen Art Gallery

MUSEUM | Northeast Scotland's most important art gallery reopened in November 2019 with the completion of its much-delayed renovation and expansion, giving it seven new exhibition spaces so that over 1,000 of its treasures can be displayed. There's also a penthouse gallery hosting three touring exhibitions each year. The collection contains excellent paintings, prints, drawings, sculptures, porcelain, costumes, and more, from 18th-century art to major contemporary British works by Lucien Freud and Henry Moore. Scottish artists are well represented in the permanent collection and special exhibits. Local stone has been used in the interior walls, pillars, and the central fountain, all designed by the acclaimed British sculptor Barbara Hepworth. ⊠ Schoolhill ☎ 030000/200293 ⊕ www.aagm.co.uk ⊠ Free.

★ Aberdeen Maritime Museum

MUSEUM | FAMILY | This excellent museum, which incorporates the 1593 Provost Ross's House, tells the story of the city's relationship with the sea, from early inshore fisheries to tea clippers and the North Sea oil boom. The information-rich exhibits include the bridge of a fishing boat and the cabins of a clipper, in addition to models, paintings, and equipment associated with the fishing, shipbuilding, and oil and gas industries. The Gateway to the North gallery on the top floor is a lively introduction to the archaeology of the region, with exhibits spanning the years 1136–1660. ⊠ Ship Row ☎ 01224/337700 ⊕ www.aagm. co.uk ⊠ Free ۝ Closed Mon.

Brig o'Balgownie

BRIDGE/TUNNEL | Until 1827, the only northern route out of Aberdeen was over the River Don on this single-arch bridge. It dates from 1314 and is thought to have been built by Richard Cementarius, Aberdeen's first provost. ⊠ Seaton Park.

Cruickshank Botanic Garden

GARDEN | Built on land bequeathed by Miss Anne Cruickshank in memory of her beloved brother, Alexander, the 11-acre Cruickshank Botanic Garden at the heart

of Old Aberdeen has a peaceful water garden and lush greens ideal for lounging—when the weather allows—and beautifully tended subtropical and alpine collections. Botanical tours are available. ⊠ St. Machar Dr., at the Chanonry ☎ 01224/272704 ⊕ www.abdn.ac.uk/botanic-garden ⊠ Free.

Duthie Park

CITY PARK | FAMILY | These 44 acres were donated to the people of Aberdeen by a Miss Elizabeth Crombie Duthie in 1880. An excellent place to while away an afternoon, whether it be the sunniest or foulest day, it has a boating pond, a bandstand, playgrounds, and a popular conservatory café selling creamy ice cream. In the beautifully tended Winter Gardens (tropical and arid conservatories), you'll find fish ponds and free-flying birds among the luxuriant foliage and flowers. The park borders Aberdeen's other river, the Dee. ⊠ Polmuir Rd. ✛ About 1 mile south of city center ⊠ Free.

King's College

BUILDING | Founded in 1494, King's College is now part of the University of Aberdeen. Its **chapel,** built around 1500, has an unmistakable flying (or crown) spire. That it has survived at all was because of the zeal of the principal, who defended his church against the destructive fanaticism that swept through Scotland during the Reformation, when the building was less than a century old. Today the renovated chapel plays an important role in university life. Don't miss the tall oak screen that separates the nave from the choir, the ribbed wooden ceiling, and the stalls, as these constitute the finest medieval wood carvings found anywhere in Scotland. ⊠ 25 High St. ☎ 01224/272137 ⊕ www.abdn. ac.uk ۝ Closed weekends.

King's Museum, Old Aberdeen Townhouse

COLLEGE | Across from the archway leading to King's College Chapel, this plain but handsome Georgian building was the center of all trading activity in

Aberdeen

KEY
1 *Exploring Sights*
1 *Restaurants*
1 *Quick Bites*
1 *Hotels*

Perhaps Aberdeen's best museum, the Aberdeen Maritime Museum explores the city's history with the sea, from shipbuilding to fishing.

the city before it became a grammar school, a Masonic lodge, and then a library. Now housing the university's museum, it hosts constantly changing exhibitions. It presents some impressive and often strange curiosities from the university's collection, from prehistoric flints to a tiger's penis. ⊠ *17 High St.* ☎ *01224/274300* ⊕ *www.abdn.ac.uk/ kingsmuseum* ▣ *Free* ⊙ *Closed Sun. and Mon.*

Mariscal College
BUILDING | Founded in 1593 by the Earl Mariscal (the keeper of the king's mares), Mariscal College was a Protestant alternative to the Catholic King's College in Old Aberdeen. The two joined to form the University of Aberdeen in 1860. The spectacularly ornate work of the main university building is set off by the gilded flags, and this turn-of-the-20th-century creation is still one of the world's largest granite buildings. ⊠ *Broad St.*

Mercat Cross
LOCAL INTEREST | Built in 1686 and restored in 1820, the Mercat Cross

(the name stems from "marketplace"), always the symbolic center of a Scottish medieval burgh, stands just beyond King Street. Along its parapet are 12 portrait panels of the Stewart monarchs. ⊠ *Justice and Mariscal Sts.*

Rosemount Viaduct
LOCAL INTEREST | Three silvery, handsome buildings on this bridge are collectively known by all Aberdonians as Education, Salvation, and Damnation. The **Central Library** and **St. Mark's Church** date from the last decade of the 19th century, and **His Majesty's Theatre** (1904–08) has been restored inside to its full Edwardian splendor. If you're taking photographs, you can choose an angle that includes the statue of Scotland's first freedom fighter, Sir William Wallace (1270–1305), in the foreground pointing majestically to Damnation. ⊠ *Aberdeen.*

★ St. Machar's Cathedral
RELIGIOUS SITE | It's said that St. Machar was sent by St. Columba to build a church on a grassy platform near the sea, where a river flowed in the shape of

a shepherd's crook. This beautiful spot, now the still-beating heart of Old Aberdeen, fits the bill. Although the cathedral was founded in AD 580, most of the existing building dates from the 15th and 16th centuries. Built as a fortified kirk, its twin towers and thick walls give it a sturdy standing. The former can be seen up close by climbing the spiral staircases to the upper floors, which also affords an admirable view of the "body of the kirk" inside and graveyard outside. It lost its status as a cathedral during the Reformation and has since been part of the Church of Scotland. The stained-glass windows depicting the martyrdom of the saints and handsome heraldic ceiling are worth noting. ✉ *Chanonry* ☎ *01224/485988* ⊕ *www.stmachar.com.*

St. Nicholas Kirk

RELIGIOUS SITE | The original burgh church, the Mither Kirk, as this edifice is known, is not within the bounds of the early town settlement; that was to the east, near the end of present-day Union Street. During the 12th century the port of Aberdeen flourished, and there wasn't room for the church within the settlement. Its earliest features are its pillars—supporting a tower built much later—and its clerestory windows: both date from the 12th century. The East Kirk is closed for renovation work, which has been extended due to the discovery of numerous skeletons, mainly children, that date back to the 12th century; the post-excavation work can be viewed from a large window in the Drum's Aisle. In the chapel, look for Shona McInnes's stained-glass window commemorating the victims of the 1989 Piper Alpha oil-rig disaster and a glass case containing two books. One lists the names of all those who've lost their lives in the pursuit of oil exploration in the North Sea; the second is empty, a testament to the many "unknown" workers whose deaths were never officially recorded. ✉ *Union St.* ☎ *01224/643494* ⊕ *www.kirk-of-st-nicholas.org.uk* ✉ *Free, but donations welcome.*

Tolbooth Museum

MUSEUM | **FAMILY** | The city was governed from this 17th-century building, which was also the burgh court and jail, for 200 years. Now a museum of crime and punishment, its highly entertaining tour guides take you around its cells and dungeons and bring life and death to the various instruments of torture—including the "Maiden," a decapitating machine—making it a must-see for older kids. ✉ *Castle St.* ☎ *01224/621167* ⊕ *www. aagm.co.uk* ✉ *Free.*

Union Street

NEIGHBORHOOD | This great thoroughfare is to Aberdeen what Princes Street is to Edinburgh: the central pivot of the city plan and the product of a wave of enthusiasm to rebuild the city in a contemporary style in the early 19th century. ✉ *Aberdeen.*

Union Terrace

NEIGHBORHOOD | In the 19th-century development of Union Terrace stands a statue of Robert Burns (1759–96) addressing a daisy. Behind Burns are the Union Terrace Gardens. Proposals for a £140 million "transformation" of this much-loved public green space were dropped after a public outcry in 2013, but in 2017 the city council approved a scaled-down £25.7 million development that aims to improve access to the gardens and make it a more attractive space for corporate events. Work is not expected to be complete before summer 2021. ✉ *Aberdeen.*

🍴 Restaurants

Ashvale

$ | **BRITISH** | **FAMILY** | Ask anyone about this long-established place and the response will probably be overwhelmingly positive. Fish-and-chips is the specialty, and the secret-recipe batter is now the stuff of legend. **Known for:** "The Whale," a giant 1-pound haddock fillet; tender locallysourced steaks; free meals for those under age five. ⓢ *Average* *main: £13* ✉ *42–48 Great Western Rd.* ☎ *01224/575842* ⊕ *theashvale.co.uk.*

Café 52

$ | **MODERN BRITISH** | This artsy café-restaurant has an innovative menu, an atmospheric dining room with open kitchen, and covered outdoor seating. The menu features veggie options such as mushroom falafel, grilled halloumi with crushed walnuts, and barley fricassee, as well as lots of imaginative Middle Eastern-fusion meat and seafood choices. **Known for:** marinated beef with chermoula; Moroccan potatoes with kale, fennel, coconut, and candied orange; all local produce. ⑤ *Average main: £13* ✉ *52 The Green* ☎ *01224/590094* ⊕ *www. cafe52onthegreen.co.uk* ◷ *No dinner Sun.*

Foodstory

$ | **VEGETARIAN** | **FAMILY** | A bright, breezy vegetarian and vegan café-eatery, Foodstory pulls in a loyal crowd to graze on its healthy, freshly made breakfasts, lunches, and wonderful cakes. Expect organic breakfast and brunch choices such as superfood porridge, scones, and filling dishes such as vegetarian hot pot. **Known for:** oatmeal enriched with nuts, fruit, and berries; eco-friendly ethos; vegan breakfast and lunches. ⑤ *Average main: £7* ✉ *13–15 Thistle St.* ☎ *01224/611717* ⊕ *www.foodstorycafe.co.uk.*

Moonfish

$$ | **BRITISH** | This elegant yet relaxed seafood restaurant can be found along a medieval lane next to St. Nicholas Kirk. Mains may include freshly caught sea trout, halibut, or hake served with imaginative accompaniments such as celeriac with seaweed. **Known for:** halibut with roast chicory, leeks, and yeast crumble; craft gin cocktails; sophisticated setting. ⑤ *Average main: £16* ✉ *9 Correction Wynd* ☎ *01224/644166* ⊕ *www.moonfishcafe.co.uk* ◷ *Closed Sun. and Mon.*

★ Silver Darling

$$$ | **SEAFOOD** | Huge windows overlook the harbor and beach at this quayside favorite in a former customhouse, long one of Aberdeen's most acclaimed restaurants. The French-inspired menu focuses on fish: try the crab bisque with samphire to start, then move on to a lavish seafood platter of scallops, mussels, langoustes, prawns, and cockles. **Known for:** classic seafood platters; prawn and crab linguine; steak fillet with king prawns in garlic butter. ⑤ *Average main: £25* ✉ *North Pier, Pocra Quay* ☎ *01224/576229* ⊕ *thesilverdarling.co.uk* ◷ *Closed Sun. No lunch Sat.*

Yatai Izakaya

$ | **JAPANESE** | The slick facade and glowing red interior might be a little intimidating at first, but the smiling staff is approachable and happy to help you choose the right blend of flavors and textures. The menu includes dishes like *kushiyaki*-style skewers of aged sirloin steak, sushi, miso soup, and salad. **Known for:** octopus balls; sushi platters; cash-only policy. ⑤ *Average main: £10* ✉ *53 Langstane Pl.* ☎ *01224/592355* ⊕ *www.yatai.co.uk.*

Coffee and Quick Bites

★ Aitkens

FOOD/CANDY | You can't leave Aberdeen without trying one of its famous *rowies* (or *butteries*), the fortifying morning roll. Aitkens Bakery is considered the finest purveyor of this local specialty. ✉ *14–16 Menzies Rd.* ☎ *01224/899124* ⊕ *www. aitkens-bakery.co.uk/the-bakery.*

Hotels

Atholl Hotel

$ | **HOTEL** | With its many turrets and gables, this granite hotel recalls a bygone era but has modern amenities that now include an elevator and two rooms specially designed for people with disabilities. **Pros:** family-run establishment;

outdoor garden seating for sunny days; private parking. **Cons:** rooms are blandly decorated; popular with locals for wedding and funeral receptions; unexciting bar. ⑤ *Rooms from: £99* ✉ *54 Kings Gate* ☎ *01224/323505* ⊕ *www.atholl-aberdeen. com* ⇨ *34 rooms* ﷽ *Free breakfast.*

★ Chester Hotel

$$$ | **HOTEL** | Contemporary style meets original 19th-century architectural detail within this gracious hotel. **Pros:** fine dining at on-site restaurant; ultracomfortable accommodations; lively bar. **Cons:** gym is small and basic; popular for meetings and events; bar can get crowded and noisy on weekends. ⑤ *Rooms from: £229* ✉ *59–63 Queen's Rd.* ☎ *01224/327777* ⊕ *www.chester-hotel.com* ⇨ *50 rooms* ﷽ *Free Breakfast.*

Craibstone Suites

$ | **HOTEL** | **FAMILY** | On one of Aberdeen's most attractive squares, these 18 modern and comfortable suites come with fully equipped kitchens. **Pros:** great central location; feels more like an apartment than a hotel room; good self-catering facilities. **Cons:** executive suites are small—go for the grand or superior suites if you need elbow room; breakfast is pretty basic; devoid of character. ⑤ *Rooms from: £59* ✉ *15 Bon Accord Sq.* ☎ *01224/857950* ⊕ *www. craibstone-suites.co.uk* ⇨ *18 suites* ﷽ *Breakfast.*

The Jays Guest House

$ | **B&B/INN** | Alice Jennings or her husband, George, will greet you at the front door of this granite house, a homey bed-and-breakfast they've run for more than 30 years. **Pros:** immaculate rooms; expert advice on city's sights; near Old Aberdeen and the university. **Cons:** no public areas; popular, so book ahead; not for those looking for a full-service hotel. ⑤ *Rooms from: £80* ✉ *422 King St.* ☎ *01224/612771* ⊕ *www.jaysguesthouse. co.uk* ⇨ *10 rooms* ﷽ *Free breakfast.*

★ Malmaison

$$ | **HOTEL** | Part of a British minichain, this boutique hotel with fabulously comfy rooms and suites—some with terraces from which you can watch the sunset—sets the standard by which all rivals in Aberdeen are judged. **Pros:** stylish rooms; excellent restaurant; delightful staff. **Cons:** not very central; no pool; meat-heavy restaurant could do more for vegetarians. ⑤ *Rooms from: £125* ✉ *45–93 Queen's Rd.* ☎ *01224/507097* ⊕ *www.malmaison. com/locations/aberdeen* ⇨ *77 rooms* ﷽ *All-inclusive.*

Marcliffe Hotel and Spa

$$ | **HOTEL** | Offering a perfect combination of town and country outside the city center, this elegant hotel stands on 11 acres of wooded grounds and combines old and new to impressive effect. **Pros:** the wooded environs means a stunning dawn chorus of birds; big rooms; well-regarded restaurant. **Cons:** if you struggle to sleep, the dawn chorus; a little out of town; popular with wedding parties. ⑤ *Rooms from: £170* ✉ *N. Deeside Rd.* ☎ *01224/861000* ⊕ *www.marcliffe.com* ⇨ *39 rooms* ﷽ *Breakfast.*

▼ Nightlife

Aberdeen has a fairly lively nightlife scene revolving around pubs and clubs. Theaters, concert halls, arts centers, and cinemas are also well represented. The principal newspapers—the *Press and Journal* and the *Evening Express* can fill you in on what's going on anywhere in the northeast. Aberdeen's tourist information center has a monthly publication with an events calendar.

Although it can't hold a candle to Edinburgh or Glasgow when it comes to sophisticated nightlife, Aberdeen has a very lively, even sometimes raucous, clubbing scene with numerous venues that are popular with students and other young locals but are less appealing to more mature visitors or anyone over 30.

Belmont Street is a lively bar-hopping neighborhood with bars to suit all tastes. Pubs close at midnight on weekdays and 1 am on weekends; clubs go until 2 or 3 am.

The Blue Lamp

BARS/PUBS | This is Aberdeen's coolest jazz venue, with brilliant acoustics and a laid-back atmosphere. The intimate vibe attracts all age groups with performances by world-class jazz talents and by local bands. On evenings when jazz is not in the cards, there's often live comedy. ⊠ *121 Gallowgate* ☎ *01244/647472* ⊕ *www.jazzatthebluelamp.com.*

BrewDog

BREWPUBS/BEER GARDENS | Aberdeen's pioneering craft brewery–turned–global brand runs its flagship bar with suitable gusto and no lack of style. A bare-brick warehouse interior with lots of steel means there's lots of noise and chatter flying around the cavernous space, oiled by a choice of over 100 craft beers. ⊠ *17 Gallowgate* ☎ *01224/631223* ⊕ *www. brewdog.com.*

CASC Bar

BARS/PUBS | A fine selection of malt whiskies and Cuban cigars (which can be smoked in the outside seating area) makes this one of Aberdeen's more sophisticated watering holes. CASC, which stands for cigars, ale, Scotch, and coffee, is popular for its craft beers (more than 150 of them) and cool industrial interior. It can seem a bit crowded and noisy on weekends. ⊠ *7 Stirling St.* ☎ *01224/212373* ⊕ *www.cascbar.co.uk.*

Illicit Still

BARS/PUBS | The old-fashioned Illicit Still is named after the 18th-century practice of brewing your own beer to avoid the malt tax. A beautifully fitted-out drinking establishment, it's popular with local students and has live music on weekends. ⊠ *Guest Row, Broad St.* ☎ *01224/623123* ⊕ *www.illicit-still.co.uk.*

Musa

GATHERING PLACES | With a mission statement of "food, art, music," Musa combines postindustrial chic with a hint of heresy—it's housed in adjoining buildings that were once, respectively, a warehouse and a church. It also offers live music, cutting-edge art exhibitions, and quirky dining options in atmospheric surroundings. ⊠ *33 Exchange St.* ☎ *01224/571771* ⊕ *www.musaaberdeen. com.*

The Prince of Wales

BARS/PUBS | Dating from 1850, the Prince of Wales has retained its paneled walls and wooden tables. Still regarded as Aberdeen's most traditional pub, it's hardly regal, but good-quality food and reasonable prices draw the regulars back. ⊠ *7 St. Nicholas La.* ☎ *01224/640597* ⊕ *www.princeofwales-aberdeen.co.uk.*

The Tippling House

BARS/PUBS | Youthful Aberdonian *bon viveurs* have taken this subterranean and sophisticated (by Belmont Street standards) late-night drinking den to their hearts and stomachs. It's a great place to escape and mingle and offers casual dining, innovative cocktails, craft beers, and spirits. ⊠ *4 Belmont St.* ⊕ *www. thetipplinghouse.com.*

Performing Arts

Aberdeen is a rich city, both financially and culturally.

ARTS CENTERS

Lemon Tree

ARTS CENTERS | This intimate theater has an innovative and international program of dance, stand-up comedy, and puppet theater, as well as folk, jazz, and rock music. ⊠ *5 W. North St.* ☎ *01224/641122* ⊕ *www.aberdeenperformingarts.com.*

Peacock Visual Arts

ARTS CENTERS | This gallery displays photographic, video, and slide exhibits of contemporary art and architecture.

✉ *21 Castle St.* ☎ *01224/639539* ⊕ *www. peacockvisualarts.com.*

CONCERT HALLS

His Majesty's Theatre

CONCERTS | The Edwardian His Majesty's Theatre hosts performances on par with those in some of the world's biggest cities. It's a regular venue for musicals and operas, as well as classical and modern dance. The restaurant, called 1906, is popular with audiences and cast members alike. ✉ *Rosemount Viaduct* ☎ *01224/641122* ⊕ *www.aberdeenperformingarts.com.*

Music Hall

CONCERTS | The Scottish National Orchestra and the Scottish Chamber Orchestra are regulars here, as are shows with a vibrant mix of Scottish traditional, folk, jazz, and roots. ✉ *Union St.* ☎ *01224/641122* ⊕ *www.aberdeen-performingarts.com.*

FILM

The Belmont

FILM | Independent, foreign language, and classic films are screened at the Belmont. The basement café bar is a stylish place to hang out. ✉ *49 Belmont St.* ☎ *01224/343500* ⊕ *www.belmont-filmhouse.com.*

Shopping

There's little to inspire visitors on Union Street, Aberdeen's main shopping thoroughfare or in Union Square and the bland Bon Accord & St. Nicholas Mall, where big British chain stores predominate, but Aberdeen does have a few good specialty shops. Rosemount Viaduct and Belmont Street are worth a meander.

Books and Beans

BOOKS/STATIONERY | This independent bookshop has its own Internet café (one of the few surviving such places in the city center) and sells a good range of flavored coffees. You're welcome to browse, sip, and surf the web at the same time. ✉ *22 Belmont St.* ☎ *01224/646438* ⊕ *www.booksand-beans.co.uk.*

Cocoa Ooze

FOOD/CANDY | Enjoy a cup of tea and a chocolate fondue before tasting and buying handmade chocolate gifts, such as chocolate-drenched cinder toffee and hand-rolled truffles. ✉ *24/28 Belmont St.* ☎ *01224/467212* ⊕ *www.cocoa-ooze. co.uk.*

Colin Wood Antiques

ANTIQUES/COLLECTIBLES | This shop is the place to go for small antiques, interesting prints, and regional maps. ✉ *25 Rose St.* ☎ *01224/643019* ⊕ *www.colinwood-antiques.com.*

Peapod

ANTIQUES/COLLECTIBLES | Check out vintage and retro clothing and housewares: think Bakelite, chichi cups and saucers, and 1920s cocktail dresses. ✉ *144 Rosemount Pl.* ☎ *01224/635710.*

★ Teasel & Tweed

CRAFTS | If you are in need of a Harris tweed iPhone cover, a Scottish golf map pinafore, or a set of Glencairn crystal tumblers, this is your place. All manner of housewares and accessories, all made by designers and craftspeople who live in Scotland, are on offer. ✉ *85 Rosemount Viaduct* ☎ *01224/652352.*

Activities

GOLF

With challenging dunes links swept by North Sea breezes, northeast Scotland is known for good golf.

You can expect to pay more than £100 for a round of world-class golf at courses in and around Aberdeen.

Murcar Links Golf Club

GOLF | Sea views and a variety of rugged terrain—from sand dunes to tinkling burns—are the highlights of this course, founded in 1909. It's most famous for breathtaking vistas at the 7th hole, appropriately called the Serpentine. Designer Archibald Simpson considered this course to be one of his finest. ✉ *Bridge of Don* ☎ *01224/704354* ⊕ *www.murcarlinks.com* ✉ *£110 weekdays, £135 weekends* ⚲. *18 holes, 6314 yards, par 73.*

★ Royal Aberdeen Golf Club

GOLF | This venerable club, founded in 1780, is the archetypal Scottish links course: tumbling over uneven ground, with the frequently added hazard of sea breezes. Prickly gorse is inclined to close in and form an additional hurdle. The two courses are tucked behind the rough, grassy sand dunes, and there are surprisingly few views of the sea. One historical note: in 1783 this club originated the five-minute-search rule for a lost ball. A handicap certificate and letter of introduction are required. Visitors are allowed only on weekdays. ✉ *Links Rd., Bridge of Don* ☎ *01224/702571* ⊕ *www.royalaberdeen-golf.com* ✉ *Balgownie, £190; Silverburn, £70* ⚲. *Balgownie: 18 holes, 6900 yards, par 71; Silverburn: 18 holes, 4021 yards, par 64* ♟ *Reservations essential.*

Stonehaven

15 miles south of Aberdeen.

Stonehaven's golden sands made this historic town near spectacular Dunnottar Castle a popular holiday destination, until Scots began vacationing in sunnier climates. The surrounding red-clay fields were made famous by Lewis Grassic Gibbon (real name James Leslie Mitchell), who attended school in the town and wrote the seminal Scottish trilogy *A Scots Quair,* about the people, the land, and the impact of World War I. Stonehaven is now famous for its Hogmanay (New Year's Eve) celebrations, where local men swing huge balls of fire on chains before tossing them into the harbor, and as the

birthplace of a quirky Scots delicacy, the deep-fried Mars bar.

GETTING HERE AND AROUND

Most trains heading south from Aberdeen stop at Stonehaven; there's at least one per hour making the 15-minute trip. Stagecoach Bluebird runs bus services between Stonehaven and Aberdeen; the fastest, the X70, takes around 40 minutes. Drivers should take A90 south and turn off at A957.

 Sights

★ Dunnottar Castle

CASTLE/PALACE | It's hard to beat the cinematic majesty of the magnificent cliff-top ruins of Dunnottar Castle, with its panoramic views of the North Sea. Building began in the 14th century, when Sir William Keith, Marischal of Scotland, decided to build a tower house to demonstrate his power. Subsequent generations added to the structure, and important visitors included Mary, Queen of Scots. The castle is most famous for holding out for eight months against Oliver Cromwell's army in 1651 and 1652, thereby saving the Scottish crown jewels, which had been stored here for safekeeping. Reach the castle via the A90; take the Stonehaven turnoff and follow the signs. Wear sensible shoes, and allow about two hours. ✉ *Off A92* ☎ *01569/766320* ⊕ *www.dunnottarcastle. co.uk* ✉ *£7.*

Stonehaven Tolbooth Museum

MUSEUM | Crime and punishment in days gone by are the central themes at this community-run museum in a 16th-century building that was once Stonehaven's jail and courthouse. Exhibits include the wooden stocks, where up to seven miscreants at a time could be publicly humiliated, and the crank, an appalling torture machine. There's also an eclectic collection of old farming tools and household utensils. ✉ *Old Pier, Stonehaven*

Royal Deeside

NORTH SEA

MORAY

ABERDEENSHIRE

ANGUS

GRAMPIAN MOUNTAINS

LADDER HILLS

HOWE OF ALFORD

GLEN GAIRN

GLEN GELDER

GLEN MUICK

GLEN CLUNIE

River Dee

Aberdeen
see detail map

Newburgh
Ellon
Pitmedden
Oldmeldrum
Kirkton of Bourtie
Hatton of Fintray
Balmedie
Belhelvie
Potterton
Footdee
Dyce
Blackburn
Westhill
Portlethen
Newtonhill
Muchalls
Stonehaven
Dunnottar Castle
Crawton
Catterline
Inverurie
Newmachar
Kinto
Kirkton of Skene
Dunecht
Elrick
Drum Castle
Whiteford
Old Rayne
Insch
Kennethmont
Rhynie
Lumsden
Port Elphinstone
Kemnay
Castle Fraser
Lyne of Skene
Monymusk
Alford
Bridge of Alford
Keig
Crathes Castle
Banchory
Royal Deeside Railway
Torphins
Kincardine O'Neil
Muir of Fowlis
Craigievar Castle
Lumphanan
Aboyne
Finzean Village
Heugh Head
Ordie
Dinnet
Tarfside
Cabrach
Strathdon
Corgarff Castle
Ballater
Tomintoul
Crathie
Balmoral Castle
Loch Muick
Braemar Castle
Braemar

5 mi
5 km

A90
A947
A96
A944
A93
A979
A957
A92
A90
B974
A97
B992
A944
A941
A939
B976
A93

Harbour ⊕ www.stonehaventolbooth. co.uk ✉ Free ⊘ Closed Tues.

Restaurants

The Ship Inn

$$ | SEAFOOD | This former coaching inn is exactly where you want to take nourishment after a bracing walk from Dunnottar Castle. Refurbishment has taken away much of the history, but wood paneling and rattan chairs make it comfortable, and huge new windows provide views of the harbor. **Known for:** traditional Cullen skink; nice views; splurge-worthy fritto misto. ⑤ *Average main: £16* ✉ *5 Shore Head* ☎ *01569/762617* ⊕ *www.shipinn-stonehaven.com.*

🛏 Hotels

Bayview B&B

$$ | B&B/INN | This contemporary bed-and-breakfast couldn't be in a more convenient location or have better views. **Pros:** spic-and-span rooms; right on the beach; fresh, modern design. **Cons:** standard rooms are smallish; narrow driveway not great for larger cars; not all rooms have sea views. ⑤ *Rooms from: £125* ✉ *Beachgate La.* ✛ *On the beach, down the lane from the town square* ☎ *07791/224227* ⊕ *www.bayviewbandb.co.uk* ✉ *7 rooms* ⑩ *Free breakfast.*

👜 Shopping

Aunty Betty's

FOOD/CANDY | FAMILY | Even if the weather is lousy, this coffee, sweets, and ice-cream shop confirms you are on your summer holidays. Grown-ups will love the gin-and-tonic or champagne sorbets, kids the complimentary sprinkles. ✉ *The Promenade* ☎ *01569/763656.*

Banchory

15 miles west of Stonehaven, 19 miles west of Aberdeen.

Banchory is an immaculate town filled with pinkish-granite buildings. It's usually bustling with ice-cream-eating strollers, out on a day trip from Aberdeen. Nearby are Crathes and Drum castles.

GETTING HERE AND AROUND

A car is by far the best way to get around the area; A93 is one of the main roads connecting the towns.

For those reliant on public transport, Stagecoach buses operate a number of services for towns along or just off A93 (Drum Castle, Banchory, Kincardine, Aboyne, Ballater, Balmoral, and Braemar).

ESSENTIALS

VISITOR INFORMATION Banchory Visitor Information Centre. ✉ *Bridge St.* ☎ *01330/822000* ⊕ *www.visitbanchory.com.*

👁 Sights

★ Crathes Castle

CASTLE/PALACE | FAMILY | About 16 miles west of Aberdeen, Crathes Castle was once the home of the Burnett family and is one of the best-preserved castles in Britain. Keepers of the Forest of Drum for generations, the family acquired lands here by marriage and later built a castle, completed in 1596. The National Trust for Scotland cares for the castle, which is furnished with many original pieces and family portraits. The castle is open for guided tours only. Outside are grand yet lovingly tended gardens with calculated symmetry and flower-rich beds. Make sure you browse the Horsemill bookshop and sample the tasty baked goods in the tearoom. There's an adventure park for kids, and the staff organizes activities that are fun and educational. ✉ *Off A93* ☎ *01330/844525* ⊕ *www.nts.org.uk* ✉ *£13* ⊘ *Closed weekdays Nov.–Mar.*

The gardens and trails of Crathes Castle are home to a wide variety of plants and flowers, as well as buzzards, herons, and kingfishers.

★ Drum Castle

CASTLE/PALACE | This foursquare tower has an evocative medieval chapel that dates from the 13th century; like many other castles, it also has later additions up to Victorian times. Note the tower's rounded corners, said to make battering-ram attacks more difficult. Nearby, fragments of the ancient Forest of Drum still stand, dating from the days when Scotland was covered by great stands of oak and pine. The Garden of Historic Roses, open from April to October, lays claim to some old-fashioned roses not commonly seen today. ⊠ *Drumoak by Banchory* ✛ *Off the A93, 8 miles east of Banchory and 11 miles west of Aberdeen* ☎ *01330/700334* ⊕ *www.nts.org.uk* ✉ *£13* ⊙ *Closed weekdays Oct.–Mar.; closed Tues. and Wed. in Apr.–June and Sept.*

Royal Deeside Railway

SCENIC DRIVE | **FAMILY** | Built for Queen Victoria, this historic station and its railway line now serve passengers using veteran steam and diesel locomotives to haul vintage carriages along a short scenic route; the journey takes only 15–20 minutes. ⊠ *Milton of Crathes* ☎ *01330/844416* ⊕ *www.deeside-railway.co.uk* ✉ *Round-trip £7.50.*

Hotels

★ Banchory Lodge

$$ | **HOTEL** | Right on the River Dee, this Georgian lodge offers the lovely touches you expect at a luxury hotel, but at a moderate cost. **Pros:** a warm welcome; great bar; excellent food and afternoon teas. **Cons:** popular for weddings; room sizes vary; no elevators so might be an issue for those with mobility issues. ⑤ *Rooms from: £185* ⊠ *Dee St.* ☎ *01330/822625* ⊕ *www.banchorylodge. com* ⇌ *28 rooms* ⁑⊙⁑ *Free breakfast.*

Tor Na Coille Country House

$ | **HOTEL** | Built as an Edwardian plutocrat's Highland retreat, this mock-baronial mansion hosted Charlie Chaplin and a clutch of small-time European bluebloods in its heyday. **Pros:** very classy restaurant; incredibly good value at times;

salmon fishing on the River Dee. **Cons:** slightly corporate feel; often overrun with wedding guests; some way from town center. ⓢ *Rooms from: £115* ⊠ *Inchmarlo Rd.* ☎ *01330/822242* ⊕ *www.tornacoille. com* ⇨ *25 rooms* �101 *Free Breakfast.*

Nightlife

★ Woodend Barn

GATHERING PLACES | Holding art exhibitions, film nights, and live performances, this arts venue packs a mean cultural punch for a renovated barn. Its excellent café-bar serves simple modern dishes. ⊠ *Burn O'Bennie* ☎ *1330/825431 box office* ⊕ *www.thebarnarts.co.uk.*

Ballater

25 miles west of Banchory, 43 miles west of Aberdeen.

The handsome holiday resort of Ballater, once noted for the curative properties of its waters, has profited from the proximity of the royals nearby at Balmoral Castle. The Old Royal Station, purpose-built to pander to Victoria and her hangers-on, has been handsomely restored. You might be amused by the array of "by royal appointment" signs proudly hanging from many of its various shops (even monarchs need bakers and butchers).

The locals have long taken the town's royal connection in stride. To this day, the hundreds who line the road when the Queen and her family arrive for services at the family's parish church at Crathie are invariably visitors to Deeside—one of Balmoral's attractions for the monarch has always been the villagers' respect for royal privacy.

GETTING HERE AND AROUND

There's good train service to Aberdeen, but you'll need to catch a bus to get to this and other towns near A93. Stagecoach Bluebird Buses 201 and 202 operate hourly to all the main towns,

including Ballater. Otherwise, it's an easy car trip.

ESSENTIALS

VISITOR INFORMATION **Ballater Visitor Information Centre.** ⊠ *Old Royal Station, Station Sq.* ☎ *01339/755306* ⊕ *www. visitscotland.com.*

Sights

★ Balmoral Castle

CASTLE/PALACE | The British royal family's favorite vacation spot is a fabulous fake-baronial pile, with emphasis on the "fake." Compared with Scotland's most authentic castles, Balmoral is a right royal upstart, designed in the 19th century by Queen Victoria's German-born consort, Prince Albert. That doesn't stop it being one of Scotland's most visited castles, though only the formal gardens, the ballroom, and the carriage hall, with their exhibitions of royal artifacts, commemorative china, and stuffed native wildlife, are on view.

When members of the royal family are in residence, usually from mid-August to the end of September, Balmoral is closed to visitors, including the grounds. You can take a guided tour in November and December; if the weather is crisp and bright, the estate is at its most dramatic and romantic. You're only allowed a peek inside, but the Royal Cottage is where Queen Victoria spent much of her time. You can see the table where she took breakfast and wrote her correspondence.

Around and about Balmoral are some notable spots—Cairn O'Mount, Cambus O'May, and the Cairngorms from the Linn of Dee—that are home to golden eagles, red squirrels, red deer, black and red grouse, snow bunting, and the United Kingdom's only free-roaming reindeer, some of which may be seen on the quintessentially royal Land Rover Safari Tour. Tempted by the setting? Balmoral Castle has a number of cottages (some very large) for rent by the week at certain times. These are atmospheric but can be basic (which, believe it or not, is how the royal family likes its holidays to be—though the late Diana, Princess of Wales, who vacationed here before the breakup of her marriage to Prince Charles, hated Balmoral's lack of luxury). ⊠ *A93 ⊹ 7 miles west of Ballater* ☎ *01339/742534* ⊕ *www.balmoralcastle.com* ⊠ *£15* ⊘ *Closed when royals are in residence.*

Loch Muick

BODY OF WATER | A three- or four-hour walk takes you around glorious Loch Muick (Gaelic for "pig") and past Glas-alt Shiel, a favorite retreat of Queen Victoria's that you might recognize from the film *Mrs. Brown.* From Ballater, take the B976 over the River Dee before turning off at the sign for Glen Muick. Park at the Spittal of Loch Muick car park. The path around the loch is well signposted, although good boots are necessary for the stony beach at the far side of the loch. ■**TIP→The native red deer are quite common throughout the Scottish Highlands, but here is one of the best places to see them.** ⊠ *Ballater.*

Restaurants

The Carriage

$ | **BRITISH** | The Old Royal Station, built for Queen Victoria and restored after a disastrous fire in 2015, now houses this combination café, tearoom, and bistro. There's something here for everyone at almost any time of day, from coffee and cakes to high tea, lunch, and dinner. **Known for:** mushroom risotto with sage, squash, and ricotta; deep-fried haddock in Deeside batter; local regional produce. ⑤ *Average main: £13* ⊠ *Ballater Station, Station Square* ☎ ⊕ *www.thecarriageballater.co.uk* ⊘ *Closed Sun.–Tues.*

Hotels

Auld Kirk

$$ | **B&B/INN** | **Pros:** private lounge bar; pin-tidy bedrooms and public rooms; family-friendly vibe. **Cons:** showers are small, and most rooms have no tub; no restaurant; not a full-service hotel. ⑤ *Rooms from: £125* ⊠ *Braemar Rd.* ☎ *01339/755762* ⊕ *www.theauldkirk.com* ⊠ *7 rooms* ⦿| *Breakfast.*

★ Hilton Grand Vacations at Craigendarroch Suites

$$$ | **HOTEL** | **FAMILY** | This grand mansion has been turned into a resort with a luxury spa and country club, combining Victorian style with modern comforts. **Pros:** great pool and gym facilities; no smoking anywhere inside or out; rooms and suites have kitchenettes. **Cons:** if there's a conference, nonattending guests can feel lost among the crowds; incongruously corporate atmosphere; a bit pricey for this area. ⑤ *Rooms from: £211* ⊠ *Braemar Rd.* ☎ *01339/755558* ⊕ *www.hiltongrandvacations.com/scotland/hgvc-craigendarroch-suites* ⊠ *51 suites* ⦿| *Free breakfast.*

No 45

$ | **B&B/INN** | With touches of period charm, this Victorian-era house offers old-fashioned hospitality and simple, understated comfort. **Pros:** unpretentious feel; good price; relaxing lounge. **Cons:** a few bedrooms on the small side; slightly garish decor; not for those seeking a full-service hotel. ⑤ *Rooms from: £115* ⊠ *45 Braemar Rd.* ☎ *01339/755420* ⊕ *www.no45.co.uk* ⊠ *8 rooms* ⦿| *Breakfast.*

Shopping

Deeside Books

BOOKS/STATIONERY | Beyond the gifts section, veer to the right and you will find an interesting collection of old, out-of-print, and hard-to-find books about Scotland, which make splendid gifts for lovers of all things Scottish. ⊠ *18–20 Bridge St.* ☎ *01339/754080* ⊕ *www.deesidebooks.com.*

McEwan Gallery

ART GALLERIES | A mile west of Ballater, the McEwan Gallery displays fine

Balmoral, Queen Victoria's Retreat

Some credit Sir Walter Scott with having opened up Scotland for tourism through his poems and novels. But it was probably Queen Victoria (1819–1901) who gave Scottish tourism its real momentum when, in 1842, she first came to Scotland and when, in 1847—on orders of a doctor, who thought the relatively dry climate of upper Deeside would suit her—she bought Balmoral. The pretty little castle was knocked down to make room for a much grander house designed by her husband, Prince Albert (1819–61), in 1855. In full-blown Scottish baronial style, the new structure had a veritable rash of tartanitis. Before long the entire Deeside and the region north were dotted with country houses and mock-baronial châteaux.

"It seems like a dream to be here in our dear Highland Home again," Queen Victoria wrote. "Every year my heart becomes more fixed in this dear Paradise." Victoria loved Balmoral more for its setting than its house, so be sure to take in its pleasant gardens. Year by year Victoria and Albert added to the estate, taking over neighboring houses, securing the forest and moorland around it, and developing deer stalking and grouse shooting here.

In consequence, Balmoral is now a large property, with grounds that run 12 miles along the Deeside road. Its privacy is protected by belts of pinewood, and the only view of the castle from the A93 is a partial one, from a point near Inver, 2 miles west of the gates.

There's an excellent bird's-eye view of Balmoral from an old military road, now the A939, which climbs out of Crathie, northbound for Cockbridge and the Don Valley. This view embraces the summit of Lochnagar, in whose *corries* (hollows) the snow lies year-round and whose boulder fields the current Prince of Wales, Charles Windsor, so fondly and frequently treads.

paintings, watercolors, prints, and books (many with a Scottish or golf theme) in an unusual house built by the Swiss artist Rudolphe Christen in 1902. ⊠ *A939* ☎ *01339/755429* ⊕ *www.mcewangallery. com.*

Braemar

17 miles west of Ballater, 60 miles west of Aberdeen, 51 miles north of Perth via A93.

Synonymous with the British monarchy, due to its closeness to Balmoral, and with the famous Highland Games, this village is popular year-round as a base for walkers and climbers enjoying the Grampian Mountains.

GETTING HERE AND AROUND
The town is on A93; there's bus service here and to other towns on the road.

ESSENTIALS
VISITOR INFORMATION Braemar Visitor Information Centre. ⊠ *The Mews, Mar Rd.* ☎ *01339/741600* ⊕ *braemarscotland. co.uk.*

Sights

Braemar Castle
CASTLE/PALACE | On the northern outskirts of town, Braemar Castle dates from the 17th century, although its defensive

walls, in the shape of a pointed star, came later. At Braemar (the *braes,* or slopes, of the district of Mar), the standard, or rebel flag, was first raised at the start of the unsuccessful Jacobite rebellion of 1715. About 30 years later, during the last Jacobite rebellion, Braemar Castle was strengthened and garrisoned by government troops. From the early 1800s the castle was the clan seat of the Farquharsons, who hold their clan reunion here every summer.

Thanks to the commitment of local volunteers, a remarkable 2008 renovation restored Braemar to the home it would have been in the early 20th century, complete with all the necessary comforts and family memorabilia. A dozen rooms are on view, including the laird's day room with a plush daybed and the kitchen. ✉ *Off A93* ☎ *01339/741219* ⊕ *www. braemarcastle.co.uk* 🎟 *£8* ⏱ *Closed Nov.–Easter. Closed Mon. and Tues. in Apr.–June, Sept., and Oct.*

Braemar Highland Games Centre
LOCAL INTEREST | This unabashedly royalist visitor attraction is devoted to the tartan heritage of the Braemar Royal Highland Society, the organizers of the original Highland Gathering. It also dedicates time to the British royal family's connection to the event and with Braemar from the days of Queen Victoria and Prince Albert through the 21st century. ✉ *Duke of Rothesay Highland Games Pavilion, Princess Royal and Duke of Fife Memorial Park, Broombank Terrace* ☎ ⊕ *www. highlandgamescentre.org.*

Braemar Highland Gathering
FESTIVAL | FAMILY | The village of Braemar is associated with the Braemar Highland Gathering, held the first Saturday in September. Although there are many such gatherings celebrated throughout Scotland, this one is distinguished by the presence of the royal family. Competitions and events include hammer throwing, caber tossing, and bagpipe playing. If you plan to attend, book your accommodations months in advance and be sure to buy tickets and, if necessary, your car parking ticket about six months in advance, as they do sell out. ✉ *Princess Royal and Duke of Fife Memorial Park, Broombank Terr.* ⊕ *www.braemargathering.org.*

Linn of Dee
VIEWPOINT | Although the main A93 slinks off to the south from Braemar, a little unmarked road will take you farther west into the hilly heartland. The road offers views over the winding River Dee and the blue hills before passing through the tiny hamlet of Inverey and crossing a bridge at the Linn of Dee. *Linn* is a Scots word meaning "rocky narrows," and the river's gash here is deep and roaring. Park beyond the bridge and walk back to admire the sylvan setting.

🍴 Restaurants

Taste
$ | CAFÉ | Tasty and fresh soups and sandwiches made with local ingredients like venison pâté and Cambus O' May artisanal cheeses adorn the menu at this chalet-style café. You can order moist cakes and tasty lattes here, too. **Known for:** homemade soups; fresh-baked bread; artisan cheeses. $ *Average main: £7* ✉ *Auchendryne Sq.* ☎ *01339/741425* ⊕ *www.taste-braemar.co.uk* ⏱ *Closed Sun. and Mon. and two weeks in mid-July.*

🛏 Hotels

★ The Fife Arms
$$$$ | HOTEL | This opulently quirky, art-filled boutique hotel is a much-needed addition to Braemar's rather thin lodging portfolio. **Pros:** fabulous, art-filled rooms; locally sourced game, salmon, and seafood on the dining menu; great cocktails. **Cons:** very expensive; overwhelmingly arty; some may find taxidermied animals in rooms and public areas distasteful. $ *Rooms from: £318* ✉ *Mar Rd.*

The Highland Games

They might not all be as royally attended as the Braemar Highland Gathering, but from spring to late summer across a wide swath of northern Scotland competitors gather to toss, pull, fling, and sing at various Highland events. No two games are the same, but many incorporate agricultural shows, sporting competitions, clan gatherings, or just beer in the sun. VisitScotland (⊕ *www. visitscotland.com*) has a list of them.

Which one to attend? Braemar stands tall on ceremony and tradition, and the chance of seeing royalty up close means it attracts visitors from far and wide. Dufftown Games (⊕ *www. dufftownhighlandgames.org*) is the most competitive, with its race up the nearby Ben Rinnes, while the most picturesque is the Lochcarron Games (⊕ *www.lochcarrongames.org. uk*), which are played and danced out under the massif of the Torridon hills.

☎ *01339/720200* ⊕ *www.fifearms.com* ⌂ *46 rooms* ⦵ *Free Breakfast.*

Ivy Cottage

$ | **B&B/INN** | Everything at this 19th-century inn, from the silky bedding to the bright bathroom fittings, is of the highest standard and done with good taste. **Pros:** relaxing rooms; owners who go out of their way to make you feel at home; facilities for walkers and cyclists. **Cons:** no bar or restaurant; no check-in before 4 pm; two-night minimum stay. ⑤ *Rooms from: £83* ✉ *Cluniebank Rd.* ☎ *01339/741642* ⊕ *www.ivycottagebraemar.co.uk* ⌂ *5 rooms* ⦵ *Free breakfast.*

Activities

Braemar Golf Course

GOLF | It's worth playing the tricky 18-hole Braemar Golf Course if only to say you've played the highest 18-hole course in Scotland. Founded in 1902, it is laden with foaming water hazards. ✉ *Cluny Bank Rd.* ☎ *01339/741618* ⊕ *www. braemargolfclub.co.uk* 🎫 *£25 weekdays, £30 weekends* 🏌 *18 holes, 4935 yards, par 65.*

Corgarff Castle

23 miles northeast of Braemar, 14 miles northwest of Ballater.

This castle has a striking setting on the moors and some rebuilt military features that recall its strategic importance.

GETTING HERE AND AROUND
By car, take A939 and then follow signs.

Sights

Castle Trail

SCENIC DRIVE | If you return east from Corgarff Castle to the A939/A944 junction and make a left onto the A944, the signs indicate that you're on the Castle Trail. The A944 meanders along the River Don to the village of Strathdon, where a great mound by the roadside turns out to be a *motte,* or the base of a wooden castle, built in the late 12th century. Although it takes considerable imagination to become enthusiastic about a grass-covered heap, surviving mottes have contributed greatly to the understanding of the history of Scottish castles. The A944 then joins the A97, and a few minutes later a sign points to **Glenbuchat Castle,** a plain Z-plan tower house. ⊕ *www.*

visitscotland.com/see-do/attractions/
castles/scotland-castle-trail.

Corgarff Castle

CASTLE/PALACE | Eighteenth-century soldiers paved a military highway north from Ballater to Corgarff Castle, an isolated tower house on the moorland with a star-shaped defensive wall that's a curious replica of Braemar Castle. Corgarff was built as a hunting lodge for the earls of Mar in the 16th century. After an eventful history that included the wife of a later laird being burned alive in a family dispute, the castle ended its career as a garrison for Hanoverian troops. The troops were responsible for preventing illegal whisky distilling. Reconstructed barracks show what the castle must have been like when the redcoats arrived in 1746. ⊠ *Off A939, Corgarff* ☎ *0131/668–8600* ⊕ *www.historicenvironment.scot* 🖃 *£6* ⏲ *Closed Oct.–Mar.*

Alford

28 miles west of Aberdeen, 41 miles northeast of Braemar.

A plain and sturdy settlement in the Howe (Hollow) of Alford, this town gives those who have grown somewhat weary of castle-hopping a break: it has a museum instead. Craigievar Castle and Castle Fraser are nearby, though.

GETTING HERE AND AROUND

The town is on A944.

 Sights

★ Castle Fraser

CASTLE/PALACE | The massive Castle Fraser is the ancestral home of the Frasers and one of the largest of the castles of Mar; it's certainly a contender as one of the grandest castles in the northeast. Although the well-furnished building shows a variety of styles reflecting the taste of its owners from the 15th through the 19th century, its design

is typical of the cavalcade of castles in the region, and for good reason. This—along with many others, including Midmar, Craigievar, Crathes, and Glenbuchat—was designed by a family of master masons called Bell. There are plenty of family items, but don't miss the two Turret Rooms—one of which is the trophy room—and Major Smiley's Room. He married into the family but is famous for having been one of the escapees from Colditz (a high-security prisoner-of-war camp) during World War II. The walled garden includes a 19th-century knot garden, with colorful flower beds, box hedging, gravel paths, and splendid herbaceous borders. Have lunch in the tearoom or the picnic area. ⊠ *Off A944* ✛ *8 miles southeast of Alford* ☎ *01330/833463* ⊕ *www.nts.org. uk* 🖃 *£12* ⏲ *Closed mid-Dec.–Feb. and weekdays in Mar. and Nov.–mid-Dec.*

Craigievar Castle

CASTLE/PALACE | Pepper-pot turrets make Craigievar Castle an outstanding example of a tower house. Striking and well preserved, it has many family furnishings, and the lovely grounds are worth exploring, too. Craigievar was built in relatively peaceful times by William Forbes, a successful merchant in trade with the Baltic Sea ports (he was also known as Danzig Willie). ⊠ *A980* ✛ *5 miles south of Alford* ☎ *01339/883635* ⊕ *www.nts.org. uk* 🖃 *£13* ⏲ *Closed Oct.–Mar.*

Grampian Transport Museum

MUSEUM | FAMILY | The entertaining and enthusiastically run Grampian Transport Museum specializes in road-based means of locomotion, backed up by archives and a library. Its collection of buses and trams is second to none, but the Craigievar Express, a steam-driven creation invented by the local postman to deliver mail more efficiently, is the most unusual. Look out for the Hillman Imp: if Scotland has a national car, this is it. There's a small café that offers tea, baked goods, and ice cream. ⊠ *Montgarrie Rd.*

Language and the Scots

Until quite recently, many Scots were made to feel uncomfortable—even within Scotland—about using their native regional dialects. After the Union of England and Scotland in 1707, Scotland's professional middle class, including its politicians, adopted an only mildly accented form of "standard English." Even today, the voices of the Scottish aristocracy—usually educated in elite English schools—are almost indistinguishable from those of their English counterparts. But in recent generations, Scots urban accents and rural dialects have become accepted once again. The creation of the post of Makar (first held by Edwin Morgan from 2004 to 2010 and now by Jackie Kay) signaled that Scots is once again to be taken seriously. Taking up the mantle of Robert Burns, whose poems drew on the *Lallans* (Lowlands) of his native southwest, contemporary authors such as Irvine Welsh and William McIlvanney and others write in the voices of working-class Scots city dwellers.

Lowland Scots

The Scots language (that is, Lowland Scots, not Gaelic), a northern form of Middle English influenced by Norse, Gaelic, French, and Dutch, was used in the court and in literature until the late 16th century. After the Scottish court moved to London in 1603 it declined as a literary or official language. But Scots survives in various forms, some of which—like the broadest urban accents of Dundee and Glasgow—are almost impenetrable to an ear used to "standard" English.

Some Scottish words are used and understood across the entire country (and world), such as *wee* (small), *aye* (yes), *lassie* (girl), and *bonny* (pretty). You may even find yourself exporting a few useful words, such as *dreich* (gloomy), *glaikit* (acting and looking foolish), or *dinna fash* (don't worry), all of which are much more expressive than their English equivalents. Doric, the regional dialect of Aberdeenshire, is the purest direct descendant of the old Scots tongue. It's loaded with borrowings from Norse, such as *quine* (a young woman) and *loon* (a young man), while "what" becomes "fit," "who" becomes "faa," and "which" becomes "fitna." The local version of "How do you do?" is "Fit like?" A country dweller might refer to an urban Aberdonian as a *toonser*; his city cousin might call him a *teuchter*. Neither term is entirely complimentary.

Gaelic

Scottish Gaelic—an entirely different language—is not, despite what many still think, Scotland's national tongue. This Celtic language is incomprehensible to 99% of Scots and spoken by fewer than 60,000 people. Most live in the Western Isles (*Eilean Siar* in Gaelic), with a handful in the Highlands and Argyll. All speak English as well as their mother tongue. Gaelic was frowned upon after the failure of the 1745 Jacobite rebellions, and numbers of Gaelic speakers have declined ever since, though the decline has slowed in recent years.

☎ 01975/562292 ⊕ www.gtm.org.uk
🎫 £10 (includes two children) ⊗ Closed
Nov.–Mar.

Dufftown

54 miles west of Aberdeen.

On one of the Spey tributaries, Dufftown was planned in 1817 by the Earl of Fife. Its simple cross layout with a square and a large clock tower (originally from Banff and now the site of the visitor center) is typical of a small Scottish town built in the 19th century. Its simplicity is made all the more stark by the brooding, heather-clad hills that rise around it. Dufftown is convenient to a number of distilleries.

GETTING HERE AND AROUND

To get here from Aberdeen, drive west on A96 and A920; then turn west at Huntly. It's not easy or quick, but you can take the train to Elgin or Keith and then the bus to Dufftown.

 Sights

Balvenie Castle

CASTLE/PALACE | On a mound just above the Glenfiddich Distillery is this grim, gray, and squat curtain-walled castle. This ruined fortress, which dates from the 13th century, once commanded the glens and passes toward Speyside and Elgin. ⊠ A941 ☎ 01856/761616 ⊕ www. historicenvironment.scot 🎫 £6 ⊗ Closed Oct.–Mar.

Balvenie Distillery

WINERY/DISTILLERY | As soon as you step into the old manager's office at Balvenie Distillery—now gently restored and fitted with knotted-elm furniture—you realize Balvenie wants to make sure that all visitors get to see, smell, and feel the magic of the making of this malt. Balvenie is unusual because it has its own cooperage with six coopers hard at work turning the barrels. Tours show the mashing, fermentation, and distillation process

and end with a tasting. ■TIP→ **Visitors must be 18 or older.** ⊠ Balvenie St. ☎ 01340/822210 ⊕ www.thebalvenie. com 🎫 £40 ⊗ Closed weekends.

★ Glenfiddich Distillery

WINERY/DISTILLERY | Many make Glenfiddich Distillery their first stop on the Malt Whisky Trail. The independent company of William Grant and Sons Limited was the first to realize the tourist potential of the distilling process. The company began offering tours around the typical pagoda-roofed malting buildings and subsequently built an entertaining visitor center. Besides a free 20-minute tour of the distillery there are various tours for more discerning visitors that include nosing and tasting sessions. Check out the Malt Barn Bar, serving a limited but tasty menu, and look out for viewings of the current Glenfiddich Distillery Artists in Residence's work. ⊠ A941 ⊹ ½ mile north of Dufftown ☎ 01340/820373 ⊕ www.glenfiddich.com 🎫 Tours from £10.

Keith and Dufftown Railway

TRANSPORTATION SITE (AIRPORT/BUS/FERRY/TRAIN) | FAMILY | Leaving from Dufftown three times a day on weekends then returning from Keith, this restored locomotive lets you return to the age when trains were exciting, chugging 11 miles through forests, fields, and across rivers. It passes Drummuir Castle on its way to Keith, home of the Strathisla Distillery. The Sidings Cafe at Dufftown Station serves breakfast, light lunches, snacks, and afternoon tea. ⊠ Dufftown Station, Station Rd. ☎ 01340/821181 ⊕ keith-dufftown-railway.co.uk 🎫 £7 ⊗ Closed Mon.–Thurs. and Oct.–Easter.

Strathisla Distillery

WINERY/DISTILLERY | Whisky lovers should take the B9014 11 miles northeast from Dufftown—or alternatively, ride the Keith Dufftown Railway—to see one of Scotland's most iconic distilleries, the Strathisla Distillery, with its cobblestone courtyard and famous double-pagoda

roofs. Stretching over the picturesque River Isla, the Strathisla Distillery was built in 1786 and now produces the main component of the Chivas Regal blend. Guided tours, for those 18 and over only, take you to the mash house, tun room, and still house—all pretty much the same as they were when production began. The tour ends with a tasting session. ⊠ *Seafield Ave., Keith* ☎ *01542/783044* ⊕ *www.chivas.com* ⊒ *£7.50* ⊗ *Closed weekends mid-Nov.–mid.-Mar.*

 ## Hotels

The Fife Arms Hotel
$ | B&B/INN | This 18th-century coaching inn offers a whiff of atmosphere and acceptable accommodations for a one-night stay in motel-style rooms attached to an old-school pub popular with locals. **Pros:** great full Scottish breakfast; off-street parking; very central. **Cons:** some noise from adjoining pub; unexciting decor; basic amenities. $ *Rooms from: £70* ⊠ *2 The Square* ☎ *01340/820220* ⊕ *www.fifearmsdufftown.co.uk* ⊐ *6 rooms* ⊙I *Free breakfast.*

 ## Shopping

Collector's Cabin
ANTIQUES/COLLECTIBLES | Two adjoining shops—one with Scottish silver, fossils, and book illustrations, the other with kilts, ceramics, and other curiosities—are filled with conversation starters. This is truly a trove worth delving into. ⊠ *22 and 24 Balvenie St.* ☎ *01340/821393* ⊕ *www. collectorscabin.vpweb.co.uk.*

Dufftown Glassworks
CRAFTS | This light and airy gallery sells interesting fused and painted glass, as well as prints and crafts by local makers. The adjoining café sells the best coffee in Dufftown, leaf tea, and a good selection of cakes from scones to lemon drizzle to gooey chocolate. ⊠ *16 Conval St.* ☎ *01340/821534* ⊕ *dufftownglassworks. com.*

Craigellachie

4 miles northwest of Dufftown via A941.

Renowned as an angling resort, Craigellachie, like so many settlements on the River Spey, is sometimes enveloped in the malty reek of the local industry. Glen Grant is one of the distilleries nearby. The Spey itself is crossed by a handsome suspension bridge, designed by noted engineer Thomas Telford (1757–1834) in 1814 and now bypassed by the modern road.

GETTING HERE AND AROUND
The town is on A491; it's best to drive here, as public transportation is infrequent and complicated.

 ## Sights

★ Glen Grant Distillery & Garden
WINERY/DISTILLERY | This historic distillery on the northern edge of Rothes has been producing award-winning single malts since 1840, and it's still going strong today. An impressive visitor center provides guided tours of the distillery, revealing its distinctive blend of centuries-old traditions and cutting-edge technology, as well as offering private tastings. There's a shop and café, too. But the biggest draw here is the stunning Victorian gardens; walk along the snaking path and pass pristine lawns, rare blooming flowers, gently flowing streams, and pretty pagodas. On your walk look out for a small cave and a locked safe; these were used to store founder Major Grant's private whisky collection, so he could share a dram with his walking companions. ⊠ *A941, Rothes* ⊹ *North of town, left at junction of A941 and B9015* ☎ *01340/832118* ⊕ *www.glengrant.com* ⊒ *£5 tour and tasting* ⊙ *Closed Sun. Nov.–Mar.*

★ Macallan Distillery
WINERY/DISTILLERY | Beneath a vast, undulating, turf-covered roof that mimics

Whisky, the Water of Life

Conjured from an innocuous mix of malted barley, water, and yeast, malt whisky is for many synonymous with Scotland. Lowlanders and Highlanders produced whisky for hundreds of years before it emerged as Scotland's national drink and major export. Today those centuries of expertise result in a sublimely subtle drink with many different layers of flavor. Each distillery produces a malt with—to the expert—instantly identifiable, predominant notes peculiarly its own.

Whisky Types and Styles

There are two types of whisky: malt and grain. Malt whisky, generally acknowledged to have a more sophisticated bouquet and flavor, is made with malted barley—barley that is soaked in water until the grains germinate and then is dried to halt the germination, all of which adds extra flavor and a touch of sweetness to the brew. Grain whisky also contains malted barley, but with the addition of unmalted barley and maize.

Blended whiskies, which make up many of the leading brands, usually balance malt- and grain-whisky distillations; deluxe blends contain a higher percentage of malts. Blends that contain several malt whiskies are called "vatted malts." Whisky connoisseurs often prefer to taste the single malts: the unblended whisky from a single distillery.

In simple terms, malt whiskies may be classified into "eastern" and "western" in style, with the whisky made in the east of Scotland, for example in Speyside, being lighter and sweeter than the products of the Western Isles, which often have a taste of peat smoke or even iodine.

The production process is, by comparison, relatively straightforward: just malt your barley, mash it, ferment it, and distill it, then mature to perfection. To find out the details, join a distillery tour, and be rewarded with a dram. Check out ⊕ *www.scotland-whisky.com* for more information.

Tasting Whisky

When tasting whisky, follow these simple steps. First, pour a dram. Turn and tilt the glass to coat the sides. Smell the whisky, "nosing" to inhale the heady aromas. If you want, you can add a little water and turn the glass gently to watch it "marry" with the whisky, nosing as you go. Take a wee sip and swirl it over your tongue and sense what connoisseurs call the mouthfeel. Swallow and admire the finish. Repeat until convinced it's a good malt.

the outlines of the surrounding moorland, the Macallan Distillery and Visitor Centre is now an exciting tourism hub for Speyside. The Six Pillars tour lasts around 90 minutes and includes nosing and tasting of some of the distillery's distinctively sherry-tinctured malts. ⊠ *Easter Elchies* ⊹ *About 1 mile west of Craigellachie, off B9102* ☏ *01304/318000* ⊕ *www.themacallan.com* ⊠ *£15.*

Speyside Cooperage and Visitor Centre
FACTORY | Situated four miles south of Rothes, this working cooperage is the only place left in the U.K. where you can see coopers hard at work making wooden whisky casks. Since 1947, coopers here have been using American oak, along with traditional tools and methods, to create the casks for distilleries across Scotland and beyond. This visitor center

gives you the chance to see the coopers at work and learn more about the life cycle of a cask, with tours throughout the working week. There's also a well-stocked gift shop and barrel-themed café. ⊠ *Dufftown Rd.* ☎ *01340/871108* ⊕ *www.speysidecooperage.co.uk* 🖭 *£4* ⊘ *Closed weekends.*

Restaurants

Copper Dog

$$ | BRITISH | With its reclaimed wood-work and mismatched wooden chairs, rows of malt whisky bottles, decorative oak barrel-ends, and walls hung with prints, the Craigellachie Hotel's bar-restaurant is an edgy blend of cozy and shabby chic. The menu is equally relaxed, with dishes such as locally produced gourmet sausages, rumbledethumps (a casserole of baked potato, cabbage, and onions), and an outstanding platter of Scottish cheeses with homemade chutney, all of which can be matched with regional craft beers. **Known for:** Portsoy fish stew; local produce; local craft beers. ⑤ *Average main: £15* ⊠ *Craigellachie Hotel, Victoria St.* ☎ *01340/881204* ⊕ *www.craigellachiehotel.co.uk.*

Hotels

Craigellachie Hotel

$$ | HOTEL | Who would expect a rock-chic hideaway in the heart of sleepy Speyside? But that's what this stylish old town house has become. **Pros:** stylish decor down to the details; perfectly pitched service; huge range of malt whiskies. **Cons:** popular for wedding parties; pretentious to a fault; booked up months or years in advance. ⑤ *Rooms from: £150* ⊠ *Victoria St.* ☎ *01340/881204* ⊕ *www.craigellachiehotel.co.uk* 🛏 *26 rooms* ⑩ *Some meals.*

Highlander Inn

$ | B&B/INN | Don't be fooled by the rather alpine exterior: this very-Scottish hotel prides itself on its whisky bar and its

friendly welcome. **Pros:** simple and cozy accommodations; warm atmosphere; great bar. **Cons:** uninspired decor; could be rather too lively for some; very whisky-focused, so might not be for everyone. ⑤ *Rooms from: £110* ⊠ *Victoria St.* ☎ *01340/881446* ⊕ *www.whiskyinn.com* 🛏 *8 rooms* ⑩ *Free breakfast.*

★ The Station Hotel

$$ | HOTEL | This historic yet contemporary hotel in the heart of Rothes is renowned for its luxury designer rooms and suites, its excellent café restaurant serving hearty pub grub, and its enormous selection of world whiskies and gins, to be enjoyed in the comfort of the stunning Spirit Safe bar. **Pros:** chic contemporary decor; incredible whisky selection; free car parking. **Cons:** breakfast buffet a little sparse; no elevator; expensive for the area. ⑤ *Rooms from: £170* ⊠ *51 New St.* ☎ *01340/832200* ⊕ *www.stationhotelspeyside.com* 🛏 *14 rooms* ⑩ *Free Breakfast.*

Aberlour

2 miles southwest of Craigellachie.

Aberlour, often listed as Charlestown of Aberlour on maps, is a handsome little burgh, essentially Victorian in style, though actually founded in 1812 by the local landowner. The names of the noted local whisky stills are Cragganmore, Aberlour, and Glenfarclas; Glenlivet and Cardhu are also nearby. Also in Aberlour is Walkers, famous for producing short-bread, tins of buttery, crumbly goodness, since 1898.

GETTING HERE AND AROUND

Aberlour is on A95; public transportation here is infrequent.

Sights

Ballindalloch Castle

CASTLE/PALACE | The family home of the Macpherson-Grants since 1546,

Ballindalloch Castle is every visitor's idea of what a Scots laird's lair should look like. You can wander around the beautifully kept rooms and meticulously tended gardens at your leisure; you may even bump into the lord and lady of the manor, who live here all year. There's also a splendid tea shop offering large slices of cake. ⊠ *Off A95* ✛ *8 miles southwest of Craigellachie* ☎ *01807/500205* ⊕ *www. ballindallochcastle.co.uk* ⊠ *£12* ⊗ *Closed Oct.–Easter.*

Cardhu Distillery

WINERY/DISTILLERY | The striking outline of Cardhu Distillery, whose main product lies at the heart of Johnnie Walker blends, is set among the heather-clad Mannoch Hills. Established by John and Helen Cumming in 1811, it was officially founded in 1824 after distilling was made legal by the Excise Act of 1823. Guides take you to the mashing, fermenting, and distilling halls, and they explain the malting process, which now takes place on the coast at Burghead. ⊠ *B1902, Knockando* ✛ *10 miles north of Glenlivet and 7 miles west of Aberlour* ☎ *01340/875635* ⊕ *www.discovering-distilleries.com/cardhu/find-us/* ⊠ *£8* ⊗ *Closed Sun. Jan.–Mar. and Oct.–Dec. and Sat. Nov.–Dec.*

Glenfarclas

WINERY/DISTILLERY | Glenfarclas is one of Scotland's few remaining family-owned distilleries, passed down from father to son since 1865. That link to the past is most visible among its low buildings, where the retired still sits outside: if you didn't know what it was, you could mistake it for part of a submarine. The tours end with tastings in the superlative Ship Room, the intact lounge of an ocean liner called the *Empress of Australia*. ⊠ *Off A95, Ballindalloch* ☎ *01807/500345* ⊕ *www.glenfarclas.com* ⊠ *£7.50; tasting tours from £40* ⊗ *Closed weekends Oct.–June and Sun. July–Sept.*

Glenlivet

WINERY/DISTILLERY | The famous Glenlivet was the first licensed distillery in the Highlands, founded in 1824 by George Smith. Today it produces one of the best-known 12-year-old single malts in the world. The 75-minute Classic Tour offers an introduction to malt whisky making, explains the distillery's history, and includes a free dram; more in-depth tours are available. There's a coffee shop with baked goods and, of course, a whisky shop. Visitors must be 18 or over. ⊠ *Off B9008, Ballindalloch* ✛ *10 miles southwest of Aberlour via A95 and B9008.* ☎ *01340/821720* ⊕ *www.glenlivet.com* ⊠ *£12.50* ⊗ *Closed mid-Nov.–mid-Mar.*

Hotels

Cardhu Country House

$ | **B&B/INN** | This once-abandoned manse (minister's house) looks as if it has always been loved and lived in: huge bedrooms with wooden floors, antique fireplaces, and large beds dressed in Harris tweed throws are married to contemporary bathrooms. **Pros:** period charm and modern comforts; tasty meals on request; great breakfasts. **Cons:** popular with shooting parties; meals must be ordered in advance; chintzy setting not for everyone. **$** *Rooms from: £120* ⊠ *Off B9102, Knockando* ☎ *01340/810895* ⊕ *www.cardhucountryhouse.co.uk* ⇌ *6 rooms* ⦿ *Breakfast* ☞ *No children under eight.*

Mash Tun

$$ | **B&B/INN** | Curvy yet sturdy, this former station hotel, now a smart bed-and-breakfast with a popular restaurant, is the social hub of the village. **Pros:** superb accommodations; tasty meals; great atmosphere in the restaurant and bar. **Cons:** often booked up in summer; small bedrooms; on the more expensive side for this area. **$** *Rooms from: £125* ⊠ *8 Broomfield Sq.* ☎ *01340/881771* ⊕ *www. mashtun-aberlour.com* ⇌ *5 rooms* ⦿ *Free breakfast.*

Elgin

15 miles north of Craigellachie, 69 miles northwest of Aberdeen, 41 miles east of Inverness.

As the center of the fertile Laigh (low-lying lands) of Moray, Elgin has been of local importance for centuries. Sheltered by great hills to the south, the city lies between two major rivers, the Spey and the Findhorn. Beginning in the 13th century, Elgin became an important religious center, a cathedral city with a walled town growing up around the cathedral and adjacent to the original settlement.

Elgin prospered, and by the early 18th century it became a mini-Edinburgh of the north and a place where country gentlemen spent their winters. It even echoed Edinburgh in carrying out wide-scale reconstruction in the 18th century. Many fine neoclassical buildings survive today despite much misguided demolition in the late 20th century for better traffic flow. Nevertheless, the central main-street plan and some of the older little streets and *wynds* (alleyways) remain.

GETTING HERE AND AROUND

Elgin is on the A96 road from Aberdeen to Inverness. The A941 runs north from the distillery area to the city. There's a train stop here on the line that links Aberdeen and Inverness: Aberdeen is 90 minutes away.

ESSENTIALS

VISITOR INFORMATION Elgin Visitor Information Point. ☒ *Elgin Library, Cooper Park* ☏ *01343/562608* ⊕ *www.morayspeyside. com.*

Sights

Elgin Cathedral

RELIGIOUS SITE | Cooper Park contains a magnificent ruin, the Elgin Cathedral, consecrated in 1224. Its eventful story included devastation by fire: a 1390 act of retaliation by warlord Alexander

Stewart (circa 1343–1405), the Wolf of Badenoch. The illegitimate son of King David II (1324–71) had sought revenge for his excommunication by the bishop of Moray. The cathedral was rebuilt but finally fell into disuse after the Reformation in 1560. By 1567 the highest authority in the land, the regent earl of Moray, had stripped the lead from the roof to pay for his army. Thus ended the career of the religious seat known as the Lamp of the North. Some traces of the cathedral settlement survive—the gateway Pann's Port and the Bishop's Palace—although they've been drastically altered. ☒ *Cooper Park* ☏ *01343/547171* ⊕ *www. historicenvironment.scot* ☒ *£9; £12 with Spynie Palace.*

Pluscarden Abbey

RELIGIOUS SITE | Given the general destruction caused by the 16th-century upheaval of the Reformation, abbeys in Scotland tend to be ruinous and deserted, but at the 13th-century Pluscarden Abbey the ancient way of life continues. Monks from Prinknash Abbey near Gloucester, England, returned here in 1948, and the abbey is now a Benedictine community. Daily mass is at 8 am (10 am on Sunday) and is sung by the monks using Gregorian chant. ☒ *Off B9010* ✛ *6 miles southwest of Elgin* ⊕ *www.pluscarden-abbey.org.*

Spynie Palace

CASTLE/PALACE | Just north of Elgin sits Spynie Palace, the impressive 15th-century former headquarters of the bishops of Moray. It has now fallen into ruin, though the top of the tower has good views over the Laigh of Moray. Find it by turning right off the Elgin–Lossiemouth road. ☒ *Off A941* ☏ *01343/546358* ⊕ *www.historicenvironment.scot* ☒ *£9, £12 with Elgin Cathedral* ☉ *Closed Oct.–Mar.*

St. Giles Church

RELIGIOUS SITE | At the center of Elgin, the most conspicuous structure is St. Giles Church, which divides High Street. The grand foursquare building, constructed in 1828, exhibits the Greek Revival style: note the columns, the pilasters, and the top of the spire, surmounted by a representation of the Monument of Lysicrates. ⊠ *High St.* ⊕ *www.elginstgileschurch.co.uk.*

 ## Hotels

Mansefield Hotel

$ | **HOTEL** | Four-poster beds add a touch of class to the very comfortable double rooms and suites in this modern hotel in the center of Elgin. **Pros:** comfortable rooms; free off-street parking; good food and beverage options. **Cons:** bland decor; popular wedding and conference venue; not much atmosphere. Ⓢ *Rooms from: £115* ⊠ *2 Mayne St.* ☎ *01343/540883* ⊕ *www.themansefield.com* ↝ *42 rooms* ⦶ *Breakfast.*

 ## Shopping

Gordon and MacPhail

FOOD/CANDY | An outstanding delicatessen and wine merchant, Gordon and MacPhail also stocks rare malt whiskies. This is a good place to shop for gifts for your foodie friends. ⊠ *58–60 South St.* ☎ *01343/545110* ⊕ *www.gordonandmacphail.com* ☉ *Closed Sun.*

Johnstons of Elgin

LOCAL SPECIALTIES | This woolen mill has a worldwide reputation for its luxury fabrics, especially cashmere. The large shop stocks not only the firm's own products, but also top-quality Scottish crafts. There's a coffee shop on the premises. ▪**TIP**→ **Tours of the mill are free and must be booked in advance.** ⊠ *Heritage Centre, Newmill Rd.* ☎ *01343/554099* ⊕ *www.johnstonscashmere.com.*

 ## Activities

Moray Golf Club

GOLF | Discover the relatively mild microclimate of what vacationing

Victorians dubbed the Moray Riviera, as Tom Morris did in 1889 when he was inspired by the lay of the natural links. Henry Cotton's New Course (1979) has tighter fairways and smaller greens. A handicap certificate is required for the Old Course. ⊠ *Stotfield Rd., Lossiemouth* ☎ *01343/812018* ⊕ *www.moraygolf.co.uk* ✉ *Old Course, £100; New Course, £50* 🏌 *Old Course: 18 holes, 6752 yards, par 71; New Course: 18 holes, 6068 yards, par 69.*

Fochabers

9 miles east of Elgin.

With its hanging baskets of fuchsia in summer and its perfectly mowed village square, Fochabers has a cared-for charm that makes you want to stop here, even just to stretch your legs. Lying just to the south of the River Spey, the former market town was founded in 1776 by the Duke of Gordon. The duke moved the village from its original site because it was too close to Gordon Castle. Famous today for being home to the Baxters brand of soups and jams, Fochabers is near some of the best berry fields: come and pick your own in the summer months.

GETTING HERE AND AROUND

Fochabers is not on the Inverness-to-Aberdeen train line, but there is an hourly bus service (Stagecoach Bluebird No. 10) from Fochabers to Elgin. It's near the junction of A98 and A96.

 ## Sights

Baxters Highland Village

STORE/MALL | Legendary Scottish food brand Baxters of Fochabers makes gourmet products here on the banks of the River Spey for worldwide export. From Tokyo to New York, upmarket stores stock the company's soups, jams, and chutneys. Watch cooking demonstrations, have a look at a re-creation of the Baxters' first grocery shop, or browse around the Best of Scotland, specializing in all kinds of Scottish products. A restaurant serves up an assortment of delectables. ✉ *A96* ☎ *01343/820666* ⊕ *www.baxters.com.*

Fochabers Folk Museum & Heritage Centre

MUSEUM | FAMILY | Once over the Spey Bridge and past the cricket ground (a very unusual sight in Scotland), you can find the symmetrical, 18th-century Fochabers village square. The old Pringle Church is now the home of the Fochabers Folk Museum, which boasts a fine collection of items relating to past life of all types of residents in the village and surrounding area. Exhibits include carts and carriages, farm implements, domestic labor-saving devices, and an exquisite collection of Victorian toys. ✉ *High St.* ☎ *01343/821204* ⊕ *www.fochabers-heritage.org.uk* ⊗ *Closed Mon. and Oct.–mid-May.*

Gordon Chapel

RELIGIOUS SITE | One of the village's lesser-known treasures is the Gordon Chapel, which has an exceptional set of stained-glass windows by Pre-Raphaelite artist Sir Edward Burne-Jones. Look out for the Good Shepherd, carrying a newborn lamb around his neck. ✉ *Church of St. Elizabeth, 40 Castle St.*

🍴 Restaurants

Gordon Castle Walled Garden Cafe

$$ | BRITISH | With light streaming through the large windows onto the wooden tables and rattan chairs, there is an airiness and freshness to this eatery. Fish landed just a few miles away on the Moray coast is a good bet, as are the long-aged steaks. **Known for:** mushroom and rarebit toast; fresh summer fruit desserts; pretty walled garden. ⑤ *Average main: £15* ✉ *Fochabers* ✛ *Just off A96, Fochabers Bypass Rd.* ☎ *01343/612317* ⊕ *www.gordoncastlescotland.com.*

The Quaich

$ | BRITISH | The friendly Quaich is a local favorite, serving great cakes and other baked goods, outstanding full Scottish breakfasts, warming porridge, and a plethora of snacks and sandwiches. Unusual dishes include a salmon omelet and haggis panini. **Known for:** imaginative omelets; stovies with pickled beets; tempting cakes and pastries. ⑤ *Average main: £6* ✉ *85 High St.* ☎ *01343/820981* ⊗ *Closed Mon.*

Cullen

21 miles east of Elgin, 13 miles east of Fochabers.

Look for some wonderfully painted homes at Cullen, in the old fishing town below the railway viaduct. The real attractions of this charming little seaside resort, however, are its white-sand beach (the water is quite cold, though) and the fine view west toward the aptly named Bowfiddle Rock. In summer Cullen bustles with families carrying buckets and spades and eating ice cream and chips.

A stroll past the small but once busy harbor reveals numerous fishers' cottages, huddled together with small yards where they dried their nets. Beyond these the vast stretch of beach curves gently round the bay. Above are the disused Victorian viaduct—formerly the Peterhead train line—and the 18th-century town.

GETTING HERE AND AROUND

Cullen is on A98, on Cullen Bay.

Sights

Seafield Street

NEIGHBORHOOD | The town has a fine *mercat* (market) cross and one main street—Seafield Street—that splits the town. It holds numerous specialty shops—antiques and gift stores, an ironmonger, a baker, a pharmacy, and a locally famous ice-cream shop among them—as well as several cafés. ✉ *Cullen.*

Restaurants

Cullen Ice Cream Shop

$ | **FAST FOOD** | **FAMILY** | In summer it can seem as if everyone you see in Cullen is licking a cone from the Ice Cream Shop. There's only a handful of flavors but they are all made on-site. **Known for:** homemade ice cream; weird vintage candies; creamy cakes. ⑤ *Average main: £8* ✉ *40 Seafield St.* ☎ *01542/840484* ▭ *No credit cards.*

Linda's Fish & Chips

$ | **SEAFOOD** | **FAMILY** | This casual place serves the freshest fish, caught in nearby Buckie and cooked to crispy perfection (gluten-free batter is available, too). There's a seating area inside, but it's best for takeout. **Known for:** fish battered to perfection; crispy fries; deep-fried squid rings. ⑤ *Average main: £10* ✉ *54 Seafield St.* ☎ *01542/840202.*

Rockpool

$ | **SEAFOOD** | This modish fish restaurant has remarkably reasonable prices for the quality of the food and size of the servings. Try the rich Cullen skink (a creamy smoked-haddock soup), a pint glass of fat prawns served with mayo and oat bread, or some freshly fried squid with a lime sauce, all beautifully presented on wooden boards. **Known for:** Cullen skink; smoked-fish platter; pan-fried herring in oatmeal. ⑤ *Average main: £10* ✉ *10 The Square* ☎ *01542/841397* ⊕ *www. rockpool-cullen.co.uk* ⊘ *Closed Mon. No dinner.*

🛏 Hotels

Seafield Arms

$ | **HOTEL** | Built in 1822, this gallant old coaching inn has retained much of its period character through its rebirth as a modern boutique hotel. **Pros:** local atmosphere; excellent value; casual

bar and elegant dining room. **Cons:** slightly pretentious; used for business meetings, so can feel a bit too businesslike; popular with wedding parties. ⑤ *Rooms from: £92* ✉ *17–19 Seafield St.* ☎ *01542/841604* ⊕ *www.seafieldarmscullen.co.uk* ➥ *16 rooms* ⦿ *No meals.*

Shopping

Cullen Antiques Centre

ANTIQUES/COLLECTIBLES | Housed in a former church, this is a treasure-trove for anyone looking for quirky vintage trinkets, Victoriana items, and Scottish-heritage bits and bobs. There's also a friendly on-site café serving fresh-brewed tea, coffee, and cakes. ✉ *Seafield St.* ☎ *01486/821034* ⊕ *www.cullenantiquescentre.co.uk.*

Banff

36 miles east of Elgin, 47 miles north of Aberdeen.

Midway along the northeast coast, overlooking Moray Firth and the estuary of the River Deveron, Banff is a dour fishing town, huddled around a small harbor, with a bleak but sometimes lovely coastline of crags, cliffs, and sandy coves to either side. Sixteenth-century houses huddle around the harbor, while surprisingly grand Georgian streets are reminders of its glory years as a hub of the fishing industry.

GETTING HERE AND AROUND

Banff is on the A98 coastal road and at the end of the tree-lined A947 to Aberdeen. If you are relying on public transportation, Bus 325 from Aberdeen bus station takes two hours and gets you into Low Street, just five minutes from Duff House.

⊙ Sights

★ Duff House

HOUSE | The jewel in Banff's crown is the grand mansion of Duff House, a splendid William Adam–designed (1689–1748) Georgian mansion. It's now an annex of the National Galleries, housing works by El Greco, Sir Henry Raeburn, and Thomas Gainsborough. A good tearoom and a gift shop are on the ground floor. ✉ Off A98 ☎ 01261/818181 ⊕ www.historicenviron-ment.scot 🎫 £9 ⊙ Closed Mon.–Thurs. Oct.–Mar.

Macduff Marine Aquarium

ZOO | **FAMILY** | Across the river in Banff's twin town, Macduff, on the shore east of the harbor, stands the conical Macduff Marine Aquarium. A 250,000-gallon central tank and many smaller display areas and touch pools show the sea life of the Moray Firth and North Atlantic. This place wouldn't be half as good without the staff, who are knowledgea-ble, inventive, and engaging, especially with children, and there's always some creature to admire—the stingrays cause the most excitement—or watch being fed by divers. ✉ 11 High Shore ☎ 01261/833369 ⊕ www.macduff-aquar-ium.org.uk 🎫 £7.50 ⊙ Closed Thurs. and Fri. in Nov.–Mar.

🏃 Activities

Duff House Royal Golf Club

GOLF | Just moments from the sea, this club combines a coastal course with a parkland setting. Close to the center of Banff, it's on the grounds of Duff House, a country-house art gallery in a William Adam–designed mansion. The club has inherited the ancient traditions of seaside play; golf records here go back to the 17th century. ✉ The Barnyards, Off A98 ☎ 01261/812062 ⊕ www.duffhouseroyal.com 🎫 £70 ⛳ 18 holes, 6031 yards, par 68 ⛳ Reservations essential.

Fyvie Castle

18 miles south of Banff.

This castle mixes ancient construction with Edwardian splendor and includes excellent art. The grounds are also worth exploring.

GETTING HERE AND AROUND

If you're driving from Banff, take the A947 south for 20 minutes or so until you see the turnoff.

⊙ Sights

★ Fyvie Castle

CASTLE/PALACE | In an area rich with castles, Fyvie Castle stands out as the most complex. Five great towers built by five successive powerful families turned a 13th-century foursquare castle into an opulent Edwardian statement of wealth. Some superb paintings are on view, including 12 works by Sir Henry Raeburn. There are myriad sumptuous interiors—the circular stone staircase is considered one of the best examples in the coun-try—and delightfully laid-out gardens. A former lady of the house, Lillia Drum-mond, was apparently starved to death by her husband, who entombed her body inside the walls of a secret room. In the 1920s, when the bones were disrupted during renovations, a string of such terri-ble misfortunes followed that they were quickly returned and the room sealed off. Her name is carved into the windowsill of the Drummond Room. ✉ Off A947, Turriff ☎ 01651/819226 ⊕ www.nts.org.uk 🎫 £13 ⊙ Closed mid-Dec.–Mar.

Ellon

32 miles southeast of Banff, 14 miles north of Aberdeen.

Formerly a market center on what was then the lowest bridging point of the River Ythan, Ellon, a bedroom suburb of

Aberdeen, is a small town at the center of a rural hinterland. It's also well placed for visiting Fyvie Castle and Haddo House.

GETTING HERE AND AROUND

To get to Ellon, take the A947 from Banff or the A90 from Aberdeen; both routes take half an hour.

 Sights

Haddo House

HOUSE | Built in 1732, this elegant mansion has a light and graceful Georgian design, with curving wings on either side of a harmonious, symmetrical facade. The interior is late-Victorian ornate, filled with magnificent paintings (including works by Pompeo Batoni and Sir Thomas Lawrence) and plenty of objets d'art. Pre-Raphaelite stained-glass windows by Sir Edward Burne-Jones grace the chapel. Outside is a terrace garden with a fountain, and a few yards farther is Haddo Country Park, which has walking trails leading to memorials about the Gordon family. ■ TIP➔ Visits to the house are by prebooked tour only, which are held at 11 and 2. ⌂ Off B999 ✛ 8 miles northwest of Ellon ☏ 01651/851440 ⊕ www.nts.org. uk ⛌ £12 ⏱ Closed mid-Dec.–mid-Jan.

Pitmedden Garden

GARDEN | Five miles west of Ellon, at Pitmedden Garden is an exquisite re-creation of a 17th-century garden. It is best visited in summer, from July onward, when annual bedding plants—framed by precision-cut box hedging—form intricate formal patterns. The 100-acre estate also has woodland and farmland walks, as well as the Museum of Farming Life. ⌂ Off A920, Pitmedden ☏ 01651/ 843188 ⊕ www.nts.org.uk ⛌ £8 ⏱ Closed Oct.–Apr.

 Performing Arts

Haddo House

ARTS CENTERS | Aristocratic Haddo House hosts a range of events in summer, from performances by the Haddo Choral and Operatic Society to opera, recitals, ballet, Shakespearean drama, and puppet shows on the grounds and in the salons of the mansion. The season runs from spring through fall. ⌂ Off B999, Tarves ✛ 8 miles northwest of Ellon ☏ 01651/851440 ⊕ www.nts.org.uk.

🏃 Activities

Cruden Bay Golf Club

GOLF | This historic golf course, sheltered among extensive sand dunes, offers a quintessential Scottish golf experience. Narrow channels and deep valleys on challenging fairways ensure plenty of excitement, making Cruden Bay one of the northeast's most outstanding courses. ⌂ Aulton Rd., Cruden Bay ☏ 01779/812285 ⊕ www.crudenbay-golfclub.co.uk ⛌ Championship: £135; St. Olaf: weekdays £30, weekends £40 ⚑ Championship: 18 holes, 6287 yards, par 70; St. Olaf: 9 holes, 2463 yards, par 32 ⚑ Reservations essential ⚐ Book months in advance for a round on weekends.

ARGYLL AND THE ISLES

Updated by
Robin Gauldie

⦿ **Sights** 🍴 **Restaurants** 🛏 **Hotels** 🛍 **Shopping** 🍸 **Nightlife**

★★★★☆   ★★☆☆☆   ★★★☆☆   ★☆☆☆☆   ★☆☆☆☆

WELCOME TO ARGYLL AND THE ISLES

TOP REASONS TO GO

★ **Whisky:** With 14 distilleries—9 on Islay, 1 each on Jura and Mull, and just 3 on the mainland—the region has been nicknamed Scotland's whisky coast.

★ **Iona and its abbey:** Maybe it's the remoteness that creates the almost mystical sense of history on Iona. From this early center of Scottish Christianity, evangelists traveled throughout Europe from the 6th century onward. It was also the burial place of Scottish kings, including Macbeth.

★ **The great outdoors:** Salmon and trout fill the lochs and rivers, while even bigger trophy fish await farther out to sea. Golfers have more than two dozen courses to choose from, and cyclists and walkers will find every kind of terrain at hand.

★ **Castles:** Often poised on cliffs overlooking the sea, the region's castles tell the story of eight centuries of occupations, sieges, and conflicts between warring clan chiefs and nobles.

1 Oban. Argyll's gateway to the isles.

2 Appin. Remote, lovely, and steeped in clan history.

3 Loch Awe. Island-dotted and flanked by forested hills.

4 Inveraray. The storied seat of Campbell chieftains.

5 Crinan. A picturesque canalside village loved by yacht owners.

6 Kintyre Peninsula. A charming strip of land with beaches and wildlife.

7 Brodick. The largest town in Arran.

8 Lamlash. Arran's lively seaside resort.

9 Machrie. A Moorland village surrounded by ancient stone circles

10 Lochranza. Home to a renowned distillery and a castle that sheltered Robert the Bruce.

11 Islay and Jura. Islay is a place of pilgrimage for whisky connoisseurs while Jura is rugged, hilly, and perfect for walkers and whisky lovers alike.

12 Isles of Mull and Iona. The Isle of Mull has great fishing, a spectacular castle, and the colorful village of Tobermory. Iona is a tranquil isle with a famed ancient abbey.

13 Tiree. Upscale island retreat famed for surf, sand, and a mellow microclimate.

14 Coll. A rarely visited isle where flocks of seabirds wheel above the shores.

15 Colonsay. A dazzlingly beautiful and utterly unspoiled isle.

Argyll's rocky seaboard looks out onto islands that were once part of a single prehistoric landmass. Its narrow roads slow travel but give time to admire its lochs and woods, and the ruins that recall the region's dramatic past. Here, too, are grand houses like Brodick and Inveraray castles and elegant gardens such as Crarae. This is whisky country, too: the peaty aroma of Islay's malts is unmistakable. Yet all this is within three hours of Glasgow.

Western Scotland has a complicated, splintered coastline where you'll observe the interplay of sea, loch, and rugged green peninsula. The islands are breathtakingly beautiful, though they often catch the extremely wet weather arriving here from the Atlantic. It is common to experience four seasons in a day, as cliffs and woods suddenly and dramatically disappear in sea mists, then reappear just as suddenly.

Ancient castles like Dunstaffnage and the ruined towers on the islands of Loch Awe testify to the region's past importance. Prehistoric peoples left their mark here in the stone circles, carved stones, and Bronze and Iron Age burial mounds around Kilmartin and on Islay and Arran. The gardens of Inveraray and Brodick castles, nourished by the temperate west-coast climate, are the pride of Argyll, while the paths of Crarae's, south of Inveraray, wind through plantings of magnolias and azaleas.

The working people of Glasgow traditionally spent their family holidays on the Clyde estuary, taking day trips by steamer down the Firth, or making longer journeys to Rothesay on the Isle of Bute or to Arran and the Ayrshire coast. From Ardrossan, farther down the coast, ferries cruise to the prosperous and varied Isle of Arran.

Western Scotland's small islands have jagged cliffs or tongues of rock, long white-sand beaches, fertile pastures where sheep and cattle graze, fortresses, and shared memories of clan wars and mysterious beasts. Their cliff paths and lochside byways are a paradise for walkers and cyclists, and their whisky the ideal reward after a long day outside. While the islands' western coasts are dramatic, their more sheltered eastern seaboards are the location for pretty harbor towns like brightly painted Tobermory on Mull, or Port Ellen on Islay, with its neat rows of low whitewashed houses.

MAJOR REGIONS

Argyll. Topographical grandeur and rocky shores are what make Argyll special. Try to take to the water at least once, even if your time is limited. The sea and the sea lochs have played a vital role in the history of western Scotland since the time of the war galleys of the clans. Oban is the major ferry gateway and transport hub, with a main road leading south into the Kintyre Peninsula. The linked peninsulas of Knapdale and Kintyre—separated by the Crinan Canal at Tarbert—are areas of moorland and forest dotted with small lochs. From Inveraray at the head of Loch Fyne, you can take in Auchindrain's re-created fishing village on the way to the Arran ferry. Or turn west toward Crinan and the prehistoric sites around Kilmartin, then travel northward toward Loch Awe and its intriguing island ruins.

Arran. Touring this island will give you a glimpse in a day or two of the whole of Scotland in miniature. In the north the forbidding Goatfell (2,868 feet) is a challenge that draws walkers and climbers. The island's wilder west coast attracts bird-watchers and naturalists, while the fertile south of the island contains nine lovely golf courses, leisurely walks, and Brodick Castle. A temperate microclimate attracted ancient settlers whose stone circles still stand on the island. This weather also explains why it has long been a favorite getaway for Glaswegians, who come here to walk, climb Goatfell, or play golf.

Islay and Jura. The smell of peat that hangs in the air on Islay is bottled in its famous whiskies. Aside from distilleries, the island's historical sites evoke a past in which these islands were far less remote. The whitewashed cottages along the coast of Islay line clean and beautiful beaches, many of them visited by a variety of wildlife. Jura is wilder and more dramatic, its twin mountains (the Paps) dominating its infertile moorland.

Isle of Mull and Iona. The pretty harbor of Tobermory, with its painted houses, is a relaxing base from which to explore the varied and beautiful island of Mull. Along Mull's west coast, spectacular cliffs and rocky beaches look out onto the Atlantic. From Craignure the road crosses the sweeping green valleys of the Ross of Mull to Fionnphort and the ferry to the meditative island of Iona.

The Smaller Islands. The region's smaller islands, sometimes known as the Southern Hebrides, may seem quite remote but were once important centers of power and production. Successively depopulated by force or by emigration to Glasgow's industries or the promise of the Americas, the islands still survive on fishing, cattle and sheep raising, and tourism. Their populations remain small, though, and many residents are "incomers" from the mainland or from England. They are havens for birdlife, particularly Coll's giant dunes or the cliffs of Tiree. For the visitor the experience is one of open, often barely populated landscapes and a slightly brooding sense of history. Colonsay's Kiloran Bay is open to the Atlantic's breakers, while Tiree's waves draw surfers from around the world.

Planning

When to Go

This part of the mainland is close enough to Glasgow to make it accessible year-round. Oban is just over two hours from the city by car (three hours by bus), but getting to the isles via ferries takes longer, and the crossings are less frequent out of season. You can take advantage of quiet roads and plentiful accommodations in early spring and late autumn. The summer months of July and August can get very busy indeed; book accommodations and restaurants in advance during high season. In winter short daylight hours and winds can make island stays rather bleak, but add allure to the prospect of sipping malt whisky by a log fire. Birding enthusiasts can observe vast flocks of migrant Arctic wildfowl arriving and leaving Islay in autumn and spring. At any time come prepared with adequate clothing for fast-changing weather.

Getting Oriented

With long sea lochs carved into its hilly, wooded interior, Argyll is a beguiling interweaving of water and land. The Mull of Kintyre, a narrow finger of land, points south towards nearby Ireland, separating the Firth of Clyde and its islands from the Atlantic and the isles of the Inner Hebrides. Arran, largest of the Clyde isles, looms near the mouth of the Clyde, separated from Kintyre by Kilbrannan Sound. Ferry services allow all kinds of interisland tours and can shorten mainland trips as well.

Linking the region with Glasgow, the A82 runs along the west shore of Loch Lomond to connect with the A83. That road follows the north shore of Loch Fyne, a long fjordlike inlet known for some of Scotland's finest seafood, all the way to Campbeltown near the tip of Kintyre. Along the way is Kennacraig, departure point for ferries to Islay and Jura. Coming from the east, the A85 runs through equally spectacular scenery between Perth and Oban, the main port for ferries to Mull and other islands. From Oban the A828 runs north to Fort William and the Great Glen.

Planning Your Time

You could easily spend a week exploring the islands alone, so consider spending at least a few nights in this region. Argyll and some island excursions make pleasant and easy side trips from Glasgow and Loch Lomond. Driving anywhere

here takes a little longer than you'd think, so allow ample travel time. A leisurely day will take you to Inveraray, its castle, and the surrounding gardens (don't miss the folk museum at Auchindrain) before driving on to Kennacraig to take the ferry for Islay and Jura. Two or three days here will give you a sense of the history and varied landscapes of these stunning islands—and time for a distillery or two. If you have time to visit just one island, sail from Oban to Mull, returning the same day or the next to take in the Scottish Sea Life Sanctuary. If you can, drive around beautiful Loch Awe on your way back to Glasgow. If time is really tight, consider flying from Glasgow to Islay or Tiree.

Plan ahead: car ferries fill up in the summer months (there is usually no problem for foot passengers), and some of the smaller islands are served only once or twice a week. Bear in mind that it is not easy to find places to eat after 9 pm at any time of year—though you can usually find a place that will sell you a whisky until much later.

Getting Here and Around

AIR

The closest major airport to Argyll and the Isles is Glasgow. Hebridean Air Services flies from Oban to Islay, Coll, Colonsay, and Tiree.

CONTACTS Hebridean Air Services.
☎ 0845/805–7465 ⊕ www.hebrideanair. co.uk.

BOAT AND FERRY

Caledonian MacBrayne (CalMac) operates car-ferry and passenger services to and from the main islands. It is important to plan ahead when traveling to the islands in order to coordinate the connecting ferries; CalMac can advise you on this. Multiple-island tickets are available and can significantly reduce the cost of island-hopping.

CalMac ferries run from Oban to Mull, Lismore, Coll, and Tiree; from Kennacraig to Islay, Jura, and Gigha; from Ardrossan to Arran; and from Port Askaig on Islay to Feolin on Jura; as well as a number of shorter routes. Western Ferries operate between Dunoon, in Argyll, and Gourock, west of Glasgow. The ferry passage between Dunoon and Gourock is one frequented by locals; it saves a lot of time, and you can take your car across as well. Jura Passenger Ferry operates between Tayvallich (on the mainland) and Craighouse on Jura.

Ferry reservations are needed if you have a car; passengers traveling by foot do not need to make reservations.

CONTACTS Caledonian MacBrayne. (*CalMac*) ☎ *0800/066–5000* ⊕ *www. calmac.co.uk.* **Jura Passenger Ferry.** ☎ *07768/450000* ⊕ *www.jurapassengerferry.com.* **Western Ferries.** ☎ *01369/704452* ⊕ *www.western-ferries. co.uk.*

BUS
You can travel throughout the region by bus, but service here tends to be less frequent than elsewhere in Scotland. Scottish Citylink runs daily service from Glasgow's Buchanan Street station to the mid-Argyll region and Kintyre; the trip to Oban takes about three hours. Several other companies provide local services within the region.

CONTACTS Garelochhead Coaches. ☎ *01436/810200* ⊕ *www.garelochheadcoaches.co.uk.* **Islay Coaches.** ☎ *01496/840273* ⊕ *www.bmundell. co.uk.* **Scottish Citylink.** ☎ *0871/266–3333* ⊕ *www.citylink.co.uk.* **Stagecoach West Scotland.** ☎ *01770/302000* ⊕ *www. stagecoachbus.com.* **West Coast Motors.** ☎ *01586/552319* ⊕ *www.westcoastmotors.co.uk.*

CAR
Negotiating this area is easy except in July and August, when the roads around Oban may be congested. A number of single-lane roads, especially on the east side of the Kintyre Peninsula and on the islands, require special care. Remember that white triangles indicate places where you can pass. You'll probably have to board a ferry at some point during your trip; nearly all ferries take cars as well as pedestrians.

From Glasgow take the A82 and the A85 to Oban, the main ferry terminal for Mull and the islands (about 2½ hours by car). From the A82 take the A83 at Arrochar; it rounds Loch Fyne to Inveraray. From there you can take the A819 from Inveraray around Loch Awe and rejoin the Glasgow–Oban road. Alternatively, you can stay on the A83 and head down Kintyre to Kennacraig, the ferry terminal for Islay. Farther down the A83 is Tayinloan, the ferry port for Gigha. You can reach Brodick on Arran by ferry from Ardrossan, on the Clyde coast (M8/ A78 from Glasgow); in summer you can travel to Lochranza from Claonaig on the Kintyre Peninsula, but there are very few crossings.

TRAIN
Oban and Ardrossan are the main rail stations; it's a three-hour trip from Glasgow to Oban. For information call ScotRail. All trains connect with ferries.

CONTACTS ScotRail. ☎ *0871/200–2233* ⊕ *www.scotrail.co.uk.*

Restaurants

Argyll and the Isles have earned a reputation for excellent gastropubs and restaurants (many of which also offer accommodations) that use superb locally sourced produce, including luscious seafood, lamb, wild and farmed venison, and game of many kinds. Most hotels and many guesthouses offer evening meals, and it may often be your best option to look to hotel restaurants, though the quality can vary. Most restaurants and pubs stop serving food by 9 pm; lunch usually ends at 2:30.

Hotels

Accommodations in Argyll and on the Isles range from country-house hotels to private homes offering a bed and breakfast. Most small, traditional, provincial hotels in coastal resorts have been updated and modernized, while still retaining personalized service. And though hotels often have a restaurant offering evening meals, the norm is to offer breakfast only.

Restaurant and hotel reviews have been shortened. For full information, visit Fodors.com. Restaurant prices are the average cost of a main course at dinner or, if dinner is not served, at lunch. Hotel prices are the lowest cost of a standard double room in high season, including 20% V.A.T.

WHAT IT COSTS in Pounds			
$	$$	$$$	$$$$
RESTAURANTS			
under £15	£15–£19	£20–£25	over £25
HOTELS			
under £125	£125–£200	£201–£300	over £300

Tours

BOAT TOURS

Getting out on the water is a wonderful way to see the landscape of the islands and also sea life.

★ Sea Life Surveys

BOAT TOURS | FAMILY | Dolphins, seals, porpoises, and (if you're fortunate) minke whales and basking sharks are among the stars of the show on a Sea Life Surveys cruise from pretty Tobermory. Seabirds abound, too, and you may spot

huge white-tailed eagles, once extinct here but reintroduced to this part of Scotland in recent years. Several cruises are offered: if time is short, choose the 90-minute Ecocruz. ⊠ *A848, Tobermory* ⊕ *Cruises leave from floating pontoons opposite Mull Aquarium* ☎ *01688/302916* ⊕ *www.sealifesurveys.com* ⛟ *From £20.*

Staffa Tours

BOAT TOURS | FAMILY | This company organizes a number of tours to the smaller islands, with the emphasis on wildlife. Tours run from Mull, Ardnamurchan on the mainland, or from Iona. The three-hour trip to uninhabited Staffa includes Fingal's Cave, commemorated by Mendelssohn in his famous overture. With luck you may encounter dolphins on the way. Staffa also runs tours to the Treshnish islands, famous for the puffin colonies on Lunga. ⊠ *The Boat Shed, Iona, Iona* ☎ *07732/912370* ⊕ *www.staffatours.com* ⛟ *From £35.*

Turus-Mara

BOAT TOURS | FAMILY | Based on the island of Mull, Turus-Mara runs trips to Staffa, Iona, and the Treshnish islands, with an emphasis on wildlife. There are puffins and guillemots through the summer, seals until late in the year, and sometimes even basking sharks. Tours depart from Ulva Ferry on the west coast of Mull, but there is a courtesy bus from Tobermory. ⊠ *Penmore Mill, Dervaig* ☎ *01688/400242* ⊕ *www.turusmara.com* ⛟ *From £32.50.*

BUS TOURS

Many of the bus companies in the area also arrange sightseeing tours, so check with them.

West Coast Tours

BUS TOURS | A range of bus tours in and around Oban and on Mull are available through West Coast Tours. The company can also arrange combined bus and boat tours. ⊠ *George St., Oban* ☎ *01631/552319* ⊕ *www.westcoasttours.co.uk* ⛟ *From £7.*

As Argyll's biggest town, Oban greets visitors to the region with its seaside charm.

Visitor Information

The only year-round visitor information offices are in Bowmore, Craignure, and Oban.

Oban

96 miles northwest of Glasgow, 125 miles northwest of Edinburgh, 50 miles south of Fort William, 118 miles southwest of Inverness.

It's almost impossible to avoid Oban when touring the west. Its waterfront has some character, but the town's main role is as a launch point for excursions into Argyll and for ferries to the islands. A traditional Scottish resort town, Oban has many music festivals, *ceilidhs* with Highland dancing, as well as all the usual tartan kitsch and late-night revelry in pubs and hotel bars. The Oban Distillery offers tours and a shop. Still, there are more exciting destinations just over the horizon, on the islands, and down into Kintyre.

GETTING HERE AND AROUND

From Glasgow the A82 along Loch Lomond meets the A85 at Crianlarich. Turn left and continue to Oban. In summer the center of Oban can become gridlocked with ferry traffic, so leave yourself time for the wait. Alternatively, the A816 from Lochgilphead enters Oban from the less-crowded south. Train services run from Glasgow to Oban (ScotRail); Scottish Citylink runs buses from Glasgow to Oban several times a day.

ESSENTIALS

VISITOR INFORMATION Oban Tourist Information Centre. ⊠ *3 North Pier* ☎ *01631/563122* ⊕ *www.oban.org.uk.*

Sights

Dunstaffnage Castle

CASTLE/PALACE | Standing high atop volcanic rock, Dunstaffnage commands the hills and lochs that surround it. That is why this 13th-century castle was so strategic and contested by those battling for control of Argyll and the Isles. From the

walk along the walls you have outstanding views across the **Sound of Mull** and the **Firth of Lorne**. A small well-illustrated guidebook (£2.50) lets you take your own guided tour, but there are storyboards throughout the building that give you a sense of how it was used across the ages. In the woods is the ruined chapel of St. Cuthbert, built by the Macdougall clan at the same time as the castle. ⊠ *Off A85* ☎ *01631/562465* ⊕ *www. historicenvironment.scot* 🖼 *£6* ⊙ *Closed Thurs. and Fri. Oct.–Mar.*

Oban Distillery

WINERY/DISTILLERY | One of Scotland's oldest and smallest distilleries was founded in 1794, several years before the town where it now stands. It produces a well-known 14-year-old malt which, according to those who know, has a taste somewhere between the smoky Islay whiskies and the softer, sweeter Highland varieties—a distinctive West Highland flavor. ⊠ *Stafford St.* ✛ *Opposite North Pier* ☎ *01631/572004* ⊕ *www. obanwhisky.com* 🖼 *Basic tour £12* ⊙ *Closed weekends in Dec.*

Oban War and Peace Museum

MUSEUM | **FAMILY** | This free museum recalls Oban's history through peace and war in photographs and other exhibits. Always a fishing harbor and a ferry port, during the Second World War the town became a key naval command center. ⊠ *Old Oban Times Building, Corran Esplanade* ☎ *01631/570007* ⊕ *www.obanmuseum.org.uk* 🖼 *Free* ⊙ *Closed Nov.–Feb.*

Ocean Explorer Centre

MUSEUM | **FAMILY** | On the Firth of Lorn, this imaginative venture lets you get a look under the sea. Hands-on exhibits include microscopes where you can observe tiny algae and a live undersea camera where you can see what's happening below the waves. Part of a scientific research center, it's educational but also accessible and fun. There is a bright little café and a shop with books on marine science and other topics. It's 2 miles from Oban—follow the signs for nearby Dunstaffnage Castle. ⊠ *Kirk Rd.* ☎ *01631/559123* ⊕ *www.ocean-explorercentre.org* 🖼 *Free* ⊙ *Closed weekends and late Dec.–early Jan.*

 Restaurants

★ Ee-usk

$$$ | **SEAFOOD** | This clean-lined restaurant's name means "fish" in Gaelic, and it has earned quite a reputation for serving excellent dishes made with the freshest fish and shellfish delivered directly from Oban's harbor. The signature creations use appealingly simple sauces; try oven-baked wild halibut with creamed leeks or the full-scale seafood platter. **Known for:** Mull scallops; Loch Linnhe oysters and langoustines; island views. ⑤ *Average main: £25* ⊠ *North Pier* ☎ *01631/565666* ⊕ *www.eeusk.com.*

Hawthorn Restaurant

$ | **BRITISH** | Fish shares the menu here with local lamb, pork, and game. Although it's just a few miles from Oban (whence it sources its seafood), the setting is rural, surrounded by crofts that are still working farms. **Known for:** freshly caught haddock; Argyll lamb; tasty steak pies. ⑤ *Average main: £12* ⊠ *Keil Crofts, Benderloch* ✛ *6 miles north of Oban off the main A816, after crossing the Connel Bridge* ☎ *01631/720777* ⊙ *Closed Mon. and Oct.–Mar.*

Oban Seafood Hut

$ | **SEAFOOD** | Serving arguably the best-value seafood in Oban, ex-fisherman John Ogden's quayside fish shack is a local legend. Look for a green-painted shed on the pier, then join the line of cognoscenti waiting for simply sautéed scallops, grilled langoustine and lobster, oysters, and mussels. **Known for:** king prawn sandwiches and scallops in garlic butter; cash or debit card only; only a few tables, so eating while standing a possibility. ⑤ *Average main: £8* ⊠ *CalMac*

Pier ☎ *07881/418565* ⊘ *Closed Nov.–Apr.* ⊟ *No credit cards.*

Hotels

Glenburnie House

$ | **B&B/INN** | At this typical seafront guesthouse in a Victorian building with fine views over Oban Bay, most rooms are spacious and comfortable, if slightly overdecorated in traditional style. **Pros:** centrally located; good sea views; lots of local atmosphere. **Cons:** too many flowery fabrics for some tastes; no bar on-site; only meal available is breakfast. ⓢ *Rooms from: £100* ✉ *Esplanade* ☎ *01631/562089* ⊕ *www.glenburnie.co.uk* ⊘ *Closed Dec.– Feb.* ⇴ *12 rooms* ⦿ *Breakfast.*

Kilchrenan House

$ | **B&B/INN** | Just a few minutes from the town center, this Victorian-era stone house has been transformed into a lovely bed-and-breakfast. **Pros:** great sea views; tasteful attention to detail; cozy rooms. **Cons:** some bedrooms may be too colorfully decorated for some tastes; attic rooms have a slanting roof; credit cards not accepted for one-night stays. ⓢ *Rooms from: £80* ✉ *Corran Esplanade* ☎ *01631/562663* ⊕ *www.kilchrenan- house.co.uk* ⊘ *Closed Dec. and Jan* ⇴ *13 rooms* ⦿ *Free breakfast.*

★ Manor House Hotel

$$ | **HOTEL** | On the coast near Oban, this 1780 stone house—once the home of the Duke of Argyll—has sea views and a convenient location. **Pros:** excellent restaurant; complimentary golf at local course; free use of local gym. **Cons:** smallish bedrooms; no children under 12; pretty expensive by local standards. ⓢ *Rooms from: £185* ✉ *Gallanach Rd.* ☎ *01631/562087* ⊕ *www.manorhouse- oban.com* ⇴ *11 rooms* ⦿ *Free Breakfast.*

Activities

BICYCLING
Oban Cycles

BICYCLING | This shop rents bikes of various sorts starting at £25 for a full day. The area round Oban is good cycling country, and the staff is happy to advise you on routes. ✉ *89 George St.* ☎ *01631/566033* ⊕ *www.obancyclescot- land.com.*

Appin

17 miles north of Oban.

The little peninsula of Appin, a 20-minute drive from Oban, is a charming, well-kept secret. Just 2 miles along a narrow road from the main Fort William route (A828), the bay opens to Lismore and the sea. Castle Stalker, a privately owned castle on the water, sits magnificently in the center of the picture, a symbol of ancient coastal Scotland. This is an excellent, uncrowded base for walking, fishing, water sports, and cycling.

GETTING HERE AND AROUND

From Oban follow the A828 around Loch Creran and take the left turn to Port Appin just beyond Tynribbie. Continue for just over 2 miles to the old pier. From the port the passenger ferry runs to the island of Lismore throughout the year. Steamers once plied the waters of Loch Linnhe, but today the largest boats here are those taking workers to the quarries of Kingairloch.

Restaurants

★ Pierhouse Hotel and Restaurant

$$$ | **SEAFOOD** | The round towers of the old pier mark the entrance to this restaurant, appealingly situated on the water's edge. The restaurant serves the freshest seafood; try its signature platter of lobster, scallops, mussels, and langoustines. **Known for:** delicious lobster thermidor;

While you can't actually visit Appin's Castle Stalker, it makes for a lovely backdrop to a sunset.

rib-eye steak with langoustines; lively atmosphere. $ *Average main: £25* ✉ *Port Appin* ☎ *01631/730302* ⊕ *www.pierhousehotel.co.uk.*

Hotels

Airds Hotel and Restaurant
$$$$ | HOTEL | This luxurious small hotel (once a travelers' inn) has rooms with superb views. **Pros:** fabulous views from the breakfast room; lots of outdoor activities available; beautiful location. **Cons:** decor a bit too pretentious; rooms too small for some tastes; very expensive. $ *Rooms from: £365* ✉ *A828, Port Appin* ☎ *01631/730236* ⊕ *www.airds-hotel.com* ⤴ *11 rooms* ❏ *Some meals.*

★ Isle of Eriska
$$$$ | HOTEL | FAMILY | On one of Scotland's few private islands, this sybaritic enclave conceals luxury facilities like a spa, pool, gym, golf course, and a Michelin-starred restaurant behind a severe baronial facade. **Pros:** exceptional food; gorgeous views; superb leisure facilities. **Cons:** usually booked out at least one year ahead in high season; dining out not an easy option; very popular with wedding parties. $ *Rooms from: £300* ✉ *Off A828, Benderloch ✧ Island signposted from Benderloch village and connected to mainland by short bridge* ☎ *01631/720371* ⊕ *www.eriska-hotel.co.uk* ⤴ *34 rooms* ❏ *Free breakfast.*

Loch Awe

18 miles east of Oban.

Measuring more than 25 miles long, Loch Awe is Scotland's longest stretch of freshwater. Its northwest shore is quiet; forest walks crisscross the Inverliever Forest here. At the loch's northern end, tiny islands, many with ruins, pepper the water. One, Inishail, is home to a 13th-century chapel.

GETTING HERE AND AROUND
From Oban the A85 will bring you to the head of Loch Awe and the small village of the same name. Turn onto the B845

at Taynuilt to reach the loch's northern shore, or continue through the forbidding Pass of Brander and turn onto the A819 to get to the southern shore. From here you can continue on to Inveraray, or drive along the loch on the B840.

Sights

★ Bonawe Iron Furnace

HISTORIC SITE | FAMILY | Seemingly out of place in this near-wilderness setting, Bonawe is a fascinating relic from the dawn of Britain's Industrial Revolution. In the mid-18th century, Argyll's virgin forests attracted ironmasters from England, where such valuable fuel sources were harder to find. Business boomed when wars with France boosted demand for pig iron and cannonballs, and in its heyday Bonawe employed up to 600 unskilled local wood gatherers and skilled southern foundrymen. ⊠ *Off B845, Bonawe* ☎ *01866/822432* ⊕ *www. historicenvironment.scot* 🖃 *£6* ⏀ *Closed Sat.–Tues. and Oct.–Mar.*

Cruachan

FACTORY | FAMILY | Like the lair of a classic James Bond villain, this triumph of 20th-century British technology lurks deep within a vast man-made cavern. Hidden 3,000 feet beneath the slopes of Ben Cruachan, the colossal water-driven turbines of this subterranean power station, completed in 1965, supply clean energy to much of Scotland. The ½-mile bus ride from the surface to the generating hall is a surreal experience, made all the more so by the subtropical plants that thrive under artificial light in the warm, humid atmosphere. ⊠ *A85, Dalmally* ☎ *01866/822618* ⊕ *www. visitcruachan.co.uk* 🖃 *£7.50* ⏀ *Closed weekends and Jan.*

Duncan Ban Macintyre Monument

MEMORIAL | The monument was erected in honor of this Gaelic poet (1724–1812), sometimes referred to as the Robert Burns of the Highlands. He fought at Culloden and wrote poetry and song in the language of the clans. The view from here is one of the finest in Argyll, taking in Ben Cruachan and the other peaks nearby, as well as Loch Awe and its scattering of islands. To find the monument from Dalmally, just east of Loch Awe, follow an old road running southwest toward the banks of the loch. You can see the round, granite structure from the road's highest point, often called Monument Hill. ⊠ *Dalmally*.

Kilchurn Castle

ARCHAEOLOGICAL SITE | This is one of Argyll's most evocative ruins, with its crumbling lochside towers and high ramparts. Built by the Campbells in the 15th century, Kilchurn was rebuilt as a government garrison after the troubles of the late 17th century. The castle was abandoned after peace came to the Highlands following the final defeat of the Jacobite cause in 1746. ⊠ *Lochawe, Dalmally* ✛ *2½ miles west of Dalmally* ⊕ *www.historic-scotland.gov.uk/places* ⏀ *Closed Oct.–Mar.*

Rest and Be Thankful

VIEWPOINT | This viewpoint at the highest point of the route from Loch Lomond to Inveraray is one of the few places where you can pull off the road to enjoy the spectacular panorama. It's an ideal place to take some selfies, and it's easy to imagine how it earned its name in the days when the only travelers on this trail went on foot or on horseback. ⊠ *A83* ✛ *10 miles northwest of Tarbert.*

St. Conan's Kirk

RELIGIOUS SITE | St. Conan's may look medieval, but in fact, it's less than 100 years old. Built in 1930 from local boulders, it features modern stained glass and wood and stone carvings, including an effigy of Robert the Bruce. ⊠ *A85, Lochawe* ✛ *About 18 miles from Oban* ⊕ *www.stconanskirk.org.uk* 🖃 *Free.*

Hotels

★ Taychreggan Hotel
$ | HOTEL | Peace and quiet are the big selling points of this lovely country-house hotel beside Loch Awe. Once a drovers' inn, the whitewashed building is surrounded by lawns and wooded gardens. **Pros:** lovely setting; activities including fishing and kayaking; wonderful meals. **Cons:** six miles from main road; limited restaurant menu; isolated location. *⑤ Rooms from: £99 ⊠ Off B845, Kilchrenan ☎ 01866/833211 ⊕ www.taychregganhotel.co.uk ⇥ 18 rooms ❢⊙❢ Free breakfast.*

Inveraray

21 miles south of Loch Awe, 61 miles north of Glasgow, 29 miles west of Loch Lomond.

Inveraray's star attraction is the grandiose seat of the Campbell Dukes of Argyll, for centuries the most powerful magnates of the Highlands. It's a trim little township, planned and built in the mid-18th century at the behest of the third duke. There are fine views of Loch Fyne, and there are gardens and museums to see nearby.

GETTING HERE AND AROUND
Driving from Oban take the A85 and the A819 beyond Loch Awe (the village). From Glasgow take the A82, turn onto the A83 at Arrochar, and make the long drive around Loch Fyne.

 # Sights

Ardkinglas Woodland Garden
GARDEN | Rambling over 12,000 acres, one of Britain's finest collections of conifers is set off by rhododendron blossoms in early summer. You can find the garden around the head of Loch Fyne, about 10 miles east of Inveraray. There's a wild woodland walk beyond the garden; both are open all year. The house, regarded as

architect Sir Robert Lorimer's masterpiece, is open to visitors only on Fridays between April and October. ⊠ *Ardkinglas Estate, Cairndow ☎ 01499/600261 ⊕ www.ardkinglas.com ✍ £5.*

★ Auchindrain Museum
MUSEUM VILLAGE | FAMILY | Step a few centuries back in time at this open-air museum, a rare surviving example of an 18th-century communal-tenancy farm. About 250 years ago, there were several thousand working communities like Auchindrain. Auchindrain was the last of them, its final tenant leaving in 1963. Today the bracken-thatch and iron-roof buildings, about 20 in all, give you a feel for early farming life in the Highland communities. Several houses are furnished and tell the story of their occupants. A tearoom is open morning to afternoon. ⊠ *Auchindrain ⊹ Off A83 about 6 miles south of Inveraray ☎ 01499/500235 ⊕ auchindrain.org.uk ✍ £8 ⊙ Closed Nov.–Mar.*

Crarae Garden
GARDEN | Exotic Himalayan plants flourish in the gentle microclimate of this 100-acre garden, where the Crarae Burn, a small stream, cascades through a rocky gorge. Rhododendrons, azaleas, and magnolias lend color, and native flowers and trees attract birds and butterflies. ⊠ *A83 ⊹ 10 miles southwest of Inveraray ☎ 01546/886614 ⊕ www.nts.org.uk ✍ £7.50 ⊙ Closed Nov.–Mar.*

Inveraray Castle
CASTLE/PALACE | The current seat of the Chief of the Clan Campbell is a smart, grayish-green turreted stone house with a self-satisfied air. Set among well-tended grounds, it contains displays of luxurious furnishings and interesting art, as well as a huge armory. Built between 1743 and 1789, the castle has spires on the four corner turrets that give it a vaguely French look. Tours of the castle follow the history of the powerful Campbell family and how it acquired its considerable wealth. There is a tearoom

for snacks and light lunches. You can hike around the extensive estate grounds, but wear sturdy footwear. ✉ *Off A83* ☎ *01499/302203* ⊕ *www.inveraray-castle.com* ✈ *£12.50* ⊘ *Closed Nov.–Mar.*

Inveraray Jail

JAIL | FAMILY | In this old jail, realistic courtroom scenes, carefully re-created cells, and other paraphernalia give you a glimpse of life behind bars in Victorian times—and today. Actors represent some of the jail's most famous occupants. The site includes a Scottish crafts shop. ✉ *Main St.* ☎ *01499/302381* ⊕ *www.inverarayjail.co.uk* ✈ *£12.25.*

🍴 Restaurants

★ Loch Fyne Oyster Bar and Restaurant

$$ | SEAFOOD | The legendary flagship of a chain of seafood restaurants that now stretches across the United Kingdom, this restaurant continues to please with its emphasis on ultrafresh, locally sourced seafood, simply prepared. Oysters, are, of course, a keynote, but the menu also features mussels, lobster, prawns, salmon, and much more from the sea, accompanied by perfect crunchy green vegetables such as peas, beans, and asparagus. **Known for:** plump oysters perfectly prepared; meltingly tender smoked salmon; seafood tapas. ⑤ *Average main: £19* ✉ *Clachan Farm, A83, Cairndow* ☎ *01499/600482* ⊕ *www.lochfyne.com.*

Samphire Seafood Restaurant

$$ | SEAFOOD | This small, cozy, unpretentious restaurant in the center of Inveraray has earned a reputation for excellently prepared seafood, though it also serves meat and vegetarian dishes. Favorites include the seafood pie, and the Taste of the Loch medley of shellfish and crustaceans is a special treat. **Known for:** lavish seafood platters; hearty seafood pie; roast cod loin. ⑤ *Average main: £18* ✉ *6A Arkland* ☎ *01499/302321* ⊕ *www.samphireseafood.com* ⊘ *Closed Sun. and Mon.*

Hotels

★ The George Hotel

$ | HOTEL | The George has been Inveraray's social hub since the 18th century, when it was a coaching inn, and it still exudes history. **Pros:** excellent restaurant; atmospheric bars; live music on weekends. **Cons:** too much tartan for some; extra charge for child beds; live music makes some rooms noisy. ⑤ *Rooms from: £90* ✉ *Main St. E* ☎ *01499/302111* ⊕ *www.thegeorgehotel.co.uk* ⇥ *25 rooms* ❦ *Free breakfast.*

Crinan

32 miles southwest of Inveraray.

Crinan is synonymous with its canal, the reason for this tiny community's existence and its mainstay. The narrow road beside the Crinan Hotel bustles with yachting types waiting to pass through the locks, bringing a surprisingly cosmopolitan feel to such an out-of-the-way corner of Scotland.

GETTING HERE AND AROUND

To reach Crinan, follow the A83 from Inveraray along the north shore of Loch Fyne through Lochgilphead, take the A816 Oban road north for about a mile, then turn left onto the B841 at Cairnbaan.

👁 Sights

Carnasserie Castle

ARCHAEOLOGICAL SITE | The tower house of Carnasserie Castle is all that remains of this Renaissance structure. It has the distinction of having belonged to the writer of the first book printed in Gaelic. John Carswell, Bishop of the Isles, translated a text by the Scottish reformer John Knox into Gaelic and published it in 1567. ✉ *Off A816* ⊕ *2 miles north of Kilmartin* ⊕ *www.historic-scotland.gov.uk* ✈ *Free.*

Castle Sween

CASTLE/PALACE | The oldest stone castle on the Scottish mainland, this 12th-century structure sits on a rocky bit of coast about 12 miles south of Crinan. From the northwest tower, known as the Latrine Tower, you can enjoy the dramatic views of the Paps of Jura. ⊕ *www.historicenvironment.scot.*

Crinan Canal

BODY OF WATER | This canal opened in 1801 to let fishing vessels reach Hebridean fishing grounds without making the long haul south around the Kintyre Peninsula. At its western end the canal drops to the sea in a series of locks, the last of which is beside the Crinan Hotel. Today it's popular with pleasure boats traveling to the west coast. ✉ *Crinan.*

Kilmartin Museum

MUSEUM | To see a little of the region's prehistoric past, start at this museum 8 miles north of Crinan and then explore some of the more than 300 ancient remnants within a 6-mile radius. Exhibits provide information about stone circles, burial mounds, and carved stones dating from the Bronze Age and earlier. Sometime in 2020, work is expected to begin on an exciting £6.7 million extension to the museum, which will display many ancient finds from the collection that the museum currently doesn't have the space to exhibit. ✉ *A816, Kilmartin* ☎ *01546/510278* ⊕ *www.kilmartin.org* 🎫 *£7* ◷ *Closed Jan.–Mar.*

 ## Hotels

Allt-Na-Craig

$ | **B&B/INN** | Overlooking Loch Fyne, this stone Victorian house is set in lovely gardens. **Pros:** traditional and atmospheric decor; great views; interesting literary heritage. **Cons:** children not allowed; pricey for what it is; not a full-service hotel. ⑤ *Rooms from: £120* ✉ *Tarbert Rd., Ardrishaig* ✛ *9 miles southeast of Crinan* ☎ *01546/603245*

⊕ *www.allt-na-craig.com* 🛏 *6 rooms* ❡◎❡ *Breakfast.*

Crinan Hotel

$$$ | **HOTEL** | A dramatic location overlooking the Sound of Jura is this hotel's big selling point, along with bright, maritime-themed public areas and guest rooms. **Pros:** good dining; some rooms with private balconies; interesting art gallery. **Cons:** not all rooms have showers; popular for wedding receptions; no satellite TV. ⑤ *Rooms from: £215* ✉ *Off B841* ☎ *01546/830261* ⊕ *www.crinanhotel.com* 🛏 *20 rooms* ❡◎❡ *Breakfast.*

Kintyre Peninsula

57 miles south of Crinan (to Campbeltown).

Rivers and streams crisscross this long, narrow strip of green pasturelands and hills stretching south from Lochgilphead.

GETTING HERE AND AROUND

Continue south on the A83 (the road to Campbeltown) to Tarbert. Some 4 miles farther along the A83 is Kennacraig, where you catch the ferry to Islay. Beyond that is the pier at Tayinloan; CalMac ferries run from here to the Isle of Gigha.

Flybe operates flights from Glasgow to Campbeltown.

ESSENTIALS

AIR TRAVEL CONTACT Campbeltown Airport. ✉ *Off A83, Campbeltown* ✛ *At Machrihanish, 3 miles west of Campbeltown* ☎ *01586/553797* ⊕ *www.hial.co.uk.*

 ## Sights

Achamore House Gardens

GARDEN | Visit Achamore House Gardens in late spring to see its azaleas and its prize collection of rhododendrons ablaze with color. The island's mellow microclimate fosters these lush shrubberies.

The charming Crinan Canal has been popular with fishing vessels and royals alike; Queen Victoria took a trip up it in 1873.

✉ *Achamore House, Isle of Gigha* ☎ *01583/505390* ✉ *Free, donations welcome.*

Isle of Gigha

ISLAND | Barely 7 miles long, this sheltered island between Kintyre and Islay has sandy beaches and rich wildlife. Ferries make the 20-minute trip from Tayinloan on the mainland. ✉ *Isle of Gigha* ☎ *01583/505390* ⊕ *www.gigha.org.uk.*

🏃 Activities

Machrihanish Golf Club

GOLF | For many Scots golfers (and they should know) Machrihanish's out-of-the-way location makes it a place of pilgrimage. Laid out in 1876, it's an intimidatingly memorable links course by a sandy bay. There is also a 9-hole course, The Pans. The historic clubhouse, devastated by fire in December 2018, is currently under restoration. ✉ *Off B843, Machrihanish* ☎ *01586/810213* ⊕ *www. machgolf.com* ✉ *£75 Apr.–Oct., £30 Nov.–Mar.* 🏌 *Championship Course: 18 holes, 6235 yards, par 70; The Pans: 9 holes (out), 2376 yards, par 34* ⛳ *Reservations essential.*

Arran

Approaching Arran by sea, you'll first see forbidding Goatfell (2,868 feet) in the north, then the green fields of the south. These varied landscapes earn the island its sobriquet: "Scotland in Miniature." A temperate microclimate attracted ancient settlers whose stone circles still stand on the island. This weather also explains why it has long been a favorite getaway for Glaswegians, who come here to walk, climb Goatfell, or play golf.

GETTING HERE AND AROUND

Caledonian MacBrayne runs regular car and passenger ferries that cross the Firth of Clyde from Ardrossan (near Saltcoats) to Brodick throughout the year; crossing takes just under an hour. There is also a small ferry from Claonaig on the Kintyre

Peninsula to Lochranza during the summer months.

Connecting trains run to the ferry at Ardrossan from Glasgow's Queen Street station. Stagecoach runs regular local bus services around the island. Exploring the island by car is easy, as the A841 road circles it.

Brodick

1 hour by ferry from Ardrossan.

Arran's largest village, Brodick, has a main street that is set back from the promenade and the lovely bay. Beyond that, it is really little more than a gateway to the rest of the island.

GETTING HERE AND AROUND
You can reach Brodick from Ardrossan by ferry. From Brodick the A841 circles the island; head south to reach Lamlash, north to reach Lochranza. The String Road crosses the island between Brodick and Machrie.

ESSENTIALS
The information center, opposite the landing point for the Ardrossan Ferry, has an accommodation desk as well as tourist information.

 ## Sights

Brodick Castle and Country Park
CASTLE/PALACE | FAMILY | On the north side of Brodick Bay, this red-sandstone mansion with typical Scottish-baronial features was built in the 16th century and was the seat of the dukes of Hamilton, who added to it extensively throughout the 19th century. It reopened in 2019 after a £1.5 million renovation, and now features an adventure park and an exciting visitor experience where costumed performers bring the past to life. In summer the expansive gardens are ablaze with azalea and rhododendron blossoms.

The country park that surrounds the castle embraces Arran's most striking scenery, rising to the 2,867-foot summit of Goatfell, the island's highest peak. The beautiful upland landscape is more challenging to explore than it seems, so it's important to go prepared with sturdy footwear and waterproof clothing. From the summit there is a stunning panoramic view of the Firth, Kintyre, and the Ayrshire coast, and on a clear day you can just see Ireland. ⊠ *Off A841, 1 mile north of Brodick Pier* ☎ *01770/302202* ⊕ *www. nts.org.uk* ⊗ *Castle closed Jan.–Mar.*

Isle of Arran Heritage Museum
MUSEUM | A typical Arran cottage, a re-created 1940s schoolroom, and farm buildings filled with antiquated implements that were in use within living memory make this lively little museum a must-see for anyone interested in the island's social history. ⊠ *Rosaburn, A841* ☎ *01770/302636* ⊕ *www.arranmuseum. co.uk* ☜ *£4* ⊗ *Closed Nov.–Mar.*

 ## Restaurants

Brodick Bar and Brasserie
$$$ | BRITISH | This lively bar and restaurant serves fixed-price lunch and dinner menus featuring popular if unadventurous seafood favorites such as monkfish, halibut, and scallops, and adds spice to the mix with an array of Asian-influenced dishes. Like many places in the west of Scotland, hours are restricted, so it is well worth booking ahead. **Known for:** Sunday roast with all the trimmings; Brodick bouillabaisse of local langoustines and shellfish; Gigha halibut with roasted gnocchi. ⑤ *Average main: £20* ⊠ *Alma Rd.* ☎ *01770/302169* ⊕ *www. brodickbar.co.uk.*

 ## Hotels

★ Auchrannie Resort
$$$ | RESORT | FAMILY | With outstanding indoor and outdoor leisure facilities (including two pools and a spa),

well-designed modern rooms, and three restaurants and bars, Auchrannie is by far the best place to stay on Arran. **Pros:** indoor leisure facilities including spa and pool; good for families; excellent outdoor activities. **Cons:** could-be-any-where atmosphere; lacks character; not for anyone looking for peace and quiet. $ *Rooms from: £215* ⊠ *Auchrannie Rd.* ☎ *01770/30234* ⊕ *www.auchrannie.co.uk* ⇥ *115 rooms* ⦿ *Free breakfast.*

 ## Shopping

Arran's shops are well stocked with locally produced goods. The Home Farm is a popular shopping area with several shops and a small restaurant.

Arran Aromatics

PERFUME/COSMETICS | This is one of Scotland's best-known suppliers of scents, soaps, and perfumes of every kind. The shop is filled with pleasant smells, and between May and September a tour of the soap factory is available every Thursday evening. ⊠ *Home Farm, A841* ☎ *01770/302595* ⊕ *www.arran.com.*

Isle of Arran Cheese Company

FOOD/CANDY | Arran is famous for its cheeses, especially its cheddar and its Arran blue; stop here to sample and buy handmade Scottish cheeses. ⊠ *The Home Farm, A841* ☎ *01770/302788* ⊕ *www.arranscheeseshop.co.uk.*

 ## Activities

Arran Adventure at Auchrannie Resort

BICYCLING | Mountain biking, sea kayaking, hill and gorge walking, and climbing are among the activities offered by Arran Adventure. Segway tours and guided strolls along the coast and on the slopes of Goatfell are also on offer. ⊠ *Shore Rd.* ☎ *01770/302244* ⊕ *auchrannie.co.uk* ⊠ *From £15* ⊗ *Closed Nov.–Mar.*

Lamlash

4 miles south of Brodick.

With views offshore to Holy Isle, which is now a Buddhist retreat, Lamlash has a breezy seaside-holiday atmosphere. To reach the highest point accessible by car, go through the village and turn right beside the bridge onto Ross Road, which climbs steeply from a thickly planted valley, **Glen Scorrodale**, and yields fine views of Lamlash Bay. From Lamlash you can explore the southern part of Arran: 4 miles to the southwest, **Whiting Bay** has a pleasant well-kept waterfront and a range of hotels and guesthouses. If you travel another 6 miles, you'll reach the little community of **Lagg**, which sits peacefully by the banks of the Kilmory Water.

GETTING HERE AND AROUND

You can reach Lamlash by driving south from Brodick on the A841. The town is also served by Stagecoach buses.

 ## Hotels

Lagg Hotel

$ | **B&B/INN** | Arran's oldest inn is an 18th-century lodge with fireplaces in the common rooms and 11 acres of gardens and grounds that meander down to the river. **Pros:** beautiful gardens; warming fireplaces; nice local feel. **Cons:** floral designs everywhere; some rooms are small; Wi-Fi in public areas only. $ *Rooms from: £110* ⊠ *A841, Kilmory* ⊹ *12 miles south of Lamlash* ☎ *01770/870255* ⊕ *www.lagghotel.com* ⇥ *13 rooms* ⦿ *Breakfast.*

Machrie

10 miles west of Brodick, 11 miles north of Lagg.

The area surrounding Machrie, home to a popular beach, is littered with prehistoric sites: chambered cairns, hut circles, and standing stones dating from the Bronze Age.

GETTING HERE AND AROUND

The quick route to Machrie is via the String Road (B880) from Brodick; turn off onto the Machrie Road 5 miles outside Brodick. A much longer but stunning journey will take you from Brodick, north to Lochranza, around the island to Machrie, and down the island's dramatic west coast, a distance of some 28 miles.

 ## Sights

Machrie Moor Stone Circles

ARCHAEOLOGICAL SITE | Six ancient circles of boulders and head-high sandstone pillars are scattered across Machrie Moor. These relics of a prehistoric culture are as old as Egypt's pyramids, if not quite as impressive, and the site evokes a dim and distant past. ✛ *1½ miles north of Machrie* ⊕ *www.historicenvironment. scot.*

 ## Restaurants

Cafe Thyme

$ | TURKISH | This bright and pleasant restaurant offers a combination of Scottish and Turkish flavors (an expression of the owners' backgrounds) as well as fine views out to sea. Look for meze as well as *pides* (Turkish pizza)—try the haggis-and-cheese or crayfish-and-olive combinations. **Known for:** Mediterranean meze; unusual East–West fusion dishes; Turkish-style haggis pizza. ⑤ *Average main: £13* ⊠ *Machrie* ✛ *Next to Old Byre Visitor Centre* ☎ *01770/840608* ⊕ *www. oldbyre.co.uk/cafethyme.irs* ⊗ *No dinner.*

 ## Shopping

Old Byre Showroom

CLOTHING | This shop sells sheepskin goods, hand-knit sweaters, leather goods, and rugs. ⊠ *Auchencar Farm, A841* ✛ *2 miles north of Machrie* ☎ *01770/840227* ⊕ *www.oldbyre.co.uk.*

Lochranza

13 miles north of Machrie, 14 miles north of Brodick.

Lochranza shows Arran's wilder northern side, with rocky seashores and sweeping slopes leading to the stark granite peaks of Goatfell and Caisteal Abahail (2,735 feet), which dominate the skyline.

The respected Isle of Arran Distillery nestles in the hills overlooking Lochranza Bay. Until recently, this was Arran's only distillery, but in 2019 it gained a baby sister, the Lagg Distillery at Kilmory; however, due to the length of time required for the distilling process, Lagg won't be producing its own malts until several years from now.

GETTING HERE AND AROUND

Lochranza is north of Brodick via the A841.

 ## Sights

★ Isle of Arran Distillery

WINERY/DISTILLERY | The open aspect and closeness to the sea explain the taste of Arran's well-respected single malt, light and airy and with the scent of sea and fields. The round white building housing the distillery sits comfortably among fields and hills in the northernmost part of the island. The tours take the visitor through the process of creating whisky, with a small or slightly larger tasting depending on the level. The basic tour ends with a dram. The CASKS café-restaurant is a comfortable place for a long lunch. ⊠ *Distillery Visitor Centre* ☎ *01770/830264* ⊕ *www.arranwhisky. com* ⊡ *Tours from £10.*

★ Lochranza Castle

CASTLE/PALACE | Perched above the bay, Lochranza is Arran's most picturesque ruin and occupies a special place in Scotland's history. It was here that Robert the Bruce, after years of dithering, returned from exile to commit himself to the war for Scotland's independence. ✉ *Off A841* ☎ *0131/668–8800* ⊕ *www.historicenvironment.scot* ⊗ *Closed Oct.–Mar.*

 ## Hotels

Butt Lodge

$ | B&B/INN | Set in 2 acres of private woods and gardens overlooking Kilbrannan Sound, this onetime Victorian shooting lodge offers a personalized welcome from owners who really make guests feel at home with hearty (but healthy) Scottish breakfasts and complimentary afternoon tea, served in a cozy lounge. **Pros:** peace and quiet; luxurious rooms and suites; great views. **Cons:** a little hard to find; no bar; up a winding farm road that can be tough on cars. ⑤ *Rooms from: £95* ✉ *Off Newton Rd.* ⊹ *½ mile east of Lochranza* ☎ *01770/830333* ⊕ *www.buttlodge.co.uk* ⇄ *6 rooms* ⑩ *Free breakfast.*

Islay and Jura

Islay is an island of rolling fields and pastures, heather-covered uplands where red deer roam and rutting stags clash antlers in spring, and white-sand beaches that on a summer day can look as enticing as any Caribbean strand. Huge flocks of Arctic wildfowl migrate to Islay in fall, leaving again in spring, when their wings literally darken the sunset sky. This was the long-ago seat of the Macdonald Lords of the Isles, a mongrel Celtic-Norse dynasty that held sway over the southern Hebrides for almost three centuries. Some of their heritage can still be seen. But it's a different inheritance that draws many visitors, namely the smoky, peaty malt whisky produced here by eight world-famous distilleries. Upstart Ardnahoe joined their ranks in 2018, with the stated aim of producing its own take on the classic Islay malt, but you won't be able to sample its wares for some years yet. In sharp contrast to Islay's gaggle of

villages set among rolling moorland and fertile pastures, thinly populated Jura is ruggedly beautiful, with a hilly landscape dominated by twin summits, the Paps of Jura.

Bowmore

On Islay: 11 miles north of Port Ellen.

Bowmore, Islay's capital, is a good base for touring because it's central to Islay's main routes. A tidy town, its grid pattern was laid out in 1768 by local landowner Daniel Campbell, of Shawfield. Main Street stretches from the pier head to the commanding parish church, built in 1767 in an unusual circular design—so the devil could not hide in a corner.

GETTING HERE AND AROUND

Loganair flights from Glasgow and Edinburgh to Islay Airport take 40–50 minutes; the airport is 5 miles north of Port Ellen. Hebridean Air links Islay with Colonsay and Oban. The trip by CalMac ferry from Kennacraig to Port Ellen takes about 2½ hours; ferries also travel less frequently to Port Askaig. From Port Ellen it is 10 miles on the A846 to reach Bowmore; drivers should use caution during the first mile out of Port Ellen, as the road is filled with sharp turns. The rest of the route is straight but bumpy, because the road is laid across peat bog.

Local bus services 450 and 451 connect the main island communities of Bowmore and Port Ellen with points around Islay. Timetables are available from the tourist information center.

AIR TRAVEL CONTACTS Islay Airport.
✉ *A846, Glenegedale* ☎ *01496/302361* ⊕ *www.hial.co.uk.*

VISITOR INFORMATION Bowmore
Visitor Information Centre. ✉ *The Square* ☎ *01496/305165* ⊕ *www.visitscotland. com.*

Sights

★ Bowmore Distillery

WINERY/DISTILLERY | Bowmore is the grand old lady of Islay's distilleries, and a tour is a must for any visitor. In business since 1779, the distillery, like all Islay whisky makers, stands by the sea. Standard tours include a walk around the malting areas and the stills, and connoisseurs can opt for in-depth tours that include tutored tastings. ⊠ *School St.* ☎ *01496/810441* ⊕ *www.bowmore.com* ✉ *From £10* ⊗ *Closed Sun. Nov.–Mar.*

Islay Woollen Mill

FACTORY | Gorgeous tweed, plaid, and tartan clothing, wraps, and throws—woven at this historic mill and dyed in subtle, traditional tones—are sold here. ⊠ *A846* ✛ *4 miles outside Bowmore on the A846* ☎ *01496/810563* ⊕ *www.islaywoollenmill.co.uk* ✉ *Free* ⊗ *Closed Sun.*

🍴 Restaurants

★ Harbour Inn

$$$ | SEAFOOD | An adjunct of the Bowmore distillery, the Harbour Inn has a bar frequented by locals and a more upscale restaurant with a menu that emphasizes oysters, langoustines, mussels, and other local seafood. The elegant dining room looks out onto the water. **Known for:** classic Islay oysters; North African–influenced vegetarian dishes; seafood paired with malt whiskies. $ *Average main: £25* ⊠ *The Square* ☎ *01496/810330* ⊕ *www.bowmore.com/harbour-inn.*

🛍 Shopping

Islay Whisky Shop

WINE/SPIRITS | If you don't have time to visit all of Islay's distilleries, let alone those elsewhere, you can do worse than visit this shop with its enormous collection of whiskies. ⊠ *Shore St.* ☎ *01496/810684* ⊕ *www.islaywhiskyshop.com.*

Islay's Whiskies

With 3,500 inhabitants and eight working distilleries—with two more due by the 2020s—Islay claims more stills per person than anywhere in the world. Yet, considering the island's size, there's remarkable variety here. Malts from the southeast coast, like Laphroaig, Lagavulin, and Ardbeg, reek of peat and iodine. Peat is still the keynote of malts from the western distilleries, such as Bowmore, Bruichladdich, and Caol Ila, but old-school aging in sherry casks gives these a lighter, more floral nose.

Port Charlotte

On Islay: 11 miles west of Bowmore.

Planned by a benevolent 19th-century laird (and named after his mom), Port Charlotte is an unusually (for Scotland) pretty village, with wild landscapes and sandy beaches nearby. South of the village, the A847 road leads to **Portnahaven** and **Port Wemyss**, where pleasing white cottages stand in a crescent around the headland.

GETTING HERE AND AROUND

To reach Port Charlotte from Bowmore, take the A846 via Bridgend and then the A847, Portnahaven Road. Local buses also connect Port Charlotte and Bowmore.

Sights

Museum of Islay Life

MUSEUM | A converted church is home to this local museum, a haphazard collection of local artifacts, photographs, and memorabilia. There is also a local

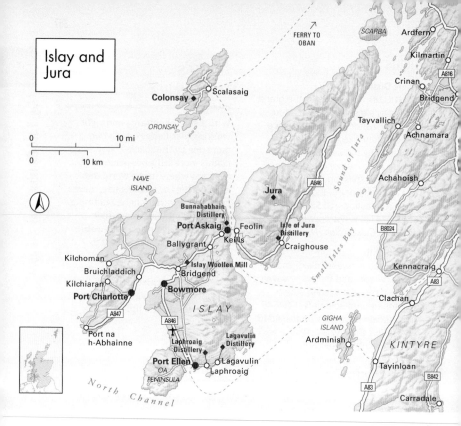

history archive. ✉ *A847* ☎ *01496/850358* ⊕ *www.islaymuseum.org* ✉ *£4* ⊙ *Closed weekends and Nov.–Mar.*

Natural History Centre

MUSEUM | FAMILY | With its exhibits about the island's wildlife, the Natural History Centre has lots of hands-on activities for kids. It's a great stop on rainy days, and tickets are valid for a week. On Monday and Friday there are nature rambles, and family activities are offered throughout July and August. ✉ *Main St.* ☎ *01496/850288* ⊕ *www.islaynaturalhistory.org* ✉ *£3.50* ⊙ *Closed Oct.–Apr.*

Hotels

★ Port Charlotte Hotel

$$$ | HOTEL | Once a row of fishermen's cottages and with views over a sandy beach, this whitewashed Victorian hotel has been lovingly restored. **Pros:** beautiful location; lovely restaurant; views over the water. **Cons:** can be a little noisy from the bar; rooms are quite small; not as luxurious as it claims. ⑤ *Rooms from: £250* ✉ *Main St.* ☎ *01496/850360* ⊕ *www.portcharlottehotel.co.uk* ⌂ *10 rooms* ⑪ *Free breakfast.*

Port Ellen

On Islay, 11 miles south of Bowmore.

Islay's sturdy community of Port Ellen was founded in the 1820s, and much of its architecture dates from the following decades. It has a harbor (ferries stop here), a few shops, and a handful of inns. The road traveling east from Port Ellen (the A846 to Ardbeg) passes three top distilleries and makes a pleasant afternoon's "whisky walk." All three distilleries offer tours, but you should call ahead for an appointment; there may be no tours on weekends at times. The last week in May, large numbers of whisky lovers descend on the island for the Islay Festival of Music and Malt, the heart of which is Port Ellen.

GETTING HERE AND AROUND
It is likely that Port Ellen will be your port of arrival on Islay. From here you can travel north to Bowmore, along the A846 before turning northwest towards Bridgend and Port Askaig.

 Sights

Islay Festival of Music and Malt
FESTIVAL | The last week in May, large numbers of whisky lovers descend on the island for this festival, the heart of which is Port Ellen. Distilleries offer special events, and traditional music performances and ceilidhs take place all over Islay. Book lodgings and distillery tours at least six months ahead. ⊠ *Port Ellen* ☎ *07914/675228* ⊕ *www.islayfes-tival.com.*

Kildalton Cross
RELIGIOUS SITE | Of interest only to anyone fascinated by Celtic heritage, this rock slab, engraved with elaborate 8th-century designs that meld pagan and early Christian motifs, stands in the kirkyard of a ruined medieval chapel. ⊠ *Port Ellen* ✛ *About 8 miles northeast of Port Ellen* ⊕ *www.historicenvironment.scot.*

Lagavulin Distillery
WINERY/DISTILLERY | Many malt whisky connoisseurs say the Lagavulin is the strongest nosed of all Islay's peaty malt whiskies. You can find out why, and how, with a distillery tour and tasting here. ⊠ *A846* ☎ *01496/302400* ⊕ *www.malts. com* 🥃 *Tours from £6.*

Laphroaig Distillery
WINERY/DISTILLERY | Laphroaig (say la-froig) is Islay's most distinctive malt,

redolent of peat, seaweed, and iodine. You can take a tour of the distillery, then settle in for a spell of sipping at the whisky bar. ⊠ *A846* ☎ *01496/302418* ⊕ *www. laphroaig.com* 🥃 *From £10.*

 Hotels

The Islay Hotel
$$ | HOTEL | This charming hotel overlooking Port Ellen's harbor has large, bright rooms decorated in muted contemporary colors. **Pros:** central location; bright, welcoming interior; good restaurant. **Cons:** can get crowded; some noise at weekends from live music in bar; no lounge or sitting area. ⑤ *Rooms from: £165* ⊠ *Charlotte St.* ☎ *01496/300109* ⊕ *www.theislayhotel.com* 🛏 *13 rooms* ❍| *Free Breakfast.*

Port Askaig

On Islay, 11 miles northeast of Bowmore.

Serving as the ferry port for Jura and receiving ferries from Kennacraig, Port Askaig is a mere cluster of cottages. Uphill, just outside the village, a side road travels along the coast, giving impressive views of Jura on the way. There are distilleries near here, too; make appointments for tours.

GETTING HERE AND AROUND
Traveling from Bowmore, you can reach Port Askaig (where the road ends) via A846. The village is also served by local buses.

 Sights

★ Bunnahabhain Distillery
WINERY/DISTILLERY | Established in 1881, the Bunnahabhain (pronounced *Boon-a-ha-bin*) Distillery sits on the shore, with dramatic views across to the Paps of Jura. This is one of Scotland's most picturesque and evocative malt whisky distilleries, redolent of a preindustrialized

era. ✉ A846 ☎ 01496/840557 ⊕ www.
bunnahabhain.com 🖃 From £7 ⊗ Closed
Nov.–Mar.

 Hotels

Kilmeny Country House
$$ | **B&B/INN** | This luxurious bed-and-
breakfast is on a 300-acre farm, but the
rooms are so elegantly furnished that the
place feels more like a hotel. **Pros:** elegant and quiet; great breakfast; afternoon
tea tray on arrival. **Cons:** easy to miss;
harsh cancellation policy; hotel prices but
without all hotel facilities. ⑤ Rooms from:
£150 ✉ A846, Ballygrant ✛ Signposted
off the A846 to Port Askaig, just before
the village of Ballygrant ☎ 01496/840668
⊕ www.kilmeny.co.uk ⇱ 5 rooms
✦○✦ Free breakfast.

Jura

5 minutes by ferry from Port Askaig.

The rugged, mountainous landscape of
the island of Jura—home to only about
200 people—looms immediately east
of Port Askaig, across the Sound of
Islay: a perfect landscape for walkers.
Jura has only one single-track road (the
A846), which begins at Feolin, the ferry
pier. It climbs across moorland, providing scenic views of the island's most
striking feature, the Paps of Jura, three
breast-shaped rounded peaks. The ruined
Claig Castle, on an island just offshore,
was built by the Lords of the Isles to
control the sound. The island has no cash
machines, so plan ahead.

GETTING HERE AND AROUND
The Port Askaig–Feolin car ferry takes
five minutes to cross the Sound of Islay,
and there is a passenger-only ferry during
the summer from Tayvallich on Argyll to
Craighouse. Bus service is also available
from Craighouse and Inverlussa.

 Sights

Isle of Jura Distillery
WINERY/DISTILLERY | The community of
Craighouse has the island's only distillery,
producing malt whisky since 1810. Tours
must be booked in advance by phone or
online. ✉ Craighouse ☎ 01496/820385
⊕ www.jurawhisky.com 🖃 Tours from £6
⊗ Closed mid-July–mid-Aug., weekends
in Oct.–Mar., and Sun. in Mar.–Oct.

 Hotels

Jura Hotel
$ | **HOTEL** | Jura's only hotel, next to the
island's renowned distillery, has simple
but cozy no-frills rooms, and its pleasant
gardens are attractive on a summer day.
Pros: convenient location; good, unpretentious restaurant; lively bar. **Cons:** some
shared bathrooms; no in-room TVs; the
only hotel on the island, so almost always
full. ⑤ Rooms from: £110 ✉ A846, Craighouse ☎ 01496/820243 ⊕ www.jurahotel.
co.uk ⇱ 17 rooms ✦○✦ Free breakfast.

Isle of Mull and Iona

Mull is one of the most beguiling of
Scotland's isles, and happily it's also one
of the easiest to get to. The island's landscapes range from the pretty harbor of
Tobermory and the gentle slopes around
Dervaig to dramatic Atlantic beaches on
the west. In the south the long road past
the sweeping green slopes of the Ross
of Mull leads to Iona, Scotland's holy
island and a year-round attraction.

GETTING HERE AND AROUND
Ferries to Mull are run by the ubiqui-
tous Caledonian MacBrayne. Its most
frequent car-ferry route to Mull is from
Oban to Craignure (45 minutes). Two
shorter routes are from Lochaline on the
Morvern Peninsula to Fishnish (15 min-
utes), or Kilchoan (on the Adrnamurchan
Peninsula) to Tobermory (15 minutes). The
Kilchoan-Lochaline ferry is not bookable.

Isle of Mull and Iona

West Coast Tours serves the east coast, running between Tobermory, Craignure, and Fionnphort (for the ferry to Iona).

Craignure

On Mull, a 40-minute ferry crossing from Oban, 15-minute ferry crossing to Fishnish (5 miles northwest of Craignure) from Lochaline.

Craignure, little more than a pier and some houses, is close to the well-known Duart Castle. Reservations for the year-round ferries that travel from Oban to Craignure are advisable in summer. The ferry from Lochaline to Fishnish, just northwest of Craignure, does not accept reservations and does not run on Sunday.

GETTING HERE AND AROUND

The arrival point for the 40-minute ferry crossing from Oban, Craignure is the starting point for further travel on Mull northwest toward Salen and Tobermory, or toward Fionnphort and the Iona ferry to the southwest.

VISITOR INFORMATION Craignure Information Centre. ⊠ *The Pierhead* ☏ *01680/812377* ⊕ *www.visitscotland. com.*

Sights

★ Duart Castle

CASTLE/PALACE | The 13th-century Duart Castle stands dramatically atop a cliff overlooking the Sound of Mull. The ancient seat of the Macleans, it was ruined by the Campbells, their archenemies, in 1691 but restored by Sir Fitzroy

Home to the Maclean Clan, Duart Castle is one of the country's last privately owned clan castles.

Maclean in 1911. Inside you can visit the dungeons and state rooms, then climb the keep for a view of the waterfront. Nearby stands the **Millennium Wood,** planted in 2000 with indigenous trees. To reach Duart by car, take the A849 and turn left around the shore of Duart Bay. From Craignure's ferry port, there is a direct bus that takes you to the castle in about 10 minutes. ⊠ *A849 ⊕ 3 miles southeast of Craignure* ☎ *01680/812309* ⊕ *www.duartcastle.com* ✉ *£6.50* ⊗ *Closed Nov.–Mar.*

Hotels

Craignure Inn
$ | **B&B/INN** | Snug bedrooms with exposed beams, polished wood furniture, and views of the Sound of Mull make this 18th-century inn very appealing. **Pros:** lively bar scene; hearty local food; expansive views. **Cons:** live music can get loud; bar can get very busy; rooms on the small size. ⑤ *Rooms from: £95* ⊠ *A849 ⊕ Near the ferry pier* ☎ *01680/812305*

⊕ *www.craignure-inn.co.uk* ⇥ *3 rooms* ⧉ *Free breakfast.*

Dervaig

On Mull, 27 miles northwest of Craignure, 60 miles north of Fionnphort.

A pretty riverside village, Dervaig has a circular, pointed church tower that is reminiscent of the Irish-Celtic style of the 8th and 9th centuries. The Bellart is a good trout- and salmon-fishing river, and Calgary Bay, 5 miles away, has one of the best beaches on Mull.

GETTING HERE AND AROUND
You can reach Dervaig from Craignure via the A849. From Salen take the B8073, and from Tobermory take the B8073.

Sights

Old Byre Heritage Centre
MUSEUM | At this museum, an audiovisual presentation on the history of the region is one of the highlights. The tearoom's

wholesome fare, particularly the home-made soup, is a boon to travelers, as is the craft shop. You'll see signs for the center on the B8073, just before Dervaig. ⊠ Off B8073 ☎ 01688/400229 ⊕ www.old-byre.co.uk ⊠ £4 ⊗ Closed weekends and Nov.–Easter.

Tobermory

On Mull, 5 miles northeast of Dervaig, 21 miles north of Craignure.

With its rainbow crescent of brightly painted harborside houses, Tobermory is the most photogenic village in the Isles and among the prettiest in all Scotland. Unsurprisingly, it's a lively tourist center and a popular base for exploring Mull, its smaller neighbors, and the sea-life-filled surrounding waters.

GETTING HERE AND AROUND
The most frequent service to Mull is via the Oban-Craignure ferry. Tobermory is 21 miles from Craignure along the A849/848 (via Salen).

VISITOR INFORMATION Mull Information Centre. ⊠ Ledaig Car Park ☎ 01683/302875 ⊕ www.exploremull.com.

 Sights

Mull Eagle Watch
TOUR—SIGHT | White-tailed sea eagles, extinct in Scotland since 1916, were reintroduced to the Hebrides in 1975. There are now around 80 breeding pairs, and on a Mull Eagle Watch trip you have an excellent chance of seeing these magnificent raptors on their nests and feeding their young at nesting sites around the island. Guides are paid directly in cash. From October to March, tours are by request only. ⊠ Tobermory ⊕ Several different nest sites around Mull. Locations change each year ☎ 01680/812556 ⊕ www.mulleaglewatch.com ⊠ £10.

★ Tobermory Distillery
WINERY/DISTILLERY | Tobermory's cute little distillery has been making distinctive malts (the peaty Ledaig and the unpeated, lighter-tasting Tobermory) since 1798, though there have been intervening decades when it was "silent" and produced no whisky. It was relaunched in 1993, and a tour here is a more personal experience than is offered by some bigger, better-known distilleries. Starting in 2020, visitors will be able to sample the distillery's newest product: its own gin. ⊠ Bad-Daraich House, Ledaig ⊕ Off Main St. on south side of harbor ☎ 01688/302647 ⊕ www.tobermorydistillery.com ⊠ Tours from £8.

★ Whale Watch With Us
TOUR—SIGHT | High-speed boats carrying 12 passengers leave from Tobermory's harbor on scenic cruises, wildlife sea safaris, and whale-watching trips lasting up to four hours. You'll have a good chance of spotting dolphins, porpoises, and minke whales. If you're lucky, basking sharks and some of the sound's orcas may also put in an appearance. ⊠ Raraig House, Raeric Rd. ⊕ Ledaig pontoons, opposite car park and Tobermory Harbor Authority on Tobermory waterfront ☎ 01688/302875 ⊕ whalewatchwithus.com ⊠ From £30.

Restaurants

★ Café Fish
$$$ | **SEAFOOD** | This restaurant's location has certainly contributed to its success—it's perched on the pier at the end of Tobermory. The owners pride themselves on the freshness of their fish; they have their own boat and bring in their own seafood each day. **Known for:** roast shellfish platters; Glengorm rib-eye steaks; Mull lobster grilled with garlic butter. ⑤ Average main: £20 ⊠ The Pier ☎ 01688/301253 ⊕ www.thecafefish.com ⊗ Closed Jan.–mid-Mar.

Hotels

Highland Cottage
$$ | B&B/INN | Set on the hill above the harbor, this family-run hotel prides itself on its elegant rooms and the imaginative dishes in its dining room. **Pros:** comfortable rooms; attentive owners; high-quality dining and a good wine list. **Cons:** rooms are a bit small; a bit pricey for what you get; not for those looking for full-service hotel amenities. ⑤ *Rooms from: £170* ⊠ *Breadalbane St.* ☎ *01688/302030* ⊕ *www.highlandcottage.co.uk* ⤴ *6 rooms* ⦿ *Breakfast.*

Tobermory Hotel
$$ | HOTEL | FAMILY | Made up of five former fishermen's cottages, this lodging on Tobermory's waterfront has a warm, intimate feel. **Pros:** adorable cottage setting with fireplace; good restaurant; very pet- and child-friendly. **Cons:** small rooms; tiny bathrooms; not all rooms have both shower and tub. ⑤ *Rooms from: £175* ⊠ *Main St.* ☎ *01688/302091* ⊕ *www.the-tobermoryhotel.com* ⊗ *Closed Nov.–Mar* ⤴ *18 rooms* ⦿ *Breakfast.*

Western Isles Hotel
$$ | HOTEL | This grand hotel from the Victorian era looks down on Tobermory from its idyllic location overlooking the Sound of Mull. **Pros:** brilliant views; spacious public rooms; great food. **Cons:** some rooms look onto the car park; rooms vary in size; overall lackluster atmosphere. ⑤ *Rooms from: £130* ⊠ *Off B882* ☎ *01688/302012* ⊕ *www.westernisleshotel.co.uk* ⤴ *26 rooms* ⦿ *Free breakfast.*

⊙ Performing Arts

Mull Theatre
THEATER | The renowned Mull Theatre, founded in 1966, once prided itself on being the smallest theater in the United Kingdom. Today it has grown in size and in stature, and its productions tour not only the islands, but the whole of Scotland. It's wise to book ahead. ⊠ *Druimfin,* *Salen Rd.* ☎ *01688/302828* ⊕ *www.comar.co.uk/about/mull-theatre.*

Iona

5 minutes by ferry from Fionnphort (Mull), which is 36 miles west of Craignure.

The ruined abbey on Iona gives little hint that this was once one of the most important Christian religious centers in the land. The priceless *Book of Kells* (now in Dublin) was illustrated here, and it was the monks of Iona who spread Christian ideas across Scotland and the north. The abbey was founded in the year 563 by the fiery and argumentative Columba (circa 521–97) after his expulsion from Ireland. Until the 11th century, many of Scotland's kings and rulers were buried here, their tombstones still visible inside the abbey. Although few visitors venture beyond the pier and the abbey, there are several tranquil paths around the island.

GETTING HERE AND AROUND
Caledonian MacBrayne's ferry from Fionnphort departs at regular intervals throughout the year (£4.50 round-trip). Timetables are available on the Caledonian MacBrayne website. Note that cars are not permitted; there's a parking lot by the ferry at Fionnphort.

Sights

★ Iona Abbey
RELIGIOUS SITE | Overseen by St. Columba, who traveled here from Ireland, Iona was the birthplace of Christianity in Scotland in the 6th century. It survived repeated Norse sackings before falling into disuse around the time of the Reformation. Restoration work began at the beginning of the 20th century. Today the restored buildings serve as a spiritual center under the jurisdiction of the Church of Scotland. Guided tours by the Iona Community, an ecumenical religious group, begin every

half hour in summer and on demand in winter. ✉ *Iona* 🕾 *01681/700404* ⊕ *www. iona.org.uk* 🎫 *£7.50.*

 Hotels

St. Columba Hotel

$ | HOTEL | As befits a religious retreat, rooms in this 1846 minister's home are simple to the point of being spartan, but those in the front make up for it with glorious views across the Sound of Iona to Mull. **Pros:** impressive views; nice log fires; eco-friendly. **Cons:** no televisions; few home comforts; basic meals. ⑤ *Rooms from: £115* ✉ *Next to cathedral* ⊹ *About ¼ mile from the ferry pier* 🕾 *01681/700304* ⊕ *www.stcolumba-hotel.co.uk* ⊗ *Closed Nov.–Mar.* 🛏 *27 rooms* ¶◯¶ *Free breakfast.*

Tiree

4-hour sail from Oban, via Coll.

Blue seas, white sands, a microclimate warmed by the Gulf Stream, and good surfing make this windy island popular in summer.

GETTING HERE AND AROUND

Caledonian MacBrayne runs ferries to Tiree via Coll, four times a week (Tuesday, Thursday, Saturday, and Sunday). You can also fly here from Glasgow on Loganair or from Oban on Hebridean Air Services. Tiree has a shared taxi service (🕾 *01879/220311*), which you should book ahead of your arrival. An alternative is to rent a bike from **Tiree Fitness** (🕾 *07867/304640*).

ESSENTIALS

AIR TRAVEL CONTACTS Tiree Airport. ✉ *Off B8065* 🕾 *01879/220456* ⊕ *www. hial.co.uk.*

 Sights

Tiree

ISLAND | A fertile, low-lying island with its own microclimate, Tiree is windswept, but has long hours of sunshine in summer. Long, rolling Atlantic swells make it a favorite with surfers, and in summer, when an influx of wealthy visitors arrives, the posh accents of southern England sometimes drown out native voices. Among Tiree's several low-key archaeological sites are a large boulder near Vaul covered with more than 50 Bronze Age cup marks, and an excavated *broch* (stone tower) at Dun Mor Vaul. Tiree has two hotels and an assortment of self-catering accommodations, including a hostel with shared dorm rooms. The island is served by CalMac ferry from Oban.

Coll

3-hour sail from Oban.

Good birding and a number of ancient sites are among the attractions on Coll.

GETTING HERE AND AROUND

Caledonian MacBrayne runs ferries to Coll on Tuesday, Thursday, Saturday, and Sunday. You can also fly here from Oban on Hebridean Air Services. There is no public transportation or taxi service on Coll, but you can rent a bike at the post office (🕾 *01879/230–3395*).

 Sights

Coll

ISLAND | Unlike their neighbors in nearby Tiree, Coll's residents were not forced to leave the island in the 19th century. Today half of the island's sparse population lives in its only village, Arinagour. Its coasts offer extraordinarily rich birdlife, particularly along the beautiful sandy beaches of its southwest. Coll is even lower lying than Tiree but also rockier and less fertile. There are prehistoric standing stones at

Totronald, a cairn at Annagour, and scant remains of several Iron Age forts around the island, though it takes some imagination to visualize what they must have looked like many centuries ago. ⊕ *www.visitcoll.co.uk.*

Colonsay

2½-hour sail from Oban.

Less bleak than Coll and Tiree, Colonsay is one of Scotland's quietest, most unspoiled, and least populated islands. It is partly wooded, with a fine 20-acre rhododendron garden surrounding Colonsay House, private home of Baron Strathcona. The island also boasts a great variety of wildlife on land and in the surrounding waters.

GETTING HERE AND AROUND

CalMac ferries run to Colonsay on Monday, Wednesday, Friday, and Sunday. The island of Oronsay lies half a mile away and can be reached at certain times across a natural causeway. There is no public transport on Colonsay; bikes can be rented from **Archie's Bike Hire** (☎ *07970/673942*).

 ## Sights

Colonsay

ISLAND | The beautiful beach at Kiloran Bay on Colonsay is an utterly peaceful place even at the height of summer. The standing stones at Kilchattan Farm are known as Fingal's Limpet Hammers. Fingal, or Finn, MacCool (Fionn mac Cumhaill) is a warrior of massive size and strength in Celtic mythology. Standing before the stones, you can imagine Fingal wielding them like hammers to cull equally large limpets from Scotland's rocky coast. The island's social life revolves around the bar at the 19th-century Colonsay Hotel, 100 yards from the ferry pier. The adjacent island of Oronsay with its ruined cloister can be reached at low tide via a 1½-mile wade across a sandy sound. ⊕ *www.colonsay.org.uk.*

Chapter 10

INVERNESS AND AROUND THE GREAT GLEN

Updated by
Joseph Reaney

⊙ **Sights**
★★★★☆

🍴 **Restaurants**
★★☆☆☆

🛏 **Hotels**
★★☆☆☆

🛍 **Shopping**
★☆☆☆☆

🍸 **Nightlife**
★★☆☆☆

WELCOME TO INVERNESS AND AROUND THE GREAT GLEN

TOP REASONS TO GO

★ **Castles, fortresses, and battlefields:** Hear stories of the Highland people and famous figures like Bonnie Prince Charlie, and absorb the atmosphere of castles and battlefields, at Culloden Moor, Cawdor and Brodie castles, Fort George, and Glencoe.

★ **Outdoor activities:** The Great Glen is renowned for its hill walking. Some of the best routes are around Glen Nevis, Glencoe, and on Ben Nevis, the highest mountain in Britain.

★ **Wild landscapes and rare wildlife:** Spot rare plants and beasts including tiny least willow trees and golden eagles in the near-arctic tundra of Cairngorms National Park.

★ **Whisky tours:** The two westernmost distilleries on the Malt Whisky Trail are in Forres. Benromach is the smallest distillery in Speyside and has excellent tours; Dallas Dhu is preserved as a museum.

If Inverness is the center point of a compass, the Great Glen spreads out to the east, south, and west. To the east on the A96 stretches the Morayshire coast, populated with castles, beaches, and the distilleries of Speyside. Head southeast on the A9 and you hit the Cairngorms National Park and other nature preserves. The A82 heads south from Inverness, hugging the west side of Loch Ness. Nearby are the contemplative ruins at Urquhart Castle and the interesting locks of the Caledonian Canal. Farther southwest, Fort William can be a good base for day trips to the foreboding and steep mountain pass of Glencoe.

1 Inverness. The biggest city in the Highlands and a popular base for the region.

2 Culloden Moor. The scene of one of Scotland's most famous battles.

3 Narin. A former fishing village now famous for golfing and Cawdor Castle.

4 Forres. A perfect Scottish medieval town and a key stop on the Malt Whisky Trail.

5 Boat of Garten. A peaceful village home to a famous steam railway.

6 Aviemore. The gateway to Cairngorms National Park.

7 Kingussie. A more low-key base for the Cairngorms.

8 Drumnadrochit and Loch Ness. Nessie's famed hometown.

9 Fort Augustus. A good base to explore the lochs of the Caledonian Canal.

10 Fort William. Once a military outpost and now the gateway to the Great Glen.

11 Glenfinnan. Another town with lots of Jacobite history.

12 Arisaig. A gateway to the smaller Scottish isles.

13 Glencoe. One of Scotland's most beautiful regions with plenty of Highlands history.

Defined by its striking topography, the Great Glen brings together mountains and myths, history and wild nature— then lets you wash it all down with a dram of the world's finest whisky. Inverness is the gateway to an area in which the views from almost every twist and bend in the circuitous roads may take your breath away.

There's also plenty here for history buffs, including Culloden Moor, where the last battle fought on British soil ended the hopes of the tragically outgunned Jacobite rebels in 1746.

The Great Glen Fault runs diagonally through the Highlands of Scotland and was formed when two tectonic plates collided, shoving masses of the crust southwest toward the Atlantic Ocean. Over time the rift broadened into a glen, and a thin line of lochs now lies along its seam. The most famous of these is deep, murky Loch Ness, home to the elusive Loch Ness Monster.

The city of Inverness has a growing reputation for excellent restaurants, and from here nearly everything in the Great Glen is an easy day trip. Just south of the city, the 13th-century ruined Urquhart Castle sits on the shores of Loch Ness. In Fort Augustus, the Caledonian Canal joins Inverness to Fort William via a series of 29 locks. At the western end of the canal, Ben Nevis, Britain's highest mountain, rises sharply. The Nevis Range, like Cairngorms National Park to the east, is ideal for walking, climbing, and mountain biking through the hills and glens.

Fort William makes a good base for exploring Glencoe, an awe-inspiring region that was also the scene of another notoriously murky episode in Scottish history: the Glencoe Massacre of 1692. It's an area where history seems to be imprinted on the landscape, and it remains desolate, with some of the steepest, most atmospheric hills in Scotland.

Just north of Fort William, the Road to the Isles offers impressive coastal views. The Small Isles of Rum and Eigg create a low rocky skyline across the water. Near the start of this road lies Glenfinnan, where in 1745 Bonnie Prince Charlie rallied his Jacobite troops. The surrounding Morayshire coast is home to a more pastoral landscape, and 14th-century Cawdor Castle and its gardens have an opulent air. Nearby Brodie Castle has an awe-inspiring library and art collection.

Impressive long, sandy beaches stretch out along the coast from the towns of Nairn and Findhorn. Finally, the Malt Whisky Trail begins in Forres and follows the wide, fast River Spey south until it butts against the Cairngorms and the old

Caledonian forests, with their diverse and rare wildlife.

MAJOR REGIONS

Inverness and Nearby. At the center of this region is Inverness, a small but appealing city that makes a useful gateway to the Great Glen. It has an increasingly strong range of restaurants and accommodations, but its cultural offerings remain more or less limited to what is happening at the Eden Court Theatre and the live music at a few good pubs. From Inverness just about anywhere in the Great Glen is a day trip. East of Inverness, the infamous Culloden Moor still looks desolate on most days, and you can easily imagine the fierce, brief, and bloody battle that took place here in 1746 that ended in final, catastrophic defeat for the Jacobites and their quest to restore the exiled Stewarts to the British throne. Because Jacobite tales are interwoven with landmarks throughout this entire area, you will get much more out of this storied landscape if you first learn something about this thorny but colorful period of Scottish history. The Morayshire coast boasts many long beaches and some refined castles (Cawdor and Brodie) that are definitely worth a visit. Moving east along the inner Moray Firth, you might be tempted by Benromach distillery in Forres, a taste of what you can find farther south if you follow the Malt Whisky Trail.

Speyside and the Cairngorms. Speyside is best known for its whisky distilleries, and those who enjoy a good dram often follow the Whisky Trail. The Spey is a long river, running from Fort Augustus to the Moray Firth, and its fast-moving waters make for excellent fishing at many points along the way. They also give Speyside malt whiskies a softer flavor than those made with peaty island water. The area's native and planted pine forests draw many birds each spring and summer, and people come for miles to see the capercaillies and ospreys. Defining the eastern edge of the Great Glen, Cairngorms National Park provides sporty types with all the adventure they could ask for, including walking, kayaking, rock climbing, and even skiing, if the winter is cold enough. With craggy mountains, calm lochs, and swift rivers, the park has everything for lovers of the great outdoors. And while the towns and villages of Speyside and the Cairngorms are nothing special, they make great bases for heading out into nature.

Loch Ness, Fort William, and Nearby. Have a go trying to spot Nessie from the banks of Loch Ness. Compared with other lochs, Ness is not known for its beauty (although it's hardly a stain on the landscape). Instead, it draws attention for its infamous monster. Heading south from Inverness, you can travel along the loch's quiet east side or the more touristy west side. A pleasant morning can be spent at Urquhart Castle, in the tiny town of Drumnadrochit, or a bit farther south in the pretty town of Fort Augustus, where the Caledonian Canal meets Loch Ness. As you travel south and west, the landscape opens up and the Nevis Range comes into view. From Fort William you can visit the dark, cloud-laden mountains of Glencoe and the desolate stretch of moors and lochans at Rannoch Moor. Travelers drive through this region to experience the landscape, which changes at nearly every turn. It's a brooding, haunting area that's worth a visit in any season. If you dare, climb Britain's highest peak, Ben Nevis. The Road to the Isles, less romantically known as the A830, leads from Fort William to the coastal towns of Arisaig, Morar, and Mallaig, with access to the Small Isles of Rum, Eigg, Canna, and Muck.

Planning

When to Go

Late spring to early autumn is the best time to visit the Great Glen. If you catch good weather in summer, the days can be glorious. Unfortunately summer is also when you will encounter midges (tiny biting insects). Keep walking, as they can't move very fast. Winter can bring a damp chill, gusty winds, and snow-blocked roads, although many Scots value the open fires and warming whisky that make the off-season so appealing.

Planning Your Time

The Great Glen is an enormous area that can easily be broken into two separate trips. The first would be based in or near Inverness, allowing an exploration of Speyside, the Cairngorms, Cawdor and Brodie castles, and perhaps a few whisky-distillery tours. The second moves through the cloud-laden Glencoe and down through the moody Rannoch Moor, or toward the Road to the Isles; you could stay near Glencoe or in Fort William. To do the area justice you probably need at least three days.

For those with more time, a trip around the Great Glen could be combined with forays north into the Northern Highlands, east toward Aberdeen and the rest of the Malt Whisky Trail, southeastward to the Central Highlands, or south to Argyll.

Getting Here and Around

AIR

Inverness Airport has flights from London, Edinburgh, and Glasgow. Domestic flights covering the Highlands and islands are operated by LoganAir. Fort William has bus and train connections with Glasgow, so Glasgow Airport can be a good access point.

BUS

A long-distance Scottish Citylink service connects Glasgow and Fort William. Inverness is also well served from the central belt of Scotland. Discount carrier Megabus (book online to avoid phone charges) has service to Inverness from various U.K. cities.

Traveling around the Great Glen area without a car is very challenging, and all but impossible in more rural areas. Stagecoach Highlands serves the Great Glen and around Fort William.

BUS CONTACTS Megabus. ☎ *0900/160–0900* ⊕ *www.megabus.com.* **Scottish Citylink.** ☎ *0871/266–3333* ⊕ *www. citylink.co.uk.* **Stagecoach Highlands.** ☎ *01463/233371* ⊕ *www.stagecoachbus. com.*

CAR

As in all areas of rural Scotland, a car is a great asset for exploring the Great Glen, especially because the best of the area is away from the main roads. You can use the main A82 from Inverness to Fort William, or use the smaller B862/B852 roads to explore the much quieter east side of Loch Ness. Mallaig, west of Fort William, is reached via a new road, but there are still a few narrow and winding single-lane roads, which require slower speeds and greater concentration.

In the Great Glen, the best sights are often hidden from the main road, which is an excellent reason to favor peaceful rural byways and to avoid as much as possible the busy A96 and A9, which carry much of the traffic in the area.

TRAIN

ScotRail has connections from London to Inverness and Fort William (including an overnight sleeper service), as well as reliable links from Glasgow and Edinburgh. There's train service between Glasgow (Queen Street) and Inverness, via Aviemore, which gives access to the heart of Speyside.

Although there's no rail connection among towns within the Great Glen, this area has the West Highland Line, which links Fort William to Mallaig. This train, run by ScotRail, remains the most enjoyable way to experience the rugged hills and loch scenery between these two places. The Jacobite Steam Train is an exciting summer (late April to late October) option on the same route.

TRAIN CONTACTS Jacobite Steam Train.
☎ 0844/850–4685 ⊕ www.westcoastrail-ways.co.uk. **ScotRail.** ☎ 0344/811–0141 ⊕ www.scotrail.co.uk.

Restaurants

Inverness, Aviemore, and Fort William have plenty of cafés and restaurants in all price ranges. Inverness has particularly diverse dining options. Outside the towns there are many country-house hotels serving superb meals.

Hotels

In the Great Glen, towns have accommodations ranging from cozy inns to expansive hotels; in more remote areas your choice will usually be limited to smaller establishments. Book as far in advance as you can, as the area is very busy in the peak season and the best places fill up early. In Inverness you may find it more appealing to stay outside the city center or in the pretty countryside nearby.

Restaurant and hotel reviews have been shortened. For full information, visit Fodors.com. Restaurant prices are the average cost of a main course at dinner or, if dinner is not served, at lunch. Hotel prices are the lowest cost of a standard double room in high season, including 20% V.A.T.

WHAT IT COSTS in Pounds			
$	$$	$$$	$$$$
RESTAURANTS			
under £15	£15–£19	£20–£25	over £25
HOTELS			
under £125	£125–£200	£201–£300	over £300

Tours

Inverness Tours

GUIDED TOURS | This outfitter runs the occasional boat cruise, but it's mainly known for very good tours around the Highlands in well-equipped vehicles, led by expert guides and heritage enthusiasts. Nevertheless, the price is per minibus, not per person, so while it's quite a bargain for parties of six or seven, it's less appealing for small groups. It may be possible to get single tickets if another group will sell its unused space. ☎ 01667/455699 ⊕ www.invernesstours.com ✉ From £150.

J. A. Johnstone

DRIVING TOURS | At the more luxurious end of the scale, this company offers chauffeur-driven tours of the Highlands in air-conditioned Mercedes sedans. Tours are completely tailored to what you want to see, and the guides have an encyclopedic knowledge of the region. The company also runs multiday tours of the Scottish regions, and can help book accommodations along the way. ☎ 01463/798372 ⊕ www.jajcd.com ✉ Prices on request.

Inverness

176 miles north of Glasgow, 109 miles northwest of Aberdeen, 161 miles northwest of Edinburgh.

It's not the prettiest or the most charming Scottish city, but with a few attractions and some reliably good hotels and restaurants, Inverness makes a practical base for exploring a region that has a lot to offer. From here you can fan out in almost any direction for interesting day trips: east to Moray and the distilleries near Forres, southeast to the Cairngorms, and south to Loch Ness. Throughout its past, the town was burned and ravaged by Highland clans competing for dominance.

GETTING HERE AND AROUND

You can easily fly into Inverness Airport, as there are daily flights from London, Bristol, Birmingham, Manchester, and Belfast; however, there are also easy train and bus connections from Glasgow Airport. Scottish Citylink has service here, and Megabus has long-distance bus service from Edinburgh and Glasgow. ScotRail runs trains here from London, Edinburgh, Glasgow, and other cities.

Once you're here, you can explore much of the city on foot. A rental car makes exploring the surrounding area much easier. But if you don't have a car, there are bus and boat tours from the city center to a number of places in the Great Glen.

An unusual option from Inverness is a day trip to Orkney. From June through August, John O'Groats Ferries runs daily tours from Inverness to Orkney. They cost £76 for a whole day, including a six-hour tour of the island.

ESSENTIALS

AIRPORT CONTACTS Inverness Airport.
✉ *Dalcross* ☎ *01667/464000* ⊕ *www. invernessairport.co.uk.*

BOAT CONTACTS John O'Groats Ferries.
☎ *01955/611353* ⊕ *www.jogferry.co.uk.*

BUS CONTACTS Inverness Bus Station.
✉ *Margaret St.* ☎ *01463/233371.*

VISITOR INFORMATION Inverness—The City in the Highlands. ⊕ *www.inverness-scotland.com.* **VisitScotland Inverness iCentre.** ✉ *36 High St.* ☎ *01463/252401* ⊕ *www.visitscotland.com.*

 Sights

★ Fort George

MILITARY SITE | After the fateful Battle of Culloden, the nervous government in London ordered the construction of a large fort on a promontory reaching into the Moray Firth. Fort George was started in 1748 and completed some 20 years later. It's one of the best-preserved 18th-century military fortifications in Europe. At its height it housed 1,600 men and around 30,000 pounds of gunpowder; the on-site Highlanders Museum gives you a glimpse of the fort's history. The fort, 14 miles northeast of Inverness, is also a great base for spotting dolphins and whales out at sea. ✉ *Old Military Rd., Ardersier* ✛ *Off B9006* ☎ *01667/460232* ⊕ *www.historicenvironment.scot* 🖼 *£9.*

Inverness Castle

CASTLE/PALACE | One of Inverness's few historic landmarks is reddish-sandstone Inverness Castle (now the local Sheriff Court), nestled above the river off Castle Road on Castle Hill. The current structure is Victorian, built after a former fort was blown up by the Jacobites in the 1745 campaign. The castle isn't open to the public, but you are free to wander the grounds. ✉ *Inverness.*

Inverness Museum and Art Gallery

MUSEUM | **FAMILY** | The small but excellent Inverness Museum and Art Gallery covers archaeology, art, local history, and the natural environment in its lively displays. The museum is also home to the Highland Photographic Archive. ✉ *Castle Wynd* ☎ *01349/781730* ⊕ *www. highlifehighland.com* 🖼 *Free* ☉ *Closed Sun. and Mon.*

St. Andrew's Cathedral

RELIGIOUS SITE | This handsome Victorian cathedral, dating from 1869, has two unique claims to fame; in addition to being the northernmost cathedral in the British Isles, it was, more significantly, the first cathedral to be built in Britain

Inverness and Nearby

after the Reformation. The twin-turreted exterior of the building is made from characteristically reddish local Tarradale stone. Inside it follows a medieval layout, with the addition of an unusual patterned wooden floor. Check out the beautiful white marble font, carved in the shape of a seated angel. ✉ *Ardross St.* ☎ *01463/225553* ⊕ *www.morayepiscopalchurch.scot* 🎫 *Free.*

🍴 Restaurants

★ Café 1

$$ | MODERN BRITISH | Consistently recommended by locals as one of the best restaurants in the area, Café 1 really practices what it preaches in terms of sustainable, local produce. Taking inspiration from such big names as Blue Hill in New York, the restaurant rears its own herds to provide the Hebridean lamb and Highland beef on the menu, usually served with a simple order of chips (thick-cut fries) and rich garlic butter. **Known for:** castle views; melt-in-your-mouth lamb; ethically sourced ingredients. 💲 *Average main: £19* ✉ *75 Castle St.* ☎ *01463/226200* ⊕ *www.cafe1.net* 🕘 *Closed Sun.*

★ Chez Roux

$$$$ | MODERN BRITISH | The menu is as sleek as the service at this restaurant in the Rocpool Reserve Hotel, with clean modern design throughout (think monochrome walls, straight lines, and a whole lot of upholstery in tasteful accent colors). Expect creative, decadent dishes, including a signature soufflé that is far more filling than a lighter-than-air starter ought to be. **Known for:** inventive dishes; beautiful presentation; chic cocktail bar. 💲 *Average main: £26* ✉ *Rocpool Reserve*

The sandstone structure known as Inverness Castle stands guard over the small city of Inverness.

Hotel, Culduthel Rd. ☎ *01463/240089* ⊕ *www.rocpool.com.*

Dores Inn

$$ | BRITISH | Off a pretty country road on the eastern shore of Loch Ness, this low-slung, white-stone eatery is the perfect place to stop for lunch or dinner. The menu is a combination of well-prepared old favorites—fish-and-chips, perhaps, or an all-day breakfast)—together with steaks, lamb, and seafood. **Known for:** well-prepared Scottish classics; excellent range of whiskies; gluten-free options. ⓢ *Average main: £16* ✉ *B862, Dores* ☎ *01463/751203* ⊕ *www.thedoresinn. co.uk.*

Fig and Thistle Bistro

$$ | BISTRO | FAMILY | This intimate little restaurant has been packing in the crowds nightly thanks to its modern bistro fare presented stylishly but without fuss. You could start with a delicious goat cheese and fig tart, for example, followed by a sumptuous steak with a red-wine-and-thyme sauce. **Known for:** seared local salmon infused with Thai flavors;

tasty homemade desserts; reservations needed, especially on weekends. ⓢ *Average main: £16* ✉ *4A Stephens Brae* ☎ *01463/712422* ⊘ *Closed Sun. and Mon. No lunch Tues.*

River House

$$$ | SEAFOOD | Head chef and owner Alfie Little draws heavily on local inspiration to shape the menu at this tiny riverside seafood restaurant, which has an interior as stylish as its appealing gray-and-white exterior. Start with mussels or oysters from the Scottish islands, then take your pick from mains based on native fish such as Shetland halibut and Scrabster hake, and wash it all down with a local beer. **Known for:** intimate atmosphere; fresh, sustainable local seafood; riverside outdoor seating in summer. ⓢ *Average main: £23* ✉ *1 Greig St.* ☎ *01463/222033* ⊕ *www.riverhouseinverness.co.uk* ⊘ *Closed Sun. and Mon. No lunch.*

★ Rocpool Restaurant

$$$ | BRASSERIE | Another perennial favorite, the Rocpool has a frequently changing menu of modern bistro classics, with a few international twists. Local seafood is a specialty, and the wine list is excellent. **Known for:** outstanding wine selection; contemporary twists on traditional dishes; quality meat and seafood. $ *Average main: £20* ✉ *1 Ness Walk* ☎ *01463/717274* ⊕ *www.rocpool-restaurant.com* ⊗ *Closed Sun.*

 Hotels

Bluebell House

$ | **B&B/INN** | Each room at this traditional Scottish guesthouse has sturdy oak furnishings, including a downstairs bedroom with a full-curtained four-poster bed and a curved chaise lounge. **Pros:** large rooms; decadent furnishing; great hosts. **Cons:** smallish bathrooms; no windows in bathrooms; minimal technology. $ *Rooms from: £100* ✉ *31 Kenneth St.* ☎ *01463/238201* ⊕ *www.bluebell-house.com* ➷ *4 rooms* ⊙| *Free breakfast.*

Bunchrew House Hotel

$$$$ | **HOTEL** | This 17th-century baronial mansion, its turrets reflected in a glassy lake, looks like something from a Scottish fairy tale. **Pros:** beautiful setting; atmospheric building; good restaurant. **Cons:** some rooms could do with refurbishment; quite expensive; a little out of town. $ *Rooms from: £345* ✉ *Off A862* ✛ *About 3 miles west of Inverness* ☎ *01463/234917* ⊕ *www.bunchrewhousehotel.com* ➷ *16 rooms* ⊙| *Free breakfast.*

Highland Apartments by Mansley

$$ | **RENTAL** | One of three Mansley properties in Scotland (the other two are in Edinburgh), Highland Apartments offers luxurious self-catering accommodations right in the city center, many with delightful balcony views of the River Ness. **Pros:** chic modern apartments; great city center location; secure parking available. **Cons:** not all apartments have river views; quite expensive; some may find entry by code impersonal. $ *Rooms from: £175* ✉ *Bridge House, 21–23 Bridge St.*

☎ *0800/304–7160* ⊕ *www.bymansley.com* ➷ *19 rooms* ⊙| *No meals.*

Moyness House

$ | **B&B/INN** | On a quiet residential street with well-trimmed hedges a few minutes from downtown Inverness, this lovely Victorian villa was once the home of Scottish author Neil M. Gunn (1891–1973), known for short stories and novels that evoke images of the Highlands, such as *Morning Tide, Highland River,* and *Butcher's Broom.* **Pros:** beautiful building; lovely garden; great location near the river. **Cons:** public rooms a bit fussy for some; books up quickly; strict cancellation policy. $ *Rooms from: £95* ✉ *6 Bruce Gardens* ☎ *01463/233836* ⊕ *www.moyness.co.uk* ➷ *7 rooms* ⊙| *Free breakfast.*

★ Ness Walk

$$$ | **HOTEL** | This spot offers true five-star luxury in the form of spacious and stylish rooms, one of Inverness's best fine-dining restaurants (Torrish), and a verdant riverside location. **Pros:** beautiful riverside property; phenomenal afternoon tea; lounge check-in with champagne. **Cons:** walk from the city center; superattentive service can be stifling; very expensive. $ *Rooms from: £240* ✉ *12 Ness Walk* ☎ *01463/215215* ⊕ *www.nesswalk.com* ➷ *47 rooms.*

Trafford Bank

$$ | **B&B/INN** | This former Bishop's home turned boutique B&B makes for a practical and stylish base, with owner Lorraine Freel's talent for interior design seen in the bespoke dining room chairs and handmade wallpaper—as well as in the eclectic array of art throughout. **Pros:** welcoming atmosphere; stylish rooms; relaxing vibe. **Cons:** some rooms on the small side; early checkout time; a walk from the city center. $ *Rooms from: £135* ✉ *96 Fairfield Rd.* ☎ *01463/241414* ⊕ *www.invernesshotelaccommodation.co.uk* ➷ *5 rooms* ⊙| *Free breakfast.*

Nightlife

★ Hootananny

BARS/PUBS | An odd but much-loved combination of Scottish pub, concert hall, and Thai restaurant, Hootananny is one of the best places in the region to hear live music. The excellent pub has a warm atmosphere and serves food that comes highly recommended by locals. Several bands play each Saturday evening and a few during the week, too—check the website for listings. ✉ *67 Church St.* ☎ *01463/233651* ⊕ *www.hootanannyinverness.co.uk.*

Performing Arts

★ Eden Court Theatre

DANCE | The varied program at this excellent local filmhouse and theater includes movies, musical theater, comedy, ballet, and even pantomime. Check out the art gallery and the bright café, and take a walk around the magnificent Bishop's Palace. In summer, there's also regular live music on the lawn. ✉ *Bishops Rd.* ☎ *01463/234234* ⊕ *www.eden-court. co.uk.*

Shopping

Although Inverness has the usual indoor shopping malls and department stores, the most interesting goods are in the specialty outlets in and around town.

BOOKSTORES

Leakey's Bookshop

BOOKS/STATIONERY | This shop claims to be Scotland's largest secondhand bookstore. When you get tired of leafing through the 100,000 or so titles, climb to the mezzanine café and study the cavernous church interior, complete with wood-burning fire. Antique prints and maps are housed on the balcony. ✉ *Greyfriars Hall, Church St.* ☎ *01463/239947.*

CLOTHING

Duncan Chisholm

CLOTHING | This shop specializes in Highland dress and tartans. Mail-order and made-to-measure services are available. ✉ *47–51 Castle St.* ☎ *01463/234599* ⊕ *www.kilts.co.uk.*

GALLERIES

Castle Gallery

ART GALLERIES | The excellent Castle Gallery sells contemporary paintings, sculpture, prints, and crafts. It also hosts frequently changing exhibitions by up-and-coming artists. ✉ *43 Castle St.* ☎ *01463/729512* ⊕ *www.castlegallery. co.uk.*

LOCAL SPECIALTIES

Inverness Coffee Roasting Co

FOOD/CANDY | An ideal place to pick up a gift, this beautifully presented little coffee shop stocks a good selection of locally roasted beans to enjoy on the premises or take away with you. Indulgent handmade treats made in Inverness by luxury chocolatiers The Chocolate Place are also available here. ✉ *15 Chapel St.* ☎ *01463/242555* ⊕ *www.inverness-coffeeroasting.co.uk.*

SHOPPING CENTERS

Victorian Market

SHOPPING CENTERS/MALLS | Don't miss the colorful Victorian Market, built in 1870. The atmospheric indoor space houses more than 40 privately owned specialty shops. ✉ *Academy St.*

Activities

★ Castle Stuart Golf Links

GOLF | Opened in 2009, this course overlooking the Moray Firth is already considered one of Scotland's finest, hosting the Scottish Open in 2011. Expect undulating fairways and extensive bunkers that test your mettle. The 210-yard 17th hole provides perilous cliff-top play; the wind can defeat the canniest player. The art deco–inspired clubhouse offers stunning views of the water. ✉ *Off B9039*

☏ 01463/796111 ⊕ www.castlestuartgolf.com ✉ £210 May–Oct.; £155 Apr. and Nov. ⅄ 18 holes, 6553 yards, par 72 ☞ Closed Dec.–Mar.

Inverness Golf Club

GOLF | Established in 1883, and partly designed by famous British Open champion and course designer James Braid, Inverness Golf Club welcomes visitors to its parkland course 1 mile from downtown. The tree-lined course overlooking the Beauly Firth presents some unique challenges to keep even experienced golfers on their toes. ⊠ Culcabock Rd. ☏ 01463/239882 ⊕ www.invernessgolfclub.co.uk ✉ £65 May–Aug.; £50 Apr., Sept., and Oct.; £25 Nov.–Mar. ⅄ 18 holes, 6102 yards, par 69.

Culloden Moor

6 miles east of Inverness.

Culloden Moor was the scene of the last battle fought on British soil—and to this day its name is enough to invoke raw and tragic feelings in Scotland. Austere and windswept, it's also a place of outstanding natural beauty.

GETTING HERE AND AROUND

Driving along the B9006 from Inverness is the easiest way to Culloden Battlefield, and there's a large car park to handle many visitors. Stagecoach Highlands Bus 5 also runs from Inverness to the battlefield.

Sights

Clava Cairns

ARCHAEOLOGICAL SITE | Not far from Culloden Moor, on a narrow road southeast of the battlefield, are the Clava Cairns, dating from the Bronze Age. In a cluster among the trees, these stones and monuments form a large ring with underground passage graves that are reached via a tunnel. Helpful placards put

Fishing in the Great Glen

The Great Glen is laced with rivers and lochs where you can fly-fish for salmon and trout. The fishing seasons are as follows: salmon and sea trout, from early February through September or even into October and November (depending on the area); brown trout, from mid-March through September; rainbow trout year-round. Sea angling from shore or boat is also possible. Tourist centers can provide information on locations, permits, and fishing rights.

everything into historical context. ⊠ Off B851, Culloden ✉ Free.

★ Culloden Battlefield

MILITARY SITE | Here, on a cold April day in 1746, the hopelessly outgunned Jacobite forces of Bonnie Prince Charlie were destroyed by King George II's army. The victorious commander, the Duke of Cumberland (George II's son), earned the name of the Butcher of Cumberland for the bloody reprisals carried out by his men on Highland families, Jacobite or not, caught in the vicinity. In the battle itself, the duke's army—greatly outnumbering the Jacobites—killed up to 2,000 soldiers. The victors, by contrast, lost just 50. The National Trust for Scotland has re-created a slightly eerie version of the battlefield as it looked in 1746 that you can explore with a guided audio tour. An innovative visitor center enables you to get closer to the sights and sounds of the battle and to interact with the characters involved, while a viewing platform helps put things into perspective from on high (literally). Academic research and technology have helped recreate the Gaelic dialect, song, and music of the time. There's also a good on-site café.

Bonnie Prince Charlie

His life became the stuff of legend. Charles Edward Louis John Casimir Silvester Maria Stuart—better known as Bonnie Prince Charlie, or the Young Pretender—was born in Rome in 1720. The grandson of ousted King James II of England (King James VII of Scotland) and son of James Stuart, the Old Pretender, he was the focus of Jacobite hopes to reclaim the throne of Scotland. Charles was charming and attractive, and he enjoyed more than the occasional drink.

In 1745 Charles led a Scottish uprising to restore his father to the throne. He sailed to the Outer Hebrides with only a few men but with promised support from France. When that support failed to arrive, he sought help from the Jacobite supporters, many from the Highland clans, who were faithful to his family. With 6,000 men behind him, Charles saw victory in Prestonpans and Falkirk, but the tide turned when he lied to his men about additional Jacobite troops waiting south of the border. When these fictitious troops did not materialize, his army retreated to Culloden where, on April 16, 1746, they were massacred.

Charles escaped to the Isle of Benbecula, where he met and is rumored to have fallen in love with Flora MacDonald. After he had hidden there for a week, Flora dressed him as her maid and brought him to sympathizers on the Isle of Skye, who helped him escape to France.

Scotland endured harsh reprisals from the government after the rebellion. As for Charles, he spent the rest of his life in drunken exile, taking the title Count of Albany. In 1772 he married Princess Louise of Stolberg-Gedern, only to separate from her eight years later. He died a broken man in Rome in 1788.

✉ Off B9006, Culloden ☎ 0844/493–2159 ⊕ www.nts.org.uk 💷 £11.

Nairn

12 miles northeast of Culloden Moor, 16 miles northeast of Inverness, 87 miles northwest of Aberdeen.

This once-prosperous fishing village is now more likely to lure golfers than sailors. Nearby is Cawdor Castle, loaded with history. East of Nairn pier is a long beach, great for a stroll.

GETTING HERE AND AROUND
A car gives you the most flexibility, but Nairn is close to Inverness (via A96), and regular local buses serve the town.

◉ Sights

★ Cawdor Castle and Gardens
CASTLE/PALACE | FAMILY | Shakespeare's Macbeth was the Thane of Cawdor (a local officer of the crown), but the sense of history that exists within the turreted walls of Cawdor Castle is certainly more than fictional. Cawdor is a lived-in castle, not an abandoned, decaying structure. The earliest part is the 14th-century central tower; the rooms contain family portraits, tapestries, fine furniture, and paraphernalia reflecting 600 years of history. Outside the walls are sheltered gardens and woodland walks. Children will have a ball exploring the lush and mysterious Big Wood, with its wildflowers and varied wildlife. There are lots of creepy stories and fantastic tales amid the dank dungeons and drawbridges. If the castle

Legend has it that Cawdor Castle was built around a thorn tree that can still be seen in the castle's dungeon today.

sounds appealing, keep in mind that the estate has cottages to rent. ✉ *B9090, Cawdor* ✛ *5 miles southwest of Nairn* ☎ *01667/404401* ⊕ *www.cawdorcastle. com* ✍ *Castle £12.50; grounds only £7.50* ⊙ *Closed mid-Oct.–mid-Apr.*

Nairn Museum

MUSEUM | The fishing boats have moved to larger ports, but Nairn's historical flavor has been preserved at the Nairn Museum, in a handsome Georgian building in the center of town. Exhibits emphasize artifacts, photographs, and model boats relating to the town's fishing past. A genealogy service is also offered. A library in the same building has a strong local-history section. ✉ *Viewfield House, Viewfield Dr.* ☎ *01667/456791* ⊕ *www. nairnmuseum.co.uk* ✍ *£4* ⊙ *Closed Sun.*

Phoenix Sea Adventures

TOUR—SIGHT | With one- and two-hour trips by boat from Nairn Harbour into the Moray Firth, Phoenix Sea Adventures offers you the chance to see seals, porpoises, and dolphins in their breeding areas. The daily departure times for the

modern, ex-naval SWIFT vessels vary depending on the tides and the weather. Evening trips are offered on certain dates in summer. ✉ *Nairn Marina, Harbour St.* ☎ *0770/316–8097* ⊕ *www.phoenix-nairn. co.uk* ✍ *Tours from £20.*

Hotels

★ Boath House

$$$$ | B&B/INN | Built in the 1820s and refurbished in 2017, this stunning Regency manor house offers elegant, spacious rooms (some with cast-iron bathtubs), a highly renowned fine-dining restaurant with local, ethically sourced ingredients, and a stunning setting within 20 acres of lovingly nurtured gardens. **Pros:** excellent dining; gorgeous 20-acre grounds; relaxed atmosphere. **Cons:** some airplane noise; no gym or spa facilities; very pricey. $ *Rooms from: £380* ✉ *Off A96, Auldearn* ☎ *01667/454896* ⊕ *www.boath-house.com* ➽ *9 rooms* ◎ *Free breakfast.*

★ Wendy Hoose

$ | B&B/INN | Located at the bottom of the Boath House Estate, the Wendy Hoose—named for owner Wendy Matheson, who runs the property with her husband, Don—is a charming B&B, where the historic exterior gives way to a thoroughly modern interior. **Pros:** cozy contemporary interior; informal and relaxed vibe; easy access to dining at Boath House. **Cons:** accepts only cash or Bacs (U.K. payment system); minimum two nights in high season; no guests under 18 allowed. $ *Rooms from: £120* ⊠ *Boath House, Off A96, Auldearn* ☎ *07703/737530* ⊕ *www.thewendyhoose.com* ⇥ *2 rooms* ⧉| *Free Breakfast.*

🛍 Shopping

Auldearn Antiques

ANTIQUES/COLLECTIBLES | It's easy to spend an hour wandering around this old church, which is filled to the brim with furniture, fireplaces, architectural antiques, and linens. The converted farm-steads also have tempting antique chinaware and textiles. ⊠ *Dalmore Manse, Lethen Rd., Auldearn* ☎ *01667/453087* ⊕ *www.auldearnantiques.co.uk.*

🏃 Activities

Nairn's courses are highly regarded by golfers and are very popular, so book far in advance.

Nairn Dunbar Golf Club

GOLF | Founded in 1899, the difficult Championship Links Course here features gorse-lined fairways and lovely sea views. ■**TIP**→ **Ask about the special-rate Nairn ticket, which allows you to play both this and the similarly named Nairn Golf Club, for the bargain rate of £180 from April to October.** ⊠ *Lochloy Rd.* ☎ *01667/452741* ⊕ *www.nairndunbar.com* ⛳ *£40 (£30 after 1 pm) Apr. and Oct.; £55 (£45 after 2 pm) May–Sept.; £27 Nov.–Mar.* 🏌 *18 holes, 6765 yards, par 72.*

Nairn Golf Club

GOLF | Highly regarded in golfing circles, the Nairn Golf Club dates from 1887 and is the regular home of Scotland's Northern Open. Huge greens, aggressive gorse, a beach hazard for five of the holes, a steady prevailing wind, and distracting views across the Moray Firth make play on the Championship Course unforgettable. The adjoining nine-hole Cameron Course is ideal for a warm-up or a fun round for the family. ⊠ *Seabank Rd.* ☎ *01667/453208* ⊕ *www.nairngolfclub.co.uk* ⛳ *Championship Course: £160 (£110 off-peak) May–Sept.; £110 Apr. and Oct.; £50 Nov.–Mar.; Cameron Course: £20* 🏌 *Championship Course: 18 holes, 6774 yards, par 72; Cameron Course: 9 holes, 1634 yards, par 29* ⚲ *Reservations essential.*

Forres

10 miles east of Nairn.

The burgh of Forres is everything a Scottish medieval town should be, with a handsome tolbooth (the former courthouse and prison) and impressive gardens as its centerpiece. It's remarkable how well the old buildings have adapted to their modern retail uses. With two distilleries—one still operating, the other preserved as a museum—Forres is a key point on the Malt Whisky Trail. Brodie Castle is also nearby. Just 6 miles north you'll find Findhorn Ecovillage, and a sandy beach stretches along the edge of the semi-enclosed Findhorn Bay, which is excellent bird-watching territory.

GETTING HERE AND AROUND

Forres is easy to reach by car or bus from Inverness on the A96. Daily ScotRail trains run here from Inverness and Aberdeen.

◉ Sights

Benromach Distillery

WINERY/DISTILLERY | The smallest distillery in Moray, Benromach was founded in 1898. It's now owned by whisky specialist Gordon and MacPhail, and produces an array of distinctive (often slightly peaty) malts, as well as the housemade gin Red Door. An informative hourly tour will lead you through the facilities, including seeing the poignant signatures of distillery managers before and after a 15-year closure in the late 20th century; tours end with a tutored nosing and tasting. ⊠ *Inٴererne Rd.* ☎ *01309/675968* ⊕ *www.benromach.com* 💷 *From £8.*

Brodie Castle

CASTLE/PALACE | A magnificent, medieval turreted fortification, Brodie Castle was rebuilt and extended in the 17th and 19th centuries. Consequently, there are fine examples of late-17th-century plasterwork preserved in the Dining Room and Blue Sitting Room, as well as a superb collection of artworks from the Old Masters up to the modern day. You'll also find an impressive library and beautiful gardens with over 400 varieties of daffodils. The castle is around 24 miles east of Inverness, making it a popular day trip. ⊠ *Off A96, Brodie* ☎ *01309/641371* ⊕ *www.nts.org.uk* 💷 *Castle and gardens £20, castle or gardens only £11.*

Dallas Dhu Historic Distillery

WINERY/DISTILLERY | The final port of call on the Malt Whisky Trail, the Dallas Dhu Historic Distillery was the last distillery built in the 19th century and was still in operation until the 1980s. Today its distillery rooms—from malt barn to still house to bonded warehouses—make up a fascinating exhibition that tells the story of Scotland's national drink. You'll be walked through the entire whisky-making process by an audio tour guide, before eventually arriving in the bar to taste a dram and watch an entertainingly dated video presentation. ⊠ *Mannachie Rd.*

☎ *01309/676548* ⊕ *www.historicenvironment.scot* 💷 *£6* 🕒 *Closed Thurs. and Fri. Oct.–Mar.*

Findhorn Ecovillage

TOWN | This education center is dedicated to developing "new ways of living infused with spiritual values," drawing power from wind turbines, local farms, and gardens to sustain themselves. A tour affords a thought-provoking glimpse into the lives of the ultra-independent villagers. See homes made out of whisky barrels, and the Universal Hall, filled with beautiful engraved glass. The Phoenix Shop sells organic foods and handmade crafts, and the Blue Angel Café serves organic and vegetarian fare. ⊠ *The Park, Off B9011, Findhorn* ☎ *01309/690311* ⊕ *www.findhorn.org* 💷 *Free; tours £8; book for self-guided tour £7* 🕒 *No tours Tues., Thurs., and Sat.*

Sueno's Stone

ARCHAEOLOGICAL SITE | At the eastern end of town stands Sueno's Stone, a 22-foot-tall pillar of stone carved with the ranks of soldiers from some long-forgotten battle. Nobody can quite agree on how old it is or what battle it marked, but its intricate Pictish carvings suggest it is from the early medieval period, probably erected between AD 600 and 1000. ⊠ *Findhorn Rd.* ⊕ *www.historicenvironment.scot* 💷 *Free.*

Hotels

Cluny Bank Hotel

$$ | **HOTEL** | Take one look at any of this pretty Victorian hotel's unique bedrooms, filled with personal touches, and you could easily guess that this is a family-run venture. **Pros:** lovely hosts; tranquil residential area; award-winning restaurant. **Cons:** some bathrooms a bit small; a little out of town; decor tired in places. $ *Rooms from: £130* ⊠ *69 St. Leonard's Rd.* ☎ *01309/674304* ⊕ *www.clunybankhotel.co.uk* 🗝 *7 rooms* ⏍ *Free breakfast.*

394

 Shopping

Brodie Countryfare

CLOTHING | Visit Brodie Countryfare only if you're feeling flush: you may covet the unusual knitwear, quality designer clothing and shoes, gifts, and toys, but they are *not* cheap. The excellent restaurant, on the other hand, is quite inexpensive. ⊠ *On A96, Brodie* ☎ *01309/641555* ⊕ *www.brodiecountryfare.com.*

 Activities

Findhorn Bay Beach

BEACHES | Along the edge of Findhorn Bay you'll find a long stretch of beach, great for an afternoon by the sea. You can reach the beach through the dunes from the northern end of the Findhorn Ecovillage, or park at the edge of the village of Findhorn for a shorter stroll. There are public restrooms, but few other amenities. **Amenities:** toilets. **Best for:** solitude; walking. ⊠ *Off B9011, Findhorn.*

Boat of Garten

35 miles southwest of Rothes, 6 miles northeast of Aviemore.

In the peaceful village of Boat of Garten, the scent of pine trees mingles with an equally evocative smell—that of steam trains. The town is home to the historic Strathspey Steam Railway, which is currently closed due to a fire in summer 2019. Close to Cairngorms National Park, Boat of Garten has built a reputation as a great place to stay while exploring the region.

GETTING HERE AND AROUND

This charming town is an easy drive from Inverness or Aviemore via the A9 and the A95. It's also serviced by local buses, and some people travel here on the Strathspey Steam Train.

 Sights

Landmark Forest Adventure Park

AMUSEMENT PARK/WATER PARK | **FAMILY** | Situated 4 miles northwest of Boat of Garten, this park has a host of attractions, including nature trails, a heart-stopping parachute jump simulator, raft rides with varying degrees of wetness, a fire tower you can climb, and, best of all, the Wonder Wood, a place where visual tricks like forced perspective are used to befuddle your senses. You could easily spend half a day here. The park is open year-round, but most attractions close in winter (so prices are significantly lower). ⊠ *B9153, Carrbridge* ☎ *0800/731–3446* ⊕ *www.landmarkpark.co.uk* ✉ *Apr.–Oct., £21.45; Nov.–Mar., £7.25.*

Loch Garten Osprey Centre

NATURE PRESERVE | Set in the heart of Abernethy Forest, the Loch Garten Osprey Centre offers a glimpse of the large fishing birds that come here to breed. The reserve, one of the last stands of ancient Scots pines in Scotland, attracts a host of other birds, too, including the bright crossbill and the crested tit. You might also spot the rarely seen red squirrel. The sanctuary is administered by the Royal Society for the Protection of Birds. ⊠ *Off B970, Nethy Bridge* ⊹ *1 mile east of Boat of Garten* ☎ *01479/831476* ⊕ *www.rspb.org.uk* ✉ *£5* ⊙ *Closed early Sept.–Mar.*

 Hotels

The Boat Country Inn

$$ | **HOTEL** | Great views of the Strathspey Steam Railway, welcoming traditional decor, and a wide variety of room types make this hotel much more than just a base for exploring the Cairngorms. **Pros:** good views; peaceful location; garden access an option. **Cons:** not all rooms are family-friendly; some shared spaces need a lick of paint; disappointing breakfast. ⑤ *Rooms from: £130* ⊠ *Deshar Rd.*

Speyside and
the Cairngorms

☎ 01479/831258 ⊕ www.boathotel.co.uk
🛏 34 rooms ⁏◎⁏ Breakfast.

 Activities

★ Boat of Garten Golf Club

GOLF | This is one of Scotland's greatest
"undiscovered" courses. The club, which
dates to the late 19th century, was
redesigned and extended by James Braid
in 1932, and each of its 18 holes has a
strong Highland feel. Some cut through
birch wood and heathery rough, and
most have long views to the Cairngorms.
An unusual feature is the preserved
steam railway that runs alongside
part of the course. ⊠ Nethybridge Rd.
☎ 01479/831282 ⊕ www.boatgolf.com
🏷 £75 ⵗ 18 holes, 5876 yards, par 70
🖉 Reservations essential.

Aviemore
━━━━━━━━━━━━━━━

*6 miles southwest of Boat of Garten, 30
miles southeast of Inverness.*

At the foot of the Cairngorms, once-quiet
Aviemore now has all the brashness and
boxiness of a year-round holiday resort.
In the summer months it's filled with
walkers, cyclists, and rock climbers, so
it's a convenient place for stocking up
on supplies. Nevertheless, many of the
smaller villages nearby are quieter places
to stay. ■TIP➔ Be forewarned: this region
can get very cold above 3,000 feet, and
weather conditions can change rapidly,
even in the middle of summer.

GETTING HERE AND AROUND
The A9, Scotland's major north–south
artery, runs past Aviemore. From Boat
of Garten take the A95. The town is

serviced by regular trains and buses from Inverness, Edinburgh, and Glasgow.

ESSENTIALS

VISITOR INFORMATION VisitScotland Aviemore iCentre. ✉ *7 Grampian Rd.* ☎ *01479/810930* ⊕ *www.visitscotland. com.*

Sights

Cairngorm Reindeer Centre

NATURE PRESERVE | FAMILY | On the high slopes of the Cairngorms, you may see the reindeer herd that was introduced here in the 1950s. The reindeer are docile creatures that seem to enjoy human company. Ranger-led visits to the herd are offered at least once a day from mid-February to December, weather permitting. In July and August you can also accompany rangers on gentle half-day treks through the mountains. From April through December a small herd of young reindeer is cared for at a paddock near the visitor center; you can visit (and pet them) for a small fee. Bring waterproof gear, as conditions can be wet and muddy. ✉ *Reindeer House, Glenmore ✛ 6 miles east of Aviemore* ☎ *01479/861228* ⊕ *www.cairngormreindeer.co.uk* 🎫 *£16; paddock £3.50* ⊗ *Closed Jan.–early Feb.*

★ Cairngorms National Park

NATIONAL/STATE PARK | A rugged wilderness of mountains, moorlands, glens, and lochs, the sprawling Cairngorms National Park, established in 2003, takes in more than 1,700 square miles. At the heart of Britain's largest national park (nearly 1,750 square miles of countryside) is a wild arctic landscape that sits on a granite plateau. Five of Scotland's nine 4,000-foot-high mountains are found in this range, and there are 13 more over 3,000 feet. These rounded mountains, including Cairn Gorm (meaning "blue hill" in Gaelic) and Ben Macdui, the second highest in Britain at 4,295 feet, were formed at the end of the last ice age. The

Boat of Garten's Ferry

A ferry that once linked both sides of the River Spey gave its name to Boat of Garten. The first official record of the ferry is in 1662, but the village itself did not appear until the coming of the railway, in 1868, when cottages sprang up between the railway line and the ferry crossing. When it was time to pick a name, the ferry seemed like a good symbol. Not long after that, bridges were built across the River Spey, and demand for the little ferry disappeared, but the name stuck.

Lairig Ghru Pass, a stunning U-shaped glen, was carved by the retreating glacier.

Past Loch Morlich, at the high parking lot on the exposed shoulders of the Cairngorm Mountains, are dozens of trails for hiking and cycling. This is a massive park, encompassing small towns as well as countryside, but a good place to start exploring is the main visitor center in Aviemore. The staff can dispense maps, expert advice on the best trails, and also information on guided walks and other activities. Because much of the best scenery in the park is off-road—including ancient pine forests and open moorland—a particularly good way to cover ground in the park is on a pony trek. The **Rothiemurchus Estate** leads guided treks for riders of all ability levels.

The environment supports rare arctic-alpine and tundra plant and animal species (a full quarter of Britain's endangered species are found here) including flora such as the least willow and alpine blue-sow thistle, and birds such as the ptarmigan, dotterel, and Scottish crossbill—the only bird completely unique to Britain. Lower down the slopes, terrain that was once

Rugged Cairngorms National Park features many lochs and beaches, including rocky Loch Morlich.

filled with woodland is now characterized by heather, cotton grass, and sphagnum moss. This open expanse allows visitors to glimpse animals such as the golden eagle, roe deer, or red deer. Fragments of the ancient Caledonian forest (largely Scots pine, birch, and rowan) remain, offering the ideal habitat for pine martens, red squirrels, and capercaillie (a large grouse). Studding these forests are dramatic glens and the Rivers Spey, Don, and Dee, which are home to Atlantic salmon, otters, and freshwater pearl mussels.

Weather conditions in the park change abruptly, so be sure to bring cold-weather gear, particularly if you plan on hiking long distance. ⊠ *Aviemore* ⊕ *cairngorms. co.uk.*

★ Rothiemurchus Estate

TOUR—SIGHT | **FAMILY** | This excellent activity center is among the best in the Cairngorms. It offers a host of organized outdoor diversions, including guided pony rides, mountain biking, fishing, gorge swimming, and white-water rafting. It also offers ranger-guided safaris to see the park's rare and endangered wildlife, including red squirrels and "hairy heilan coos" (Highland slang for Highland cattle—docile, yaklike creatures). The Rothiemurchus Centre is the best place to get oriented and book activities; it also has a handy restaurant and a well-stocked shop selling plenty of fresh produce from the estate. One of the most beautiful parts of the estate is a nature reserve called **Loch an Eilein**. There are great low-level paths around the tree-rimmed loch—perfect for bikes—or longer trails to Glen Einich. A converted cottage beside Loch an Eilein serves as a visitor center, art gallery, and craft store. ⊠ *Rothiemurchus Centre, B970, Inverdruie* ☎ *01479/812345* ⊕ *www.rothiemurchus.net* ✉ *Free.*

🍴 Restaurants

Mountain Café

$ | **CAFÉ** | On the main street in Aviemore, the Mountain Café is a useful pit stop for a hearty lunch or afternoon snack. Regularly appearing on lists of Scotland's best cafés, this small place has a big reputation, which means it's rarely empty. **Known for:** lively atmosphere (be prepared to wait); award-winning baked goods; beautiful views. ⑤ *Average main: £12 ⊠ 111 Grampian Rd.* ☎ *01479/812473* ⊕ *mountaincafe-aviemore.co.uk* ⊘ *Closed Wed. No dinner.*

Old Bridge Inn

$$ | **MODERN BRITISH** | This old-style bar and conservatory restaurant serves what many locals call the best pub food in Aviemore. The menu changes with the seasons, but you can always expect simple dishes built around quality ingredients such as local lamb chops or Angus beef, as well as a variety of fresh fish. **Known for:** classic British fare; spirited live music; warm and welcoming vibe. ⑤ *Average main: £18 ⊠ 23 Dalfaber Rd.* ☎ *01479/811137* ⊕ *www.oldbridgeinn. co.uk.*

 Hotels

Cairngorm Hotel

$ | **HOTEL** | Walk past the suit of armor standing guard at the entrance and you should already have a good idea of what awaits within this grand old house, the first building you'll see on exiting the train station. **Pros:** practical location; simple, traditional rooms; family rooms offered. **Cons:** not scenic; interior needs a refresh; regular live bagpiper not for everyone. ⑤ *Rooms from: £110 ⊠ 77 Grampian Rd.* ☎ *01479/810233* ⊕ *www.cairngorm.com* ⤴ *31 rooms* ❑ *Free breakfast.*

★ Ravenscraig Guest House

$ | **B&B/INN** | Owned by Scottish-Swedish couple Scott and Helena, this charming little B&B offers a warm family welcome, modern rooms with bathrooms en suite, and a great location at the heart of Aviemore. **Pros:** fantastic breakfast; smart TVs in the rooms; free off-road parking. **Cons:** early checkout time; weak shower pressure; no dinner service. ⑤ *Rooms from: £95 ⊠ 141 Grampian Rd.* ☎ *01479/810278* ⊕ *www.aviemoreonline. com* ⤴ *14 rooms* ❑ *Free Breakfast.*

Rowan Tree Country Hotel

$ | **B&B/INN** | Hugging the quieter road from Aviemore to Kingussie, Rowan Tree offers a comfortable, traditional Highland stay and a practical base for exploring nature, from the on-the-doorstep Loch Alvie to the long-distance Speyside Way. **Pros:** stunning countryside location; incredibly good value; delicious breakfast porridge with cream and Drambuie. **Cons:** very old-fashioned in places; 2 miles outside Aviemore; some rooms with shared bathrooms. ⑤ *Rooms from: £70 ⊠ B9152* ⊕ *Near Alvie* ☎ *01479/810207* ⊕ *www. rowantreehotel.com* ⤴ *12 rooms* ❑ *Free Breakfast.*

 Activities

Glenmore Lodge

CLIMBING/MOUNTAINEERING | In Cairngorms National Park, this is a good center for day and residential courses on rock and ice climbing, hiking, kayaking, ski touring, mountain biking, and more. Some classes are aimed at under-18s. There are superb facilities, such as an indoor climbing wall. ⊠ *Off B970, Glenmore* ⊕ *About 9 miles east of Aviemore* ☎ *01479/861256* ⊕ *www.glenmorelodge. org.uk.*

G2 Outdoor

CLIMBING/MOUNTAINEERING | The wide range of adventures at G2 Outdoor includes white-water rafting, gorge walking, and rock climbing. The company offers a family float trip on the River Spey in summer, and in winter runs ski courses. ⊠ *The Hatchery, Alvie Estate* ⊕ *Off A9* ☎ *01540/651784* ⊕ *www.g2outdoor. co.uk.*

Mikes Bikes

BICYCLING | This small bike shop stocks all the gear you might need to take advantage of the many paths around Aviemore. It also rents and repairs bikes. Prices start at £15 for three hours. ⊠ *5A Myrtlefield Shopping Centre, Grampian Rd.* ☎ *01479/810478* ⊕ *www.aviemore-bikes.co.uk.*

Kingussie

13 miles southwest of Aviemore.

Set in a wide glen, Kingussie is a pretty town east of the Monadhliath Mountains. With great distant views of the Cairngorms, it's perfect for those who would prefer to avoid the far more hectic town of Aviemore.

GETTING HERE AND AROUND

From Aviemore, Kingussie is easy to reach by car via the A9 and the A86. Although the slightly longer drive along the B9152 is generally quieter and more pleasant. There are also good bus and train services between the two towns.

◉ Sights

★ Highland Folk Museum

MUSEUM | FAMILY | Explore reconstructed Highland buildings, including a Victorian-era schoolhouse, and watch tailors, clock makers, and joiners demonstrating their trades at this open-air museum. Walking paths (or old-fashioned buses) take you to the 18th-century township that was a setting for the hit TV show *Outlander* and includes a peat house made of turf, and a weaver's house. Throughout the museum there are hands-on exhibits like a working quern stone for grinding grain. ⊠ *Aultlarie Croft, Kingussie Rd., Newtonmore* ☎ *01349/781650* ⊕ *www.highlifehighland.com* 🆓 *Free* ☉ *Closed Nov.–Mar.*

Biking the Glen

A dedicated bicycle path, created by Scotland's National Cycle Networks, runs from Glasgow to Inverness, passing through Fort William and Kingussie. Additionally, a good network of back roads snakes around Inverness and toward Nairn. The B862/B852, which runs by the southeast side of Loch Ness, has little traffic and is a good bet for cyclists. Stay off the A9 on both sides of Aviemore and the A82 main road along the northwest bank of Loch Ness via Drumnadrochit, however, as they're both busy with vehicular traffic.

Ruthven Barracks

MILITARY SITE | Looking like a ruined castle on a mound, Ruthven Barracks is redolent with tales of "the '45" (as the last Jacobite rebellion is often called). The defeated Jacobite forces rallied here after the Battle of Culloden, but then abandoned and blew up the government outpost they had earlier captured. You'll see its crumbling, yet imposing, stone outline as you approach. ⊠ *Off B970* ✛ *½ mile southeast of Kingussie* ☎ ⊕ *www.historicenvironment.scot* 🆓 *Free.*

⊌ Restaurants

★ The Cross at Kingussie

$$$$ | BRITISH | This former tweed mill, with a narrow river running alongside its stone walls, is a haven of wooden beams, whitewashed stone walls, and open fireplaces, all set within four acres of woodlands. The intimate dining room serves sumptuous Scottish produce, from duck and halibut to lamb and sea bass, each delicately prepared with an intimate knowledge of textures and flavors. **Known for:** perfectly curated set menus; stunning location; gorgeous desserts like passion fruit cheesecake. $ Average main: £55 ⊠ Tweedmill Brae, Ardbroilach Rd. ☎ 01540/661166 ⊕ www. thecross.co.uk ⊗ Closed Jan. No dinner Sun. and Mon.

Hotels

Coig Na Shee
$ | **B&B/INN** | This century-old Highland lodge has a warm and cozy atmosphere, and each of its spacious bedrooms is unique, with well-chosen furnishings and soothing color schemes. **Pros:** quiet location; great walks from house; plenty of privacy. **Cons:** 3 miles outside Kingussie; hard to reach without a car; some rooms on the smaller side. $ Rooms from: £90 ⊠ Off Laggan Rd. (A86), Newtonmore ☎ 01540/670109 ⊕ www.coignashee. co.uk ⇆ 5 rooms ⦿ Free breakfast ⌕ No children under eight.

★ Sutherlands Guest House
$ | **B&B/INN** | Finding that sweet spot where contemporary meets cozy is no mean feat, but the husband-and-wife team behind this welcoming guesthouse make it look simple. **Pros:** lovely spacious bedrooms; stunning lounge views; great value. **Cons:** hilltop location best accessed by car; not licensed to sell alcohol; early checkout time. $ Rooms from: £110 ⊠ Old Distillery Rd. ☎ 01540/661155 ⊕ www.sutherlandskingussie.co.uk ⇆ 5 rooms ⦿ Free breakfast.

Drumnadrochit and Loch Ness

15 miles south of Inverness.

A tourist hub at the curve of the road, Drumnadrochit is not known for its style or culture, but it attracts plenty of people interested in searching for mythical monsters. There aren't many good restaurants, but there are some decent-enough hotels.

GETTING HERE AND AROUND
Drumnadrochit is an easy drive from Inverness (to the north) or Fort Augustus (to the south) on the A82. Buses run frequently, as this is a busy tourist destination.

Sights

Jacobite Cruises
TOUR—SIGHT | The company runs morning and afternoon cruises on Loch Ness to Urquhart Castle and other destinations throughout the region. Tours depart from either Clansman Harbour, 5 miles northeast of Drumnadrochit, or Dochgarroch Loch farther up the A82. ⊠ Barckla Harbour, A82 ☎ 01463/233999 ⊕ www. jacobite.co.uk ⊠ Tours from £15.

Loch Ness
BODY OF WATER | From the A82 you get some spectacular views of the formidable Loch Ness, which has a greater volume of water than any other British lake, a maximum depth of more than 800 feet, and—perhaps you've already heard?—a famous monster. Early travelers who passed this way included General Wade (1673–1748), who, prior to destroying much of Hadrian's Wall in England, came to dig a road up the loch's eastern shore; English lexicographer Dr. Samuel Johnson (1709–84), who remarked at the time about the poor condition of the population and the squalor of their homes; and travel writer and naturalist Thomas Pennant (1726–98), who noted that the loch kept the locality frost-free in winter. None of these observant early travelers ever made mention of a monster. Clearly, they had not read the local guidebooks. From Easter to October, you can also take hourly cruises of the loch, leaving from the little craft store at the Loch Ness Lodge Hotel in Drumnadrochit, and try to spot Nessie yourself; pre-booking for the cruises is not available. ⊠ Drumnadrochit.

"Nessie": The Loch Ness Monster

Tall tales involving some kind of beast inhabiting the dark waters of Loch Ness go all the way back to St. Columba in the 7th century AD—but, for the most part, the legend of "Nessie" is a disappointingly modern one. In 1933 two vacationing Londoners gave an intriguing account to a newspaper, describing a large, unidentifiable creature that slithered in front of their car before plunging into the loch. Later that year a local man, Hugh Gray, took the first purported photograph of the monster—and Nessie fever was born. The pictures kept coming—none of them *too* clear, of course—and before long the resident monster turned into a boon for the local tourism industry. Fortunately for them the age of camera phones has not dented Nessie's popularity; you don't have to search far on the Internet to find all sorts of photos of something—*anything*—that must surely be the monster, if you only squint a little. But does anybody seriously believe in it? Well... no. But like all good legends, there is just enough doubt to keep the campfire tales alive. In 2006 declassified documents even revealed that, in the 1980s, Prime Minister Margaret Thatcher considered plans to declare the Loch Ness monster a protected species, as a safeguard against the hordes of bounty hunters she feared would descend should it ever be proven to exist.

Loch Ness Centre and Exhibition
MUSEUM | FAMILY | If you're in search of the infamous monster, the Loch Ness Centre and Exhibition walks you through the fuzzy photographs, the unexplained sonar readings, and the sincere testimony of eyewitnesses. It's an entertaining way to spend an hour, even if the boasts of "high tech" and "state-of-the-art" feel overly generous. It's said that the loch's huge volume of water has a warming effect on the local weather, making the loch conducive to mirages in still, warm conditions—but you'll have to make up your own mind about that explanation. ✉ *A82* ☎ *01456/450573* ⊕ *www.loch-ness.com* 💰 *£8.45.*

★ Urquhart Castle
CASTLE/PALACE | About 2 miles southeast of Drumnadrochit, this castle is a favorite Loch Ness monster–watching spot. This romantically broken-down fortress stands on a promontory overlooking the loch, as it has since the Middle Ages. Because of its central and strategic position in the Great Glen line of communication, the castle has a complex history involving military offense and defense, as well as its own destruction and renovation. The castle was begun in the 13th century and was destroyed before the end of the 17th century to prevent its use by the Jacobites. A visitor center gives an idea of what life was like here in medieval times. ✉ *Off A82* ☎ *01456/450551* ⊕ *www.historic-scotland.gov.uk* 💰 *£12.*

Hotels

★ Loch Ness Lodge
$$$ | B&B/INN | Run by siblings Scott and Iona Sutherland, Loch Ness Lodge is an elegant and exclusive lodging option offering a traditional Highland welcome; the formalities are kept to a minimum, but nice touches like the small decanter of sherry on arrival ensure you feel pampered. **Pros:** superb views of Loch Ness; lovely rooms; complimentary afternoon tea. **Cons:** near a busy road; no restaurant; easily confused with a (lesser) hotel of the same name in Drumnadrochit.

Loch Ness, Fort William, and Nearby

Ⓢ *Rooms from: £285* ✉ *A82, Brachla* ☎ *01456/459469* ⊕ *www.loch-ness-lodge.com* ⇆ *9 rooms* ⦿ *Free breakfast.*

🛍 Shopping

An Talla by Loch Ness

CRAFTS | This appealing retail destination en-route from Inverness to Drumnadrochit sells traditional Scottish crafts, whisky, porcelain, and a whole host of other souvenirs. There's also a lovely little café; grab a take-out coffee and stroll along Dochgarroch Loch. ✉ *Dochgarrock Loch* ☎ *01463/572323* ⊕ *www.an-talla.co.uk.*

Fort Augustus

19 miles south of Drumnadrochit, 33 miles south of Inverness, 31 miles northeast of Fort William.

The best place to see the lochs of the Caledonian Canal is Fort Augustus, at the southern tip of Loch Ness. This bustling small town is a great place to begin walking and cycling excursions, or to sit by the canal watching the loch fill and empty as boats sail between Loch Lochy, Loch Oich, and Loch Ness.

Fort Augustus itself was captured by the Jacobite clans during the 1745 rebellion. Later the fort was rebuilt as a Benedictine abbey, but the monks no longer live here.

GETTING HERE AND AROUND

It's quick and easy to get here from Inverness via the A82, either by car or by local bus, and you'll pass Drumnadrochit on the way. A more leisurely alternative, however, is driving the B862 south from Inverness and along the east bank of Loch Ness. Take the opportunity to view the waterfalls at Foyers and the peaceful, reedy Loch Tarff. Descend through forests and moorland until the road runs around the southern tip of Loch Ness. Parts of the route are remnants of the military road built by General Wade.

👁 Sights

Caledonian Canal

BODY OF WATER | The canal, which links the lochs of the Great Glen—Loch Lochy, Loch Oich, and Loch Ness—owes its origins to a combination of military and political pressures that emerged at the time of the Napoleonic Wars with France. In short: Britain needed a better and faster way to move naval vessels from one side of Scotland to the other. The great Scottish engineer Thomas Telford (1757–1834) surveyed the route in 1803, taking advantage of the three lochs that lie in the Great Glen, which have a combined length of 45 miles, so that only 22 miles of canal had to be constructed to connect the lochs and complete the waterway from coast to coast. After 19 years, the canal, with its 29 locks and 42 gates, was open and ready for action. Travel along the canal today and stunning vistas open up: mountains, lochs, and glens, and to the south, the profile of Ben Nevis. At the visitor center in Fort Augustus, you can learn all about this historic engineering feat and take a picturesque walk along the towpath. ✉ *Caledonian Canal Centre, Canalside* ⊕ *www.scottishcanals.co.uk* 🎟 *Free.*

🍴 Restaurants

The Brasserie

$$$ | **BRITISH** | Food doesn't come any more photogenic than the elaborate creations of Sean Kelly, the chef at this tiny, shabby-chic restaurant housed in The Lovat hotel. The dishes might not sound overly eccentric—expect halibut with mussels and green vegetables or venison saddle with onion tart and cabbage—but when it comes to subtle flavors and inspired presentation, they're in a league of their own. **Known for:** artistic presentation; foraged ingredients; pricey mains. Ⓢ *Average main: £24* ✉ *The Lovat, Off A82* ☎ *01456/490000* ⊕ *www. thelovat.com.*

Stretching 60 miles through the Great Glen, a boat trip on the Caledonian Canal is a lovely way to see this part of Scotland.

 Hotels

Glengarry Castle Hotel

$$ | HOTEL | Tucked away in Invergarry, this rambling baronial mansion is 7 miles south of Fort Augustus and within easy reach of the Great Glen's most popular sights. **Pros:** atmospheric building and gardens; good-value take-out lunches; family rooms available. **Cons:** no elevator; a little way from Loch Ness; some may find it old-fashioned. ⑤ *Rooms from: £185* ⊠ *Off A82, Invergarry* ☎ *01809/501254* ⊕ *www.glengarry.net* ⊘ *Closed Nov.–Mar.* ⌁ *26 rooms* ⦿ *Free breakfast.*

The Lovat

$$ | HOTEL | The rooms in this charming Victorian hotel are tasteful and comfy, with some offering loch views, but the real highlights are the carefully furnished shared areas. **Pros:** excellent bar and restaurant; some dog-friendly rooms; lovely lochside location. **Cons:** inconsistency in the quality of rooms; some corridors feel sterile; expensive for the area. ⑤ *Rooms from: £190* ⊠ *Off A82* ☎ *01456/490000* ⊕ *www.thelovat.com* ⌁ *28 rooms* ⦿ *Breakfast.*

Fort William

32 miles southwest of Fort Augustus, 67 miles southwest of Inverness, 108 miles northwest of Glasgow, 132 miles northwest of Edinburgh.

As its name suggests, Fort William originated as a military outpost, first established by Oliver Cromwell's General Monk in 1655 and refortified by George I (1660–1727) in 1715 to help combat an uprising by the turbulent Jacobite clans. It remains the southern gateway to the Great Glen and the far west. It's not Scotland's most charming or authentic town, but it's got several good hotels and makes a convenient base for exploring the surrounding countryside.

GETTING HERE AND AROUND

From Glasgow (to the south) and Inverness (to the north), the A82 takes you the entire way. From Edinburgh take the M9 to the A84. This empties into the A85, which connects to the A82 that takes you to Fort William. Roads around Fort William are well maintained, but mostly one lane in each direction. They can be very busy in summer.

A long-distance Scottish Citylink bus connects Glasgow and Fort William. ScotRail has trains from London, as well as connections from Glasgow and Edinburgh. It also operates a train service three times a day between Fort William and Mallaig. For those who like to combine travel and accommodations, the Caledonian Sleeper (⊕ www.sleeper.scot) leaves most days from London Euston late in the evening, arriving at Fort William midmorning the following day.

ESSENTIALS

VISITOR INFORMATION VisitScotland Fort William iCentre. ⊠ 15 High St. ☎ 01397/701801 ⊕ www.visitfortwilliam. co.uk, www.visitscotland.com.

 Sights

Ben Nevis

MOUNTAIN—SIGHT | The tallest mountain in the British Isles, 4,411-foot Ben Nevis looms over Fort William, less than 4 miles from Loch Linnhe. A trek to its summit is a rewarding experience, but you should be fit and well prepared—food and water, map and compass, first-aid kit, whistle, hat, gloves, and warm clothing (yes, even in summer), as well as insect spray for midges—as the unpredictable weather can make it a hazardous hike. Ask for advice at the local tourist office before you begin.

★ Jacobite Steam Train

TRANSPORTATION SITE (AIRPORT/BUS/FERRY/ TRAIN) | **FAMILY** | The most relaxing way to take in the landscape of birch- and bracken-covered wild slopes is by rail, and the best ride is on the historic Jacobite Steam Train, a spectacularly scenic 84-mile round-trip that runs between Fort William and Mallaig. You'll see mountains, lochs, beaches, and islands along the way. There are two trips a day between mid-April and late October (though weekend trips are only in the height of summer). ⊠ *Fort William Travel Centre, Tom-na-Faire Station Sq.* ☎ *0844/850–4685* ⊕ *www.westcoastrailways.co.uk* ⊠ *£59.95 round-trip* ⊙ *Closed late Oct.–mid-Apr.*

★ Nevis Range Mountain Experience

VIEWPOINT | Located 6 miles outside Fort William, this fantastic outdoor center offers a range of activities in all seasons, from downhill skiing and snowboarding to exhilarating mountain-biking trails, treetop adventure obstacle courses, and mountain-top paragliding. From June to early September, you can also take a gondola up to the 2,000-foot summit of Aonach Mor, from which you can hike and explore more of the mountain range (and enjoy stunning views of Ben Nevis). There are also two good dining options; try Pinemarten Café at the foot of the gondola for its rich macaroni and cheese and local craft beer selection. ⊠ *Off A82* ☎ *01397/705825* ⊕ *www.nevisrange. co.uk* ⊠ *Gondola £19.50.*

★ West Highland Museum

MUSEUM | In the town center, the small but fascinating West Highland Museum explores the history of Prince Charles Edward Stuart and the 1745 rebellion. Included in the museum's folk exhibits are a costume and tartan display and an excellent collection of Jacobite relics. One of the most intriguing objects here is a tray decorated with a distorted image of Bonnie Prince Charlie that only becomes visible when reflected in a wine glass or goblet. This elaborate ruse enabled clandestine supporters among the nobility to raise a (treasonous) toast without fear of discovery. ⊠ *Cameron*

The famous Jacobite Steam Train doubles as the Hogwarts Express in the Harry Potter films.

Sq. ☎ *01397/702169* ⊕ *www.westhighlandmuseum.org.uk* ✉ *Free* ⊙ *Closed Mon.–Sat. in July and Aug. and Sun. in Sept.–June.*

 ## 🍴 Restaurants

★ Crannog Seafood Restaurant

$$ | **SEAFOOD** | With a reputation for quality and simplicity, this restaurant on the town pier serves outstanding seafood. Fishing boats draw up on the shores of Loch Linnhe and deliver their catch straight to the kitchen. **Known for:** small but well-curated menu; idyllic lochside location; delicious Cullen skink. ⑤ *Average main: £19* ✉ *Town Pier* ☎ *01397/705589* ⊕ *www.crannog.net.*

Lime Tree An Ealdhain

$$$ | **MODERN BRITISH** | One of Fort William's most upscale culinary spots, this restaurant is unfussy and modern inside, with low-hanging lamps, rich jewel-toned walls, and solid wood furniture. Expect filling dishes that, while not overly complex, are given an edge with embellishments such as fennel sauerkraut or marrowbone crumble. **Known for:** some of Fort William's most interesting food; inspired desserts; on-site art gallery. ⑤ *Average main: £21* ✉ *Achintore Rd.* ☎ *01397/701806* ⊕ *www.limetreefortwilliam.co.uk* ⊙ *No lunch.*

 ## 🛏 Hotels

★ Crolinnhe

$$ | **B&B/INN** | An elegant old house with colorful gardens, this exceptionally comfortable B&B overlooks Loch Linnhe, yet is only a 10-minute walk from town. **Pros:** stunning loch views; great breakfasts; comfortable rooms. **Cons:** final payment only by cash or check; short walk from town; grand decor not to everyone's tastes. ⑤ *Rooms from: £160* ✉ *Grange Rd.* ☎ *01397/703795* ⊕ *www.crolinnhe. co.uk* ▬ *No credit cards* ⊙ *Closed Nov.– Easter* ⭷ *3 suites* ⦿ *Free breakfast.*

Inverlochy Castle Hotel

$$$$ | **HOTEL** | A red-granite mansion turned luxury boutique hotel, Inverlochy

Castle stands on 50 acres of woodlands in the shadow of Ben Nevis, with striking scenery on every side; prices are high, but you could have a meal here to take in the surroundings. **Pros:** spectacular setting; excellent restaurant; beautiful location. **Cons:** extremely expensive; must dress up for dinner; a little outside Fort William. $ *Rooms from: £495* ✉ *Off A82* ☎ *01397/702177* ⊕ *www.inverlochy-castlehotel.com* ☉ *Closed Jan. and Feb.* ⤶ *17 rooms* ⧖ *Breakfast.*

Myrtle Bank Guest House

$ | **B&B/INN** | This sweet, cheerful guesthouse is in a converted Victorian villa on the banks of Loch Linnhe. **Pros:** great views; friendly owners; convenient location. **Cons:** ground-floor rooms lacking views; breakfast finishes early; some shared bathrooms. $ *Rooms from: £90* ✉ *8 Achintore Rd.* ☎ *01397/702034* ⊕ *www.myrtlebankguesthouse.co.uk* ⤶ *25 rooms* ⧖ *Breakfast.*

 Activities

GOLF

Fort William Golf Club

GOLF | This excellent course has spectacular views of Ben Nevis (indeed, it partly occupies its lower slope). The Highland course appeals to beginners and experts alike, drawn as much for the beautiful setting as the thoroughly reasonable greens fees. Watch out for the treacherous 4th hole—it looks simple, but a fierce prevailing wind will test even the most practiced swing. ✉ *North Road, Torlundy* ⊹ *Off A82* ☎ *01397/704464* ⊕ *www.fortwilliamgolfclub.com* ⊠ *£30* 🎿 *18 holes, 6217 yards, par 70.*

HIKING

This area—especially around Glen Nevis, Glencoe, and Ben Nevis—is popular with hikers; however, routes are not well marked, so contact the VisitScotland Fort William iCentre before you go. The center will provide you with expert advice based on your interests, level of fitness, and hiking experience.

★ Glen Nevis

HIKING/WALKING | For a walk in Glen Nevis, drive north from Fort William on the A82 toward Fort Augustus. On the outskirts of town, just before the bridge over the River Nevis, turn right up the road signposted Glen Nevis. About 8 miles along this road is a parking lot (Upper Glen Nevis Car Park); from here, a footpath will lead you to a steel-cable bridge (1 mile), and then to Steall Waterfall. The ruined croft beside the boulder-strewn stream is a great picnic place. You can continue up the glen for some distance without any danger of becoming lost as long as you stay on the path and keep the river to your right. Watch your step going through the tree-lined gorge. The return route is simply back the way you came. ✉ *Upper Glen Nevis Car Park.*

Glenfinnan

16 miles west of Fort William, 18 miles east of Arisaig.

Perhaps the most visitor-oriented stop on the route between Fort William and Mallaig, Glenfinnan has much to offer if you're interested in Scottish history. Here the National Trust for Scotland has capitalized on the romance surrounding the story of the Jacobites and their attempts to return a Stewart monarch and the Roman Catholic religion to a country that had become staunchly Protestant. It was at Glenfinnan that the rash adventurer Bonnie Prince Charlie gathered his meager forces for the final Jacobite rebellion of 1745–46.

GETTING HERE AND AROUND

If you're driving from Fort William, travel west via the A830. For great views, take a ride on the Jacobite Steam Train, which you can catch in Fort William.

Sights

Glenfinnan Monument

MEMORIAL | One of the most striking monuments in Britain, the Glenfinnan Monument commemorates the place where Bonnie Prince Charlie raised his standard. The tower, which was built in 1815, overlooks Loch Shiel; note, however, that the figure on the top is a Highlander, not the prince himself. The story of his ill-fated campaign is told in the nearby visitor center. ■ TIP→ **The view down Loch Shiel from the Glenfinnan Monument is one of the most photographed in Scotland.** ⊠ *Off A830* ☎ *01397/722250* ⊕ *www.nts.org. uk* ✉ *£4.*

Glenfinnan Viaduct

BRIDGE/TUNNEL | The 1,248-foot-long Glenfinnan Viaduct was a genuine wonder when it was built in 1897, and remains so today. The railway's contractor, Robert MacAlpine (known among locals as "Concrete Bob") pioneered the use of concrete for bridges when his company built the Mallaig extension, which opened in 1901. In more recent times the viaduct became famous for its appearance in the Harry Potter films. The viaduct can be seen on foot; about half a mile west of the railway station in Glenfinnan, on the A380 road, is a small parking lot. Take the footpath from here; you'll reach the viaduct in about ½ mile. If you time it right (usually at 11 am, 3 pm, and 7:30 pm, but you can confirm times at ⊕ *westcoastrailways.co.uk),* you'll see the iconic Jacobite Steam Train crossing the bridge. ⊠ *Glenfinnan Viaduct Car Park, Off A380.*

Hotels

Glenfinnan House

$$ | HOTEL | This handsome hotel on the shores of Loch Shiel was built in the 18th century as the home of Alexander MacDonald VII of Glenaladale, who was wounded fighting for Bonnie Prince Charlie; it was transformed into an even grander mansion in the 19th century. **Pros:** fabulous setting; atmospheric dining experience; beautiful views. **Cons:** some shared bathrooms; a bit fussy for some; no air-conditioning. ⑤ *Rooms from: £145* ⊠ *Off A830* ☎ *01397/722235* ⊕ *www.glenfinnanhouse.com* ⊘ *Closed mid-Nov.–mid-Mar.* ⬠ *14 rooms* ⑩ *Free breakfast.*

Arisaig

18 miles west of Glenfinnan, 34 miles west of Fort William, 52 miles northwest of Glencoe.

Considering its small size, Arisaig, gateway to the **Small Isles,** offers a surprising choice of high-quality options for dining and lodging. To the north of Arisaig, the road cuts across a headland to reach a stretch of coastline where silver sands glitter with the mica in the local rock; clear water, blue sky, and white sand lend a tropical flavor to the beaches—when the sun is shining.

From Arisaig try to visit a couple of the Small Isles: **Rum, Eigg, Muck,** and **Canna,** each tiny and with few or no inhabitants. Rum serves as a wildlife reserve, while Eigg was the world's first community where electricity was produced off-grid, solely by wind, wave, and solar energy.

GETTING HERE AND AROUND

From Glenfinnan, you reach Arisaig on the A830, the only road leading west. The Fort William–Mallaig train also stops here.

Sights

Arisaig Marine

TRANSPORTATION SITE (AIRPORT/BUS/FERRY/ TRAIN) | Along with a host of wildlife excursions offering a chance to see minke whales, basking sharks, bottlenose dolphins, killer whales, porpoises, gray seals, and lots of sea birdlife (including cute puffins), Arisaig Marine runs a boat service from the harbor at Arisaig to the Small Isles from May to September. There's also a little tearoom and gift shop here. ⊠ *Arisaig Harbour* ☎ *01687/450224* ⊕ *www.arisaig.co.uk* ⊠ *Eigg £18 round-trip.*

Loch Morar

BODY OF WATER | Take the A830 north from Arisaig, turn right onto the B8008 before Morar, then turn right again onto an even smaller, unnamed side road, and you'll find yourself driving along the northern edge of Loch Morar, the deepest of all the Scottish lochs (more than 1,000 feet). The next deepest point is miles out into the Atlantic, beyond the continental shelf. The beautifully atmospheric loch is said to have a resident monster, Morag, which undoubtedly gets less recognition than its famous cousin Nessie. Whether that means you have more chance of getting her to appear for a photograph, we can't say. ⊠ *Loch Morar, Off A830, Mallaig.*

🍴 Restaurants

The Old Library

$$ | FRENCH | On the waterfront, this 1722 barn has been converted into a lovely, reasonably priced restaurant. Expect simple but tasty plates of local fish and meats, prepared in a French-bistro style—lamb shank, sirloin, or perhaps a fillet of buttery hake, served with seasonal veggies. **Known for:** hearty meals; ultra-fresh produce; local character. ⑤ *Average main: £18* ⊠ *B8008* ☎ *01687/450651* ⊕ *www.oldlibrary.co.uk.*

🛏 Hotels

Arisaig Hotel

$ | B&B/INN | A coaching inn built in 1720, this hotel is close to the water and has magnificent views of the Small Isles. **Pros:** good-value restaurant; lots of life and music in the bar; amazing views of

The Glencoe Massacre

In 1692 Glencoe was the site of a brutal and bloody massacre, still remembered in the Highlands for the treachery with which soldiers of the Campbell clan (acting as a government militia) treated their hosts, the MacDonalds. According to Highland code, in his own home a clansman should give shelter even to his sworn enemy. In the face of bitter weather, the Campbells were accepted as guests by the MacDonalds. But apparently acting on orders from the British Crown, the Campbells turned on their hosts and murdered them. The Massacre of Glencoe has gained an unlikely resurgence of fame in recent years, since it was revealed to be the historical basis for the infamous "Red Wedding" in George R. R. Martin's popular books (and HBO series) *Game of Thrones.*

the bay. **Cons:** the main bar is noisy for some; small restaurant portions; some rooms could do with a refresh. ⑤ *Rooms from: £80* ⊠ *B8008* ☎ *01687/450210* ⊕ *www.arisaighotel.co.uk* ⊠ *13 rooms* ⊠ *Breakfast.*

★ Arisaig House

$$ | HOTEL | An open-arms welcome and stunning views of the Isle of Skye await you at this handsome stone mansion, built in the 1860s. **Pros:** beautiful views; lovely hosts; outstanding food. **Cons:** a bit isolated; expensive for the area; two-night minimum in summer. ⑤ *Rooms from: £195* ⊠ *Beasdale, Off A830* ☎ *01687/450730* ⊕ *www.arisaighouse. co.uk* ⊠ *12 rooms* ⊠ *Free breakfast.*

Glencoe

16 miles south of Fort William, 92 miles north of Glasgow, 44 miles northwest of Edinburgh.

Glencoe is both a small town and a region of stunning grandeur, with high peaks and secluded glens. Dramatic scenery is the main attraction here; it's as awesomely beautiful for a drive as it is for a hike. The A82—the main route through Glencoe—can get surprisingly crowded in high season, but it's one of the great scenic drives in Scotland. This area, where wild, craggy buttresses loom darkly over the road, has a special place in the folk memory of Scotland, as it was the site of an infamous 17th-century massacre.

GETTING HERE AND AROUND
Glencoe is easily accessed by car via the A82. ScotRail trains and regional buses arrive from most of Scotland's major cities.

 ## Sights

Glencoe Visitor Centre
INFO CENTER | This impressive visitor center tells the life story of Glencoe, from its volcanic origins to the MacDonald massacre to its current wildlife maintenance projects. There are fascinating exhibitions on the region, its landscape, and its people, as well as great hiking trails leaving from the center (you can get expert advice on longer hikes, too). There's also an excellent café and shop. ⊠ *Off A82* ✛ *1 mile south of Glencoe Village* ☎ *01855/811307* ⊕ *www.glencoe-nts.org.uk* 🅿 *Parking £4* ⊙ *Closed Mar.–mid-Apr.*

 ## Hotels

★ Glencoe House
\$\$\$\$ | **B&B/INN** | Peaceful surroundings, arresting views, and the friendliest of welcomes await you at this former Victorian hunting lodge. **Pros:** beautiful landscape; superb restoration; lovely hosts. **Cons:** very expensive; limited facilities; breakfast a little underwhelming. ⑤ *Rooms from: £425* ⊠ *Glencoe Lochan* ☎ *01855/811179* ⊕ *www.glencoe-house. com* ⌐ *14 suites* ⦵ *No meals.*

 ## Activities

★ Glencoe Activities
CLIMBING/MOUNTAINEERING | **FAMILY** | This popular outdoor center west of Ballachulish offers a long list of high-energy activities, from rock climbing to white-water rafting, and even hair-raising vertical canyon explorations complete with 500-foot descents. But there's a welcome twist here—it also caters to those with more limited mobility (or less adventurous souls). Guided Segway tours (£35) last 50 minutes and take you through some spectacular scenery, with stunning mountain views and even a trail along a stretch of Loch Leven. ⊠ *Dragon's Tooth Golf Course, Off A828* ✛ *4 miles west of Glencoe* ☎ *01855/413200* ⊕ *www. glencoeactivities.com.*

Chapter 11

THE NORTHERN HIGHLANDS AND THE WESTERN ISLES

Updated by
Joseph Reaney

⊙ **Sights**
★★★★☆

🍴 **Restaurants**
★★★☆☆

🛏 **Hotels**
★★★☆☆

🛍 **Shopping**
★★☆☆☆

🍸 **Nightlife**
★☆☆☆☆

WELCOME TO THE NORTHERN HIGHLANDS AND THE WESTERN ISLES

TOP REASONS TO GO

★ **Isle of Skye:** Scotland in miniature, the landscape of Skye ranges from the lush, undulating hills and coastal tracks of Sleat to the deep glens and saw-toothed peaks of the Cuillin Mountains. Farther north are stunning geological features like the Old Man of Storr and Kilt Rock.

★ **Seafood:** Sample fresh seafood like Bracadale crab, Dunvegan Bay langoustines, and Sconser king scallops, as well as the local smoked salmon, lobster, and oysters.

★ **Coastal walks:** There are no wilder places in Britain to enjoy an invigorating coastal walk than on the islands of the Uists, Lewis, and Harris. Expect vast swaths of golden sand set against blue bays, or—when the weather is rough—giant waves crashing against the rocks.

★ **Wildlife viewing:** Seals, deer, otters, dolphins, and an abundance of birdlife can be seen throughout the Northern Highlands and Western Isles. Don't miss a boating foray to the Handa Island bird reserve, off Scourie.

1 Dingwall. A common first stop on any journey north.

2 Dornoch. Famed for its golf courses.

3 Helmsdale. A fishing village shaped by Vikings.

4 Wick. Famed for its herring and whisky.

5 John O'Groats. Britain's northeastern tip.

6 Thurso. The north coast's biggest town.

7 Tongue. Home to a dramatic ruined castle.

8 Durness. A remote village.

9 Scourie. An ideal base for exploring Handa Island.

10 Kylesku. A tiny fishing hamlet with Britain's highest waterfall.

11 Lochinver. A pretty shoreside community.

12 Ullapool. A charming base for ferrying to Lewis and Harris.

13 Gairloch. Peaceful, picturesque, and pleasantly warm.

14 Shieldaig. A lovely lochside village.

15 Lochcarron. Lush green mountains and a shimmering blue loch.

16 Kyle of Lochalsh. The gateway to Skye.

17 Broadford. One of Skye's main towns.

18 Armadale. The ferry gateway to Sleat, Skye's southernmost peninsula.

19 Portree. Skye's main hub.

20 Trotternish Peninsula. Skye's dramatic north, home to Quiraing, Kilt Rock, and the Old Man of Storr.

21 **Waternish Peninsula.** Skye's northwestern corner, home to crofting communities and coastal views.

22 **Glendale.** A rocky coastline with dramatic castles and Skye's best restaurant.

23 **Glen Brittle and the Cuillin Mountains.** An impossibly green, fairy tale valley.

24 **Isle of Raasay.** Skye's little brother with striking scenery.

25 **Isle of Lewis.** Home to Bronze Age standing stones, Iron Age towers, and Victorian blackhouses.

26 **Isle of Harris.** Known for spectacular beaches and handwoven tweed.

27 **St. Kilda.** A unique day trip to experience colossal cliffs and swooping seabirds.

28 **North Uist.** A hidden gem with remarkable birdlife and historic ruins.

29 **South Uist.** An island steeped in royal history.

Wild and remote, the Northern Highlands and the Western Isles of Scotland have a timeless grandeur. Dramatic cliffs, long beaches, and craggy mountains that rise up out of moorland like islands in a sea heighten the romance and mystery.

Well-preserved Eilean Donan Castle marks a kind of gateway to the Isle of Skye, famous for the brooding Cuillin Mountains and forever associated with Bonnie Prince Charlie. Jurassic-era sites, prehistoric ruins, crumbling castles, and abandoned crofts (small farms) compress the whole span of history in the islands.

The Northern Highlands is a region where roads hug the coast, dipping down toward beaches and back up for stunning views over the clear ocean, across to the dramatic mountains, or along stunning heather moorland. These twisted, undulating roads—many of them single-track—demand that you shift down a gear, pause to let others pass, and take the time to do less and experience more of the rough-hewn beauty. If you're lucky, you may see a puffin fishing below the cliffs, an eagle swooping for a hare, or perhaps even a pod of dolphins or whales swimming off the coast. Adorable Highland *coos* (cows) are sure to make an appearance, too.

Sutherland was once the southern land belonging to the Vikings, and some names reflect this. Cape Wrath got its name from the Viking word *hvarth,* meaning "turning point," and Suilven translates as "pillar." The Isle of Skye and the Outer Hebrides are referred to as the Western Isles, and remain the stronghold of the Gaelic language. Skye is often called Scotland in miniature because the terrain shifts from lush valleys in the south to the rugged girdle of the Cuillin Mountains and then to the steep cliffs that define the northern coast. A short ferry journey away, the moody island of Lewis and Harris lays claim to the brilliant golden sands of Luskentyre and incredible prehistoric sites, from the lunar-aligned Calanais Standing Stones to the Iron Age Doune Broch.

Depending on the weather, a trip to the Northern Highlands and the Western Isles can feel like a tropical getaway or a blustery, rain-drenched holiday. Just remember: "There's no such thing as bad weather, just inappropriate clothing."

MAJOR REGIONS

The Northern Landscapes. The northern-most part of Scotland, from Inverness all the way up to John O'Groats in the east and Cape Wrath in the west, has some of the most distinctive mountain profiles and coastal stretches in all of Scotland. The rim roads around the wilds of Durness overlook rocky shores, and the long beaches are as dramatic as the awe-inspiring and desolate cross-country routes like Destitution Road in Wester Ross. To explore these landscapes most thoroughly, you should travel by car. You'll want to explore Stoer Point Lighthouse, the beaches north of Lochinver, and spectacular islandlike hills such as Suilven. Follow the North Coast 500 loop from Inverness to see the very best of the region. If you head counterclockwise up the east coast, along the north coast, and down the west coast, the spectacular landscape gets more and more dramatic at every turn. Travel clockwise, and you might find the east coast down from John O'Groats feels a bit anticlimactic.

Torridon. Located far to the west of Scotland, Torridon has a grand, rugged, and wild air that feels especially remote, yet it is only an hour's drive from Inverness before you reach Kinlochewe, near the east end of Glen Torridon. It has cool glens, mirrorlike lochs, impressive mountains, and tantalizing glimpses across to the Isle of Skye. The western side is equally spectacular, with walking trails and mountain panoramas galore. Torridon is a wonderful place to visit if you want to tackle one of the legendary peaks here—Beinn Alligin, Liathach, and Beinn Eighe—or if you enjoy outdoor activities like kayaking, climbing, or mountain biking. The A890, which runs from the A832 into the heart of Torridon, is a single-lane road in some stretches, with plenty of open vistas across the deserted heart of northern Scotland. Other single-track roads lead to Glen Torridon and to lighthouses on sea-lashed headlands.

Isle of Skye. Scotland's most famous island is home to the 11 peaks of the Cuillin Mountains, the quiet gardens of Sleat, and the dramatic peninsulas of Waternish and Trotternish. You can take a day trip to Skye, but it's worth spending a few days exploring its shores if you can.

The Outer Hebrides. The Outer Hebrides—the Western Isles in common parlance—stretch about 130 miles from end to end and lie roughly 50 miles from the Scottish mainland. This splintered archipelago extends from the Butt of Lewis in the north (no giggling) to Barra Head in the south, whose lighthouse has the greatest arc of visibility in the world. In the Hebrides clouds cling to the hills, and rain comes in squalls. Any trip here requires protection from the weather and a conviction that a great holiday does not require constant sunshine.

It may contain two areas called isles, but it is just one single island that makes up the isles of Lewis and Harris. The island is the third largest in the United Kingdom, in fact, after Britain and Ireland. Lewis and Harris is the term to describe the island as a whole, but people also talk about the isles individually. Lewis by itself refers to the northern two-thirds of the island, while Harris represents the southern third. The island's only major town, Stornoway, is on a nearly landlocked harbor on the east coast of Lewis, and is the most convenient starting point for a driving tour of Lewis and Harris (assuming you arrive, like most visitors, by ferry from the mainland or by plane). The island has some fine historic attractions, including the Calanais Standing Stones—a truly magical glimpse of an ancient civilization—as well as an abundance of natural beauty. It's also the jumping-off point for a day trip to the unique isolated archipelago of St. Kilda.

Just south of the Sound of Harris is the Isle of North Uist, rich in monoliths, chambered cairns, and other reminders of a prehistoric past. Benbecula, sandwiched between North and South Uist, is in fact less bare and neglected-looking than its bigger neighbors to the north. The Isle of South Uist, once a refuge of the old Catholic faith, is dotted with ruined forts and chapels; in summer its wild gardens burst with alpine and rock plants. Eriskay Island and a scattering of islets almost block the 6-mile strait between South Uist and Barra, an island you can walk across in an hour. Harris tweed is available at many outlets on the islands, including some of the weavers' homes; keep an eye out for signs directing you to weavers' workshops. Sunday on the islands is observed as a day of rest, and nearly all shops and visitor attractions are closed. This includes most restaurants, with the exception of some island hotels, so make dinner plans in advance.

Planning

When to Go

The Northern Highlands and islands are best seen from May to September. The earlier in the spring or later in the fall you go, the greater the chances of your encountering the elements in their extreme form, and the fewer attractions and accommodations you will find open (even Skye closes down almost completely by the end of October). Then again, you'll also find fewer tourists. Winter is best avoided altogether, unless taking a ferry in a relentless gale is your idea of fun.

Planning Your Time

The rough landscape of the Highlands and islands, as this region is sometimes called, means this isn't a place you can rush through. It could take eight busy days to do a coastal loop and also see some islands. Single-lane roadways, undulating landscapes, and eye-popping views will slow you down. You can base yourself in a town like Ullapool or Portree, or choose a B&B or hotel (of which there are many) tucked into the hills or sitting at the edge of a sea loch. If you have only a couple of days, head directly to the Isle of Skye and the other islands off the coast. They attract hordes of tourists, and for good reason, yet you don't have to walk far to find yourself in the wilderness. Sunday is a day of minimal activity here; restaurants, bars, and shops are closed, as are many sites.

You could combine a trip to the Northern Highlands with forays into the Great Glen (including Inverness and Loch Ness) or up to Orkney (there are day trips from John O'Groats) and the Shetland Islands.

Getting Here and Around

AIR

On a map this area may seem far from major urban centers, but it's easy to reach. Inverness has an airport with direct links to London, Edinburgh, Glasgow, and Amsterdam.

The main airports for the Northern Highlands are Inverness and Wick (both on the mainland). Loganair has direct air service from Glasgow to Inverness and from Edinburgh to Wick. You can fly from London Gatwick, London Luton, or Bristol to Inverness on one of the daily easyJet flights. British Airways also has a service from London Heathrow. Loganair operates flights to and among the islands of Barra, Benbecula, and Lewis and Harris in the Outer Hebrides.

AIRPORT CONTACTS Inverness Airport. ☎ 01667/464000 ⊕ www.invernessairport.co.uk.

BOAT AND FERRY

Ferry services are generally reliable, weather permitting. Car and passenger ferries run from Ullapool to Stornoway (Lewis and Harris), from Oban to Castlebay (Barra), from Mallaig to Lochboisdale (South Uist), and from Uig (Skye) to Tarbert (Lewis and Harris) and Lochmaddy (North Uist). The Hopscotch planned-route ticket by Caledonian MacBrayne (known locally as CalMac) gives considerable reductions on interisland ferry fares; it is worth calling ahead and asking for the best route plan.

BOAT AND FERRY CONTACTS Caledonian MacBrayne. (CalMac) ☎ 0800/066–5000 ⊕ www.calmac.co.uk.

BUS

Scottish Citylink runs two main routes in the Northern Highlands; one heading west from Inverness to Ullapool and the other up the east coast to Scrabster (via Dornoch, Wick, and Thurso). It also has a route across the Isle of Skye to Uig. These buses can be a good way to see the region, but they don't run frequently.

Once you're in the Northern Highlands, Stagecoach has some routes up the east coast of the mainland to Brora. It also has regular services on Skye. In the Outer Hebrides, several small operators run regular routes to most towns and villages. Traveline Scotland, a handy website, provides timetables and a journey planner to help you navigate around Scotland. There's an app, too.

BUS CONTACTS Scottish Citylink.
☎ *0871/266–3333* ⊕ *www.citylink.co.uk.*
Stagecoach. ☎ *01463/233371* ⊕ *www.stagecoachbus.com.* **Traveline Scotland.**
☎ *0871/200–2233* ⊕ *www.travelinescotland.com.*

CAR

Because of infrequent bus and train services, a car is definitely the best way to explore this region. The winding single-lane roads demand a degree of driving dexterity, however. Local rules of the road require that when two cars meet, whichever driver is the first to reach a passing place (a pullout, or extra patch of pavement to the side of the lane, often marked by a diamond-shaped sign), he must stop and allow the oncoming car to continue (this may entail a bit of backing up). You can also pull into passing places to allow traffic behind you to pass. Drivers always wave, as a courtesy and as a genuine greeting. Cars driving uphill have priority, and small cars tend to yield to large commercial vehicles. Never park in passing places. On bad days you can encounter trucks at the most awkward of spots. On good days single-track driving can be relaxing, with a lovely pace of stopping, waving, moving on.

Note that in this sparsely populated area distances between gas stations can be considerable, so it is wise to fill your tank when you see one. You can reach Inverness (the natural starting point for an exploration of the Northern Highlands) in 3½ hours from Edinburgh or Glasgow; it's around 4½ hours to Skye.

TRAIN

Main railway stations in the area include Oban (for ferries to Barra and the Uists) and Kyle of Lochalsh (for Skye) on the west coast, as well as Inverness (for points north to Thurso and Wick). There's direct service from London to Inverness and connecting service from Edinburgh and Glasgow. For information contact National Rail or ScotRail.

TRAIN CONTACTS National Rail.
☎ *03457/484950* ⊕ *www.nationalrail.co.uk.* **ScotRail.** ☎ *0344/811–0141*
⊕ *www.scotrail.co.uk.*

Restaurants

Northern Scotland has many fine restaurants, where talented chefs use locally grown produce. Most country-house inns and pubs serve reliable, hearty seafood and tasty meat-and-potatoes meals. The Isle of Skye has the most—and the most expensive—restaurants, many of them exceptionally good, but you can find tasty meals almost everywhere. In remote regions you may just have to drive some distance to find them. Remember that locals eat early, so most restaurants stop serving dinner at 9.

Hotels

Charming B&Bs, inexpensive inns, and a few excellent luxury hotels are all here to welcome you after a day touring the Highlands. Much of the available accommodation books up far in advance in high season, when some require a minimum two-day stay.

In the more remote parts of Scotland, your best lodging option may be to rent a cottage or house. Besides allowing you to make your own meals and to come and go as you please, it can also be less expensive. VisitScotland (⊕ *www.visitscotland.com*), the official tourism agency, lists many cottages and even rates them with stars, just like hotels.

Restaurant and hotel reviews have been shortened. For full information, visit Fodors.com. Restaurant prices are the average cost of a main course at dinner or, if dinner is not served, at lunch. Hotel prices are the lowest cost of a standard double room in high season, including 20% V.A.T.

WHAT IT COSTS in Pounds			
$	$$	$$$	$$$$
RESTAURANTS			
under £15	£15–£19	£20–£25	over £25
HOTELS			
under £125	£125–£200	£201–£300	over £300

Tours

There are fascinating boat tours from a number of places around the coast, including seal- and bird-watching trips. Inland bus tours of castles, distilleries, fishing lochs, and hill-walking routes are available locally.

Rabbie's

BUS TOURS | This popular tour operator organizes tours of various lengths throughout the Highlands, from half-day trips to 17-day epics. Tours start from Edinburgh, Glasgow, Aberdeen, or Inverness, and travel is in comfortable 16-seater minibuses. ☎ *0131/226–3133* ⊕ *www.rabbies.com* ✉ *From £19.*

Scotland Tours

BUS TOURS | Choose from a wide range of bus tours for a wide range of budgets, taking anywhere from one to eight days. The company is Highland-owned, and the guides know their region well. ☎ *0131/226–1414* ⊕ *www.scotlandtours.com* ✉ *From £42.*

Visitor Information

There has been a signficant reduction in the number of VisitScotland iCentres in the Northern Highlands and the Western Isles. From nine visitor information centers a few years ago, only four remain, in Inverness and Ullapool (Northern Highlands), Portree (Skye), and Stornoway (Lewis). They're open every day during July and August but closed the rest of the year. Some towns in the region also have independently run visitor centers.

CONTACTS VisitScotland Inverness iCentre. ✉ *36 High St., Inverness* ☎ *01463/252401* ⊕ *www.visitscotland.com.*

Dingwall

10 miles northwest of Inverness, 180 miles north of Glasgow.

This pretty market town and royal burgh (a Scottish town granted a royal charter) makes for a very pleasant stop if you're heading north from Inverness. Although it may not have the headline-grabbing attractions of some other Northern Highland towns—notwithstanding its excellent museum—Dingwall's historic center, replete with alluring architecture, charming cafés, and quaint little shops, makes it well worth a stop. What's more, it's a convenient place to stock up on fuel and supplies before venturing farther up the east coast; opportunities become scarcer after this point.

The Northern Highlands

GETTING HERE AND AROUND

From Inverness take the A9 north to Dingwall, turning off onto the A835. From the north take the A9 south, turning off onto the A862.

 Sights

Dingwall Museum

MUSEUM | Set inside the old town council building, topped by the pretty Townhouse Tower, this small museum offers real insight into local life throughout the 20th century. Exhibits include reproductions of a 1920s kitchen and a local *smiddy* (blacksmiths), a section on military life in the town, and details of historical crimes and punishments. Upstairs has a re-creation of a town council meeting with information on the walls, though the creepy mannequins around the table may make you wary of turning your back. ✉ *Town House, 65 High St., Inverness* ☎ *01349/865366* ⊕ *www.dingwallmuseum.co.uk* 🎫 *Free (donations welcome)* ⊘ *Closed Sat. and Sun. and Oct.–mid-May.*

 Hotels

Coul House Hotel

$$ | HOTEL | Situated in the countryside 8 miles west of Dingwall, this magnificent Georgian manor house offers stylish rooms with mountain views, comfortable lounges with log fireplaces, and an excellent restaurant that's open all day. **Pros:** family-run and family-friendly; free golf practice court; outdoor dining when sunny. **Cons:** hunting portraits not to all tastes; a little off the beaten path; expensive in high season. ⑤ *Rooms from: £175* ✉ *Off A835, Contin* ☎ *01997/421487* ⊕ *www.coulhousehotel.com* 🛏 *21 rooms* ⦿ *Free Breakfast.*

Tulloch Castle Hotel

$$$ | HOTEL | For hundreds of years, Tulloch Castle has watched over the town of Dingwall and the Cromarty Firth, first as the home of the Bain family and Clan Davidson, now as a grand, historic hotel. **Pros:** characterful accommodations; comfy beds and armchairs; good breakfasts. **Cons:** a whiff of faded glory; thin walls and creaking floorboards; very expensive. ⑤ *Rooms from: £235* ✉ *Tulloch Castle Dr., Inverness* ☎ *0844/815–9833* ⊕ *www.bespokehotels.com* 🛏 *20 rooms* ⦿ *Breakfast.*

Dornoch

33 miles northeast of Dingwall.

A town of sandstone houses, tiny rose-filled gardens, and a 13th-century cathedral with stunning traditional and modern stained-glass windows, Dornoch is well worth a visit. It's noted for golf (you may hear it referred to as the "St. Andrews of the North"), but because of the town's location so far north, the golf courses here are delightfully uncrowded. Royal Dornoch is the jewel in its crown, praised by the world's top golfers.

GETTING HERE AND AROUND

From Dingwall or Inverness, take the A9 north to Dornoch. Note that this stretch of the road can get busy with ferry traffic.

ESSENTIALS

VISITOR INFORMATION Dornoch Visitors Centre. ✉ *The Carnegie Courthouse, Castle St.* ☎ *01862/810594* ⊕ *www.visitdornoch.com.*

 Sights

★ Glenmorangie Distillery

WINERY/DISTILLERY | The light color and delicate floral taste of the Speyside whiskies is exemplified in Glenmorangie, one of the best known of the Highland whiskies. The picturesque distillery in Tain, 8 miles south of Dornoch, offers fascinating tours that reveal how the taste is achieved (the secret's in the exceedingly tall stills). The Original Tour includes a dram, and the Signet Tour (£35) offers a chance to sample the rare, chocolatey Glenmorangie

Signet in a unique audio tasting experience. ✉ *Off A9, Tain* ☎ *01862/892477* ⊕ *www.glenmorangie.com* 🎫 *Tours from £8.*

Dunrobin Castle

CASTLE/PALACE | **FAMILY** | Situated 12 miles north of Dornoch, flamboyant Dunrobin Castle is an ancient seat that became the home of the dukes of Sutherland, at which point it was transformed into the 19th-century white-turreted behemoth you see today. As well as its grand palatial facade and lavish interiors, the property also has summer falconry demonstrations and Versailles-inspired gardens. The first duke, who was fascinated by trains, built his own railroad in the park and staffed it with his servants. Yet for all this frivolity, the duke has a controversial legacy; he was responsible for the Sutherland Clearances of 1810 to 1820, when people were forcibly removed from their farms to make room for sheep to graze. ✉ *Off A9, Golspie* ☎ *01408/633177* ⊕ *www.dunrobincastle.co.uk* 🎫 *£12* 🕑 *Closed Nov.–Mar.*

Restaurants

★ Mac and Wild at Falls of Shin

$ | **BRITISH** | This upmarket café-restaurant, located 19 miles west of Dornoch in a modish wood-and-glass (and subtly salmon-shaped) building, serves deliciously meaty dishes, often using venison from deer hunted at the co-owner's nearby estate. It's also a two-minute stroll from the Falls of Shin, one of the Highlands' best spots to see wild salmon leaping upstream in the summer. **Known for:** fresh local produce; award-winning burgers; venison roast dinners. $ *Average main: £13* ✉ *Achany Glen* ☎ *01549/402888* ⊕ *www.macand-wild.com.*

Sutherland House

$ | **BRITISH** | Just off Dornoch's main square, Sutherland House restaurant has a feeling of intimacy in its two separate rooms, reinforced by the enthusiastic reception and delicious food. The menu is imaginative, with some unusual combinations dreamed up by the chef. **Known for:** imaginative seafood; chicken in Glenmorangie sauce; friendly service. $ *Average main: £14* ✉ *Argyle St.* ☎ *01862/811023* ⊕ *www.sutherland-house.net.*

🛏 Hotels

★ Glenmorangie House

$$$$ | **RESORT** | Situated 10 miles southeast from the distillery, Glenmorangie House offers luxurious but casual stays in a spectacular 17th-century country home. **Pros:** wonderfully rural location; superb service; extensive whisky collection. **Cons:** puny showers take a while to heat up; need a car to get here; extremely expensive. $ *Rooms from: £405* ✉ *Fearn by Tain, Tain* ☎ *01862/871671* ⊕ *www. theglenmorangiehouse.com* 🛏 *9 rooms* 🍽 *Some meals.*

Strathview Lodge

$ | **B&B/INN** | A few miles north of Dornoch, this B&B sits high above the road with a wonderful view of Loch Fleet. **Pros:** beautiful location; comfortable and warm rooms; great value. **Cons:** a little way out of Dornoch; unappealing exterior; no on-site restaurant. $ *Rooms from: £84* ✉ *Cambusavie* ☎ *01408/634286* ⊕ *www.strathview-dornoch.co.uk* 🛏 *3 rooms* 🍽 *Breakfast.*

🛍 Shopping

Jail Dornoch

CLOTHING | It's rare for people to voluntarily walk into jail, but this place is the exception, as an old prison has been converted in a popular fashion store. The one-time cells are now home to a range of elegant clothes and accessories, toiletries, housewares, and interesting gifts. It's so popular that there's now a second outlet at Inverness Airport. ✉ *Castle Street* ☎ *01862/810555* ⊕ *www. jail-dornoch.com.*

One of the most treasured properties in the Highlands, Glenmorangie House sits grandly amid expansive manicured grounds.

Activities

★ Royal Dornoch Golf Club

GOLF | The legendary Championship Course, laid out by Tom Morris in 1886, challenges even the very best golfers with its fast, raised greens. It also inspires them with views of white sandy beaches and tall mountains carpeted in wild yellow gorse each spring. The Struie Course provides even more sea views and demanding golf for players of every level. ✉ *Golf Road* ☎ *01862/810219* ⊕ *www.royaldornoch.com* ✉ *Championship: £180; Struie: £50* 🏌 *Championship: 18 holes, 6748 yards, par 70; Struie: 18 holes, 6265 yards, par 71* ⛳ *Reservations essential.*

Helmsdale

28 miles northeast of Dornoch.

Helmsdale is a fascinating fishing village with a checkered past. It was once a busy Viking settlement, later became the scene of an aristocratic poisoning plot, and then was transformed into a Victorian village, used to house some of the poor souls removed from their land to make way for sheep. These "clearances," perpetrated by the Duke of Sutherland, were among the Highlands' most inhumane.

GETTING HERE AND AROUND

Helmsdale is one of the few towns on this part of the coast that has direct train services from Inverness (four a day). But a car will allow you to see more in the surrounding area. Get here via the coastal A9 in each direction, or the inland A897.

Sights

Timespan

MUSEUM | **FAMILY** | This thought-provoking mix of displays, artifacts, and audiovisual materials portrays the history of the area, from the Stone Age to the 1869 gold rush in the Strath of Kildonan. There's a geology exhibit in the garden and a tour of the Kildonan gold-rush site. The complex also includes a café and an art gallery that often hosts visiting artists and changing exhibitions. ✉ *Dunrobin Street* ☎ *01431/821327* ⊕ *www.timespan.org.uk* 🖅 *£4* 🕤 *Closed Mon. and Tue.–Fri. in Nov.–mid-Mar.*

Wick

35 miles northeast of Helmsdale.

Wick is a substantial town that was built on its fishing industry. The town itself is not especially noteworthy, but it does have a handful of worthwhile sights.

GETTING HERE AND AROUND
From Helmsdale follow the A99 north. From Thurso take the A9 south, then the A882 that cuts diagonally southwest.

 ## Sights

Castle Sinclair Girnigoe
CASTLE/PALACE | Dramatically perched on the edge of the cliff, this ruined castle—or rather, castles—is a spectacular sight. Situated 3 miles north of Wick, this site comprises the remains of the 15th-century Castle Girnigoe and the 17th-century Castle Sinclair, set among stunning scenery. The precipitous location, with old walls teetering inches from the cliff edge, means it has a limited lifespan, so go take a look while you can. ✉ *Wick* 🖅 *Free.*

Grey Cairns of Camster
ARCHAEOLOGICAL SITE | The remarkable Grey Cairns of Camster, two Neolithic chambers made of rough stones, were built more than 5,000 years ago and are among the best preserved in Britain. **Camster Round Cairn** is 20 yards in diameter and 13 yards high, while **Camster Long Cairn** stretches an extraordinary 77 yards. Some 19th-century excavations revealed skeletons, pottery, and flint tools in the round cairn's internal chamber. They are in an isolated location, around 8 miles southwest of Wick and without a visitor center in sight, so if you feel adventurous

and don't mind dirty knees, you can crawl into the chambers (the metal grills over the entrances mean they appear locked, but they aren't). To get here, you'll need to drive 5 miles along the unnamed road from Occumster to Watten; when you're just north of Lybster on the A99, look out for the brown signposts pointing the way. ✉ *Off A9* ⊕ *www.historicenvironment.scot* 🖅 *Free.*

★ Pulteney Distillery
WINERY/DISTILLERY | Unusually for a distillery, Pulteney is situated very close to the town center, and it has been for almost 200 years. The spirit produced here, known as "gold," was once in the shadow of the town's other big "silver" industry—herring fishing. But, despite a hairy period of prohibition, it has easily outlasted its competition. The brooding brick distillery is open for tours and tastings, so join the standard one-hour tour (£10) for a behind-the-scenes look at the facilities and a taste of the award-winning 12-year-old Old Pulteney—famed for its smooth, faintly briny character with lingering butterscotch sweet finish. Or, for £25, experience all this plus additional tastings of three older expressions. ✉ *Huddart Street* ☎ *01955/602371* ⊕ *www.old-pulteney.com* 🖅 *Tours from £10* 🕤 *Closed Sun. May–Sept. and weekends Oct.–Apr.*

Wick Heritage Museum
MUSEUM | The locals who run this lovely town museum are real enthusiasts, and they will take you through Wick's history from its founding by the Vikings to its heyday in the 1860s as a leading herring port. The collection includes everything from ancient fossils and a 19th-century cooperage to the Johnston Photographic Collection, a set of 40,000 images that show more than a century of life in Wick through one local family's eyes. There's also an art gallery and lovely terraced gardens that overlook the town. ✉ *18–27 Bank Row* ☎ *01955/605393* ⊕ *www.wickheritage.org* 🖅 *£4* 🕤 *Closed Sun. and Nov.–Easter.*

John O'Groats

16 miles north of Wick.

The windswept little outpost of John O'Groats is usually taken to be the northernmost point on the Scottish mainland, though that is not strictly true, as a short drive to Dunnet Head will reveal. From the harbor you can take a boat to see the dolphins and seals that live beneath the coastal cliffs—or head farther afield with a ferry to Orkney. The little town has charms of its own, including a row of colorful wooden houses (part of the Inn at John O' Groats) and a crafts center with high-quality shops selling knitwear, candles, and gifts.

GETTING HERE AND AROUND
Traveling north from Wick, take the A99. From the east, take the coast-hugging A836.

TOURS
John O'Groats Ferries
TOUR—SIGHT | Sailing from John O'Groats Harbor, this company offers 90-minute wildlife cruises past spectacular cliff scenery and birdlife into the Pentland Firth, to Duncansby Stacks, and to the island of Stroma. Trips cost £19 and are available daily at 2:30 between mid-June and August. The company also offers a Maxi Day tour of Orkney between May and September. It leaves at 8:45 am and costs £68. ⊠ *Ferry Office, County Road, John O'Groats* ☎ *01955/611353* ⊕ *www.jogferry.co.uk* ⌨ *Tours from £19.*

◉ Sights

Duncansby Head
VIEWPOINT | Head to this lighthouse for spectacular views of cliffs and sea stacks, as well as seabirds like guillemots and (if you're lucky) puffins. It's on the coastal road east of town. There are a few parking spaces there, or you can walk (about 30 minutes) from the main road. ⊠ *John O'Groats* ⊕ *www.nlb.org.uk/lighthouses/duncansby-head* ⌨ *Free.*

Hotels

★ John O'Groats by Together Travel
$$$ | **RENTAL** | A local landmark in their own right, the brightly colored lodges here are the region's best self-catering accommodations—not to mention the most photogenic—and they provide stunning views out to sea (on a clear day, all the way to Orkney). **Pros:** very comfy beds; good Wi-Fi (a rarity here); natural light all day long. **Cons:** can feel understaffed; two nights minimum in high season; a little expensive. ⑤ *Rooms from: £210* ⊠ *John O'Groats* ✛ *West of ferry terminal* ☎ *01625/416430* ⊕ *www.togethertravel.co.uk/destinations/scotland/john-ogroats* ⇶ *23 lodges* ⦿ *No meals.*

Thurso

19 miles west of John O'Groats.

The town of Thurso is quite substantial for a community so far north. Attractions in the town include Old St. Peter's Kirk, which dates back to the 12th century; fine nearby beaches, particularly at Dunnet Bay; and great seabird spotting at Dunnet Head.

GETTING HERE AND AROUND
A car remains the best way to see this region, although local buses run most days. From John O'Groats simply follow the A836 west.

◉ Sights

Dunnet Bay Distillery
WINERY/DISTILLERY | This small north coast distillery proves that Scotland's craft distilling boom has stretched to the very edges of the mainland. It also proves that Scotland has far more to offer than just whisky. Dunnet Bay Distillery has gained

plaudits and prizes galore for its Rock Rose gin (notable for its use of sea buckthorn and other coastal botanicals), and it also produces a superb vodka called Holy Grass. You can tour the "wee" distillery every summer; reservations are advised. *Children younger than 18 are allowed to visit and are admitted on the tour free of charge with an accompanying adult.* ✉ *Off A836* ☎ *01847/851287* ⊕ *www.dunnetbaydistillers.co.uk* 🎫 *Tours £15* ◷ *Closed Dec.–mid-Mar.*

Dunnet Head

VIEWPOINT | Most people make the trip to Dunnet Head to stand at the northernmost point of mainland Britain. But it's also worth a visit for the pretty Dunnet Head Lighthouse (built 1831), the dramatic sea cliffs, and the fine views over the water to Orkney. The Royal Society for the Protection of Birds also runs a nature reserve here, due to the number of seabirds nesting in the cliffs. ✉ *Brough* ⊕ *www.dunnethead.co.uk* 🎫 *Free.*

Old St. Peter's Kirk

RELIGIOUS SITE | This roofless, ruined parish church on the banks of the River Thurso was once the principal place of worship in northeast Scotland. Dating back to (at least) the early 1100s, the church is known for its decorative window carved from a single slab of stone, as well as its atmospheric graveyard. Look for headstone emblems that represent the trade of the person buried beneath. ✉ *Back Shore Street.*

Hotels

★ Forss House

$$$ | B&B/INN | Don't be fooled by the stark exterior, as this house dating from 1810 is a charming place to stay, offering beautiful bedrooms, expansive grounds, and the area's finest dining option.
Pros: large guest rooms; lots of outdoor activities; deliciously hearty meals.
Cons: heavy old doors make a racket; River House lacking the charm of main

house; expensive option. 💲 *Rooms from: £215* ✉ *Forss* ✈ *4 miles west of Thurso* ☎ *01847/861201* ⊕ *www.forsshousehotel.co.uk* ➔ *14 rooms* �ΟΙ *Breakfast.*

Activities

The Bike Shop

BICYCLING | This cycle-repair shop has a friendly staff and a handful of hybrid bikes to rent. You can also get advice on the best local routes. ✉ *35 High St.* ☎ *01847/895385.*

Tongue

43 miles west of Thurso.

A popular pit stop between Thurso and Durness, Tongue has some worthwhile sights and good accommodations options.

GETTING HERE AND AROUND
From Thurso simply head west along the A836, which will turn into A838 just before you reach Tongue.

Sights

★ Castle Varrich

CASTLE/PALACE | Standing on a high rocky outcrop, overlooking both the town and the Kyle of Tongue, Castle Varrich (or Bharrich) was built by Clan Mackay in the 14th century—but possibly not from scratch. It's believed an old Norse fort may have previously occupied the site. Today a steel staircase and viewing platform make it easily accessible to visitors, who can walk from Tongue and back in less than an hour. The clearly signposted path gets a little steep in parts, but the climb is worth it for the spectacular views. ✉ *Tongue.*

★ Coldbackie Beach

BEACH—SIGHT | This windswept bay, 3 miles north of Tongue, is a well-kept secret, offering powder-white sands, spectacular island views, and perfect peace and quiet—so long as you don't arrive when surf's up. To get here simply park in Coldbackie and walk. **Amenities:** parking (no fee); water sports. **Best for:** solitude; surfing; walking. ⊠ *Coldbackie, Tongue* ⊹ *Off A836.*

 ## Hotels

Garvault House
$ | **HOTEL** | Billed as mainland Britain's most remote hotel (Tongue, its nearest town, is 50 minutes' drive away), the charmingly rustic and almost entirely off-grid Garvault House offers a classic countryside escape in the heart of the Highlands. **Pros:** beautiful panoramic views; dinner included; fishing and hill walking galore. **Cons:** a little fusty in places; patchy Wi-Fi; no amenities for miles. ⑤ *Rooms from: £110* ⊠ *Off B871* ☎ *07596/202171* ⊕ *www.garvaulthouse. uk* ⊗ *Closed Dec.–Mar.* ⇨ *8 rooms* ��⦿*⼁ Free Breakfast.*

The Tongue Hotel
$ | **HOTEL** | With open fireplaces, tartan rugs, and floral wallpaper, this traditional Highland hotel is a great base for exploring the northern coast of the Scottish mainland. **Pros:** warm and friendly staff; beautiful location with stunning views; deliciously creamy porridge at breakfast. **Cons:** Wi-Fi only in public areas; TV sets from the '80s; food is hit and miss. ⑤ *Rooms from: £115* ⊠ *Tongue* ☎ *01847/611206* ⊕ *www.tonguehotel. co.uk* ⇨ *19 rooms* ⡀⦿⼁ *Free breakfast.*

Durness

29 miles west of Tongue.

The sudden patches of green surrounding the village of Durness, on the north coast, are caused by the richer limestone outcrops among the acid moorlands. The town is the jumping-off point for several natural highlights, from a beautiful sandy beach to the country's highest cliff.

GETTING HERE AND AROUND
From Tongue simply head west along the A838.

 ## Sights

Balnakeil Craft Village
CRAFTS | Artisans sell pottery, leather, weavings, paintings, and more from their studios at Balnakeil Craft Village. It is a charmingly odd place consisting of rows of shabby former military buildings located on an unnamed road running northwest from Durness and framed by dramatic views of Balnakeil Bay. The village is open during the summer, with most shops open daily from 10 to 5. ⊠ *Balnakeil* ☎ *01971/511713 Nicola Poole's Wee Gallery* ⊕ *www.balnakeilcraftvillage. weebly.com* ⊗ *Closed Nov.–Mar.*

Cape Wrath
VIEWPOINT | If you've made it this far north, you'll probably want to go all the way to Cape Wrath, a rugged headland at the northwest tip of Scotland. The white-sand beaches, impressive dunes covered in marram grass, and crashing seas of nearby Balnakeil Bay make it an exhilarating place to visit. As this land is owned by the Ministry of Defence (it is listed as an area for air force training), you can't drive your own vehicle. From May through September, a small boat ferries people here from Keoldale, 2 miles outside Durness. En route look out for Clo Mor; at 920 feet, they're the highest sea cliffs in mainland Britain. Once you're across the sea inlet, a minibus will take you to the lighthouse. Call ahead or check departure times on the board at the jetty. ☎ *01971/511284* ⊕ *www. visitcapewrath.com* 🎫 *£20.50 boat/bus return* ⊗ *No boat mid-Oct.–mid-Apr.*

Ciannabeine Beach
BEACH—SIGHT | Situated 10 miles east of Durness, Ciannabeine is one of Scotland's most achingly beautiful beaches, a spectacular sweep of sand caught in the embrace of 10,000-year-old rocks. There

The dramatic Smoo Cave has one of the largest entrances to any sea cave in Britain.

is a car park opposite and a path down to the beach itself. You will recognize it by the white house just beyond, once the village school. **Amenities:** parking (no fee). **Best for:** swimming; walking. ✉ *Off A838* ✛ *Between Rispond and Sangobeg.*

★ Sandwood Bay
BEACH—SIGHT | The very definition of *off the beaten path*, Sandwood Bay is one of Scotland's most spectacular—and most isolated—beaches. The only way to reach it is to walk 4 miles each way across sheep fields and sand dunes. It's a lovely, fairly easy walk, which may just end with you having a long, sandy beach, with its dramatic sea stack Am Buachaille, all to yourself. To get here turn off the A838 onto the B801 at Rhiconich (14 miles southwest of Durness), then turn off at Kinlochbervie to Balchrick. Just before you reach the latter, look for a tiny white sign to "Sandwood," then follow this single-track lane to its end, where you can park and start walking. **Amenities:** parking (no fee). **Best for:** solitude; walking. ✉ *Durness.*

★ Sculpture Croft
ART GALLERIES | This odd garden of delights provokes a double-take from most drivers traveling along the A838, thanks to its incongruous ceramic-topped gates. Park opposite and take a stroll down into Danish artist Lotte Glob's pottery wonderland, where ceramic and metal sculptures are scattered across the gardens. Several paths lead down to the coast, and there are hundreds of pieces en route, including a library of ceramic books. Her work reflects and adds to the landscape, using natural shapes and forms and building patterns into the rocks themselves. End your visit with a trip to the studio and pottery shop. ✉ *105 Laid* ☎ *01971/511727* ⊕ *www.lotteglob. co.uk* ⊘ *Only open by appointment Oct.–mid-May.*

★ Smoo Cave
CAVE | This atmospheric cavern, hollowed out of the limestone by rushing water, feels like something out of a fantasy novel. The combined sea-and-freshwater cave, complete with gushing waterfall,

can be reached via a steep cliff stairway from the Smoo Cave car park. But don't start your descent before reading the explanatory boards at the top of the stairs, which tell the history of those who lived and used the caves in much earlier times. ⊠ Off A838 ➯ Free.

🍴 Restaurants

Cocoa Mountain

$ | **CAFÉ** | A must for those with a sweet tooth, this "chocolate bar" within the Balnakeil Craft Village serves world-class truffles and stunningly rich hot chocolate made in its specialist "chocolate factory," which sources the beans from around the world. There are also sandwiches, cakes, and coffee available. **Known for:** sublime chocolate truffles; homemade hot chocolate; friendly service. $ *Average main: £12* ⊠ *Balnakeil Craft Village, Balnakeil* ☎ *01971/511233* ⊕ *www.cocoamountain.co.uk.*

Scourie

25 miles southwest of Durness.

Scourie is a small coastal settlement catering to visitors—particularly fisherfolk—with a good range of accommodations. The bayside town makes a good base for a trip to the bird sanctuary on Handa Island.

GETTING HERE AND AROUND
From Durness head south on the A838, turning onto the A894.

👁 Sights

★ Handa Island

ISLAND | Just off the coast of Scourie is Handa Island, a bird sanctuary that shelters huge seabird colonies, especially impressive at nesting time. You can gaze at more than 200,000 birds nesting on dramatic cliffs here, including guillemots,

razorbills, great skuas, kittiwakes, and, of course, crowd-pleasingly colorful puffins. Sturdy boots, a waterproof jacket, and a degree of fitness are needed to walk the path around the island. This remarkable reserve, administered by the Scottish Wildlife Trust, is open only in spring and summer, and can be reached by a small open boat from Tarbert; contact the Assynt Visitor Centre in Lochinver for details. ■**TIP**➜ **Note that ferries don't run on Sunday.** ⊕ *scottishwildlifetrust.org.uk* ⊗ *Closed Oct.–Mar.*

🍴 Restaurants

★ Shorehouse Restaurant

$$ | **SEAFOOD** | If you're feeling peckish after a trip to Handa Island, make a stop at this exceptional seafood restaurant overlooking Tarbet Harbor. It serves freshly caught seafood specialties, from hand-dived scallops and hot smoked mackerel to whole lobsters, in a quaint, maritime-themed setting. **Known for:** spectacular seafood; gorgeous views; friendly and attentive service. $ *Average main: £17* ⊠ *Tigh Na Mara, Tarbet* ☎ *01971/502251* ⊗ *Closed Sun. and Oct.–Easter.*

🛏 Hotels

★ Eddrachilles Hotel

$$ | **B&B/INN** | With one of the most spectacular vistas of any hotel in Scotland—out toward the picturesque islands of Badcall Bay—Eddrachilles sits on a huge plot of private moorland just south of the Handa Island bird sanctuary. **Pros:** attractive garden; stunning shoreline nearby; close to bird sanctuary. **Cons:** needs a lick of paint; Wi-Fi limited to public areas; set menus only. $ *Rooms from: £145* ⊠ *Off A894* ☎ *01971/502080* ⊕ *www.eddrachilles.com* ⊗ *Closed Nov.–mid-Mar.* ⤸ *10 rooms* ⏀ *Free breakfast.*

Kylesku

10 miles southeast of Scourie.

This tiny settlement once served as a ferry crossing, before being usurped by the (incredibly photogenic) Kylesku Bridge. Today it's a lovely stop for lunch, a boat trip along Loch Glendhu and Loch Glencoul, or even an overnight stay.

GETTING HERE AND AROUND
From Scourie head south on the A894.

Sights

★ Drumbeg Loop

SCENIC DRIVE | Bold souls journeying from Kylesku to Lochinver may enjoy taking the interesting single-track B869 Drumbeg Loop. It has several challenging hairpin turns along with breathtaking views. Head 2 miles south of Kylesku on the A894 and hang a right when you see the brown sign to "An Druim Beag." Although it's only 20 miles to Lochinver, it will take around an hour without stops—but plan on longer, because you'll definitely want to stop. Just before the scattered community of Stoer, a road leads west to **Stoer Point Lighthouse.** If you're an energetic walker, you can hike across the short turf and heather along the cliff top for fine views west toward Lewis and Harris. There's also a red-sandstone sea stack: the **Old Man of Stoer** (not to be confused with the Old Man of Storr on Skye). This makes a pleasant excursion on a long summer evening.

Eas a' Chual Aluinn Waterfall

BODY OF WATER | With a drop of 685 feet, this is the longest waterfall in the United Kingdom. A rugged hike leads to the falls, which are at the head of Loch Glencoul. Start from the car park off the A894, on the bend of the road 4 miles south of Kylesku, just before you reach Loch na Gainmhich. Alternatively, between April and September, cruises from Kylesku Old

Ferry Pier offer a less-taxing alternative (£30). ⊠ *Off A894, Lochinver.*

Hotels

Kylesku Hotel

$$ | HOTEL | This charming hotel, looking out over Loch Glendhu and toward Eas Coul Aulin (Scotland's highest waterfall), has great service, excellent food, and a warm, relaxed atmosphere. **Pros:** stunning views; great staff; delicious food. **Cons:** some old-building quirks; two tiny (but cheap) attic rooms; 20-minute drive from Scourie. ⑤ *Rooms from: £130* ⊠ *Off A894* ✛ *10 miles south of Scourie* ☎ 01971/502231 ⊕ *www.kyleskuhotel. co.uk* ⮑ *11 rooms* ⦿ *Breakfast.*

Lochinver

18 miles southwest of Kylesku.

Lochinver is a pretty, quiet, shoreside community of whitewashed cottages overlooked by soaring Suilven mountain. There are lovely beaches to the north, a harbor used by the west-coast fishing fleet, and some good dining and lodging options, making it an ideal base for exploring Sutherland. Take the cul-de-sac, **Baddidarroch Road**, for scenery that makes for great photo opportunities.

GETTING HERE AND AROUND
To get to Lochinver from Kylesku in roughly 30 minutes, head south on the A894, then turn west onto the A837. If you prefer to take your time, opt for the scenic B869 (known as the "Drumbeg Loop") instead.

ESSENTIALS
VISITOR INFORMATION Assynt Visitor Centre. ⊠ *Culag New Pier* ☎ 01571/844123 ⊕ *www.discoverassynt. co.uk.*

Sights

Achmelvich Bay

BEACH—SIGHT | This beautiful white-sand beach, located 4 miles northwest of Lochinver, is a popular summer spot with water babies, from kayakers to windsurfers, as well as landlubbers who delight in the surrounding hiking trails and climbing opportunities. It's also a favorite of fishers, dog walkers, and "rockpoolers." The beach is considerably quieter outside of peak season. **Amenities:** parking (no fee); water sports. **Best for:** walking; windsurfing ⊠ *Achmelvich Beach Car Park, Off B869.*

Ardvreck Castle

CASTLE/PALACE | Beside Loch Assynt, 11 miles east of Lochinver, stands the striking ruined Ardvreck Castle, a onetime Clan MacLeod stronghold built in the late 1500s. Still highly atmospheric, it sits on an outcrop with perfect views the length of the loch in both directions. Located off the A837, just over half a mile south of the junction with the A894, it's visible as you approach from either direction. You'll find a car park located directly opposite the ruins; you can park, take the muddy path down to a stony beach, and then walk along to the castle. ⊠ *Off A837* ⊕ *www.undiscoveredscotland.co.uk* 🖼 *Free.*

★ Assynt and Coigach

NATURE PRESERVE | To the east and south of Lochinver, on the way to Ullapool, lies a different kind of landscape: a vast region of brooding mountains and languid lochs, where peaks punch their way out of heathered terrain and appear to constantly shift positions. Even their names have a more mysterious air than those of the *bens* (mountain peaks or hills) elsewhere: Cul Mor, Cul Beag, Stac Pollaidh, Canisp, Suilven. Some hark back to Norse rather than to Gaelic—a reminder that Vikings used to sail this northern shore. The highlight of the region is the eerily pretty Loch Assynt, peppered with tiny wooded isles, but the Coigach peninsula northwest of Ullapool is equally dramatic.

 Restaurants

Lochinver Mission Cafe

$ | BRITISH | An abandoned fishermen's mission (a place where fishermen stayed while in port), situated at the far end of town near the harbor, now houses this pleasant café serving lunch, soup, sandwiches, and home baking. The specials often include fish freshly delivered from the harbor. **Known for:** delicious homemade soup; great fish-and-chips; cash only. *Average main: £9* ⊠ *Culag Park* 🕿 *01571/844324* ⊕ *www.lochinvermission.org.uk* ▭ *No credit cards* ⊗ *Closed Sun.*

 Hotels

Inver Lodge Hotel

$$$ | HOTEL | In a commanding location on a hillside above Lochinver, this modern luxury hotel has stunning views of the coast, as well as smart guest rooms that are decorated in contemporary colors and traditional mahogany furniture. **Pros:** cozy public room with a fireplace; refreshing sauna; great fishing nearby. **Cons:** slightly drab exterior; not good for families with children; extremely expensive. ⓢ *Rooms from: £300* ⊠ *Iolaire Road* 🕿 *01571/844496* ⊕ *www.inverlodge.com* ⇶ *21 rooms* ⎮⊚⎮ *Free breakfast.*

Tigh Na Sith

$$ | B&B/INN | Set just above the bay at Lochinver, this family-run B&B wins rave reviews for its warm welcome. **Pros:** welcoming hosts; fantastic views; delicious breakfast. **Cons:** room at back has no view; beds can be creaky; room rates have risen significantly. ⓢ *Rooms from: £125* ⊠ *Off A837* 🕿 *01571/844588* ⊕ *www.tighnasith.com* ⇶ *3 rooms* ⎮⊚⎮ *Breakfast.*

Shopping

Highland Stoneware

HOUSEHOLD ITEMS/FURNITURE | The huge sofa and television composed entirely of broken crockery are a witty introduction to the beautiful ceramic works of art made at Highland Stoneware. The potters and decorators busy themselves in a studio behind the shop, and visitors are encouraged to watch as they create pieces incorporating Highland themes. If you miss this one, know that there's a second Highland Stoneware store in Ullapool. ⊠ *Baddidarroch* ☎ *01571/844376* ⊕ *www.highlandstoneware.com.*

Ullapool

36 miles south of Lochinver, 223 miles north of Glasgow, 58 miles northwest of Inverness.

Ullapool is an ideal base for hiking throughout Sutherland and taking wildlife and nature cruises, especially to the Summer Isles. By the shores of salty Loch Broom, the town was founded in 1788 as a fishing station to exploit the local herring stocks. There's still a smattering of fishing vessels, as well as visiting yachts and foreign ships. When their crews fill the pubs, Ullapool has a surprisingly cosmopolitan feel. The harbor area comes to life when the Lewis and Harris ferry arrives and departs.

GETTING HERE AND AROUND

A desolate but well-maintained stretch of the A835 takes you from Inverness to Ullapool, with a connection to Torridon via the A832.

ESSENTIALS

VISITOR INFORMATION VisitScotland Ullapool iCentre. ⊠ *Argyle Street* ☎ *01854/612486.*

Sights

The Ceilidh Place

ARTS VENUE | Ullapool's cultural focal point is The Ceilidh Place, an excellent venue for concerts and other events all through the year (*ceilidh* is a Scottish social gathering with traditional music and dance). It started out as a small café, but over the years it has added space for local performers, an excellent bookshop specializing in Scottish writing, and a handful of comfortable rooms (as well as a basic bunkhouse) for those who want to spend the night. It's a great place for afternoon coffee or a wee dram in the evening. ⊠ *14 W. Argyle St.* ☎ *01854/612103* ⊕ *www.theceilidhplace.com.*

Corrieshalloch Gorge

BODY OF WATER | For a thrilling touch of vertigo, don't miss Corrieshalloch Gorge, 12 miles south of Ullapool, just off the A835. Draining the high moors, the Falls of Measach plunge into a 200-foot-deep, thickly wooded gorge. There's a suspension-bridge viewpoint and a heady atmosphere of romantic grandeur, like an old Scottish print come to life. A short walk leads from a parking area to the viewpoint. ⊕ *www.nts.org.uk.*

Ullapool Museum

MUSEUM | Films, photographs, and audiovisual displays tell the story of the area from the Ice Age to modern times, including the "klondyking" period between 1970 and 1990, when foreign boats filled the loch to fish the mackerel. There's an ongoing exhibition on weather, climate change, and the environment. The building was designed by Thomas Telford and dates from the early 19th century. ⊠ *7–8 W. Argyle St.* ☎ *01854/612987* ⊕ *www.ullapoolmuseum.co.uk* 🎟 *£4* ⊘ *Closed Sun. and Nov.–Mar.*

🍴 Restaurants

The Arch Inn

$ | **BRITISH** | On the face of it, this popular restaurant isn't doing anything particularly remarkable; its simple pub-style menu of steaks, burgers, and fish-and-chips hardly pushes the envelope. But its use of fresh, local ingredients, its pretty presentation of dishes, and its appealing waterside seating make it a favorite dining spot among locals. **Known for:** fresh and tasty pub grub; waterside seating; always busy. $ *Average main: £14* ⊠ *10–11 W. Shore St.* ☎ *01854/612454* ⊕ *www.thearchinn.co.uk.*

★ The West Coast Delicatessen

$ | **CAFÉ** | This charming family-run deli serves delicious homemade sandwiches, pies, soups, salads, and hummus to a long line of locals and tourists. It also has great cakes and baked goods. **Known for:** great homemade soups; excellent coffee; an array of artisanal products. $ *Average main: £8* ⊠ *5 Argyle St.* ☎ *01854/613450* ⊕ *www.westcoastdeli.co.uk* ⊗ *Closed Sun. No dinner.*

🛏 Hotels

Tanglewood House

$ | **B&B/INN** | Sitting on a headland above a rocky beach, with spectacular views across Loch Broom toward Ullapool, one of Scotland's most unique and appealing B&Bs feels wonderfully remote while only being a short drive (or even a walk) into town. **Pros:** truly unique property; beautiful setting; fast and reliable Wi-Fi. **Cons:** steep drive down to the house; some fusty decor; a little remote. $ *Rooms from: £99* ⊠ *Off A835* ☎ *01854/612059* ⊕ *www.tanglewoodhouse.co.uk* ⊡ *3 rooms* ⍟ *Free breakfast.*

★ Westlea House

$ | **B&B/INN** | This quaint, quirky boutique B&B is one of Ullapool's undoubted gems, with bedrooms themed around

Fishing in the Highlands

The possibilities for fishing are endless in Sutherland, as a glance at the loch-covered map suggests. Brown trout and salmon are abundant. You can fish from the banks of Loch Garve, 33 miles southeast of Ullapool, or Loch Assynt, 6 miles east of Lochinver, from March to October. Boat fishing is popular on Loch Maree, southeast of Gairloch and north of Poolewe, from May to October. Fishing permits are available at local post offices and shops; some hotels have their own fishing rights but most will arrange fishing permits for you.

different natural features and cozy common rooms stuffed with comfy armchairs, colorful cushions, and off-the-wall artworks. **Pros:** wonderfully whimsical decor; superfriendly owners; great location. **Cons:** TVs are small; sea views limited; some low ceilings. $ *Rooms from: £85* ⊠ *2 Market St.* ☎ *01854/612594* ⊕ *www.westlea-ullapool.co.uk* ⊡ *5 rooms.*

🏃 Activities

Stac Pollaidh

HIKING/WALKING | For a great afternoon of walking, ascend the dramatic hill of Stac Pollaidh (pronounced "stack polly"), about 14 miles north of Ullapool. The clearly marked path climbs for a bit and then curves around to the right and takes you on a loop with incredible views over Sutherland, north to Suilven, and west to the Summer Isles. About halfway around the hill, a steeper path takes you to the start of the ridge. ⚠ **Only very experienced rock climbers should continue from here, as the route requires rock climbing**

in very exposed conditions. But not to worry, because from the west side of the looped path, you can see the pinnacled pitch of Stac Pollaidh. To get here take the A835 to Drumrunie, then a minor road off to the west (there's a sign for "Achiltibuie"). Five miles along the road, there's a car park; start your walk from here. ⊠ *Off A835, Dornie.*

Gairloch

55 miles southwest of Ullapool.

Aside from its restaurants and lodgings, peaceful Gairloch has one further advantage: it often escapes the rain clouds that can cling to the high summits. You can enjoy a round of golf here and perhaps stay dry, even when the nearby Torridon Hills are deluged.

GETTING HERE AND AROUND

From Ullapool, head south down the A835 and, after 12 miles (just after Corrieshalloch Gorge), turn west onto the winding A832 (also known as "Destitution Road").

 ## Sights

Destitution Road

SCENIC DRIVE | The road south between **Corrieshalloch Gorge** (a very worthwhile stop) and Gairloch passes through wild woodlands around Dundonnell and Loch Broom, then takes in stunning coastal scenery with views of Gruinard Bay and its white beaches. Look out for the toothed ramparts of the mountain **An Teallach** (pronounced tyel-lack), visible on the horizon for miles. The moorland route you travel is officially called the A832, but is better (and more chillingly) known as Destitution Road; a holdover from the terrible potato famines of the 1840s.

★ Inverewe Garden

GARDEN | A highlight of the area, Inverewe Garden has lush plantings tucked away behind a dense barrier of trees and shrubs. This is all thanks to the warm North Atlantic Drift, which takes the edge off winter frosts. Inverewe is sometimes described as subtropical, but this inaccuracy irritates the head gardener; do not expect coconuts and palm trees here. Instead, look for rarities like the blue Himalayan poppy. ⊠ *Off A832, Poolewe ⊹ 6 miles northeast of Gairloch* ☎ *01445/781229 ⊕ www.nts.org.uk* ⊠ *£12.50.*

★ Loch Maree

BODY OF WATER | Southeast of Gairloch stretches one of Scotland's most scenic lochs, Loch Maree. Its harmonious setting, with tall Scots pines and the mountain Slioch looming as a backdrop, is regularly visited by red deer, as well as the endangered pine marten (a member of the weasel family)—though they're just as likely to be hanging around the trash cans as in the trees. There are few official parking places along the loch, but these are nestled between the trees with limited views, so be prepared to park and climb to a better vantage point. ⊠ *Gairloch.*

 ## Hotels

The Dundonnell

$ | HOTEL | Located along "Destitution Road," around 30 miles from Gairloch, this lovely family-run hotel sits on the edge of Little Loch Broom, with the mountains of An Leachall rising up behind. **Pros:** fabulous scenery; plenty of outdoor activities; good dining options. **Cons:** bland exterior; some outdated rooms; Wi-Fi only in public areas. ⑤ *Rooms from: £110* ⊠ *A832, Dundonnell* ☎ *01854/633204 ⊕ www.dundonnellho-tel.com ⤴ 23 rooms ❏ Free breakfast.*

 ## Activities

Gairloch Golf Club

GOLF | This lovely nine-hole course is one of the few to be found on this stretch of coast, but it is the coastal location that gives it its charm—as well as its challenges. There has been a golf club here since 1898, and local records show that putters of more than a century ago played on the golden sand dunes, long since been replaced by rolling greens. While you are waiting for your turn at the tee, take a moment to drink in fine views of the Minch and Skye. ✉ *Off A832* ☎ *01445/712407* ⊕ *www.gairlochgolfclub. co.uk* ✉ *£15 for 9 holes, £25 for 18 holes* 🏌 *9 holes, 2137 yards, par 31.*

Shieldaig

37 miles south of Gairloch.

Just west of the southern coast of Upper Loch Torridon is Shieldaig, a village that sits in an attractive crescent overlooking a loch of its own, Loch Shieldaig. For an atmospheric evening foray, walk north toward Loch Torridon, at the northern end of the village by the church. The path—fairly well made, though hiking shoes are recommended—leads to exquisite views and tiny, rocky beaches.

GETTING HERE AND AROUND

From Gairloch head southeast on the A832, then turn southwest onto the A896 at Kinlochewe; Shieldaig is around 17 miles along this road.

Sights

★ Applecross

SCENIC DRIVE | The most exciting way to reach this small community facing Skye is by a twisting, turning coastal road, which leaves the A896 just a few miles south of Shieldaig; simply follow the brown sign marked "Wester Ross Coastal Trail." A series of hairpin bends corkscrew up the steep wall at the head of a corrie (a glacier-cut mountain valley) and over the **Bealach na Ba** (Pass of the Cattle). There are spectacular views of Raasay and Skye from the bare plateau

on top, and you can brag afterward that you've been on what is probably Scotland's highest drivable road.

★ Glen Torridon

VIEWPOINT | The scenic spectacle of Glen Torridon lies east of Shieldaig; if you're following the A896 from Kinlochewe to Shieldaig, you pass right through it. Some say that Glen Torridon has the finest mountain scenery in Scotland. It consists mainly of the long, gray, quartzite flanks of **Beinn Eighe** and **Liathach,** with its distinct ridge profile that looks like the keel of an upturned boat.

Hotels

The Torridon

$$$$ | **HOTEL** | The Victorian Gothic turrets of this former hunting lodge promise atmosphere and grandeur—and with its log fires, handsome plasterwork ceilings, mounted stag heads, and antique mahogany furniture, The Torridon doesn't disappoint. **Pros:** wonderful location; center for outdoor activities; more than 300 malts in the bar. **Cons:** very pricey; 6 miles out of town; activities must be booked in advance. $ *Rooms from: £400* ✉ *Off A896* ☎ *01445/791242* ⊕ *www.thetorridon.com* 🛏 *18 rooms* ♨ *Breakfast.*

Torridon Inn

$$ | **B&B/INN** | A more affordable option than the grand Torridon hotel, this bright and sparkling clean lodging makes a great base for exploring the area. **Pros:** pleasant wood-clad decor; eco-friendly vibe; reasonable rates. **Cons:** service sometimes erratic; can be noisy; some rooms lacking views. $ *Rooms from: £145* ✉ *Off A896* ☎ *01445/791242* ⊕ *www.thetorridon.com/stay/inn* 🛏 *12 rooms* ♨ *Breakfast.*

Lochcarron

14 miles southeast of Shieldaig, 25 miles northeast of Skye, 63 miles west of Inverness.

Strung along the shore, the village of Lochcarron has some attractive croft buildings, a couple of churches (one an 18th-century ruin set in a graveyard), a golf club, and some handy shops.

GETTING HERE AND AROUND

To drive here from Shieldaig, take the A896 southeast; the single-lane road skirts both steep mountains and lochs. From Skye take the A87 east, turn northwards onto the A890, then turn west onto the A896.

 Restaurants

The Bealach Cafe and Gallery

$ | CAFÉ | This lovely café offers sandwiches, soups, and fine home baking against a background of mountains and the steepest road ascent in Britain, the Bealach na Ba (from which it gets its name). All this can be viewed through the café's large windows or from the outside deck, if weather allows. **Known for:** lovely home-baked cakes; friendly hosts; views to die for. $ *Average main: £9* ⊠ *A896* ☎ *01520/733436* ⊕ *www.thebealach.co.uk* ⊗ *Closed Mon. and Tue. No dinner.*

 Shopping

Lochcarron Weavers

TEXTILES/SEWING | Watch a weaver producing pure-wool tartans that can be bought here or at the company's other outlets in the area. There's also a nice little café. ⊠ *Lochcarron* ☎ *01520/722212* ⊕ *www.lochcarron.co.uk.*

Isle of Skye

The misty Isle of Skye is awash with romance and myth, lush green gardens, and steep, magnetic mountains. Its extraordinary natural beauty and royal connections see it rank highly on most visitors' must-see lists, while its proximity to the mainland makes it one of Scotland's most easily accessible islands.

Skye has a dramatic, mysterious, and mountainous landscape, where sunsets linger brilliantly until late at night and otherworldly mists roll gently through the valleys. Much photographed are the old crofts, one or two of which are still inhabited today. It also has an impressive range of accommodations, and restaurants that showcase the best of the island's produce and culinary talent.

To reach Skye, cross over the bridge spanning the narrow channel of Kyleakin, between Kyle of Lochalsh and Kyleakin. Or, if you're visiting in the summer, take a romantic boat trip between Mallaig and Armadale or between Glenelg and Kylerhea. You can tour comfortably around the island in two or three days, but a bit longer will allow extra time for hiking or sea kayaking.

Orientation is easy: in the north, follow the roads that loop around the peninsulas of Waternish and Trotternish; in the south, enjoy the road running the length of the Sleat Peninsula. There are some stretches of single-lane road, but for careful drivers these shouldn't pose a problem.

Kyle of Lochalsh

80 miles west of Inverness, 180 miles northwest of Glasgow.

The little town of Kyle of Lochalsh is the mainland gateway to Skye. Opened in 1995, the bridge transformed not only

Isle of Skye

travel to Skye but the very seascape itself. The area's most notable—and most photographed—attraction is 8 miles farther east at Dornie—Eilean Donan Castle.

GETTING HERE AND AROUND

From the north you reach Kyle of Lochalsh via the A890; from the south take the A87. There are four direct trains a day from Inverness.

 Sights

Bright Water Visitor Centre

INFO CENTER | FAMILY | Discover *Ring of Bright Water*, Gavin Maxwell's much-loved account of his work with otters on the island of Eilean Ban. This center, in Kyleakin at the northern tip of Skye, has an exhibit illustrating his work; wildlife tours that promise otters, seals, and birdlife; and a whole host of

interactive activities. The center itself is just over the bridge from Kyle of Lochalsh, and includes a 155-year-old lighthouse designed by Robert Louis Stevenson's father. ☒ *The Pier, Kyleakin* ☎ *01599/530040* ⊕ *www. eileanban. org* ☒ *Free* ⊙ *Closed Oct.–Easter and weekends.*

★ Eilean Donan Castle

CASTLE/PALACE | Guarding the confluence of lochs Long, Alsh, and Duich stands the most picturesque of all Scottish fortifications. Eilean Donan Castle, perched on an islet connected to the mainland by a stone-arched bridge, dates from the 14th century and has all the dramatic stone walls, timber ceilings, and winding stairs you could possibly desire. Empty and neglected for years after being bombarded by frigates of the Royal Navy during an abortive Spanish-Jacobite landing in 1719, this romantic Scottish icon was almost entirely rebuilt from a ruin in the early 20th century. The kitchen re-creates the busy scene before a grand banquet, and the upper floors show how the castle was transformed into a grand house. The picturesque cover of a thousand travel brochures, Eilean Donan has also appeared in a number of Hollywood movies and TV shows, from *The Wicker Man* to *Highlander*. There's a shop and a coffeehouse for the many visitors. ✉ *Off A87, Dornie* ☎ *01599/555202* ⊕ *www. eileandonancastle.com* 🏷 *£10* ⊙ *Closed Jan.*

Plockton

TOWN | Once a fishing and crofting center, Plockton today attracts visitors for its natural beauty and its warm microclimate, which allows palms to grow all along the main Harbour Street. Situated just 6 miles northeast of Kyle of Lochalsh, its natural bay is an ideal space for the small yachts that make their leisurely way to the coast and beyond, where gray seals can often be seen. Park at the car park at the entrance to the village and stroll along the main street, ideally with an ice cream as your companion. ✉ *Kyle of Lochalsh.*

🍴 Restaurants

★ All the Goodness

$ | CAFÉ | This excellent little bakery-café serves homemade cakes, tray bakes, and pastries, along with artisan coffee and an array of tempting foodie gifts and souvenirs—all to be enjoyed with a stunning vista of Eilean Donan Castle. In summer the café also displays evocative works by local artist Lorraine Tolmie. **Known for:** delicious baked goods; superior tea and coffee; unbeatable castle views. $ *Average main: £5* ✉ *Off A87* ✛ *8 miles east of Kyle of Lochalsh* ☎ *01599/555221* ⊕ *www.allthegoodness.co.uk* ⊙ *Closed Mon.–Tues. No dinner.*

Broadford

8 miles west of Kyle of Lochalsh via Skye Bridge.

One of the larger of Skye's settlements, Broadford lies along the shore of Broadford Bay, which has been known to welcome whales to its sheltered waters.

GETTING HERE AND AROUND
Broadford is on the A87, the main road crossing the Isle of Skye.

TOURS
★ Misty Isle Boat Trips
TOUR—SIGHT | FAMILY | For fantastic views of the Cuillin Mountains and the Inner Hebrides, book a place on one of the Misty Isle Boat Trips. The expansive scenery around Loch Coruisk is some of the most spectacular in Scotland. Round-trip journeys depart from the town of Elgol, 15 miles southwest of Broadford, and booking ahead is essential. Prices vary, but a cruise to a seal colony costs £25. Private charters are also available. ✉ *Elgol jetty, Sealladh na Mara, Elgol* ☎ *01471/866288* ⊕ *www.mistyisle-boattrips.co.uk* 🏷 *From £14* ⊙ *Closed Nov.–Mar.*

Sights

Road to Elgol

SCENIC DRIVE | The B8083 leads from Broadford to one of the finest vistas anywhere in Scotland. This road passes by **Strath Suardal** and little **Loch Cill Chriosd** (Kilchrist), and also takes in breathtaking views of the mountain **Bla Bheinn** en route. As you near Elgol, look out for a gathering of traditional crofts that descends to a pier, then admire the heart-stopping profile of the Cuillin peaks from the shore. Seek out the path, around halfway down the hill, that leads across rough grasslands into the mountains. ✉ *Elgol.*

Just a glimpse at Eilean Donan Castle from a distance makes it clear why this is one of the most photographed castles in all of Scotland.

Restaurants

★ Creelers of Skye

$$ | SEAFOOD | Don't be fooled by its humble appearance; Creelers is a celebrated French seafood restaurant. From its pan-roasted sea bass to its seafood gumbo, it is a compulsory stop for all passing gourmands. **Known for:** excellent bouillabaisse; stunning sea views; tasty desserts. $ *Average main: £19* ✉ *Lower Harrapool* ☎ *01471/822281* ⊕ *www. skye-seafood-restaurant.co.uk* ⊘ *Closed Sun.*

🛏 Hotels

Broadford Hotel

$$$ | HOTEL | Watch over Broadford Bay in comfort and style with a stay at this well-appointed hotel, which takes pride in being the place where Drambuie was invented. **Pros:** quintessentially Scottish; convenient location; Drambuie-colored tartan. **Cons:** no elevator; poorly lit public areas; breakfast underwhelming.

$ *Rooms from: £205* ✉ *Torrin Road* ☎ *01471/822204* ⊕ *www.broadfordhotel. co.uk* ⇥ *11 rooms* ⦿ *Free breakfast.*

Armadale

16 miles south of Broadford, 42 miles south of Portree, 5 miles (ferry crossing) west of Mallaig.

Rolling moorlands, scattered with rivers and lochans, give way to enchanting hidden coves and scattered waterside communities. Welcome to **Sleat,** Skye's southernmost peninsula.

GETTING HERE AND AROUND

The Mallaig-Armadale ferry arrives here. There's a short (and beautiful) road to the southwest, while the main road heads east following the stunning coast.

◉ Sights

Armadale Castle, Gardens & Museum

CASTLE/PALACE | As the name suggests, this attraction has three distinct strings to its bow: a romantic, ruined castle; a lush, flower-filled estate; and a fascinating museum of local island history. The castle is a windswept 17th-century mansion house built by the influential Clan Donald, while the extensive gardens cover 40 acres, offering magnificent views across the Sound of Sleat to Knoydart and the Mallaig Peninsula. The highlight, however, is the fascinating museum, which tells the story of the clan and its proud title, the Lords of the Isles, with the help of an excellent audiovisual presentation. There's a gift shop, restaurant, library, and center for genealogy research. Also on the grounds are high-quality accommodations in the form of seven cottages, complete with kitchen facilities. Access is from Armadale Pier, where signs indicate the different forest walks that are available. ✉ Off A851 ☎ 01471/844305 ⊕ www.armadalecastle.com 🎫 £8.75 ⊙ Closed Weekends in Nov.–Mar.

Hotels

Duisdale House Hotel

$$$ | HOTEL | Set in 35 acres of mature woodlands and gardens, this former mansion with a lovely hillside location and ocean views is boutique chic at its very best. **Pros:** finely furnished rooms; expansive views; attentive staff. **Cons:** nautical decor is an acquired taste; meals are expensive; some rooms are noisy. $ Rooms from: £295 ✉ Off A851, Isleornsay ☎ 01471/833202 ⊕ www.duis-dale.com 🛏 18 rooms ¶◎¶ Breakfast.

Hotel Eilean Iarmain

$$$ | HOTEL | Built on a small peninsula dotted by a quiet lighthouse, this hotel has an unforgettable location and an enchanting collection of wood paneling, chintz fabrics, and country-style antiques. **Pros:** spectacular waterfront location; plenty of sporting activities; excellent wine list. **Cons:** temperamental Wi-Fi; service can be mixed; food a little underwhelming. $ Rooms from: £235 ✉ Off A851, Isleornsay ☎ 01471/833332 ⊕ www.eileaniarmain.co.uk 🛏 16 rooms ¶◎¶ Free breakfast.

★ Kinloch Lodge

$$$$ | HOTEL | An upmarket hotel with an equally upmarket restaurant, Kinloch Lodge peacefully overlooks the tidal Loch na Dal. The historic buildings date from the 17th century, while the newer South House has the best views, built from the ground up with comfort and relaxation in mind. **Pros:** historic property; characterful interior; sublime afternoon tea. **Cons:** expensive dining; far from amenities; some of the old porcelain is stained. $ Rooms from: £380 ✉ Off A851, Isleornsay ☎ 01471/833333 ⊕ www.kinloch-lodge.co.uk 🛏 19 rooms ¶◎¶ Breakfast.

Portree

42 miles northwest of Armadale.

Portree, the population center of the island, is a pleasant place clustered around a small and sheltered bay. Although not overburdened by historical features, it's a fine touring base with a number of good shops.

GETTING HERE AND AROUND

The biggest town on Skye, Portree is well served by local buses and by a well-maintained road, the A87.

VISITOR INFORMATION VisitScotland

Portree iCentre. ✉ Bayfield House, Bayfield Road ☎ 01478/612992 ⊕ www.visitscotland.com/info/services/portree-icentre-p333111.

Sights

Aros
ARTS VENUE | On the outskirts of town, Aros is a community center that screens films, exhibits artworks, and hosts live music, dance, and theater productions. It's the cultural hub of the Isle of Skye. ⊠ *Viewfield Road* ☎ *01478/613649* ⊕ *www.aros.co.uk* ⊠ *Free.*

Restaurants

Café Arriba
$ | **BRITISH** | Up a steep flight of stairs, the laid-back café has window seats with great views over Portree Harbour. Using only local produce (whatever is "fresh, local, and available"), this is a good option for no-frills eating. **Known for:** delicious homemade cakes; mildly treacherous stairs; there are lines. $ *Average main: £9* ⊠ *Quay Brae, Quay Street* ☎ *01478/611830* ⊕ *www.cafearriba.co.uk.*

Scorrybreac Restaurant
$$$$ | **BRITISH** | It may be tiny, but this 20-seater restaurant has made big waves since opening in 2013. The vibe is relaxed and informal, while the cooking is imaginative and varied, creating unexpected marriages such as coffee-crusted venison or hake with coconut. **Known for:** intimate dining; inventive dishes; gorgeous bay views. $ *Average main: £42* ⊠ *7 Bosville Terr.* ☎ *01478/612069* ⊕ *www.scorrybreac.com* ☉ *Closed Sun.–Mon. No lunch.*

Hotels

Cuillin Hills Hotel
$$$ | **HOTEL** | This delightful Victorian-era hunting lodge looks down on Portree and the brightly painted houses around the harbor. **Pros:** a short stroll from Portree; good breakfast menu; attentive service. **Cons:** rooms at back overpriced; restaurant can be full; no elevator. $ *Rooms from: £245* ⊠ *Off A855* ☎ *01478/612003* ⊕ *www.cuillinhills-hotel-skye.co.uk* ⤵ *34 rooms* ◯⦶ *Free breakfast.*

Shopping

Isle of Skye Soap Company
PERFUME/COSMETICS | This charming little shop handcrafts its own soaps, aromatherapy oils, candles, and other pleasingly fragranced gifts. Founder (and soap maker in chief) Fiona is an aromatherapist. ⊠ *Somerled Square* ☎ *01478/611350* ⊕ *www.skye-soap.co.uk.*

Trotternish Peninsula

5 miles north of Portree.

Travel north from Portree on the A855 and you'll see cliffs rising to the left. These are the closest edge of an ancient lava flow, set back from the road and running the length of the peninsula. Fossilized dinosaur bones have been uncovered at the base of these cliffs, while overhead you might just spot a sea eagle, identifiable by the flash of its white tail.

GETTING HERE AND AROUND
From Portree take the twisting, undulating A855 as it follows the coast.

Sights

★ Fairy Glen
NATURE SITE | What was once a hidden gem has now become just another stop on the ever-expanding Skye tourist trail. Still, come early or late to avoid the crowds and the Fairy Glen remains a magical place—an enchanting, otherworldly valley of strange green hillocks, eerily still pools, crumbling cottages, and roaming sheep. To get here, take a small road just south of Uig signed "Sheader and Balnaknock" and drive for a little over a mile. ⊠ *Free*

Kilt Rock
NATURE SITE | No drive between Portree and Staffin is complete without a sojourn at Skye's most famous sea cliff. Named for the shape of its sheer rock face,

Clans and Tartans

The Scottish clans have a long and varied history. Some clans claim Norman roots and later married into Celtic society; others were of Norse origin, the product of Viking raids on Scotland; while others still may have been descended from Pictish tribes. Whatever their origins, by the 13th century the clan system was at the heart of Gaelic tribal culture. By the 15th century clan chiefs of the Scottish Highlands were even a threat to the authority of the Stewart monarchs. The word *clann* means "family" or "children" in Gaelic, and it was customary for clan chiefs to board out their sons among nearby families, a practice that helped to bond the clan unit and create strong allegiances.

The Clan System

Gradually, by the 18th century, increasing knowledge of Lowland agricultural improvements, and better roads into the Highlands that improved communication of ideas and "southern" ways, began to weaken the clan system. The Battle of Culloden marked the death of the clan system, as the victorious English armies banned the kilt and the pipes and claimed the land of the rebellious clan chiefs. And when the new landowners introduced the hardy Cheviot breed of sheep and changed farming activity, the Highlands were transformed forever. Many Highlanders, and especially islanders, began to emigrate in the 1750s, and by the 1820s, landowners were paying people to leave.

Tartan Revival

Tartan's own origins as a part of the clan system are disputed; the Gaelic word for striped cloth is *breacan*—piebald or spotted—so even the word itself is not Highland. Nevertheless, when cloth was locally spun, woven, and dyed using plant derivatives, each neighborhood would use different colorings. In this way combinations of colors and favorite patterns of the local weavers could become associated with an area and therefore its dominant clans. Between 1746 and 1782 the wearing of tartan was generally prohibited, and by the time the ban was lifted, many recipes for dyes and weaving patterns had been forgotten.

It took the influence of Sir Walter Scott, with his romantic (and fashionable) view of Highland history, to create the "modern myth" of clans and tartan. Sir Walter engineered George IV's visit to Scotland in 1822, which turned into a tartan extravaganza. The idea of one tartan or group of tartans "belonging" to one particular clan was created at this time—literally created, with new patterns dreamed up and "assigned" to particular clans.

which is ridged like a pleated kilt and swoops out to sea at the "hem," soaring Kilt Rock (and its gushing waterfall) can be seen from a specially built viewing platform. ⊠ *Off A855, Staffin ✛ 1½ miles south of Staffin.*

Old Man of Storr

NATURE SITE | Along the dramatic road around the Trotternish Peninsula, a gate beside a car park marks the beginning of the climb to the Old Man of Storr, one of Skye's most iconic landmarks. At 2,000 feet, this volcanic pinnacle is the highest point on the peninsula, so give yourself at least three hours to explore and enjoy the spectacular views from the top. ⚠ **The weather here changes very quickly, so be prepared.** ✉ *Off A855.*

★ Quiraing

NATURE SITE | A spectacular geological formation of rocky crags and towering stacks, Quiraing dominates the horizon of the Trotternish Peninsula. It is situated about 5 miles beyond Kilt Rock, so for a closer look, make a left onto a small road at Brogaig by Staffin Bay. There's a parking lot near the point where this road breaches the ever-present cliff line. The road is very narrow and rough, so drive cautiously. The rambler's trail is on uneven, stony ground, and it's a steep scramble up to the rock formations. In ages past, stolen cattle were hidden deep within the Quiraing's rocky jaws.

Skye Museum of Island Life

MUSEUM | Discover the old crofting ways of the local population at this museum, situated close to the tip of the Trotternish Peninsula. Informative displays and exhibits show life as it was on the island merely a century ago, from reconstructed interiors with traditional tools and implements to historical photographs and documents. ✉ *Off A855, Kilmuir* ☎ *01470/552206* ⊕ *www.skyemuseum.co.uk* 🎫 *£3* ⊗ *Closed Sun. and Oct.–Easter.*

Staffin Ecomuseum

MUSEUM VILLAGE | **FAMILY** | Billed as "a museum without walls," the Staffin Ecomuseum is a collection of 13 open-air geological and social exhibits dotted along the landscape of the peninsula. Follow the map along the coastal route and you will discover dinosaur footprints, a healing well, a deserted village, and more. This is not to be confused with Staffin Museum, Dugald Ross's nearby exhibition. ✉ *Staffin Community Trust, 3 Ellishadder, Staffin* ⊕ *www.skyecomuseum.co.uk.*

Hotels

Corran House

$ | B&B/INN | Set back off the A87 near Kingsburgh, this cozy B&B is a convenient, good-value stay at the base of the Trotternish Peninsula, 8 miles northwest of Portree. **Pros:** great location between sights; splendid views; good value. **Cons:** not close to any one particular attraction; easy to miss; more expensive than it used to be. $ *Rooms from: £100* ✉ *1 Eyre, Portree* ⊹ *Set back from the road; look out for the small white sign* ☎ *01470/532699* ⊕ *www.corran-houseskye.co.uk* 🛏 *6 rooms* 🍽 *Free breakfast.*

The Flodigarry Hotel

$$$ | HOTEL | With spectacular coastal views and antique furnishings throughout, the Flodigarry Hotel retains the feel of a grand country manor. **Pros:** spectacular views; a good base for walking; free Wi-Fi. **Cons:** steep road down; expensive rooms; a long way from anywhere. $ *Rooms from: £260* ✉ *Off A855, Staffin* ☎ *01470/552203* ⊕ *www.hotelintheskye.co.uk* 🛏 *18 rooms* 🍽 *Free breakfast.*

Waternish Peninsula

20 miles northwest of Portree.

The northwest corner of Skye has scattered crofting communities and magnificent coastal views. In the Hallin area look westward for a sea loch with small cliffs rising from the water like miniature models of full-size islands.

GETTING HERE AND AROUND

From Portree follow the A87 north, then head west on the A850 to the Waternish Peninsula.

Sights

Skyeskyns

FACTORY | A 10-minute tour of this working tannery gives visitors excellent insight into the process of salting, washing, and preparing sheepskins. You'll learn the source of such phrases as "on tenterhooks" and "stretched to the limits," and you can buy sheepskins from the on-site shop. ☒ 17 Lochbay, Waternish ☎ 01470/592237 ⊕ www.skyeskyns. co.uk ⊠ Free.

Restaurants

Loch Bay Restaurant

$$$$ | SEAFOOD | Situated right on the waterfront, this distinctive black-and-white restaurant, where the island's top chefs come to unwind on their nights off, is a Skye foodie favorite. The seafood is freshly caught and simply prepared by renowned chef Michael Smith, with the aim of enhancing the natural flavors of the ingredients rather than overwhelming them with superfluous sauces. **Known for:** sublime yet simple seafood; beautiful bay views; impeccable service. ⑤ Average main: £29.50 ☒ 1 Macleods Terr., Stein ☎ 01470/592235 ⊕ www.lochbay-restaurant.co.uk ⊗ Closed Mon. Closed Jan. and Feb. No dinner Tues. Mar.–Oct. and Sun. Mar.–Dec. No lunch in Nov. and Dec. and Tues., Wed., and Sat. Mar.–Oct.

Shopping

Edinbane Pottery

ART GALLERIES | This store, which specializes in quirky handmade ceramics and watercolors of local wildlife, is a great place to pick up a distinctive souvenir from your time on Skye. ☒ Off A850, Edinbane ☎ 01470/582234 ⊕ www. edinbane-pottery.co.uk.

Glendale

14 miles southwest of Waternish.

Glendale is a region rich in flora and fauna: otters, seals, and dolphins can be spotted off its rocky coast, while white-tailed sea eagles soar overhead. Dunvegan Castle is just at the region's eastern edge.

GETTING HERE AND AROUND

From the Waternish Peninsula, take the A850 southwest, turn onto the A863 southeast at Dunvegan, then follow the twisty, turny B884 west along the coast. It can feel rather isolated in bad weather or after dark.

Sights

Dunvegan Castle and Gardens

CASTLE/PALACE | In a commanding position looming over a sea loch, Dunvegan Castle has been the seat of the chiefs of Clan MacLeod for more than 700 years. Today it's a popular (if overpriced) tourist attraction. Step inside and into the clan's illustrious past through plush interiors, fascinating photos, and, most notably, the Fairy Flag—a silk banner, thought to be originally from Rhodes or Syria, which is credited with protecting the clan from danger. And make time to explore the gardens, with their water garden and falls, fern house, walled garden, and various viewing points. There's a café beside the car park. Boat trips from the castle to the nearby seal colony run April through September. ☒ Junction of A850 and A863, Dunvegan ☎ 01470/521206 ⊕ www.dunvegancastle.com ⊠ Castle and gardens £14; gardens only £12; seal trips £9.50.

Restaurants

★ Three Chimneys

$$$$ | MODERN BRITISH | Perhaps the Isle of Skye's biggest culinary draw, this old stone-walled restaurant on the banks of Loch Dunvegan serves consistently daring, well-crafted food. The chef's belief in quality Scottish ingredients is evident in every dish, from the locally sourced game to the sublime Scottish seafood, and when aligned with the chic, minimalist interior—all crisp white walls and exposed brickwork—it makes for a luxury dining experience you won't soon forget. **Known for:** inventive seafood dishes; sublime haddock ravioli; faultless service. $ *Average main: £69* ⊠ *B884, Colbost* ☎ *01470/511258* ⊕ *www.threechimneys. co.uk* ⊗ *Closed mid-Dec.–mid-Jan.* ☞ *No children under eight at dinner.*

🛍 Shopping

Skye Silver

JEWELRY/ACCESSORIES | Distinctive gold and silver jewelry with Celtic themes is the bread and butter of Skye Silver. From pendants to rings, bracelets to earrings, the unique pieces here are inspired by the surrounding natural landscapes of sea and countryside, with motifs of island wildlife. ⊠ *The Old School, B884, Colbost* ☎ *01470/511263* ⊕ *www.skyesilver.com.*

Glen Brittle and the Cuillin Mountains

32 miles southeast of Glendale.

The gentle slopes of this valley are a gateway to the dramatic peaks and ridges of the Cuillin Mountains. Glen Brittle's lower slopes are fine for walkers and weekend climbers, but the higher ridges are strictly for serious mountaineers.

GETTING HERE AND AROUND

From Glendale follow the B884 east to Lonmore, turn south onto the A863, then after 16 miles head west on the B8009. Glen Brittle extends from here to cover the southwest corner of the island.

👁 Sights

★ Fairy Pools

BODY OF WATER | One of the most magical sights in Scotland, the Fairy Pools are a spectacularly beautiful collection of waterfalls and plunge pools in the midst of Glen Brittle. The rocky gray landscape contrasts with the vivid blue-green of the pools, the colorful plant life, and visiting wildlife (including, occasionally, red deer) to give the environment a fairy-tale feel. You can walk to the pools from a parking lot 20 minutes away. Come at sunrise or sunset for smaller crowds and the opportunity for a truly enchanting swim— just don't expect the water to be warm. ⊠ *Glenbrittle* 🎫 *Free.*

Glen Brittle

MOUNTAIN—SIGHT | Enjoy spectacular mountain scenery in Glen Brittle, including some unforgettable views of the Cuillin Mountains (these are not for the casual walker, due to steep and dangerous cliff faces). The drive from Carbost along a single-track road is one of the most dramatic in Scotland and draws outdoorsy types from across the globe. At the southern end of the glen is a murky-colored beach, a campground, and gentle foothills that were made for strolling. ⊠ *Off A863 and B8009.*

Talisker Distillery

WINERY/DISTILLERY | The only distillery on the Isle of Skye is one of the best in Scotland. Talisker produces a sweet, light single malt that has the distinctive peaty aroma of island whiskies, yet with less intensity—making it a great introductory dram for newcomers to Scotch. Robert Louis Stevenson called Talisker "the king of drinks," and the inhabitants of Skye are

The Isle of Skye's most magical walk is to the Fairy Pools, rock pools of spring water fed by waterfalls from the Cuillin Mountains.

very proud of it. Classic tours here take about 45 minutes, while tasting tours (available weekdays) take between one-and-a-half and two hours. Book ahead, as tours are very popular. ✉ *B8009, Carbost* ☎ *01478/614308* ⊕ *www.malts.com* 🎫 *Tours from £10.*

Isle of Raasay

17 miles northeast of Glenbrittle.

This beautiful and rugged isle lies a few miles off Skye's east coast and offers a pleasant escape from its tourist hordes. Although only 10 miles long, it's home to some fine coastal walks, a brooding castle ruin and an inventive, up-and-coming distillery.

GETTING HERE AND AROUND

There are regular ferries to Raasay from Sconser on Skye (20 minutes south of Portree) every day of the week, all year-round.

Sights

Calum's Road

LOCAL INTEREST | An extraordinary feat of human endeavor, this single-track, 2-mile road was conceived and constructed by a single man—local crofter Calum MacLeod. Following several failed petitions to the local council, requesting them to improve access to northern Raasay by transforming a narrow footpath into a usable road, MacLeod decided to take matters into his own hands. Using only a pick-axe, shovel, and wheelbarrow, he began laying the road in 1964. Ten years later it was finally complete. The road would later be officially adopted and surfaced by the council, and named "Calum's Road" in MacLeod's honor. It begins just beyond the atmospheric, 16th-century ruins of Brochel Castle on the northeast coast of Raasay, and ends at Arnish. ✉ *Near Brochel, Isle of Raasay.*

🛏 Hotels

★ Isle of Raasay Distillery

$$ | HOTEL | More than just Raasay's first legal distillery (look out for its single-malt Scotch launch in late 2020), this stunning building—a modern glass-and-steel structure wrapped around a Victorian-era villa—also happens to be the island's most luxurious accommodations option. **Pros:** chic minimalist design; comfy lounge with honesty bar; breathtaking views of Skye. **Cons:** no kitchen (meals at nearby Raasay House); no family rooms; whisky still in progress. ⑤ *Rooms from: £155 ✉ Borodale House, Isle of Raasay ☎ 01478/470178 ⊕ www.raasaydistillery. com ➦ 6 rooms ❐ Free Breakfast.*

Isle of Lewis

53 miles from Ullapool via ferry.

The history of Lewis stretches back 5,000 years, as archaeological sites scattered across the island attest. Here the Highland past persists in the Gaelic that is spoken everywhere, and most of its inhabitants still bear clan names. The main town on Lewis is Stornoway.

GETTING HERE AND AROUND

Three main routes radiate from Stornoway to give access to the rest of the island. The A859 leads south all the way to Harris; the A857 leads north to Port of Ness, the island's northernmost point; and the A858 leads west, looping up and round to meet the A857 near Brue.

Stornoway

2½-hour ferry trip from Ullapool.

The port capital for the Outer Hebrides is Stornoway, the only major town on Lewis. As the island's cultural center, it has a few interesting attractions and an increasing number of good restaurants.

Keep an eye out for seals bobbing about in the harbor.

The ferry docks at Stornoway, and there's an airport within easy reach of the center. It's best to have a car to explore the island, but there are also infrequent local buses to attractions including the Calanais Standing Stones and the Blackhouse at Arnol.

AIRPORT CONTACTS Stornoway Airport. ✉ *A866, Stornoway ☎ 01851/702256 ⊕ www.hial.co.uk.*

VISITOR INFORMATION Stornoway VisitScotland iCentre. ✉ *26 Cromwell St., Stornoway ☎ 01851/703088 ⊕ www. visitscotland.com.*

💿 Sights

An Lanntair

ARTS VENUE | This fabulous arts center hosts exhibitions of contemporary and traditional art and frequent traditional musical and theatrical events in the impressive auditorium. There's also a cinema, a gift shop, and a café-bar serving coffee and snacks alongside fine international and Scottish fare. ✉ *Kenneth St., Stornoway ☎ 01851/708480 ⊕ www. lanntair.com ⊗ Closed Sun.*

🍽 Restaurants

★ Digby Chick

$$$ | MODERN BRITISH | Lewis's best seafood restaurant, this informal local favorite is an ideal destination for a rainy evening's meal. The solid wood floors and white tablecloths are guaranteed to brighten your outlook, while the sublime seasonal food will lighten the spirits. **Known for:** inventive seafood dishes; informal atmosphere; reservations by phone only. ⑤ *Average main: £23 ✉ 5 Bank St., Stornoway ☎ 01851/700026 ⊕ www. digbychick.co.uk ⊗ Closed Sun.*

Hotels

Broad Bay House

$$ | B&B/INN | It may be a little out of town, but the view alone makes Broad Bay House a worthwhile detour—and it's an added bonus that the hotel is also meticulously designed and constructed. **Pros:** stunning views; great coastal walks; fine evening meals. **Cons:** no kids under 12; car required; expensive for the area. ⑤ *Rooms from: £189* ⊠ *B895, Stornoway* ⊹ *7 miles north of Stornoway* ☎ *01851/820990* ⊕ *www.broadbayhouse. co.uk* ⤳ *4 rooms* ⦿ *Breakfast*.

 Activities

BICYCLING

Alex Dan's Cycle Centre (*AD Cycle Centre*)
BICYCLING | With a range of bikes to hire, AD Cycle Centre is also a place to pick up valuable advice on where to ride, including a route to Tolsta that takes in five stunning beaches before reaching the edge of moorland. Bike rental is £5 per hour or £20 for 24 hours. ⊠ *67 Kenneth St., Stornoway* ☎ *01851/704025* ⊕ *www. ad-cycles.co.uk*.

Port of Ness

27 miles north of Stornoway.

The stark, windswept community of Port of Ness cradles a small harbor squeezed in among the rocks.

From Stornoway drive up the A857 or take bus W1.

 Sights

Butt of Lewis Lighthouse

LIGHTHOUSE | At the northernmost point of Lewis stands the Butt of Lewis Lighthouse, which was first illuminated in 1862. Designed by David and Thomas Stevenson, it's one of many Scottish lighthouses built by the prominent Stevenson engineering family, whose best-known member was not an engineer at all but novelist Robert Louis Stevenson. The adjacent cliffs provide a good vantage point for viewing seabirds, whales, and porpoises. ⊠ *Off A857, Port of Ness* ⊹ *3 miles northwest of Port of Ness* ⊕ *www.undiscoveredscotland. co.uk*.

 Shopping

Borgh Pottery

CERAMICS/GLASSWARE | Pick up a range of attractive hand-thrown studio pottery made on the premises, including lamps, vases, mugs, and dishes. It's open only on Saturdays from November through Easter. ⊠ *Fivepenny House, Off A857, Borve* ☎ *01851/850345* ⊕ *www.borgh-pottery.co.uk*.

Carloway and Callanish

17 miles west of Stornoway.

The old crofting town of Carloway is surrounded by historic sights that give real insight into island life, including the mysterious arrangement of ancient stones at Callanish; Lewis's top attraction.

Travel west on the A858 to reach Carloway directly, or take the looping A859 to get there via Callanish. The W2 bus from Stornoway stops at both Carloway and Callanish.

 Sights

★ The Blackhouse

MUSEUM VILLAGE | In the small community of Arnol, the Blackhouse is a well-preserved example of an increasingly rare type of traditional Hebridean home. Common throughout the islands as recently as the mid-20th century, these dwellings were built without mortar and thatched on a timber framework without eaves. Other characteristic features include an open central peat hearth and the absence of a chimney (hence "blackhouse," from all the soot) . Inside you'll find half the house designated for family life, complete with many original furnishings, and the other half a stable for animals. Opposite is the White House, built later when houses were no longer allowed to accommodate humans and animals together. ⊠ Off A858, Arnol ☎ 01851/710395 ⊕ www.historicenvironment.scot ⊠ £6 ⊗ Closed Sun. Also closed Wed. Oct.–Mar.

★ **Calanais Standing Stones** (Callanish Stones)

ARCHAEOLOGICAL SITE | The west coast of Lewis is rich in prehistoric sites, and the most famous of these is the Calanais Standing Stones. Believed to have been positioned in several stages between 3000 BC and 1500 BC, this arrangement consists of an avenue of 19 monoliths extending northward from a circle of 13 stones, with other rows leading south, east, and west. Ruins of a cairn sit within the circle on the east side. Researchers believe they may have been used for astronomical observations, but you're free to cook up your own theories. The visitor center has an interesting exhibit on the stones, a very pleasant tearoom, and a gift shop. ⊠ Callanish ☎ 01851/621422 ⊕ www.historicenvironment.scot ⊠ Free.

Dun Carloway Broch (Doune Broch)

ARCHAEOLOGICAL SITE | Discover one of the country's best-preserved Iron Age brochs (circular stone towers). These fortified residences are exclusive to Scotland, and Dun Carloway Broch dominates the scattered community of the same name. The mysterious tower was probably built around 2,000 years ago as protection against seaborne raiders; the nearby visitor center explains all about the broch, its history, and its setting. ⊠ Off A858, Carloway ⊠ Free.

Gearrannan Blackhouse Village (Garenin)

MUSEUM VILLAGE | Situated at the end of a side road north from Carloway, Gearrannan is an old coastal crofting village that has been brought back to life as a living museum with excellent guided tours evoking its past. You can rent one of the restored blackhouses here if you want a unique self-catering cottage stay. There is also a small gift shop and café. ⊠ 5a Gearrannan, Carloway ☎ 01851/643416 ⊕ www.gearrannan.com ⊠ Free.

Isle of Harris

36 miles southwest of Stornoway.

For most people Harris is forever linked to tweed. Woven here and on nearby islands, the tweed has colors that echo the tones of the landscape. The dramatic mountains of the northern part of Harris give way in the south to machairs, grassy plains typical of this region, and a series of spectacular sandy beaches.

GETTING HERE AND AROUND

The A859 is the main artery through Harris. From Tarbert you can follow the A859 south to Leverburgh (21 miles), where you can take a boat to St. Kilda or a ferry to North Uist. The single-track road down the east coast is known as the Golden Road.

Tarbert

38 miles south of Calanais.

The main port of Harris, Tarbert has some good shops and a few worthwhile sights. **Traigh Luskentyre,** roughly 5 miles southwest of Tarbert, is a spectacular example of a Harris beach—2 miles of pristine white sand flanked by dunes. Across the bay lies another beautiful beach, **Traigh Seilebost**; both of these would be crowded with holidaymakers if in warmer climes. The narrow Golden Road, which runs along the east coast, offers some glorious views of a rocky, otherworldly landscape.

The ferry from Uig on the Isle of Skye arrives at Tarbert once or twice daily.

At Gearrannan Blackhouse Village, you can experience traditional Scottish crofting life via the many blackhouses scattered throughout the living museum.

Having a car makes travel on Harris much easier, but with careful planning and plenty of patience, it's possible to see the area with local buses.

Sights

★ Isle of Harris Distillery

WINERY/DISTILLERY | Opened in 2015, this island distillery rapidly gained a reputation for its distinctive gin, infused with coastal botanicals including sugar kelp. Its first malt whisky, called The Hearach (the Gaelic term for an inhabitant of Harris), is currently maturing in bourbon barrels. The distillery holds guided tours (£10) every weekday from March to October—call to book in advance. ⊠ *Tarbert* ☎ *01859/502212* ⊕ *www.harrisdistillery. com* ⊠ *Free; tours £10.*

★ Traigh Luskentyre

BEACH—SIGHT | One of Scotland's most spectacular beaches, Traigh Luskentyre is flanked by rolling sand dunes on one side and the shimmering sea on the other. Add in the distant peaks, the lush grassland, and the rocky islets and there are few better places on Lewis and Harris for a windswept walk. To reach the beach, drive 8 miles south of Tarbert on the A859, then turn right at the sign to "Losgaintir" (Gaelic for Luskentyre). **Amenities:** parking (no fee); toilets. **Best for:** solitude; sunset; walking. ⊠ *Off A859, Tarbert.*

🍴 Restaurants

Skoon Art Café

$ | CAFÉ | This renovated croft house café, which is tucked just off the twisting Golden Road running south from Tarbert to Leverburgh, has a simple, delicious menu that changes daily. It has everything from filling homemade soups to sumptuous smoked salmon to mouthwatering cakes. **Known for:** simple but delicious fare; good tea and coffee; wonderfully remote. ⑤ *Average main: £8* ⊠ *4 Geocrab, Tarbert* ☎ *01859/530268* ⊕ *www.skoon.com* ⊙ *Closed Sun. and Mon. No dinner* ⊟ *No credit cards.*

Hotels

Scarista House

$$$ | HOTEL | This lovingly converted Georgian *manse* (minister's residence) offers large and comfortable bedrooms, a peaceful location with spectacular views over a pristine 3-mile-long sandy beach, and a dining experience that's unmatched anywhere else on Harris. **Pros:** magnificent setting and views; delicious food (try the tarte Tatin); friendly and attentive service. **Cons:** patchy Wi-Fi; some oppressively floral wallpaper; very expensive for Harris. $ *Rooms from: £230* ⊠ *Off A859, Borve* ☎ *01859/550238* ⊕ *www.scaristahouse.com* ⇌ *6 rooms* ❍| *Free Breakfast.*

Hotel Hebrides

$$ | HOTEL | A welcoming hotel with lovely gardens and views across the loch and harbor, Hotel Hebrides is an oasis of luxury in unassuming Tarbert. **Pros:** wonderful location; comfortable bedrooms; parking on the street right outside. **Cons:** some rooms small; sea views only from some rooms; noises from the bar can drift up. $ *Rooms from: £155* ⊠ *Pier Road, Tarbert* ☎ *01859/502364* ⊕ *www.hotel-hebrides. com* ⇌ *21 rooms* ❍| *Breakfast.*

Shopping

Essence of Harris

PERFUME/COSMETICS | This popular pierside store specializes in candles, bath products, and reed diffusers with wonderful fragrances inspired by the island. The black pomegranate Seilebost hand cream is particularly popular. ⊠ *The Pier, Tarbert* ☎ *01859/502768* ⊕ *www.essenceofharris.co.uk.*

Leverburgh

21 miles south of Tarbert.

Named after Lord Leverhulme, who bought Lewis and Harris in 1917 with an eye to developing its local industries,

Leverburgh is now the departure and arrival port for North Uist ferries, as well as day-tripping boats to St. Kilda. Nearby Northton and Rodel have several attractions, with St. Clement's Church a particular highlight.

Leverburgh is on the A859 between Tarbert and Rodel.

Sights

Seallam! Visitor Centre and Co Leis Thu Genealogical Research Centre

LIBRARY | Learn more about life in the Western Isles and trace your Hebridean ancestry at this informative visitor center. Photographs and interpretive signs reveal the long and turbulent history of Harris and its residents, with the owners organizing guided walks and cultural evenings every week between May and September. ⊠ *Off A859, Northton* ☎ *01859/520258* ⊕ *www.hebridespeople. com* ⊠ *£2.50* ⊗ *Closed Sat. and Sun. in summer and Sat.–Tue. in winter.*

★ **St. Clement's Church** (*Eaglais Roghadail*) **RELIGIOUS SITE |** At the southernmost point of Harris, in the village of Rodel, lies St. Clement's Church—the most impressive pre-Reformation House of God in the Outer Hebrides. The large cruciform church, which sits atop a small hillock, was built around 1500. Head inside to see the magnificently sculpted 16th-century wall tomb of the church's builder, clan chief Alasdair Crotach MacLeod of Dunvegan Castle. ⊠ *A859, Rodel* ⊕ *3 miles southeast of Leverburgh* ⊕ *www. historicenvironment.scot* ⊠ *Free.*

Restaurants

Anchorage Restaurant

$$ | MODERN BRITISH | Along the southern coast of Harris, looking across the Sea of Hebrides toward North Uist, this lively restaurant is a great place to grab a bite before hopping aboard the ferry. The menu ranges from burgers, sandwiches,

The Isle of Harris is home to many spectacular landscapes, like this one with St. Clement's Church in the distance.

and fish-and-chips to quality local seafood. **Known for:** cheap and tasty dishes; open until fairly late; handy harborside location. ⑤ *Average main: £18* ⊠ *The Pier, Ferry Road, Leverburgh* ☎ *01859/520225* ⊕ *www.anchoragerestaurant.co.uk* ⊗ *Closed Sun.*

 ## Hotels

Pairc an t-Srath Guest House

$ | **B&B/INN** | Set back from the main road and with splendid views of the beach, this rural B&B is comfortable and quirky, with elegant and unpretentious rooms. **Pros:** lovely views of the coast; very good breakfasts; convenient location off main road. **Cons:** rooms quite small; overkill with the animal statues; no à la carte dinner option. ⑤ *Rooms from: £108* ⊠ *Off A859, Borve* ☎ *01859/550386* ⊕ *www.paircant-srath.co.uk* ↝ *4 rooms* ¶○¶ *Breakfast.*

St. Kilda

57 miles west of Leverburgh.

The most distant corner of the British Isles, this archipelago of five islands has double World Heritage status, recognized for both its natural and cultural significance. The natural highlights are immediately obvious, with Eiffel Tower–sized cliffs, colossal sea stacks, and soaring seabirds in abundance; make the most of main island Hirta's natural highlights with a hike to Ruival in the south of the island, or to Conachair (the island's highest point) in the north. The human impact is more subtle yet equally captivating, with hillside *cleits* (stone storage huts) and a 19th-century village offering insight into the lives of the people who, until recently, called this inhospitable environment home.

GETTING HERE AND AROUND

You can get to Hirta, St. Kilda's main island, on a private tour boat from Leverburgh on Harris or from Stein on

Skye. Tours are operated by Kilda Cruises (⊕ *www.kildacruises.co.uk*) and Sea Harris (⊕ *www.seaharris.co.uk*) from Harris, and by Go to St. Kilda (⊕ *www.seaharris. co.uk*) from Skye.

TOURS
Kilda Cruises
BOAT TOURS | This popular tour operator organizes day trips to St. Kilda three times a week (allowing some leeway in case of bad weather.) Tours leave from Leverburgh on Harris and include 4½ hours on Hirta island, as well as a cruise around the archipelago's dizzyingly high cliffs and sea stacks. ✉ *Pier Road, Tarbert* ☎ *01859/502060* ⊕ *www.kildacruises. co.uk.*

Sights

St. Kilda Village
TOWN | This crumbling, wind-ravaged village is the last remaining evidence of the community that lived on Hirta for thousands of years. For most of that time, the St. Kildans lived in utter isolation, with the abundant birdlife providing the bulk of their diet. But in the 1830s, visiting missionary Reverend Neil Mackenzie decided to improve living conditions on the island and raised funds for the construction of this street of Hebridean blackhouses, along with a church, *manse* (minister's residence), and school. Today visitors to St. Kilda can walk in and around the village buildings, with one house containing an informative museum telling the incredible story of island life through pottery, textiles, and photographs. ⊕ *www.nts.org.uk.*

North Uist

7 miles southwest of Leverburgh.

Stunning coastal scenery and ancient ruins are the main draws on North Uist. There are lochs everywhere you look, and a surprising number of public artworks,

too, from the ends of roads to the top of hills to the edge of the coast.

GETTING HERE AND AROUND
You can get to North Uist by ferry from Leverburgh on Harris and from Uig on the Isle of Skye, or you can drive from South Uist and Benbecula on the A865. Public transport is infrequent, so a car (or a bike) is the most reliable way to get around.

Sights

Balranald Nature Reserve
NATURE PRESERVE | Run by the Royal Society for the Protection of Birds (RSPB), the Balranald Nature Reserve shelters large numbers of waders and seabirds who inhabit the rock foreshore and marshland. Listen for corncrakes, whose distinctive rasping cry sounds not unlike a plastic drink lid being unscrewed. ✉ *Hougharry* ✛ *3 miles northwest of Bayhead* ☎ *01876/560287* ⊕ *www.rspb. org.uk* ⊠ *Free.*

Barpa Langass
ARCHAEOLOGICAL SITE | Dating back around 5,000 years, Barpa Langass is a chambered cairn (a Neolithic burial monument), the only one in the Western Isles to retain a fully intact inner chamber. You can peek inside, but don't venture too far without a light. You'll find Barpa Langass just off the A867, two-thirds of the way between Lochmaddy and Clacheny. ✉ *Off A687, Lochmaddy.*

Dun an Sticir
ARCHAEOLOGICAL SITE | Near Port nan Long in the very north of North Uist stands the remains of Dun an Sticir, reputed to have been the last inhabited broch on the island. This defensive tower, reached by a causeway over the loch, was built in the Iron Age but abandoned when the Vikings arrived in the 9th century. In 1602 it was reoccupied by Hugh Macdonald, a descendant of Macdonald of Sleat, but since he reached an unpleasant end (starved to death in a castle dungeon on the Isle of Skye), it has been slowly

crumbling into the sea. ⊠ *Off B893* ☞ *Free.*

Taigh Chearsabhagh

MUSEUM | Set right on the shore in Lochmaddy, the well-run Taigh Chearsabhagh is an informative museum and arts center, complete with two exhibition spaces, a working printshop, and a permanent exhibition that reveals what life is really like on North Uist. The café serves a selection of cakes and soup, as well as excellent French-press coffee. ⊠ *Lochmaddy* ☎ *01870/603970* ⊕ *www.taigh-chearsabhagh.org* ☞ *£3 museum; galleries free* ⊙ *Closed Sun.*

South Uist

12 miles south of Carinish (on North Uist) via Grimsay, Benbecula, and three causeways.

Carpets of wildflowers in spring and early summer, superb deserted beaches, and historical connections to Flora Macdonald and Bonnie Prince Charlie head the list of reasons to visit this island.

GETTING HERE AND AROUND
You can travel the length of South Uist along the A865, making short treks off this main road on your way to Lochboisdale in the southeast. At Lochboisdale you can catch ferries to Barra, the southernmost of the Outer Hebrides' main islands, or to Oban on the mainland.

Sights

Kildonan Museum

MUSEUM | This small museum has a number of interesting artifacts on the Uists and their people. The small details, like how locals filled their mattresses or the names for the tools they used in their houses, are what make this place interesting. There is also a craft shop and an excellent café renowned for its filled baked potatoes and homemade cakes. ⊠ *A865, Kildonan* ☎ *01878/710343* ⊕ *www.kildonanmuseum.co.uk* ☞ *£3* ⊙ *Closed Nov.–Mar.*

Our Lady of the Isles

PUBLIC ART | This 30-foot-high granite statue of the Madonna and child is a symbol of island resistance. In the 1950s the Ministry of Defense proposed building a missile-testing facility on South Uist, but islanders opposed the plans, fearing it would destroy their way of life, culture, and language. So they raised the funds for this ambitious work of art and erected it on land earmarked for development by the MOD. Today it is a listed monument, making any future building proposals even less likely to succeed. ⊠ *Off A865.*

Hotels

Polochar Inn

$ | **B&B/INN** | Set within a 300-year-old property, this secluded inn at the southern end of South Uist offers basic but pleasant rooms with sea views, as well as a good seafood restaurant. **Pros:** reasonable rates; good food and drink; free and reliable Wi-Fi. **Cons:** some small rooms; remote location; a little old-fashioned. ⑤ *Rooms from: £90* ⊠ *Off B888, Lochboisdale* ☎ *01878/700215* ⊕ *www.polocharinn.com* ⇌ *11 rooms* ⦿❘ *Breakfast.*

Shopping

Hebridean Jewellery

JEWELRY/ACCESSORIES | Handcrafted Celtic-influenced silver and gold earrings, brooches, and pendants are the order of the day at Hebridean Jewellery. Come for a tour of the workshop and stay for an espresso and cake in the on-site café. ⊠ *Bualadubh, Iochdar* ☎ *01870/610288* ⊕ *www.hebrideanjewellery.co.uk.*

Chapter 12

ORKNEY AND SHETLAND ISLANDS

12

Updated by
Robin Gauldie

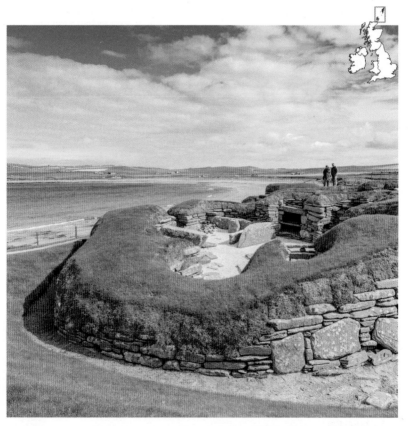

⦿ Sights	🍴 Restaurants	🛏 Hotels	🛍 Shopping	🍸 Nightlife
★★★☆☆	★☆☆☆☆	★★☆☆☆	★★☆☆☆	★☆☆☆☆

WELCOME TO ORKNEY AND SHETLAND ISLANDS

TOP REASONS TO GO

★ **Ancient sites:** Among the many Neolithic treasures in Orkney are the Ring of Brodgar, a 3,000-year old circle of standing stones, and Skara Brae, the remarkable remains of a village uncovered on the grounds of delightful Skaill House.

★ **Music and arts festivals:** The Shetland Folk Festival in late April–early May is a fiddling shindig that attracts musicians and revelers from around the world. Orkney's St. Magnus International Festival is a more high-brow celebration of classical music, poetry, and performance.

★ **Seabirds, seals, and more:** These islands have some of the planet's most important colonies of seabirds, with millions clinging to colossal cliffs. You're guaranteed to see seals and may spot dolphins, orcas, or porpoises.

★ **Outdoor activities:** The rugged terrain, beautiful beaches, and unspoiled waters make a perfect backdrop for invigorating strolls, sea fishing, diving, or exploring the coastline and sea lochs by boat.

Ten miles from Caithness in Scotland, Orkney is made up of 70 islands, of which 10 are inhabited. A number of ferries travel to ports on the Mainland, the main island of Orkney, including its administrative center, Kirkwall, where an airport serves Scotland's larger cities. The primary road is essentially a loop that passes near the key historic sites. The Mainland is linked to the southern island of South Ronaldsay by way of the Barricades.

About 125 miles north of Orkney lies the spiny outline of Shetland, comprising 100 islands. Sumburgh has the main airport, and 25 miles north is Lerwick, the island's "capital" and a port linking the island to Scotland and Orkney. South Mainland, half an hour from Lerwick, has prehistoric sites. Less than an hour north of Lerwick are dramatic landscapes such as Eshaness. Ferries go beyond the Mainland to Yell and Unst, the latter Britain's most northerly point.

1 Stromness and the Neolithic Sites. Home to some important and very ancient sites.

2 Birsay. A tiny village with Iron Age, Norse, and Pictish ruins.

3 Kirkwall. Orkney's charming capital.

4 Scapa Flow Visitor Centre. Where you can explore the role of this area in two world wars.

5 Lerwick. A handsome Shetland harbor town.

6 The South Mainland. A region of Shetland littered with prehistoric treasures.

7 Scalloway. The original capital of Shetland.

8 Weisdale. A tiny hamlet with an interesting art gallery.

9 Brae. A thriving modern village surrounded by rugged landscapes.

10 Yell. A peaceful isle covered with boggy moorland.

11 Unst. Scotland's most northerly inhabited island.

A Scandinavian heritage gives the 170 islets that make up Orkney and Shetland a history and an atmosphere different from that of any other region of Scotland. Both Orkney and Shetland are essentially austere and bleak, but they have awe-inspiring seascapes, fascinating seabirds, remarkable ancient ruins, and genuinely warm, friendly people.

An Orcadian has been defined as a crofter (farmer) with a boat, whereas a Shetlander has been called a fisherman with a croft. Orkney, the southern archipelago, is greener and is rich with artifacts that testify to the many centuries of continuous settlement here: stone circles, burial chambers, ancient settlements, and fortifications. UNESCO has recognized the key remains as a World Heritage site called the Heart of Neolithic Orkney.

North of Orkney, Shetland, with its ocean views and sparse landscapes—trees are a rarity because of ever-present wind—seems even more remote. But don't let Shetland's desolate countryside fool you: it has a wealth of historic interest and is far from being a backwater. Oil money from local mineral resources and its position as a crossroads in the northern seas for centuries have helped make Shetland a busy, thriving community that wants for little.

For mainland Scots, visiting these islands is a little like traveling abroad without having to worry about a different language or currency. Neither has yet been overrun by tourism, but the people of Orkney and Shetland will be delighted that you have come so far to see their islands and learn a little of their extraordinary past.

MAJOR REGIONS

Orkney. If you're touring the north of Scotland, the short boat trip to Orkney offers the chance to step outside the Scottish history you've experienced on the mainland. Prehistoric sites such as the Ring of Brodgar, and the remnants of Orkney's Viking-influenced past, are in dramatic contrast to that of the mainland. The Orkney Islands may have a population of just 20,000, but a visit reveals the islands' cultural richness. In addition Orkney's continued reliance on farming and fishing reminds you how some things can stay the same despite technological advances. At Maeshowe, for example, it becomes evident that graffiti is not solely an expression of today's youths: the Vikings left their marks here way back in the 12th century. The towns of Stromness and Kirkwall have sights and museums testifying to Orkney's rich past, including Kirkwall's Norman St. Magnus Cathedral. For many people though, they're a prelude to impressive Neolithic sites around the Mainland: Maeshowe, Skara Brae, the

Ring of Brodgar, and others. Beyond the Mainland, explore sights such as the Scapa Flow Visitor Centre on Hoy, which reveals the strategic role of the islands in both world wars. ■ TIP➜ **You can purchase the Historic Scotland Orkney Explorer Pass joint-entry ticket (£27) at the first site you visit; the ticket costs less than paying separately for entry into each site.**

Shetland. A descent at Sumburgh's airport provides stunning views of a shining white lighthouse, bird-crammed cliffs, and golden bays. The Shetland coastline is an incredible 900 miles because of the rugged geology and many inlets; there isn't a point on the islands farther than 3 miles from the sea. Lerwick is the primary town, but the population of 22,000 is scattered across the 15 inhabited islands. Lerwick has the excellent Shetland Museum, and nearby on the South Mainland are the prehistoric sites of Jarlshof, Old Scatness, and Mousa Broch. Worth exploring to the north are the lunarlike Ronas Hill and wave-lashed Eshaness. Unst, the island farthest north, is worth the journey for wide-open ocean views and superb bird-watching at Hermaness National Nature Reserve. Wherever your interest, you'll see and hear an island that buzzes with music, life, and history.

Planning

When to Go

Although shivering, wind-flattened visitors braving Orkney and Shetland's winter are not unheard of, the travel season doesn't really start until May, and it runs until September. June is one of the most popular months for both islands. The bird colonies are at their liveliest in early summer, which is also when the long northern daylight hours allow you plenty of sightseeing time. Shetland's northerly position means that it has only four or five hours of darkness around the summer solstice, and on a clear night it doesn't seem to get dark at all. Beware the changeable weather even in summer: it could be 75°F one day and then hail the next. Many sights close in September, and by October wilder gales will be mixed with snow flurries one minute and glorious sunshine the next. If you are determined to brave the elements, take into account that there are only six hours of daylight in winter months. More important, there can be thick mist and high winds at Sumburgh and Kirkwall airports even in July, meaning flights cannot take off for days, although they will put you on the Northlink boat if there's space. Bear this in mind when planning flight connections.

Shetland's festival of fire, Up Helly Aa, is held the last Tuesday of each January. The spectacle of Lerwick overrun by Vikings, with torches aflame and a huge Viking longship, is wildly popular. Book at least a year in advance if you want to get a bed for the night.

FESTIVALS
Orkney Blues
MUSIC FESTIVALS | This eclectic three-day festival held around the last weekend in September is billed as the most northerly blues event in the United Kingdom, attracting leading rhythm and blues performers from all over the world. It takes place in hotel bars and pubs around Stromness, and all the concerts, except the grand finale event, are free. ✉ *Stromness* ⊕ *www.orkneyblues.co.uk.*

Orkney Folk Festival
MUSIC FESTIVALS | This four-day festival held in and around Stromness in late May attracts musicians of all ages from Orkney's own vibrant folk music scene and from as far away as Canada, Latin America, Africa, and the Caribbean. ✉ *Ferry Terminal, Stromness* ☎ *01856 /851–331* ⊕ *www.orkneyfolkfestival.com.*

Shetland Accordion and Fiddle Festival

MUSIC FESTIVALS | This busy five-day event in early October is one of the biggest fixtures on Shetland's cultural calendar, with concerts by celebrated local fiddlers, squeezebox players, and visiting musicians at venues all over the islands. ⊠ *Shetland Accordion and Fiddle Club, 21 Twageos Rd., Lerwick* ☎ *01595/693162* ⊕ *www.shetlandaccordionandfiddle.com.*

Shetland Folk Festival

MUSIC FESTIVALS | Shetland fiddlers are legends in the folk music world, keeping the musical traditions of the islands alive when such folkways had all but died out in the rest of Scotland. Musicians and music fans from all over the world gather for four days and nights of foot-tapping tunes at venues in Lerwick and all over Shetland. ⊠ *Islesburgh Community Centre, King Harald St., Lerwick* ☎ *01595/694757* ⊕ *www.shetlandfolkfestival.com.*

★ St. Magnus International Festival

FESTIVALS | Usually held in the third week of June, Kirkwall's St. Magnus International Festival is a world-class celebration of classical music, opera, chamber music, ensemble and solo performances, dance, and drama, performed in inspiring venues including St. Magnus Cathedral. ☎ *01856/871445* ⊕ *www.stmagnusfestival.com.*

Up Helly Aa Festival

FESTIVALS | On the last Tuesday in January, Shetlanders celebrate their Norse heritage by dressing as Vikings, parading through the streets with flaming torches, and then burning a replica of a Viking galley. This is naturally followed by extensive feasting, carousing, and dancing. ⊠ *The Galley Shed, St. Sunniva St., Lerwick* ⊕ *www.uphellyaa.org.*

Planning Your Time

Orkney and Shetland require at least a couple of days each if you're to do more than just scratch the surface. The isles generate their own laid-back approach to life, and once here, you may want to take it slowly.

A good clutch of the key sites of Mainland Orkney can be seen in a day, if you have a car and are disciplined, but to really get the most out of them, take two days. You can do the Kirkwall sights in a morning before heading to the Italian Chapel on South Ronaldsay in the afternoon. This allows a whole day for Stomness, a town caught in the most poignant of time warps, and the archaeological sites of Maeshowe, the Ring of Brodgar, Skara Brae and Skaill House, and Gurness Broch. To include Birsay, plan your day round the tides.

Since getting to Shetland isn't easy, you may want to spend three or four days here. The sites on the South Mainland—Jarlshof, Old Scatness, the Shetland Crofhouse Museum, St. Ninian's Isle, and Mousa Broch—take the best part of a day, although sailing times for Mousa must be factored into your schedule. Lerwick, with its lanes and spectacular museum, is a good day, and can be supplemented with a trip to the Bonhoga Gallery in Weisdale. It's a good idea to take a whole day to explore the north of the islands, including Eshaness and Tangwick Haa, although a car or a guide who drives will be necessary. Ferry times allow for a mad dash round the northern islands of Yell and Unst, but you will see more if you book an overnight stay.

Getting Here and Around

AIR

Loganair flies to Sumburgh in Shetland and to Kirkwall in Orkney from Edinburgh, Glasgow, Aberdeen, Inverness, and Manchester. Tickets are very expensive. Loganair also flies to the outer islands of Eday, North Ronaldsay, Sanday, Stronsay, Westray, and Papa Westray. The flight between Westray and Papa Westray, which takes two minutes, is claimed to be the world's shortest scheduled passenger flight. Airtask flies to Fair Isle, Foula, the Outer Skerries, and Papa Stour from Lerwick.

AIRLINE CONTACTS Airtask.
☎ 01595/840246 ⊕ www.airtask.com. **Loganair.** ☎ 0344/800–2855 ⊕ www. loganair.co.uk.

BOAT AND FERRY
For those willing to travel the slow way, Northlink operates ferries—locally known as "the boat"—from Aberdeen to Kirkwall in Orkney and Lerwick in Shetland. These leave Aberdeen Harbor each evening (or every second night for Kirkwall), arriving at Kirkwall at 11 pm and Lerwick at 7:30 am the next day. These services have reclining seats for the budget traveler, pods for those wanting more comfort, and clean, compact cabins in single, double, or four-berth combinations. There's a shop, a cinema, two bars, and two restaurants (one self-service and one table service) on each boat.

If you're arriving in Aberdeen on Sunday morning and plan on meeting a train, note that the station does not open until 9 am. Northlink allows you to stay in your cabin or the restaurant until 9:30 am.

An alternate way of reaching Orkney is the Northlink ferry from Scrabster to Stromness. There is also a ferry from John O'Groats to Burwick, operated by John O'Groats Ferries, with up to three daily departures May through September. The fastest and smoothest sail is by catamaran from Gills Bay, Caithness, to St. Margaret's Hope on Orkney. Operated by Pentland Ferries, it has three daily departures.

In both Orkney and Shetland, the local council runs the interisland ferry networks (Orkney Ferries and Shetland Island Ferries) to the outer islands. Northlink Ferries has service between Lerwick on Shetland and Kirkwall on Orkney.

■ **TIP→ These are lifeline services, so not just for visitors; always book ferry tickets in advance.**

FERRY CONTACTS John O'Groats Ferries.
☎ 01955/611353 ⊕ www.jogferry.co.uk. **Northlink Ferries.** ☎ 0845/600–0449 ⊕ www.northlinkferries.co.uk. **Orkney Ferries.** ☎ 01856/872044 ⊕ www.orkneyferries.co.uk. **Pentland Ferries.** ☎ 0800/688–8998 ⊕ www.pentlandferries.co.uk. **Shetland Island Ferries.** ☎ 01595/745804 for Unst, Fetlar, Yell, Whalsay, Skerries, and Papa Stour, 01595/760363 for Fair Isle ⊕ www.shetland.gov.uk/ferries.

BUS
John O'Groats Ferries operates the Orkney Bus, a direct express coach from Inverness to Kirkwall (via ferry) that runs daily from June to early September, making a day trip to Orkney a definite—if hurried—possibility.

The main bus service on Orkney is operated by Stagecoach and on Shetland by ZetTrans (although buses are run by small operators).

BUS CONTACTS John O'Groats Ferries.
☎ 01955/611353 ⊕ www.jogferry.co.uk. **Stagecoach.** ☎ 01856/878014 ⊕ www.stagecoachbus.com. **ZetTrans.** ☎ 01595/744868 ⊕ www.zettrans.org.uk.

CAR
The most convenient way of getting around these islands is by car, especially if your time is limited. Roads are well maintained and traffic is nearly nonexistent, although speeding cars can be a problem. Orkney has causeways—the Barricades—connecting some of the islands, but in some cases these roads take fairly roundabout routes.

You can transport your rental car from Aberdeen, but for fewer than five days it's usually cheaper to rent a car from one of Shetland and Orkney's agencies. Most are based in Lerwick, Shetland, and Kirkwall, Orkney, but airport pickups are easily arranged.

LOCAL CAR RENTAL CONTACTS Bolts Car and Minibus Hire. ✉ *26 North Rd., Lerwick* ☎ *01595/693636* ⊕ *www.boltscarhire. co.uk.* **Orkney Car Hire.** ✉ *Junction Rd., Kirkwall* ☎ *01856/872866* ⊕ *www.orkney-carhire.co.uk.* **Star Rent-a-Car.** ✉ *22 Commercial Rd., Lerwick* ☎ *01595/692075 Lerwick, 01950/460444 Sumburgh Airport* ⊕ *www.starrentacar.co.uk.* **W. R. Tullock.** ✉ *Castle Garage, Castle St., Kirkwall* ☎ *01856/875500* ⊕ *www.orkney-carrental.co.uk.*

TRAIN

There are no trains on Orkney or Shetland, but you can take the train to Aberdeen or Thurso and then take a ferry to the islands.

TRAIN CONTACTS ScotRail. ☎ *0871/2002233* ⊕ *www.scotrail.co.uk.*

Restaurants

Kirkwall has an increasing number of good cafés and restaurants, as does Lerwick, but both islands now have memorable spots beyond the main towns, from cafés and fish-and-chips spots to some fancier restaurants. Orkney and Shetland have first-class seafood, and in pastoral Orkney the beef is lauded and in Shetland the heather- or seaweed-fed lamb. Orkney is famous for its cheese and its fudge; a glug of its Highland Park malt whisky or some Skull Splitter Ale is also worth trying. Shetlanders are also now brewing their own and make much of their natural edible resources of seaweed-fed lamb and mussels, while making ice cream and smoking fish in a variety of ways. Some bakeries create their own version of bannocks—a scone-type baked item you eat with salt beef, mutton, or jam—but Johnson and Wood (otherwise known as the Voe bakery),

available in shops across the islands, takes the biscuit.

Hotels

Accommodations in Orkney and Shetland are on par with mainland Scotland, with a growing range of stylish bed-and-breakfasts that might suit some travelers better than the bigger hotels that rely on, and therefore focus on, business customers, which in Shetland—with the oil and the building of a major gas plant—are many. Although standards are improving, the islands still do not offer luxury accommodations. To experience a simpler stay, check out the unique "camping *böds*" in Shetland—old cottages providing inexpensive, basic lodging (log fires, cold water, and sometimes no electricity). For details, contact the Shetland Tourist Information Centre.

Restaurant and hotel reviews have been shortened. For full information, visit Fodors.com. Restaurant prices are the average cost of a main course at dinner or, if dinner is not served, at lunch. Hotel prices are the lowest cost of a standard double room in high season, including 20% V.A.T.

WHAT IT COSTS in Pounds			
$	$$	$$$	$$$$
RESTAURANTS			
under £15	£15–£19	£20–£25	over £25
HOTELS			
under £125	£125–£200	£201–£300	over £300

Tours

★ **Island Trails**
GUIDED TOURS | Local tour guide and crofter James Tait offers tours steeped in the social history of Shetland, giving you a lively account, and no doubt many an

introduction, to Shetland and its people. Opt for a guided tour around St. Ninian's Isle or a bespoke day's tour of the island. ☎ 01950/950228 ⊕ www.island-trails. co.uk ✉ From £25.

Shetland Nature

SPECIAL-INTEREST | Here you'll find richly informed tours that cover a lot of ground while quietly tracking Shetland's otters, birds, and the unique wildflowers of the islands. Photographers are specially catered to. ☎ 01595/760333 ⊕ www. shetlandnature.net ✉ From £120.

Wildabout Orkney

GUIDED TOURS | Well-organized and informative tours, including Treasures of Orkney and Megalithic Masterpieces, run daily April to September. ☎ 01856/877737 ⊕ www.wildaboutorkney.com ✉ From £59.

Visitor Information

The official Visit Scotland visitor information centers in Kirkwall and Lerwick are open year-round. The visitor information websites, provided by the Orkney Islands Council and Shetland Islands Council, are helpful online sources.

VISITOR INFORMATION Visit Orkney. ⊠ W. Castle St. ☎ 01856/872856 ⊕ www.orkney.com. **Visit Shetland.** ☎ 01595/693434 ⊕ www.shetland.org.

Stromness and the Neolithic Sites

1¾ hrs north of Thurso on Scotland's mainland, via ferry from Scrabster.

On the southwest of the Mainland, on the shore of the old Norse anchorage Hamnavoe, is Stromness, a remarkably attractive fishing town seemingly so unsullied by modernity that it evokes an uncomplicated way of life long gone. Walk past the old-fashioned shops and austere cottages that line the main street and you'll understand why local poet and novelist George Mackay Brown (1921–96) was inspired and moved by its sober beauty.

With its ferry connection to Scrabster in Caithness, Stromness makes a good base for visiting the western parts of Orkney, and the town holds several points of interest. It was once a key trading port for the Hudson's Bay Company, and the Stromness Museum displays artifacts from those days. Nearby are three spectacular ancient sites, the Ring of Brodgar, Maeshowe, and Skara Brae at Skaill House.

GETTING HERE AND AROUND
Stromness is at the end of the A965 and can be reached by one of the many buses from Kirkwall.

Stagecoach Buses 7 and 8S link Kirkwall, the Ring of Brodgar, and Skara Brae and Skaill House with Kirkwall. Altogether there are three bus services there and three back per day except Sunday, so plan accordingly.

 Sights

Maeshowe

ARCHAEOLOGICAL SITE | The huge burial mound of Maeshowe, circa 2500 BC, measures 115 feet in diameter and contains an enormous burial chamber. It was raided by Vikings in the 12th century, and Norse crusaders found shelter here, leaving a rich collection of runic inscriptions. Outside you see a large, grassy mound; the stunning interior of the chambered tomb has remarkably sophisticated stonework. This site is 6 miles northeast of Stromness and 1 mile from the Ring of Brodgar. The site is open for guided tours only, which start at the visitor center at Stenness. ■TIP→ **As space is limited, buy tickets for guided tours online or call to check availability.** ⊠ A965, Stromness ☎ 01856/851266 ⊕ www.historicenvironment.scot ✉ £9.

Orkney

ATLANTIC OCEAN

NORTH RONALDSAY
Hollandstoun

PAPA WESTRAY
Aikerness
Backaskaill
Pierowall
Braehead
WESTRAY
Midbea

SANDAY
Lady Village
Kettletoft

EDAY
Backaland

Whitehall
STRONSAY
Aith

ROUSAY
EGILSAY
Brinian

Brough of Birsay
Birsay
Broch of Gurness
(Aikerness Broch)

Marwick Head
Nature
Reserve
Quoyloo
A986
Dounby
A967
Mirbister
A966
MAINLAND
Skara Brae
and Skaill
House
Tenston

SHAPINSAY
Balfour

FERRY TO
SCALLOWAY,
SHETLAND ISLANDS

AUSKERRY

Ring of Brodgar
Unstan Chambered Tomb
Maeshowe
Stenness
Stromness
Finstown
Kirkwall

A964
Kirbister
A961
A360
Skaill

Houton
St Mary's
COPINSAY

Moaness
Scapa Flow
FERRY TO
ABERDEEN

Rackwick
Italian Chapel
Northtown
BURRAY

HOY
**Scapa Flow
Visitor Centre**
Lyness
FLOTTA
Uppertown
Southtown
St Margaret's Hope
*NORTH
SEA*

Longhope
Wyng
Herston
A961

Sandwick
*SOUTH
RONALDSAY*

SWONA
Burwick
Tomb of the Eagles
Old Head

Pentland Firth

FERRY TO
SCRABSTER
STROMA
*PENTLAND
SKERRIES*

Dunnet Head
Duncansby Head
Scarfskerry
Brough
A836
John O'Groats
Dunnet
Castletown
A99

| 0 | | 10 mi |
| 0 | | 10 km |

★ Pier Arts Centre

MUSEUM | At the striking Pier Arts Centre, a gallery in a former merchant's house and adjoining buildings, huge sheets of glass offer tranquil harborside views and combine with space-maximizing design to make the best use of every shard of natural light and inch of wall to display the superb permanent collection. The more than 100 20th- and 21st-century paintings and sculptures include works by Barbara Hepworth and Douglas Gordon, and edgy temporary exhibitions showcase international contemporary artists such as Damien Hirst. A chic shop sells design products and art books. ⊠ 28–30 Victoria St., Stromness ☎ 01856/850209 ⊕ www.pierartscentre. com 🖾 Free 🕓 Closed Sun. and Mon.

★ Ring of Brodgar

ARCHAEOLOGICAL SITE | About 5 miles northeast of Stromness, the Ring of Brodgar is a magnificent circle of 36 Neolithic standing stones (originally 60) surrounded by a henge, or deep ditch. When the fog descends over the stones—a frequent occurrence—their looming shapes seem to come alive. The site dates to between 2500 and 2000 BC. Though the original use of the circle is uncertain, it's not hard to imagine strange rituals taking place here in the misty past. The stones stand between Loch of Harray and Loch of Stenness. ⊠ B9055, Stromness ☎ 01856/841815 ⊕ www.historicenvironment.scot 🖾 Free.

★ Skara Brae and Skaill House

ARCHAEOLOGICAL SITE | After a fierce storm in 1850, the laird of Breckness, William Graham Watt, discovered this cluster of Neolithic houses at the bottom of his garden. The houses, first occupied around 3000 BC and containing stone beds, fireplaces, dressers, and cupboards, are the most extensive of their kind in northern Europe and provide real insight into this ancient civilization. A reconstruction of one house can be seen in the visitor center, which displays artifacts from the site and hosts an excellent café. Skara Brae stands on the grounds of **Skaill House,** a splendid, intriguing mansion built by the Bishop of Orkney in the 1600s. His descendants, the lairds of Breckness, along with the various ladies of the manor, added to the house and to the eclectic furnishings. These sites offer a joint ticket in summer months that's well worth the price: the juxtaposition of different societies thousands of years apart that shared the same corner of Orkney makes a fascinating visit. ⊠ B9056, Sandwick, Stromness ✢ 8 miles north of Stromness ☎ 01856/841815 ⊕ www.historicenvironment.scot 🖾 Skara Brae £7, Skara Brae and Skaill House £9 🕓 Skaill House closed Oct.–Mar.

★ Stromness Museum

MUSEUM | FAMILY | The enchanting Stromness Museum has the feel of some grand Victorian's private collection but has, in fact, been community owned since it opened in 1837. Its crammed but utterly fascinating exhibits on fishing, shipping, and whaling are full of interesting trinkets from all over the world that found their way to this small Orcadian town because of its connections with the Hudson's Bay Shipping Company. The company recruited workers in Stromness between the late 18th and 19th century as they were considered more sober and therefore more reliable than other Scots. Also here are model ships and displays on the German fleet that was scuttled on Scapa Flow in 1919. Upstairs don't miss the beguiling, traditionally presented collection of birds and butterflies native to the British Isles. ⊠ 52 Alfred St., Stromness ☎ 01856/850025 ⊕ www. stromnessmuseum.org.uk 🖾 £5 (allows as many visits as you like within a week) 🕓 Closed Sun. Nov.–Mar.

The stone circles that make up the Ring of Brodgar are part of the Heart of Neolithic Orkney, a UNESCO World Heritage Site.

Restaurants

★ Julia's Café Bistro

$ | CAFÉ | Right on the quayside, this casual spot serves the cakes that make you forget about calories. Expect huge slices of lemon drizzle, coffee layer, raspberry cream, and other cakes, as well as scones and traybakes (cakes baked in pans and cut up). **Known for:** Orkney crab sandwiches; full Scottish breakfasts; vibrant decor and sunny harbor views. ⑤ *Average main: £8* ⊠ *20 Ferry Rd., Stromness* ☎ *01856/850904* ⊕ *www. juliascafe.co.uk* ⊘ *No dinner.*

Hotels

Ferry Inn

$ | HOTEL | This traditional inn with rooms and a restaurant is handy for the ferry and other transport links for Orkney's sights. **Pros:** good restaurant; friendly pub; handy location for ferry. **Cons:** no elevator; can get very busy; uninspired decor. ⑤ *Rooms from: £110* ⊠ *10 John St., Stromness* ☎ *01856/850280* ⊕ *www. ferryinn.com* ⇥ *20 rooms* � | *Breakfast.*

Merkister Hotel

$$ | HOTEL | Popular with anglers, this family-run hotel overlooks the gentle lap of Loch Harray—its experienced *ghillies* (guides) know the choicest spots and provide instruction for novices. **Pros:** endless coffee in the lounge and library; notable restaurant; fishing experts. **Cons:** some small rooms; dated decor; bar can get crowded. ⑤ *Rooms from: £140* ⊠ *A965, Harray, Birsay* ☎ *01856/771366* ⊕ *www.merkister.com* ⇥ *16 rooms* � | *Breakfast.*

★ Mill of Eyrland

$$ | B&B/INN | White-painted stone walls, country antiques, and the rippling sound of a stream running beneath the windows make for an evocative stay at this former mill dating from 1861. **Pros:** the old grinding stones are a stunning focal point in the lounge; beautiful views out to Scapa Flow; notable breakfasts and packed lunches. **Cons:** difficult to find; breakfast is served at one big table, so be prepared to socialize; 25% nonrefundable deposit required for all bookings. ⑤ *Rooms from: £130* ✉ *Off A964, Stenness* ☎ *01856/850136* ⊕ *www.millofeyrland.co.uk* ⇨ *4 rooms* ⑩ *Breakfast.*

Activities

The cool, clear waters of Scapa Flow and eight sunken ships that were part of Germany's fleet during World War I make for an unparalleled diving experience. Several companies organize trips to Scapa Flow—including shore and offshore dives among the Churchill Barriers—and other nearby dive sites.

Scapa Scuba

SCUBA DIVING | Dives with Scapa Scuba are from its boat, the MV *Radiant Queen*. Two dives around wrecks near the Churchill Barriers cost £170 including full equipment hire. ✉ *Lifeboat House, Dundas St., Stromness* ☎ *01856/851218* ⊕ *www.scapascuba.co.uk.*

Birsay

12 miles north of Stromness, 25 miles northwest of Kirkwall.

Birsay itself is a small collection of houses, but some interesting historic and natural sites are nearby.

GETTING HERE AND AROUND
The village is on A966; a car is the easiest way to see the nearby sites.

◉ Sights

Broch of Gurness (Aikerness Broch)
ARCHAEOLOGICAL SITE | An Iron Age tower built between 500 BC and 200 BC, the Broch of Gurness stands more than 10 feet high and is surrounded by stone huts, indicating that this was a village.

The tower's foundations and dimensions suggest that it was one of the biggest brochs in Scotland, and the remains of the surrounding houses are well preserved. ✉ *A966* ⊕ *8 miles east of Birsay* ☎ *01856/751414* ⊕ *www.historicenvironment.scot* ▨ *£6* ⊙ *Closed Oct.–Mar.*

Brough of Birsay
ARCHAEOLOGICAL SITE | A Romanesque church can be seen at the Brough of Birsay, a tidal island with the remains of an early Pictish and then Norse settlement. (*Brough* is another word for fort.) The collection of roofless stone structures on the tiny island, close to Birsay, is accessible only at low tide by means of a concrete path that winds across the seaweed-strewn bay. The path is slippery, so boots are essential. To ensure you won't be swept away, check the tides with the tourism office in Kirkwall or Stromness before setting out. ⚠ **The cliffs at the far side of the island are stunning but be very careful as you look for puffins.** ✉ *A966* ☎ *01856/841815* ⊕ *www.historicenvironment.scot* ▨ *£6* ⊙ *Closed Oct.–mid-June.*

Marwick Head Nature Reserve
NATURE PRESERVE | The Royal Society for the Protection of Birds tends the remote Marwick Head Nature Reserve, where in spring and summer the cliffs are draped in wildflowers such as campion and thrift, and resound with thousands of nesting seabirds including cormorants, kittiwakes, and guillemots. The Kitchener Memorial, recalling the 1916 sinking of the cruiser HMS *Hampshire* with Lord Kitchener aboard, sits atop a cliff. Access to the reserve, which is unstaffed, is along a path north from Marwick Bay. ✉ *Off B9056* ⊕ *4 miles south of Birsay* ☎ *01856/850176* ⊕ *www.rspb.org.uk* ▨ *Free, donations welcome.*

Kirkwall

16 miles east of Stromness.

In bustling Kirkwall, the main town on Orkney, there's plenty to see in the narrow, winding streets extending from the harbor. The cathedral and some museums are highlights.

GETTING HERE AND AROUND

Kirkwall is a ferry port and also near Orkney's main airport. Its sights are all near one another, though visitors to the Highland Park Distillery might want to hop on the T11 Kirkwall Circular or get a taxi (about £7).

ESSENTIALS

VISITOR INFORMATION Kirkwall Visitor Information Centre. ⊠ *Travel Centre, W. Castle St.* ☎ *01856/872856* ⊕ *www. visitscotland.com.*

 Sights

Bishop's and Earl's Palaces

CASTLE/PALACE | The Bishop's Palace dates to the 12th century when St. Magnus Cathedral was built. In 1253 this was the site of King Hakon IV of Norway's death, marking the end of Norwegian rule over Sudreyjar (the Southern Hebrides). It was rebuilt in the late 15th century, and a round tower was added in the 16th century. The nearby Earl's Palace was built in 1607 for Earl Patrick Stewart, the much despised Earl of Orkney and Shetland who bound the people of both into terrible, inescapable poverty. While his name is still mud, his Orcadian residence is considered one of the finest examples of Renaissance architecture in Scotland. The great hall with its magnificent fireplace may be a ruin, but it evokes the splendor of its age. ⊠ *Palace Rd.* ☎ *01856/871918* ⊕ *www.historicenvironment.scot* 🎫 *£6* ⊗ *Closed Nov.–Mar.*

★ Highland Park Distillery

WINERY/DISTILLERY | Having come this far, you'll have earned a dram of the local single malt at one of Scotland's northernmost distilleries. It was founded around the turn of the 19th century by Magnus Eunson, a church officer who dabbled in illicit stilling. The Viking Soul tour is highly recommended and takes you through the essential aspects of this near-sacred process, from the ingredients to the hand-turning of the malt, the peating in the peat kilns, the mashing, and finally the maturation in oak casks. This smoky, peaty malt can be purchased all over Orkney, as well as from the distillery's austere shop. ⊠ *Holm Rd.* ☎ *01856/874619* ⊕ *www.highlandpark-whisky.com* 🎫 *Tours from £10* ⊗ *Closed weekends Oct.–Mar.*

★ Italian Chapel

RELIGIOUS SITE | During World War II, 550 Italian prisoners of war were captured in North Africa and sent to Orkney to assist with the building of the Churchill Barriers, four causeways that blocked entry into Scapa Flow, Orkney's great natural harbor. Using two corrugated-iron Nissan huts, the prisoners, led by Domenico Chiocchetti, a painter-decorator from the Dolomites, constructed this beautiful and inspiring chapel in memory of their homeland. The elaborate interior frescoes were adorned with whatever came to hand, including bits of metal, colorful stones, and leftover paints. ⊠ *A961* ✛ *7 miles south of Kirkwall* ☎ *01856/781580* ⊕ *www.facebook.com/italianchapelorkney* 🎫 *£3.*

Orkney Museum

MUSEUM | FAMILY | With artifacts from the Picts, the Vikings, and other ancient peoples, this museum—the former townhouse of the prosperous Bakie family of Tankerness—has the entire history of Orkney crammed into a rabbit warren of rooms. It's not easily accessible for those with disabilities, but with the help of staff, can be done. The setup may be old-fashioned, but some artifacts—especially those from everyday Orcadian life in the 19th century—are riveting. Lovely gardens around the back provide a spot to recoup after a history lesson. ⊠ *Broad St.* ☏ *01856/873191* ⊕ *www.orkney.gov. uk* 🖅 *Free* ⏰ *Closed Sun.*

Orkney Wireless Museum

MUSEUM | Vintage radio buffs will find this oddball museum fascinating. Amassed by the late Jim MacDonald, a radio operator during World War II, it tells the story of wartime communications at Scapa Flow, where thousands of service members were stationed; they used the equipment displayed to protect the Home Fleet. Run by volunteers, the museum also contains many handsome 1930s wireless radios and examples of the handicrafts produced by Italian prisoners of war. ⊠ *Kiln Corner, Junction Rd.* ☏ *01856/871400* ⊕ *www.owm.org.uk* 🖅 *£3* ⏰ *Closed Oct.–Mar.*

St. Magnus Cathedral

RELIGIOUS SITE | Founded by the Norse earl Jarl Rognvald in 1137 and named for his uncle, this grand red-and-yellow-sandstone cathedral was mostly finished by 1200, although more work was carried out during the following 300 years. The cathedral is still in use and contains some fine examples of Norman architecture, although traces of later styles are found here and there. The ornamentation on some of the tombstones in the church is particularly striking. At the far end to the left is the tomb of the tragically discredited Dr. John Rae, the Victorian-era Orcadian adventurer and unsung hero who discovered the final section of the Northwest Passage in Canada but was decried for his reporting that the British men of the Franklin expedition, overwhelmed by starvation, had resorted to cannibalism: an assertion that has since been proved true. ⊠ *Broad St.* ☏ *01856/874894* ⊕ *www.stmagnus.org* 🖅 *Free* ⏰ *Closed Sun. Oct.–Mar.*

Tomb of the Eagles

ARCHAEOLOGICAL SITE | In 1958, while looking for stones for diking, local farmer Ronnie Simison found and excavated this chambered cairn, packed with 340 human skulls that were 5,000 years old. The lack of other bones suggests that the skulls were taken after the bones had been picked clean by birds. The tomb, however, gets its name from the 70 talons of sea eagles and their remains found among the skulls. The walk to the tomb is a mile through fields and then along spectacular cliffs. Access to the tomb is by way of a trolley. This can be messy if it's muddy and a no-go for those with mobility problems, but it's not as uncomfortable or claustrophobic as you'd imagine. The visitor center, still run by Ronnie Simison's family, is full of exhibits. ⊠ *Off A961, St. Margaret's Hope* ✛ *22 miles south of Kirkwall* ☏ *01856/831339* ⊕ *www.tomboftheeagles.co.uk* 🖅 *£7.80* ⏰ *Closed Nov.–Feb.*

Unstan Chambered Tomb

ARCHAEOLOGICAL SITE | This intriguing burial chamber lies within a 5,000-year-old cairn. Excavations here uncovered a collection of similarly designed pottery bowls, subsequently found in other Orcadian Neolithic tombs. Access to the tomb by trolley can be awkward for those with mobility problems. ⊠ *A964* ✛ *7½ miles west of Kirkwall* ☏ *01856/841815* ⊕ *www.historicenvironment.scot* 🖅 *Free.*

🍴 Restaurants

★ Lucano

$$$ | **ITALIAN** | **FAMILY** | This modern trattoria-style Italian restaurant has been taken to the heart of Orcadians, and rightly so, as it delivers an abundant menu of good Italian food. From pizza to classic pasta dishes—with fulsomely meaty carbonara and Bolognese and very tasty vegetarian *burro e salvia* (butter and sage) and pesto—to excellent *secondi piatti* such as chicken in rosemary, it's got something for every appetite. **Known for:** healthy choice of classic Italian dishes; pizza Lucano with tomato, mushrooms, olives, peppers, and Parma ham; ice-cream pudding for dessert. $ *Average main: £20* ✉ *31–33 Victoria St.* ☎ *01856/875687.*

The Reel

$ | **CAFÉ** | Orkney's musical tradition is alive and fiddling, but never more so than at this café and restaurant. The eating is cheap and hearty: expect big bowls of soup, doorstop-size sandwiches with inventive fillings, and slices of sponge cake. **Known for:** Orcadian craft beer; chicken salsa sandwiches; on-site music school that leads to live music nights. $ *Average main: £7* ✉ *3 Castle St.* ☎ *01856/871000* ⊕ *www.wrigleyandthereel.com* ☾ *No dinner.*

 # Hotels

Ayre Hotel

$$ | **HOTEL** | This large, functional hotel by the harbor offers ample accommodation choices—including a wing of nine spacious, self-catering apartments—plus a good bar-restaurant. **Pros:** great for families and groups; some rooms have great sea views; location near the harbor. **Cons:** uninspiring parking lot views from some rooms; feels like a chain hotel; used by tour groups often. $ *Rooms from: £130* ✉ *Ayre Rd.* ☎ *01856/873001* ⊕ *www.ayrehotel.co.uk* ⇨ *60 rooms* ❏ *Breakfast.*

Foveran Hotel

$$ | **HOTEL** | About 34 acres of grounds surround this modern, ranch-style hotel overlooking Scapa Flow, about 3 miles southwest of Kirkwall. **Pros:** expansive grounds; charming, family-run vibe; food that's cooked to perfection. **Cons:** exterior looks a bit institutional; you must book the popular restaurant ahead of time; restaurant serves only dinner. $ *Rooms from: £125* ✉ *Off A964* ☎ *01856/872389* ⊕ *www.thefoveran.com* ⇨ *8 rooms* ❏ *Breakfast.*

The Shore

$$ | **B&B/INN** | Right on the harbor, this friendly hotel above a pub has surprisingly modern bedrooms, some with chic bathrooms. **Pros:** clean and well-maintained bedrooms; sleek, minimalist decor; popular restaurant. **Cons:** pricey for an inn; bars can be noisy; cars tearing up the main road outside may disturb sleep. $ *Rooms from: £140* ✉ *Shore St.* ☎ *01856/872200* ⊕ *www.theshore.co.uk* ⇨ *10 rooms* ❏ *Breakfast.*

West End Hotel

$ | **B&B/INN** | Built in 1824 by a retired sea captain, the West End Hotel once served as Kirkwall's first hospital and is now a small, affably run hotel. **Pros:** great location; friendly owners; on-site restaurant and beer garden. **Cons:** no tubs, just showers; some rooms are small; basic furnishings. $ *Rooms from: £120* ✉ *Main St.* ☎ *01856/872368* ⊕ *www.westendkirkwall.co.uk* ⇨ *10 rooms* ❏ *Breakfast.*

◔ Shopping

Beyond its famed silversmiths, Orkney's others crafts, from textiles to furniture making to ceramics, have been given a boost by the Orkney Craft Trail (⊕ *www.orkneydesignercrafts.com*), which encourages customers with an interest in these crafts to go straight to the makers, visit their workshops, and buy direct. If you don't have time to do the trail, some of these wares can be found in Kirkwall shops, along with specialty foods and books particular to Orkney and its history.

Judith Glue

CLOTHING | Not only can you purchase designer knitwear with traditional patterns, as well as handmade crafts and hampers of local produce at Judith Glue, the shop is also home to the Orkney Real Food Café. ✉ *25 Broad St.* ☎ *01856/874225* ⊕ *www.judithglue.com.*

The Longship

JEWELRY/ACCESSORIES | Don't miss this eclectic shop, open since the 19th century, which sells a huge array of Ola Gorrie's original designs in gold and silver jewelry with Celtic and Norse themes. It also stocks knitwear, under-the-radar designer clothes labels, and quirky housewares. Its wineshop in the courtyard has a large selection, plus locally brewed craft beers and quality deli staples from Italy. ⊠ *11 Broad St.* ☎ *01856/888790* ⊕ *www.thelongship. co.uk.*

 # Activities

Largely flat and with lovely stretches of quiet road, Orkney is the perfect place for cycling, so long as you pack water-proof gear and can deal with the wind in your face as well as your hair. The Visit Orkney tourist information office has information on interesting routes. The brown-trout-filled lochs of Orkney have all the makings of a spectacular day's fishing. Visit ⊕ *www.orkneytroutfishing. co.uk* for the lowdown on the lochs and how to fish them.

Cycle Orkney

BICYCLING | For £20 a day bicycles can be rented from Cycle Orkney, which is open year-round. For less energetic visitors, Cycle Orkney also rents e-bikes for £35 a day. ⊠ *Tankerness La.* ☎ *01856/875777* ⊕ *www.cycleorkney.com.*

Merkister Hotel

FISHING | The Merkister Hotel, on Loch Harray, arranges fishing trips. All your equipment, including boats, is available to rent, and ghillies provide instruction. ⊠ *A965, Harray, Birsay* ☎ *01856/771366* ⊕ *www.merkister.com.*

Scapa Flow Visitor Centre

On Hoy, 14 miles southwest of Kirkwall, 6 miles south of Stromness.

On the beautiful island of Hoy, Scapa Flow Visitor Centre explores the strategic and dramatic role that this sheltered anchorage played in two world wars.

GETTING HERE AND AROUND

The car ferry from Houton (7 miles east of Stromness) takes 25 minutes to reach Lyness on Hoy and the visitor center. The ferry costs around £28 round-trip for a regular-size car and £8.80 round-trip per passenger.

ESSENTIALS

FERRY CONTACTS Orkney Ferries. ☎ *01856/872044* ⊕ *www.orkneyferries. co.uk.*

 # Sights

Scapa Flow Visitor Centre

INFO CENTER | Military history buffs will appreciate the Scapa Flow Visitor Centre, which displays military vehicles and guns from both world wars. You'll also find equipment salvaged from the German boats scuttled off the coast. In the plain but poignant graveyard here, British and German personnel both rest in peace. If you want to take your car over to Hoy, book well in advance with Orkney Ferries, as this is a popular route. The visitor center is a short walk from the ferry terminal on the island of Hoy. ⊠ *Off B9047, Lyness* ☎ *01856/791300* ⊕ *www. scapaflow.co.uk* ⊠ *Free* ☉ *Closed Nov.– Feb. and weekends in Mar., Apr., and Oct.*

Shetland

ATLANTIC OCEAN

NORTH SEA

St Magnus Bay

MAINLAND

The South Mainland

0   10 mi
0   10 km

Hermaness National Nature Reserve
Saxa Vord
Unst Heritage Centre
Unst Boat Haven
Baltasound
BALTA
Unst
A968
Cullivoe
Clivocast
Muness Castle
Dalsetter
Colvister
FETLAR
Mid Yell
Funzie
North Roe
A970
Yell
A968
Otterswick
Housetter
Ronas Hill
Ollaberry
Old Haa
Eshaness
Urafirth
Ulsta
Burravoe
Tangwick Haa Museum
Hillswick
Mossbank
OUT SKERRIES
Mavis Grind
Brae
Vidlin
Voe
WHALSAY
Symbister
PAPA STOUR
Sandness
Aith
A970
Weisdale
A971
Hellister
Walls
Haggersta
Whiteness
Veensgarth
Holmsgarth
Aberdeen Ferry Dock
Noss National Nature Reserve
Clickimin Broch
Lerwick
ISLE OF NOSS
Scalloway
Hoswick Visitor Centre
Gulberwick
FOULA
Hamnavoe
Quarff
Bridge End
Aithsetter
Ferry
Mousa Broch
MOUSA
Sandwick
Bigton
Levenwick
St. Ninian's Isle
A970
Dunrossness
Shetland Crofthouse Museum
Toab
FERRY TO FAIR ISLE
FERRY TO KIRKWALL, ORKNEY ISLANDS
Old Scatness
Jarlshof
Sumburgh Head Lighthouse and Visitor Centre
TO FAIR ISLE
FERRY TO ABERDEEN

Lerwick

14 hrs by ferry from Aberdeen.

Founded by Dutch fishermen in the 17th century, Lerwick today is a busy town and administrative center. Handsome stone buildings—known as lodberries—line the old harbor; they provided loading bays for goods, some of them illegal. The town's twisting flagstone lanes once heaved with activity, and Lerwick is still an active port today. This is also where most visitors to Shetland dock, spilling out of cruise ships to walk around the town.

GETTING HERE AND AROUND
The town center of Lerwick is 1 mile south of Holmsgarth, the terminal for the ferry from Aberdeen. You can take a bus from Holmsgarth to the center or to the bus station for travel to Sumburgh or Scalloway. Car rentals can be arranged to meet you at the ferry terminal. Lerwick is small and compact, and the bus network, overseen by ZetTrans, offers hourly bus service around town.

ESSENTIALS
TRANSPORTATION CONTACTS Boddam Cabs. ☎ *01950/460111* ⊕ *www.boddam-cabs.co.uk.*

VISITOR INFORMATION Lerwick Visitor iCentre. ✉ *Market Cross* ☎ *01595/693434* ⊕ *www.shetland.org.*

Sights

★ Clickimin Broch
MILITARY SITE | A stone tower on the site of what was originally an Iron Age fortification, Clickimin Broch makes a good introduction to these mysterious buildings. It was possibly intended as a place of retreat and protection in the event of attack. South of the broch are vivid views of the cliffs at the south end of the island of Bressay, which shelters Lerwick Harbor. ✉ *Off A970* ✛ *1 mile south of Lerwick* ⊕ *www.historicenvironment.scot* 🎫 *Free.*

Fort Charlotte
MILITARY SITE | This artillery fort was built in 1665 to protect the Sound of Bressay from the invading Dutch. They seized it in 1673 and razed the fort to the ground. They were soon chased out of Shetland and the fort was rebuilt in 1781. ✉ *Market St.* ⊕ *www.historicenvironment.scot* 🎫 *Free.*

★ Mareel
ARTS VENUE | Next to the Shetland Museum, the bold and beautiful—although somewhat brutal around the back—Mareel is Shetland's adventurous and ambitious arts center. It has a live performance space attracting national and international musicians, two cinemas showing art-house and mainstream films, and a café and bar area that showcases local crafts, acoustic musicians, and some very drinkable Shetland beers. ✉ *North Ness* ☎ *01595/745500* ⊕ *www.mareel.org.*

Noss National Nature Reserve
NATURE PRESERVE | The island of Noss (which means "nose" in old Norse) rises to a point called the Noup. The smell and noise of the birds that live on the vertiginous cliffs can assault the senses. Residents nest in orderly fashion: black-and-white guillemots (45,000 pairs) and razorbills at the bottom; gulls, gannets, cormorants, and kittiwake in the middle; fulmars and puffins at the top. If you get too close to their chicks, some will dive-bomb from above. To get here, take a ferry from Lerwick to Bressay, then (weather permitting) an inflatable boat to Noss. It's a four- to five-hour walk around the reserve, so allow plenty of time if the walk is the draw. Mid-May to mid-July is the best time to view breeding birds. No matter when you visit, be sure to wear waterproof clothing and sensible shoes. ✉ *Noss* ☎ *01595/693345* ⊕ *www.nature.scot* 🎫 *Free* ⊙ *Visitor center and inflatable ferry closed Sept.–Apr.*

★ Shetland Museum

MUSEUM | FAMILY | On the last remaining stretch of the old waterfront at the restored Hay's Dock, the striking Shetland Museum, with its sail-like tower, is the area's cultural hub and a stimulating introduction to local history. The two-story space is filled with displays about archaeology, textiles, and contemporary arts. Standout exhibits include depictions of the minutiae of everyday Shetland life across the centuries, the last remaining *sixareen* (a kind of fishing boat), and the collection of lace shawls donated by Shetland families. Its informal spaces make this a wonderful place to hang out; look for vintage vessels moored in the dock and seals that pop up to observe everyone at the glass-fronted café-restaurant terrace. The museum shop is a must-visit, with a beautiful selection of nicely priced postcards and useful things inspired by the museum's collection. ⊠ *Hay's Dock, Commercial Rd.* ☎ *01595/695057* ⊕ *www.shetlandmuseumandarchives.org.uk* ✉ *Free.*

🍴 Restaurants

★ Fjarå

$$ | CAFÉ | Sitting on rocks on the ebb (or *fjara* in Faroese) of Brewick Bay, the views from this large wood-and-glass house allow you to look at otters and seals between courses. The menu is very simple: big breakfasts, coffees, and cake—including an array of gluten-free items—soup and huge salads, as well as Shetland mussels or fish-and-chips for lunch. **Known for:** delicious local lamb; gorgeous views; handmade burgers. $ *Average main: £16* ⊠ *Sea Rd.* ☎ *01595/697388* ⊕ *www.fjaracoffee.com.*

★ The Peerie Shop Cafe

$ | CAFÉ | Who would believe you could get such good cappuccino at 60 degrees north? In back of the popular Lerwick knitwear shop is a modish, consistently good café that sells filled sponge cakes, lip-smackingly good soups, and, yes, the best coffee on the islands. **Known for:** excellent coffee; full Scottish breakfast; crowds of locals. $ *Average main: £6* ⊠ *Esplanade* ☎ *01595/692817* ⊕ *www.peerieshop.co.uk* ⊗ *Closed Sun. No dinner.*

Hotels

Alder Lodge Guest House

$ | B&B/INN | Occupying a bank building dating from the 1830s, this family-run guesthouse sits on a quiet street within easy reach of Lerwick's shops, pubs, and harbor. **Pros:** comfortable beds; superb location; charming patio. **Cons:** booked solid in the summer months; dull motel-style exterior; bedrooms very basic. $ *Rooms from: £80* ⊠ *8 Clairmont Pl.* ☎ *01595/695705* ⊕ *www.alderlodge-guesthouse.com* ⤴ *10 rooms* ⓘⓞⓘ *Breakfast.*

Kveldsro House Hotel

$$ | B&B/INN | Tucked away behind the town's main thoroughfare is this unfussy small hotel with comfortable, if rather expensive, rooms. **Pros:** minutes from the city center; cheery bar; excellent staff. **Cons:** slightly pretentious decor scheme; noise from the bar in some rooms; expensive for what it offers. $ *Rooms from: £145* ⊠ *Greenfield Pl.* ⊹ *Off Commercial St.* ☎ *01595/692195* ⊕ *www.shetlandhotels.com* ⤴ *17 rooms* ⓘⓞⓘ *Breakfast.*

🛍 Shopping

Shetland's tradition of knitting and knitted lace is still going strong. You can still buy the traditional Fair Isle knitwear, but also look out for the new wave of Shetland knitters. The Shetland Museum shop is perhaps one of the best in the islands for cards, books, and souvenirs, but there are a number of other independent sellers who stock interesting knitwear, gifts, and books. The island's artisans have, like Orkney, opened their studios to visitors and are selling their work directly:

look on the Shetland Craft Trail (⊕ *www. shetlandartsandcrafts.co.uk* and, as you tour the island, fit in a visit to a craftsman who takes your fancy. Appointments are generally required.

Anderson & Co.

CLOTHING | On Commercial Street, Anderson & Co. carries hand-knitted cardigans, jumpers, Shetland lace scarves, sheepskin slippers, and woven throws. ✉ *60–62 Commercial St.* ☎ *01595/693714* ⊕ *www.shetlandknitwear.com* ⊙ *Closed Sun.*

Ninian

CLOTHING | Tempting 21st-century interpretations of traditional Fair Isle clothing, scarves, and throws as well as ceramics, gifts, and beautiful children's toys are found at Ninian. ✉ *80 Commercial St.* ☎ *01595/696655* ⊕ *www.ninianshetland. co.uk.*

★ Peerie Shop

BOOKS/STATIONERY | The Peerie (Shetland for small) Shop sells a colorful mix of knitwear, cards, ceramics, and interesting—and, yes, small—miscellanea. ✉ *Esplanade* ☎ *01595/692816* ⊕ *www. peerieshop.co.uk.*

The South Mainland

14 to 25 miles south of Lerwick via A970.

The narrow 3- or 4-mile-wide stretch of land that reaches south from Lerwick to Sumburgh Head has a number of fascinating ancient sites (and an airport) as well as farmland, wild landscapes, and dramatic ocean views.

GETTING HERE AND AROUND

Arriving in Sumburgh by plane offers stunning views of Sumburgh Head and its golden sands. A fairly regular bus makes the hour-long trip between the airport and Lerwick, and it's also easy to drive here if you're based in Lerwick. You can rent a car from the airport or take a

---

Shetland Ponies

The squat and shaggy Shetland pony has been a common sight for more than 12 centuries. Roaming wild over the hills, the pony evolved its long mane and dense winter coat. The animals stand between 28 and 42 inches tall, which made them ideal for working in cramped coal-mine tunnels in the 1850s, when child labor was restricted. They became a popular pet for the aristocracy in the late 19th century; many believe this helped save the breed. Today you'll see ponies at equine events and all over the island, chomping the grass.

---

taxi. Jarlshof and Scatness are both within walking distance of the terminal.

◉ Sights

Hoswick Visitor Centre

MUSEUM | This café has an unmanned museum space that heaves with an impressive collection of vintage radios (hugely important to an island community), knitting, spinning, and fishing paraphernalia. The café is popular with locals and visitors alike and sells cakes and soups while trading in knitted and crafty keepsakes made by entrepreneurial Shetlanders. In the mezzanine room is an interesting exhibition on the historic Hoswick whale case, when in 1888 the local fishermen took on an oppressive laird (estate owner) and won. ✉ *Hoswick* ☎ *01950/431406* ⊕ *www.shetlandheritageassociation.com/members/south-mainland/hoswick-visitor-centre* ✑ *Free* ⊙ *Closed Oct.–May.*

The stone tower of Mousa Broch dates back 2,000 years and is impressively preserved.

★ Jarlshof

ARCHAEOLOGICAL SITE | FAMILY | In 1897 a huge storm blew away 4,000 years of sand to expose the multilayered remains of Bronze Age, Iron Age, Pictish, and Viking buildings; prehistoric wheelhouses; and earth houses that represented thousands of years of continuous settlement. It's a large and complex site, and you can roam—and photograph—the remains freely. The small visitor center is packed with details of the lives of former residents and illustrates Jarlshof's more recent history as a medieval farmstead and home of the 16th-century Earl of Orkney and Shetland, "cruel" Patrick Stewart, who enslaved the men of Scalloway to build Scalloway Castle. ✉ *Sumburgh Head, Virkie* ✛ *Off A970* ☎ *01950/460112* ⊕ *www.historicenvironment.scot* 🖃 *£6* ⊗ *Closed Oct.–Mar.*

★ Mousa Broch

ARCHAEOLOGICAL SITE | Sandsayre Pier in Sandwick is the departure point for the passenger ferry to the tiny isle of Mousa, where you can see Mousa Broch, a fortified Iron Age stone tower rising about 40 feet high. The massive walls give a real sense of security, which must have been reassuring for islanders subject to attacks from ship-borne raiders. Exploring this beautifully preserved, curved-stone structure, standing on what feels like an untouched island, makes you feel as if you're back in 100 BC. From April to September, the ferry (£16 round-trip) departs for the island once or twice each afternoon. From May to July there are dusk boat trips (£25 round-trip) to catch the tiny storm petrels as they return from their day feeding at sea to their nests in the walls of the broch. The sight—and feel—of them swarming in the half-light is something you'll never forget. Note that you must pay in cash for the ferry rides and boat trips. ✉ *Sandsayre Pier, Sandwick* ✛ *Off A970, 14 miles south of Lerwick* ☎ *07901/872339 ferry* ⊕ *www.mousa.co.uk* ⊗ *Closed Oct.–Mar.*

Old Scatness

ARCHAEOLOGICAL SITE | FAMILY | This ongoing excavation of an Iron Age village is a worthwhile stop. Enthusiastic and entertaining guides, most in costume, tell stories that breathe life into the stones and the middens, showing how its former residents made their clothes and cooked their food, including their staple dish: the ghastly seaweed porridge. ⊠ *Off A970, Virkie* ☎ *01595/694688* ⊕ *www.shetland-heritage.co.uk/old-scatness* 🖃 *£6* ⊗ *Closed Sat.–Mon. and Sept.–mid-May.*

★ Shetland Crofthouse Museum

MUSEUM | FAMILY | Nine miles south of Sandwick this 19th-century thatched house reveals the way of life of rural Shetlanders, which the traditionally attired attendant will be delighted to discuss with you. The peat fire casts a glow on the box bed, the resting chair, and the wealth of domestic implements, including a hand mill for preparing meal and a straw "keshie" for carrying peat. One building made from an upturned boat was used for storing and drying fish and mutton; huts like this inspired the design of the new Scottish Parliament. ⊠ *East of A970, South Voe, Dunrossness* ☎ *01590/460557* ⊕ *www.shetlandheritageassociation.com* 🖃 *Free (donations welcome)* ⊗ *Closed Oct.–Apr.*

★ St. Ninian's Isle

ISLAND | It was on St. Ninian's Isle that a schoolboy helping archaeologists excavate the ruins of a 12th-century church discovered the St. Ninian treasure, a collection of 28 silver objects dating from the 8th century. This Celtic silver is housed in the Museum of Scotland in Edinburgh (a point of controversy), but good replicas are in the Shetland Museum in Lerwick. Although you can't see the silver, walking over the causeway of golden sand (called a tombolo or *ayre*) that joins St. Ninian's Isle to the Mainland is an unforgettable experience. From Sumburgh head 8 miles north on A970 and B9122, then turn left at Skelberry.

Puffins and More

Every summer more than a million birds alight on the cliff faces in Shetland to nest. Bird-watchers can spot more than 20 species, from tiny storm petrels to gannets with 6-foot wingspans. Popular with visitors are the puffins, with their short necks, striped beaks, and orange feet. Look for them on the cliffs at Sumburgh Head near the lighthouse, 2 miles south of Sumburgh Airport. The visitor center has information about nesting sites, as well as live puffin cams during breeding season.

★ Sumburgh Head Lighthouse and Visitor Centre

LIGHTHOUSE | FAMILY | Perhaps one of northern Europe's most stunning locations, this Robert Stevenson—grandfather of the writer Robert Louis—designed lighthouse, built in 1921, was the first lighthouse in Shetland. Sir Walter Scott was very taken with the location and based his novel *The Pirate* on the nearby landmarks of Jarlshof and Fitful Head. The stories of the Old Radar Hut—crucial during WWII—and the engine room with its deep booming foghorn are brought back to life here, while a Marine Life Centre has excellent displays on the birds, fish, and sea mammals found around the cliffs. If you walk round the dry-stone dikes, you will hear and probably see puffins, guillemots, and fulmars breeding, feeding, and fighting on the rocks, but if it's wet and wild, the circular café and Education Suite with its jaw-dropping panorama will provide enough drama. ⊠ *Sumburgh Head, Sumburgh* ☎ *01595/694688* ⊕ *www.sumburghhead.com* 🖃 *£6* ⊗ *Closed Oct.–Mar.*

Hotels

★ Hayhoull B&B

$ | B&B/INN | FAMILY | This lively bed-and-breakfast offers the chance to slip into the life of the buzzing Shetland community of Bigton. **Pros:** in friendly village next to the magical St. Ninian's Isle; children welcomed warmly; beautiful views. **Cons:** shared bathroom in two rooms; 4 miles to the nearest pub or restaurant; expensive meals. ⓈⒹ *Rooms from: £80* ✉ *Off B9122, Bigton* ☎ *01950/422206* ⊕ *www.hayhoull.co.uk* ▤ *No credit cards* ⌐⊃ *4 rooms* ⎩◯⎧ *Breakfast.*

Shopping

★ Nielanell

CLOTHING | The designs here are rich in texture, color, and shape, but it's the philosophy behind the knitwear—she makes it for the day you feel your worst—that makes it so desirable. Most of the pieces are made to be worn in multiple ways, meaning you get three pieces for the price of one. ✉ *Hoswick* ☎ *01950/431413* ⊕ *www.nielanell.com.*

Scalloway

6 miles west of Lerwick, 21 miles north of St. Ninian's Isle.

On the west coast of Mainland Island is Scalloway, which preceded Lerwick as the capital of the region. During World War II Scalloway was the port for the "Shetland Bus," a secret fleet of boats that carried British agents to Norway to perform acts of sabotage against the Germans, who were occupying the country. On the return trips, the boats would carry refugees back to Shetland. As you approach the town from the A970, look for the information board, which overlooks the settlement and its castle.

GETTING HERE AND AROUND

The town is 10 minutes by car from Lerwick, or you can get one of the fairly regular buses or even a taxi (£12).

Sights

Scalloway Castle

CASTLE/PALACE | This waterfront fortress was built in 1600 by Patrick Stewart, Earl of Orkney and Shetland. He was hanged in 1615 for his cruelty and misdeeds, and the castle was never used again. To enter, retrieve the key from the Scalloway Museum. You may explore these handsome ruins to your heart's content. ✉ *A970* ☎ *01856/841815* ⊕ *www.historicenvironment.scot* ⎙ *Free* ⊙ *Closed Oct.–mid-Apr.*

Scalloway Museum

MUSEUM | This modern museum tells some fascinating stories about Scalloway and its well-traveled locals. There is a section dedicated to the exploits of the Shetland Bus, the WWII resistance movement that operated between Norway and Shetland, and cabinet upon cabinet of maritime artifacts and *proil* (sailors' booty) donated by locals. ✉ *Castle St.* ☎ *01595/880734* ⊕ *www.scallowaymuseum.org* ⎙ *£3* ⊙ *Closed Oct.–mid-Apr.*

Restaurants

The Cornerstone

$ | CAFÉ | The unfussy menu here features dishes such as soups, quiche, and sandwiches by day or steaks and lasagna by night. It isn't fancy, but it is made and served with great enthusiasm and generosity. **Known for:** mammoth scones; tasty quiches; friendly, welcoming atmosphere. ⓈⒹ *Average main: £12* ✉ *Burn Beach, Main St.* ☎ *01595/880346* ⊕ *www.thecornerstonebandb.com* ⊙ *No dinner Sun.–Thurs.*

Hotels

★ Scalloway Hotel

$$ | B&B/INN | Facing the harbor, this traditional stone lodging has fine views, especially at sunset. **Pros:** thoughtfully put together bedrooms; memorable meals from the restaurant; lots of local charm. **Cons:** can get booked up in advance; some noise from bar on weekends; chintzy decor. ⓢ *Rooms from: £140 ✉ Main St.* ☎ *01595/880444* ⊕ *www.scallowayhotel.com* ⇌ *4 rooms* ⵏⵔ *Breakfast.*

Weisdale

9 miles north of Lerwick.

This tiny place is less a village than a group of houses, but it does have a worthwhile gallery.

GETTING HERE AND AROUND

Take A971 from Lerwick. The No. 9 bus runs three times a day weekdays; the trip from Lerwick is 20 minutes.

 Sights

Bonhoga Gallery

MUSEUM | Built in 1855 using stones from the Kergord estate's "cleared" (forcibly evicted) crofts, Weisdale Mill is now the Bonhoga Gallery, a contemporary art space showing quirky exhibitions by local, national, and international artists. Downstairs is a small but cake-laden café that looks over the Weisdale burn. An excellent shop sells artist-made housewares. ✉ *B9075* ☎ *01595/745750* ⊕ *www.shetlandarts.org.*

 Shopping

Shetland Jewellery

JEWELRY/ACCESSORIES | This shop sells gold and silver Nordic- and Celtic-inspired jewelry, desk knives, and belt buckles made in the on-site workshop. ✉ *Sound*

Side ☎ *01595/830275* ⊕ *www.shetland-jewellery.co.uk.*

Brae

15 miles north of Weisdale, 24 miles north of Lerwick.

A thriving community, Brae is where you can see the spoils of Shetland's oil money. The rugged moorland and tranquil *voes* (inlets) of Brae are the home of Busta House, one of the best hotels on the island.

GETTING HERE AND AROUND

There are buses from Lerwick to Brae, but the spread-out sights make it impossible to really see this area without a car. A970 is the main road, and B9078 will take you through Hillswick and to Eshaness.

 Sights

Eshaness and Ronas Hill

VIEWPOINT | About 15 miles north of Brae are the rugged, forbidding cliffs around **Eshaness**; drive north and then turn left onto B9078. On the way, look for the defiant Drongs, striking sandstone stacks or pillars battered into shape by thousands of years of crashing seas. Then return to join the A970 at Hillswick, but before reaching Ura Firth, turn left toward the old crofting community of Heylor on Ronas Voe, beautifully documented by the pioneer filmmaker Jenny Gilbertson in the 1930s. Providing a front-on vista of rounded, red **Ronas Hill,** the highest hill in Shetland, Heylor's delightful sandy beach is known as the Blade. Beware: arctic terns—which Shetlanders call Tirricks—nest among the pebbles in May and June.

Mavis Grind

BEACH—SIGHT | North of Brae the A970 meanders past Mavis Grind, a strip of land so narrow you can throw a stone—if you're strong—from the Atlantic, in one inlet, to the North Sea, in another. Keep an eye out for sea otters, which sometimes cross here.

★ Tangwick Haa Museum

MUSEUM | After viewing the cliffs at Eshaness, call in at Tangwick Haa Museum, the 17th-century home of the Cheynes, now packed full with photographs, household items, and knitting, farming, and fishing equipment from the 18th to early 20th century. Upstairs is the Laird's Room—a traditional sitting room of the 19th century and a room of curiosities, including whale eardrums. Downstairs—next to the help-yourself café—there are rows of folders; ask one of the staff to let you hear what's in them and you will be rewarded with the soft, gentle voices of local elders telling you of life lived in Shetland. ☒ Off B9078, Tangwick ☎ 01806/503389 ⊕ www.tangwickhaa. org.uk ☒ Free ۞ Closed. Oct.–Mar.

 Restaurants

Braewick Café

$ | BRITISH | With a stunning position overlooking the Drongs (rocky columns standing in the sea), this eatery serves famously large portions popular with visitors and Shetlanders alike. Browse the local crafts in the shop while waiting for a crispy battered-fish supper, or just sit back on the sofas by the huge picture window and watch the dramatic sea and sky. **Known for:** Shetland roast lamb; lovely cakes; wonderful ocean view. ⑤ Average main: £10 ☒ Off B9078, Eshaness ☎ 01806/503345 ⊕ www.eshaness. moonfruit.com ۞ Closed Tues. and Wed. No dinner.

★ Frankie's Fish & Chips

$ | SEAFOOD | Proudly claiming to be the northernmost fish-and-chips shop in Britain, this "chipper" is also the best of its kind on the islands. The combination of superfresh seafood—skate wings, squid, and crab legs—and light and crispy batter (including a gluten-free option) means Frankie's is everything a chip shop could be. **Known for:** Shetland mussels; king scallops in garlic butter; early closing at 8 pm. ⑤ Average main: £11 ☒ A970 ☎ 01806/522700 ⊕ www.frankiesfishandchips.com.

 Hotels

★ Busta House

$$ | HOTEL | Dating from the 16th century, Busta House—built by the well-heeled but ill-fated Gifford family—is one of the few grand houses of Shetland. **Pros:** truly haunting atmosphere; charming public rooms; lovely grounds. **Cons:** noisy plumbing; some rooms are a tight fit; popular with wedding parties. ⑤ Rooms from: £125 ☒ Off A970 ☎ 01806/522506 ⊕ www.bustahouse.com ⮑ 22 rooms ۞ Breakfast.

Yell

11 miles northeast of Brae, 31 miles north of Lerwick.

A desolate-looking blanket bog cloaks two-thirds of the island of Yell, creating an atmospheric landscape to pass through on the way to Unst to the north.

GETTING HERE AND AROUND

Although you will see the odd walker or cyclist, a car is needed to explore the northern isles. To get to Yell, take A970 or B9076 and catch the ferry from Toft to Ulsta. On Yell, B9081 runs through Burravoe and up the east side and joins the A968, which leads to Gutcher and the ferry to Unst.

 Sights

Old Haa

MUSEUM | The oldest building on the island, Burravoe's Old Haa is known for its crowstepped gables (the stepped effect on the ends of the roofs), typical of an early-18th-century Shetland merchant's house. There's an earnest memorial to Bobby Tulloch, the great Shetland naturalist and champion of Shetland's bird population (1929–96), and the displays in the upstairs museum tell the story of the wrecking of the German ship, the *Bohus,* in 1924. A copy of the ship's figurehead is displayed outside the building. The Old Haa serves light meals with home-baked bannocks, cakes, and other goodies and also acts as a kind of unofficial information center. A crafts shop is on the premises, too. ✉ *Burravoe* ☎ *01957/702431* ⊕ *www.oldhaa.com* ✉ *Free* ⊘ *Closed Fri.–Sun. and Oct.–Mar.*

Unst

49 miles north of Lerwick.

Unst is the northernmost inhabited island in Scotland, a remote and special place, especially for nature lovers and those who want to experience a community on the edge of faraway. On a long summer evening, views north to Muckle Flugga, with only the ocean beyond, are incomparable. If you're a bird-watcher, head to the Hermaness and Keen of Hamar nature reserves.

GETTING HERE AND AROUND
A ferry (take the A968 at the village of Mid Yell to Gutcher) crosses the Bluemull Sound to Unst. A car is best for exploring, though there is limited bus service, including from Lerwick; taxis are an option.

◉ Sights

Hermaness National Nature Reserve
NATURE PRESERVE | A bleak moorland ending in rocky cliffs, the Hermaness National Nature Reserve is prime bird-watching territory. About half the world's population (6,000 pairs) of great skuas, called "bonxies" by locals, are found here. These sky pirates attack anything that strays near their nests, including

humans, so keep to the paths. Thousands of other seabirds, including more than 50,000 puffins, nest on the cliffs, about an hour's walk from the reserve entrance. Gray seals haul out at the foot of the cliffs in fall, and offshore, dolphins and occasionally whales (including orcas) can be seen on calm days.

A path meanders across moorland and climbs up a gentle hill, from which you can see, to the north, a series of tilting offshore rocks; the largest of these sea-battered protrusions is **Muckle Flugga**, meaning "big, steep-sided island," on which stands a lighthouse. The lighthouse was built by engineer Thomas Stevenson, whose son, the great Scottish writer Robert Louis Stevenson, used the outline of Unst for his map of Treasure Island. Muckle Flugga is the northernmost point in Scotland.

The visitor center has leaflets that outline a walk; mid-May to mid-July is the best time to visit. To get here from Haroldswick, follow the B9086 around the head of Burrafirth to the signposted car park. ✉ *B9086, Burrafirth* ☎ *01957/693345* ⊕ *www.nature. scot* ✉ *Free* ⊘ *Visitor center closed mid-Sept.–mid-Apr.*

Muness Castle
ARCHAEOLOGICAL SITE | Scotland's northernmost castle was built in 1598 by Laurence Bruce of Cultmalindie, uncle of "cruel" Patrick Stewart. Despite being a ruin it is rather fetching, with circular corner towers and a scale-and-platt (that is, not circular but straight on) staircase. ✉ *B9084, Uyeasound* ⊕ *www.historicenvironment.scot* ✉ *Free.*

Unst Boat Haven
MUSEUM | Reflecting Shetland's intimacy with the sea, Unst Boat Haven displays a beautiful collection of traditional small fishing and sailing boats. ✉ *Beach Rd., Haroldswick* ☎ *01957/711528* ⊕ *www. unstheritage.com* ✉ *£3, includes Unst Heritage Centre* ⊘ *Closed Oct.–Apr.*

Unst Heritage Centre

MUSEUM | The unique and colorful history of the people of Unst is told in this fascinating assemblage of artifacts, tools, photographs, and reconstructions, including a classroom and a *ben* or "good" end (sitting room) of a croft house. It will leave you with an enduring visual memory of the ways in which the locals learned, crofted, knitted, fished, and worshipped through the last two centuries. ✉ *Haroldswick* ☎ *01957/711528* ⊕ *www.unstheritage.com* 🎫 *£3, includes Unst Boat Haven* ⊘ *Closed Oct.–Apr.*

Restaurants

Victoria's Vintage Tea Rooms

$ | **CAFÉ** | **FAMILY** | Run by a Devon girl, who knows a thing or two about cream teas, this vintage-style café does a roaring trade right on the water at Haroldswick. The Shetland smoked salmon on Skibhoul (the local baker) bread is a sandwich worth getting excited about, as are the cakes, especially the Victoria Sponge and scones. **Known for:** Devon cream teas; great coffee; seal and otter spotting. ⑤ *Average main: £6* ✉ *Old Haroldswick Shop, Haroldswick* ☎ *01957/711885* ⊕ *victoriasvintagetearooms.co.uk* ⊘ *Closed Mon. No dinner.*

Hotels

Gardiesfauld Hostel

$ | **B&B/INN** | With options limited for an overnighter in Unst, this quiet and spacious youth hostel will appeal to travelers who want more than a quick day trip and take an interest in others who end up in the same remote location. **Pros:** perfect for travelers on a shoestring; quiet (especially outside school holidays); family rooms en suite available. **Cons:** communal facilities; you can't guarantee silence; private rooms must be booked well in advance. ⑤ *Rooms from: £32* ✉ *B9084, Uyeasound* ☎ *01957/755279* ⊕ *www.gardiesfauld.shetland.co.uk* ▤ *No credit cards* ⊘ *Oct.–Mar. by arrangement only* *6 rooms* ⦿ *No meals.*

Shopping

Skibhoul Stores and Bakery

FOOD/CANDY | The bread from Skibhoul is so popular that large shipments of it head south to the rest of the Isles on Thursdays. It's also famous for the Oceanic sea-salt oatcakes and Balta biscuits that are perfect for picnics. There's a small self-serve café so you can taste the wares. ✉ *Northside* ☎ *01957/711444*.

Index

Photo Credits

Front Cover: Maurizio Rellini/SIME/eStock Photo [Description: Maurizio Rellini / SIME / eStock Photo, Scotland.]. **Back cover, from left to right:** Martin M303/Shutterstock, f11photo/Shutterstock David Lyons/age fotostock. **Spine:** Shaiith/Dreamstime. **Interior, from left to right:** Buccleuch Estate (1), Paul Tomkins/VisitScotland (2). **Chapter 1: Experience Scotland:** Heartland/Shutterstock (8-9). W. McKelvie 2005 (10). Kenny Lam/VisitScotland (11). Tomas Rebro/Shutterstock (11). A. Karnholz/Shutterstock (12). Jaime Pharr/Shutterstock (12). Brendan Howard/Shutterstock (12). John A Cameron/Shutterstock (12). Paul Tomkins/VisitScotland (13). Kenny Lam/VisitScotland (13). Kenny Lam/VisitScotland (14). Hufton Crow/V&A Dundee (14). kawhia/Shutterstock (14). jimmcdowall/iStockphoto (14). Kenny Lam/VisitScotland (15). Ben Queenborough/Shutterstock (16). Kenny Lam/VisitScotland (16). Kenny Lam/VisitScotland (16). Kenny Lam/VisitScotland (16). Ian Rutherford/VisitScotland (17). Findlay Rankin / age fotostock (17). Kenny Lam/VisitScotland (18). Monkey Business Images/Shutterstock (18). Mitch Gunn/Shutterstock (18). Kenny Lam/VisitScotland (19). David Lyons / age fotostock (19). Tana888/Shutterstock (24). vertmedia/iStockphoto (24). Jag_cz/iStockphoto (24). Joerg Beuge/Shutterstock (25). yingko/Shutterstock (25). Paolo Gallo/Shutterstock (26). Courtesy The Quaich Company (27). Jeff Whyte/Shutterstock (28). Elinor Staniforth (28). Anton_Ivanov/Shutterstock (28). CSG CIC Glasgow Museums Collection (28). James McDowall/Shutterstock (29). HuftonCrow (29). Scottish Fisheries Museum (29). Timawe/Dreamstime (29). Kenny Lam/VisitScotland (30). Klodien/Dreamstime (30). Kenny Lam/VisitScotland (30). Kenny Lam/VisitScotland (30). Kenny Lam/VisitScotland (30). Simon Taylor/Dreamstime (31). Craig Duncanson/Shutterstock (31). Damian Shields/North East 250/VisitScotland (31). Targn Pleiades/Shutterstock (31). Kenny Lam/VisitScotland (31). Kenny Lam/VisitScotland (32). Kenny Lam/VisitScotland (32). JeniFoto/Shutterstock (32). TreasureGalore/Shutterstock (32). Heartland Arts/Shutterstock (32). Kenny Lam/VisitScotland (33). Paul Tomkins/VisitScotland (33). Paul Tomkins/VisitScotland (33). Kenny Lam/VisitScotland (33). Moomusician/Shutterstock (33). Damian Shields/North East 250/VisitScotland (34). 13threephotography/Shutterstock (34). Glen Grant (34). JASPERIMAGE/Shutterstock (34). Søren Solkær/Highland Park (34). Robert Porter/Dreamstime (35). Tyler W. Stipp/Shutterstock (35). JOHN PAUL/The Glenmorangie Company (35). 13threephotography/Shutterstock (35). Christian Jordi/Dreamstime (35). **Chapter 3: Edinburgh and the Lothians:** Kenny Lam/VisitScotland (65). Kenny Lam/VisitScotland (70). Kenny Lam/VisitScotland (83). Matteo Provendola/Shutterstock (86). Anton_Ivanov/Shutterstock (89). Harald Lueder/Shutterstock (91). lou armor/Shutterstock (117). Alexey Fedorenko/Shutterstock (121). SergeBertasiusPhotography/Shutterstock (123). PhotoFires/Shutterstock (127). **Chapter 4: Glasgow:** Kenny Lam/VisitScotland (133). Leonid Andronov/Shutterstock (145). cornfield/Shutterstock (149). Anton_Ivanov/Shutterstock (159). Roman Babakin/Shutterstock (164). Stefano_Valeri/Shutterstock (179). Ulmus Media/Shutterstock (191). **Chapter 5: The Borders and the Southwest:** David Bostock/Shutterstock (193). WApted/Shutterstock (206). Keith K/Shutterstock (222). **Chapter 6: Fife and Angus:** HuftonCrow (229). Julietphotography/Shutterstock (238). James McDowall/Shutterstock (254). HuftonCrow (256). MagSpace/Shutterstock (265). **Chapter 7: Stirling and the Central Highlands:** Kenny Lam/VisitScotland (267). HeroToZero/Shutterstock (281). Khirman Vladimir/Shutterstock (287). cornfield/Shutterstock (303). **Chapter 8: Aberdeen and the Northeast:** Paul Tomkins/VisitScotland (305). Kenny Lam/VisitScotland (316). Francesco Dazzi/Shutterstock (325). **Chapter 9: Argyll and the Isles:** Lukasz Pajor/Shutterstock (345). Lukassek/Shutterstock (353). Nick Fox/Shutterstock (357). Dmitry Naumov/Shutterstock (362). Joost van Uffelen/Shutterstock (372). **Chapter 10: Inverness and Around the Great Glen:** George KUZ/Shutterstock (377). Iowsun/Shutterstock (386). chbaum/Shutterstock (391). johnbraid/Shutterstock (397). dnaveh/Shutterstock (404). Samot/Shutterstock (406). **Chapter 11: The Northern Highlands and the Western Isles:** Helen Hotson/Shutterstock (411). JOHN PAUL/The Glenmorangie Company (422). Boris Edelmann/Shutterstock (427). Lukassek/Shutterstock (438). EyesTravelling/Shutterstock (445). M. Vinuesa/Shutterstock (450). Helen Hotson/Shutterstock (452). **Chapter 12: Orkney and Shetland Islands:** Kenny Lam/VisitScotland (455). Colin Keldie/VisitScotland (466). Marcin Kadziolka/Shutterstock (476). **About Our Writers:** All photos are courtesy of the writers except for the following.

*Every effort has been made to trace the copyright holders, and we apologize in advance for any accidental errors. We would be happy to apply the corrections in the following edition of this publication.

Notes

Notes

Fodor's ESSENTIAL SCOTLAND

Publisher: Stephen Horowitz, *General Manager*

Editorial: Douglas Stallings, *Editorial Director;* Jill Fergus, Jacinta O'Halloran, Amanda Sadlowski, *Senior Editors;* Kayla Becker, Alexis Kelly, Rachael Roth, *Editors*

Design: Tina Malaney, *Director of Design and Production;* Jessica Gonzalez, *Graphic Designer;* Mariana Tabares, *Design & Production Intern*

Production: Jennifer DePrima, *Editorial Production Manager;* Carrie Parker, *Senior Production Editor;* Elyse Rozelle, *Production Editor;* Jackson Pranica, *Editorial Production Assistant*

Maps: Rebecca Baer, *Senior Map Editor;* David Lindroth and Mark Stroud (Moon Street Carography), *Cartographers*

Photography: Viviane Teles, *Senior Photo Editor;* Namrata Aggarwal, Ashok Kumar, Carl Yu, *Photo Editors;* Rebecca Rimmer, *Photo Intern*

Business and Operations: Chuck Hoover, *Chief Marketing Officer;* Robert Ames, *Group General Manager;* Devin Duckworth, *Director of Print Publishing;* Victor Bernal, *Business Analyst*

Public Relations and Marketing: Joe Ewaskiw, *Senior Director Communications & Public Relations;* Esther Su, *Senior Marketing Manager*

Fodors.com: Jeremy Tarr, *Editorial Director;* Rachael Levitt, *Managing Editor* Teddy Minford, *Editor*

Technology: Jon Atkinson, *Director of Technology;* Rudresh Teotia, *Lead Developer;* Jacob Ashpis, *Content Operations Manager*

Writers: Nick Bruno, Robin Gauldie, Mike Gonzalez, Joseph Reaney

Editors: Amanda Sadlowski, Debbie Harmsen

Production Editor: Jennifer DePrima

2nd Edition

ISBN 978-1-64097-246-9

ISSN 2574–0636

SPECIAL SALES
This book is available at special discounts for bulk purchases for sales promotions or premiums. For more information, e-mail SpecialMarkets@fodors.com.

PRINTED IN THE UNITED STATES OF AMERICA

10 9 8 7 6 5 4 3 2 1

Scotland About Our Writers

 Based in Dundee, **Nick Bruno** is a travel writer, journalist, and a Fodor's contributor for over a decade. He has authored many books and features about both Italy and Scotland, and also works for the BBC. An interest in history has led to a project researching the lives of Italians—including his paternal family—before, during, and after Il Ventennio Fascista. For this edition, he contributed to Experience Scotland and updated Travel Smart and Fife and Angus.

 Robin Gauldie was born in Dundee and studied history at Edinburgh University before training as journalist on local newspapers in Tayside. Since 1990 he has been a freelance journalist specializing in travel and the tourism industry, and is the author of more than 30 travel guidebooks to destinations in Europe, Asia, Africa, and South America. When not traveling he divides his time between his home in Edinburgh's New Town and a village house in Languedoc, southern France. This edition, Robin updated Aberdeen and the Northeast, Argyll and the Isles, and Orkney and Shetland Islands.

Mike Gonzalez is emeritus professor of Latin American Studies at Glasgow University and also writes regularly for the *Herald* and other publications on politics and culture. This edition, Mike updated the Glasgow, the Borders and the Southwest, and the Stirling and the Central Highlands chapters. His travels took him to places familiar and less familiar, and included exploring a tiny island on Islay whose houses were once an imperial center and walking in a hidden sculpture park in the hills near Dumfries.

 Joseph Reaney is an experienced travel writer and editor based part-time in Scotland and part-time in the Czech Republic—and regularly writes about both. He contributes to *National Geographic, Forbes Travel Guide*, and *USA Today*, among others, and runs his own travel content writing agency, World Words. When he has the time, he also writes and directs short films and comedy sketches. He updated three chapters for this edition: Edinburgh and the Lothians, Inverness and Around the Great Glen, and the Northern Highlands and the Western Isles as well as contributing to the Experience chapter.